Ellis Wasson
The British and Irish Ruling Class 1660-1945
Volume 2

Ellis Wasson

The British and Irish Ruling Class 1660-1945

Volume 2

Managing Editor: Katarzyna Michalak

Associate Editor: Łukasz Połczyński

DE GRUYTER
OPEN

ISBN 978-3-11-056238-5
e-ISBN 978-3-11-056239-2

Published by De Gruyter Open Ltd, Warsaw/Berlin
Part of Walter de Gruyter GmbH, Berlin/Boston
The book is published with open access at www.degruyter.com.

Library of Congress Cataloging-in-Publication Data
A CIP catalog record for this book has been applied for at the Library of Congress.

Managing Editor: Katarzyna Michalak
Associate Editor: Łukasz Połczyński

www.degruyteropen.com
Cover illustration: © Thinkstock/bwzenith

Contents

The Entries

"ORIGINS": Where reliable information is available about the first entry of the family into the gentry, the date of the purchase of land or holding of office is provided. When possible, the source of the wealth that enabled the family's election to Parliament for the first time is identified. Inheritance of property that supported participation in Parliament is delineated. The date of the election of the first MP (or peer), if this occurred before 1660, is given and the number and dates of subsequent MPs elected before 1660 follow. **These are printed in bold**. The information available about pre-1660 MPs varies considerably in quality. When possible, data are taken from the printed volumes of the Histories of Parliament for England and Wales, Scotland, and Ireland (see "Reference Works" in the Bibliography). Other sources include the printed list of MPs issued by Parliament in the nineteenth century, Stenton and Lees, *Who's Who*, online sources, and local and family histories. The dates and numbers of pre-1660 MPs in such sources are not always accurate, so that data should be used with caution.

"SEAT(S)": This category does not necessarily include all residences that belonged to a family. Most seats sold or abandoned before 1660 or inherited or purchased after 1945 are not included. Some houses were only used temporarily or by junior members of the family. Information about many seats was difficult to trace and no heroic efforts were made to find out about every building associated with a family. Information concerning current ownership was accumulated at various times over the past twenty years and, therefore, is sometimes out of date. The architectural data is as accurate as I can make it, but the quality of sources varies enormously and even respected authorities often contradict each other about dates. However, following the history of country houses is one of the surest means of keeping track of landed families.

"ESTATES": Data about wealth is drawn from the Bateman compendium of great landowners published in the 1870s (John Bateman, *The Great Landowners of Great Britain and Ireland*, 1876, 1883). Bateman based his numbers on a government survey of landownership. The first figure in the entry lists acreage, the initials in parentheses identify the location of estates, and the second figure is income in pounds (the entry usually does not include urban property or some other non-landed sources of wealth). Data has also been collected from Rubinstein's *Who Were the Rich*, the History of Parliament volumes, the *ODNB*, obituaries, magazines and, sometimes polemical, books, and works of reference. Families extinct before the survey of landowners was conducted often passed their estates on to other parliamentary families via heiresses. In that case data may be included further down the entry in the section on estates of a successor family. However, in some cases estates were sold or divided up among multiple heirs.

"TITLES": The dates of creation and extinction of all subsidiary peerages and all baronetcies are included in this category. The highest rank in the peerage achieved by a member of the family (1660-1945) is placed at the head of the entry, even if it was not held for long.

"PEERS": Dates (1660-1945) when peerages were held provide years of legal access to the Houses of Lords (in London and Dublin - the Scottish Parliament was unicameral but included title holders) and do not mean a seat in the chamber was actually occupied unless direct evidence shows it was not assumed (due, for example, to insanity, religious disqualification, exile, imprisonment, or other known causes). Years served by elected Irish or Scottish Representative Peers in the British House of Lords are included.

"LD LT": The number of family members appointed to serve as Lord Lieutenant of a county after 1660. Until the twentieth century the office retained a considerable amount of power as well as prestige, especially in times of emergency or war. The power to nominate JPs was used to exercise control over the gentry by the magnates.

"CABINET": Dates provided for senior office holders, including Secretaries of State, etc. before the modern Cabinet emerged.

"KG, KT, KP": The number of family members who were holders of the most prestigious orders of knighthood in England and Wales, Scotland and Ireland after 1660: Knight of the Garter, Knight of the Thistle, and Knight of St. Patrick. The "Garter" was of considerable significance. An eighteenth-century magnate could be thrown into a rage and even move into political opposition by being denied one. Nineteenth-century magnates were so enamored of membership in these orders that they could be seen wearing the insignia on their dressing gowns. The Garter was the nation's reward to Winston Churchill for his service in the Second World War.

Brackets

Brackets are used to differentiate members of the English/Welsh Parliament from the Scottish and Irish Parliaments. The dates of service of English and Welsh MPs are not enclosed in brackets.

[dates] = membership in the Scottish Parliament in Edinburgh

{dates} = membership in the Irish Parliament in Dublin or TDs after 1922

Abbreviations

acq.	acquired
add.	addition
BLG	*Burke's Landed Gentry*
BP	*Burke's Peerage*
Bt	Baronet
c.	*circa* or century
CL	*Country Life*
CP	*Complete Peerage*
cr.	creation
d.	died
DNB	*Dictionary of National Biography*
E	England
EI	East India
fl.	flourishing
GB	Great Britain
HP	*History of Parliament*
I	Ireland
IoW	Isle of Wight
inher.	inherited
KC	King's Counsel
KG	Knight of the Order of the Garter
KP	Knight of the Order of St. Patrick
KT	Knight of the Order of the Thistle
Kt	Knight
Kted	Knighted
Ld Lt	Lord Lieutenant
mar.	marriage, married
MP	Member of the House of Commons
NT	National Trust
ODNB	*Oxford Dictionary of National Biography*
pa	*per annum*
PC	Privy Councilor
purch.	purchased
QC	Queen's Counsel
r.	reign
Rep	Representative
RE	Royal Engineers
remod.	remodeled
repurch.	repurchased
RN	Royal Navy

S	Scotland
TD	Member of the Irish *Dáil*
UK	United Kingdom of Great Britain and Ireland
W	Wales
WI	West Indies

Corrections or Additions

Please forward any suggestions for corrections or additions to:
Ellis Wasson ewasson@udel.edu or ewasson@towerhill.org

List of Parliamentary Families

MACARTHUR

Origins: The first two MPs were sons of a Wesleyan minister in Londonderry. Alexander went to Australia for many years as a banker and colonial merchant. Sir William was in banking, insurance, and a merchant, Lord Mayor of London 1880.

1. Sir William MacArthur – Lambeth 1868-85
2. Alexander MacArthur – Leicester 1874-92
3. William MacArthur – St. Austell Div. Cornwall 1887-1908

Estates: No landed estate. Sir William MacArthur left £480,000 in 1887.
Notes: One in ODNB.

MACARTNEY [Ellison] *IRELAND*

Origins: Emigrated from Scotland to Belfast in 1630 where they set up as merchants. A son was a lt. general under the 1 Duke of Marlborough. Sheriff 1690. His brother acquired a large estate. A granddaughter of William Macartney married 1815 Thomas Ellison. Their son took the name Ellison-Macartney. The Ellisons were merchants from Newcastle-upon-Tyne (see Carr Ellison). A younger son went to Ireland c. 1620s.

1. William Macartney – {Belfast 1747-60}
2. Sir John Macartney 1 Bt – {Fore 1792-97 Naas 1798-1800}
3. John Ellison-Macartney – County Tyrone 1874-85
4. William Ellison-Macartney – S. Antrim 1885-1903

Seats: Mountjoy Grange, Antrim (purch. 19th c., resident into 20th c.); Lish, Armagh
Estates: 1439 (I) 1681 in 1878
Title: Baronet 1799-
Notes: Family has been in Australia since the 3 Bt emigrated in the 19th c. One in ODNB.

MCBRIAR (M'Brear) *SCOTLAND*

Origins: The first MP was a burgess in Dumfries and Provost in 1454. **First [MP 1469 for Dumfries]. Three additional [MPs 1504-1630, for Dumfries, the last for Dumfriesshire].**

1. David McBriar – [Dumfriesshire 1646-47 1648-51 Kirkcudbright Stewartry 1661-63]

Seats: Almagill, Dumfriesshire (acq. 1427, forfeited 1746); Netherwood, Dumfriesshire (acq. mid-15th c., forfeited 1746)

MACCARTY *IRELAND*

Earl of Clancarty (1658-91 I)

Origins: Ancient Irish family. "Cormac Oge", Charles MacCarty, was created Viscount Muskerry in 1628. His son was made Earl of Clancarty as a reward for his military service on the royalist side in the Civil War. {**First MP 1634 for County Cork.**} The title was lost through attainder in 1691.

No post-1660 MPs

Seat: Blarney Castle, Cork (built 1446, forfeited 1691)
Estates: Vast estates, forfeited in 1691.
Titles: Baron Blarney and Viscount Muskerry 1628-91; Viscount Mountcashel 1689-90
Peers: {3 peers 1660-65 1662-65 1666-76}
Notes: The 3 Earl was a Roman Catholic monk in France, but conformed to the Protestant faith on sucession to the Earldom and married. His widow married Sir William Davys (see Davys I). Although under age the 4 Earl was summoned to James II's Parliament in 1689 and later went into exile with the Jacobite court. 1 and 4 Earls and 1 Viscount Mountcashel in ODNB.

MCCAUSLAND (M'Auslane) [Hamilton] *IRELAND*

Origins: Came from Scotland to Ireland in the army. Settled in Tyrone. Sheriff 1687. Succeeded to a large property in Londonderry c. 1700.

1. Oliver M'Auslane – {Strabane 1692-93 1695-99 1703-23}
2. John McCausland – {Strabane 1725-29}
3. Oliver McCausland – {Strabane 1729-33}
4. John McCausland – {County Donegal 1768-76}

Seats: Woodbank House, Londonderry (acq. by mar. c. 1700, resident at least until 1935, sold); Drimbawn, Mayo (acq. 19th c., resident 20th c.); Roe Park (Mullagh, Daisy Hill), Londonderry (built early 18th c., acq. 1729, rebuilt 1743, add. c. 1782, sold c. 1800, now hotel); Castlefinn, Donegal (acq. by mar. 1748, sold early 19th c.)
Estates: Owned 898 acres worth £385 in 1870s.
Notes: McCauslands of Drenagh, Londonderry were cousins. Founded by an agent to the famous William Conolly of Castletown, who left him Drenagh in 1729 in his will. In Bateman 17685 (I) 9168. One in ODNB.

Hamilton

Origins: Very little is known about the MP. Sheriff 1683.

1. John Hamilton – {Donegal 1692-93 St. Johnstown 1713-14}

Seat: Castlefinn, Donegal (passed by marriage 1748 to the McCauslands).

MCCULLOCH *SCOTLAND*

Origins: Acquired landed estates in the 14th century. **First [MP 1612 for Kirkcudbrightshire]. An additional [MP 1641 Wigtownshire].**

1. Sir Godfrey McCulloch 2 Bt – [Wigtownshire 1678]

Seat: Myrton Castle, Wigtownshire (built 12th c., acq. by 1330, rebuilt c. 1500, add. early 17th c., abandoned 1697, ruin)
Title: Baronet 1664-97
Notes: The 2 Bt was executed for murdering a neighbor.

MACDONALD *SCOTLAND & ENGLAND*

Baron MacDonald (1776- I)

Origins: Descended from a son of the ancient line of the Lords of the Isles (15th c.). After the main branch died out, this cadet descended from a natural son took the appellation "of the Isles" and "of Sleat". **Summoned to the Parliament at Inverness in 1427.**

1. Sir Archibald MacDonald 1 Bt – Hindon 1777-80 Newcastle-under-Lyme 1780-93
2. Alexander MacDonald 2 Baron MacDonald – Saltash 1796-1802
3. Sir James MacDonald 2 Bt – Tain Burghs 1805-06 Newcastle-under-Lyme 1806-12 Sutherland 1812-16 Calne 1816-31 Hampshire 1831-32

Seats: Armadale Castle, Inverness-shire (built 1650s, rebuilt c. 1790, add. 1815, fire 1855, family abandoned 1925, mostly ruin, museum); Thorpe Hall, Yorkshire (built 1690s, rebuilt early 18th c., add. c. 1750, inher. 1813, add. late 19th c., still own); Gunthwaite Hall, Yorkshire (acq. by Bosvilles later 15th c., passed by mar. to MacDonalds 1813)
Estates: Bateman 132480 (S & E) 16613 and 8949 (E) 8993
Title: Baronet 1625- ; 1813-1919
Peers: {2 peers 1776-1800}
1 Ld Lt 20th

Notes: The Bosvilles of Thorpe and Gunthwaite, whose estates passed to the MacDonalds in 1813, produced an **MP in the Long Parliament**. The MacDonalds of Sleat have an entry in the ODNB.

MCDOUGAL [Brisbane] *SCOTLAND*

McDougal

Origins: The family traced descent from a Norse lord d. 1164. **First [MP 1560]. Two additional [MPs 1597-1625, one kt of the shire].**

1. Henry McDougal – [Roxburghshire 1665 1667 1678 1681]

Seat: Makerstoun (Mackerston), Roxburghshire (acq. c. 1390, destroyed 1545, rebuilt 1590, remod. 1725 and 1828, fire 1970, remod. 1973-74)
Notes: One in ODNB.

Brisbane

Origins: The daughter and heiress of the last McDougal married c. 1700 Sir George Hay of Adderstone. In 1819 a Hay heiress married Thomas Brisbane 1 Bt, who inherited the McDougal estates in 1825 and took the name McDougal. **First [MP 1644].**

1. John Brisbane – [Ayrshire 1704-07]

Seats: Bishopton (Bishoptoun) House, Renfrewshire (acq. 15th c., sold 1671, institutional use); Brisbane House (Kelso-land), Ayrshire (built 1636, purch. 1671, demolished c. 1920)

MCKAY (Mackay) *SCOTLAND*

Baron Reay (1628- S)

Origins: Emerged as lairds in the 13th century. Baron 1628.

1. George McKay – Sutherlandshire 1747-61
2. Alexander McKay – Sutherland 1761-68

Seats: House of Tongue, Sutherlandshire (acq. and built 16th c., add. 1620s, rebuilt 1678, add. 1750, add. 1841, sold 19th c.); Balnakeil House, Sutherlandshire (medieval house, acq. 16th c., rebuilt 1720s-44, sold 19th c.); Carolside, Berwickshire (built c. 1800, acq. by mar. mid-19th c., sold early 20th c.)

Estates: Bateman 15321 (S) 12470. Sold estates (perhaps 150,000 acres) worth £300,000 to the Duke of Sutherland in 1828 and even after that were still heavily indebted. (Richards, *Leviathan of Wealth*, 290)
Title: Baron Reay 1881-1921 UK
Peers: [2 peers 1660-80 1699-1707] 1 Scottish Rep peer 1806-07 1835-47 1 peer 1881-1921
1 Ld Lt 19th-20th
1 KT 20th
Notes: Deep financial difficulties in the 19th century. The 10 Baron lived in the Netherlands and was a government minister there (d. 1876). The 11 Baron returned to the UK. 1, 2, and 11 Barons in ODNB.

MACKAY

Earl of Inchcape (1929- UK)

Origins: The 1 Earl was the son of a small ship captain, apprenticed to a ropemaker, and then a clerk in London. Later in business in India. Became shipowners.

No MPs

Seats: Glenapp Castle, Ayrshire (built 1870, purch. 1917, add. 1922-24, sold 1982, still own estate); Carlock House, Ayrshire; Chinthurst Hill, Surrey (built 1893, purch. 1937, sold 1953)
Estates: 1 Earl left £552,000 in 1932 and the 3 Earl three million in 1994. Owned 14,000 acres in 1996.
Titles: Baron Inchcape 1911- UK; Viscount Inchcape 1924- UK
Peers: 3 peers 1911-45
Notes: 1 and 3 Earls in ODNB.

MACKENZIE [Fraser] *SCOTLAND*

Earl of Seaforth (1623-1716 S; 1771-81 I)

Origins: The family descended from Colin Mackenzie of Kintail (d. 1278). The 1 Baron (Earls of Seaforth) was the 12th chief of the clan. From his brother descended the Earls of Cromartie and the Mackenzies of Scatwell. From a third brother, Alexander of Coul, descended most of the other cadet lines. The Earldom was attainted in 1715 and estates confiscated, but the land was repurchased in the 1740s. The daughter of the 1 Baron Seaforth (d. 1815) married James Stewart, a grandson of the 6 Earl of Galloway and continued to be seated at Brahan Castle. He took the additional name Mackenzie and one of his descendents was created Baron Seaforth in 1921.

1. John Mackenzie – [Fortrose 1703-04]
2. Kenneth Mackenzie Lord Fortrose (but for attainder 6 Earl of Seaforth) – Inverness Burghs 1741-47 Ross-shire 1747-61
3. Kenneth Mackenzie 1 Earl of Seaforth – Caithness 1768-74
4. Francis Mackenzie 1 Baron Seaforth – Ross-shire 1784-90 1794-96
5. William Mackenzie – Ross-shire 1812-14

Seats: Seaforth, Ross-shire; Brahan Castle, Ross-shire (built 1611, forfeited 1716, repurch., passed to Stewart Mackenzies 1815, requisitioned WWII, demolished 1951, stables converted into a house, but main line of the family extinct and it is held by a trust)
Estates: Bateman 8051 (S) 7905. At one time the Earls owned the island of Lewis.
Titles: Baron Mackenzie 1609-1716 S; Viscount Fortrose 1766-81 I; Baron Seaforth 1797-1815 GB; Baron Seaforth 1921-23 UK
Peers: [1 peer 1660-78] 2 peers 1797-1815 1921-23
1 Ld Lt 18th-19th
1 KT 17th
Notes: Mackenzie family and 1, 2, 3, 4 and 5 Earls of first cr., 1 Baron (1797) and three others in ODNB.

Mackenzie

Origins: Cadet line of the Earls of Seaforth.

1. John Mackenzie – Tain Burghs 1806-08 Sutherland 1808-09

Seat: Suddie, Ross-shire

Mackenzie

Origins: Cadet of the Earls of Seaforth.

1. Sir Roderick Mackenzie – [Dingwall 1672-74 Ross-shire 1678 1681]

Seat: Findon, Ross-shire

Mackenzie

Origins: Cadet of the Earls of Seaforth.

1. John Mackenzie – [Ross-shire 1665]

Seat: Inverlaul, Ross-shire

Mackenzie

Origins: Cadet of the Earls of Seaforth. **First [MP 1598]. One additional [MP 1640-41].**

1. Thomas Mackenzie – [Elgin & Forfarshire 1645 1661-63]

Seats: Kintail, Inverness-shire; Pluscardine, Elginshire; Lochslin, Inverness-shire

Earl of Cromartie (1702-46 S 1861- UK)

Origins: See Earl of Seaforth above. **First [MP 1628, Inverness-shire]**. First Earl was a highly successful lawyer. The Earldom was attainted in 1746. The estates were restored in 1784. The daughter of the last Earl succeeded to the estates in 1796. She married the 6 Baron Elibank. Their daughter married the brother of the 7 Marquis of Tweeddale (see Hay). Their son took the name Hay-Mackenzie. The Earldom was revived by Queen Victoria in 1861 for his daughter, the Countess of Stafford, in her own right. Her younger son, and then his daughter, succeeded to the title (see Leveson Gower).

1. George Mackenzie 1 Earl of Cromatie – [Ross-shire 1661-63 1678 1681]
2. Sir Kenneth Mackenzie 1 Bt – [Cromartyshire 1693-1702 1703-07]
3. Sir Roderick Mackenzie – [Cromartyshire 1700-02 Fortrose Burgh 1705-07]
4. Sir Kenneth Mackenzie 3 Bt – Scotland 1707-08 Cromartyshire 1710-13 1727-28
5. Sir George Mackenzie 4 Bt – Cromartyshire 1729-34
6. John Mackenzie Lord MacLeod – Ross-shire 1780-84

Seats: Cromarty House (Castle), Cromartyshire (built 1470, add. 1632, acq. by 1680s, sold 1741, castle demolished 1772); Castle Leod, Ross-shire (acq. and built 1605-16, add. 1854, add. 1914, still own); Tarbat House, Ross-shire (castle, rebuilt c. 1690, rebuilt 1787, sold 1962, house ruinous from 1980s); Ballone Castle, Ross-shire (built late 16th c., abandoned late 17th c., ruin); Caroline Park House (House of Royston), Edinburghshire (acq. and built 1685, add. 1696, sold 1739, flats)
Estates: See Leveson Gower (Cromartie share 149,999 (S) 56937)
Titles: Viscount Tarbat 1685-1746 S; Baron MacLeod and Viscount Tarbat 1861- UK; Baronet 1628-1746; 1704-46
Peer: [1 peer 1685-1707] 1 peer 1888-93
1 in Cabinet 1702-04
Notes: The 2 Earl was a Roman Catholic and Jacobite. 1 and 3 Earls of 1st cr. in ODNB.

Mackenzie

Origins: Descended from the uncle of the 1 Earl of Cromartie. Successful lawyer in the Restoration period purchased estates. Succeeded in the 19th century to the Suddie estates (see above).

1. Sir Kenneth Mackenzie 1 Bt – [Ross-shire 1703-07]
2. Sir James Mackenzie 5 Bt – Ross-shire 1822-31

Seats: Scatwell, Ross-shire (sold c. 1850); Rosehaugh House, Ross-shire (castle, acq. 1660s, rebuilt 1790s, sold 1864, demolished 1959)
Title: Baronet 1703-
1 Ld Lt 19th
Notes: In financial difficulties in the mid-19th century. One in ODNB.

Mackenzie-Fraser

Origins: Descended from the Coul line (see Earl of Seaforth above). Colin Mackenzie 6th of Kilcoy married Martha Fraser of Castle Fraser. Their younger son succeeded to the Fraser estates and took the additional name Fraser (see Fraser II).

1. Alexander Mackenzie-Fraser – Cromartyshire 1802-06 Ross-shire 1806-09
2. Charles Mackenzie-Fraser – Ross-shire 1814-18

Seats: Castle Fraser, Aberdeenshire (built 1575-1636, remod. late 18th c. and mid-19th c., sold 1921); Inverallochy Castle, Aberdeenshire (medieval, rebuilt early 16th c., acq. 1666, passed out of the family 1792, ruin)
Estates: Bateman 4247 (S) 3697; at Kilcoy Castle 24658 (S) 7257 (built c. 1620, ruin by 1890, restored c. 1900); at Mountgerald House, Ross-shire 5804 (S) 4022
Notes: Male line extinct 1897. One of Kilcoy line in ODNB.

Mackenzie

Origins: Cadet line. See above, Earl of Seaforth.

1. Sir Alexander Mackenzie 2 Bt – [Ross-shire 1693-1701]

Seat: Coul House, Ross-shire (castle, ruin by mid-18th c., rebuilt mid-18th c., rebuilt 1819-21, add. 1860, now a hotel)
Estates: Bateman 43189 (S) 5214
Title: Baronet 1673-1715
Notes: One in ODNB.

Baron Muir Mackenzie (1915-30 UK)

Origins: Cadet of the Coul line.

No MPs

Seat: Delvine (Dalvine), Perthshire (demolished)
Estates: Bateman 4241 (S) 6419
Title: Baronet 1805-1930
Peer: 1 peer 1915-30
Notes: The father of the 1 Bt succeeded to Delvine by inheritance from a maternal uncle. 1 Baron in ODNB.

Mackenzie

Origins: A cadet of the 1st chief of Kintail.

1. Sir Kenneth Mackenzie 1 Bt – [Ross-shire 1703]

Seats: Flowerdale (Gairloch) House, Ross-shire (acq. 15th c., rebuilt 1738, add. 1904, still own); Conon House, Ross-shire (built 1790-99, add. c. 1805)
Estates: Bateman 164680 (S) 9344. Owned 56,900 acres in 1996.
Title: Baronet 1703-
3 Lds Lt 19th, 20th
Notes: Three in ODNB.

Mackenzie

Origins: Cadet of Gairloch line, see above.

1. William Mackenzie – Peeblesshire 1837-52 Liverpool 1852

Seat: Portmore House, Peeblesshire (built 1850, fire 1883, rebuilt 1884, restored 1982)
Estates: Bateman 9685 (S) 4859

Mackenzie

Origins: Cadet of the Earl of Cromartie in the 16th century. The MP below married the heiress of Lord Lovat (see Fraser II). His son succeeded as Lord Lovat but died in 1730 without an heir.

1. Alexander Mackenzie – Inverness-shire 1710-15

Seat: Fraserdale, Inverness-shire

Mackenzie

Origins: Cadet of Fraser of Rosehaugh (see above) 17th century.

1. Sir George Mackenzie – [Ross-shire 1669-74 Forfarshire 1689 1689-90]
2. George Mackenzie – [Ross-shire 1705-07]
3. George Mackenzie – Inverness Burghs 1710-13

Seat: Inchcoulter, Ross-shire
Notes: The last MP died in debt. The estate passed in 1790 to a granddaughter whose widower sold it. One in ODNB.

MACKIE (Mackye) *SCOTLAND*

Mackie

Origins: An old Galloway family. Acquired Larg during the time of Robert Bruce. **First [MP 1628].**

1. Alexander Mackie – [Kirkcudbright Stewartry 1705-07]
2. John Mackye – Linlithgow Burghs 1742-47 Kirkcudbright Stewartry 1747-68

Seats: Larg, Kirkcudbrightshire; Palgown, Kirkcudbrightshire

Mackie

Origins: Cadets of the Mackies of Larg.

1. John Mackie – Kirkcudbrightshire 1850-57
2. James Mackie – Kirkcudbrightshire 1857-68
3. John Mackie – Galloway Div. Kirkcudbrightshire and Wigtownshire 1931-58

Seats: Bargaly, Kirkcudbrightshire; Ernespie Castle, Kirkcudbrightshire; Auchencairn House, Kirkcudbrightshire (built late 18th c., purch. and add. c. 1860, sold later 19th c.)
Estates: Bateman 10850 (S) 2532 and 4167 (S) 4794

MACKINNON

Mackinnon

Origins: Ancient Scottish clan. The 30th Chief went to Antigua and acquired wealth in the 18th century. Ancestral lands were then repurchased. The first MP below succeeded as 33rd Chief of the clan in 1809.

1. William A. Mackinnon – Dunwich 1819-20 Lymington 1831-32 1835-52 Rye 1853-65
2. William A. Mackinnon – Rye 1852-53 Lymington 1857-68
3. Lauchlan Mackinnon – Rye 1865-68

Seats: Acryse (Acrise) Park (Place), Kent (built 16th c., remod. 18th c., purch. 1861, sold 1911); Newton (Newtown) Park, Hampshire (built 1792); Portswood House, Hampshire (built c. 1772, purch. c. 1800, demolished by 1860)
Estates: Bateman 5746 (E) 6474
Notes: Three in ODNB.

Mackinnon

Origins: An East India Company official. His pedigree was not recorded but the clan Chief was this MP's executor.

1. Charles Mackinnon – Ipswich 1827-31

MACKWORTH [Backwell, Dolben Praed, Tyringham] *ENGLAND & WALES*

Mackworth

Origins: An old Rutland family first mentioned in the 13th century. Involved in smelting ventures in South Wales with cousins. **First MP 1424 for Derbyshire**. Granted arms 1430s.

1. Sir Thomas Mackworth 3 Bt – Rutland 1679-81 1685-87 1689-94
2. Sir Thomas Mackworth 4 Bt – Rutland 1694-95 1701-08 Portsmouth 1713-15 Rutland 1721-27

Seats: Normanton Hall, Rutland (acq. by mar. 15th c., sold 1729); Mackworth Castle, Derbyshire (built 14th c., rebuilt 15th c., sold 1655)
Title: Baronet 1619-1803
Notes: Ruined by election expenses in 1727. The last Bt died in poverty. One in ODNB.

Mackworth

Origins: A cadet line in Shropshire. **First MP 1646. Two additional MPs 1654-59.** Acquired wealth from exploiting collieries and copper smelting works by marriage 1686 to the heiress to Gnoll Castle.

1. Sir Humphrey Mackworth – Cardiganshire 1701-05 Totnes 1705-08 Cardiganshire 1710-13
2. Herbert Mackworth – Cardiff Boroughs 1739-65
3. Sir Herbert Mackworth 1 Bt – Cardiff Boroughs 1766-90

Seats: Gnoll Castle, Glamorganshire (built early 17th c., acq. by mar. 1696, rebuilt as Gnoll House 1776-78, demolished 1956); Bretton Grange, Shropshire (acq. 16th c., held into 18th c.); Pencrug House, Monmouthshire; Buntingsdale Hall, Shropshire (acq. 1501, built 1719-25, sold mid-18th c., derelict, repurch. by Mackworths 1991)
Estates: Bateman 3203 (W) 3649
Title: Baronet 1776-
Notes: The 2 Bt left his estates to his wife, who married a Hanbury of Pontypool (see Hanbury). Two in ODNB.

Mackworth-Praed

Origins: A younger son of Sir Humphrey Mackworth MP (above) took the name Praed on his adoption as part of a financial deal by John Praed of Trevethoe in 1715. The Praeds became gentry later 16th century. High Sheriff 1653. Sir Humphrey paid Praed's debts and gave Praed an annuity for life in exchange for the reversion of the Trevethoe estate and parliamentary interest in St. Ives. Became involved in banking in the 18th century (bought out by Lloyd's 1891).

1. James Praed – St. Ives 1660-79
2. James Praed – St. Ives 1681 1689-1705
3. John Praed – St. Ives 1708-13
4. William Mackworth Praed – St. Ives 1734-41
5. Humphrey Mackworth-Praed – St. Ives 1761-68 Cornwall 1772-74
6. William Mackworth-Praed – St. Ives 1774-75 1780-1806 Banbury 1806-08
7. Winthrop Mackworth-Praed – St. Germans 1830-32 Great Yarmouth 1835-37 Aylesbury 1837-39
8. James Backwell Praed – Buckinghamshire 1835-37
9. William Tyringham Praed – St. Ives 1838-46
10. Charles Tyringham Praed – St. Ives 1874-80

Seats: Trevethoe, Cornwall (acq. by Praeds early 17th c., passed to Mackworths 1715, rebuilt 19th c., resident in 19th c.); Tyringham Hall, Buckinghamshire (medieval, acq. by mar. 1778, new house, built 1792-97, sold 19th c.)
Estates: Bateman 7757 (E) 14941
Note: One in ODNB.

Mackworth Praed

Origins: A cadet line descended from a younger son of the banker William Mackworth Praed. Sir Herbert was also a banker.

1. Sir Herbert Mackworth Praed 1 Bt – Colchester 1874-80

Seat: Ousden (Owsden) Hall, Suffolk (built later 16th c., add. 1760, add. mid-19th c., purch. 1863/4 for £85,000 – Roberts, *Lost Country Houses of Suffolk*, 116 – sold 1954, demolished 1955)
Estates: Bateman 2198 (E) 3055
Title: Baronet 1905-20

Tyringham Backwell

Origins: The Tyringhams held the manor of that name from the reign of King John. **First MP 1295 for Buckinghamshire. Four further MPs 1386-1614, one for the county**. The daughter and heiress of Sir William Tyringham married in 1678 John Backwell. The Backwells were naval victuallers in the mid-17th century and then bankers. The grandson of William Mackworth Praed (MP 1734-41) married Elizabeth Tyringham daughter of Barnaby Backwell (MP 1754) and heiress of her brother Tyringham Backwell of Tyringham.

1. Sir William Tyringham – Buckinghamshire 1660-79
2. Edward Backwell – Wendover 1673-81
3. John Backwell – Wendover 1685-87 1690-1701
4. Barnaby Backwell – Bishop's Castle 1754

Seat: Tyringham, Buckinghamshire (acq. 1165 by Tyringhams, acq. by mar. by Backwells 1678, passed by mar. to Backwell heiress to Praeds 1778)
Notes: One Backwell in ODNB.

Dolben

The founder was Archbishop of York (d. 1686). His son, 1 Bt, was a lawyer. The daughter and heiress of the last Bt married 1835 William Mackworth, son of Sir Digby Mackworth 3 Bt, who took the additional name Dolben.

1. Sir Gilbert Dolben 1 Bt – Ripon 1685-87 Peterborough 1689-98 1701-10 Yarmouth (IoW) 1710-15
2. John Dolben – Liskeard 1707-10
3. Sir William Dolben 3 Bt – Oxford University 1768 1780-1806 Northamptonshire 1768-74

Seat: Finedon Hall, Northamptonshire (acq. by mar. 1682, built c. 1700, passed by mar. to Mackworths 1835, built c. 1851-59, sold 1912, flats)
Title: Baronet 1704-1837
Notes: 1 and 2 Bts and four others in ODNB.

MCLAREN [Pochin] *SCOTLAND, ENGLAND, & WALES*

Baron Aberconway (1911- UK)

Origins: The founder was the son of a farmer. Duncan McLaren was apprenticed to a draper in 1812 and became a successful merchant, Provost of Edinburgh, and MP 1865. The 1 Baron married an industrial heiress, and he ran the company after his father in law's death in 1895.

1. Duncan McLaren – Edinburgh 1865-81
2. John McLaren – Wigtown District 1880 Edinburgh 1881
3. Charles McLaren 1 Baron Aberconway – Stafford 1880-86 Bosworth 1892-1910
4. Walter McLaren – Crewe Div. Cheshire 1886-95 1910-12
5. Henry McLaren 2 Baron Aberconway – W. Staffordshire 1906-10 Bosworth 1910-22
6. Francis McLaren – Spalding Div. Lincolnshire 1910-17
7. Martin McLaren – Bristol N. W. 1959-66 1970-74

Seat: Bodnant, Denbighshire (acq. by mar. 1895, NT 1949)
Estates: Family worth at least three-quarters of a million pounds in the 1930s. One of the 2 Baron's children left 52 million pounds in 2008. Owned 6,700 acres in 2001.
Title: Baronet 1902-
Peers: 2 peers 1911-45
Notes: 1 and 2 Barons and four others in ODNB.

Pochin

Origins: The first MP was the son of a famer. He became a manufacturing chemist and manufacturer. He left his company and landed property to his daughter who married the 1 Baron Aberconway.

1. Henry Davis Pochin – Stafford 1868

Seat: Bodnant, Denbighshire (purch. 1874, remod. 1876, passed to McLarens 1895)

MACLEOD *SCOTLAND*

MacLeod

Origins: MacLeod of MacLeod. The family is of very ancient descent probably stretching back to the 800s. Sons of the Kings of Man in the 13th century. Clan chiefs from the mid-13th century. **First [MP 1640 for Inverness-shire].**

1. John McLeod – [Inverness-shire 1678 1681]
2. Norman McLeod – Inverness-shire 1741-54
3. Norman McLeod – Inverness-shire 1790-96
4. John McLeod – Sudbury 1828-30

Seat: Dunvegan Castle, Inverness-shire (acq. and built c.1200, add. 1623, 1684-90, and 1790, remod. 1810-15 and 1840-50, fire 1938, rebuilt 1940, still own)
Estates: Bateman 141679 (S) 8464. Owned 30,600 acres in 1996.
Notes: Dunvegan is the oldest inhabited castle in Scotland, The family finances were rocky in the 18th century. Norman McLeod MP 1790-96 worked for the East India Company and returned to Scotland in 1790 with £100,000, although the estates remained indebted. Four in ODNB.

MacLeod

Origins: A cadet line from the 14th century.

1. Aeneas MacLeod – [Cromartyshire 1703-07]
2. Robert MacLeod – Cromarty 1807-12
3. Roderick MacLeod – Cromarty 1818-20 Sutherland 1831-37 Inverness Burghs 1837-40

Seats: Cadboll Castle (House), Cromartyshire (built 16th c., ruin, new house built c. 1700, add. later); Invergordon Castle, Cromartyshire (medieval castle, fire early 19th c., rebuilt 1873, purch. later 19th c., demolished 1928)
Estates: Bateman 11827 (S) 10761
2 Lds Lt 18th, 19th
Notes: One in ODNB.

MCCLINTOCK [Bunbury] *IRELAND*

Baron Rathdonnell (1868- I)

Origins: Came from Scotland to Ireland in the late 16th century and purchased estates in Donegal 1597.

1. John McClintock – {Enniskillin 1783-90 Belturbet 1790-97}
2. John McClintock – Athlone 1820 County Louth 1830-31
3. William McClintock-Bunbury – County Carlow 1846-62
4. John McClintock 1 Baron Rathdonnell – County Louth 1857-59

Seats: Drumcar House, Louth (acq. early 18th c., built 1777-78, add. 19th c., family depart 20th c., monastery); Lisnavagh, Carlow (built 1847, acq. by mar. 1874 and became principal seat, reduced in size 1953, still own); Moyle, Carlow (passed by mar. of 1797 to McClintocks from Bunburys 1874); Seskinore Lodge, Tyrone (built 1834, acq. by mar. before 1860, new house 1862, resident into 20th c.)
Estates: Bateman 19923 (I) 15400
Peers: 1 Irish Rep peer 1889-1929
2 Lds Lt 19th, 20th

Bunbury

Origins: Thomas Bunbury settled in County Carlow in the early 18th century. First MP was a Clerk of the Court of Chancery. Sheriff 1769. John McClintock married 1797 the daughter of William Bunbury of Moyle. On the death of Kane Bunbury in 1874 the estates passed to his grandnephew John McClintock of Drumcar.

1. Walter Bunbury – {Clomines 1703-13}
2. William Bunbury – {County Carlow 1776-88}
3. George Bunbury – {Thomastown 1786-97 Gowran 1797-1800}
4. Thomas Bunbury – County Carlow 1841-46

Seats: Moyle, Carlow (acq. early 18th c., passed by mar. to McClintocks 1874); Lisnavagh, Carlow (acq. early 18th c., rebuilt 1847, passed by mar. to McClintocks 1874)
Notes: One in ODNB.

MACNAGHTEN *IRELAND*

Origins: To Ireland from Scotland in the 1570s. The father of the first MP was manager of the Marquess of Hertford's Irish estates. Sheriff 1793. The 1 Bt was a judge in Madras. Nabob fortune.

1. Edmund MacNaghten – County Antrim {1797-1800} 1801-12 Orford 1812-26 County Antrim 1826-30
2. Sir Edmund MacNaghten 2 Bt – County Antrim 1847-52
3. Sir Edward MacNaghten 3 Bt – County Antrim 1880-85 N. Antrim 1885-87
4. Sir Malcolm MacNaghten – N. Londonderry 1922 County Londonderry 1922-28

Seats: Dunderave (Dundarave)(Bushmills House), Antrim (purch. and built c. 1808, rebuilt 1847, for sale 2014); Runkerry, Antrim (built 1883, now institutional use); Roe Park (Daisy Hill), Antrim (built c. 1744, add. 1782, purch. and add. 1826, remod. later 19th c., sold early 20th c.); Beardiville, Antrim (acq. 1709, built c. 1710, remod. mid-18th c., sold 1845)
Estates: Bateman 8281 (I) 8937 (still owned 550 acres in Antrim in 2014)
Titles: Baronet 1836- ; 1840-41
1 Ld Lt 19th
Notes: The 3 Bt served as a judge in the House of Lords as Lord MacNaghten. One of the younger sons of the 1 Bt was Chairman of the East India Company. 1 and 3 Bts and one other in ODNB.

MACNAMARA *IRELAND*

Origins: Old native Irish, hereditary marshals of Thomond; head of the family The Macnamara Fionn. This branch emerged in the 17th century. The first at Doolen was born 1714. He married the daughter and heiress of Francis Sarsfield of Doolen.

1. Francis MacNamara – {Ardee 1776-83 County Clare 1790-97 Killybegs 1798-1800}
2. William MacNamara – County Clare 1830-52
3. Francis MacNamara – Ennis 1832-35

Seats: Doolen (Doolin) Castle, Clare (acq. by mar. 18th c., built 1778, burned early 1920s); Knoppogue (Knappogue) Castle, Clare (tower house built 1467, sold 1800); Moyriesk (Mooreask), Clare (acq. 16th c., built mid-18th c., sold late 18th c.); Ennistymon House, Clare (acq. by mar. from O'Briens 18th c., add. 19th c., sold c. 1945, hotel)
Estates: Bateman 15246 (I) 6932

MADOCKS *WALES*

Origins: Sheriff 17th c. The first MP was a rich barrister earning £3,800 a year in fees in the 1780s.

1. John Madocks – Westbury 1786-90
2. William Madocks – Boston 1802-20 Chippenham 1820-26
3. John Madocks – Denbigh Boroughs 1832-34

Seats: Tan-yr-allt, Caernarvonshire (purch. 1798, sold c. 1828); Dolmelynllyn, Merionethshire (purch. c. 1790, sold c. 1830); Vron Iw (Fron Yw), Denbighshire (resident 17th - 19th c., sold); Mount Mascal (and Vale Mascal), Kent (purch. 1782, sold c. 1806, demolished 1957); Llay Hall (Place), Denbighshire (owned in 18th c., sold early 20th c.); Glan-y-wern (Glanywern) Hall, Denbighshire (built 18th c., purch. c. 1800, remod. and add. 1810, sold mid-19th c., institutional use); Tregunter Hall, Breconshire (acq. by mar. 1818, passed out of family 1828)
Notes: One in ODNB.

MAHER *IRELAND*

Origins: Emerged 18th century. Business wealth in Cashel (flower mills). Sheriff 1853.

1. John Maher – County Wexford 1835-41
2. Valentine Maher – County Tipperary 1841-44
3. Nicholas Maher – County Tipperary 1844-52

Seats: Ballinkeele, Wexford (built 18th c., purch. 1825, rebuilt c. 1840, still own); Turtulla, Tipperary (purch. by 1837, sold c. 1871); Tullamaine Castle, Tipperary (purch. by 1837, sold 1871)
Estates: Bateman 6559 (I) 4477. In addition 4,452 acres in Tipperary sold 1856-71.

MAINWARING (Maynwaring) *ENGLAND & WALES*

<u>Mainwaring</u>

Origins: The family held Over Peover from the 12th century and possibly the 11th. **First MP 1553. Two additional MPs 1559-1621, one for Shropshire.**

1. Sir Philip Mainwaring – Boroughbridge 1624 1625 1626 Derby 1628 Morpeth 1640 Newton 1661
2. Sir Thomas Mainwaring 1 Bt – Cheshire 1660
3. Sir John Mainwaring 2 Bt – Cheshire 1689-1702

Seats: Peaover Hall (Over Peover), Cheshire (acq. by early 12th c., new hall built 1585, remod. 1760s, sold 1919, partially demolished c. 1965); Baddiley Hall, Cheshire (medieval? or 16th c., sold 1797); Kermincham Hall, Cheshire (built 1718, demolished c. 1860)
Estates: Worth £1,000 pa in 1660. Estate worth c. £25,000 in 1689. Peover estate consisted of 1,700 acres in 1919.
Titles: Baronet 1660-1797; 1804-1934
Notes: On the death of the 4 Bt in 1797, the estates passed to his step-brother Thomas Wetenhall, who took the name Mainwaring and a new Btcy was granted in 1804. Family died out in male line 1934. 1 Bt and two others in ODNB.

Mainwaring

Origins: Descended from a younger son of Sir John Mainwaring of Over Peover who established a cadet line by a fortunate marriage in the 15th century. **First MP 1572. Three further MPs 1601-26.** Several branches of this line were seated at Whitmore, Bwlchyberdy, and Oteley Park.

1. Edward Mainwaring – Newcastle-under-Lyme 1625 1661-74
2. Edward Mainwaring – Newcastle-under-Lyme 1685-87
3. George Mainwaring – Chester 1689-90
4. Arthur Mainwaring – Preston 1706-10 West Looe 1710-12
5. Townshend Mainwaring – Denbigh Boroughs 1841-47 1857-68

Seats: Oteley Park, Shropshire (Knyastons acq. by mar. from the Oteleys in the 16th c., the Mainwarings inher. by mar. from the Knyastons in 1781, rebuilt 1826-30, demolished 1959); Galltfaenan Hall, Denbighshire (built early 16th c., remod. c. 1810, acq. by mar. mid-19th c., remod. 1860s, sold 1926, institutional use); Bromborough Court, Cheshire (built c. 1680, purch. mid-18th c., demolished 1969); Whitmore Hall, Staffordshire (held since 12th c. by Whitmores, acq. by mar. to heiress 1546, rebuilt early 17th c., rebuilt 1670s, still own); Ightfield Hall, Shropshire (acq. and built mid 15th c., add. 1579, sold 1707); Bwlchyberdy, Denbighshire
Estates: Bateman 5706 (E & W) 9203; 10685 (W) 4327; 2666 (E) 4053
Notes: 34 generations by descent have lived at Whitmore. Four in ODNB.

MAITLAND I [Gibson, Ramsay] *SCOTLAND*

Duke of Lauderdale (1672-82 S)

Origins: Settled in Berwickshire in the late 12th century. Secretary of State 1560, Lord of Session 1561, Privy Seal 1567 and other high posts led to peerages. Baron 1590.

1. Charles Maitland 3 Earl of Lauderdale – [Edinburghshire 1669-70]
2. Richard Maitland 4 Earl of Lauderdale – [Edinburghshire 1678]
3. John Maitland 5 Earl of Lauderdale – [Edinburghshire 1685-86 1689-95]
4. Alexander Maitland – Scotland 1707-08
5. John Maitland – Haddington Burghs 1774-79
6. James Maitland 8 Earl of Lauderdale – Newport 1780-84 Malmesbury 1784-89
7. Sir Thomas Maitland – Haddington Burghs 1790-96 1802-05 1812-13
8. James Maitland 9 Earl of Lauderdale – Camelford 1806-07 Richmond 1818-20 Appleby 1826-32
9. Anthony Maitland 10 Earl of Lauderdale – Haddington Burghs 1813-18 Berwickshire 1826-32
10. Patrick Maitland 17 Earl of Lauderdale – Lanark Div. Lanarkshire 1951-59
11. Lady Olga Maitland – Sutton & Cheam 1992-97

Seats: Thirlestane Castle, Berwickshire (acq. some land mid-13th c., purch site 1563, rebuilt 1670-77, remod. 1840-41, given to charitable foundation 1984); Haltoun (Hatton House), Edinburghshire (medieval keep, rebuilt c. 1515, acq. by mar. 1653 and rebuilt 1664-92, sold 1792, fire 1952, demolished 1955); Lethington Hall (Castle) (aka Lennoxlove), Haddingtonshire (acq. 1345, built 14th and 15th c., add. 17th c., sold 1703); Brunstane House (Gilberton), Edinburghshire (built 1565, acq. by mar. 1593, remod. c. 1639, add. 1672, passed to Dukes of Argyll by mar. early 18th c.)
Estates: Bateman 25512 (S) 17318. Rubinstein - Sir Alexander Maitland 1 Bt left £120,000 in probate in 1820.
Titles: Baron Maitland 1590- S; Viscount Lauderdale 1616- S; Earl of Lauderdale 1624- S; Earl of Guildford 1674-82 E; Baron Lauderdale 1806-63 UK; Baronet 1680-
Peers: [4 peers 1660-1707] 7 Scottish Rep peers 1741-44 1747-61 1784-84 1790-96 1867-78 1889-1920 1920-31 4 peers 1664-82 1806-63
2 Lds Lt 19th, 20th
1 in Cabinet 1661-80
1 KG 17th
1 KT 19th
Notes: The 3 Earl of Lauderdale married in 1652 the daughter and heiress of Richard Lauder of Haltoun. That family was represented in Parliament [**first in 1504 and two additional members 1560-1621.**] 1 Baron and 3, 4, 5, 8, 10, and 11 Earls and 1 Duke and seven others in ODNB.

Ramsay-Gibson-Maitland

Origins: The 1 Baronet was the fifth son of the 6 Earl of Lauderdale.

1. Sir Alexander Ramsay-Gibson-Maitland 3 Bt – Edinburghshire 1868-73

2. Sir Arthur Ramsay-Steel-Maitland 1 Bt – Birmingham East 1910-18 Birmingham Erdington 1918-29 Tamworth 1929-35

Seats: Clifton Hall, Edinburghshire (old house, acq. by inher. 1786, rebuilt 1850, sold 1930); Barnton House (Kings Cramond), Edinburghshire (built c. 1640, Ramsays purch. c. 1780, add. 1794, remod. 1810, passed to Maitlands in 19th c., demolished c. 1920); Rose Hill, Hertfordshire; Sauchie, Stirlingshire (Ramsay estate, passed to Maitlands in the 19th c.)
Estates: Bateman 10228 (S) 20657
Title: Baronet 1818- ; 1918-65
1 in Cabinet 1924-29
Notes: Arthur Drummond-Steel married the heiress of the 4th Ramsay-Gibson-Maitland Bt in 1901, took the name Maitland, and succeeded to the family estates. 1 Bt sec. cr. and one other in ODNB.

MAITLAND II [Fuller] *ENGLAND & WALES*

Origins: Began as Presbyterian ministers in Scotland. Then merchants in London in the 18th century. The first MP was a wholesale clothier and Director of the Bank of England. Ebenezer Maitland MP succeeded in 1810 to a £500,000 banking fortune via marriage to a Fuller heiress in 1800. He took the additional name Fuller. He purchased Stansted Hall. High Sheriff 1825. A younger brother succeeded to Loughton Hall by inheritance from the Whitakers. The 20th century MP descended from that line.

1. John Maitland – Chippenham 1803-12 1817-18
2. Ebenezer Fuller-Maitland – Lostwithiel 1807-12 Wallingford 1812-20 Chippenham 1826-30
3. William Fuller-Maitland – Breconshire 1875-95
4. Sir John Whitaker Maitland – Horncastle 1945-66

Seats: Stansted (Stansted Mountfitchet) Hall, Essex (built c. 1625, purch. c. 1808, rebuilt 1875-76, sold 1923); Shinfield Park, Berkshire (purch. 1810, sold 1939); Woodford Hall, Essex (purch. c. 1801, demolished 1900); Loughton Hall, Essex (built early 16th c., add. early 17th c., purch. by Whitakers in 1745, Maitlands inher. 1825, fire 1836, rebuilt 1878, sold 1919, derelict); Garth House, Breconshire (purch. c. 1830)
Estates: Bateman 7645 (E & W) 6622
Notes: Two in ODNB.

MALCOLM *SCOTLAND & ENGLAND*

Baron Malcolm (1896-1902 UK)

Origins: Lairds at Poltalloch from 1562. The 11th laird was a West Indian merchant in the later 18th and early 19th centuries. He acquired a large plantation in Jamaica. Used West Indian wealth to expand estates in Argyllshire.

1. Neill Malcolm – Boston 1826-31
2. John Malcolm 1 Baron Malcolm – Boston 1860-78 Argyllshire 1886-92
3. Sir Ian Malcolm – Stowmarket Div. Suffolk 1895-1906 Croydon 1910-18 S. Croydon 1918-19

Seats: Poltalloch, Argyllshire (acq. 1562, built 1849-53, dismantled 1957); Duntrune (Duntroon) Castle, Argyllshire (built 15th c., add. c. 1600, rebuilt late 18th c., purch. 1792, rebuilt 1833-35, renovated 1954, still own)
Estates: Bateman 85611 (S & E) 24989. Rubinstein – Neil Malcolm left £500,000 in probate in 1837. Sold a large operation in South Australia in 1873 for £175,000.
Peer: 1 peer 1896-1902
Notes: Two in ODNB.

MALET (Mallet)

Origins: A prominent Anglo-Norman family in the 11th-12th centuries. This cadet line was prominent in the 16th and 17th centuries. Judge early 17th century. **First MP 1554. Three further MPs 1571-1626.**

1. Michael Malet – Milborne Port 1660-79
2. Sir John Malet – Minehead 1666-79 Bridgwater 1681

Seat: Poyntington, Somerset (now in Dorset) (medieval house, leased, probably from 1566, from the Lords Willoughby de Broke, the owners)
Estates: Owned at least eight manors in 1665.
Title: Bt 1663 but not assumed.
Notes: The family lapsed into obscurity in the late 17th century. One in ODNB.

MALLALIEU

Origins: Cotton manufacturers later 19th century.

1. Frederick Mallalieu – Colne Valley Div. Yorkshire 1916-22

2. Sir Edward Mallalieu – Colne Valley Div. Yorkshire 1931-35 Brigg Div. Linconshire 1948-74
3. Sir Joseph Mallalieu – Huddersfield 1945-50 E. Div. Huddersfield 1950-79

Seat: Larkwood, Oldham, Lancashire

MALLOCK

Origins: Merchants in Exeter. **First MP 1553.**

1. Rawlin Mallock – Ashburton 1677-79 Totnes 1689
2. Richard Mallock – Torquay Div. Devon 1886-95

Seat: Cockington Court, Devon (purch. 1654, sold 1933)
Notes: One in ODNB.

MALONE *IRELAND*

Baron Sunderlin (1785-1816 I)

Origins: Successful barrister in the later 17th century. His son was Chancellor of the Exchequer in Ireland 1757. His brother was Judge of the Common Pleas 1766.

1. Edmond Malone – {Ardfert 1743-58}
2. Richard Malone – {Fore 1741-59}
3. Anthony Malone – {County Westmeath 1727-60 Castlemartyr 1761-68 County Westmeath 1768-76}
4. Edmund Malone – {Askeaton 1753-60 Granard 1761-67}
5. Richard Malone 1 Baron Sunderlin – {Granard 1769-76}
6. Richard Malone – {Banagher 1783-85}

Seats: Baronstown (Baronston), Westmeath (acq. c. 1700, built 1755, fire and rebuilt 1889, fire and rebuilt 1903, sold 1929, demolished); Ballynahown (Ballynahowen), Westmeath (acq. by mid-18th c., built 1746, sold c. 1830)
Estates: Bateman 13715 (I) 10203. Income £6,000 pa or less c. 1800.
Peer: {1 peer 1785-1800}
Notes: On the death of the 1 Baron succession to the estates was disputed. 1 Baron and three others in ODNB.

MANATON

Origins: The Manatons were seated at Manaton since at least the 15th century. This branch was a cadet line. **First MP 1621.**

1. Ambrose Manaton – Newport 1678-81 Camelford 1689-96 Tavistock 1696
2. Henry Manaton – Camelford 1689-95 1698-1703 Tavistock 1703-11 Camelford 1711 Callington 1713

Seats: Trecarrell, Cornwall (medieval, add. c. 1500-11, acq. 16th c., sold 18th c.); Kilworthy, Devon (built 16th c., acq. later 17th c., sold 18th c.); Harewood, Cornwall

MANGLES

Origins: The first MP was a ship chandler and East India proprietor, but the family business was founded in the first half of the 18th century. Ross Mangles MP was Chairman of the East India Company. Charles was a chairman of railway companies.

1. James Mangles – Guildford 1831-37
2. Ross Mangles – Guildford 1841-58
3. Charles Mangles – Newport 1857-59

Seats: Poyle Park, Surrey (acq. 1st half 19th c., estate broken up 20th c., demolished); Woodbridge House, Surrey (purch. 1803)
Estates: Rubinstein – John Mangles left £100,000 in probate in 1837.
Notes: Two in ODNB.

MANLEY *WALES*

Origins: Lineage traces back to the 13th century. First MP was a London brewer.

1. John Manley – Denbigh Boroughs 1659 Bridport 1689
2. John Manley – Bossiney 1695-98 1701-08 Camelford 1708-10 Bossiney 1710-13
3. Issac Manley – {Downpatrick 1705-13 Newtown Limavady 1715-35}

Seat: Bryn y Ffynnon (Brynyffynnon), Denbighshire (leased mid-17th c.)
Notes: Two in ODNB.

MANNERS [Nelthorpe, Sutton, Tollemache]

Duke of Rutland (1703- UK)

Origins: The Manners were settled at Etal in Northumberland in or before the 12th century. Governors of Norham Castle 14th century. Inherited Haddon Hall from the Vernons by marriage to the heiress 1565, who in turn had inherited it from an Avenel heiress. (The Avenels held Haddon possibly from Saxon times.) Succeeded by marriage 1469 to an heiress as 11 Lord Roos and inherited the Roos seat at Belvoir in c. 1508. The Roos family held manorial land from at least the 12th century. The First Roos was summoned to Parliament in 1299. Lord Roos was at Agincourt. (Payling, *Political Society in Lancastrian England*, 93-95 and Acheson, *A Gentry Community*, 95) **First Roos MP 1555. One further MP 1597. First Manners MP 1340. Thirteen further MPs 1421-1640, ten of them kts of the shire.**

1. John Manners 1 Duke of Rutland – Leicestershire 1661-79
2. John Manners 2 Duke of Rutland – Derbyshire 1701 Leicestershire 1701-02 Grantham 1705-10 Leicestershire 1710-11
3. Thomas Manners – Grantham 1701
4. John Manners 3 Duke of Rutland – Rutland 1719-21
5. Lord William Manners – Leicestershire 1719-34 Newark 1738-54
6. John Manners Marquess of Granby – Grantham 1741-54 Cambridgeshire 1754-70
7. Lord Sherard Manners – Tavistock 1741-42
8. Lord Robert Manners – Kingston-upon-Hull 1747-82
9. George Manners – Scarborough 1768-72
10. Charles Manners 4 Duke of Rutland – University of Cambridge 1774-79
11. Lord Robert Manners – Cambridgeshire 1780-82
12. Robert Manners – Great Bedwyn 1784-90 Cambridge 1791-1820
13. Lord Charles Manners – Cambridgeshire 1802-30 N. Leicestershire 1835-52
14. Lord Robert Manners – Scarborough 1802-06 Leicestershire 1806-31 N. Leicestershire 1832-35
15. Russell Manners – Grantham 1806-07
16. Charles Manners 6 Duke of Rutland – Stamford 1837-52 N. Leicestershire 1852-57
17. John Manners 7 Duke of Rutland – Newark 1841-47 Colchester 1850-57 N. Leicestershire 1857-85 Melton Div. Leicestershire 1885-88
18. Lord George Manners – Cambridgeshire 1847-57 1863-74
19. Henry Manners 8 Duke of Rutland – Melton Div. Leicestershire 1888-95
20. Lord Edward Manners – Melton Div. Leicestershire 1895-1900
21. Lord Cecil Manners – Melton Div. Leicestershire 1900-06

Seats: Belvoir Castle, Leicestershire (pronounced "beaver", built later 11th c., inher. 1508, rebuilt 1523-55, rebuilt 1654-68, remod. c. 1750 and 1801, fire 1816 and rebuilt

1816-20, still own); Cheveley Park, Cambridgeshire (built 1670, acq. by mar. 1750, remodol. 1850, sold 1892, demolished later 19th c.); Haddon Hall, Derbyshire (house built 11th c., the Vernons acq. by mar. in c. 1171, rebuilt late 12th c., add. c. 1370-77, c. 1450, acq. by Manners family by mar. 1565, remod. early 17th c., restored 1912, still own); Croxton Park, Lincolnshire (acq. 1534, built c. 1730, demolished 1860s, ruin); St. Mary's Tower, Perthshire (acq. mid-19th c., built 1861, demolished, ruin); Stanton Woodhouse, Derbyshire (built 1530, purch. 1760, sold 1962); Longshaw Lodge, Yorkshire (built 1827, sold 1927); Bloxholm Hall, Lincolnshire (built mid-17th c., purch. 1721, remod. 1772, add. 1827, passed by mar. to Nisbet Hamiltons (Hamilton I) c. 1830, demolished after 1973)
Estates: Bateman 70137 (E) 97486. Worth at least £2,485 pa in c. 1563 and £20,000 pa in 1721. 27,000 acres sold in 1920. Owned 26,000 acres worth 150 million pounds in 2001.
Titles: Earl of Rutland 1525- E; Baron Manners 1679- E; Marquess of Granby 1703- E; Baron Roos 1896- UK
Peers: 11 peers 1660-1787 1799-1906 1896-1945
9 Lds Lt 17th, 18th, 19th, 20th
4 in Cabinet 1727-36 1763-72 1783-87 1852 1858-59 1866-68 1874-80 1885-92
7 KG 18th, 19th, 20th
Notes: 1, 2, 3, 5, 6, and 8 Earls and 1, 4, 6, and 7 Dukes and ten others in ODNB.

<u>Viscount Canterbury</u> (1835-1941 UK)

Origins: Lord George Manners inherited the estates of his maternal grandfather, Robert Sutton, 2 Baron Lexinton, on the death of his brother, Lord Robert Manners, in 1772 and took the additional name Sutton. The 3 Viscount married in 1838 the daughter and heiress of Charles Thompson of Witchingham Hall. Lord George's fifth son was created Baron Manners 1807.

1. Lord Robert Manners Sutton – Nottinghamshire 1747-62
2. Lord George Manners Sutton – Grantham 1754-80 Newark 1780-83
3. George Manners Sutton – Newark 1774-80 Grantham 1780-1802 Bramber 1802-04
4. John Manners Sutton – Newark 1783-96
5. Thomas Manners Sutton 1 Baron Manners – Newark 1796-1805
6. Charles Manners Sutton 1 Viscount Canterbury – Scarborough 1806-32 University of Cambridge 1832-35
7. John Manners Sutton 3 Viscount Canterbury – Cambridge 1839-40 1841-47
8. John Manners Sutton – Newark 1847-57

Seats: (Great) Witchingham Hall, Norfolk (medieval, rebuilt 1812, remod. 1872, purch. by Thompsons through whom it passed by mar. to the Manners Suttons, sold c. 1890); Kelham Hall, Nottinghamshire (purch. by father of 1 Baron Lexinton, passed by mar. of

1717 to the Duke of Rutland, rebuilt 1728-31, remod. 1844-46, fire 1857, new house 1859-61 for £50,000 – Franklin, *The Gentleman's Country House*, 263 - mortgage foreclosed 1898, institutional use); Mistley Hall, Essex (add. c. 1780, leased?, demolished 1835 or 1844); Avon Tyrrell, Hampshire (acq. by mar. 1885 from Fanes, rebuilt 1890-92, family departed 1939, house donated to institutional use 1949, still own estate)
Estates: Bateman 5177 (E) 8399. Charles Manners Sutton, Archbishop of Canterbury left £180,000 in probate in 1828.
Titles: Baron Manners 1807- UK; Baron Bottesford 1835-1941 UK
Peers: 10 peers 1807-64 1835-1941 1873-1945
Notes: 1 Baron and 1 and 3 Viscounts and one other in ODNB.

Baron Lexinton (1645-1723 E)

Origins: Descended from a younger son of Rowlande de Sutton, ancestor of the Sutton Lords Dudley (acq. land 12th c.). Henry de Sutton, Lord of Sutton, married the sister and co-heir of the Lord of Dudley and their son was summoned to Parliament 1342. (For Dudleys see Ward I) **First MP 1414 for Nottinghamshire. Another MP 1624 for Nottinghamshire.** The daughter of the last Baron married the 3 Duke of Rutland. Their younger sons inherited the Sutton estates and name (see Viscount Canterbury above). Descendents of a younger brother of the 1 Baron were created Baronets and seated at Norwood Park.

1. Richard Sutton – Newark 1708-10 1712-37
2. Sir Robert Sutton – Nottinghamshire 1722-32 Great Grimsby 1734-41
3. Sir Richard Sutton 1 Bt – St. Albans 1768-80 Sandwich 1780-84 Boroughbridge 1784-96

Seats: Benham-Valence (Benham Park or Place), Berkshire (built 1775, purch. late 19th c., sold 1983); Norwood Park, Nottinghamshire (built 1650s, purch. 1764, rebuilt 1760s, sold 19th c.)
Estates: Bateman 9340 (E) 15500. Owned 9,474 acres worth over 700 million pounds in 2001 (due to a substantial London estate inherited from the Pulteneys, see).
Title: Baronet 1772-
Peers: 2 peers 1660-68 1683-1723
Notes: 1 Bt and 1 and 2 Barons and one other in ODNB.

Nelthorpe

Origins: A yeoman from Yorkshire came to London (d. 1580) for a business career. His son established himself in Lincolnshire. Mayor of Beverley 1611. **First MP 1645 for Beverley.** A cadet was created Baronet in 1666, extinct 1865. Robert Sutton of a cadet line of the Barons Lexinton (see above) married the Nelthorpe heiress.

1. James Nelthorpe – Tiverton 1728-34

Seats: Lynford Hall, Norfolk (purch. 1717, built 1720, sold 1856); Scawby Hall, Lincolnshire (acq. by mar. and built c. 1603, remod c. 1795, add. 1913, still own); Little Grimsby, Lincolnshire (built early 18th c., passed by mar. to the Duke of St. Albans)
Estates: Bateman 7263 (E) 9044. Some land sold 1914/15, but 1,500 acres around Scawby was purchased and added to the estate in 1917. (Leach, *Lincolnshire Country Houses*, *Part Two*, 112)
Title: Baronet 1666-1865

Earl of Dysart (1643- S)

Origins: The Tollemaches owned manorial land in Suffolk by 1338. They greatly increased their estates in the 16th century. **First MP 1621**. Sir Lyonel Tollemache 3 Bt married the daughter and heiress of the 1 Earl of Dysart and their son succeeded to the title and Ham House. William Murray 1 Earl of Dysart was the son of a minister in Fife and served as whipping boy to Charles I. John Manners (kinsman of the Duke of Atholl), illegitimate son of Lord William Manners (son of the 2 Duke of Rutland) assembled the Buckminster estate in the later 18th century, married Lady Louisa Tollemache, daughter of the 4 Earl of Dysart. Their grandson succeeded as 8 Earl of Dysart.

1. Thomas Tollemache – Malmesbury 1689-90 Chippenham 1692-94
2. Lionel Tollemache 3 Earl of Dysart – Orford 1679-81 1685-87 Suffolk 1698-1707
3. John Manners – Newark 1754-74
4. Wilbraham Tollemache 6 Earl of Dysart – Northampton 1771-80 Liskeard 1780-84
5. William Manners Tollemache Lord Huntingtower – Ilchester 1803-04 1806-07
6. John Manners – Ilchester 1804-06
7. Frederick Manners Tollemache – Grantham 1826-31 1837-52 1857-65 1868-74
8. Felix Tollemache – Ilchester 1827-30
9. Lionel Tollemache 8 Earl of Dysart – Ilchester 1827-30
10. Algernon Tollemache – Grantham 1832-37

Seats: Buckminster Park, Leicestershire (purch. by John Manners 1763, built 1794-98, house demolished 1964, still own estate); Ham House, Surrey (built 1608-10, purch. by 1 Earl of Dysart 1626, remod. 1637, passed by mar. to Tollemaches, who became Earls of Dysart 1698, family departed 1935, NT 1948); Grantham Grange, Lincolnshire (acq. 18th c.); Hanby Hall, Lincolnshire (built early 18th c., add. late 18th c., acq. c. 1800)
Estates: Bateman 27190 (E) 44500
Titles: Baron Huntingtower 1643- S; Baronet 1611-1821 1793-
Peer: [1 peer 1698-1706]
2 Lds Lt 18th, 19th, 20th

1 KT 18th

Notes: The 1 Earl of Dysart was a cadet of the family of the Dukes of Atholl (William Murray **MP 1626-28**). The 2 Earl succeeded to the Wilbraham estates in Cheshire – Woodheay and Tilstone. On the death of the 6 Earl in 1821, Ham House went to the elder sister and the Cheshire estates to the younger sister, married to John Delap Halliday. His son took the name Tollemache. In 1935 the title passed to the 9 Earl's niece, Wenefryde Scott, while the estates passed to Sir Lyonel Tollemache. 1 Earl and four others in ODNB.

<u>Baron Tollemache</u> (1876- UK)

Origins: Lady Jane Tollemache, daughter of the 4 Earl of Dysart, married John Halliday of Leasowes, Shropshire. They succeeded to part of the original Tollemache patrimony and took the name Tollemache. Their grandson was created 1 Baron Tollemache.

1. John Tollemache 1 Baron Tollemache – S. Cheshire 1841-68 W. Cheshire 1868-72
2. Wilbraham Tollemache 2 Baron Tollemache – W. Cheshire 1872-85
3. Henry Tollemache – W. Cheshire 1881-85 Eddis Div. Cheshire 1885-1906

Seats: Peckforton Castle, Cheshire (built 1841-50, family departed by 1945, sold 1988, hotel); Helmingham Hall, Suffolk (built 14th c., acq. by marriage 1487, rebuilt soon after, add. c. 1750, 1800, and 1841, still resident); Dorfold Hall, Cheshire (built 1616, remod. 1824, purch. by Tomkinsons 1754, passed by mar. to Tollemaches mid-19th c., add. 1862, descendents still own)
Estates: Bateman 39030 (E & W) 53375. Worth £30,000,000 with 13,000 acres in 1990.
Peers: 3 peers 1876-1945
Notes: The Tollemache Cobbold brewery was active 1730-1989 in Ipswich. One in ODNB.

MANSFIELD (originally Manfield)

<u>Viscount Sandhurst</u> (1917-21 UK)

Origins: Gentry 18th century. Barrister 1758, Solicitor General 1780.

1. Sir James Mansfield – University of Cambridge 1779-84

Seat: Edgebrook, Norfolk
Estates: Rubinstein – Sir James Mansfield MP left £100,000 in probate 1821.
Title: Baron Sandhurst 1871- UK
Peers: 4 peers 1871-1945
Notes: Commander-in-Chief in India 1870. 1 Baron and one other in ODNB.

MARJORIBANKS [Robertson] *SCOTLAND & ENGLAND*

Baron Marjoribanks (1873-73 UK)

Origins: The 1 Bt was an Edinburgh banker. His brother was a partner in Coutts.

1. Sir John Marjoribanks 1 Bt – Buteshire 1812-18 Berwickshire 1818-26
2. Stewart Marjoribanks – Hythe 1820-37 1841-47
3. Charles Marjoribanks – Berwickshire 1832-33
4. David Marjoribanks Robertson 1 Baron Marjoribanks – Berwickshire 1859-73

Seats: The Lees (House), Berwickshire (built c. 1770, demolished 1975); Hallyards, Linlithgowshire (built 1630, purch. 1696, add. 19th c., remod. 1897)
Estates: Bateman 4152 (S & E) 6913 and 6832 (S) 11754
Title: Baronet 1815-73
Peer: 1 peer 1873
1 Ld Lt 19th

Baron Tweedmouth (1881-1935 UK)

Origins: Cadet line.

1. Dudley Marjoribanks 1 Baron Tweedmouth – Berwick-on-Tweed 1853-68 1874-81
2. Edward Marjoribanks 2 Baron Tweedmouth – Berwickshire 1880-94
3. Edward Marjoribanks – Eastbourne Div. Sussex 1929-32

Seats: Guisachan House, Inverness-shire (old house, purch. 1856, remod. 1860s, sold 1908, ruin by 1986, demolished); Hutton Hall (Castle), Berwickshire (built 16th c., sold 1915); Ninewells House, Berwickshire (built 1839-41, demolished 1964)
Estates: Bateman 23246 (S) 9146
Title: Baronet 1866-1935
Peers: 3 peers 1881-1945
1 in Cabinet 1894-95 1905-08
1 KT 20th
Notes: 2 Baron and one other in ODNB. The family met a financial crisis due to business losses c. 1905, and much property was sold.

MARKHAM

Markham

Origins: A genuine Conquest family (Bindoff, *The House of Commons*, II, 565) long settled at Markham, Nottinghamshire. By the 12th century a leading family in the county, castellans of Nottingham Castle. Judge of the Common Pleas 1396. Lord Chief Justice of the King's Bench 1461. The profits of office used to add to estates. Also a series of marriages to heiresses assisted their rise. (Payling, *Political Society in Lancastrian England*, 39-41) **First MP in the senior line 1467 for Nottinghamshire. One additional MP 1554 for the county.**

1. Sir Robert Markham 2 Bt – Grantham 1678-79 Newark-on-Trent 1679-81
2. Sir George Markham 3 Bt – Newark-on-Trent 1695-98 1701

Seats: Markham, Nottinghamshire (by 12th c., sold 1606); Sedgebrook Manor, Lincolnshire (acq. by mar. 1461 to Sedgebrooke heiress, held since 1225, sold c. 1716)
Estates: Worth £1,600 pa in c. 1667.
Title: Baronet 1642-1779
Notes: The 3 Bt sold Sedgebrook c. 1716 and purchased estates in Essex. A cadet branch seated at Cotham and Ollerton, Nottinghamshire produced **four MPs 1529-86**. Six in ODNB.

Markham

Origins: Cadet line descended from the eldest son of William Markham of Creaton, Northamptonshire (d. 1602).

1. Sir Arthur Markham 1 Bt – Mansfield Div. Nottinghamshire 1900-16

Seats: Creaton, Northamptonshire (acq. 16th c., built c. 1604, resident 18th c.); Beachborough Park, Kent (old house, rebuilt 17th c., rebuilt 1813, acq. 19th c., sold early 20th c.)
Title: Baronet 1911-

Markham

Origins: Cadet descended from a younger son of William Markham (see above). The first MP, an Admiral, was a son of an Archbishop of York.

1. John Markham – Portsmouth 1801-18 1820-26
2. Osborne Markham – Calne 1806-07

Seats: Ades, Sussex (purch. 1802 for £9,826, property divided 1827); Rochetts, Essex (medieval, rebuilt 18th c., leased, fire 1975)
Estates: Rubinstein – William Markham left £150,000 in probate 1814
Notes: Three in ODNB.

MARSHALL

Origins: Leeds linen and flax-spinning magnates beginning in the second half of the 18th century. High Sheriff 1821.

1. John Marshall – Yorkshire 1826-30
2. William Marshall – Petersfield 1826-30 Leominster 1830-31 Beverley 1831-32 Carlisle 1835-47 E. Cumberland 1847-68
3. John Marshall – Leeds 1832-35
4. James Marshall – Leeds 1847-52

Seats: Patterdale Hall, Westmorland (built 17th c., rebuilt c.1800, purch. 1824, ad. 1845-50, sold 1937); Enholmes Hall, Yorkshire (purch. and built 1858, still owned into 20th c.); Hallsteads, Cumberland (acq. and built 1815); Headingly House, Yorkshire (resident 19th c.); Castlerigg Manor, Cumberland (purch. and built 1832, sold 1913); Derwent Isle, Cumberland (built 1778, purch. mid-19th c., rebuilt 1850, remod. 1913, this branch of the family died out 1936); Monk Coniston Hall, Lancashire (built c. 1800, purch. c. 1840, sold after 1918)
Estates: Bateman 4729 (E) 3549. John Marshall MP 1826-30 was worth £400,000 by 1815. He left between one and a half and two and a half million pounds at his death in 1845.
Notes: The company was sold in 1886. Three in ODNB.

MARSHAM [Onley, Savill, Shovell]

Earl of Romney (1801- UK)

Origins: Settled at Marsham in the 14th century. A grocer was Mayor of Norwich 1518. **First MP 1553 for Norwich**. Merchant in London 1620s. Purchased landed estate 1630. Kt 1660.

1. Sir John Marsham 1 Bt – Rochester 1660
2. Sir Robert Marsham 4 Bt – Maidstone 1698-1702
3. Robert Marsham 1 Baron Romney – Maidstone 1708-16
4. Charles Marsham 1 Earl of Romney – Maidstone 1768-74 Kent 1774-90
5. Charles Marsham 2 Earl of Romney – Hythe 1798-1802 Downton 1803-06 Hythe 1806-07
6. Charles Marsham 3 Earl of Romney – W. Kent 1841-45

Seats: The Mote (Park, House), Kent (medieval, purch. 1690, rebuilt 1793-1801, sold 1895); Whorn's Place (Whorne's), Kent (built 15th c., rebuilt early 17th c., purch. 1630, demolished 1782, farm house); Gayton Hall, Norfolk (built 19th c., purch. c. 1891, still own)
Estates: Bateman 4923 (E) 12750 and at Caversfield, Oxfordshire 2211 (E) 3619
Titles: Baron Romney 1716- GB; Baronet 1663-
Peers: 8 peers 1716-24 1733-1945
1 Ld Lt 18th-19th
Notes: 1 Bt and 2 Baron in ODNB.

Savill-Onley

Origins: Henry Marsham of Rippon Hall, Norfolk (built c. 1600, acq. by 1845, sold 1937), a younger son of the senior line of the Marshams descended from John Marsham, ancestor of the Earls of Romney, married Caroline Savill-Onley, daughter and heiress of that family seated at Stisted Hall. Their son took the name Savill-Onley and became an MP. The Savills were mercers in Colchester in the late 17th and early 18th century. The Onleys were gentry, barrister.

1. Samuel Savill – Colchester 1742-47
2. Charles Savill-Onley (Harvey) – Norwich 1812-18 Carlow 1818-26

Seat: Stisted Hall, Essex (purch. 18th c., built 1823, sold later 19th c.?)
Estates: Bateman 3062 (E) 4617 and at Stratton Strawless, Norfolk (acq. before 1560, sold 1900) 2122 (E) 2606
Notes: Charles Savill-Onley MP was the son of Robert Harvey, a Norwich banker who (Rubinstein) left £300,000 in probate in 1816. He succeeded his maternal uncle at Stisted and took the name Savill-Onley 1822. Charles Onley left £250,000 in probate 1822.

Shovell

Origins: The 1 Baron Romney married the daughter and heiress of Sir Cloudsley Shovell, who rose from cabin boy to admiral. His family were merchants in Norwich in the 16th century, and small gentry in the 17th. Became a naval family.

1. Sir Cloudsley Shovell – Rochester 1695-1701 1705-07

Seat: May Place, Kent (medieval, acq. early 18th c., sold 18th c.)
Notes: Sir Cloudsley was famous for drowning in the midst of shipwrecking his squadron. One in ODNB.

MARTIN I

Origins: Mayors of Evesham in the 17th century. London bankers from the early 18th century, purchased landed estates, and kept involved in business into the 20th century. Martin's Bank merged into the Bank of Liverpool 1918. Family name changed to Holland-Martin 1923.

1. William Martin – {Gowran 1725-27}
2. Thomas Martin – Wilton 1727-34
3. John Martin – Tewkesbury 1741-47
4. James Martin – Cambridge 1741-44
5. John Martin – Tewkesbury 1754-61
6. Joseph Martin – Gatton 1768-74 Tewkesbury 1774-76
7. James Martin – Tewkesbury 1776-1807
8. John Martin – Tewkesbury 1812-32
9. John Martin – Tewkesbury 1832-35 1837-59
10. John Martin – Tewkesbury 1859-65
11. Sir Richard Martin 1 Bt – Tewkesbury 1880-85 Droitwich Div. Worcestershire 1892-1906
12. Christopher Holland-Martin – Ludlow Div. Shropshire 1951-60

Seats: Overbury Court, Worcestershire (leased 1723, purch. and built c. 1735, fire and rebuilt c. 1739, add. 1890s, still own); Quy Hall, Cambridgeshire (medieval, rebuilt late 15th c., add. early 17th c., purch. 1722, remod. c. 1810, sold 1855); Ham Court, Worcestershire (acq. by mar. 1761, rebuilt 1772, sold and demolished 1925)
Estates: 2377 (E) 3799 plus Cambridgeshire estate of c. 1,100 acres. James Martin (d. 1744) left £300,000.
Title: Baronet 1905-16
Notes: Martin family has entry in ODNB and one other.

MARTIN II

Origins: The grandfather of the first MP was an Ulster royalist who fled to the West Indies and gained plantations in Antigua and then returned to England. His son was Speaker of the Antigua Assembly 1753. They were officials, merchants, and planters. The second MP was a Captain RN and the third MP an admiral.

1. Samuel Martin – Camelford 1747-68 Hastings 1768-74
2. Sir Henry Martin 1 Bt – Southampton 1790-94
3. Sir Thomas Martin – Plymouth 1818-32

Seats: Little Farm, Surrey; Lockynge House, Berkshire (built 1750, leased only)
Title: Baronet 1791-1910
Notes: Two in ODNB.

MARTON

Origins: Minor gentry and a barrister in the 18th century.

1. Edward Marton – Lancaster 1747-58
2. George Marton – Lancaster 1837-47
3. George Marton – Lancaster Div. Lancashire 1885-86

Seat: Capernwray Hall, Lancashire (purch. early 18th c., rebuilt 1844, sold 1945, demolished 1946)
Estates: Bateman 4693 (E) 6354

MARTYN I (Martin)

Martyn

Origins: Gentry in the 14th century, but younger sons in law and trade. **First MP 1363 for Plympton Erle. Ten additional MPs 1397-1648 in two branches, four kts of the shire**. The family represented Plympton Erle over three centuries.

1. Christopher Martyn – Plympton Erle 1647 Devon 1653 Plymtpon Erle 1659 1660

Martyn

Origins: A cadet line.

1. Thomas Martyn – Dartmouth 1722-27

Notes: Pre-1660 seats included Oxton, Devon and Athelhampton, Dorset.

MARTYN II [Hemphill] *IRELAND*

Martyn

Origins: To Ireland late 16th century.

1. Oliver Martyn – {Galway town 1689}

Seats: Tulira (Tullira, Tullyra) Castle, Galway (old castle, purch. 1598, new house 18th c., demolished 19th c. add. to castle 1882, passed by mar. to Hemphills 1922); Dungaoty Castle, Galway (acq. c. 1607, fell into disuse 19th c., sold 20th c.)
Estates: 4932 (I) 2424

Note: A Roman Catholic family. Edward Martyn was President of Sinn Féin 1905-08. He disposed of his estates to his tenants retaining Tulira and 1,000 acres. One in ODNB.

Baron Hemphill (1906- UK)

Origins: To Ireland from Scotland c. 1600. Professional family. Clerics and lawyers. 1 Baron was a politician and lawyer, Solicitor General of Ireland 1892-95.

1. Charles Hemphill 1 Baron Hemphill – County Tyrone 1895-1906

Seats: Tulira Castle, Galway (old Castle, add. 1882, inher. by mar. from Martyns 1922, sold 1962); Renville Hall, Galway (acq. 20th c.)
Estates: 1,000 acres. 1 Baron died in 1908 worth over £100,000. Owned 700 acres in 2001.
Peers: 4 peers 1906-45
Notes: 1 Baron in ODNB.

MASHAM

Baron Masham (1712-76 GB)

Origins: Gentry by 15th century but the grandfather of the 1 Bt was also a London merchant and Alderman (d. 1525). His father (d. 1605) purchased Otes. Baronet 1621. **First MP 1624**. Member of Cromwell's Council of State.

1. Sir Francis Masham 3 Bt – Essex 1690-98 1701-10
2. Samuel Masham 1 Baron Masham – Ilchester 1710-11 New Windsor 1711-12

Seat: Otes, Essex (purch. late 16th c., sold 1766)
Estates: Property worth £1,200 pa in 1656.
Title: Baronet 1621-1776
Peers: 2 peers 1712-76
Notes: The barony was acquired by royal favor. The 2 Baron was a wastrel too indebted even to appear in the House of Lords. (Laslet, "The Rise and Fall of an English Family", 535-43.) 1 and 2 Barons and two others in ODNB.

MASON

Origins: Prominent in the borough of Bishop's Castle from the 1570s. Clerk Comptroller of the Royal Household and Kt 1671.

1. Sir Richard Mason – Yarmouth (IoW) 1679-81 Bishop's Castle 1681

2. Richard Mason – Bishop's Castle 1690
3. Charles Mason – Bishop's Castle 1695-1705 Montgomery Boroughs 1705-08 Bishop's Castle 1708-10 1715-22 1726-27

Seats: Rockley Hall, Shropshire; Worcester Park, Surrey; Church Stoke, Shropshire
Estates: One of Sir Richard Mason MP's daughters had a marriage portion of £12,000 and £25,000 in 1683.
Notes: A son-in-law was also MP for Bishop's Castle 1701. One in ODNB.

MASSEY (Massie)

Origins: Cheshire family in the 14th century. **First MP 1547, kt of shire for Flint. Two further MPs 1553-63, one for Cheshire**. Sir Edward Massey MP 1646-74, was an apprentice in London and then a soldier in Ireland. Granted a 99 year lease on Abbey Leix 1660.

1. Sir Edward Massey – Wootton Bassett 1646 Gloucester 1660-74

Seats: Coddington Hall, Cheshire (medieval, acq. by mar. 14th c., fire mid-18th c., sold 20th c.); Abbey Leix, Queen's County (acq. 1660, sold 1674)
Notes: One in ODNB.

MASSY (Massey) [Dawson, Mainwaring] *IRELAND*

Baron Massy (1776- I)

Origins: An old Cheshire family. The first to appear in Ireland was a general in Cromwell's army during the rebellion 1641. His son settled in Limerick.

1. Hugh Massy 1 Baron Massy – {County Limerick 1759-76 Old Leighlin 1776}
2. Hugh Massy 2 Baron Massy – {Askeaton 1776-83 County Limerick 1783-88}
3. John Massy – {County Limerick 1790-97}

Seats: The Hermitage, Limerick (built c. 1800, purch. mid-19th c., burned early 1920s, demolished); Killakee House, Dublin (built 1806, inher. 1880 from White family, lost to family 1924, demolished)
Estates: Bateman 33003 (I) 12101. Worth £7,000 pa c. 1800. Much of the estate sold to tenants in the 1890s for £100,000. Family bankrupt 1924. (Blake, *Abandoned Mansions of Ireland II*, 78-80).
Peers: {3 peers 1776-1800} 1 Irish Rep peer 1876-1915

Notes: The Massys inherited very large blocks of land in Leitrim and Dublin and Killakee House from two younger sons of Luke White (see White I), uncles of the 6 Baron, in 1874 and 1880.

Massy-Dawson

Origins: Massys descended from a younger brother of the 1 Baron Massy, who married the Dawson heiress of Ballynacourty. Dawsons emerged in the later 17th c. through the career of a soldier who purchased confiscated lands. Sheriff 1697.

1. James Dawson – {County Tipperary 1703-14}
2. James Massy-Dawson – Clonmel 1820-30 County Limerick 1830

Seat: Ballynacourty (Ballynacourte), Tipperary (Dawsons acq. late 17th c., passed by mar. to Massys 18th c., rebuilt early 19th c., demolished 20th c.)
Estates: Bateman 19258 (I) 6528. Dawson estates worth £1,500 pa in 1713.

Massy

Origins: Descended from an uncle of the 1 Baron Massy, a younger son who became a Church of Ireland Dean and married a Dillon heiress.

1. Sir Hugh Dillon Massy 1 Bt – {County Clare 1783-90}
2. Sir Hugh Dillon Massy 2 Bt – {County Clare 1797-1800} 1801-02

Seats: Doonass (Donas) Castle (House, Lodge), Clare (old castle acq. 1739, remodeled c. 1820, sold c. 1920s); Summerhill, Clare (acq. and built 18th c., passed by mar. Vincent family 19th c.)
Estates: Bateman 4623 (I) 3173. Held 11,208 acres worth £4,010 pa in 1858.
Title: Baronet 1782-1870
Notes: Doonass originally belonged to the Earls of Thomond. Financial difficulties obliged a partial sale of estates in 1858 and the rest in 1910.

Baron Clarina (1800-1952 I)

Origins: Descended from a younger son of Hugh Massy ancestor of the Barons Massy.

1. Eyre Massey 1 Baron Clarina – {Swords 1790-97}
2. William Massey – Newport (IoW) 1855-57 Salford 1857-63 Tiverton 1872-81
3. William Massey-Mainwaring – Finsbury 1895-1906

Seat: Elm Park (Elmgove), Limerick (built early 19th c., demolished 20th c.)

Estates: Bateman 2012 (I) 2497
Peers: 2 Irish Rep peers 1849-72 1888-97
Nores: 1 Baron and one other in ODNB.

MASTER [Chester]

Master

Origins: The founder was a physician to Elizabeth I. The first MP was a merchant and brewer. Purchased estates in Kent 1544. **First MP 1545. Three additional MPs 1586-1624, two for Cirencester.**

1. Thomas Master – Cirencester 1660
2. Thomas Master – Cirencester 1685-87 1689-90
3. William Master – Cirencester 1701-05
4. Thomas Master – Cirencester 1712-47
5. Thomas Master – Cirencester 1747-49
6. Thomas Master – Gloucestershire 1784-96
7. Richard Master – Cirencester 1785-92
8. Thomas Chester-Master – Cirencester 1837-44
9. Thomas Chester-Master – Cirencester 1878-85 1892-93

Seats: The Abbey House, Cirencester, Gloucestershire (acq. 1564, built early 17th c., demolished and rebuilt 1774-76, remod. 1817-25, add. c. 1868, leased out from 1897, demolished 1964, still own estate); Knole Park, Gloucestershire (acq. by mar. 1799 from Chesters, see below, remod. early 19th c., sold 1931, demolished 1970)
Estates: Bateman 7190 (E) 13722
Notes: Five in ODNB.

Master

Origins: Kinsmen. **First MP 1640 for Canterbury.**

1. Sir Edward Master – Canterbury 1661-79

Chester

Origins: The Chesters were prominent burgesses in Bristol in the 15th century. Overseas merchants in wool and sugar. Mayor of Bristol 1559. Purchased land 1569. By 1573 living as gentry. Also owned coal mines. **First MP 1555 for Bristol. Two further MPs 1563-72, one kt of the shire.** On the death of Thomas Chester his estates passed to his niece and her husband, William Bromley, who took the name Chester. She died in 1799 when the estates passed to Thomas Master MP.

1. Thomas Chester – Gloucester 1727-28 Gloucestershire 1734-63

Seat: Knole Park, Gloucestershire (purh. 1569, house built late 16th c., passed by mar. to Master family 1799)
Notes: Three in ODNB.

MATHESON *SCOTLAND*

Origins: Purchased an estate 1730. Lairds in the 18th century. Founded Jardine Matheson, opium traders, with Dr. William Jardine c. 1820 in Macao, China, which became one of the largest trading firms in the world. Purchased vast estates.

1. Sir James Matheson 1 Bt – Ashburton 1843-47 Ross & Cromarty 1847-68
2. Thomas Matheson – Ashburton 1847-52
3. Sir Alexander Matheson 1 Bt – Inverness District 1847-68 Ross & Cromarty 1868-84

Seats: Ardross Castle, Ross-shire (old house, purch. 1840s, sold 1880); Rose Hall (Rosehall House), Sutherlandshire (built 1818-25, purch. later 19th c., sold 1920s, derelict)
Estates: Bateman 220663 (S) 26461 and 424560 (S) 20346 (Alexander Matheson 1 Bt spent over £2 million on purchase and improvement of estates 1840-80)
Title: Baronet 1850-78; 1882-
1 Ld Lt 19th
Notes: Much land sold after 1 Bt's death. Both 1 Bts in ODNB.

MATHEW (Mathews) *IRELAND & ENGLAND*

Earl of Landaff (1797-1833 I)

Origins: An old Glamorganshire family. At Llandaff since the reign of Richard II. Standard bearer for Edward IV. Father of first MP fought at Bosworth. **First MP 1553 for Glamorganshire. One additional MP 1572 also for the county**. Financial difficulties led to emigration to Ireland c. 1620. Married the widowed Viscountess Thurles, mother of the Duke of Ormonde. Acquired substantial estates. The head of the family conformed to the Established Church in 1755 but other family members remained Roman Catholic.

1. George Mathew – {County Tipperary 1713-14 1728-38}
2. Francis Mathew 1 Earl of Landaff – {County Tipperary 1768-83]

3. Francis Mathew 2 Earl of Landaff – {Callan 1796 County Tipperary 1796-1800} 1801-06
4. Montague Mathew – {Ballynakill 1797-1800} County Tipperary 1806-19

Seats: Thomastown Castle, Tipperary (acq. and built c. 1670, add. 1711, remod. 1812, abandoned 1872, sold, ruin, repurch. 1938); Thurles Castle, Tipperary (built 15th c., acq. 17th c., sold 19th c.); Annefield, Tipperary (acq. 17th c., sold 1859?)
Estates: Worth £1,500 pa in 1713 and £6,000 pa in 1779. 32,000 acres worth £28,000 pa c. 1805. Part of estate sold to pay debts early and mid-19th c.
Titles: Baron Landaff 1783-1833 I; Viscount Landaff 1793-1833 I
Peers: 2 Irish Rep peers 1801-06 1806-33
1 KP 19th
Notes: Remaining Welsh estates sold 1818. On the death of the 2 Earl of Landaff's sister in 1841 the estates passed to his cousin on his mother's side, Viscomte de Rohan Chabot, and his son Comte de Jarnac. They inhabited Thomastown until 1872 when it became derelict. Seven in ODNB.

Mathews

Origins: Glamorganshire branch of the family.

1. Thomas Mathews – Glamorgan 1745-47 Carmarthen 1747-51
2. Thomas Mathews – Glamorgan 1756-61

Seat: Llandaff Court, Glamorganshire (acq. 15th c., built 16th c., rebuilt 1744-46 sold 1798, became residence of Bishop of Llandaff 1850, now school)
Notes: Extinct in male line 1798 and estates dispersed.

Mathew

Origins: Cornish branch of the family.

1. George Mathew – Athlone 1835-37 Shaftesbury 1838-41

MAUDE *IRELAND*

Earl de Montalt (1886-1905 UK)

Origins: Moved from Yorkshire to Ireland c. 1640 and purchased estates. **First {MP 1639}.** Sheriff 1686.

1. Anthony Maude – {Cashel 1695-99}

2. Sir Robert Maude 1 Bt – {Gowran 1703-13 St. Canice 1713-27 Bangor 1727-50}
3. Thomas Maude 1 Baron de Montalt – {County Tipperary 1761-76}
4. Cornwallis Maude 1 Viscount Hawarden – {Roscommon 1783-85}

Seat: Dundrum (House), Tipperary (acq. c. 1640s, built mid- 18th c., add. c. 1890, sold 20th c., institution)
Estates: Bateman 15272 (I) 8781. Worth £1,200 pa in 1805.
Titles: Baron de Montalt 1776-77 I; Baron de Montalt 1785- I; Viscount Hawarden 1793- I; Baronet 1705-
Peers: {1 peer 1791-1900} 2 Irish Rep peers 1836-56 1862-86
1 peer 1886-1905
1 Ld Lt 19th-20th
Notes: Claimed a rather unlikely descent from a "Conquest" family. Two in ODNB.

MAUNSELL *IRELAND*

Origins: Moved from Buckinghamshire to Ireland 1609 as a soldier. The second MP made a fortune in the East India Company service and returned home a nabob and became a banker.

1. Richard Maunsell – {Limerick 1741-60}
2. Thomas Maunsell – {Kilmallock 1769-76}
3. Thomas Maunsell – {Thomastown 1768-76 Granard 1776-83}

Seats: Plassey House, Limerick (acq. 18th c., sold 19th c.); Rathleigh, Dublin; Ballywilliam, Limerick (acq. 18th c., resident into 20th c.)

MAXWELL [Barry, Heron, Stewart, Stirling] *SCOTLAND, IRELAND, & ENGLAND*

<u>Earl of Nithsdale</u> (1620-1716 S)

Origins: Perhaps a Norman family. Witnessed an inquest 1116. High Sheriff 1207. Great Chamberlain of Scotland 1231. The common ancestor of the family, Aymer Maxwell, lived in the 13th century. From the senior line descended the Earls of Morton, Traquair, and Nithsdale as well as the Barons Herries and the Constable-Maxwells. From the junior line sprung the Stirling-Maxwells and the Earls of Farnham. The senior line was created Baron Maxwell in 1445. The 7 Baron was created Earl of Morton in 1581. His son was 1 Earl of Nithsdale. On the death of the 2 Earl in 1667 the Earldom passed to a cousin the 6 Baron Herries, who married a sister of the 1 Earl. This led to the interconnected small group of Roman Catholic families, which explains the paucity of post-1660 MPs. Winifred Maxwell, daughter of the 5 Earl married William Constable of Everingham Park, Yorkshire. The Constables (not connected to the Constables of

Burton Constable - see Clifford) where a major producer of MPs (**eleven MPs 1319-1653**). They suffered financially due to their recusant status, although they managed to hold Everingham until 1982. The brother of the 10 Baron succeeded to the estates of another ancestor of the Earl of Traquair in 1876 (see below). **Two Maxwell [MPs 1525-1585].**

No post-1660 MPs.

Seats: Terregles House (Castle), Dumfriesshire (built 1789, add. 1831, demolished 1964); Everingham Park, Yorkshire (acq. 12th c., rebuilt mid-16th c., rebuilt 1757-64, remod. 19th c., sold 1982); Carlaverock Castle, Dumfriesshire (acq. and built 13th c., add. c. 1634, slighted and abandoned 1640, ruin); Traquair House, Peebleshire (see below, acq. by mar. 1876)
Estates: Bateman - Baron Herries 18995 (E & S) 19152. Owned 5,200 acres in 1996; Constable-Maxwell 12396 (S) 14430; 1 Earl of Nithsdale rental £3,000 pa.
Titles: Baron Maxwell 1445-1716 S; Baron Herries 1491-1716, attainder reversed 1858 S; Earl of Morton 1581-93 S; Baron Herries 1884-1908 UK
Peers: [6 peers 160-83 1661-65 1680-1706 1697-1706] 1 peer 1884-1908
1 Ld Lt 19th-20th
Notes: A cadet line of Maxwells seated at Newark produced an [MP 1639]. 1, 2, 4, 5, and 9 Barons Maxwell and 4 and 5 Barons Herries and 1 Earl of Morton and 1 and 5 Earls of Nithsdale in ODNB.

Maxwell

Origins: A cadet line of the Earls of Nithsadle.

1. Sir Robert Maxwell 2 Bt – [Kirkcudbright Stewartry 1669-74 1681]

Seat: Orchardtoun Castle (House), Kirkcudbrightshire (purch. 1616, built 1761, sold 1785)
Title: Baronet 1633-
Notes: 7 Bt a Roman Catholic "out" in 1745, exiled. Returned to estates 1753 and conformed.

Earl of Traquair (1633-1861 S)

Origins: James VI's uncle, the Earl of Buchan, gave Traquair to his son Sir James Stewart. A dedicated Roman Catholic family. **First [MP 1593 for Peeblesshire]. Two further [MPs 1612-25 both for the county].** Estates passed to the Maxwells in 1876, (see above).

No post-1660 MPs

Seat: Traquair House, Peeblesshire (medieval, rebuilt 15th c., acq. 1478, add. 16th and 17th c., still own)
Estates: Bateman 22221 (S & E) 8681
Titles: Baron Stewart 1628-1861 S
Peers: [2 peers 1660-65 1686-89]

Maxwell

Origins: Descended from the senior line.

1. Sir William Maxwell 1 Bt – [Wigtownshire 1667 1669-72]
2. Sir Alexander Maxwell 2 Bt – Wigtown Burghs 1713-15
3. Sir William Maxwell 5 Bt – Wigtownshire 1805-12 1822-30
4. Sir Herbert Maxwell 7 Bt – Wigtownshire 1880-1906

Seat: Monreith House, Wigtownshire (acq. 15th c., built 1791, add. 1821, add. 1878, still own)
Estates: Bateman 16877 (S) 15569
Title: Baronet 1681-
1 Ld Lt 20th
1 KT 20th
Notes: Two in ODNB.

Stirling-Maxwell

Origins: Descended from the junior line. One fought at Otterburn 1388. On the death of the 8 Bt in 1865 his sister and heiress, who had married Archibald Stirling of Keir, succeeded to the estates. Their son succeeded by special patent of 1707 as 9 Bt and took the additional name Maxwell. A younger son inherited Keir. **First [MP 1560]. Four additional [MPs 1593-1650, all kts of the shire].**

1. Sir John Maxwell 1 Bt – [Renfrewshire 1689-98]
2. Sir John Maxwell 8 Bt – Renfrewshire 1818-30 Lanarkshire 1832-37
3. Sir John Maxwell 7 Bt – Paisley 1832-34
4. Sir William Stirling-Maxwell 9 Bt – Perthshire 1852-68 1874-78
5. Sir John Stirling-Maxwell 10 Bt – Coll Div. Glasgow 1895-1906
6. Archibald Stirling – W. Perthshire 1917-18

Seats: Pollock House, Renfrewshire (acq. and built c. 1269, rebuilt 1752, donated 1966, institutional use); Haggs Castle, Renfrewshire (built later 16th c., became a ruin 19th c.)
Estates: Bateman 20814 (S) 34233
Title: Baronet 1682-dormant from 1956 - active again as of 2005
2 KT 19th, 20th

Notes: This baronetcy is unusual in having passed twice through the female line by special remainder, upheld in 2005. Two Maxwells and one Stirling-Maxwell in ODNB.

Stirling

Origins: Sir William Stirling Kt 1460. At Keir mid-15th century. The grandson of Sir William was guardian of James V. Attainted 1715 but recovered the estates. Younger sons merchants, went to Jamaica and made fortunes. Plantations worth £5,000 pa in the 18th century. (Alistair Rowen, *Country Life*, 157, p. 391). **First [MP 1525]. Five additional [MPs 1560-1641, three of them kts of the shire].** Acquired Maxwell estates 1865

1. Sir Archibald Stirling – [Linlithgowshire 1646-47 1661-63 1667]
2. Sir John Stirling – [Stirlingshire 1669-74 1678]

Seats: Keir House, Stirlingshire (acq. 1448, rebuilt mid-18th c., add. 1820, remod. 1845-51, sold c. 1982); Garden, Stirlingshire (acq. 17th c., built 1749, rebuilt 1824, still resident early 20th c.); Cawder, Perthshire (acq. by mar. 1541, remod. 18th c.)
Estates: Bateman 3239 (S) 2767
Notes: Two in ODNB.

Earl of Farnham (1763-79 I; 1785-1823 I)

Origins: The common ancestor of the Pollock lines was Sir John Maxwell of Pollock (15th c.). His eldest son was the ancestor of the Stirling-Maxwells. A younger son, Sir Robert Maxwell of Calderwood, the ancestor of the Baronets seated at Cardoness, Kirkcudbrightshire and by a younger line leading to the 1 Baron Farnham. The Farnhams went to Ireland in the late 16th century. Bishop 1643. Bt 1627. The latter married Judith, daughter and heiress of James Barry of Newton Barry. In 1800 the 5 Baron Farnham succeeded to the Barry estates and took the additional name Barry.

1. Henry Maxwell – {Bangor 1698-99 1703-13 Killybegs 1713-14 Donegal 1715-30}
2. John Maxwell 1 Baron Farnham – {County Cavan 1727-56}
3. Robert Maxwell 1 Earl of Farnham – {Lisburn 1743-59} Taunton 1754-68
4. Barry Maxwell 1 Earl of Farnham – {County Cavan 1756-60 Armagh 1761-68 County Cavan 1768-79}
5. John Barry Maxwell 2 Earl of Farnham – {County Cavan 1780-83 1793-1800}
6. John Maxwell-Barry 5 Baron Farnham – {Doneraile 1792-97 Newtown Limavady 1798-1800} County Cavan 1806-23
7. Henry Maxwell 7 Baron Farnham – County Cavan 1824-38
8. Somerset Maxwell 8 Baron Farnham – County Cavan 1839-40
9. James Maxwell 9 Baron Farnham – County Cavan 1843-65
10. Somerset Maxwell – Kings Lynn Div. Norfolk 1935-42

Seats: Farnham House, Cavan (purch. 1641, built c. 1645, fire 1688, new house c. 1700, remod. c. 1780, rebuilt 1802, add. 1839, remod. and partially demolished 1961, house and final 1,200 acres sold 2002); Newtown (Newton) Barry (Newtownbarry) (aka Woodfield), Wexford (built early 17th c., passed from Barrys to Maxwells 1719, sold 1854)
Estates: Bateman 25920 (I) 18250. Worth £3,764 pa 1714 and £5,000 pa in 1779. Estates sold between 1903 and 1931 excepting 2,800 acres of untenanted land (Hicks, *Irish Country Houses*, 189). Owned 1,200 acres in 2000 (*Country Life*, 197, p. 31) Owned 3,000 acres in 2001 (Cahill, *Who Owns Britain*, 330).
Titles: Baron Farnham 1756- I; Viscount Farnham 1760-79 I; Viscount Farnham 1781-1823 I; Baronet 1627-
Peers: {3 peers 1756-1800} 5 Irish Rep peers 1816-23 1825-38 1839-68 1898-1900 1908-45
1 Ld Lt 20th
1 KP 19th
Notes: Cadet married into the Waring family (see Waring).

Maxwell-Heron

Origins: Descended from a younger line of the Maxwells of Pollock. John Maxwell 4 Bt of Springkell married in 1802 Mary, daughter and heiress of Patrick Heron of Heron. A younger son took the additional name Heron. Became bankers in 18th century.

1. Patrick Heron – Kirkcudbright Stewartry 1727-41
2. Patrick Heron – Kirkcudbright Stewartry 1795-1803
3. Sir John Maxwell 4 Bt – Dumfries Burghs 1807-12
4. John Maxwell-Heron – Kirkcudbrightshire 1880-85

Seats: Springkell House, Dumfriesshire (built 1734, add. 1818, add. 1840, sold 1893, hotel); Kirroughtrie (Kirroughtree) House (aka Heron), Kirkcudbrightshire (acq. early 15th c., rebuilt 1719, sold 1952, hotel)
Estates: Bateman 13391 (S) 8758
Title: Baronet 1683-

Barry

Origins:

1. James Barry – {Naas 1695-99 1711-13 Kildare 1715-25}

Seat: Newtown (Newton) Barry (Newtownbarry) (aka Woodfield), Wexford (acq. and built early 17th c., passed from Barrys to Maxwells 1719)

MAY *IRELAND & ENGLAND*

Origins: The founder was a merchant tailor who bought landed property in Sussex in 1581. Two lines were established. The English one merged with the Knights (see Peachey). Another son became Master of the Rolls 1629, seated at Carrow Abbey (Priory) Norfolk. **First MP 1605. Two other MPs 1621-1640.** The father of first MP was granted land in Ireland after 1688. Edward May MP was a Revenue Commissioner and Commissioner of Forfeited Estates 1694. Sheriff 1705.

1. Edward May – {Gowran 1695-99}
2. Humphrey May – {St. Johnstown 1695-99 Charlemont 1715-22}
3. Edward May – {County Waterford 1715-29}
4. James May – {County Waterford 1725-27 1733-35}
5. Sir James May 1 Bt – {County Waterford 1759-97}
6. Sir Edward May 2 Bt – {Belfast 1800} 1801-14
7. Sir Stephen May – Belfast 1814-16

Seat: Mayfield House, Waterford (acq. late 17th c., rebuilt 1740s, sold early 19th c., ruin)
Estates: Worth £1,500 pa in 1775.
Title: Baronet 1763-1834

MAYNARD I

Origins: The first MP was a successful barrister, Councilor of State 1660.

1. Sir John Maynard – Totnes 1640-48 Plymouth 1656 Newtown (IoW) 1659 Plymouth 1660 Exeter 1660 Bere Alston 1661-79 Plymouth 1679-81 Bere Alston 1685-87 Plymouth 1689-90
2. John Maynard – Bere Alston 1660
3. Joseph Maynard – Bere Alston 1665-79

Seat: Clifton Reynes, Buckinghamshire (purch. 1673 for £13,500, passed to Hobarts by mar. 1690 and sold 1750)
Notes: One in ODNB.

MAYNARD II *IRELAND*

Origins: Merchants in London early 17th century. To Ireland mid-17th century (?). Arms granted 1714. Sheriff 1718.

1. Sir Boyle Maynard – {Youghal 1661-66}
2. Samuel Maynard – {Tallow 1692-93 1695-99 1703-12}

3. William Maynard – {Tallow 1713-34}

Seat: Curryglass (Curriglass), Cork (sold by early/mid-18th c.)
Estates: Worth £1,500 pa in 1713.

MEADE [Hawkins, Johnston, Magill, Whitshead] *IRELAND*

Earl of Clanwilliam (1776- I)

Origins: The Meades claimed medieval native Irish descent. First MP a judge. Kt 1623. 1 Bt was a judge and Attorney General. **First {MP 1559}.** The 1 Earl of Clanwilliam married 1765 Theodosia Magill, heiress to Gill Hall, the daughter of John Hawkins of Rathfriland, who had taken the name Magill on inheriting Gill Hall from his mother, Mary Magill, sister and heiress of Sir John Magill 1 Bt (see below).

1. Sir John Meade 1 Bt – {County Tipperary 1692-93 1695-99 1703-07
2. Sir Richard Meade 3 Bt – {Kinsale 1725-44}
3. John Meade 1 Earl of Clanwilliam – {Banagher 1764-66}
4. John Meade – County Down 1805-17

Seats: Gill Hall, Down (built 1670-80, acq. by mar. 1774, abandoned 1909, derelict, fire, demolished 1990s); Ballintober, Cork (acq. later 16th c., built sec. half 17th c., sold 1787 to another branch of Meade family, demolished 1940s); Montalto, Down (built mid-18th c., remod. early 19th c., add. 1837, add. later 19th c., purch. 1912, part demolished 1952, sold c. 1980); Burrenwood, Down (built mid 18th c., add. 1837, add. later 19th c., purch. 1910, part demolished 1952, fire 1985)
Estates: Bateman 17076 (I) 18024. Worth £14,000 pa in 1799. Property divided among brothers in early 19th c. and some land sold.
Titles: Baron Gillford and Viscount Clanwilliam 1766- I; Baron Clanwilliam 1828- UK; Baronet 1703-
Peers: {1 peer 1767-1800} 3 peers 1828-1945
Notes: 3 and 4 Earls and two others in ODNB.

Hawkins-Magill

Origins: See Meade above. William Hawkins was Ulster King of Arms (son of an Alderman of Dublin d. 1680). Sheriff 1659. His son was also Ulster King of Arms (d. 1787). His son was Bishop of Raphoe (d. 1807). The Magills were of Irish descent.

1. Sir John Magill – {Hillsborough 1692-93 Downpatrick 1695-99}
2. John Hawkins-Magill – {County Down 1703-13}
3. Robert Hawkins-Magill – {County Down 1724-45}

Seats: Gill Hall, Down (built 1670-80, add c. 1736, passed by mar. to Clanwilliams 1774, see above); Rathfriland, Down (castle demolished mid-17th c., acq. by Magills mid-17th c., passed by mar. 1774 to Earl of Clanwilliam, see above)
Title: Baronet 1680-1700

Johnston

Origins: Sheriff 1765. Sir John Magill 1 Bt (see Meade) was the son of William Johnston of Gillford and Susanna Magill, daughter of John Magill of Gill Hall.

1. Sir Richard Johnston 1 Bt – {Kilbeggan 1776-83 Blessington 1783-95}

Seat: Gillford (Gilford) Castle, Down (acq. 18th c., sold c. 1855, demolished)
Estates: Held 6,053 acres worth £1,065 pa in 1731. Worth £948 pa in 1840.
Title: Baronet 1772-1841

Whitshed

Origins: The first Whitshed MP was a successful barrister in the later 17th century. The granddaughter of Thomas Whitshed married in 1755 James Hawkins of Rathfriland (see above), whose great uncle married Mary Magill of Gill Hall. The son of this marriage, Admiral James Hawkins-Whitshed, succeeded to Killincarrig in 1791 and was created a Baronet.

1. Thomas Whitshed – {Carysfort 1692-93}
2. William Whitshed – {County Wicklow 1703-14}
3. Samuel Whitshed – {Wicklow 1715-46}
4. James Whitshed – {Wicklow 1723-35}
5. James Whitshed – {Wicklow 1747-60} St. Ives 1754-61 Cirencester 1761-83
6. William Whitshed – {Wicklow 1761-71}

Seat: Killincarrig, Wicklow (acq. early 18th c., acq. by mar. 1791, built early 19th c., passed out of family by mar. 1879, sold 1895, now golf club)
Estates: Bateman 5938 (I) 5039. Worth £1,000 pa in 1690s, £2,000 pa in 1779.
Title: Baronet 1834-71
Notes: 1 Bt in and three others ODNB.

MEDLYCOTT

Origins: Moved from Shropshire to London and built a fortune as a dyer in the early 17th century. The first MP was a barrister.

1. Thomas Medlycott – Abingdon 1689-90
2. Thomas Medlycott – {Kildare 1692-93 1695-99 Clonmell 1703-13} Milbourne Port 1705-08 Westminster 1708-15 {Ballynakill 1713-14 Downpatrick 1715-27 Newtown Limavady 1728-38} Milbourne Port 1727-34
3. James Medlycott – Milbourne Port 1710-22
4. Thomas Medlycott – Milbourne Port 1734-42 1747-63
5. Thomas Hutchings-Medlycott – Milbourne Port 1763-70 1780-81
6. Sir William Medlycott 1 Bt – Milbourne Port 1790-91

Seat: Ven House, Somerset (built 16th c., purch. 1696, rebuilt 1698-1700, add. 1720-31, add. 1836, leased out from 1906, sold 1957)
Estates: Bateman 3809 (E) 7730. Much land sold off in 1918.
Title: Baronet 1808-

MELLISH

Origins: London family long prominent in the Merchant Taylors Company. Married a Nottinghamshire heiress in the late 16th century. Purchased a landed estate 1635. High Sheriff 1630s. Oporto merchant late 17th century. Bankers in the 18th century. Though a landed dynasty, even the head of the family remained active in business and commerce into the 19th century.

1. Reason Mellish – Nottinghamshire 1685-87
2. William Mellish – East Retford 1741-51
3. Joseph Mellish – Great Grimsby 1761-80
4. Charles Mellish – Pontefract 1774-80 Aldborough 1780-84
5. William Mellish – Great Grimsby 1796-1802 1803-06 Middlesex 1806-20

Seats: Blyth(e) Hall, Nottinghamshire (purch. 1635, rebuilt 1684, sold 1806, demolished 1972); Bush Hill Park, Middlesex (acq. by mar. 1794, sold c. 1838, demolished 1927)
Notes: Serious financial difficulties early 19th c. Two in ODNB.

MELLOR

Origins: A legal family. QC 1851. Judge 1861. PC 1879. Son also QC and PC and a judge 1886. 1 Bt Solicitor General.

1. Sir John Mellor – Yarmouth 1857-59 Nottingham 1859-61
2. Sir John Mellor – Grantham 1880-86 Sowerby Div. Yorkshire 1892-1904
3. Sir John Mellor 2 Bt – Tamworth Div. Warwickshire 1935-45 Sutton Coldfield Div. Warwickshire 1945-55

Seat: Culmhead House, Somerset (acq. and built c. 1850, sold after 1945, hotel)
Title: Baronet 1924-90
Notes: One in ODNB.

MENZIES *SCOTLAND*

Origins: Granted lands in the 12th century. Chamberlain of Scotland 1249. At Menzies by the 14th century. **First [MP 1560]. Another [MP 1625 for Perthshire].**

1. Sir Alexander Menzies 1 Bt – [Perthshire 1693]

Seat: Castle Menzies, Perthshire (acq. and built 14th c., rebuilt 1488, fire 1502 and rebuilt, add. 1571-77, add. early 18th c., add. 1839-40, family departed 1910, sold and derelict, purch. by Clan Menzies 1957 and repaired 1970s, museum)
Estates: Bateman 98284 (S) 11467
Title: Baronet 1665-1910
Notes: Extinct in principal male line 1910.

MEREDITH I *IRELAND*

Origins: Claimed ancient Welsh descent. Moved from Denbighshire to Ireland as a chaplain to the Lord Deputy 1584. Bishop of Ferns and Leighlin 1589. His son settled at Dollardstown. Chancellor of the Exchequer in Ireland and Kt 1635. **First {MP 1613}. Two further {MPs 1634-39}.** Several lines are combined here.

1. Sir Robert Meredith – {Augher 1634 Athy 1639-49 Jamestown 1661-66}
2. Sir Amos Meredith – {Ballynakill 1661-66}
3. Sir Charles Meredith – {Old Leighlin 1661-66 Gowran 1692-93}
4. Sir Charles Meredith – {County Meath 1692-93 Kells 1695-99 1703-10}
5. Arthur Meredith – {Navan 1692-93 1695-99 1703-14 1715-27}
6. Richard Meredith – {Athy 1703-13}
7. Thomas Meredith – {Navan 1703-13 1715-19} Midhurst 1709-10
8. Henry Meredith – {Kells 1710-13 Navan 1713-14}
9. Thomas Meredith – {Wexford 1713-14 New Ross 1715-27 Navan 1727-32}
10. Arthur Meredith – {County Meath 1751-60}
11. Henry Meredith – {Armagh 1776-89}

Seats: Dollardstown, Meath (acq. early 17th c., built late 17th c., passed to Somervilles in the 18th c., demolished 1986); Greenhills, Kildare (acq. early 17th c., departed early/mid-18th c.); Shrowland, Kildare (acq. mid-17th c.); Norelands, Kilkenny (resident 19th c.); Carlanstown (Carlandstown), Meath (resident 19th c.); Madalee, Kilkenny
Estates: Bateman 6416 (I) 6509

Titles: Baronet 1660-65; 1795-1923
Notes: The Meredith Baronets eventually inherited Hollymount House, Down from the Savage family (see Price II) by mar. via the Baylys in the mid-19th c. One in ODNB.

MEREDITH II

Origins: Welsh origin. Settled at Leeds Abbey c. James I. **First MP 1656, for Kent.**

1. Thomas Meredith – Kent 1701
2. Sir Roger Meredith 5 Bt – Kent 1727-34

Seat: Leeds Abbey, Kent (acq. early 17th c., sold 1765)
Title: Baronet 1622-1739

MERVYN (Marvyn) [Richardson] *IRELAND*

Mervyn

Origins: Gentry from the 15th century. Judge under Henry VIII acquired more landed property mid-16th c. The first MP was the son of an English admiral from Hampshire who acquired land in Ulster c. 1603-04. **First MP 1584. Three further MPs 1584-1621.** Speaker of the Irish House of Commons 1661. Sheriff 1686.

1. Sir Audley Mervyn – {County Tyrone 1639 1661-66}
2. Henry Mervyn – {Augher 1661-66 County Tyrone 1692-93 1695-96}
3. Audley Mervyn – {Strabane 1695-99 County Tyrone 1703-17}
4. Henry Mervyn – {Augher 1713-27 County Tyrone 1727-48}
5. Audley Mervyn – {County Tyrone 1717-27}

Seats: Trelick (Trillick, Trillie or Castle Touchett) (Castle Mervyn), Tyrone (acq. 1611, castle built by 1628, passed to Archdalls (see) by inher. mid-18th c., abandoned early 19th c.)
Estates: Worth £1,500 pa in 1713. Part of estates sold 1720.
Notes: Two in ODNB.

Richardson

Origins: Emigrated to Ireland and gained estates by 1619. Sheriff 1662. James Richardson married in 1739 Ann, daughter and heiress of Audley Mervyn of Castle Mervyn and took the name Mervyn. Richardsons also took the name Bunbury in 1775 after marrying an heiress.

1. Archibald Richardson – {Augher 1692-93}
2. William Richardson – {Augher 1737-55}
3. St. George Richardson – {Augher 1755-60}
4. Sir William Richardson 1 Bt – {Augher 1783-90 Ballyshannon 1798-1800}

Seats: Springtown, Tyrone (acq. later 17th c.); Kilfeacle Kilfeakle), Tipperary (acq. from Bunburys by mar. of 1749, sold later 18th c., ruin); Augher Castle (Spur Royal, Castle Hill), Tyrone (built 1615, acq. 1641, burned 1689, rebuilt 1832)
Estates: 1424 (I) 1079 in the 1870s.
Title: Baronet 1787-
Notes: Resident in England in 20th c.

METGE *IRELAND*

Origins: Huguenot settlers in Ireland c. 1685. Merchants. Grandson of first settler an MP 1776. Held civil offices in the 19th century.

1. Peter Metge – {Ardee 1776-83 Ratoath 1783-84}
2. John Metge – {Ratoath 1784-90 Banagher 1790-97 Tallow 1797-1800} Dundalk 1806-07 1812 1820
3. Robert Metge – County Meath 1880-83

Seat: Athlumney House, Meath (acq. late 18th c., resident into 20th c.)
Estates: 788 (I) 1168 in the 1870s.

METHUEN

Baron Methuen (1838- UK)

Origins: Probably founded by a clergyman who emigrated from Scotland in the mid-16th century for religious reasons. (Wagner, *English Genealogy*, 214-15) Became very wealthy clothiers in the 17th century, intermixing business and a gentry style of life. One left £10,000 in cash in 1667. The first MP was a successful lawyer, Lord Chancellor of Ireland in 1694, and an ambassador in 1703. His son also amassed a large fortune (£250,000) from the stock market and office (d. 1757). The last clothier in the family died in 1733. His son inherited money and estates. (Ladd, *Architects at Corsham Court*, 23-33, 156)

1. John Methuen – Devizes 1690-1706
2. Sir Paul Methuen – Devizes 1708-10 Brackley 1713-14 1715-47
3. Paul Methuen – Westbury 1747-48 Warwick 1762-74 Great Bedwyn 1774-81
4. Pal Methuen – Great Bedwyn 1781-84

5. Paul Methuen 1 Baron Methuen – Wiltshire 1812-19 N. Wiltshire 1832-37

Seat: Corsham Court, Wiltshire (medieval, ruin by 1541, rebuilt 1582, purch. 1745, add. 1761-64 and 1797, remod. 1844-49, still own)
Estates: Bateman 5542 (E) 10208
Peers: 4 peers 1838-1945
1 in Cabinet 1716-17
Notes: 3 and 4 Barons and four others in ODNB.

MEYNELL [Ingram, Villiers]

Origins: An old family established in Derbyshire since the 12th century. At Langley Hall by 1176. Summoned as a Baron by writ 1327. **First MP 1295. Five additional MPs 14th and 15th centuries.** The main stem of the family continued at Meynell Langley down to the present. The cadet line here was founded by the father of the first MP, who created a large fortune by "play", an unsavory gambler and racing man. The Meynells were descended in the female line from the Viscounts Ingram (extinct 1778), but the estates passed to the Marquess of Hertford (see Seymour). The Meynells took the name Ingram anyway.

1. Hugo Meynell – Lichfield 1762-68 Lymington 1769-74 Stafford 1774-80
2. Henry Meynell – Lisburn 1826-47
3. Frederick Meynell Villiers – Saltash 1831-32 Canterbury 1835 Sudbury 1841-42 (an illegitimate son)
4. Hugo Meynell Ingram – W. Staffordshire 1869-71

Seats: Hoar Cross, Staffordshire (built later 16th, new house 1871, add. 1897, sold 1970); Bradley Hall, Derbyshire (purch. 1655, old house demolished, rebuilt 1772, sold 19th c.); Meynell Langley, Derbyshire (acq. by 1176, passed out of the family, repurch. later by junior line, still own); Quorndon Hall, Leicestershire (purch. 1754, sold 1800)
Estates: Bateman 25205 (E) 45491
Notes: Hugo Meynell Ingram, the last of the main line, died in 1871. His wife was the sister of the 2 Viscount Halifax (see Wood). Hoar Cross passed to a younger son who took the name Meynell in 1904. One in ODNB.

MEYRICK [Charlton, Gervis, Mews (Meux), Tapps] *WALES & ENGLAND*

<u>Meyrick</u> (Meyricke)

Origins: The Meyricks claimed descent from ancient Welsh kings and that they had held Bodorgan for 1000 years. They became prominent after Bosworth, where one fought for Henry VII. His son was taken into the royal household as an official. High Sheriff of

Anglesey under Henry VIII. **First MP 1589, kt of the shire. One additional MP 1614.** They succeeded to the estates of the last Earl of Londonderry in 1765 (see Pitt).

1. Edmund Meyricke – Merioneth 1660
2. Owen Meyrick – Anglesey 1715-22
3. Owen Meyrick – Angelsey 1761-70

Seat: Bodorgan (Bodwrgan), Angelsey (acq. and built mid-16th c., demolished and rebuilt 1779-82, still own)
Estates: Owen Morgan MP (d. 1825) owned London property and was said to have had an income of £11,000 pa from his Welsh estates. Rubinstein - Owen Morgan left £140,000 in probate in 1825. See Tapps-Gervis below. One of the largest estates on Anglesey.
Notes: Four in ODNB.

Tapps-Gervis

Origins: The daughter and heiress of Owen Meyrick married August Fuller of Rosehill, Sussex (see Elliot). On his death in 1876 he was succeeded by his nephew Sir George Meyrick-Tapps-Gervis of Hinton Admiral (see below). Gained wealth in 19th century developing Bournemouth as a resort.

1. Sir George Tapps-Gervis 2 Bt – New Romney 1826-30 Christchurch 1832-37

Seats: Hinton Admiral (Hinton Park), Hampshire (built 1720, fire 1777, rebuilt 1777, acq. by mar. later 18th c., remod. c. 1905, still own); Bodorgan, Anglesey (see above)
Estates: Bateman 21204 (E & W) 16641
Title: Baronet 1791-
Notes: 3 Bt in ODNB.

Mews

Origins: The Meux or Mews were gentry in the 14th century. One married the heiress of the Kingstons of Kingston Manor, Isle of Wight, in the 15th century. **First MP 1584. Two further MPs 1604-44**. Lydia Gervis married in 1719 Sir Peter Mews of Hinton Admiral. Her sister and heiress had a son Benjamin Clerke who succeeded in 1759. Sir George Tapps, cousin of the last Clerke who died childless, inherited. Sir George Meyrick-Tapps-Gervis was his grandson.

1. Sir Peter Mews – Christchurch 1710-26

Seat: Hinton Admiral, Hampshire (purch. 1708, built 1720, passed to Tapps-Gervis later 18th c., see above)

Meux

Origins: This cadet line descended in the 17th century from the Mews family (see above). They became successful brewers in London in the second half of the 18th century but continued to marry into the gentry and aristocracy.

1. Sir Henry Meux 1 Bt – Hertfordshire 1847-59

Seats: Theobalds Park, Hertfordshire (built later 18th c., purch. 1820s/30s, passed to Lambtons 1910/11, sold 1929, institutional use); Dauntsey, Wiltshire (medieval, remod. 17th and 18th c., purch. 1877, sold 1913/14)
Estates: Bateman 15110 (E) 23507. Rubinstein – Richard Meux left £125,000 in probate in 1813. The 1 Bt was worth £700,000 with £40,000 pa. in 1857.
Titles: Baronet 1641-1706; 1831-1900
Notes: The Meux estates were inherited by the Earls of Durham in 1911 (see Lambton), and passed in 1929 to the Gilmour Bts. Meux family has an entry in ODNB.

Charlton-Meyrick

Origins: Descended from a cadet line of the Meyricks of Bodorgan. **First MP 1640.** Sir John Charlton of Apley Castle married (1820) the daughter and heiress of Thomas Meyrick of Bush. The Charltons were landowners in Shropshire from the 13th century (Lord Charlton 1313), a cadet of the Charltons of Whitton (see Lechmere). **First Charlton MP 1554 for Shropshire. One other MP 1645**. They took the name Meyrick in 1880.

1. John Meyrick – Pembroke 1702-08 Cardigan 1710-12
2. St. John Charlton – Bridgnorth 1725-34
3. Sir Thomas Charlton Meyrick 1 Bt – Pembroke District 1868-74

Seats: Bush, Pembrokeshire (acq. c. 1600, burned 1866, rebuilt 1906, now a home for the elderly); Apley Castle, Shropshire (medieval, Charltons acq. early 14th c., rebuilt 1567-1620, new house built 1791-94 by Charltons, sold late 1840s, demolished 1955)
Estates: Bateman 8164 (W & E) 30105. Worth £3,000 p.a. in 1642.
Title: Baronet 1880-
Notes: One Meyrick and one Charlton in ODNB.

MICHELL (Michel)

Michell

Origins: Merchants in Lyme Regis in the 16th century. A lawyer settled at Kingston Russell c. 1600. **First MP 1554. Another MP 1610.**

1. John Michel – Bridport 1681 1690-95 St. Ives 1695-98
2. Robert Michell – Petersfield 1689-1705
3. David Michell – Lyme Regis 1780-84
4. John Michel – Belfast 1816-18

Seats: Kingston Russell House, Dorset (acq. and built early 17th c., rebuilt c. 1730, sold 1862); Dewlish House, Dorset (built 1702, purch. c. 1756, passed to the Montmorencys 1886)
Estates: Worth £1,500 pa in 1660.
Notes: A mid-19th c. Michel was a field marshal, responsible for the great cultural atrocity of burning the Imperial Summer Place at Beijing in 1860. The Michel estates passed via an heiress to the 3 Viscount Franfort de Montmorency in 1886 (see Morres). One in ODNB.

Michell

Origins: Another line in Sussex. **First MP 1529. Two other MPs 1529-53.**

1. John Michell – Horsham 1679-81

Seat: Field Place, Sussex (medieval, acq. early 16th c., add. 1678, sold 1729)

MICKLETHWAIT [Cropley]

Viscount Micklethwait (1727-34 I)

Origins: Thomas Micklethwait, the grandson of an eminent physician, purchased the manor of Swine in the mid-17th century. In 1713 his friend, Sir John Cropley 2 Bt, left his estate worth £4,000 pa to Micklethwait. The Cropley 1 Bt was the son of a London mercer.

1. Sir John Cropley 2 Bt – Shaftesbury 1701-10
2. Thomas Micklethwait – Arundel 1715-18
3. Joseph Micklethwait 1 Viscount Micklethwait – Arundel 1718-27 Kingston-upon-Hull 1727-34

Seat: Swine Hall, Yorkshire (medieval, purch. by Cropleys 1639, remod. 17th c., passed to Micklethwaites 1713, passed out of the family 1734, demolished c. 1868)
Estates: Worth at least £4,000 pa 1713. 2,200 acres at Swine in 1734.
Title: Baron 1724-34 I
Notes: The 1 and last Viscount left his estates to his mistress and hence, eventually, to the Earls of Shaftesbury.

MIDDLETON I *SCOTLAND*

Earl of Middleton (1660-95 S)

Origins: A Scottish gentry family that traced back to the 12th century and were gentry by the 15th. Soldiers in the 17th century. The 1 Earl was Captain General of the Forces 1653.

1. Charles Middleton 2 Earl of Middleton – Winchelsea 1685-87
2. John Middleton – Aberdeen Burghs 1713-39

Seat: Fettercairn House (Middleton), Kincardineshire (resident since 12th c., gained full estate 1648, built 1666-70, estates confiscated and/or sold late 17th and mid-18th century)
Peers: [2 peers 1660-92]
1 in Cabinet 1684-88
Notes: Indebted in 17th c. The 2 Earl of Middleton was a Jacobite and went into exile after 1688, and estates confiscated 1695 (but 2 Earl continued to receive the income in exile). 1 and 2 Earls in ODNB.

MIDDLETON II

Origins: Married a Scottish heiress to Belsay c. 1226. Chancellor under Henry III. **First MP 1324. Three other MPs 1414-75.**

1. Sir William Middleton 3 Bt – Northumberland 1722-57
2. Sir William Middleton 5 Bt – Northumberland 1774-95
3. Sir Charles Middleton Monck 6 Bt – Northumberland 1812-20
4. Sir Arthur Middleton 7 Bt – Durham 1874-80

Seats: Belsay Castle and Hall, Northumberland (acq. c. 1226, tower house built 14th c., add. 1614, ruin, new house built 1809-17, family departed 1962, decayed, restored 1984, still own); Caneby (Caenby), Lincolnshire (acq. by Moncks later 18th c., passed to Middletons by inher. 1798, sold 1871, demolished)
Estates: Bateman 9079 (E) 9712

Title: Baronet 1662-
Notes: 6 Bt in ODNB.

MIDDLETON III

Origins: The first MP's father built up an estate fom the profits of the iron industry in the mid-16th century and the family became gunfounders. **First MP 1614**.

1. Thomas Middleton – Horsham 1640-48 1660
2. John Middleton – Bramber 1703-04 Horsham 1710-15

Seats: Hills Place, Sussex (built 15th-16th c., purch. 1608, add. 1610, sold 1668, part demolished 1925); Muntham Court, Sussex (medieval, acq. 16th c., sold 1734, demolished 1961, crematorium)
Notes: The family fortunes waned at the end of the 17th century.

MILBANKE [Byron, Johnson, King, Lovelace, Pye]

Milbanke

Origins: Prominent merchants in Newcastle-upon-Tyne in the 17th century. Mayor 1630s. Married a merchant heiress and acquired estates from c. 1600 onwards.

1. Sir Mark Milbanke 2 Bt – Richmond 1690-95
2. Ralph Milbanke – Northallerton 1697-1701
3. Sir Ralph Milbanke 5 Bt – Scarborough 1754-61 Richmond 1761-68
4. Sir Ralph Milbanke-Noel 6 Bt – County Durham 1790-1812
5. Mark Milbanke – Camelford 1818-19 1820-32
6. Sir Frederick Milbanke 1 Bt – N. R. Yorkshire 1865-85
7. Sir Powlett Milbanke 2 Bt – Radnorshire 1895-1900

Seats: Thorp Perrow, Yorkshire (medieval house, add. 16th c., purch. 1798, rebuilt c. 1800, sold 1897); Halnaby Hall, Yorkshire (purch. 1649, rebuilt post 1660 and c. 1729, sold 1842, demolished 1952); Barningham Park, Yorkshire (purch. and built c. 1690s, remod. 1790s, add. 19th c., still own); Dalden Tower and Seaham Hall, Durham (medieval, purch. 1676/8, tower a ruin in 18th c., sold 1821); Norton Manor, Radnorshire; Kirkby Mallory, Leicestershire (built early 17th c., rebuilt c. 1750, acq. by mar. from Noels 1816, passed to Lord Lovelace 1860, demolished 1953)
Estates: Bateman 14456 (E) 27594. Worth £2,000 pa c. 1660. Owned 5,500 acres in the 1980s.
Title: Baronet 1661-1949; 1882-
1 Ld Lt 20th
Notes: Three in ODNB.

Baron Byron (1643- E)

Origins: The 6 Lord Byron married Anne Milbanke, Baroness Wentworth in her own right (see Wentworth), daughter of Sir Ralph Milbanke-Noel 6 Bt. The Byrons claimed to have come over with the Conqueror. Held land in Nottinghamshire 1086. They acquired Clayton in Lancashire in the 12th century. Kt 14th century. **First MP 1322 for Lincolnshire. Six further MPs 1421-1628, all kts of the shire.**

1. William Byron – Morpeth 1775-76

Seats: Newstead Abbey, Nottinghamshire (late 13th c. abbey buildings, purch. 1540 and house built, sold 1817, now a museum); Colwick Hall, Nottinghamshire (acq. by marriage 1380, sold mid-18th c., rebuilt 1776, became part of race course 1898, now hotel)
Estates: Sold in 1817 for £94,000 (3,200 acres). Junior lines 4326 (E) 6225
Peers: 10 peers 1660-1736 1743-98 1809-70 1882-1945
Notes: Estates much diminished due to the Civil War and extravagance. The 6 Baron was a great poet. 1 and 6 Barons and five others in ODNB.

Earl of Lovelace (1838- UK)

Origins: The father of the 1 Baron was a grocer and dry salter in Exeter. The 1 Baron served as a shop boy (Mingay, *English Landed Society in the Eighteenth Century*, 75) and became a barrister, Lord Chief Justice of the Common Pleas 1714, and Lord Chancellor 1725. William King married Ada Byron and succeeded to the Noel-Wentworth-Lovelace estates. He was created Earl of Lovelace. His son Byron Noel succeeded his maternal grandmother as 12 Baron Wentworth.

1. Peter King 1 Baron King – Bere Alston 1701-15
2. John King 2 Baron King – Launceston 1727-34
3. Peter King – E. Surrey 1847-74

Seats: (East) Horsley Towers, Surrey (built 1834, purch. c. 1847, add. 1847-c.1860, sold, conference center); Ockham Park, Surrey (built early 17th c., purch. 1711, rebuilt 1725-29, remod. 1830, fire 1946, demolished 1950); Brooklands House, Surrey (built 1862, motor racing track opened there 1907); Ben Damph Forest, Ross-shire (built 1884-87, now hotel); Kirkby Mallory, Leicestershire (built early 17th c., rebuilt c. 1750, acq. by mar. from the Milbankes 1860, sold 1918, demolished 1953)
Estates: Bateman 23112 (E) 29413
Titles: Baron Wentworth 1529- E; Baron King 1725- GB
Peers: 11 peers 1725-93 1796-1893 1864-1945
1 Ld Lt 19th

1 In Cabinet 18th
Notes: 1 and 7 Barons King and 2 Earl and two others in ODNB.

Baron Lovelace (1627-1736 E)

Origins: The Lovelace family rose as soldiers and officials under the Tudors. Granted arms 1577. **First MP 1554. Two further MPs 1601-21, one for Berkshire**. The 2 Baron Lovelace married in 1638 Anne Baroness Wentworth in her own right, daughter of the 4 Baron Wentworth and 1 Earl of Cleveland. Margaret Lovelace, daughter of the 2 Baron Lovelace married Sir William Noel of Kirkby Mallory (see Noel) and their descendents succeeded to the Barony of Wentworth and were created Viscounts Wentworth and Earls of Lovelace.

1. John Lovelace 3 Baron Lovelace – Berkshire 1661-70

Seats: Hurley (Lady Place), Berkshire (purch. 1545, sold 1924); Water Eaton, Oxfordshire (built 1586, purch. 1624, remod. 1670s, sold 1692)
Estates: Worth £7,000 pa c. 1735.
Peers: 4 peers 1660-1709 1729-36
1 Ld Lt 17th
Notes: 3 and 4 Barons and one other in ODNB.

Pye

Origins: The grandfather of the first MP was a butcher. The father was a wealthy scrivener. Bt 1641. John 3 Baron Lovelace married Martha Pye, heiress of Bradenham. Their daughter succeeded as 8 Baroness Wentworth in her own right.

1. Sir Edmund Pye 1 Bt – Chipping Wycombe 1661-73

Seat: Bradenham, Buckinghamshire (purch. 1642, passed by mar. to the Lovelaces late 17th c.)
Estates: Worth £1,050 pa c. 1650.
Title: Baronet 1641-73

Johnson

Origins: Merchants and ship builders and owners in the 16th century. **First MP 1597**. The second MP was the greatest ship owner of his day. Kt 1680. Captain General of the Royal Africa Company at Cape Coast Castle in later 17th c. Sir Henry Johnson married Martha 8 Baroness Wentworth in her own right (see above).

1. Sir Henry Johnson – Aldeburgh 1679
2. Sir Henry Johnson – Aldeburgh 1689-1719
3. William Johnson – Aldeburgh 1689-1718

Seats: Friston Hall, Suffolk (built c. 1570, purch. 1680s, passed to Wentworths (Strafford) by mar. of 1711, estate broken up in 1791); Bradenham, Buckinghamshire (inherited from Lovelaces first half 18th c., sold 1787, see above)
Notes: The daughter and heiress of the 8 Baroness and Sir Henry Johnson married in 1711 the 1 Earl of Strafford of the second creation, whose family inherited some of the estates. One in ODNB.

MILBORNE-PILKINGTON

Pilkington

Origins: At Pilkington, Lancashire by c. 1200. **First MP 1316 for Lancashire. Three additional MPs 1316-1478, all kts of the shire**. One knighted at Agincourt.

1. Sir Lionel Pilkington 5 Bt – Horsham 1748-68

Seats: Chevet Park (Hall), Yorkshire (inher. by the Pilkingtons 1749, demolished 1955); Stanley Hall, Yorkshire (purch. 1603, moved seat to Chevet 1750s, leased out, fire 1759, sold 1802 for £23,500, rebuilt, institutional use); Wonastow Court, Monmouthshire (see below)
Estates: Bateman 8744 (E & W) 13597
Title: Baronet 1635-
Notes: The estates of the main line of the family were forfeited after Bosworth and the male line extinct 1502. The branch discussed above descended from an illegitimate son. The family name became Milborne-Swinnerton-Pilkington in the 19th century. See below. Pilkington family has an entry in ODNB.

Milborne

Origins: Medieval family that greatly enlarged their estates under Henry VIII. The 8 Pilkington Baronet married the heiress of Wonastow.

1. William Milborne – Milborne Port 1660
2. Clayton Milborne – Monmouth 1708-15

Seat: Wonastow Court, Monmouthshire (built 16th c., acq. by Milbornes 1630s by mar., add. 17th c., passed by mar. to Swinnertons 1775, rebuilt 1803, to Pilkington Bts by mar. 19th c., see above, derelict mid-20th c.)

Notes: The Swinnertons (Swynnerton, Swinnarton) of Wonastow produced a number of MPs. **First MP 1322. Three others 1402-1604.**

MILES

Origins: Plantation owners in Jamaica from the early 18th century and Bristol shipowners, merchants and then bankers later in the century. Used a great fortune to purchase estates in the 19th century. Mayor of Bristol 1780. Two lines are combined here.

1. Sir William Miles 1 Bt – Chippenham 1818-20 New Romney 1830-32
2. Philip Miles – Westbury 1820-26 Corfe Castle 1829-32 Bristol 1835-37
3. Philip Miles – Bristol 1837-52
4. John Miles – Bristol 1868
5. Sir Philip Miles 2 Bt – E. Somerset 1878-85
6. Charles Miles – Malmesbury 1882-85

Seats: Kings Weston, Gloucestershire (built 1580s, rebuilt 1707-19, purch. 1833 for £210,000, sold 1937, institutional use); Leigh Court, Somerset (built 16th c., purch. 1811, rebuilt 1814, sold 1916, institutional use); Forde Abbey, Dorset (in Devon until 1844) (medieval, remodeled 16th c., purch. 1649, remodeled 1650s, purch. 1846 for £55,000, sold 1864)
Estates: Bateman 3207 (E) 9092 and 5484 (E) 6868. Worth £1,000,000 in 1845.
Title: Baronet 1859-
Notes: The first four MPs were all actively engaged in business and the plantations were still in the family's possession in the later 19th century.

MILLER I *SCOTLAND*

Origins: The founder was a lawyer in the early 18th century. Lord President of the Court of Session 1761. Lord of Session 19th century. Banking later 18th c.

1. Sir Thomas Miller 1 Bt – Dumfries Burghs 1761-66
2. Sir William Miller 2 Bt – Edinburgh 1780-81
3. Patrick Miller – Dumfries 1790-96

Seats: Glenlee Park, Kirkcudbrightshire (purch. and built 18th c., sold, remod. 1822, remod. c. 1860); Barskimming, Ayrshire (purch. and built 1771, sold, rebuilt 1883); Dalswinton House, Dumfriesshire (castle 13th c., purch. 1785 and built, demolished 1788, rebuilt 1788-1802, sold 1818)
Estates: Bateman 4453 (S) 3823
Title: Baronet 1788-
Notes: 1 and 2 Bts and two others in ODNB.

MILLER II (Meller, Mellor)

Origins: Rising gentry building up an estate 1550-1600. **First MP 1601.** Kt 1603. **Another MP 1628.**

1. Edward Meller – Dorchester 1685-87

Seats: Little Bredy, Dorset (purch. 1590s and built c. 1600, sold early 18th c.); Winterborne Came, Dorset (purch. c. 1560, sold by 1700); Upcerne Manor House, Dorset (purch. c. 1600, built early 17th c., sold 1685)
Notes: Family heavily indebted by 1685.

MILLER III

Origins: Clothiers and maltsters prominent in Chichester from the mid-16th century.

1. Sir Thomas Miller 1 Bt – Chichester 1689-95
2. Sir John Miller 2 Bt – Chichester 1698-1700 Sussex 1701 Chichester 1701-05 1710-13
3. Sir Thomas Miller 3 Bt – Chichester 1715-27
4. Sir Thomas Miller 5 Bt – Lewes 1774-80 Portsmouth 1806-16

Seats: Froyle Place, Hampshire (medieval, add. 1588, remod. 17th, 18th, purch. 1765-82, remod. 1867, sold 1947); Lavant, Sussex (purch. later 17th c., sold mid-18th c.)
Estates: Bateman 4008 (E) 4667
Title: Baronet 1705-

MILLS

<u>Baron Hillingdon</u> (1886-1982 UK)

Origins: Rose as merchants and bankers in the 18th century continuing in the 19th century. East India Company Chairman and married an heiress of a Lord Mayor of London. Five generations were partners in Glyn's Bank 1753-1939.

1. Charles Mills – Warwick 1802-26
2. William Mills – St. Ives 1790-96 Coventry 1805-12
3. John Mills – Rochester 1831-34
4. Arthur Mills – Taunton 1852-53 1857-65 Exeter 1873-80
5. Charles Mills 1 Baron Hillingdon – Northallerton 1865-66 W. Kent 1868-85
6. Charles Mills 2 Baron Hillingdon – Sevenoaks Div. W. Kent 1885-92
7. Charles Mills – Uxbridge Div. Middlesex 1910-15
8. Arthur Mills 3 Baron Hillingdon – Uxbridge Div. Middlesex 1915-18

9. Sir John Mills – New Forest Div. Hampshire 1932-45

Seats: Hillingdon Court, Middlesex (acq. and built c. 1854, sold 1919); Bisterne, Hampshire (built later 16th c., add. 1652, remod late 17th c., purch. 1792 for £46,000, remod. c. 1840, still own); Overstrand Hall, Norfolk (built 1899-1901, sold 1932); Barford Hill House, Warwickshire (purch. c. 1800, built c. 1805, sold 1837, demolished 1955); The Wildernesse House, Kent (leased 1860, purch. 1885, sold 1921, housing estate, institutional use)
Estates: Bateman 2710 (E) 6118; 4316 (E) 4867; 2630 (E) 3992. The Hillingdon Court estate was 3,185 acres in 1920. Rubinstein - Charles Mills left £120,000 in probate in 1826. The 1 Baron left a million and a half pounds in 1898.
Title: Baronet 1868-1982
Peers: 3 peers 1886-1945
Notes: Mills family has an entry in ODNB.

MILNE (Mylne) *SCOTLAND*

Origins: Surgeons and merchants in the 16th and 17th centuries. Provost 1616. **First [MP 1617].**

1. Sir Robert Milne 1 Bt – [Linlithgow 1667 1669-74 1678]
2. Alexander Milne – [Linlithgow 1681 1685-86]

Seat: Barnton, Dumfriesshire
Title: Baronet 1686-1791

MILNER

Origins: Exceptionally successful merchants in Leeds in the 17th and 18th centuries. Mayor 1697. Granted arms 1710. The father of the first MP purchased landed estates and severed connections with trade by 1740. High Sheriff 1747. (Roebuck, *Yorkshire Baronets*, 26, 309).

1. Sir William Milner 1 Bt – York 1722-34
2. Sir William Milner 3 Bt – York 1790-1811
3. Sir William Milner 5 Bt – York 1848-57
4. Sir Frederick Milner 7 Bt – York 1883-85 Bassetlaw Div. Nottinghamshire 1890-1906

Seat: Nun Appleton Hall, Yorkshire (purch. for £17,000 in 1708, rebuilt soon after, add. c. 1864, sold c. 1890, partially demolished and derelict c. 2000)

Estates: Bateman 5491 (E) 8977. Income in 1800 was £12,000 pa over half of which came from canal stock. (R. G. Wilson, *Gentlemen Merchants*, 221)
Title: Baronet 1717-
Notes: 1 Bt in ODNB.

MITCHELLHILL *SCOTLAND*

Origins: Unknown. Burgesses? **First [MP 1579 for Selkirk. Two additional [MPs for Selkirk 1612-40].**

1. William Mitchellhill – [Selkirk 1665 1667]

MITFORD [Edwards, Freeman]

Mitford

Origins: Old gentry family. **First MP 1658.**

1. William Mitford – Midhurst 1859-74

Seats: Mitford Castle, Northumberland (built by 1138, acq. c. 1556, rebuilt early 17th c., in ruins); Mitford Hall, Northumberland (built 1828, sold 1992)
Estates: Bateman 12672 (E) 14353
Notes: One in ODNB.

Earl of Redesdale (1877-86 UK)

Origins: A younger son of the senior line became a merchant in London and acquired land in Hampshire. A younger son married a Freeman (see below) heiress. His grandson became a barrister, Speaker of the House of Commons 1801, and Lord Chancellor of Ireland 1802. On the extinction of the younger line, the title was recreated for Mitford cousins at Exbury.

1. John Mitford 1 Baron Redesdale – Bere Alston 1788-99 East Looe 1799-1802
2. Sir William Mitford – Newport 1785-90 Bere Alston 1796-1806 New Romney 1812-18
3. Algernon Freeman Mitford 1 Baron Redesdale – Stratford-on-Avon Div. Warwickshire 1892-95

Seats: Batsford, Gloucestershire (built 16th c., remod. c. 1700, 1760s, acq. by mar. 1808, remod. 1809-16, demolished 1890, rebuilt 1887-92, sold 1918); Exbury House, Hampshire (Mitfords purch. 1718, sold c. 1881)
Estates: Bateman 26497 (E) 15467; Baron Redesdale 2120 (E) 2019

Titles: Baron Redesdale 1802-86 UK; Baron Redesdale 1902-
Peers: 4 peers 1802-86 1902-45
Notes: 1 Baron of first cr. and 1 Baron sec. cr. and 1 Earl and five others in ODNB.

Edwards Freeman

Origins: The Freemans were settled at Batsford by 1490. Modest gentry until a prominent lawyer became Lord Chancellor of Ireland 1707-10. The Freeman estates passed by marriage to the Edwards family 1745. The first MP was the son of a Bristol attorney. He was also a lawyer and married the heiress of a great Bristol merchant (Hayman). William Mitford, grandfather of the first Baron Redesdale, married the daughter and heiress of Robert Edwards Freeman of Wingfield.

1. Thomas Edwards – Bristol 1713-15 Wells 1719-35
2. Thomas Edwards Freeman – Steyning 1768-80
3. Thomas Edwards Freeman – Steyning 1785-88

Seats: Wingfield Park, Berkshire (Edwards acq. by mar. 1737, sold later 18th c.); Filkins, Oxfordshire (purch. 1703, sold 1737)
Notes: William Mitford married Margaret Edwards, heiress of Wingfield, Berkshire, to which he succeeded in 1737. One in ODNB.

MOHUN

Origins: Bridport merchants in the 16th century. **First MP 1539, for Bridport. Two additional MPs for Bridport 1559-86.**

1. Francis Mohun – Weymouth & Melcombe Regis 1685-87

Seat: Fleet, Dorset (acq. 1563, passed out of the family by mar. 1758)
Estates: Worth £300 pa c. 1650.

MOLESWORTH [St. Aubyn] *ENGLAND & IRELAND*

Viscount Molesworth (1716- I)

Origins: An old Northamptonshire family. High Sheriff 1304. Declined in wealth in the 16th century due to prodigality. A younger son went to Ireland as a soldier during the Civil War, and gained a 2,500 acre estate. He then set up as a merchant in Dublin and amassed a fortune.

1. Robert Molesworth 1 Viscount Molesworth – {County Dublin 1695-99} Camelford 1695-98 {Swords 1703-14} Lothwithiel 1705-06 East Retford 1706-08 Mitchell 1715-22
2. Richard Molesworth 3 Viscount Molesworth – {Swords 1715-26}
3. William Molesworth – {Philipstown 1717-60}
4. Brysse Molesworth – {Swords 1727-60}

Seats: Brackenstown House, Dublin (acq. by mar. mid-17th c., rebuilt mid-18th c., passed to heiresses 1793); Edlington, Yorkshire (acq. c. 1700, sold c. 1730)
Estates: Worth £2,825 pa in 1689; £3,739 pa in 1795; under 2,000 acres in Bateman. Substantial urban property in Dublin in the 18th c.
Peers: {5 peers 1719-58 1769-93 1795-1800}
Notes: A substantial portion of the 3 Viscount's estates passed by mar. to the Stewarts of Killymoon in 1794 (see Stewart II). 1, 2, and 3 Viscounts and three others in ODNB.

<u>Molesworth</u>

Origins: A cadet line that broke off in the late 16th century. Married an heiress in Cornwall. A younger son married a Jamaican heiress. Governor of Jamaica in the 1680s.

1. Sir John Molesworth 2 Bt – Bossiney 1701-02 Lostwithiel 1701 1702-05
2. Sir John Molesworth 4 Bt – Newport 1734-41 Cornwall 1744-61
3. Sir John Molesworth 5 Bt – Cornwall 1765-75
4. Sir William Molesworth 6 Bt – Cornwall 1784-90
5. Sir William Molesworth 8 Bt – Cornwall 1832-37 Leeds 1837-41 Southwark 1845-55
6. Walter Molesworth-St. Aubyn – Helston 1880-85
7. Sir Lewis Molesworth 11 Bt – Bodmin Div. Cornwall 1900-06

Seats: Pencarrow, Cornwall (leased late 16th c., purch. 1626, rebuilt c. 1760, still own); Clowance, Cornwall (acq. by mar. 1839, fire 1843, rebuilt, sold 1923, holiday village); Trewarthenick, Cornwall (sold 1640); Tetcott House, Devon (rebuilt c. 1700, acq. by mar. from Arscott family 1788, demolished 1831, rebuilt, still own)
Estates: Bateman 17034 (E) 10997 and 6299 (E) 8796
Title: Baronet 1689-
1 in Cabinet 1853-58
Notes: 8 Bt in ODNB.

<u>Baron St. Levan</u> (1887- UK)

Origins: Claimed Norman descent. The family emerged in the 14th century. The first MP married an heiress. **First MP 1414 for Devon. Four additional MPs 1554-1658**. The 5 Molesworth Bt married the daughter of Sir John St. Aubyn of Clowance and the

Molesworths succeeded to the Clowance estates in 1839. The illegitimate son of the 5 St. Aubyn Bt succeeded to St. Michael's Mount, and his son was created a peer.

1. John St. Aubyn – Tregony 1640 Cornwall 1656 St. Ives 1660
2. Sir John St. Aubyn 1 Bt – Mitchell 1679-81
3. Sir John St. Aubyn 2 Bt – Helston 1689-95
4. Sir John St. Aubyn 3 Bt – Cornwall 1722-44
5. Sir John St. Aubyn 4 Bt – Launceston 1747-54 1758-59 Cornwall 1761-72
6. Sir John St. Aubyn 5 Bt – Truro 1784 Penryn 1784-90 Helston 1807-12
7. John St. Aubyn 1 Baron St. Levan – W. Cornwall 1858-85 St. Ives Div. Cornwall 1885-87

Seats: St. Michael's Mount, Cornwall (medieval monastic buildings, purch. 1659, rebuilt 18th c., expanded 1874-78, NT 1956); Clowance, Cornwall (acq. by mar. 1380, fire 1837, passed by mar. to Molesworths 1839); Trekenning, Cornwall (built 17th c., acq. by mar. 1665, remod. 18th and 19th c., became farm house, now holiday park)
Estates: Bateman 6555 (E) not known. Still own 5,000 acres 2016.
Titles: Baronet 1671-1839; 1866-
Peers: 3 peers 1887-1945
Notes: 3 and 5 Bts and one other in ODNB.

MOLYNEUX I [More]

<u>Earl of Sefton</u> (1771-1972 I)

Origins: Genuine Norman ancestry. Arrived at or soon after the Conquest. Held Sefton from c. 1100. Fought in Scotland with Edward II. A hero at Agincourt. **First MP 1312 for Lancashire. Seven further MPs 1397-1628, three kts of the shire**.

1. Charles Molyneux 1 Earl of Sefton – Lancashire 1771-74
2. William Molyneux 2 Earl of Sefton – Droitwich 1816-31
3. Charles Molyneux 3 Earl of Sefton – S. Lancashire 1832-35

Seats: Croxteth Hall, Lancashire (acq. 1446, built 1575, main seat and add. from 1702, add. 1790 and 1874, add. 1902-04, fire 1952, donated to City of Liverpool 1972); Sefton Hall, Lancashire (acq. c. 1100, medieval house, demolished 1702, held estate until 1972); Abbeystead, Lancashire (purch. and built 1886-88, gradually became the principal seat, sold with 19,000 acres 1979); Woolton Hall, Lancashire (built c. 1704, add. c. 1770s, add. 1865, institutional use)
Estates: Bateman 20250 (E) 43000. Held 40,000 acres c. 1600 with in addition industrial enterprises in Liverpool worth £2,000 pa. Income of £1,300 pa. in 1694. Rubinstein – 2 Earl left £100,000 in probate in 1838.

Titles: Viscount Molyneux 1628-1972 I; Baron Sefton 1831-1972 UK; Baronet 1611-1972
Peers: {2 peers 1769-1800} 5 peers 1831-97 1904-45
3 Lds Lt 17th, 19th
1 KG 19th
Notes: One of the two most prominent families in the history of Lancashire. Involved in the development of Liverpool, whose expansion brought them great wealth. The family remained Roman Catholic until 1768, which accounts for the absence of MPS 1628-1771. 1, 2, and 3 Viscounts and two others in ODNB.

More-Molyneux

Origins: The father of the first More MP was a London fishmonger. His son was a legal official and Kt under Henry VIII, purchased a landed estate 1508. **First MP 1539 for Surrey. Four further MPs 1539-1649, three for the county**. The grandfather of James Molyneux of the Sefton family married the daughter and heiress of the 1 More Bt of Loseley Park. He succeeded to Loseley in 1704 and took the additional name More.

1. Sir William More 2 Bt – Haslemere 1675-81
2. James More-Molyneux – Haslemere 1754-59
3. Thomas More-Molyneux – Haselemere 1759-76

Seat: Loseley Park (House), Surrey (purch. 1508, built 1562-68, add. early 17th c., still own)
Estates: Bateman 2406 (E) 3249. Owned 1,400 acres in 2012.
Title: Baronet 1642-84
Notes: *Country Life*, 206, 79-83. One in ODNB.

Molyneux

Origins: Cadet line descended from the Sefton family settled in Nottinghamshire in the 15th century. **First MP 1563 for Nottinghamshire. One additional MP 1572.**

1. Sir John Molyneux 3 Bt – Wigan 1660
2. Sir Francis Molyneux 4 Bt – Newark-on-Trent 1693-1700 Nottinghamshire 1701-05
3. Thomas Molyneux – Preston 1695-1702

Seats: Teversal(l) Manor, Nottinghamshire (built 16th c., acq. by mar. 1562 – from Barre family which held it from 1154 – remod. late 17th c., passed out of family via an heiress 1830, sold 1929); Kneeton (Kneveton), Nottinghamshire (medieval, acq. mid-16th c., demolished 1781, passed out of family via an heiress 1830)
Estates: coal mines at Teversall 18th-19th c.
Title: Baronet 1611-1812

Notes: Male line extinct 1812. The estates then passed to Lord Henry Howard (son of the Duke of Norfolk) who took the additional name Molyneux in 1817 and conformed to the Established Church. In 1830 the property passed to the Earl of Carnarvon. Two in ODNB.

MOLYNEUX II [Shuldham] *IRELAND*

Molyneux

Origins: Huguenots who fled from Calais to Flanders and then from the Duke of Alba's persecution to Ireland 1576. Chancellor of the Exchequer in Ireland under Elizabeth I. Gentry by the 1640s. **First {MP 1586}. One further {MP 1613}.**

1. Adam Molyneux – {County Londonderry 1661-66}
2. William Molyneux – {Dublin University 1692-93 1695-98}
3. Sir Thomas Molyneux 1 Bt – {Ratoath 1695-99}
4. Samuel Molyneux – Bossiney 1715-22 St. Mawes 1726-27 Exeter 1727-28 {Dublin University 1727-28}
5. Sir Capel Molyneux 3 Bt – {Clogher 1761-68 Dublin University 1768-76 Clogher 1776-83}
6. George Molyneux – {Granard 1783-90}

Seats: Castle Dillon, Armagh (old house, purch. 1664, new house mid-18th c., rebuilt 1845, sold 1926, hospital); Moig(h) House (Ballymulvey), Longford (acq. 16th c., passed to Shuldhams by mar. 18th c.)
Estates: Bateman 16560 (I) 10000
Title: Baronet 1730-1940
Notes: Family resident in England by 1930s. 1 Bt and two others in ODNB.

Baron Shuldham (1776-98 I)

Origins: Claim to have descended from old gentry in Norfolk. First notable family member was a Crown Solicitor in Dublin 1713. His son Lemuel was a clergyman who married Elizabeth Molyneux, heiress 1772 to Ballymulvey (see above), which passed to her son the 1 Baron Shuldham, an admiral.

1. Molyneux Shuldham 1 Baron Shuldham – Fowey 1774-84

Seats: Moig(h) House (Ballymulvey), Longford (built 16th c., acq. by mar. 18th c., resident into 20th c.); Dunmanway, Cork (resident 18th-19th c.)
Estates: Bateman 2571 (I) 3681
Peer: {1 peer 1776-98}
Notes: 1 Baron in ODNB.

MOMPESSON

Origins: Established in Wiltshire since the 15th century. **First MP 1453 for Wilton. Two additional MPs 1593-1621.**

1. Sir Thomas Mompesson – Wilton 1661-79 Salisbury 1679-81 Old Sarum 1681 1685-87 Wiltshire 1689-90 Old Sarum 1690-95 Salisbury 1695-98 1701
2. Roger Mompesson – Southampton 1698-1701
3. Charles Mompesson – Old Sarum 1698-1708 Wilton 1708-13

Seats: Mompesson House, Wiltshire (purch. and built by 1701 late 17th c., passed out of the family by mar. c. 1740, NT); Bathampton House, Wiltshire (acq. 15th c., built 1694, sold before 1760)
Notes: One in ODNB.

MONCK [Stanley] *ENGLAND & IRELAND*

Duke of Albemarle (1660-88 E)

Origins: The family emerged in Devon in the 12th century. The senior line was seated at Great Potheridge. **First MP 1626.**

1. George Monck 1 Duke of Albemarle – Devon 1653 1660
2. Christopher Monck 2 Duke of Albemarle – Devon 1667-70

Seats: Great Potheridge, Devon (acq. 12th c., sold 1734); New Hall, Essex (built 13th c., new house c. 1518, add. c. 1573, acq. 1660, passed by mar. to Montagus 1691, sold 1713)
Estates: 1 Duke died worth £60,000.
Peers: 2 peers 1660-70 1674-88
2 Lds Lt 17th
1 in Cabinet 1660-70
2 KG 17th
Notes: The 1 Duke engineered the Restoration of the monarchy in 1660. 1 and 2 Dukes and one other in ODNB.

Earl of Rathdown (1822-48 I)

Origins: Descended from a younger son of the Devon family in the 15th century. A lawyer went to Ireland as Surveyor General of the Customs 1618, acquired land in Westmeath and was elected an **{MP 1634}.** (Batt, *The Moncks and Charleville*).

1. Charles Monck – {Newcastle 1711-13 Innistioge 1713-14 Newcastle 1715-27}

2. George Monck – {Philipstown 1703-13}
3. Henry Monck – {Dunleek 1755-60 1761-68}
4. George Monck – {Coleraine 1763-68}
5. Thomas Monck – {Old Leighlin 1768-72}
6. Charles Monck 1 Viscount Monck – {Gorey 1790-97}
7. William Monck – {Coleraine 1795-97 Gorey 1797-1799}
8. Charles Monck 4 Viscount Monck – Portsmouth 1852-57

Seats: Charleville, Wicklow (built c. 1700, inher. by mar. to Hitchcock heiress 1705, fire 1792, rebuilt 1797, sold 1941); Grange Gorman, Dublin (acq. by mar. 1744, sold 1946)
Estates: Bateman 14144 (I) 10466. Stanley estates worth £1,500 pa in 1713.
Titles: Baron Monck 1797- I; Viscount Monck 1801- I; Baron Monck 1866- UK
Peers: {1 peer 1797-1800} 3 peers 1866-1945
1 Ld Lt 19th
Notes: 4 Viscount in ODNB.

Monck

Origins: Descended from a younger son of Henry Monck in the late 17th century, ancestor of the Earls of Rathdown. Several generations of barristers in the 18th century.

1. John Monck – Reading 1820-30

Seat: Coley Park (aka Vachel House), Berkshire (built c. 1555, remod. c. 1651, derelict, new house 1802, purch. 1810, family depart 1905, sold 1937, Reading CC)
Estates: Rubinstein £125,000 probate 1809. About 600 acres in 1937.

Stanley

Origins: The Stanleys arrived in Ireland as officials in the later 17th century and rose through marriage to the heiress of John Bisse, Lord Chancellor of Ireland. Sheriff 1688. Bt 1699. The 1 Baronet was secretary to the Earl of Dorset and the Earl of Sunderland, Lord Chamberlain of the Household, and Warden of the Mint. The sister of the 1 Bt had a son, Charles Monck MP, who inherited the Stanley estates in 1744. His descendent became Earl of Rathdown.

1. Sir Thomas Stanley – {County Louth 1661-66}
2. Sir John Stanley 1 Bt – {Gorey 1713-14}
3. Stephen Stanley – {County Waterford 1715-25}

Seat: Grange Gorman, Dublin (acq. later 17th c., passed to Moncks by mar. 1744, see above)
Title: Baronet 1699-1744

MONCKTON [Arundell, Mauleverer]

Viscount Galway (1727- I)

Origins: Acquired original estate by marriage to an heiress in 1454. **First MP 1559.** The second son of the 1 Viscount inherited Fineshade Abbey, which later passed to a younger son of the third son of the 1 Viscount. The 3 Viscount inherited Allerton Park from the Arundells, relatives by marriage, in 1769. The third son established his own line seated at Somerford Hall founded on a fortune he made in India. The three lines are combined here.

1. Sir Philip Monckton – Scarborough 1670-79
2. Robert Monckton – Pontefract 1695-98 Aldborough 1701-13
3. John Monckton 1 Viscount Galway – Clitheroe 1727-34 Pontefract 1734-47 1749-51
4. William Monckton 2 Viscount Galway – Pontefract 1747-48 Thirsk 1749-54 Pontefract 1754-72
5. Robert Monckton-Arundell – Pontefract 1751-54 1774 Portsmouth 1778-82
6. Henry Monckton-Arundell 3 Viscount Galway – Pontefract 1772-74
7. Robert Monckton-Arundell 4 Viscount Galway – Pontefract 1780-83 York 1783-90 Pontefract 1796-1802
8. Edward Monckton – Stafford 1780-1812
9. George Monckton-Arundell 6 Viscount Galway – East Retford 1847-76
10. Francis Monckton – W. Staffordshire 1871-85
11. George Monckton-Arundell 7 Viscount Galway – N. Nottinghamshire 1872-85
12. Edward Monckton – N. Northamptonshire 1895-1900

Seats: Serlby Hall, Nottinghamshire (purch. 1724, built c. 1754-60, remod. c. 1812 and early 20th c., sold 1981, decayed); Cavill Hall, Yorkshire (medieval, acq. by mar. 1454, demolished 18th c., rebuilt, demolished 1950s); Somerford Hall, Staffordshire (built c. 1730, purch. 1779, remod. later 18th c., sold 1945, institutional use); Stretton Hall, Staffordshire (rebuilt 1720, purch. c. 1795, remod. 1860s, still own); Fineshade Abbey, Northamptonshire (built c. 1749, purch. 1759, add. early 19th c. and 1856, demolished 1956); Allerton Park, Yorkshire (inher. by mar. 1769, sold 1786); Hodroyd Hall, Yorkshire (acq. by mar. c. 1655, sold 1911)
Estates: 16169 (E) 27792. Worth £50,000,000 (combined with the Earl of Ilchester) with 3,000 acres in 1990.
Title: Baron Monckton 1887- UK
Peers: {1 peer 1727-51} 2 peers 1887-1943
Notes: See Baron Houghton under Crewe. Three in ODNB.

Baron Arundell of Trerice (1644-1768 E)

Origins: Settled at Trerice since the 14th century. One of the richest families in Cornwall in the 17th century. **First MP 1555. Three additional MPs 1597-1648, one for the county**. With the extinction of the Mauleverers in 1692, the last member of the family's widow remarried and left Allerton to the son of her second marriage, Richard Arundell. The 3 Viscount Galway succeeded to the estates of his maternal aunt Lady Frances Arundell of Allerton Mauleverer in 1769 and the Moncktons took the additional name Arundell.

1. Richard Arundell 1 Baron Arundell – Lostwithiel 1640-44 Bere Alston 1660 1662-65
2. Nicholas Arundell – Truro 1661-66
3. John Arundell 2 Baron Arundell – Truro 1666-79 1685-87
4. Richard Arundell – Knaresborough 1720-58

Seats: Trerice, Cornwall (acq. by mar. 14th c., rebuilt 1570-73, passed by mar. to Wentworth family of Hembury in the 18th c., NT 1953); Allerton (Park) Mauleverer, Yorkshire (medieval house, inher. by mar. early 18th c., rebuilt 1740s, passed to the Galways 1769)
Estates: Owned over 10,000 acres in 1560. Trerice estate 1,500 acres in 19th c.
Peers: 4 peers 1664-1706 1722-68
Notes: Arundell family has an entry in ODNB. 1 Baron and one other also in ODNB.

Baron Arundell of Wardour (1605-1944 E)

Origins: Claimed Norman descent. Emerged in the 13th century. High Sheriff 1260. Descended from the eldest son of Sir John Arundell of Lanherne, Cornwall (acq. by mar. 1231) in the 16th century. The Trerice line (see above) were descended from a younger son of Sir John. **First MP 1340 for Cornwall. Ten further MPs 1397-1558, nine kts of the shire**.

No post-1660 MPs

Seats: Wardour Castle, Wiltshire (built 1343, purch. 1547, remod. 1578, damaged 1643-44, new house 1768-76 and 1788, sold post 1944, now flats); Lanherne, Cornwall (acq. by mar. 1231, donated as a religious house for French exiles 1794 and is still a convent)
Estates: 6219 (E) 9174
Peers: 7 peers 1660-78 1684-89 1827-1944
1 in Cabinet 1687-89
Notes: This line was Roman Catholic, which accounts for the absence of MPs after 1558. The Lanherne line lost influence and wealth in Cornwall by the end of the 16th

century. Counts of the Holy Roman Empire cr. 1595. Arundell family has an entry in the ODNB. 1 and 3 Barons and seven additional also in ODNB.

Arundell

Origins: A cadet line that inherited in 1645 the estates of Sir Richard Crane, whose older brother Sir Francis (**MP 1614-24**) had been secretary to Charles I as Prince of Wales and Auditor General, granted Stoke Park by the King in 1617.

1. Francis Arundell – Northampton 1704-10

Seat: Stoke Bruerne Park, Northamptonshire (old house, acq. by Cranes 1627, passed by mar. to Arundells after 1636, rebuilt 1635, passed to Vernons 1786, remod. late 18th c., sold 1928, fire 1886, demolished soon after)

Mauleverer

Origins: Seated at Allerton since the 13th century. **First MP 1334, for Yorkshire. Four additional MPs 1388-1653, two kts of the shire**. The 2 Baron Arundell of Trerice married in 1692 Barbara, widow of Sir Richard Mauleverer 4 Bt of Allerton Mauleverer, and the Arundells succeeded to the Mauleverer estates.

1. Sir Richard Mauleverer 2 Bt – Boroughbridge 1661-75
2. Sir Thomas Mualeverer 3 Bt – Boroughbridge 1679-81 1685-87

Seat: Allerton Mauleverer, Yorkshire (acq. 13th c., medieval house, passed by mar. to Arundells early 18th c., see above)
Estates: Over 3,000 acres worth £1,500 pa in the 1650s.
Title: Baronet 1641-1713
Notes: 1, 2, and 3 Bts and one other in ODNB.

MONCREIFF(E) *SCOTLAND*

Baron Moncreiff (1874- UK)

Origins: Emerged in the 13th century. Lord of Council 1450s. **First [MP 1597]. Two further [MPs 1605-41].**

1. James Moncreiff 1 Baron Moncreiff – Leith 1851-59 Edinburgh 1859-68 Glasgow & Aberdeen Universities 1868-69

Seats: Tulliebole (Tullibole) Castle, Kinross-shire (built later 16th c., add. 1608, rebuilt 1679, acq. by mar. 1722, still own); Moncreiffe House, Perthshire (built 1679, fire 1957, demolished 1962, new house 1962, still own)
Estates: 4743 (S) 7247. Owned 60,000 acres in 1970.
Title: Baronet 1626- ; 1871-
Peers: 5 peers 1874-1945
1 Ld Lt 20th
Notes: The 2 Bt sold the family estates in 1633. The 5 Bt was a physician. The 9, 10, and 11 Bts were judges. The Hallidays acquired Tulliebole in 1598. Their heiress brought it to the Moncreiffs. 1 Baron in ODNB.

Moncreiff

Origins: Cadet line.

1. George Moncreiff – [Fife 1690-1702]
2. Patrick Moncreiff – [Kinghorn 1706-07] Scotland 1707-08 Fifeshire 1708-10

Seats: Reidie (Reedie), Fife (acq. by mar. c. 1620 and built, later demolished); Myres Castle (House of Myres), Fife (medieval, built c. 1530, add. 1616, acq. by mar. c. 1620, add. 1750, sold 1820, business use)

Moncreiff

Origins: Cadet line. **First [MP 1644]. One additional [MP 1645].**

1. George Moncreiff – [Crail 1678 1681 1689 1689-1702 1703-07]

Seat: Sauchop(e), Fife
Notes: Acquired estates in the West Indies in 18th c. Male line died out 1793. One in ODNB.

Moncreiff

Origins: Cadet of the Sauchope line.

1. James Moncreiff – [Kirkwall 1669-74]

Seat: Seater, Fife

MONOUX

Origins: Merchants in Bristol and then a draper in London. Lord Mayor 1514, 1523. Granted arms 1514 and acquired estates. **First MP 1523**.

1. Sir Humphrey Monoux 2 Bt – Bedfordshire 1679-81
2. Sir Philip Monoux 3 Bt – Bedford 1705-07
3. Sir Humphrey Monoux 4 Bt – Tavistock 1728-34 Stockbridge 1734-41

Seat: Wootton, Bedfordshire (acq. 1514, rebuilt 17th c., passed to Paynes – under Frankland – 1792 by mar.)
Title: Baronet 1660-1814
Notes: One in ODNB.

MONSELL *IRELAND*

Baron Emly (1874-1932 UK)

Origins: Emerged in the 16th century in Dorset. A son went to London and then to Limerick in 1612. He returned to England in 1634. His son owned estates in Somerset and Limerick. The first MP married a merchant heiress.

1. W. T. Monsell – {Dunleer 1776-83 Dingle 1798-1800}
2. William Monsell 1 Baron Emly – Limerick 1847-74

Seat: Tervoe, Limerick (built c. 1690, purch. 1715, rebuilt 1776, add. c. 1830, family departed 1951, demolished 1953)
Estates: Bateman 2710 (I) 2638
Peers: 2 peers 1874-1932
1 Ld Lt 19th
Notes: 1 Baron in ODNB.

Viscount Monsell (1935-93 UK)

Origins: Cadet of Trevoe line. 1 Viscount married 1904 the Eyers heiress of Dumbleton Hall, Worcestershire

1. Bolton Eyres Monsell 1 Viscount Monsell – Evesham 1910-35

Seat: Dumbleton Hall, Worcestershire (built c. 1534, rebuilt c. 1690, part demolished 1779 and the rest in 1830, rebuilt c. 1850, purch. by Eyres 1875, sold 1959, hotel)
Estates: 5,000 acres. 1 Viscount left over £100,000 in 1969.

1 peer 1935-45
1 in Cabinet 1931-36
Notes: 1 Viscount and two others in ODNB

MONTAGU I [Blair, Douglas, Fountayne, Hussey, Robinson, Scott, Stuart, Wilson, Winwood, Wortley] *ENGLAND & SCOTLAND*

Duke of Montagu (1705-49 E)

Origins: Yeomen in the 14th and 15th centuries. A successful attorney in the late 15th c. Landed status achieved by a Lord Chief Justice of Common Pleas 1539, Sir Edward Montagu, who speculated in monastic land and was the common ancestor of the various branches of the family listed below. **First MP 1559, for Northamptonshire. Five additional MPs 1584-1644, three of them kts of the shire.**

1. William Montagu – Huntingdon 1640 University of Cambridge 1660 Stamford 1661-76 Amersham 1690-95
2. Edward Montagu – Sandwich 1661-65
3. Ralph Montagu 1 Duke of Montagu – Northampton 1678-81 Huntingdonshire 1679
4. William Montagu – Midhurst 1681 Stockbridge 1689-91

Seat: Boughton House, Northamptonshire (medieval, purch. 1528, add. late 16th c. and 1685-1709, passed by mar. 1749 to the Buccleuchs below)
Estates: £17,000 pa in 1749
Titles: Baron Monatgu 1621-1749 E; Viscount Monthermer and Earl Montagu 1689-1749 E; Marquess of Monthermer 1705-49 E
Peers: 4 peers 1660-1709 1711-49 1797-1845
2 Lds Lt 17th, 18th
1 KG 18th
Notes: 1 and 2 Barons and 1 and 2 Dukes and and four others in ODNB.

Duke of Buccleuch and Queensberry (1663- S and 1684- S)

Origins: On the death of the 2 Duke of Montagu his estates passed to two heirs. The eldest daughter, Lady Mary, married the 4 Earl of Cardigan (see Brudenell). Their daughter, Lady Elizabeth Brudenell Montagu married the 3 Duke of Buccleuch and 5 Duke of Queensberry (see Douglas). Their eldest son succeeded to the Buccleuch estates while the younger son succeeded as Baron Montagu. Eventually the two lines were reunited. Anne Scott, Countess of Buccleuch in her own right married in 1662 the Duke of Monmouth, illegitimate son of King Charles II, who was created Duke of Buccleuch. He was attainted and executed after his rebellion in 1685, but the Dukedom was restored to his grandson. The 2 Duke married Lady Jane Douglas, the daughter of the 2 Duke of Queensberry. The 3 Duke of Buccleuch succeeded to the Queensberry titles and estates on the death of the 4 Duke of Queensberry in 1810. The Scotts "of Buccleuch" were a medieval family, recorded in the 12th century, created Barons in 1606. **First [MP 1597]. Several cadet lines elected [MPs 1568, 1630].**

1. Francis Scott Earl of Dalkieth – Boroughbridge 1746-50
2. Charles Montagu-Scott 4 Duke of Buccleuch – Marlborough 1793-96 Ludgershall 1796-1804 St. Michael 1805-06 Marlborough 1806-07
3. John Douglas-Scott – Roxburghshire 1835-37
4. William Douglas-Scott – 6 Duke of Buccleuch – Midlothian 1853-68 1874-80
5. John Douglas-Scott 7 Duke of Buccleuch – Roxburghshire 1895-1906
6. Walter Douglas-Scott 8 Duke of Buccleuch – Roxburgh & Selkirk 1923-35
7. Lord William Douglas-Scott – Roxburgh & Selkirk 1935-50
8. Walter Montagu-Douglas-Scott 9 Duke of Buccleuch – Edinburgh N. 1960-73

Seats: Dalkeith Palace (House), Edinburghshire (built 12th c., rebuilt 1570s, purch. 1642, rebuilt 1701-11, remod. 1780s, family departed 1914, still own but leased out); Boughton House, Northamptonshire (acq. by mar. 1749, still own); Drumlanrig Castle, Dumfriesshire (acq. by Douglas family 15th c., medieval, rebuilt mid-16th c., rebuilt 1675-91, passed by mar. 1810 to the Scotts, still own); Bowhill, Selkirkshire (acq. by Scotts c. 1550, built c. 1708, rebuilt 1812-14, add. 1819, remod. 1831-32, add. 1874-76, still own); Eildon Hall, Roxburghshire (built 1802-06, acq. mid-19th c., add. 1862, still own); Branxholme Castle, Roxburghshire (Scott house, acq. 1420, built 15th c., burned 1532, new house 1571-76, inher. by Dukes of Buccleuch, add. 1836, still own)
Estates: Bateman 460108 (E & S) 217163. Rubinstein – the Dowager Duchess of Buccleuch left £160,000 in probate 1821. Worth £300,000,000 with 277,000 acres in 1990 (some of the wealth is due to an exceptional collection of European art).
Titles: Baron Scott of Buccleuch 1606- S; Earl of Buccleuch 1619- S; Earl of Doncaster 1662-85, restored 1743- E; Earl of Dalkeith 1663- S; Earl of Drumlanrig and Marquis of Dumfriesshire 1684- S; Baron Goldielands, Viscount of Hermitage, and Earl of Delorains 1706-1807 S
Peers: 2 Scottish Rep peers 1715-30 1734-41 8 peers 1743-51 1767-1812 1807-19 1827-1945
7 Lds Lt 18th, 19th, 20th
1 in Cabinet 1842-46
4 KG 17th, 18th, 19th
6 KT 18th, 19th ,20th
Notes: Lady Alice Montagu-Douglas-Scott married a younger son of King George V, becoming Princess Alice, Duchess of Gloucester. Princess Alice, the Duchess of Monmouth, and 1, 3, and 5 Dukes and 1 Baron Scott and three others in ODNB.

Baron Montagu of Beaulieu (1885- UK)

Origins: The younger son of the 5 Duke of Buccleuch inherited The Palace House at Beaulieu and was created Baron Montagu in 1885.

1. Henry Douglas Scott-Montagu 1 Baron Montagu – Selkirkshire 1861-68 S. Hampshire 1868-84
2. John Douglas Scott-Montagu 2 Baron Montagu – New Forest Div. Hampshire 1892-1905

Seat: The Palace House (Beaulieu Palace House), Beaulieu, Hampshire (medieval, purch. 1538 by Earl of Southampton, passed by mar. to Montagus 1667, remod. 1730s, given to a younger son 1867, add. 1871-74, still own)
Estates: Bateman 8946 (E) 7386
Peers: 2 peers 1885-1929
Notes: 2 Baron in ODNB.

Scott

Origins: Cadet of Scott of Buccleuch. **First [MP 1644 for Selkirkshire]**.

1. William Scott – [Selkirkshire 1667]

Seat: Hartwoodmyres, Selkirkshire

Scott

Origins: Cadet of Scott of Buccleuch. **First [MP 1639 for Selkirkshire]. An additional [MP 1645 for Selkirkshire].**

1. Thomas Scott – [Selkirkshire 1661-63]

Seat: Whitslade (Whitslaid), Selkirkshire

Scott-Blair

Origins: William Scott of Malleny, Edinburghshire, a cadet of the Scotts of Buccleuch married 1666 the daughter and heiress of William Blair of Blair and took the additional name Blair. The Blairs were at Blair by 1200, possibly earlier and prominent in the affairs of Ayrshire for 600 years. **First Scott [MP 1650]. First Blair [MP 1572]. One additional [MP 1621].**

1. William Blair – [Ayrshire 1669-74 1678 1685-86 1689]
2. William Blair – Ayrshire 1829-32

Seat: Blair (Castle) House, Ayrshire (acq. by 1200, built 15th c., add. 1617, remod. 1668, sold 2012)
Estates: Bateman 7280 (S) 5828

Earl of Beaulieu (1784-1802 GB)

Origins: The second co-heir of the 2 Duke of Montagu (see above) married Edward Hussey of Westown House, Dublin who took the name Montagu and was created Earl of Beaulieu. The Husseys were lawyers in the 18th century, cadets of the Husseys of Rathkenny, Meath. On the extinction of the family the estates passed to the Dukes of Bucceluch consolidating the entire Montagu inheritance.

1. Edward Hussey Montagu 1 Earl of Beaulieu – Tiverton 1758-62
2. John Hussey Montagu Baron Montagu – New Windsor 1772-87

Seats: Ditton Park, Buckinghamshire (now in Berkshire) (acq. by mar. 1691, passed to the Montagus of this line, passed to D. of Buccleuch, fire 1812, sold 1917 for £20,000, business use); Westown House, Dublin (stayed with Hussey family) (tower house built c. 1600, new house early 18th c., sold 1942, ruin)
Estates: Bateman 4700 (I) 3320
1 Ld Lt 19th

Winwood

Origins: The family came to prominence with a landless secretary to Charles Brandon, Duke of Suffolk in the 16th century. His son was a Secretary of State 1614, Kt, and purchased an estate. **First MP 1614**. On the death of Richard Winwood of Ditton Park his estates passed to his nephew the 1 Duke of Montagu (see above).

1. Richard Winwood – New Windsor 1641-48 1679-81

Seats: Ditton Park, Buckinghamshire (built c. 1500, purch. 1632, passed to Montagus by mar. 1691); Quainton, Buckinghamshire (purch. 1615, passed to Montagus by mar. 1688 in 1691, sold 1718)
Estates: Worth £1,500 pa in 1617.
Notes: One in ODNB.

Duke of Manchester (1719- GB)

Origins: A younger son of Sir Edward Montagu (see under Duke of Monatgu) was Lord Chief Justice in 1616. Created a Viscount 1620 and Earl 1626. **First MP 1593. Four additional MPs 1624-54, two for Huntingdonshire**.

1. Robert Montagu 3 Earl of Manchester – Huntingdonshire 1660-71
2. Robert Montagu – Huntingdonshire 1689-93
3. Heneage Montagu – Huntingdonshire 1695-98
4. Edward Montagu – Chippenham 1698-1700
5. James Montagu – Chippenham 1702-05
6. Robert Montagu 3 Duke of Manchester – Huntingdonshire 1734-39
7. John Montagu – Huntingdon 1748-54
8. George Montagu 4 Duke of Manchester – Huntingdonshire 1761-62
9. Lord Charles Montagu – Huntingdonshire 1762-65
10. Lord Frederick Montagu – Huntingdonshire 1796-1806 1818-20
11. George Montagu 6 Duke of Manchester – Huntingdonshire 1826-37
12. William Montagu 7 Duke of Manchester – Bewdley 1847-52 Huntingdonshire 1852-55
13. Lord Robert Montagu – Huntingdonshire 1859-74 Westmeath 1874-80
14. George Montagu 8 Duke of Manchester – Huntingdon 1877-80

Seats: Kimbolton Castle, Huntingdonshire (medieval, remod. 1521-25, purch. 1615, rebuilt 1617-20, rebuilt 1690-96 and 1707-20, add. 1869, house sold 1950, estate sold 1978, school); Brampton Park, Huntingdonshire (rebuilt 1821-22, fire 1907, rebuilt, purch. 1930, sold 1945, RAF); Lackham House, Wiltshire (medieval, acq. by mar. 1635, rebuilt 1793-95, sold 1835, institutional use); Cromore, Londonderry (built mid-18th c., add. 1834, inh. by mar. from Cromies in mid-19th c., sold 20th c., institutional use); Kylemore Castle, Galway (built c. 1860, purch. 1900, sold 1920, school); Tandragee Castle, Armagh (old castle, acq. by mar. 1812, rebuilt 1830-37, remod. 1850s, 1860s, contents sold 1925, house sold 1955, became a factory, shell standing)
Estates: Bateman 34383 (E & I) 47578. £4,000 pa in 1739. In 1977 the estate still covered 3,250 acres, with additional land in Ireland and Kenya. The Duke's income in 1978 was c. £100,000 pa. (Scriven, *Splendour and Squalour*, 181) Owned no land in 2001.
Titles: Baron Kimbolton and Viscount Mandeville 1620- E; Earl of Manchester 1626- E
Peers: 11 peers 1660-71 1673-83 1685-1788 1792-1892 1898-1945
7 Lds Lt 17th, 18th, 19th
1 in Cabinet 1702-04
1 KG 17th
1 KP 19th
Notes: A younger son established a junior line at Lackham, Wiltshire. Lord Robert Montagu succeeded by marriage to the Cromie estates in Northern Ireland. Acquired

Stanstead Park via an heiress from the Earls of Scarborough (see Lumley). 1, 2, and 3 Earls and 1, 4, and 5 Dukes and eight others in ODNB.

Earl of Halifax (1714-15 GB; 1715-71 GB)

Origins: Two younger sons of the 1 Earl of Manchester established the "Halifax" family at Horton. The 2 Earl took the additional name Dunk on inheriting a fortune from a Dunk heiress he married in 1741. The first prominent Dunk was a clothier who left £110,000 (*Country Life*, 171, p. 346).

1. George Montagu – Huntingdonshire 1640-48 Dover 1660-79
2. Edward Montagu – Seaford 1681 Northamptonshire 1685-87 1689-90
3. Charles Montagu 1 Earl of Halifax – Maldon 1689-95 Westminster 1695-1700
4. Christopher Montagu – Northampton 1695-1702
5. Irby Montagu – Maldon 1695-1701
6. Sir James Montagu – Tregony 1695-98 Bere Alston 1698-1700 Carlisle 1705-13
7. George Montagu 1 Earl of Halifax – Northampton 1705-15
8. Edward Montagu – Northampton 1722-34
9. George Monatgu – Northampton 1744-54

Seats: Horton Hall (House), Northamptonshire (built 16th c., purch. early 17th c., remod. 1740s, sold 1781, demolished c. 1935); Stanstead Park, Sussex (succ. by mar. 1766, sold 1781)
Titles: Baron Halifax 1700-71 E; Viscount Sunbury 1714-15 GB; Viscount Sunbury 1715-71 GB
Peers: 3 peers 1700-71
2 Lds Lt 18th
2 in Cabinet 1691-99 1714-15 1748-65 1771
2 KG 18th
Notes: 1 Earl of 1st cr. and two others in ODNB.

Montagu

Origins: Charles Montagu MP below was the son of a brother of the 1 Earl of Halifax. His daughter Anne married John Fountayne. Their daughter Elizabeth Fountayne married Richard Wilson of Rudding Park. Their grandsons took the name Montagu in 1826.

1. Charles Montagu – Westminster 1722-27 St. Germans 1734-41 Camelford 1741-47 Northampton 1754-59
2. Frederick Montagu – Northampton 1759-68 Higham Ferrers 1768-90
3. Richard Fountayne-Wilson – Yorkshire 1826-30

Seats: Papplewick Hall, Nottinghamshire (inher. 1770, built c. 1787, sold 1920); Ingmanthorpe, Yorkshire (built early 19th c., sold early 20th c.); Melton Park (Hall, House), Yorkshire (Fountayne property) (Wilson acq. by inher. 1802 from Fountaynes, built early 19th c., demolished 1957); Shortgrove Hall, Essex (built early 17th c., add. c. 1684 and 1712, purch. 1924, sold 1938, fire 1966)
Estates: Bateman 27265 (E) 53034
Notes: Two in ODNB.

Wilson

Origins: The Wilsons (see above) were Leeds merchants in the 17th century. An elder son established the line at Rudding that succeeded to the Fountayne/Montagu inheritance. A younger son was a Danzig merchant who purchased a landed estate in the mid-18th century and entered the gentry. A stranger, William Wright (d. 1814), left his estates in Hampshire and elsewhere to Lady Frances Wilson, the wife of the MP below and they took the additional name Wright in 1814.

1. Sir Henry Wright Wilson – St. Albans 1821-26

Seats: Crofton Hall, Yorkshire (purch. and built 1750, sold 1935, demolished 1980s); Drayton Lodge, Hampshire (Wright property)
Estates: Bateman 2015 (E) 3229

Earl of Sandwich (1660- E)

Origins: Descended from the youngest son of Sir Edward Montagu (see Duke of Montagu above). **First MP of this line at Hinchingbrooke 1593.**

1. Edward Montagu 1 Earl of Sandwich – Huntingdonshire 1645-48 1653 1654 1656 Dover 1660
2. Edward Montagu 2 Earl of Sandwich – Dover 1670-72
3. Oliver Montagu – Huntingdon 1685-87
4. Charles Montagu – Durham 1685-87 1695-1702
5. Richard Montagu 3 Earl of Sandwich – Huntingdon 1690-97
6. James Montagu – Chippenham 1708-10 Camelford 1715-22
7. Edward Montagu Viscount Hinchingbrooke – Huntingdon 1713-22 Huntingdonshire 1722
8. John Montagu – Stockbridge 1734
9. Edward Montagu – Huntingdon 1734-68
10. William Montagu – Huntingdonshire 1745-47 Bossiney 1752-54
11. John Montagu 5 Earl of Sandwich – Brackley 1765-68 Huntingdonshire 1768-92
12. William Montagu – Huntingdon 1774-76

13. John Montagu Viscount Hinchingbrooke – Huntingdon 1790
14. George Montagu 6 Earl of Sandwich – Huntingdonshire 1794-1814
15. William Montagu – Huntingdon 1818-20
16. Edward Montagu 8 Earl of Sandwich – Huntingdon 1876-84
17. George Montagu 9 Earl of Sandwich – S. Div. Huntingdonshire 1900-06
18. Alexander Montagu 10 Earl of Sandwich – S. Dorset 1941-62

Seats: Hinchingbrooke House, Huntingdonshire (medieval, remod. c. 1540-50 and additional work later in the c., add. 17th c., purch. 1627, add. 1660s, fire 1830, rebuilt 1832, remod. 1894-96, departed 1955, sold 1962, school); Allerthorpe Hall, Yorkshire (purch. 1590 by Robinsons - see below - built 1608, passed to Montagus by mar. of 1742, then to 4 Lord Rokeby, passed out of family 1904); Sandleford, Berkshire (leased 1730 until 1st half 19th c.); Hooke Court, Dorset (medieval, estate descended via many heiresses from the family holding it in 1281 to the the Earls of Sandwich in the early 19th c., became a shooting box, sold 1919)
Estates: Bateman 11377 (E & I) 16423. The 10 Earl left £2,267,000 in 1995
Titles: Baron Montagu 1660- ; Viscount Hinchingbrooke 1660-
Peers: 9 peers 1660-88 1691-1729 1739-1818 1832-1945
6 Lds Lt 17th, 18th, 19th, 20th
1 in Cabinet 1748-51 1763-65 1770-82
1 KG 17th
Notes: The 1 Earl was an admiral and courtier. When the Earls of Sandwich left their principal seat in 1955, they purchased Mapperton House in Dorset as a replacement, which they still own. 1, 4, 5, and 10 Earls and five others in ODNB.

Baron Rokeby (1777-1883 I)

Origins: Descended from a merchant in the City of London. Acquired an estate early 17th century. (*Country Life*, 47, p. 279 countering entry in DNB) Elizabeth Robinson married a grandson of the 1 Earl of Sandwich. Her nephew, the 4 Baron Rokeby, changed his name to Montagu on inheriting her estates in 1800.

1. Thomas Robinson 1 Bt – Morpeth 1727-34
2. Matthew Robinson Morris 2 Baron Rokeby – Canterbury 1747-61
3. Charles Robinson – Canterbury 1780-90
4. Matthew Robinson Montagu 4 Baron Rokeby – Bossiney 1786-90 Tregony 1790-96 St. Germans 1806-12
5. Morris Robinson 3 Baron Rokeby – Boroughbridge 1790-96

Seats: Hazelwood House (aka Hunton Park), Hertfordshire (purch. 1838, sold 1886, demolished 1908 and rebuilt, hotel); Rokeby Hall, Louth (built 1785 for 1 Baron, passed by inher. 1794 to Freind family, see below); Rokeby Park, Yorkshire (purch. early 17th

c., built 1725-35, sold 1769); (East) Denton Hall, Northumberland (built early 17th c., passed to Montagus by mar. of 1748, passed to Lord Rokeby in 1801, institutional use later 20th c.); Mount Morris, Monks Horton, Kent (acq. by inher. early 18th c., sold first half 19th c., demolished?)
Estates: 4863 (E) 9180
Title: Baronet 1731-1883
Peers: {2 peers 1777-1800}
1 in Cabinet 1787
Notes: Rokeby Hall was sold in 1769 due to financial difficulties, to the outrage of the brother and heir of the seller, who was Archbishop of Armagh and had just taken the name Rokeby for his new peerage. (*Country Life*, 42, p. 279) 1 Bt and 1, 2, 3, and 6 Barons and five others in ODNB.

Freind (Friend) [Robinson]

Origins: First MP was a successful physician. His fortune passed to a nephew, Sir John Friend 1 Baronet, who took the name Robinson on inheriting 1794 the 1 Baron Rokeby's estates (see above under Robinson) estates through his mother, daughter of the 1 Robinson Baronet of Rokeby.

1. John Freind – Launceston 1722-27

Seats: Rokeby Hall, Louth (inher. by mar. 1794, passed out of family 1910 and estate broken up, sold 1912); Hall Barn, Buckinghamshire (leased?)
Estates: Bateman 2941 (I) 2733. Rubinstein – 1 Bt left £120,000 in probate in 1832
Title: Baronet 1819-1910

Earl of Wharncliffe (1876- UK)

Origins: The Wortleys emerged in the 12th century. **First MP 1497. Two additional MPs 1621-26**. The second son of the 1 Earl of Sandwich married Anne Wortley, illegitimate daughter and heiress of Sir Francis Wortley 2 Bt. Their granddaughter married the 3 Earl of Bute. The senior line became Marquises of Bute (see Stuart) while a younger son succeeded to the Wortley-Montagu estates. A junior line were created Barons Wortley.

1. Sidney Wortley-Montagu – Huntingdon 1679-81 1689-95 Camelford 1696-98 Peterborough 1698-1710 Huntingdon 1713-22 Peterborough 1722-27
2. Francis Wortley-Montagu – Huntingdon 1697-1702
3. Edward Wortley-Montagu – Huntingdon 1705-13 Westminster 1715-22 Huntingdon 1722-34 Peterborough 1734-61
4. Edward Wortley-Montagu – Huntingdonshire 1747-54 Bossiney 1754-68

5. John Stuart-Wortley – Bossiney 1796-97
6. James Stuart-Wortley 1 Baron Wharncliffe – Bossiney 1802-18 Yorkshire 1818-26
7. John Stuart-Wortley 2 Baron Wharncliffe – Bossiney 1823-30 Perth Burghs 1830 Bossiney 1831-32 W. R. Yorkshire 1841-45
8. Charles Stuart-Wortley-Mackenzie – Bossiney 1830-31
9. James Stuart-Wortley – Halifax 1835-37 Buteshire 1842-59
10. Archibald Stuart-Wortley – Honiton 1857-59
11. Charles Stuart-Wortley 1 Baron Stuart of Wortley – Sheffield 1880-85 Hallam Div. Sheffield 1885-1916

Seats: Wortley Hall, Yorkshire (acq. 13th c., passed to Montagus by mar. 1665, contents sold 1948, house sold 1954); Newbold Verdon, Leicestershire (acq. by mar. 1721, passed out of family by mar. 1761); Boreham Wood, Hertfordshire; Simonstone Hall, Yorkshire (built 1733, purch. 1870, sold 1947, hotel); Belmont Castle, Perthshire (built c. 1500, add. 1752, remod. early 19th c., fire 1884, rebuilt soon after, sold later 19th c., now institution); Highcliffe Castle, Hampshire (built 1773, rebuilt 1830-34, inher. by Stuart-Wortleys 1894, sold 1949, fire 1967, public ownership)
Estates: Bateman 33449 (E & S) 50823
Titles: Baron Wharncliffe 1826- UK; Baron Stuart of Wortley 1917-26 UK; Baronet 1611-65
Peers: 6 peers 1826-1945 1917-26
1 Ld Lt 19th
1 in Cabinet 1834-35 1841-45
Notes: 1 Bt and Baron Stuart and 1 and 2 Barons Wharncliffe and five others in ODNB.

MONTAGU II [Samuel]

Baron Swaythling (1907- UK)

Origins: Father of the 1 Baron was a silversmith and watchmaker (d. 1859). Merchant bankers in Liverpool and London (family bank founded 1853).

1. Montagu Samuel Montagu 1 Baron Swaythling – Whitechapel Div. Tower Hamlets 1885-1900
2. Sir Stuart Montagu Samuel 1 Bt – Whitechapel Div. Tower Hamlets 1900-16
3. Edwin Samuel Montagu – Chesterton Div. Cambridgeshire 1906-22

Seat: Townhill Park, Hampshire (built 1793, purch. 1897, remod. 1912, sold 1948, school)
Estates: 1 Baron left £1,150,000 in 1911. The Samuels owned 11,300 aces in Scotland in 1996.
Title: Viscount Samuel 1937- UK; Baronet 1894-
Peers: 4 peers 1907-1945

1 in Cabinet 1916-22
Notes: Family continued in the bank (sold 1973) through the life of the 4 Baron, who then headed Rothmans until 1998. 1 and 4 Barons and six others in ODNB.

MONTGOMERIE (Montgomery) [Foster, Graham, Leslie, Molineux, Moore, Pigott, Seton, Tichborne, Tipping] *SCOTLAND, IRELAND, & ENGLAND*

Earl of Eglinton & Winton (1507- S; 1859- UK)

Origins: Emerged in the 12th century. Baron 1448. **First [MP 1560]. Three further [MPs 1560-1644]**. The Baronets of Skelmorie were descended from a younger son of the 1 Baron Montgomerie. The Skelmorlie heiress married the father of the 12 Earl of Elington. The 1 Earl of Winton (6 Baron Seton) married the daughter of the 3 Earl of Eglinton. A younger son took the name Montgomerie and succeeded as 6 Earl of Eglinton. On the extinction of the main line of the Earls of Winton, the title passed to the Eglintons.

1. Sir James Montgomerie 4 Bt – [Ayrshire 1689-90]
2. Sir Hugh Montgomerie 6 Bt – [Glasgow 1703-07] Scotland 1707-08
3. Francis Montgomerie – [Ayrshire 1690-1707] Scotland 1707-08 Ayrshire 1708-10
4. John Montgomerie – Ayrshire 1710-27
5. Archibald Montgomerie 11 Earl of Eglinton – Ayrshire 1761-68
6. Hugh Montgomerie 12 Earl of Eglinton – Ayrshire 1780-81 1784-89 1796
7. James Montgomerie – Ayrshire 1818-29
8. Roger Montgomerie – N. Ayrshire 1874-80

Seats: Eglinton Castle, Ayrshire (acq. by mar. 14th c., built medieval period, rebuilt 1796-1803, unroofed 1925, demolished 1973); Skelmorlie Castle, Ayrshire (acq. 1453, built 1502, sold to a Glasgow merchant, John Graham, mid-19th c.); Coilsfield (Coylfield) Castle (House), Ayrshire (acq. c. 1640, rebuilt early 19th c., sold 1838, fire 1969, demolished 1971); Giffen Castle, Ayrshire (acq. 1370, built 15th c., sold 1722, became a ruin); Seagate Castle, Ayrshire (acq. 1366, built 1562-85, unroofed and abandoned 1746, ruin)
Estates: Bateman 30168 (S) 50830. Indebted and some estates sold 1819. Owned 2,000 acres in 1996.
Titles: Baron Montgomerie 1448- S; Baron Ardrossan 1806- UK; Baronet 1628-1735
Peers: [4 peers 1660-1707] 4 Scottish Rep peers 1710-14 1761-69 1776-96 1798-1806 5 peers 1859-1945
4 Lds Lt 18th, 19th, 20th
1 in Cabinet 1852-53 1858-59
2 KT 19th

Notes: The 6 Bt was a pioneer in developing the American trade. (Anderson, *Members of Parliament for Glasgow*, 4-5) Montgomery family has an entry as well as 1, 3, 6, 7, 9, 10, 11, 12, and 13 Earls and five others in ODNB.

Earl of Winton (Wintoun) (1660-1716 S)

Origins: The Setons emerged in the 12th century. Baron 1451. (see above) A younger son of the 5 Baron Seton was created Earl of Dunfermline in 1605 (forfeited 1690). A younger son of the 3 Earl became Viscount Kingston. This title was also attainted. **First [MP 1558]. Two other [MPs 1598-1617**].

No post-1660 MPs

Seats: Seton Palace, East Lothian (medieval, rebuilt c. 1400, remod. 1599, decayed by 1716); Pinkie House, Edinburghshire (acq. mid-16th c., built 16th c., rebuilt c. 1613, forfeited 1690); Fyvie Castle, Aberdeenshire (medieval, purch. 1596, add. 1598-1603, forfeited 1690); Winton (Wintoun) Castle (House), Haddingtonshire (built 1620-32, forfeited 1716)
Titles: Baron Seton 1451-1716 S; Baron Fyvie 1598-1690 S; Earl of Dunfermline 1605-1690 S; Viscount Kingston 1651-1716 S
Peers: [4 peers 1660-90 1663-1704]
Notes: Many members of the family remained Roman Catholic after the Reformation. The titles were forfeited in 1690 and 1715 and exile ensued. Estates sold 1716. The last Earl of Dunferline died in Rome in 1749. Seton family has an entry in the ODNB. 1 Viscount and 1 and 2 Earls of Dunfermline and 3 and 5 Earls of Winton and 4 and 5 Barons and two others also in ODNB.

Montgomerie

Origins: Cadet of the Earls of Eglinton. **First [MP 1560].**

1. Robert Montgomerie – [Ayrshire 1661-63]

Seat: Hessilheid (Hesilheid, Hazelhead) Castle, Ayrshire (medieval, acq. by mar. c. 1380, add. c. 1660s, sold 1722, abandoned c. 1776, ruin)
Notes: Family became heavily indebted in the early 18th c., One in ODNB.

Molineux-Montgomerie

Origins: Descended from a younger son of the 1 Earl of Eglinton. A Montgomerie heiress married in 1756 Crisp Molineux of Garboldisham.

1. John Montgomerie – [Linlithgowshire 1704-07] Buteshire 1710
2. George Montgomerie – Ipswich 1759-61
3. Crisp Molineux – Castle Rising 1771-74 King's Lynn 1774-90

Seats: Garboldisham Hall (Manor), Norfolk (acq. by mar. 1756, built 1868-69, sold 1919, demolished post-1945); Garboldisham Old Hall (built 16th c., acq. by mar. 1756, sold c. 1873, fire 1955); Thundersley Hall, Essex (built c. 1600)
Estates: Bateman 2588 (E) 2798

Montgomery

Origins: Descended from a younger son of the 1 Earl of Eglinton. The 1 Bt was Solicitor General, Lord Advocate, and Chief Baron of the Exchequer in Ireland. Other members of the family were also legal officials. Sir James Montgomery 2 Bt married the daughter and heiress of Thomas Graham of Kinross.

1. Sir William Montgomery 1 Bt – {Ballynakill 1768-88}
2. Sir James Montgomery 1 Bt – Dumfries Burghs 1766-68 Peeblesshire 1768-75
3. William Montgomery – Peeblesshire 1790-1800
4. Sir James Montgomery 2 Bt – Peeblesshire 1800-31
5. Sir George Montgomery 2 Bt – Peeblesshire 1831
6. Sir Graham Graham-Montgomery 3 Bt – Peebles 1852-68 Selkirk & Peeblesshire 1868-80

Seats: Stobo Castle, Peeblesshire (acq. 1767, built 1805-11, remod. 1849, sold 1905, now a health farm); Stanhope, Peeblesshire (purch. 1767); Kinross House, Kinross-shire (built c. 1554, new house built 1685-93, old house demolished 1723, purch. by Grahams 1777, passed to Montgomerys 1819, restored 1902-28, still own); Magbiehill (Macbie/ Magbie Hill), Peeblesshire (old tower house, add. 1835, demolished c. 1950)
Estates: Bateman 20626 (S) 11885. Owned 1,100 acres in 1996.
Titles: Baronet 1774-1831; 1801-
3 Lds Lt 19th, 20th
Notes: The 3 Bt was deputy governor of a linen company and active in insurance companies (Whiteley, *The Social Composition of the House of Commons*, 334). One in ODNB.

Graham

Origins: The founder was a merchant in Jamaica and then Calcutta. He returned to Scotland and purchased the Kinross estate in 1777. His brother's daughter married Sir James Montgomery 2 Bt above. A nephew of James Graham of Kinross, Graham

Graham, married in 1794 the niece and heiress of William Foster-Pigott and succeeded to the Pigott estates in 1824. His son took the name of Graham-Foster-Pigott.

1. George Graham – Kinross-shire 1780-84 1790-96
2. Thomas Graham – Kinross-shire 1811-12 1818-19
3. George Graham-Foster-Pigott – Kinross-shire 1819-20 1826-30

Seats: Kinross House, Kinross-shire (built c. 1554, new house built 1685-93, purch. 1777, passed to Montgomerys by mar. 1819); Abington Pigotts Hall, Cambridgeshire (acq. by mar. 1802, built c. 1829, passed to heiress, still own); Chayley, Sussex
1 Ld Lt 18th-19th

Pigott

Origins: The Pigotts were wool merchants in Hertfordshire. They purchased an estate in Cambridgeshire in the first half of the 15th century.

1. Granado Pigott – Cambridge 1690-95 Cambridgeshire 1702-05

Seat: Abington Pigotts Hall, Cambridgeshire (acq. c. 1428, passed by mar. to Graham-Foster-Pigotts 1802)

Earl of Mount Alexander (1661-1757 I)

Origins: The 1 Viscount was born in Scotland and went to Ireland in the 17th century with the assistance of the Earl of Eglinton, a distant kinsman (he was descended from a younger son of the 1 Baron Montgomerie) and accumulated estates from 1605. (Stevenson, *Two Centuries in Life in Down 1600-1800*, 30-31.) **First {MP 1613}. Four further {MPs 1613-40}**. Sherifff 1702. The estates passed in 1757 to a junior line at Grey Abbey.

1. William Montgomery – {Newtown 1661-66}
2. Hugh Montgomery 4 Earl of Mount Alexander – {Antrim 1703-13}
3. William Montgomery – {Hillsborough 1761-99}

Seats: Mount Alexander House, Down (built c. 1625, sold c. 1675); Grey Abbey (Rosemount), Down (acq. 1607 and built 1626, fire, rebuilt 1762, remod. 1782, still own); Newtown Priory, Down (acq. 1605, built house in ruins of priory c. 1606)
Estates: Bateman 5580 (I) 5907
Title: Viscount Montgomery of the Ards 1622-1757
Peers: {5 peers 1661-63 1692-1745 1751-57}

Notes: Sales of land in the later 17th c. due to the Civil War. In the 1730s the Earl of Mount Alexander was very hard up financially. (Moody and Vaughan, *A New History of Ireland*, IV, 72) 1 Earl and two others in ODNB.

Montgomery

Origins: Descended from a junior line of the Earls of Mount Alexander. Bishop 17th century.

1. Sir John Montgomery – {Lifford 1692-93 1695-98}
2. Alexander Montgomery – {County Monaghan 1713-22}
3. John Montgomery – {County Monaghan 1727-33}
4. Alexander Montgomery – {County Donegal 1727-29}
5. Thomas Montgomery – {Lifford 1729-60}
6. John Montgomery – {County Monaghan 1741}
7. Alexander Montgomery – {County Monaghan 1743-60 1768-83}
8. John Montgomery – {County Monaghan 1783-97}

Seats: Ballyleek House, Monaghan (old castle, acq. by mar. 1699, demolished mid-18th c., new house begun c. 1750, completed later 18th c., sold early 19th c.); Beaulieu, Louth (built 1660-67, acq. by mar. early 19th c., passed by mar. to Waddingtons 1939, still own); Blessingborne (Manor), Tyrone (acq. by mar. from Tichbornes early 19th c., cottage built 1810, house built 1870-74, passed to Lowry family after WWII); Derrygonnelley Castle, Fermanagh (old castle, acq. 17th c., fire 18th c., ruin, moved to Blessingborne)
Estates: Bateman 12548 (I) 4925. Worth £800 pa in 1730 and £1,772 pa in 1794.
Notes: One in ODNB.

Baron Ferrard (1715-31 I)

Origins: The Tichbornes were at Tichborne in Hampshire by 1135. **First MP 1314 for Hampshire. Seven additional MPs 1491-1628, three for Hampshire**. Hampered by remaining loyal Roman Catholics in the 17th century. A younger son went to Ireland as a soldier in the Civil War and became Lord Justice of Ireland in 1642. Charles II granted the family estates in Ireland. In 1731 the property was left by marriage to William Aston MP (see Clifford) and later passed in the early 19th century to the Montgomerys of Ballyleek via the Tippings.

1. Sir William Tichborne 3 Bt – {Swords 1661-66 County Louth 1692-93}
2. Sir Henry Tichborne – {County Tyrone 1630 Sligo 1661-66}
3. Henry Tichborne 1 Baron Ferrard – {Ardee 1692-93 County Louth 1695-99 1710-13}
4. William Tichborne – {Philipstown 1715-17}

Seats: Beaulieu, Louth (purch. 1650, built 1660-67, passed by mar. to Tippings 1776); Blessingborne, Tyrone (acq. mid 17th c., passed by mar. to Tippings 18th c.)
Title: Baronet 1697-1731
Peer: {1 peer 1715-31}
Notes: 1 Baron and one other in ODNB.

Tichborne

Origins: Cadet of the Tichbornes of Tichborne.

1. White Tichborne – Haslemere 1689-90

Seats: Frimley Park, Surrey (acq. by mar. 1599, rebuilt 1699, sold 1789 for £20,000, institutional use); Aldershot, Hampshire (acq. by mar. 1599, built late 17th c., house lost via mortgage from 1712)

Tipping

Origins: Tippings acquired land in Ireland from 1666. Sheriff 1745. Tichborne Aston MP (see Clifford) of Beaulieu left his estates to his brother-in-law, Thomas Tipping. A Tipping heiress married a Montgomery of Ballyleek.

1. Thomas Tipping – {County Louth 1755-60 Kilbeggan 1761-68}

Seats: Bellurgan Park, Louth (purch. 1723, still own – commercial use); Beaulieu, Louth (built 1660-67, acq. by mar. 18th c., passes to Montgomeries by mar. early 19th c.)
Estates: 4,276 acres worth £2,905 in 1855.

Montgomery-Moore

Origins: A daughter and heiress of the Montgomerys of Ballyleek married Acheson Moore MP of Garvey. Their son took the name Montgomery. The Moores were lairds from Renfrewshire who moved to Ireland in the 1660s. Sheriff 1664. The grandfather of Acheson Moore MP was attainted by James II in 1688, and his father wounded in the siege of Derry.

1. Acheson Moore – {Bangor 1716-60}
2. Nathaniel Montgomery – {County Tyrone 1781-90 Strabane 1797-1800}

Seats: Garvey House, Tyrone (acq. and built by Moores 1667, rebuilt 1800-12, dismantled 1820s, now a ruin); Fassaroe Castle, Wicklow (built 1536, ruin); Aughnacloy, Tyrone (acq. 17th c.)

Estates: Bateman 2686 (I) 2110
Notes: The rebuilding of Garvey 1800-12 was said to have cost £70,000. The builder fled to France in deep debt 1815 and the house was pulled down.

Leslie-Montgomery

Origins: Margaret Montgomery, an heiress of the Ballyleek line, married George Leslie, a clergyman, of Ballyconnell. Their son took the name Leslie-Montgomery. The Leslies emerged in the 17th century. Bishop of Raphoe.

1. George Leslie-Montgomery – {Strabane 1765-68 County Cavan 1768-87}
2. Sir Edward Leslie 1 Bt – {Old Leighlin 1787-90}

Seats: Ballyconnell House, Cavan (old castle, burned, new house acq. and built by Leslie-Montgomerys 1764, sold early 19th c.); Tarbert House, Kerry (acq. late 17th c., built c. 1701, add. 19th c., sold estate 1904 but retained house and demesne); Bingfield, Cavan (acq. 17th c., sold mid-18th c.)
Estates: 1747 (I) 1738 in 1878. Worth £3,000 to 4,000 pa c. 1818. Estates divided between a daughter and a cousin 1818.
Title: Baronet 1787-1818

Montgomery

Origins: Cadet of the Ballyleek line.

1. Alexander Montgomery – {Donegal 1715-27}
2. Alexander Montgomery – {County Donegal 1768-1800}

Seat: Convoy House, Donegal (purch. 1719, rebuilt early-mid 19th c., passed by mar. 19th c., to Boytons, still resident 1950s)
Estates: Bateman 8861 (I) 3640

MOORE I [Bury, Palliser] *IRELAND & ENGLAND*

Marquess of Drogheda (1791-1892 I)

Origins: Gentry in Kent, to Ireland c. 1550 as an official. Acquired 50,000 acres of monastic land near Drogheda. (Malcolmson, *John Foster*, 12) Sheriff 1571. Kt 1579. Acquired more land in the early 17th century. **First {MP 1613). Three {MPs 1634-44}.**

1. Charles Moore 2 Earl of Drogheda – {Drogheda 1692-99 1703-13}
2. Brabazon Moore – {Ardee 1695-99}

3. Robert Moore 3 Earl of Drogheda – {Belfast 1713-14 County Louth 1715-27}
4. Capel Moore – {Bangor 1713-14}
5. William Moore – {Ardee 1715-27}
6. Henry Moore 4 Earl of Drogheda – Camelford 1722-27
7. Edward Moore 5 Earl of Drogheda – {Dunleer 1725-27}
8. Charles Moore 1 Marquess of Drogheda – {St. Canice 1756-58} Horsham 1776-80
9. Ponsonby Moore – {Lismore 1759-60}
10. Lord Henry Moore – Orford 1806-12 Lisburn 1812-18

Seats: Moore Abbey, Kildare (medieval buildings, acq. by Loftus famly later 16th c., house built 17th c., passed by mar. to Moores 1699, remod. 1767, sold mid-20th c., hospital); Mellefont (Mellifont) Abbey, Louth (acq. early 17th c., sold 1927)
Estates: Bateman 19297 (I) 10466. Indebted 18th-19th c. 11 Earl left £819,000 in 1989.
Titles: Baron Moore 1616- I; Viscount Moore 1622- I; Earl of Drogheda 1661- I; Baron Moore 1801-92 UK; Baron Moore 1954- UK
Peers: {6 peers 1661-79 1692-1714 1721-1800} 2 Irish Rep peers 1899-1908 1913-45 3 peers 1801-22 1801-37 1846-92
2 Lds Lt 19th, 20th
2 in Cabinet 1696 1764-65
2 KP 18th, 19th
Notes: Much of the family land was sold in the 18th century to pay debts. 11 Earl was a leading newspaper proprietor (d. 1989). 1 and 2 Viscounts, 11 Earl, and 1 Marquess and one other in ODNB.

Moore

Origins: Descended from an uncle of the 1 Earl of Drogheda.

1. John Moore – {Charlemont 1727-52}
2. Henry Moore – {Charlemont 1761-62}
3. John Moore – {Ballynakill 1768-83}
4. John Moore – {Ballynakill 1783-90 Lisburn 1791-97 Newry 1799-1800} 1801-02

Seat: Drumbanagher, Armagh (acq. 17th c., rebuilt c. 1837, sold 1818, demolished 1962)
Estates: Held 4,000 acres in 1800, sold house and estate for £86,000 in 1818 to pay debts.

Earl of Charleville (1758-64 I; 1806-75 I)

Origins: A younger brother of Sir Edward Moore, ancestor of the Marquesses of Drogheda, established a line that was raised to the Barony of Moore of Tullamore in 1715 and the Earldom of Charleville in 1758. The sister and heiress of the 1 Earl married

William Bury of Shannon Grove. Their grandson was created Earl of Charleville in 1806. The Bury family acquired estates in Limerick in 1666. Sheriff 1672.

1. John Moore 1 Baron Moore – {Philipstown 1703-13 King's County 1713-14}
2. John Bury – {Askeaton 1715-22}
3. Charles Bury 1 Earl of Charleville – {Kilmallock 1790 1792-97}
4. Charles Bury 2 Earl of Charleville – Carlow 1826-32 Penryn 1832-34

Seats: Charleville Forest (Castle), King's County (Moores purch. 1731, passed by mar. of 1764 to Burys 1785, built 1800-09, passed by mar. 1875 to Howards who took name Bury, family departed 1912, leased from 1931 on, contents auctioned 1947, sold 1971, held by a trust); Shannon Grove, Limerick (Burys acq. by 1666, built 1709-23, sold 1844)
Estates: Bateman 20032 (I) 10052. Worth £5,000 pa in 18th c. Still owned 2,000 acres in the 1970s.
Titles: Baron Moore of Tullamore 1715-64 I; Baron Tullamore 1797-1875 I; Viscount Charleville 1800-75 I
Peers: {3 peers 1715-25 1733-64 1797-1800} 2 Irish Rep peers 1801-35 1838-51
Notes: Finances "embarrassed" in the 1840s. Limerick estates sold 1844. Contents of Charleville Forest auctioned 1848. One in ODNB.

Moore

Origins: A cadet (late 16th century) with shared ancestor with Earl of Charleville. **First {MP 1634}. One additional {MP 1639}**.

1. Roger Moore – {Mullingar 1692-93 1695-99}

Seat: Croghan, King's County

Palliser

Origins: A modest Yorkshire family. The 1 Bt went to sea as a boy and ended up an admiral and Governor of Newfoundland. Jane Palliser married John Bury. Their great-grandson became Earl of Charleville of the second creation. A senior line was created Baronets in 1773 and a junior line was seated at Comragh. These are combined here.

1. Sir Hugh Palliser 1 Bt – Scarborough 1774-79 Huntingdon 1780-84
2. Sir William Palliser – Taunton 1880-82

Seats: The Vache (Vatch), Buckinghamshire (medieval, remod. 18th c., purch. 1778, sold 1826, institutional use); Comragh, Waterford (acq. 18th c., resident 19th c.)

Estates: Bateman 13846 (I) 6800
Title: Baronet 1773-1868
Notes: Much of 1 Bt's estate passed to an illegitimate son and not to the 2 Bt. 1 Bt and one other in ODNB.

Palliser

Origins: Cadet line.

1. Thomas Palliser – {Fethard 1703-27}

MOORE II *IRELAND*

Earl of Mount Cashel (1781-1915 I)

Origins: Moved from Shropshire to Ireland in 1620 and settled in Clonmell 1654. Sheriff 1666. Purchased 40,000 acres in 1684. A son purchased further estates c. 1700.

1. Stephen Moore – {County Tipperary 1692-93 1695-99}
2. Richard Moore – {Clonmell 1692-93 1695-99}
3. Stephen Moore 1 Viscount Mount Cashel – {County Tipperary 1738-60}
4. Richard Moore – {Clonmell 1761}
5. Colvill Moore – {Clonmell 1761-76}
6. Stephen Moore 1 Earl of Mount Cashel – {Lismore 1761-66}
7. William Moore – {Clogher 1765-76 Clonmell 1781-97 St. Johnstown 1798-99}
8. Stephen Moore 2 Earl of Mount Cashel – {Clonmell 1790}
9. John Moore – {Clonmell 1792-97}
10. Stephen Moore – {Clonmell 1797-1800}

Seats: Moore Park, Cork (old castle, purch. 1684, rebuilt late Georgian, add. 19th c., sold 1903, fire 1908); Kilworth, Cork (purch. 1684, principal residence of the Earls of Mount Cashel in the 18th c.); Galgorm Castle (Mount Colville), Antrim (old castle, house built c. 1645, purch. 1744, remod. c. 1830, sold 1851); Moore Hill, Waterford (built later 18th c., passed 1856 by mar. of 1839 to Perceval-Maxwells)
Estates: Bateman 12344 (I) 3725
Titles: Baron Kilworth 1764-1915 I; Viscount Mount Cashel 1766-1915 I
Peers: {2 peers 1764-90} 3 Irish Rep peers 1815-22 1826-83 1815-22

Moore

Origins: Descended from a younger son (17th c.) of Richard Moore, ancestor of the Earls of Mount Cashel. Several lines are combined here.

1. Stephen Moore – {Clonmell 1713-27}
2. Guy Moore – {Fethard 1715-27}
3. Stephen Moore – {Fethard 1719-27}
4. Richard Moore – {Kells 1757-68}
5. Guy Moore – {Clonmell 1757-83}
6. Stephen Moore – {Fethard 1761-68}
7. Thomas Moore – {Kells 1768-81}
8. Stephen Moore – {Clonmell 1776-81}
9. Stephen Moore – {Clonmell 1783-90 Lanesborough 1790-97 Kells 1797-1800}
10. Stephen Moore – County Tipperary 1875-80

Seats: Barne, Tipperary (acq. and built early 18th c., remod. 19th c., resident at least until 1940s); Moore Hall, Cork; Marlfield, Tipperary (sold 1784)
Estates: Bateman 2141 (I) 2184. £2,000 pa in 1775.

MORDAUNT (Carey, Cary)

<u>Earl of Peterborough</u> (1628-1814 E)

Origins: Founded by Robert St. Giles, a follower of the Conqueror who was rewarded with land in Bedfordshire at the time of the Conquest. (Roskell, Clark, and Rawcliffe, *The House of Commons*, III, 767) Steadly expanded estates during the Middle Ages. **First MP 1341 for Bedfordshire. Six further MPs 1421-1584, three of them for the county**. The estates became separated from the title in 1697. The daughter of the 2 Earl of Peterborough succeeded as 7 Baroness Mordaunt and settled her estates, including Drayton House, on her second husband Sir John Germain (see Sackville). The younger brother of the 2 Earl, John Viscount Mordaunt married Elizabeth Carey, daughter and heiress of Thomas Carey, second son of Robert Carey 1 Earl of Monmouth (see below). Their son, the 3 Earl of Peterborough, was created Earl of Monmouth and succeeded as 8 Baron Mordaunt. The Barony of Mordaunt survived the extinction of the earldoms in 1814. It passed by marriage to the Dukes of Gordon and fell into abeyance in 1836 (see Gordon).

1. Harry Mordaunt – Brackley 1692-98 1701-02 1705-08 Richmond 1708-20
2. John Mordaunt Baron Mordaunt – Chippenham 1701-08
3. Henry Mordaunt – Malmesbury 1705-08
4. Sir John Mordaunt – Pontefract 1730-34 Whitchurch 1735-41 Cockermouth 1741-68
5. John Mordaunt – Nottinghamshire 1739-47 Winchelsea 1747-54 Christchurch 1754-61

Seats: Turvey House, Bedfordshire (acq. by mar. 1197, from a family that held it from before 1086, rebuilt c. 1605, sold 1786-87, rebuilt 1792); Drayton House, Northamptonshire

(built 1328, add. late 14th c., inher. 1515 by mar. to an heiress whose ancestors held the estate in the 13th c., rebuilt late 16th c. and c. 1670s, house separated from title and passed to dau. of 2 Earl 1697 and hence by mar. to the Sackvilles (see that family) 1769, still own)
Titles: Baron Mordaunt 1532-1836 E; Viscount Mordaunt 1659-1814 E; Earl of Monmouth 1689-1814 E
Peers: 5 peers 1660-88 1660-75 1680-1814 1690-97
3 Lds Lt 17th, 18th
1 in Cabinet 1689-90
2 KG 17th, 18th
Notes: 1 and 2 Barons, 1 Viscount, and 2 and 3 Earls and five others in ODNB.

Mordaunt

Origins: Cadet line in the 15th century. Soldier under Elizabeth I.

1. Sir John Mordaunt 5 Bt – Warwickshire 1698-1715
2. Sir Charles Mordaunt 6 Bt – Warwickshire 1734-74
3. Sir John Mordaunt 7 Bt – Warwickshire 1793-1802
4. Sir Charles Mordaunt 8 Bt – Warwickshire 1804-20
5. Sir John Mordaunt 9 Bt – S. Warwickshire 1835-45
6. Sir Charles Mordaunt 10 Bt – S. Warwickshire 1859-68

Seats: Walton D'Eiville Hall (later Walton Hall), Warwickshire (medieval house, acq. 1st half 16th c., often remodeled, rebuilt 1858-62, now country club, family still own); Massingham Parva, Norfolk (acq. by mar. 1517, sold 1807)
Estates: Bateman 7448 (E) 12792
Title: Baronet 1611-

Earl of Dover (1628-77 E)

Origins: The Careys were an old family (see below). **First MP 1547. Nine further MPs 1571-1629, four of them kts of the shire**. A younger son of the 1 Baron Hunsdon was created Earl of Monmouth in 1626. His heiress married the 3 Earl of Peterborough (see above). The son of the 1 Baron's second son was created Earl of Dover.

No post-1660 MPs

Seats: Hunsdon House, Hertfordshire (built 1446-48, acq. later 16th c., remod. 1630s, decayed 18th c., sold 1745); Conisborough Castle, Yorkshire (medieval, ruin, acq. 16th c., sold 1737)
Estates: Income of £4,000 pa in 1559. 1 Earl of Monmouth worth £1,350 in 1639

Titles: Baron Hunsdon 1559-1765 E; Viscount Rochford 1621-77 E; Baron Carey 1622-61 E; Earl of Monmouth 1626-61 E
Peers: 6 peers 1660-61 1660-1702 1708-65
Notes: The 1 Baron Hunsdon married a sister of Anne Boleyn, and was hence a cousin of Queen Elizabeth I. 1, 2, and 3 Barons Hunsdon and 1 and 2 Earls of Monmouth and three others in ODNB.

Viscount Falkland (1620- S)

Origins: Medieval family. The grandfather of the 1 Baron Hunsdon had an elder son whose great-grandfather was created 1 Viscount Falkland. **First MP 1572. Six additional MPs 1601-1654, two of them kts of the shire**.

1. Henry Cary 4 Viscount Falkland – Oxfordshire 1659 Oxford 1660 Oxfordshire 1661-63 {Fore 1662-63}
2. John Carey – New Windsor 1679-80
3. Anthony Carey 5 Viscount Falkland – Oxfordshire 1685-87 Great Marlow 1689-90 Great Bedwyn 1690-94
4. Edward Cary 6 Viscount Falkland – Colchester 1690-92
5. Nicholas Carey – Bridport 1695-97 (probable kinsman)
6. Lucius Carey – Bridport 1774-80

Seats: Scutterskelfe, Yorkshire (acq. later 16th c., sold c. 1900); Great Tew Park, Oxfordshire (built early 17th c., passed by mar. to the Careys 1626, add. later 17th c., sold 1698, demolished c. 1800)
Estates: Bateman 3011 (E) 4464
Title: Baron Hunsdon 1832-84 UK
Peers: 3 Scottish Rep peers 1831-32 1894-1922 1922-31 1 peer 1832-84
1 Ld Lt 17th
1 in Cabinet 1693-94
Notes: The 6 Viscount Falkland was a Jacobite. The Falklands were very poor in the later 17th century. The Tanfields of Burford Priory, Oxfordshire **elected four MPs 1449-1606.** The 2 Viscount Falkland inherited Burford from them 1625 but sold it in 1634. 1, 2, 4, and 5 Viscounts in ODNB.

Cary

Origins: The most senior line of the Cary family. Held land in Devon since the 12th century. The first MP was Chief Baron of the Exchequer 1387. **First MP 1358 for Devon. Seven additional MPS 1358-1628, three for the county**.

1. Sir George Cary – Okehampton 1681

2. William Cary – Okehampton 1685-87 1689-95 Launceston 1695-1701

Seat: Clovelly Court, Devon (acq. by mar. 1370, sold by heirs 1738)
Notes: The family became extinct in the 18th century leaving an encumbered estate.

MORE I (Moore)

Origins: Settled in Lancashire with extensive estates near Liverpool in the 13th century. Several stewards of the Earl of Derby. **First MP 1306 for Liverpool. Five further MPs 1404-1650, three for Liverpool**. Remained part of the merchant elite of the city into the 17th century as well as large landowners.

1. Sir Cleave More 2 Bt – Bramber 1709-10

Seats: Bank Hall (Kirkdale), Lancashire (built 16th c., sold to Earl of Derby by 2 Bt 1725, demolished 1778); Swinestead Abbey, Lincolnshire (acq. by 2 Bt, sold later 18th c.)
Title: Baronet 1675-1810
Notes: Nearly bankrupt early 18th century. One in ODNB.

MORE II (Moore)

<u>More</u>

Origins: Minor gentry or yeomen since the 14th century. Played the land market after the Dissolution as Tudor officials. One a London merchant in the 17th century. **First MP 1547. Three further MPs 1610-59**.

1. Richard More – Bishop's Castle 1681 1689-90 1695-98
2. Robert More – Bishop's Castle 1727-41 Shrewsbury 1754-61
3. Robert More – S. Shropshire 1865-68 Ludlow Div. Shropshire 1885-1903
4. Sir Jasper More – Ludlow 1960-79

Seat: Linley Hall, Shropshire (purch. 1583, rebuilt 1742, still own)
Estates: Bateman 6089 (E) 5020 plus 3200
Notes: Four in ODNB.

<u>Moore</u>

Origins: Probable kinsmen. **First MP 1572.**

1. Thomas Moore – Heytesbury 1640-48 1660 Lyme Regis 1679-81

Seats: Hawkchurch, Somerset (acq. and built 1593, estates divided among multiple heirs 1695); Spargrove, Somerset (built 16th c., acq. and remod. 17th c., estates divided among heirs 1695)
Notes: Male line extinct 1695.

MORETON [Langston, Reynolds]

Earl of Ducie (1837- UK)

Origins: A Moreton from a family seated at Moreton since the 13th century married Elizabeth Ducie daughter and heiress of Robert Ducie and niece of William Ducie 1 Viscount Downe of Tortworth. On the death of the 2 Baron Ducie, his title passed to his sister's son, Thomas Reynolds by special remainder. Reynolds took the name Moreton. Sir Robert Ducie was a rich merchant in London early 17th century. Banker to Charles I. Sheriff and Alderman 1620, Lord Mayor 1631.

1. Matthew Moreton 1 Baron Ducie – Gloucestershire 1708-13 1715-20
2. Matthew Moreton 1 Baron Ducie – Cricklade 1721-22 Calne 1723-27 Tregony 1729-34 Losthwithiel 1735
3. Francis Reynolds – Lancaster 1745-73
4. Francis Moreton 3 Baron Ducie – Lancaster 1784-85
5. Henry Moreton 2 Earl of Ducie – Gloucestershire 1831-32 E. Gloucestershire 1832-35
6. Augustus Moreton – W. Div. Gloucestershire 1832-35 E. Gloucestershire 1835-41
7. Henry Moreton 3 Earl of Ducie – Stroud 1852-53
8. Henry Moreton Lord Moreton – W. Gloucestershire 1880-85

Seats: Tortworth Court, Gloucestershire (built 16th c., purch. 1620, remod. late 18th c., rebuilt 1849-52 at a cost of about £45,000 – Kingsley, *The Country Houses of Gloucestershire*, III, 243 – requisitioned 1940, never a residence again, fire and house sold 1991, still own estate); Moreton, Staffordshire (acq. 13th c.); Spring Park (Woodchester), Gloucestershire (purch. 1631, built 16th or 17th c., remod. C. 1830, sold 1845)
Estates: Bateman 13992 (E) 21971. Still own 4,000 acres 2016.
Titles: Viscount Downe 1675-79 I; Baron Ducie 1720-70 GB; Baron Ducie 1763- GB; Baronet 1629-1703
Peers: {1 peer 1675-79}
9 peers 1720-1945
2 Lds Lt 18th, 19th
Notes: 2 Earl and two others in ODNB.

Langston

Origins: The father of the first Langston MP was a wine merchant and banker said to have been worth £500,000 at his death. On the death of James Langston MP in 1863 his estates went to his daughter and heiress, who married the 3 Earl of Ducie.

1. John Langston – Sudbury 1784-90 Bridgwater 1790-96 Minehead 1796-1802 Portarlington 1806 Bridgwater 1806-07
2. James Langston – New Woodstock 1820-26 Oxford 1826-34 1841-63

Seat: Sarsden House, Oxford (old house, fire, rebuilt 1689, purch. 1791, add. c. 1823-25, passed to Earls of Ducie later in century)
Estates: Rubinstein – John Langston MP left £250,000 probate in 1812.

MORGAN I [Bray, Gould] *WALES & ENGLAND*

Viscount Tredegar (1905-13 UK; 1926-49 UK)

Origins: The Morgans were territorial magnates in south Wales before the Normans moved into the region. (Hasler, *The House of Commons*, III, 95) Seated at Tredegar before 1402. Kt 15th century. **First MP 1559 for Monmouthshire. Six additional MPs 1589-1655, four for the county.** On the death of John Morgan in 1792 the estates passed to his sister Jane who married Charles Gould. Their son took the additional name Morgan.

1. William Morgan – Monmouthshire 1659 1660-80
2. Thomas Morgan – Brecon 1689-90 Monmouthshire 1690-1700
3. John Morgan – Monmouthshire 1701-05
4. John Morgan – Monmouthshire 1701-20
5. William Morgan – Monmouthshire 1722-31
6. Thomas Morgan – Brecon 1723-34 Monmouthshire 1734-47 Breconshire 1747-69
7. William Morgan – Monmouthshire 1747-63
8. Thomas Morgan – Brecon 1754-63 Monmouthshire 1763-71
9. Charles Morgan – Brecon 1763-69 Breconshire 1769-87
10. John Morgan – Brecon 1769-71 Monmouthshire 1771-92
11. Sir Charles Gould Morgan 1 Bt – Brecon 1778-87 Breconshire 1787-1806
12. Sir Charles Gould Morgan 2 Bt – Brecon 1787-96 Monmouthshire 1796-1831
13. Charles Morgan 1 Baron Tredegar – Brecon 1812-18 1830-32 1835-47
14. George Gould Morgan – Brecon 1818-30
15. Charles Morgan – Monmouthshire 1840-74
16. Charles Morgan – Brecon 1852-54
17. Godfrey Morgan 1 Viscount Tredegar – Breconshire 1858-75
18. Frederick Morgan – Monmouthshire 1874-85 S. Div. Monmouthshire 1885-1906

Seats: Tredegar Park (House), Monmouthshire (acq. and built early 15th c., rebuilt 1664-72, family departed 1951, sold to town council 1974); Ruperra Castle (Rhiwperra), Glamorganshire (medieval house, rebuilt 1626, purch. 1706, fire and remod. 1785, fire 1942, sold, ruin)
Estates: Bateman 39157 (W & E) 60000; worth £7,000 pa in the early 18th century; worth £40,000 pa by 1820.
Titles: Baron Tredegar 1859-1962 UK; Baronet 1792-1962
Peers: 4 peers 1859-1945
8 Lds Lt 18th, 19th, 20th
Notes: Two cadet lines at Penhaw, Monmouthshire and Penllwyn Sarth, Monmouthshire produced **four MPs 1601-49, two for the county**. John Morgan MP 1701-20 is a good example of a not uncommon phenomenon, a younger son who made a fortune as a merchant, had no children, and left his estates back to the head of the main line of the family. 1 and 2 Bts and 1 Viscount and five others in ODNB.

Bray

Origins: The Brays emerged in the late 15th century. The first rose as a favorite of Henry VII. Edmund Bray MP 1701-20 inherited the estates of Sir Edward Morgan 3 Bt of Llantarnam Abbey by marriage to a Morgan heiress. The Morgans of Llantarnam were a cadet line of the Morgans of Tredegar (14th century) and had accumulated the estates of several other Morgan lines at Pencoed, Monmouthshire and Pentrebach, Monmouthshire that also produced MPs. **First MP 1547 for Monmouthshire. Five additional MPs 1547-86, two for the county**.

1. Edmund Bray – Tewkesbury 1701-08 Gloucestershire 1720-22
2. William Bray – Monmouth 1715-20

Seats: Barrington Park, Gloucestershire (built 16th c., purch. by Brays 1553, sold 1735); Llantarnam Abbey, Monmouthshire (medieval, purch. and built by Morgans 1554, passed to Brays 1728, passed out of family later 18th c.)
Title: Baronet 1642-1728
Notes: The Morgans remained staunch Roman Catholics in the later 16th and the 17th c.

MORGAN II

Origins: The 1 Baronet was a famous soldier (Major General 1655) who purchased landed estates.

1. Sir John Morgan 2 Bt – New Radnor 1681 Herefordshire 1685-87
2. James Morgan – Weobley 1689-90 Hereford 1695-98
3. Sir Thomas Morgan 3 Bt – Herefordshire 1712-16
4. Sir John Morgan 4 Bt – Hereford 1734-41 Herefordshire 1755-67

Seats: Kinnersley Castle, Herefordshire (medieval, add. 16th c., purch. 1675, sold 1801); Chanston Court, Herefordshire; Henbury, Staffordshire (purch. 1650); Braham Hall, Yorkshire (purch. 1670s)
Title: Baronet 1661-1767
Notes: 1 Bt in ODNB.

MORICE

Origins: Chancellor of the Diocese of Exeter (d. 1605). London merchants and bankers, purchased a landed estate 1651. First MP a key figure in the Restoration and Secretary of State under Charles II.

1. Sir William Morice – Devon 1648 1654 1656 Newport 1659 Plymouth 1660-76
2. Nicholas Morice – Newport 1667-79
3. William Morice – Newport 1681 1685-87
4. Sir William Morice 1 Bt – Newport 1689-90
5. John Morice – Newport 1690-98 Saltash 1698-1700
6. Sir Nicholas Morice 2 Bt – Newport 1702-26
7. Humphrey Morice – Newport 1713-22 Grampound 1722-31
8. John Morice – Newport 1722-27
9. Sir William Morice 3 Bt – Newport 1727-34 Launceston 1734-50
10. Humphrey Morice – Launceston 1750-80

Seat: Werrington Park, Devon (now in Cornwall) (medieval, rebuilt c. 1630s, purch. 1651, rebuilt 1730s, sold 1775)
Estates: 11,000 acres in the 18th c.
Title: Baronet 1661-1750
Notes: Four in ODNB.

MORLEY I

<u>Baron Hollenden</u> (1912- UK)

Origins: Samuel Morley MP of modest origins amassed a fortune in the stockings and underwear business in the mid-19th century (2 million pounds of sales in 1871), and became a politician and owner of the *Daily News*. The 1 Baron was Governor of the Bank of England 1903.

1. Samuel Morley – Nottingham 1865-66 Bristol 1868-85
2. Arnold Morley – Nottingham 1880-85 E. Div. Nottingham 1885-95
3. Charles Morley – Breconshire 1895-1906

Seat: Hall Place, Leigh, Kent (purch. 1870, new house built 1871-76 at a cost, with the layout of the park, of £70,000 - Quiney, *Kent Houses*, 249-50 - fire 1940, for sale 2015)
Estates: Hall Place estate began with 398 acres. The 1 Baron built it up to 1,400 acres. First MP left half a million pounds plus landed property in 1886.
Peers: 2 peers 1912-45
1 in Cabinet 1892-95
Notes: One in ODNB.

MORLEY II

Origins: The father of the first MP was a Captain of Foot in the Civil War. Rising gentry? The first MP's brother was Bishop of Winchester.

1. Francis Morley – Winchester 1689
2. Charles Morley – Hindon 1695-97
3. George Morley – Hindon 1701-02 1705-08 1710-11

Seat: Droxford, Hampshire (built 17th c., Bishops of Winchester owners, lease?)

MORRES [de Montmorency, Pratt] *IRELAND*

Viscount Mountmorres (1763-1951 I)

Origins: The family claimed descent from the great house of de Montmorency in France and that the founder of the family in Ireland was Herve de Marisco, Constable of Leinster c. 1175. The family converted to Protestantism in the 1640s and served with Cromwell after which they acquired grants of land. (Burtchael, *Genealogical Memoirs of the Members of Parliament for the County and City of Kilkenny*, 76) A nephew of the 1 Viscount was created Viscount Frankfort in 1816. The family changed its name from Morres to de Montmorency in 1815.

1. Henry Morres 1 Viscount Mountmorres – {St. Canice 1734-56}
2. Sir William Morres 1 Bt – {Kilkenny 1752-68 Newtown 1769-74}
3. Redmond Morres – {Thomastown 1755-60 Newtown 1761-68 Dublin 1773-76}
4. Lodge Morres 1 Viscount Frankfort de Montmorency – {Innistiogue 1768-76 Bandon 1776-96 Ennis 1796-97 Dingle 1797-1800}
5. Sir Heydock Morres 2 Bt – {Kilkenny 1768-76}
6. Sir William de Montmorency 3 Bt – {Newtown 1785-90}

Seats: Castle Morres, Kilkenny (acq. c. 1667-84, built mid-18th c., remod. early 19th c., passed by mar. to Pratts 1831, sold 1924, part demolished 1940, rest demolished late

20th c.); Ebor Hall, Galway (built early 19th c., purch. mid-19th c., sold 1880s); Knockagh Castle, Tipperary (acq. and built 17th c., ruin)
Estates: Bateman 7953 (I) 3805; 4845 (I) 2849. Estate of 2 Viscount worth £5,000 pa in 1797.
Titles: Baron Mountmorres 1756-1951 I; Baron Frankfort 1800-1917 I; Viscount Frankfort de Montmorency 1816-1917 I; Baronet 1631-1951; 1758-1829
Peers: {3 peers 1756-1800} 1 Irish Rep peer 1900-02
1 in Cabinet 1795-1800
Notes: The 3 Viscount Frankfort de Montmorency inherited Dewlish House and the Michel estates in 1886 (see Michel), which the family retained until after WWII. The 5 Viscount was murdered in 1880. 2 Viscount and one other in ODNB.

Pratt

Origins: To Ireland during the Cromwellian period when estates were acquired. Sheriff 1698. The 2 Viscount Mountmorres left his estates to his sisters and not his half brother the 3 Viscount. His sister Sarah Morres married John Pratt of Cabra Castle. They succeeded to Castle Morres in 1831.

1. John Pratt – {Dingle 1713-27}
2. Mervyn Pratt – {County Cavan 1715-27}
3. James Pratt – {Navan 1781-83}

Seats: Cabra Castle, Cavan (purch. later 17th c., built early 18th c. - demolished 1950 - new house c. 1830, passed by mar. to Sheppards 20th c., sold c. 1966, hotel); Castle Morres, Kilkenny (see above)
Estates: Bateman 27064 (I) 9471

MORRIS *IRELAND*

Baron Killanin (1900- UK)

Origins: Claimed descent from baliffs and mayors of Galway in the 16th century. Gentry 17th and 18th centuries. Sheriff 1841. Rose as a barrister in the 19th c. Lord Chief Justice of Ireland 1887.

1. Michael Morris 1 Baron Killanin – Galway 1865-67
2. George Morris – Galway 1867-68 1874-80
3. Martin Morris 2 Baron Killanin – Galway 1900-01

Seats: Spiddal House, Galway (partly acq. by mar. 1684, rebuilt 18th c., partly purch. 1860s, rebuilt 1910, fire 1923, rebuilt 1931, sold c. 1960); Wellpark, Galway (built 18th c., acq. mid-19th c., sold by 1914, demolished 2007)
Estates: 1 Baron left £127,000 in 1901. Sold 2,557 acres in 1914.
Titles: Baron Morris 1889-1901 UK; Baronet 1885-
Peers: 3 peers 1889-1927 1935-45
1 Ld Lt 20th
Notes: 3 Baron was President of the International Olympic Committee 1972-80. Roman Catholic family. 1 Baron in ODNB.

MORRISON

Baron Margadale (1964- UK)

Origins: James Morrison was the son of an innkeeper. He was a textile wholesaler from 1809 onwards. He had five sons who were worth a total of £15,000,000 at their deaths. Their warehouse firm had a turnover of £650,000 pa in 1871. (Rubinstein "New Men of Wealth and the Purchase of Land in the Nineteenth-Century Britain", 132.) Later involved in banking. Purchased estates. High Sheriff 1857.

1. James Morrison – St. Ives 1830-31 Ipswich 1831-34 1835-37 Inverness Burghs 1840-47
2. Walter Morrison – Plymouth 1861-74 Skipton Div. Yorkshire 1886-92 1895-1900
3. James Morrison – Wilton Div. Wiltshire 1900-06 E. Nottingham 1910-12
4. Hugh Morrison – Salisbury Div. Wiltshire 1918-23 1924-64
5. John Morrison 1 Baron Margadale – Salisbury Div. Wiltshire 1942-64
6. Charles Morrison – Devizes Div. Wiltshire 1964-92
7. Peter Morrison – Chester 1974-92

Seats: Basildon Park, Berkshire (built 1776, purch. 1838 for £97,000, family departed 1910, sold 1928 – *Country Life*, 161, pp. 1230 and 1238); Fonthill House, Wiltshire (built 16th c., remod, 1745, fire 1755, rebuilt, purch. c. 1829, remod. 1848, old house demolished 1921, new house 1902-04, add. 1921, demolished 1971-72, new house 1972-74, still own); Hole Park, Kent (built 17th c., remod. 18th c., add. 1830, purch. 1854, sold 1911); Islay House, Argyll (built 1677, purch. 1726, add. c. 1731, add. c. 1760, add. 1841-45, purch. 1852, remod. 1909-11, sold 1985, still own estate)
Estates: Bateman 106915 (E & S) 53740; worth £2,000,000 in 1857. The first MP was worth £4,000,000 to £6,000,000 and owned 100,000 acres. Charles Morrison, a banker, left over ten million pounds at his death in 1909; worth £45,000,000 in 1990. Owned 9,000 acres in Wiltshire and up to 73,000 acres on Islay 2001.
Notes: Active in the leadership of the Conservative party. Four in ODNB.

MOSLEY

Origins: The founder was a clothier and Lord Mayor of London 1599. Purchased the manor of Manchester. **First MP,** a successful lawyer, **1614.** He invested heavily in land. **Another MP who was probably related 1547-59**. A younger son of the 3 Bt was created Baron Anslow 1916. The wife of the 6 Bt (Lady Cynthia Mosley) was an MP 1929-31 but is listed under Curzon.

1. Sir Edward Mosley 2 Bt – Mitchell 1661-65
2. Sir Oswald Mosley 2 Bt – Portarlington 1806-07 Winchelsea 1807-12 Midhurst 1817-18 N. Staffordshire 1832-37
3. Sir Oswald Mosley 6 Bt – Harrow Div. Middlesex 1918-24 Smethwick 1926-31

Seats: Rolleston Hall, Staffordshire (medieval, purch. 1617 and rebuilt, fire 1871, rebuilt, estate sold 1923, house demolished 1928); Ancoats Hall, Lancashire (purch. and built 1609, sold later 18th c., demolished 1820s and rebuilt, demolished 1960s); Strangeways Hall, Lancashire (medieval, purch 17th c.?, sold 18th c.?, demolished 19th c., rebuilt as a prison); Hough End Hall, Lancashire (built 1596, sold 18th c.)
Estates: Bateman 3703 (E) 7500. Worth £3,000 pa in 1638.
Titles: Baron Anslow 1916-23 UK; Baronet 1640-65; 1720-79; 1781-
Notes: Sir Oswald Mosley 6 Bt was the founder and leader of the fascist party in Britain during the interwar years. Imprisoned WWII. 6 Bt and one other in ODNB.

MOSSOM [Hewetson] *IRELAND*

Mossom

Origins: An English family. To Ireland as a Dean 1660 and became Bishop of Derry (d. 1679). His son was Master of Chancery in Dublin. The first MP was Recorder of Kilkenny.

1. Eland Mossom – {St. Canice 1759-74}
2. Eland Mossom – {Kilkenny 1777-83}

Seat: Mount Eland, Kilkenny (acq. by mar. from the Elands c. 1700, sold c. 1870)
Estates: Worth £1,500 pa in 1775.
Notes: One in ODNB.

Hewetson

Origins: An English family settled in Ireland later 16th c. The first MP was a son of a clergyman, Treasurer of Christchurch Cathedral, Dublin 1596. **First {MP 1642}.** A Hewetson heiress married in 1799 Colonel Eland Mossom.

1. Christopher Hewetson – {Thomastown 1695-99}

Estates: First MP acq. 500 acres in 1666.
Notes: Family fortunes declined mid-18th c. One in ODNB.

MOSTYN [Lloyd, Owen] *WALES & ENGLAND*

Baron Mostyn (1831- UK)

Origins: An ancient Welsh family prominent before the English conquest. The wealth of the family was created by Iorwerth Ddu ab Ednyfed Gam of Chirkland an urban merchant in the late 14th century. (R. R. Davies, *The Age of Conquest: Wales 1063-1415*, 429). Marriages to heiresses in the 14th and 15th centuries also contributed to their wealth. **First MP 1545 for Flintshire. Four further MPS 1554-1644, all for the county**.

1. Sir Thomas Mostyn 2 Bt – Caernarvon 1679-81
2. Thomas Mostyn – Flint 1698-1702 Flintshire 1702-05
3. Sir Roger Mostyn 3 Bt – Flintshire 1701-02 Cheshire 1702-05 Flint Boroughs 1705-08 Flintshire 1708-13 Flint Boroughs 1713-15 Flintshire 1715-34
4. Sir Thomas Mostyn 4 Bt – Flintshire 1734-41 1747-58
5. John Mostyn – Malton 1741-68
6. Savage Mostyn – Weobley 1747-57
7. Sir Roger Mostyn 5 Bt – Flintshire 1758-96
8. Sir Thomas Mostyn 6 Bt – Flintshire 1796-97 1799-1831
9. Edward Lloyd 1 Baron Mostyn – Flint Boroughs 1806-07 Beaumaris 1807-12 Flint Boroughs 1812-31
10. Edward Lloyd-Mostyn 2 Baron Mostyn – Flintshire 1831-37 1841-42 Lichfield 1846-47 Flintshire 1847-54
11. Thomas Lloyd-Mostyn – Flintshire 1854-61

Seats: Mostyn Hall, Flintshire (acq. 1432, built c. 1470, remod. 1631-32, still own); Gloddaeth Hall, Flintshire (acq. 15th c., built early-mid-16th c., add. c. 1700, add. 19th c. and 1889, sold 1965, school); Pengwern, Flintshire (Lloyd seat, acq. and built 18th c., estate sold 1919-21, school); Bodfach Hall, Montgomeryshire (medieval, add. 17th c., acq. by Lloyds by mar. 1758, sold 1840s)

Estates: Bateman 7779 (W) 14752. Income £1,678 pa in 1619. Worth £25,000,000 in 1990. Owned 2,000 acres in 2001.
Title: Baronet 1660-1831; 1778-
Peers: 4 peers 1831-1945
3 Lds Lt 18th, 19th
Notes: The Mostyn family has an entry in the ODNB. The 1 and 3 Bts and three others also in ODNB.

Mostyn-Owen

Origins: Cadet of the Mostyns of Mostyn. Succeeded to the Owen estates by marriage and took name Owen 1774. The Owens were Tudor gentry.

1. William Mostyn Owen – Montgomeryshire 1774-95

Seats: Woodhouse, Shropshire (acq. and built 16th c., rebuilt 1773-74, still own); Bryngwyn Hall, Montgomeryshire (old house, Mostyn seat from at least early 18th c., rebuilt 1773, fire 1793, passed out of family late 18th c., rebuilt 1813)
Estates: Bateman 2174 (E) 3459

Baron Vaux of Harrowden (1523- E)

Origins: The Vauxes were territorial magnates by the 12th century. Attainted in 1461. Restored by Henry VII. **First MP 1442 for Northamptonshire. An additional MP 1515 for the county**. On the death of the 5 Baron Vaux in 1663 the title fell into abeyance. It descended through the female line to George Mostyn of the Talacre line. He succeeded as 6 Baron on the termination of the abeyance in 1838. The 7 Baron repurchased Harrowden Hall in 1895.

No post-1660 MPs

Seats: (Great) Harrowden Hall, Northamptonshire (acq. by 15th c., passed 1662 by inher. to the Knollys family, rebuilt c. 1687-1712, repurch. 1895, sold to golf club 1966); Boughton Hall, Northamptonshire (medieval, inher. by mar. 1506 from a family that held it in the 14th c., passed to another family 1662); Kiddington Hall, Oxfordshire (built 1673, acq. by mar. 18th c., sold 1840); Rosmead House, Westmeath (built 18th c., purch. 1852, sold 1880 for £35,000, burned 1923, ruin)
Estates: Bateman 4323 (I) 2401; at Talacre, Flintshire 4184 (W) 9000
Peers: 2 peers 1838-1935
Notes: The 1 Baron Vaux inherited Boughton Hall from the Greenes (MP for **Northamptonshire 1336-38**). The 4 Baron Vaux, who died in 1662, left his estates away from the family. He made the claimant to the Banbury Earldom (see Knollys)

his heir. He may have been his real son, hence the case about Banbury's legitimacy. Harrowden was sold by Banbury in 1694. A Roman Catholic family. 1, 2, 3, and 4 Barons and five others in ODNB.

MOUNT

Origins: Businessmen in London in the later 17th century. Master of the Stationers Company in London 1717. His son held the same office. They became squires in the mid 18th century. The grandson of the founder was High Sheriff of Berkshire 1770.

1. William Mount – Yarmouth (IoW) 1818-19 Newport 1831-32
2. William Mount – Newbury Div. Berkshire 1885-1900
3. Sir William Mount 1 Bt – Newbury Div. Berkshire 1900-06 1910-22

Seat: Wasing Place, Berkshire (acq. 1759 and built 1770, fire and demolished c. 1943, new house built, still own, commercial use)
Estates: Bateman 4197 (E) 5163. Own 4,000 acres 2016
Title: Baronet 1921-

MOYLE [Copley, Purcell] *ENGLAND & WALES*

Moyle

Origins: A leading gentry family of Cornwall from the 14th century. **First MP 1388. Six further MPs 1410-1640.**

1. Walter Moyle – Cornwall 1654 1656 Lothwithiel 1659 1660 St. Germans 1689-90
2. Walter Moyle – Saltash 1695-98
3. Joseph Moyle – Saltash 1705-08

Seat: Bake, Cornwall (acq. by mar. mid-15th c., see below)
Notes: Five in ODNB.

Copley

Origins: Emerged in Yorkshire in the 15th century. The 1 Copley Bt of the second creation was born a cadet of the Moyles of Bake. He took the name Copley on succeeding through his mother to the Copley estates in 1766. The Copleys also succeeded to Bake.

1. Sir Godfrey Copley 1 Bt – Aldborough 1679-81 Thirsk 1695-1709
2. Sir Lionel Moyle Copley 2 Bt – Tregony 1796-1802

Seats: Sprotborough Hall, Yorkshire (acq. by mar. first half 16th c. from the Fitzwilliams who had held it since the early medieval period, then passed to the Copleys by mar. 1709, rebuilt 1696-1700, passed to Moyles 1766, sold 1925, demolished 1926); Bake, Cornwall (acq. by mar. 1766, fire 1808, sold)
Estates: Bateman 5942 (E) 7620
Titles: Baronet 1661-1709; 1778-1883
Notes: The Copleys of Batley, Yorkshire inherited Sprotborough from the senior line of the Fitzwilliams (acq. 13th century), junior line at Milton, Northamptonshire see Wentworth. 2 Bt first cr. and one other in ODNB.

Purcell

Origins: The Purcells held land in Shropshire from 1240. **First MP 1539. One further MP 1563**. A cadet acquired estates after the Dissolution in Wales. Sir Godfrey Copley 1 Bt (above) married the heiress of John Purcell (below).

1. John Purcell – Montgomeryshire 1660 Montgomery Boroughs 1661-65

Seat: Nantcribba, Montgomeryshire (acq. mid 16th c., sold c. 1670)

MULLHOLLAND *IRELAND*

Baron Dunleath (1892- UK)

Origins: Modest businessmen in Belfast in the 18th century. Rose very rapidly to great wealth as linen and cotton manufacturers in the 19th century (first mill purchased 1815). Lord Mayor of Belfast 1845. Purchased estates 1840s-60s and became country gentlemen. Sheriff 1866.

1. John Mullholland 1 Baron Dunleath – Downpatrick 1874-85
2. Henry Mullholland 2 Baron Dunleath – N. Londonderry 1885-95
3. Sir Henry Mullholland – County Down 1921

Seats: Ballywalter Park, Down (built 1810, purch. 1846 for £23,500, add. 1846, remod. 1863, add. 1902, still own); Craigavad, Down (purch. 1847, built 1852, sold 1883, golf club)
Estates: Bateman 14688 (I) 19424. The 1 Baron died worth £600,000.
Peers: 3 peers 1892-1945
Notes: 1 Baron and one other in ODNB.

MULLINS (de Moleyns) [Everleigh] *IRELAND*

Baron Ventry (1800- I)

Origins: A colonel settled in Ireland in 1666. Sheriff 1690. Changed name to Everleigh de Moleyns in 1841.

1. Frederick Mullins – {Dingle 1692-93 Tralee 1695-99}
2. William Mullins 2 Baron Ventry – {Dingle 1800}
3. Frederick Mullins – Kerry 1831-37

Seats: Burnham House, Kerry (purch. 1666, rebuilt c. 1790 for £4,000, add. mid-19th c., sold 1922, institution); Beaufort House, Kerry (castle, acq. and house built in ruins of castle c. 1666, sold 1847)
Estates: Bateman 93626 (I) 17067. Worth £20,000 pa 1804.
Title: Baronet 1797-
Peers: {1 peer 1800} 1 Irish Rep peer 1871-1914

MUNDY [Bisset, Popham]

Mundy

Origins: First prominent Mundy was a goldsmith, Lord Mayor of London 1522. Purchased estates. **First MP 1545 for Derbyshire**.

1. Wrightson Mundy – Leicestershire 1747-54
2. Francis Mundy – Derbyshire 1822-31
3. William Mundy – S. Derbyshire 1849-57 1859-65

Seats: Markeaton Hall, Derbyshire (medieval, purch. 1516, rebuilt soon after, rebuilt 1753-55, add. 1792, donated to Derby 1929, demolished 1964); Osbaston Hall, Leicestershire (built c. 1600, acq. by mar. early 18th c., rebuilt c. 1720, sold 1766)
Estates: Bateman 2765 (E) 7749
Notes: Male line extinct 1903, but heirs held the estates until 1964. Osbaston acquired by marriage to a Wrightson heiress.

Mundy

Origins: Cadet line.

1. Edward Mundy – Derby 1711-15
2. Edward Mundy – Derbyshire 1784-1822

3. George Mundy – Boroughbridge 1818-30
4. Edward Mundy – S. Derbyshire 1814-49

Seats: Shipley Hall, Derbyshire (built c. 1322, rebuilt 1631-36, acq. by mar. 1713, rebuilt 1749, rebuilt 1778-79, add. 1895, sold 1922, demolished 1948); Allestree Hall, Derbyshire (purch. 1516, sold 1781)
Estates: Bateman 2879 (E) 6810 and 7395 (E) 9264. Very productive coal mines on the estate in the 19th c.
Notes: One in ODNB.

Popham

Origins: Old and widespread family in Hampshire and Somerset. Many kts of the shire. Sir John Popham MP served at Agincourt and another Sir John was Lord Chief Justice 1592. **First MP 1295. At least 16 other MPs 1299-1651.** A Mundy of Shipley married the Popham heiress to Littlecote in the 19th century.

1. Alexander Popham – Bath 1640-53 Minehead 1654 Somerset 1656 Wiltshire 1559 Bath 1661-69
2. Sir Francis Popham – Bath 1669-74
3. Alexander Popham – Chippenham 1690-98 Bath 1698-1705
4. Francis Popham – Wootton Bassett 1706-10 Chippenham 1710-13
5. John Popham – Winchester 1714-15
6. Edward Popham – Great Bedwyn 1738-41 Wiltshire 1741-72

Seats: Littlecote, Wiltshire (medieval, rebuilt late 15th c., add. mid-16th c., inher. by mar. 1589, remod. c. 1810, held until 1922); Hunstrete (Huntstreet, Houndstrete) House, Somerset (medieval, purch. c. 1600, rebuilt 1760s-70s, rebuilt 1820, sold 1956, hotel); Bourton House, Gloucestershire (built later 16th c., purch. 1680, rebuilt c. 1710, sold 1727); Russley Park, Wiltshire (resident later 17th and early 18th c.)
Estates: Bateman 3341 (E) 5753 (Said to have been worth £10,000 pa in c. 1600.)
Notes: Littlecote was built c. 1200 by the de Calston family and passed by marriage 1415 to the Darrells. On the death of the last Darrell in 1589 it went to cousins, the Pophams. (Negus, *A Tour of Twelve Great Country Houses*, 12-13) Heavily indebted 17th c. Six in ODNB.

Popham

Origins: Senior line of the Pophams (separated in the 16th century).

1. Alexander Popham – Taunton 1768-96
2. William Popham – Milborne Port 1787-1790

3. Sir Hume Popham – Yarmouth 1804-06 Shaftesbury 1806-07 Ipswich 1807-12

Seat: Winterbourne Monkton, Somerset (acq. by mar. c. 1630, sold c. 1899)

<u>Bisset</u>

Origins: Mordaunt Bisset married 1851 Susan Popham the daughter and heiress of Francis Popham of Huntstrete.

1. Mordaunt Bisset – W. Somerset 1880-83

Seat: Bagborough House, Somerset (medieval, acq. later 17th c., rebuilt 1739, add. 1820, add. 1900, Brooke-Pophams still own)
Estates: Bateman 9949 (E & I) 6314

MUNRO (Monro) *SCOTLAND*

Origins: Old Scottish family. The first laird at Foulis died in 1126. **First [MP 1560]. Another [MP 1649].** Related to the Munros of Novar (see Butler I).

1. Sir George Munro – [Ross-shire 1661-67 Sutherland 1669-74 Ross-shire 1685-86 1689-90]
2. Sir John Munro 4 Bt – [Ross-shire 1689-96]
3. Sir Robert Munro 5 Bt – [Ross-shire 1698]
4. Sir Robert Munro 6 Bt – Tain Burghs 1710-41
5. John Munro – Ross-shire 1733-34
6. Sir Harry Munro 7 Bt – Ross-shire 1746-47 Tain Burghs 1747-61

Seats: Foulis Castle, Ross-shire (acq. by 1126, built 1164, sacked and burned 1746, rebuilt 1754-92, still own); Obsdale House (Dalmore), Ross-shire (acq. 16th c., still resident 19th c.)
Estates: Bateman 4458 (S) 3780. Owned 1,300 acres in 1980s.
Title: Baronet 1634-
1 Ld Lt 19th-20th
Notes: 6 Bt and two others in ODNB.

MUNTZ

Origins: Emigrated from Poland to France to England and settled in Birmingham in 1793. Became successful industrialists (metal manufacturing).

1. George Muntz – Birmingham 1840-57

2. Philip Muntz – Birmingham 1868-85
3. Sir Philip Muntz 1 Bt – N. Warwickshire 1884-1908

Seats: Umberslade Hall, Warwickshire (built 1693-8, leased 1850, purch. 1858, offices from 1940, sold c. 1970, now flats); Dunsmore House, Warwickshire (acq. and built 1881, sold 20th c., institutional use); Briton Ferry House, Glamorganshire (leased early and mid-19th)
Estates: Bateman 2561 (E) 4212
Title: Baronet 1902-40
Notes: One in ODNB.

MURE (Muir) *SCOTLAND*

Origins: Landowners and Kt 14th c. The first MP was a lawyer and official.

1. William Mure – Renfrewshire 1742-61
2. William Mure – Renfrewshire 1846-55
3. Dabid Mure – Bute 1859-65
4. William Mure – Renfrewshire 1874-80

Seat: Caldwell House, Renfrewshire (acq. before 1328, medieval castle, new house c. 1712, rebuilt 1773, family departed 1909, sold 1927, hospital, fire 1995, derelict)
Estates: Bateman 5024 (S) 6248 + 997
Notes: Three in ODNB.

MURRAY I [Keith, Pulteney] *SCOTLAND*

Duke of Atholl (1703- S) (Athole)

Origins: The Murrays of Tullibardine became prominent at the end of the 13th century. **First [MP 1560]. One additional [MP 1593]**. Created Earl of Tullibardine in 1606. The 2 Earl married Lady Dorothea Stewart the heiress of the 5 Earl of Atholl and succeeded to Blair Castle in 1629. The Stewarts descended from a half brother of King James II.

1. Mungo Murray – [Perthshire 1661-63 1669-70]
2. Charles Murray 1 Earl of Dunmore – Wigan 1685-87
3. John Murray – [Perthshire 1704-07]
4. Lord James Murray – Perthshire 1710-15
5. James Murray 2 Duke of Atholl – Perthshire 1715-24
6. Lord John Murray – Perthshire 1734-61
7. John Murray 3 Duke of Atholl – Perthshire 1761-64
8. James Murray – Perthshire 1773-94

9. Lord George Murray – Perth Burghs 1790-96
10. Lord James Murray – Perthshire 1807-12
11. John Stewart-Murray 8 Duke of Atholl – W. Perthshire 1910-17
12. Katherine Murray Duchess of Atholl – Kinross & W. Div. Perth & Kinross 1923-38

Seats: Blair Castle, Perthshire (built 1269, add. 1530, add. early 17th c., acq. by mar. 1629, remod. 1736, add. 1743-45, remod. 1869-71, remod. 1886, held in a trust from 1996); Pitnacree, Perthshire (built 18th c., still own?); Dunkeld House, Perthshire (acq. by 1529, old house, destroyed 1654, rebuilt 1676-84, add. 1758, demolished 1827, new house 1899-1901, sold 1930s, hotel); Castle Mona, Isle of Man (built 1801-04, became a hotel by 1832); Tullibardine Castle, Perthshire (castle, dismantled 1747, demolished c. 1830); House of Nairne, Perthshire (built 1710 by Lord William Murray, Lord Nairne, forefeited 1745, purch. by duke, demolished 1764); Eastwood House, Perthshire (acq. 16th c., built 1831, add. 1861-62, sold 1950s); Huntingtower, Perthshire (medieval, remod. 16th and 17th c., acq. 1663, decayed, sold 1805, state ownership)
Estates: Bateman 201640 (S) 42030. Atholl estates worth £143,000,000 in 1990; 148,000 acres in 1996.
Titles: Baron Innermeath 1439-1625 S; Earl of Atholl 1457-1595 S; Earl of Atholl 1596-1625 S; Baron Murray 1604- S; Earl of Tullibardine 1606- S; Baron Strange of Knocklyn 1628- E; Earl of Atholl 1629- S; Marquis of Atholl 1676- S; Earl of Tullibardine 1696- S; Baron Percy 1722- GB; Earl Strange 1786- E; Baron Glenlyon 1821-1957 UK
Peers: [4 peers 1660-1703 1661-70 1690-1707 1696-1707] 4 Scottish Rep peers 1710-15 1733-36 1766-74 1780-86 7 peers 1736-64 1786-1830 1835-1945
4 Lds Lt 18th, 19th, 20th
1 in Cabinet 1696-98
8 KT 17th, 18th, 19th, 20th
Notes: Inherited the Sovereignty of the Isle of Man in the 18th c. The park and gardens at Blair extend to 2,500 acres. Current Duke lives in South Africa. 1 Earl of Dunmore and 1 Marquis of Atholl and 1, 2 [and 2 Duke], 3, and 8 Dukes and twelve others in ODNB.

Earl of Dunmore (1686- S)

Origins: The 1 Earl was the second son of the 1 Marquis of Atholl.

1. Robert Murray – Wootton Bassett 1722-27 Great Bedwyn 1734-38
2. George Murray 4 Earl of Dunmore – Liskeard 1800-02
3. Charles Murray – Hastings 1880-83 Coventry 1895-1906

Seat: Dunmore Park, Stirlingshire (built 1820-25, empty since 1972, ruin)
Estates: Bateman 78620 (S) 10411 + 4000
Title: Baron Dunmore 1831- UK

Peers: [1 peer 1686-90] 2 Scottish Rep peers 1713-14 1727-52 1761-74 1776-90 4 peers 1831-45 1862-1945
1 Ld Lt 19th
Notes: Held large property in Virginia in 18th c. Family in deep financial trouble later 1860s. 2, 4, and 7 Earls and one other in ODNB.

Earl of Mansfield and Mansfield (1776- and 1792- GB)

Origins: Descended from (1498) younger son of William Murray ancestor of the Dukes of Atholl. **First [MP 1572]. Two additional [MPs 1599-1607].**

1. Sir John Murray – [Perthshire 1685-86]
2. James Murray – Dumfriesshire 1711-13 Elgin Burghs 1713-15
3. William Murray 1 Earl of Mansfield – Boroughbridge 1742-56
4. William Murray 4 Earl of Mansfield – Aldborough 1830-31 Woodstock 1831-32 Norwich 1832-37 Perthshire 1837-40
5. Mungo Murray 7 Earl of Mansfield – Perth Div. Perth & Kinross 1931-35

Seats: Scone Palace, Perthshire (medieval, rebuilt c. 1580, acq. 1604, remod. early 17th c., remod. 1793, rebuilt 1803-12, still own); Kenwood House, Middlesex (built 1616, purch. 1754, remod. 1764, add. early 19th c., sold 1925, now English Heritage museum); Comlongan Castle, Dumfriesshire (acq. and built 15th c., derelict 17th c., restored and add. 1890-1902, family departed 1939, sold 1984, hotel)
Estates: Bateman 49074 (S & E) 42968. Owned 33,800 acres in 2001.
Titles: Baron Mansfield 1605- S; Viscount Stormont 1621- S; Baron Balvaird 1641- S; Baron Mansfield 1756-93 GB
Peers: [2 peers 1661-68 1683-1707] 1 Scottish Rep peer 1754-96 6 peers 1756-93 1796-1945
2 Lds Lt 19th
2 in Cabinet 1757 1767 1779-1801
3 KT 17th, 18th
Notes: The 8 Earl was a member of the first British delegation to the European Parliament and later Minister of State for Scotland in 1979 and for Northern Ireland in 1983. 1 Baron Balvaird and 1 Viscount Stormont and 1 and 2 Earls of Mansfield in ODNB.

Murray

Origins: This cadet of the Mansfield (above) family shared a common ancestry with the Earls of Annandale.

1. Richard Murray – [Wigtownshire 1661-63 Kirkcudbright Stewartry 1678]
2. John Murray – [Kirkcudbrightshire 1703]

3. Alexander Murray – Kirkcudbright Stewartry 1715-27
4. James Murray – Wigtownshire 1762-68 Kirkcudbrightshire 1768-74
5. Horatio Stewart-Murray – Kirkcudbrightshire 1802-12
6. Alexander Murray – Kirkcudbrightshire 1838-45

Seats: Cally House, Kirkcudbrightshire (old house, acq. by mar. 1658 from Lennox family medieval owners, rebuilt 1763-65, add. 1795, remod. 1833, sold 1933, now hotel); Broughton House, Wigtownshire (built 1734, purch. 1740, sold 1756)
Estates: Bateman 47451 (S) 16322 and 50818 (I) 6500

Viscount Elibank (1911- UK)

Origins: Descended from a junior line of the Mansfield family in the 16th century. Lord of Session 1613. **First [MP 1605]. Five additional [MPs 1608-41, all for county seats].**

1. Sir Archibald Murray 3 Bt – [Peeblesshire 1661-63 1665 1667 1669-74 1678 1681 1685-86 1689 1689-98]
2. William Murray – [Stirlingshire 1665]
3. Patrick Murray – [Linlithgowshire 1686 1689 1689-1702]
4. Alexander Murray – [Peeblesshire 1693-98]
5. Sir Alexander Murray 4 Bt – [Peeblesshire 1700-01]
6. Sir Robert Murray Keith – Peeblesshire 1775-80
7. Alexander Murray 7 Baron Elibank – Peeblesshire 1783-84
8. James Murray – Yarmouth (IoW) 1802-03
9. Alexander Murray 1 Baron Murray – Midlothian 1900-06 Peeblesshire 1906-12
10. Arthur Murray 3 Viscount Elibank – Kincardineshire 1908-18
11. Charles Murray 2 Viscount Elibank – St. Rollex Div. Glasgow 1918-22

Seats: Black Barony (Blackbarony, Barony Castle) (aka Darn Hall or Darnhall), Peeblesshire (acq. and built 16th c., rebuilt late 17th c., add. 18th c. and 1855 and 1877, sold 1930s, hotel); Elibank (Eliburn) Castle (Tower), Selkirkshire (acq. 1595, built late 16th c., a ruin by 1722); Halmyre House (Murrayshall), Peeblesshire (purch. 1617, built early 17th c., passed to Keiths by mar. 1743, who took the additional name Murray); Ballencrieff, Haddingtonshire (built 1507, burned, rebuilt 1586, purch. 1632, add. 1730, fire 1868, ruin, sold, rebuilt 1990s)
Estates: Bateman 6690 (S) 10098
Titles: Baron Elibank 1643- S; Baron Murray of Elibank 1912-20 UK; Baronet 1628-
Peers: [2 peers 1660-61 1698-1707] 4 peers 1911-45
3 Lds Lt 18th, 19th, 20th
Notes: Earl of Westminster in the Jacobite peerage. 1 [Earl] of Westminster and 1 Baron Murray of Elibank (1912) and 5 Baron Elibank and two others in ODNB.

Murray

Origins: David Murray of Murrayfield was a grandson of the 4 Baron Elibank.

1. Alexander Murray – Peeblesshire 1780-83
2. David Murray – Peeblesshire 1784-90 New Radnor Boroughs 1790-94
3. Sir John Murray – Leith District 1832-39

Seats: Murrayfield, Edinburghshire (built 1735, add. 1780); Hattenknowe, Peeblesshire (a farm on the Blackbarony/Darn Hall estate); Henderland, Peeblesshire (purch. c. 1750, sold 1862)
Notes: Lord Henderland and Lord Murray in ODNB.

Murray

Origins: A cadet of the Elibank Murrays.

1. Alexander Murray – Peeblesshire 1715-22 1741-47

Seat: Cringletie House, Peeblesshire (purch. 1666, built 1861-63, now hotel)
Estates: Bateman 5838 (S) 2950
Title: Baronet 1628-
Notes: One in ODNB.

Murray

Origins: The most junior cadet line of the Elibank Murrays. Sir James Murray 7 Bt married in 1794 Henrietta Pulteney Countess of Bath in her own right, daughter and heiress of Sir William Pulteney 5 Bt. (See Johnstone under Hope and Pulteney)

1. Sir James Murray-Pulteney 7 Bt – Weymouth & Melcombe Regis 1790-1811
2. Sir John Murray 8 Bt – Wootton Bassett 1807-11 Weymouth & Melcombe Regis 1811-18

Seats: Dunerne, Fife (acq. 16th c.); Murrayshall (Halmyre), Peeblesshire (see above); Clermont, Fife (held 17th, 18th, and 19th c.)
Estates: Thanks to his wife's fortune the 7 Bt was able to leave £600,000 to the 8 Bt and £200,000 to a younger brother in 1811.
Title: Baronet 1630- ; Baroness Bath 1792-1808; Countess of Bath 1803-1808; Baronet 1630-
Notes: 7 and Bts in ODNB.

Murray

Origins: Descended from a younger son of Sir David Murray, ancestor of the Dukes of Atholl.

1. Sir William Murray 1 Bt – [Perthshire 1673-74]
2. Sir Patrick Murray 2 Bt – [Perthshire 1703-07]
3. Sir Patrick Murray 6 Bt – Edinburgh 1806-12
4. Sir George Murray – Perthshire 1824-32

Seat: Ochtertyre, Perthshire (acq. 15th c., built 1750, rebuilt 1784-90, family departed 1939, sold c. 1945)
Estates: Bateman 17876 (S) 11051
Title: Baronet 1673-
1 in Cabinet 1828-30
Notes: One in ODNB.

MURRAY II *SCOTLAND & ENGLAND*

Murray

Origins: May have been related to Murray I family. Originally seated at Falahill, they acquired estates in the 14th century. Lord of Session 17th century. **First [MP 1612 for Selkirkshire]. Another [MP 1628, also for the county].**

1. John Murray – [Selkirkshire 1661-63]
2. Sir James Murray – [Selkirkshire 1678 1681]
3. John Murray – [Selkirk Burgh 1689-1702 Selkirkshire 1703-07] Scotland 1707-08
4. John Murray – Linlithgow Burghs 1725-34 Selkirkshire 1734-54
5. John Murray – Linlithgow Burghs 1754-61

Seats: Philiphaugh, Selkirkshire (acq. 1528, old house remod. 1874, sold c. 1960, demolished 1965-70 and rebuilt 1964); Falahill, Selkirkshire (acq. 14th c.)
Estates: Bateman 2799 (S) 3035
Titles: Baronet 1704-1882
Notes: One in ODNB.

Murray

Origins: Descendent of a younger son of John Murray of Philiphaugh.

1. Charles Scott Murray – Buckinghamshire 1832-35 1841-45

Seat: Danesfield, Buckinghamshire (built mid-18th c., Scotts purch. 1787, Murrays succed by mar., rebuilt late 18th c., add. 1845, sold 1897, business)
Estates: Bateman 2528 (E) 4231

Murray

Origins: Descended from a younger son of the Falahill family in the 16th century. **First [MP 1639 for Peeblesshire].**

1. Sir William Murray 1 Bt – [Peeblesshire 1661-63 1665 1667]
2. Sir David Murray 2 Bt – [Peeblesshire 1681 1689-93]
3. Sir Alexander Murray 3 Bt – Peeblesshire 1710-13

Seat: Stanhope, Peeblesshire (purch. 1634, forfeited 1746)
Estates: Sold in 1767 for £84,000.
Title: Baronet 1664-1878
Notes: The 4 Bt was a Jacobite "out" in 1745. His estates were sold, and he died in exile. The family was allowed to resume the title late in the 18th century.

MURRAY III *SCOTLAND*

Origins: Merchants in Edinburgh. Acquired estates 1650s-60s. **First [MP 1650 for Peeblesshire].**

1. Sir Robert Murray – [Edinburgh 1661-63]
2. Patrick Murray – [Selkirkshire 1665 1667 1669-74]

MURRAY IV *SCOTLAND*

Origins: Landowners in the 14th century. Provost of Stirling 1595. Kt 1624. **First [MP 1609, sat for Stirlingshire 1625]. One additional [MP 1639 for the county].**

1. John Murray – [Stirlinghsire 1645-46 1648 1661-63]

Seats: Touchadam Castle, Stirlingshire (acq. 1369, abandoned in favor of Polmaise 17th c., now ruin); Polmaise Castle, Stirlingshire (acq. by mar. 1569, built 1691, remod. 18th c., new house 1865, family departed 1956, demolished 1966)
Estates: Exploited coal mines in 19th c.
Notes: Male line extinct c. 1915.

MUSGRAVE [Perrot]

Musgrave

Origins: J. B. Burke called the Musgraves a "martial and warlike family." (Burke, *A Visitation of Seats*, I, 264) Held the manor of Musgrave from 1204 and sustained an unbroken line of male succession from the 12th century to the 20th. Baron 1358, although descendents not summoned to Parliament. **First MP 1339 for Westmorland. Ten additional MPs 1399-1604, eight kts of the shire**.

1. Sir Philip Musgrave 2 Bt – Westmorland 1640-43 1661-78
2. Sir Christopher Musgrave 4 Bt – Carlisle 1661-81 1685-87 1689-90 Westmorland 1690-95 Appleby 1695-98 University of Oxford 1698-1700 Westmorland 1701 Totnes 1701-02 Westmorland 1702-04
3. Philip Musgrave – Appleby 1685-87 1689
4. Christopher Musgrave – Carlisle 1690-95 1702-05
5. Sir Christopher Musgrave 5 Bt – Carlisle 1713-15 Cumberland 1722-27
6. Joseph Musgrave – Cockermouth 1713-15
7. Sir Philip Musgrave 6 Bt – Westmorland 1741-47
8. George Musgrave – Carlisle 1768-74
9. Sir Philip Musgrave 8 Bt – Petersfield 1820-25 Carlisle 1825-27
10. Sir Richard Musgrave 11 Bt – E. Cumberland 1880-81

Seats: Edenhall (Eden Hall), Cumberland (old house, remod. 1723, rebuilt 1821-24, sold and demolished 1934); Kempton Park, Middlesex (acq. by mar. 1755, sold 1798); Hartley Castle, Westmorland (medieval, purch. 1353 and rebuilt 1361, rebuilt late 16th c., remod. c. 1670, demolished 1720)
Estates: Bateman 15449 (E) 15016 exclusive of mines
Titles: Baron 1358-85; Baronet 1611-
1 Ld Lt 19th
Notes: 2 Bt declined a peerage in 1660. The Musgraves inherited Scaleby Castle, Cumberland from the Tilliols (at Scaleby before 1130) by marriage in 1435. The Tilliols elected **three MPs 1352-1426 for Cumberland**. Thus the two families elected MPs from Cumberland from 1352 to 1881. 2 and 4 Bts and two others in ODNB.

Musgrave

Origins: Descended from a common ancestor with the Musgraves of Edenhall. **First MP 1559 for Cumberland. One MP 1604 also for the county**. Hayton Castle passed to the daughter of the 5 Bt, who had inherited the Hylton estates (see Joliffe). A younger line held the Baronetcy and was seated at Barnsley Park.

1. Sir Richard Musgrave 3 Bt – Cumberland 1701-08

Seats: Hayton Castle, Cumberland (acq. by mar. second half 15th c., built 15th c., rebuilt 1609, remod. c. 1665, 18th c. work, passed to Joliffes in the 18th c. by mar.); Barnsley Park, Gloucestershire (built 1697, rebuilt 1720-31, acq. by mar. in 1778, remod. 1806-13, passed to Wykehams (see that family) 1875, sold 1935)
Title: Baronet 1638-1875
Notes: Barnsley Park was acquired by Anthony Bourchier in 1548. The source of his wealth is a mystery. A Bouchier heiress (whose mother was a sister of the Duke of Chandos) married Henry Perrot (see below). Their daughter Cassandra died in 1778 leaving Barnsley to distant kin. Her aunt Perrot had married a younger brother of Sir Richard Musgrave. Late in the 19th century Barnsley passed to the Wykeham Musgraves by a sister's son (see Wykeham under Wenman). 6 and 7 Bts and one other in ODNB.

Perrot

Origins: Acquired wealth at the Dissolution of the monasteries. Long connected with Oxford University. For the connection with the Musgraves see notes above.

1. Charles Perrot – Oxford University 1679-81 1685-86
2. Henry Perrot – Oxfordshire 1721-40

Seats: Northleigh (North Leigh), Oxfordshire (medieval, purch. 1676, demolished later 18th c., sold 1765); Barnsley Park, Gloucestershire (built 1697, Henry Perrot MP above married the Bouchier heiress to Barnsley, whose family acq. it in 1548, rebuilt 1720-31, passed to cousins the Musgraves in 1778)

MUSSENDEN [Leathes] *IRELAND & ENGLAND*

Origins: The Mussendens were Belfast merchants and bankers. Carteret Mussenden succeeded to his uncle Leathes estates and took the name Leathes 1727.

1. Carteret Mussenden Leathes – Sudbury 1727-34 Harwich 1734-41 Sudbury 1741-47
2. Hill Mussenden – Harwich 1741-47
3. Daniel Mussenden – {Killyleagh 1800}

Seats: Herringfleet Hall, Suffolk (acq. by mar. 1727, built c. 1730, add. 1778-88, remod. c. 1830s, add. 1873, sold 1919); Larchfield, Down (purch. 1749, built c. 1750, sold 1868)
Estates: Bateman 2125 (E) 2888; 3098 (I) 3520

MYDDELTON (Middleton) [Biddulph, Trollope] *WALES & ENGLAND*

Myddelton

Origins: A Welsh family settled in Oswestry in the 12th century. Acquired estates in Denbighshire in the 15th century. A younger son acquired a fortune in trade (Lord Mayor of London 1613). Purchased estates in the late 16th century. Became the greatest landed magnates in North Wales by the 18th century. **First MP 1542. Four additional MPs 1547-1628.**

1. Sir Thomas Myddelton – Weymouth & Melcombe Regis 1624 Denbighshire 1625 1640-48 1660
2. Sir Thomas Myttelton 1 Bt – Flint Boroughs 1646 Montgomery 1660 Denbighshire 1661-63
3. Sir Thomas Myddelton 2 Bt – Denbighshire 1679-81
4. Sir Richard Myddelton 3 Bt – Denbighshire 1685-87 1689-1716
5. Robert Myddelton – Denbigh Boroughs 1722-23
6. John Myddelton – Denbigh Boroughs 1733-41 Denbighshire 1741-42
7. Richard Myddelton – Denbigh Boroughs 1747-88
8. Richard Myddelton – Denbigh Boroughs 1788-96
9. Robert Myddelton-Biddulph – Herefordshire 1796-1802 Denbigh Boroughs 1806-12
10. Robert Mydddelton-Biddulph – Denbigh Boroughs 1830-32 Denighshire 1832-34 1852-68

Seats: Chirk Castle, Denbighshire (medieval, purch. 1595, rebuilt soon after, demolished 1659, reconstructed soon after, remod. 1777, remod. 19th c., still own); Burghill House (Court), Herefordshire (acq. by Biddulphs and built 1773-6, passed by mar. to Myddeltons 1801, sold 1874) Estates: Bateman 8338 (E & W) 11742. 18,000 acres in the 1640s. 60,000 acres worth £5,000 pa. by 1660s. Rubinstein – Robert Myddleton Biddulph left £100,000 in probate 1814.
Titles: Baronet 1622- ; 1660-
Notes: Robert Myddelton-Biddulph MP made a fortune worth £70,000 pa in the East India Company and banking (Fisher, *The House of Commons*, VI, 471) 1 Bt. first cr. and two others in ODNB.

Baron Biddulph (1903- UK)

Origins: Mercers in Lichfield in the 16th century and drapers in London in the 17th. **First MP 1646**. The eldest son of Michael Biddulph of Ledbury and Crofton married in 1801 Charlotte, sister and heiress of Richard Myddelton of Chirk Castle. His descendents took the additional name Myddelton (until 1899) and were seated at Chirk. The junior line was made Barons Biddulph. A senior line, silk merchants in London in the 17th century, descended from Simon Biddulph (ancestor of Michael) was seated at Westcombe and created Bts in 1664 is included here. Active in the family bank in London into the twentieth century.

1. Sir Theophilus Biddulph 1 Bt – London 1656 1659 Lichfield 1661-79
2. Michael Biddulph – Lichfield 1660
3. Sir Michael Biddulph 2 Bt – Lichfield 1679-81 1689-90 1695-1710
4. Michael Biddulph – Tamworth 1690-95
5. Robert Biddulph – Hereford 1832-37
6. Michael Biddulph 1 Baron Biddulph – Herefordshire 1865-85 S. Herefordshire 1885-86 Ross 1886-1900

Seats: Ledbury Park, Herefordshire (built late 16th c., inher. by mar. from Hall family 17th c., add. c. 1820, sold 1950s); Kemble House, Gloucestershire (built late 17th c., acq. by inher. 1884, sold 1948); Elmhurst, Staffordshire (old house, acq. 17th c., rebuilt c. 1683, sold 1765, demolished 1921); Westcombe Park, Kent (medieval, purch. 1652, sold c. 1720); Crofton Hall, Worcestershire (acq. by mar. 1791 from families by descent that had held it since 1594, sold 1812); Birdingbury Hall, Warwickshire (built 1st half 17th c., acq. by mar. from the Whelers (see Wheler) 1687, fire 1859, rebuilt late 19th c., sold 1914, now offices); Dingwood Park, Herefordshire (medieval, purch. 1680s, rebuilt c. 1690, became a farm house in 18th c., sold 20th c.); Rodmarton Manor, Gloucestershire (medieval, demolished later 18th c., acq. 1894, rebuilt 1909-29, said to have cost £100,000 – Kingsley, *The Country Houses of Gloucestershire*, III, 214 – still own)
Title: Baronet 1664-
Peers: 2 peers 1903-45
Notes: Three in ODNB.

Middleton

Origins: Cadet line descended from Sir Thomas Myddelton of Chirk in the 17th century.

1. Sir Thomas Middleton – Harwich 1679-81 1689-1700
2. Thomas Middleton – Essex 1707-13 1715

Seat: Stansted Hall (Stansted Mountfitchet), Essex (purch. c. 1615, built c. 1625, sold 1710)
Estates: Worth £1,500 pa in 1702.
Notes: On the death of Thomas Middleton MP above in 1715 the estate was divided among five daughters.

Middleton

Origins: Descended from a brother of Sir Thomas Myddelton of Chirk. The **first MP of this branch in 1601** was a skinner in London.

1. Peter Middleton – Weymouth & Melcombe Regis 1659 1660

Baron Kesteven (1868-1915)

Origins: The daughter and heiress of Thomas Middleton of Stansted Hall married Sir Thomas Trollope 4 Bt of Casewick. The Trollopes made an undramatic rise in the town of Bourne in the 1560s-80s perhaps as sheep farmers or in trade (*Country Life*, 136, p. 1764). Acquired estates 1621. High Sheriff 1642.

1. John Trollope 1 Baron Kesteven – S. Lincolnshire 1841-68

Seat: Casewick, Lincolnshire (purch. 1621, rebuilt early 17th c., turned into flats after 1975)
Estates: Bateman 6291 (E) 10856
Title: Baronet 1642-1915
Peers: 3 peers 1868-1945
Notes: See Carew I. Seven in ODNB.

MYTTON

Origins: Emerged as clothiers in Shrewsbury in the fourteenth century, a city where they were citizens from the early medieval period. **First MP 1354 for Shrewsbury. Eight additional MPS 1447-1654, five of them for Shrewsbury and three kts of the shire.** The Myttons succeeded to the Pride estates. The Prides elected **three MPs in the 14th century**.

1. Richard Mytton – Shrewsbury 1690-95 1698-1713
2. John Mytton – Shrewsbury 1819-20

Seats: Halston Hall, Shropshire (acq. late 15th c., rebuilt 18th c., sold 1847); Dinas Mawddwy, Merionethshire (acq. 15th c., divested 16th c.); Shipton Hall, Shropshire (Lutwyche acq. 1580, built 1587-98, passed by mar. to Myttons early 17th c., passed to Moores 1874)
Estates: Worth £5,000 pa. c. 1820
Notes: Most property sold to pay debts 1820s-1840s. The last male Mytton died 1874. Three in ODNB.

NAPIER I (Naper, Napper) [Alington, Scott, Sturt] *SCOTLAND & ENGLAND*

Baron Napier and Ettrick (1627- S and 1872- UK)

Origins: The founder of the family made a fortune in the wool trade. Provost of Edinburgh 1403. His son, a merchant adventurer and courtier, was Kted 1452. Began purchasing estates in the 1530s. One family member fought at Flodden and another at Pinkie. Master of the Mint 1576. **First [MP 1471 for Edinburgh]. Another [MP 1463, also for Edinburgh].**

1. Alexander Napier – [Stirlingshire 1690-1700]
2. Francis Napier – [Stirling Burgh 1698-1702]
3. Sir Charles Napier – Marylebone 1841-47 Southwark 1855-60
4. Sir Joseph Napier 1 Bt – Dublin University 1848-58
5. Mark Napier – Roxburghshire 1892-95

Seats: Thirlestane Castle (House, Tower), Selkirkshire (built late 16th c., rebuilt 1816-20, remod. 1872, demolished 1965); Merchistoun (Merchiston) (Hall), Edinburghshire (purch. and built 1436, add. 16th c., remod. 18th c., sold 1914, later a school)
Estates: Bateman 6991 (S) 2316
Titles: Baronet 1627-83; 1637- ; 1867-
Peers: [2 peers 1660-86] 2 Scottish Rep peers 1796-1806 1807-23 1824-32 3 peers 1872-1945
1 Ld Lt 18th-19th
1 KT 19th
Notes: John Napier of Merchistoun invented logarithms. 1, 2, 8, 9, and 10 Barons and seventeen others in ODNB.

Scott

Origins: Sir William Scott 2 Bt of Thirlestane married the daughter of the 5 Baron Napier. Their son took the name Napier and inherited the Barony and Thirlestane. The Scotts were cadets of the Scotts of Harden (see Home). Granted arms 1542 and acquired estates in the first half of the 16th century. **First [MP 1607 for Selkirkshire]. Another [MP 1648 also for the county].**

1. Sir Francis Scott 1 Bt – [Selkirkshire 1669-74 1685-86 1693-1702]

Seat: Thirlestane Castle, Selkirkshire (acq. c. 1535, see above)
Title: Baronet 1666-

Napier (Napper)

Origins: A younger son of the Napiers of Merchistoun settled in Dorset in the reign of Henry VII. The eldest son established the Napers of Luton Hoo (see Herne). The son of a younger son was an eminent lawyer under Elizabeth I and Chief Baron of the Exchequer in Ireland 1593-1602. He purchased Middlemarsh in 1606. His son, Sir Nathaniel Napier, built More Crichel House and was elected an MP for Dorset. His eldest son succeeded to Middlemarsh (see below), a middle son to Puncknowle (see below), and a younger son emigrated to Ireland and settled at Loughcrew (see Legge). **First MP of the Puncknowle line 1586. Another MP 1626.**

1. Sir Robert Napier 1 Bt – Weymouth & Melcombe Regis 1689-90 Dorchester 1690 1698-1700

Seat: Puncknowle, Dorset (built 16th c., acq. early 17th c., sold 1743)
Estates: Worth £2,000 pa in 1653.
Title: Baronet 1682-1743
Notes: Roman Catholic in the 18th century. 1 Bt in ODNB.

Napier

Origins: See above. **First MP 1625 for Dorset. Another MP 1628-44.**

1. Sir Nathaniel Napier 2 Bt – Corfe Castle 1679-81 1685-87 Poole 1689-98 Dorchester 1702-05
2. Gerard Napier – Dorchester 1689
3. Sir Nathaniel Napier 3 Bt – Dorchester 1695-1708 1710-22
4. Sir Gerard Napier 6 Bt – Bridport 1761-65

Seats: Middlemarsh Hall (House, Grange), Dorset (medieval, purch. 1606, demolished c. 1774); [More] Crichel (Critchell) House, Dorset (purch. and built early c. 1615, fire 1742, rebuilt 1740s, passed to Sturts 1765, add. c. 1765 and c. 1775, sold 2013)
Estates: 18,000 acres in 1765 (Legg, *Dorset Families*, 46)
Title: Baronet 1641-1765
Notes: Male line extinct 1765. 1 and 2 Bts and two others in ODNB.

Baron Alington (1642-1723 I; 1682-91 GB; 1876-1940 UK)

Origins: The Alingtons may have begun as wine traders in the 1380s. Acquired Horseheath 1397. They exploited court office, royal favor, and marriage to heiresses (most notably the Argentine estates acquired by that family in the 11th century that passed to the Alingtons in the 15th century via an heiress). (Roskell, Clark, and

Rawcliffe, *The House of Commons*, II, 28, and III, 381). Two Speakers of the House of Commons in the 15th century. **First MP 1410 for Cambridgeshire. Three further MPs 1433-1558, all for the county**. One was killed at Bosworth fighting for Richard III. Barons 1642. The family became extinct in the male line in 1723. The daughter of the 3 Baron Alington married Sir Nathaniel Napier 3 Bt. Their daughter, the heiress of the Alingtons and the Napiers, married in 1717 Humphrey Sturt of Horton. The Sturts rose via a City fortune made as merchants and victuallers to the Royal Navy. One was an Alderman of London late 17th century. His son was granted arms 1691, Kted, and High Sheriff of Hampshire. His son married the Napier an Alington heiress.

1. William Alington 3 Baron Alington – Cambridge 1664-81
2. Sir Anthony Sturt – Stockbridge 1695-1701 Hampshire 1713-15
3. Humphrey Sturt – Dorset 1754-84
4. Charles Sturt – Bridport 1784-1802
5. Henry Sturt – Bridport 1817-20 Dorchester 1830 Dorset 1835-46
6. Henry Sturt 1 Baron Alington – Dorchester 1847-56 Dorset 1856-76
7. Charles Sturt – Dorchester 1856-74
8. Humphrey Sturt 2 Baron Alington – E. Dorset 1891-1904

Seats: [More] Crichel, Dorset (built c. 1615, rebuilt 1740s, passes by mar. to Sturts 1765, add. c. 1765 and c. 1775, school post 1940, sold 2013); Horseheath Hall, Cambridgeshire (acq. 1397, built 16th c., rebuilt 1663-65, sold 1701, demolished 1792); Horton, Dorset (built c. 1718, add. mid 18th c., became farm house post 1765); Heckfield Park (later known as Highfield Park), Hampshire (purch. and built 1691, sold before 1778); Brownsea (Branksea) Castle, Dorset (built 1547, purch. 1765, rebuilt 1760s, sold 1817, fire c. 1896, NT 1962)
Estates: Bateman 17500 (E) 23624. 8,000 acres in 1970.
Peers: 3 peers 1682-85 1876-1940
1 Ld Lt 17th
Notes: 1 Baron third cr. and one other in ODNB.

NAPIER II *SCOTLAND*

Baron Napier of Magdala (1868- UK)

Origins: Son of a major. 1 Baron Commander in Chief in India.

No MPs

Seat: Lynedale House, Inverness-shire (built c. 1760, purch. 1900, sold 1970s)
Estates: Bateman under 2000
Peers: 4 peers 1868-1945
Notes: 1 Baron and one other in ODNB.

NEEDHAM (Nedham) *IRELAND & ENGLAND*

Earl of Kilmorey (1822- I)

Origins: At Shavington by the 15th century. The first MP was a Kt and judge. **First MP 1442. Three additional MPs 1593-1648**. The father of the 1 Viscount was a military commander in Ireland (d. 1603) and acquired estates there, but the family resided frequently in England. It was, however, most active electorally in Ireland in the 18th and 19th centuries.

1. Robert Needham – {Newry 1727-53}
2. George Needham – {Newry 1761-67}
3. William Needham – {Athenry 1800}
4. Francis Needham 1 Earl of Kilmorey – Newry 1806-18
5. Francis Needham 2 Earl of Kilmorey – Newry 1819-26
6. Francis Needham Viscount Newry and Mourne – Newry 1841-51
7. Francis Needham 3 Earl of Kilmorey – Newry 1871-74
8. Richard Needham 6 Earl of Kilmorey – Chippenham 1979-83 Wiltshire N. 1983-97

Seats: Shavington Hall, Shropshire (acq. 1438, built 1685, sold 1884, demolished 1959); Mourne Park, Down (acq. 1806 possibly by inher. and rebuilt, add. 1820s, add. 1859, remod. late 19th c., add. 1904, add. 1919-21, fire 2013, family still own); Wareseley Park, Huntingdonshire (purch. 1788, sold 1833, demolished 1934)
Estates: Bateman 52412 (E & I) 34022. Irish estates worth £4,000 pa in 1779. Owned 12,000 acres in 2001.
Titles: Viscount Kilmorey 1625- I
Peers: {5 peers 1680-87 1704-10 1724-1800} 2 Irish Rep peers 1881-1915 1916-45
1 KP 19th-20th
Notes: The 6 Earl of Kilmorey was Minister of State for Northern Ireland 1985-92. 4 Viscount and 1 Earl and three others in ODNB.

Nedham

Origins: Descended from a younger son of the Kilmorey family. Went to Jamaica after the Civil War.

1. Robert Nedham – Old Sarum 1734-41 {Newry 1753-60}
2. William Nedham – {Newry 1767-76} Winchelsea 1774 Pontefract 1780-84 Winchelsea 1784-90

Seat: Howbery Park, Oxfordshire (resident 18th c.)

NESBITT *IRELAND & ENGLAND*

Origins: Scottish soldier to Ireland under Charles I. The first MP was High Sheriff 1715 and Collector of Revenue in Cavan 1730. He succeeded to the Cosby estates at Lismore by marriage in 1722. Albert Nesbitt MP emigrated from Ireland to London in c. 1717 and became a Baltic merchant. Several younger sons were great merchants and bankers in London in the 18th century.

1. Thomas Nesbitt – {Cavan 1715-50}
2. Alexander Nesbitt – {Newton Limavady 1736-60}
3. Albert Nesbitt – Huntingdon 1741-47 Mitchell 1747-53
4. Cosby Nesbitt – {Cavan 1750-68}
5. Arnold Nesbitt – Mitchell 1753-54 Winchelsea 1754-61 Cricklade 1761-68 Winchelsea 1770-74 Cricklade 1774-79
6. Thomas Nesbitt – {Cavan 1768-1800}
7. John Nesbitt – Winchelsea 1780-90 Gatton 1790-96 Bodmin 1796-1802

Seats: Lismore House, Cavan (acq. 1722, built c. 1730, passed by mar. to Burrrowes family 1854, demolished c. 1952); Keston Park, Kent (acq. 1750, sold c. 1802); Ringmer, Sussex (purch. 1741)
Estates: Bateman 11497 (I & E) 6444. Worth £1,200 pa in 1743.
Notes: The family businesses in London became insolvent late 18th c., bankrupt 1802. Nesbitt family has an entry in ODNB. Two others in ODNB.

NETTERVILLE *IRELAND*

<u>Viscount Netterville</u> (1622-1882 I)

Origins: Archbishop of Armagh 13th c.? Irish judge and Kt 1559. **First {MP 1585 for County Meath}. Another {MP 1585 for County Dublin}.** The title was dormant 1812-34 and 1854-67.

No post-1660 MPs

Seats: Dowth Castle, Louth (acq. castle medieval period, rebuilt mid-18th c., sold c. 1882); Cruicerath, Meath (resident 19th-20th c.); Coarsefeild (Oory House), Mayo (purch. 18th c., sold by 1830)
Estates: Bateman 3332 (I) 2153
Peers: {3 peers 1660-89 1730-51 1765-1800}
Notes: A Roman Catholic family. Most estates confiscated under Cromwell. 1 and 2 Viscounts and two others in ODNB.

NEVILL [Jones] *IRELAND*

Origins: Richard Nevill claimed to be a grandson of the Hon. Francis Neville of Kyner, second son of Edward Lord Abergavenny, who fled to Ireland after a duel in 1649 and settled in Kildare and purchased estates. (*Burke's Landed Gentry*, 1879, II, 1159) There is no proof of this connection. Not listed under Abergavenny in *Burke's Peerage*. Sheriff 1674. Mary Nevill married Edward Jones, who took the name Nevill and succeeded to the Nevill estates. The first Jones emigrated to Ireland in the 1640s as a soldier. In the next generation a lawyer. Richard Nevill MP 1771-1819 was a banker.

1. Richard Nevill – {Naas 1695-99}
2. Edward Jones – {New Ross 1713-14 Wexford 1715-35}
3. Arthur Jones Nevill – {Wexford 1751-53 1761-71}
4. Richard Nevill – {Wexford 1771-1800} 1802-19

Seats: Furness (Phornauts, Phornace) House, Kildare (acq. by Nevills c. 1649, rebuilt c. 1731, add. 1780, passed by mar. to Derings 1822); Borrismore House (Marymount), Kilkenny (acq. 18th c., built c. 1765, owned into 20th c.)
Estates: Held 3,650 acres worth £2,880 pa in 1794. Much of the estate sold by 1810 to pay heavy indebtedness. Held 1095 (I) 786 in 1878.

NEVILLE (Nevill, Nevile) [Aldworth, Griffin, Rainsford, Robinson]

Marquess of Abergavenny (1876- UK)

Origins: The Nevilles were declared by one genealogist to be "the most illustrious house in the peerage". (Shirley, *The Noble and Gentle Men of England*, 102) Even a modern scholar declared it "one of the oldest families in England". (Roskell, Clark, and Rawcliffe, *The House of Commons*, III, 824) The Marquesses of Abergavenny have a male pedigree "without parallel among English noble families". (*DNB*, xiv, 249) The family claimed Saxon descent, held land in the Domesday Book, and became barons in 1294. One of the first Baron's sons was made Baron Furnivalle, a title that passed through the Talbot and Howard families. **First MP 1290. At least eleven further MPs 1318-1603, many kts of the shire**. Another line derived from the Earl of Westmorland (1397-1570) from who were descended the Earls of Salisbury, Kent, and Warwick and the Dukes of Bedford (all now extinct), and the cadet lines listed below. The Nevilles of Eridge would, but for an attainder, be the heirs to the medieval Earldom of Westmorland. The line began with a son of the 1 Earl of Westmorland by a daughter of John of Gaunt who was created Baron Abergavenny in 1450. Eridge, which is the oldest still stocked deer park in England - probably established before the Conquest - came to the Nevilles through a line of heiresses beginning in 1290. The daughter of the 24 Baron Abergavenny by tenure married the younger son of the 1 Earl of Westmorland. The 1 Neville Baron Abergavenny became 27 Baron by tenure. **First MP 1515 for Kent. Five further MPs 1555-1624, one other for Kent**. The family was Roman Catholic for a time.

1. Henry Nevill 2 Earl of Abergavenny – Seaford 1784 Monmouthshire 1784-85

Seats: Eridge Castle, Sussex (by descent from 1290, medieval, rebuilt 1787, demolished 1937, rebuilt, still own); Birling Manor (Place), Kent (medieval, acq. by mar. 1435, remod 16th, 18th and 19th c., fire 1917, restored, still own); Kidbrooke Park, Sussex (built 1733, sold 1803)
Estates: Bateman 28534 (E & W) 30235
Titles: Baron Bergavenny 1450- E; Earl of Abergavenny 1784- GB
Peers: 15 peers 1660-66 1685-1744 1748-1945
2 Lds Lt 18th, 19th, 20th
1 KG 19th-20th
1 KT 19th
Notes: No other great English family has produced so few MPs, in part due to recusancy. The Neville family has an entry in ODNB. 1, 2, 4, 5, and 6 Earls of Westmorland, 1, 3, Barons Bergavenny and twenty-eight other additional biographies in ODNB.

Robinson

Origins: Began as yeomen, a son a merchant and his son, steward of the Lowther estates, attorney, and a Treasury official. His daughter and heiress married the 2 Earl of Abergavenny. (Christie, *Myth and Reality in Late Eighteenth-Century British Politics*, 145-82)

1. John Robinson – Westmorland 1764-74 Harwich 1774-1802

Seat: Winder Hall, Westmorland (medieval, rebuilt c. 1612, purch. 1697, passed to Nevills by mar. 1802 and sold, became a farm house, now hotel)
Notes: One in ODNB.

Baron Braybrooke (1788- GB)

Origins: The descent of the Neville estates and lineage in this branch of the family became unusually complex. The Nevilles of Billingbear were descended from a younger son of the Barons Abergavenny in the 16th century. **First MP 1553 for Berkshire. Four further MPs 1584-1659, one a kt of the shire**. Anne Neville married Richard Rainsford of Dallington (see below). Their daughter, Anne Rainsford married the 2 Baron Griffin of Braybrooke Castle and Dingley Hall Northamptonshire. The 1 Baron Griffin had married the heiress to Audley End (see Howard I - Suffolk). The

Griffins emerged in Leicestershire in the 14th century. One married a Favel heiress of Weston Favel, Northamptonshire in 1315. Prominent at court under the Tudors. Attorney General 1546. **First MP 1640.** Their son, the 3 Baron Griffin, died in 1742, when the title became extinct. Their daughter, Elizabeth, became Countess of Portsmouth and left Audley End to her nephew John Griffin Whitwell, who took the name Griffin and was created 1 Baron Braybrooke with a special remainder to Richard Aldworth Neville of Billingbear. The Barony of Howard de Walden was revived in the 1 Baron Braybrooke's favor in 1784 but it later wandered into other families. Anne Neville's (see above) brother, Richard Neville of Billigbear married the daughter and heiress of Ralph, Lord Grey of Warke. Their son, Henry Neville, took the name Grey. Their daughter, Catherine, married Richard Aldworth of Stanlake (see below). Their son took the name Neville. His son succeeded as 2 Baron Braybrooke and inherited Audley End from his kinsman in 1797. Ralph Neville, a younger son of the 2 Baron, inherited Butleigh Court and took the name Grenville (see Baron Glastonbury under Grenville).

1. Richard Neville – Berkshire 1670-76
2. James Griffin – Brackley 1685-87
3. Richard Neville – Berkshire 1695-1710
4. Grey Neville – Abingdon 1705-08 Wallingford 1708-10 Berwick-on-Tweed 1715-23
5. Henry Neville Grey – Wendover 1709-13 Wallingford 1719-22 Berwick-on-Tweed 1723-27 Reading 1734-40
6. Richard Neville Aldworth – Reading 1747-54 Wallingford 1754-61 Tavistock 1761-74
7. Richard Griffin 2 Baron Braybrooke – Grampound 1774-80 Buckingham 1780-82 Reading 1782-97
8. Richard Neville Griffin 3 Baron Braybrooke – Thirsk 1805-06 Saltash 1807 Buckingham 1807-12 Berkshire 1812-25
9. Ralph Neville Grenville – Windsor 1841-47 E. Somerset 1865-68 Mid Div. Somerset 1868-78

Seats: Audley End, Essex (medieval, acq. by Audley 1538, inher. by Howards mid-century, rebuilt 1603-14, remod. 17th and 18th c., part demolished c. 1720 and 1750, purch. by Cts. of Portsmouth 1745, Whitwell Griffins inher. 1761, remod. 1763, inher. by Nevilles 1797, remod. 1820-40, house sold to government 1948, family retained the estate); Billingbear, Berkshire (acq. by the Neville 1552, built 1567, remod. 18th c., fire and demolished 1924); Stanlake, Wiltshire (acq. by mar. 1765, add. later 18th c., park sold 1847, manor held into 20th c.); Dingley Hall, Northamptonshire (purch. by Griffins 1549, built mid-16th c., remod. 1681-88, sold c. 1742, part demolished 1972)
Estates: Bateman 13511 (E) 18713. Owned 7,000 acres in 2001.
Peers: 8 peers 1797-1945
1 Ld Lt 18th-19th

Notes: The Lords Braybrooke exercised the hereditary right to appoint the Master of Magdalene College, Cambridge until 2012. The 1 Baron Braybrooke spent £100,000 on the reconstruction of Audley End. 1, 2, 3, and 4 Barons and seven others in ODNB.

Aldworth

Origins: The first important Aldworth was descended from a line of clothiers, Mayor of Reading in 1551. One who was a London grocer purchased Stanlake in 1610. Also merchants in Bristol, Mayor of Bristol 1582. **First MP 1558 for Reading. Three further MPs 1586-1653.** Richard Aldworth married Catherine Neville of Billigbear (see above). Their grandson succeeded as 2 Baron Braybrooke.

1. Robert Aldworth – Bristol 1654 1656 1659 Devizes 1660
2. Richard Aldworth – Reading 1661-79
3. William Aldworth – Reading 1685
4. Charles Aldworth – Windsor 1712-14

Seats: Stanlake, Wiltshire (built later 16th c., purch. 1610, passed to Nevilles (Griffin) by mar. 1762, see above); Frogmore House, Berkshire (built 1680, leased 1687, lapsed early 18th c.)
Notes: One in ODNB.

Rainsford (Raynsford)

Origins: Late medieval early Tudor gentry. Chief Justice in the 1660s. **First MP 1640.** Anne Neville married Richard Rainsford (see above).

1. Sir Richard Rainsford – Northampton 1660 1661-63
2. Richard Rainsford – Northampton 1685-87

Seat: Dallington, Northamptonshire (purch. 1630s, sold 1720)
Estates: £600 pa in 1650s
Notes: One in ODNB.

Nevile

Origins: Cadet of the Earls of Westmorland.

1. Sir Christopher Nevile – Lincoln 1689-90

Seats: Wellingore Hall, Lincolnshire (acq. 1692 by mar. to Ellis family, built 18th c., family abandoned after 1946, now flats and offices); Haddington Hall, Lincolnshire

(medieval, acq. 1575, became derelict 17th c. then ruinous); Aubourn Hall, Lincolnshire (old house, purch. 1628 and rebuilt c. 1628, add. 1660, farm house 18th and 19th c., restored 1903, became principal seat 1946, still own)
Estates: Bateman 6531 (E) 9717

Neville

Origins: Cadet of the Neville settled in Nottinghamshire in the 13th century. **First MP 1363.**

1. Sir Edward Neville 1 Bt – East Retford 1679-81 1685

Seat: Grove Hall, Nottinghamshire (medieval, acq. by mar to a Hercy heiress 14th c., rebuilt 16th c., acq. by mar. 1570, sold late 17th c.)
Estates: Worth £1,000 pa in 1660.
Title: Baronet 1675-86
Notes: Two in ODNB.

NEWCOMMEN (Newcomen) [Gleadowe] *IRELAND*

Viscount Newcommen (1803-25 I)

Origins: Rose as an official in the Exchequer in London in the 16th century. Founder's son went to Ireland c. 1600. Kt 1605. High Sheriff 1612. His son an admiral. Bt 1623. **First {MP 1613}. Three further {MPs 1613-46}.** Two lines of the family are combined here: the Baronets seated at Mosstown and the Newcommens of Carrigglas, who were created Viscounts. The 1 Viscountess married Sir William Gleadowe 1 Bt of Killester, who took the name Newcommen. The Gleadowes were bankers in Dublin in the 18th century. **First {MP 1781}.**

1. Sir Robert Newcommen 4 Bt – {Mullingar 1661-66}
2. Sir Robert Newcommen 6 Bt – {County Longford 1692-93 1695-99 1703-14 1727-35}
3. Brabazon Newcommen – {Kilbeggan 1713-27}
4. Thomas Newcommen – {St. Johnstown 1727-60}
5. Sir Arthur Newcommen 7 Bt – {County Longford 1735-59}
6. Sir Thomas Newcommen 8 Bt – {County Longford 1759-60 Longford 1761-68}
7. Charles Newcommen – {St. Johnstown 1761-73}
8. Sir William Gleadowe-Newcommen 1 Bt – {County Longford 1790-1800} 1801-02
9. Thomas Gleadowe-Newcommen 2 Viscount Newcommen – County Longford 1802-06

Seats: Carrigglas (Carrickglas) Manor, Longford (leased by Newcommens 18th c., departed 1825); Mosstown, Longford (built 17th c., sold by 1798, demolished 1962); Killester House, Dublin (built early 18th c., demolished c. 1910, new house built, demolished also)
Estates: Newcommens owned property worth £7,000 pa in 1800.
Titles: Baron Newcommen 1800-25 I; Baronet 1623-1789; 1781-1825
Notes: The Gleadowe/Newcommen bank crashed in 1825 and the Viscount shot himself. The 2 Viscount left his estates to his eight illegitimate children.

NEWDIGATE (Newdegate)

Origins: Rose through a combination of good management of agricultural land, the law, fortunate marriages, royal favor, and coal. (Larmine, *Wealth, Kinship and Culture: The Seventeenth-Century Newdigates of Arbury and Their World*) Acquired Newdigate, Surrey in the early 13th century. **First MP 1360 for Surrey. Nine additional MPs 1386-1628, four kts of the shire**. The family elected an MP in every century between the 14th and the 20th except for the 15th. A judge acquired the Warwickshire property in the 16th century. Another lawyer and judge made a fortune at the bar in the 17th century.

1. Sir Richard Newdigate 1 Bt – Tamworth 1660
2. Sir Richard Newdigate 2 Bt – Warwickshire 1681 1689-90
3. Richard Newdigate – Newark-on-Trent 1710-15
4. Sir Roger Newdigate 5 Bt – Middlesex 1742-47 University of Oxford 1757-80
5. Charles Newdigate – Warwickshire 1843-85
6. Sir Francis Newdigate-Newdegate – Nuneaton Div. Warwickshire 1892-1906 Tamworth Div. Warwickshire 1909-17

Seats: Arbury Hall, Warwickshire (built 1560s, acq. 1585, add. 1670s, remod. 1771-79, still own); Harefield Place, Middlesex (medieval, acq. c. 1440, sold 1585, repurch. 1677, rebuilt 1786, demolished 1813, rebuilt, sold house 1877, still owned some land in 1920s, golf club); West Hallam, Derbyshire (acq. 1822, built 1876, sold 1913, demolished 1938); Astley Castle, Warwickshire (medieval, rebuilt later 16th c., purch. 1674, often leased out in 19th c., then a hotel, fire 1981, ruin)
Estates: Bateman 10989 (E) 19089. Estates worth £15,000 pa in the 1780s due to exploitation of coal mines (Tyack, *Warwickshire Country Houses*, 11) The first mines were sunk as early as 1603.
Title: Baronet 1677-1806
Notes: The estates passed through the Parker family by marriage 1806, who took the name Newdigate. Viscount Daventry (see Fitzroy) inherited from his mother after 1936. 1, 2, and 5 Bts and five others in ODNB.

NEWENHAM [Devonsher] *IRELAND*

Newenham

Origins: The family claimed descent from the Newenham family of Gloucestershire. In the early 17th century John Newenham emigrated to Ireland and settled in County Cork. Mayor of Cork 1671. Purchased landed estates in the 1690s.

1. Thomas Newenham – {Cork 1751-60}
2. John Newenham – {Fore 1761-68}
3. Sir Edward Newenham – {Enniscorthy 1769-76 County Dublin 1776-97}
4. Thomas Newenham – {Clonmel 1797-1800}

Seats: Belcamp Hall, Dublin (built c. 1786, sold 1893, now derelict); Coolmore, Cork (purch. 1680, new house built 1701, rebuilt 1788, sold 1984)
Estates: Bateman 2740 (I) 3643. Worth £4,000 pa c. 1769 and £10,000 pa c. 1804.
Notes: One in ODNB.

Devonsher

Origins: Quaker merchants and bankers in Cork from the mid-17th c. Sheriff 1762. Abraham Devonsher of Kilshannig left his estates to his sister's grandson, John Newenham, who took the name Devonsher c. 1837.

1. Abraham Devonsher – {Rathcormack 1757-76}

Seat: Kilshannig, Cork (estate acq. c. 1660, built c. 1765, sold mid-19th c.)

NEWLAND

Origins: The first Newland MP was the son of a poor miller. He married a Turgis heiress in 1677. The first prominent Turgis was Mayor of Chichester c. 1600. His son made a fortune as a London grocer.

1. Thomas Turgis – Gatton 1659-81 1685-87 1689-1702
2. Sir George Newland – Gatton 1705-10 London 1710-14
3. William Newland – Gatton 1710-38
4. George Newland – Gatton 1738-49

Seat: Gatton Park, Surrey (medieval, Turgis acq. 1654, passed by mar. 1703 to Newlands, sold c. 1749)
Estate: Turgis left an estate worth £100,000 in 1703.

NEWMAN

Baron Mamhead (1931-45 UK)

Origins: Merchants in Devon from the 15th century onwards. Had interests in Newfoundland fish and the Portugal wine trade into the 20th century. (*Country Life*, 117, p. 1428) **First MP 1553.**

1. Sir Robert Newman 1 Bt – Bletchingley 1812-18 Exeter 1818-26
2. Robert Newman 1 Baron Mamhead – Exeter 1918-31

Seat: Mamhead Park, Devon (old house, rebuilt c. 1700, purch. 1822, new house 1826-33, after 1945 a school)
Estates: Bateman 5290 (E) 6587
Title: Baronet 1836-
Peer: 1 peer 1931-45

NEWNHAM

Origins: Founder a Nonconformist merchant, Director of the East India Company. His son the first MP.

1. Thomas Newnham – Queenborough 1741-54
2. Nathaniel Newnham – Aldborough 1743-54 Bramber 1754-61
3. George Newnham – Arundel 1774-80
4. Nathaniel Newnham – London 1780-90 Ludgershall 1793-96

Seat: Newtimber Place, Sussex (medieval, rebuilt 16th c., rebuilt 1681, purch. 1741, sold 1832)

NEWTON

Origins: A husbandman acquired Woolsthorpe in the mid-16th century. Inherited money and land from a moneylender.

1. Sir John Newton 2 Bt – Grantham 1660 1661-81
2. Sir Isaac Newton – University of Cambridge 1689 1701-02
3. Michael Newton 4 Bt – Beverley 1722-27 Grantham 1727-43
4. Michael Newton – Beverley 1761-68

Seats: Barr's Court (Baronscourt or Barscote), Gloucestershire (acq. 17th c.); Culverthorpe Hall, Lincolnshire (built 1680, add. c. 1704-05, add. 1734, passed out of

family 1743); Woolsthorpe, Lincolnshire (built early 17th c., purch. 1623, passed out of family 18th c., NT)
Title: Baronet 1660-1743
Notes: Woolsthorpe is where Sir Isaac first had his insight into the laws of gravity. One in ODNB.

NICHOLAS

Nicholas

Origins: An old Wiltshire family that held land since 1362 raised to prominence by a lawyer who was steward of the Pembroke estates. Granted arms 1612. His son was a Secretary of State 1641. **First MP 1558. Two others 1589 and 1621, cousins**.

1. Sir Edward Nicholas – Old Sarum 1661-79
2. Sir John Nicholas – Ripon 1661-79 Wilton 1679-81
3. Edward Nicholas – Shaftesbury 1689-1726
4. George Nicholas – Morpeth 1692-98
5. William Nicholas – Wilton 1705-08

Seat: West Horsley Place, Surrey (medieval, rebuilt 16th c., purch. 1664 for £9,750, passed out of family 1749)
Notes: Male line extinct 1749. Two in ODNB.

Nicholas

Origins: Cousins of the above. **First MP 1640**.

1. John Nicholas – Devizes 1713-15
2. Robert Nicholas – Cricklade 1785-90

Seats: Ashton Keynes, Wiltshire (acq. by mar. and rebuilt c. 1780, still owned 19th c.); Roundway Park, Wiltshire (owned since mid-15th c., sold c. 1790)
Estates: Worth c. £300 pa in 1670.
Notes: Two in ODNB.

Nicholas

Origins: Probably related to the above family.

1. Oliver Nicholas – Wilton 1685-87

Seat: Aldbourne, Wiltshire (purch. 1631, owned into 18th c.)

NICHOLSON

Origins: Gin distillers. Company founded in the 1730s.

1. William Nicholson – Petersfield 1866-74 1880-85
2. William Nicholson – Petersfield Div. Hampshire 1897-1935
3. John Nicholson – Abbey Div. Westminster 1921-24
4. Otho Nicholson – Abbey Div. Westminster 1924-32
5. Sir Godfrey Nicholson 1 Bt – Morpeth 1931-35 Farnham Div. Surrey 1937-66
6. Emma Nicholson Baroness Nicholson – Torridge and West Devon 1987-97

Seats: Basing Park, Hampshire (purch. 1863, estate sold 1944, demolished 1964); Bordean House, Hampshire (built 1611, purch. 1878, family departed 1939, sold 1947, institutional use)
Estates: Bateman 3014 (E) 2323
Title: Baroness Nicholson 1997- UKLife; Baronet 1958-
Notes: The family firm was sold in the 1970s.

NICOLL

Origins: Burgesses in Bodmin in the 14th and 15th centuries, Mayor 1402. Purchased landed estates in the 15th century. **First MP 1402 for Bodmin. Two further MPs 1628-59 both for Bodmin.**

1. Humphrey Nicoll – Bossiney 1689-90 1694-95
2. Anthony Nicoll – Tregony 1708-10

Seat: Penvose, Cornwall (acq. by 1446, sold 1720s, became a farm house)
Estates: Held 2,500 acres in 1597. Worth £800 pa in the 1660s.
Notes: Estates sold to pay debts 1720s. One in ODNB.

NOEL (Nowell) [Edwards, Hicks, Middleton]

Earl of Gainsborough (1682-1798 E; 1841- UK)

Origins: The Noels were minor gentry in the 15th century, acquired estates after the Dissolution and married heiresses in the mid-16th century. Kt 1585. **First MP 1553 for Rutland. Eight further MPs 1553-1643, three for Rutland**. Baptist Hicks 1 Viscount Campden left his estates to his son-in-law and the title also passed to the Noels by special remainder. The Earldom created for the later in 1682 became extinct in 1798. Sir Baptist Hicks, son of a yeoman, became a mercer, and rose to wealth and a viscountcy through banking (see also Hicks-Beach). Purchased estates in the early 17th century.

First MP 1584. Two further MP 1621-26. On the extinction of the Noel male line the estates passed to the Edwards family for whom the earldom was recreated. Francis Edwards (d. 1729) was the son of a clergyman. His daughter bore an illegitimate son to Lord Anne Hamilton (see Hamilton I), who succeeded to the Edwards estates and married in 1754 the sister and heiress of the 6 Earl of Gainsborough. Their son succeeded to Exton.

1. Edward Noel 1 Earl of Gainsborough – Rutland 1661-79 Hampshire 1679
2. Henry Noel – Stamford 1677
3. Wriothesley Noel 2 Earl of Gainsborough – Hampshire 1685-86
4. Baptist Noel – Rutland 1685-87
5. John Noel – Rutland 1710-11 1715-18
6. John Noel – Rutland 1727-28
7. Thomas Noel – Rutland 1728-41 1753-88
8. James Noel – Rutland 1734-52
9. Gerard Edwards Noel 2 Bt – Maidstone 1784-88 Rutland 1788-1808 1814-38
10. Charles Noel 1 Earl of Gainsborough – Rutland 1808-14
11. William Noel – Rutland 1838-40
12. Charles Noel 2 Earl of Gainsborough – Rutland 1840-41
13. Gerard Noel – Rutland 1847-83
14. Ernest Noel – Dumfries Burghs 1874-86

Seats: Exton Park, Rutland (purch. and built by Hicks early 17th c., fire 1810, rebuilt, add. mid-19th c., still own); The Hall, North Luffenham, Rutland (built 1635, demolished 1806); Walcot Hall (House), Northamptonshire (old house, rebuilt 1674-8, acq. c. 1700, sold late 18th c.); Campden Manor, Gloucestershire (purch. 1608 by Hicks, built 1613 – said to have cost £44,000 - Kingsley, *Country Houses of Gloucestershire*, I, 69 - burned 1645); Campden House (Combe Manor), Gloucestershire (built 16th c., purch. 1608, add. 1845-48, sold 1934); Barham Court, Kent (acq. by mar. 1813, sold 1846, fire 1930, offices); Welham Grove, Leicestershire (acq. by mar. 1754, sold 1854); Moxhull Hall, Warwickshire (acq. by Hackets mid-17th c., house built later 17th c., passed by mar. to Noels 1827, sold 1881, demolished c. 1920)
Estates: Bateman 18568 (E) 28991. Owned 4,500 acres in 2001.
Titles: Baron Noel 1617-1798 E; Baron Hicks and Viscount Campden 1628-1798 E; Baron Noel 1681-1798 E; Baron Barham 1805- UK; Baron Noel and Viscount Campden 1841- UK; Baronet 1617- ; 1620-29 1781-
Peers: 11 peers 1660-90 1707-14 1729-51 1764-98 1823-1927 1944-45
4 Lds Lt 17th, 19th
Notes: The Noel claim to have come over with the Conqueror and received grants of lands from Henry I is false (Morris, *A Series of Picturesque Views of Seats*, IV, 6). 2 and 3 Viscounts first cr. and seven others in ODNB.

Viscount Wentworth (1762-1815 GB)

Origins: Sir William Noel of Kirkby Mallory shared a common ancestor in the 16th century with the Earls of Gainsborough. He married Margaret, Baroness Wentworth in her own right (see Wentworth).

1. William Noel – Stamford 1722-47 West Looe 1747-57
2. Sir Clobery Noel 5 Bt – Leicestershire 1727-33
3. Thomas Noel 2 Viscount Wentworth – Leicestershire 1774

Seat: Kirkby Mallory Hall, Leicestershire (acq. by 1622, rebuilt c. 1750, passed by mar. to Milbankes 1816, demolished 1953)
Titles: Baron Wentworth 1529- E; Baronet 1660-1815
Peers: 2 peers 1745-1815
Notes: On the death of the 2 Viscount Wentworth the Barony of Wentworth and estates passed to his sister, who married Sir Ralph Milbanke and thence to the Byrons and Earls of Lovelace (see Milbanke). 4 Bt and one other in ODNB.

Baron Barham (1805- UK)

Origins: The 1 Baron, an admiral, was the son of a collector of customs at Bo'ness, Linlithgow and a cousin of the Earl of Middleton (see Middleton). The 1 Baron's daughter and heiress married the 1 Earl of Gainsborough of the second creation.

1. Charles Middleton 1 Baron Barham – Rochester 1784-90

Seat: Barham Court, Kent (old house, rebuilt 18th c., purch. late 18th c., passed to Noels 1813, see above)
Estates: Rubinstein – 1 Baron left £150,000 probate in 1813.
Title: Baronet 1781-
Peer: 1 peer 1805-13
1 in Cabinet 1805-06
Notes: Related to the Barhams of Trecwn, Pembrokeshire (see Foster II). 1 Baron and one other in ODNB.

NORRIS I (Norreys, Nores) [Cleivland (Cleveland)]

Norris

Origins: Settled at Speke in the 13th century. **First MP 1324 for Lancashire. One further MP 1554 for Liverpool.** A Norris served at Bosworth under Lord Stanley. Roman Catholic until 1689. Male line extinct 1731.

1. Thomas Norris – Liverpool 1689-95
2. Sir William Norris 1 Bt – Liverpool 1695-1701
3. Richard Norris – Liverpool 1708-10
4. Edward Norris – Liverpool 1715-22

Seats: Utkinton Hall, Cheshire (medieval house, rebuilt early 17th c., remod. c. 1700, leased early 18th c.?, now a farm house); Speke Hall, Lancashire (acq. by mar. by late 13th c., built c. 1490, add. 16th c., passed by mar. to Beauclerks 1731, sold 1797, NT 1943)
Estates: Worth £700 pa in 1616. Held 2,400 acres 18th c.
Title: Baronet 1698-1702
Notes: A Beauclerk married the Norris heiress on the extinction of the male line c. 1736 and sold the Norris estates. 1 Bt and two others in ODNB.

Cleiveland (Cleveland)

Origins: John Cleiveland was a younger son of a Leicestershire gentry family adopted by an uncle who was a rich Liverpool merchant in the 17th century. On the death of William Cleiveland in 1724 the family estates passed to his daughter and heiress who married Edward Norris MP.

1. John Cleiveland – Liverpool 1710-13
2. William Cleiveland – Liverpool 1722-24

Seat: Cleiveland Place, Liverpool, Lancashire

NORRIS II

Origins: The first MP was of unknown parentage. He rose to become an admiral of the fleet 1734.

1. Sir John Norris – Rye 1708-22 Portsmouth 1722-34 Rye 1734-49
2. John Norris – Rye 1727-32
3. Matthew Norris – Rye 1733-34
4. John Norris – Rye 1762-74

Seat: Hemsted Park, Kent (medieval, purch. 1718, sold by 1786, school)
Estates: The Hemsted estate was purch. for £157,000 in 1857.

NORTH [Bunbury, Furnese, Hanmer, Moore, Pope] *ENGLAND & WALES*

Earl of Guildford (1752- GB)

Origins: A younger son of a Nottinghamshire gentry family became a London merchant c. 1500. His son was a lawyer, Chancellor of the Court of Augmentations and executor of Henry VIII's will. Baron 1554. **First MP 1542 for Cambridgeshire. Five further MPs 1555-1651, all kts of the shire**. The Barony of North and Earldom of Guildford were separated, united and separated again over the course of several centuries. All the Norths are combined here.

1. Dudley North 4 Baron North – Horsham 1628 Cambridgeshire 1640-48 Cambridge 1660
2. Sir Henry North 1 Bt – Suffolk 1661-71
3. Francis North 1 Baron Guildford – Kings Lynn 1673-74
4. Roger North – Dunwich 1685-87
5. Sir Dudley North – Banbury 1685-87
6. Sir Henry North 2 Bt – Suffolk 1685-87
7. Charles North – Banbury 1701-13
8. Dudley North – Thetford 1710-22 Oxford 1722-30
9. Francis North 1 Earl of Guildford – Banbury 1727-29 {Dunleer 1727-38}
10. Frederick North 2 Earl of Guildford – Banbury 1754-90
11. George North 3 Earl of Guildford – Harwich 1778-84 Wootton Bassett 1784-90 Petersfield 1790 Banbury 1790-92
12. Frederick North 5 Earl of Guildford – Banbury 1792-94
13. Frederick North – Hastings 1831-37 1854-65 1868-69
14. John Doyle North – Oxfordshire 1852-85

Seats: Waldershare Park, Kent (built 1702-12, acq. by mar. from Furnese family 1766, fire 1913, rebuilt 1913-14, leased out as flats c. 1977); Wroxton Abbey, Oxfordshire (acq. by mar. 1668, sold 1933); Kirtling Tower, Cambridgeshire (castle built early 13th c., acq. and built 1533, enlarged 1578, demolished 1801, new house 1872, sold 1940s); Glemham Hall, Suffolk (medieval house, rebuilt 16th c., purch. 1690, sold c. 1920); Mildenhall, Suffolk (purch. 1586/1614, built c. 1614, passed later in the 17th c. to the Hanmers, demolished 1934); Rougham Hall, Norfolk (built pre-1690, purch. 1690, rebuilt soon after 1690, largely dismantled c. 1780, still own)
Estates: Bateman 23673 (E) 35378. Rubinstein – Brownlow North left £180,000 in probate 1820.
Titles: Baron North 1554- E; Baron Grey of Rolleston 1673-1734 E); Baron Guildford 1683- E; Baronet 1660-95; 1707-35
Peers: 17 peers 1660-77 1673-91 1685 1694-1861 1699-1722 1872-85 1884-1945 1899-1945
3 Lds Lt 18th

3 in Cabinet 1682-85 1713-14 1766-83
1 KG 18th
Notes: 1, 2, 3, 4, and 6 Barons North, 1 Baron Guildford, 1, 2, 3, 4, and 5 Earls and thirteen others in ODNB.

Earl of Downe (1628-68 I)

Origins: The 1 Earl of Downe was a nephew of Sir Thomas Pope (see Alexander). **First MP 1621 for Oxfordshire**. The sister and heiress of the 4 Earl (d. 1668) married Francis North Baron Guildford, and the Norths succeeded to Wroxton Abbey.

No post-1660 MPs

Seat: Wroxton Abbey, Oxfordshire (acq. 1537, passed by mar. to Norths 1668 see above)
Estates: £2,200 pa in 1645.
Titles: Baron Pope of Belturbet 1628-68 I; Baronet 1611-68
Peers: {2 peers 1660-68]
Notes: 2 and 3 Earls in ODNB.

Furnese

Origins: Founder a Cromwellian sergeant of dragoons turned tallow chandler. His son was an East India merchant and important financier in London. The 2 Earl of Guildford married the daughter and heiress of the 2 Furnese Baronet.

1. Sir Henry Furnese 1 Bt – Bramber 1698-99 Sandwich 1701-12
2. Sir Robert Furnese 2 Bt – Truro 1708-10 New Romney 1710-27 Kent 1727-33
3. Henry Furnese – Dover 1720-34 Morpeth 1738-41 New Romney 1741-56

Seats: Waldershare Park, Kent (built 1702-10, passed by mar. to the Norths 1766, see above); Gunnersbury Park, Middlesex (built 1658-63, purch. 1739, sold 1761)
Title: Baronet 1707-35
Notes: 1 and 2 Bts in ODNB.

Baron Hanmer (1872-81 UK)

Origins: Settled in Wales after Edward I's conquest. Kt c. 1300 and judge under Richard II. At Bettesfield since the 13th century. Rose higher under the patronage of the Stanleys in the second half of the 16th century. **First MP 1553 for Flintshire. Four further MPs 1559-1624, two for the county**. Sir Thomas Hanmer 4 Bt succeeded to the North estate of Mildenhall through the heiress of the last Baronet of that place.

1. Sir Thomas Hanmer 2 Bt – Flintshire 1640 1669-78
2. Sir John Hanmer 3 Bt – Flint 1659 Evesham 1669-79 Flintshire 1681 Flint 1685-87 1689-90 {Carlingford 1695-99}
3. Thomas Hanmer – Ludlow 1690
4. Sir Thomas Hanmer 4 Bt – Thetford 1701-02 Flintshire 1702-05 Thetford 1705-08 Suffolk 1708-27
5. Thomas Hanmer – Castle Rising 1734-37
6. Sir Walden Hanmer 1 Bt – Sudbury 1768-74 1775-80
7. Henry Hanmer – Westbury 1831 Aylesbury 1832-37
8. John Hanmer 1 Baron Hanmer – Shrewsbury 1832-37 Hull 1841-47 Flint 1847-72

Seats: Hanmer Hall, Flintshire (acq. 14th c., demolished mid-19th c.); Mildenhall, Suffolk (built early 17th c., acq. by mar. later in the 17th c., passed to Bunburys 1746, see below); Bettisfield Park (Hall), Flintshire (acq. 13th c., rebuilt 16th c., rebuilt c. 1787, add. 1844, family departed 1977, sold 1989); Fenns (Fens) Hall, Flintshire (acq. 14th c., demolished mid-18th c.); Simpson Place, Buckinghamshire (acq. by mar. 1701, sold 1806, demolished soon afterwards); Stockgrove House (Park), Buckinghamshire (old house, purch. 1792, rebuilt c. 1835, sold 1928, demolished and rebuilt, now flats); Barton Hall, Suffolk (built c. 1600, acq. 1724, passed to Bunburys 1746, see below)
Estates: Bateman 11660 (E & W) 14823. In 1600 the family held 4,500 acres and in addition the main part of Flintshire.
Title: Baronet 1620-1746; 1774-
Peers: 1 peer 1872-81
Notes: Margaret Hanmer married Owen Glyndwr in 1383. 2 and 4 Bts and 1 Baron and one other in ODNB.

<u>Bunbury</u>

Origins: Claimed Norman descent. Established at Stanney since the 12th century and rose very gradually. The Bunburys succeeded by marriage to a Hanmer heiress in 1746 to the North estates in Suffolk.

1. Sir Henry Bunbury 3 Bt – Chester 1701-27
2. Sir Charles Bunbury 4 Bt – Chester 1733-42
3. Sir Thomas Bunbury 6 Bt – Suffolk 1761-84 1790-1812
4. Sir Henry Bunbury 7 Bt – Suffolk 1830-32
5. Sir Edward Bunbury 9 Bt – Bury St. Edmunds 1847-52

Seats: Barton Hall, Suffolk (acq. by mar. 1746, add. 1767-68, rebuilt 19th c., burned 1914, sold 1915); The Manor House, Mildenhall, Suffolk (acq. by mar. 1746, became main seat 1901, sold 1932, demolished 1934); Bunbury, Cheshire; Stanney Hall (Rake Hall) (Little Stanney), Cheshire (acq. and built 12th c., derelict and demolished 17th c., rebuilt

17th c. as Rake Hall, family departed 1746, now pub); Hoole Hall, Cheshire (medieval, purch. 14th c., burned 1640s, sold c. 1757 and rebuilt, hotel)
Estates: Bateman 9831 (E) 11924
Title: Baronet 1681-
1 in Cabinet 1765
Notes: 6, 7, 8, and 9 Bts and one other in ODNB.

Moore

Origins: The first MP was an Irish adventurer who began life as a footman. Became a Director of the East India Company and important financier. William Moore MP left Polesden Lacy to Prime Minister Lord North in 1746, which he sold.

1. Arthur Moore – Great Grimsby 1695-1715 1721-22
2. William Moore – Banbury 1740-46

Seats: Polesden Lacy, Surrey (built 1632, purch. 1723, passed to Norths 1746 and sold immediately, NT); Fetcham Park, Surrey (built 1699, purch. 1705 for £8,250, sold 1737, now offices)
Notes: One in ODNB.

NORTHCOTE

Earl of Iddesleigh (1885- UK)

Origins: A landed family that could trace their ancestry to 1103. Clothiers in Crediton in the early 16th century. A son married an heiress to Hayne and entered the gentry.

1. Sir John Northcote 1 Bt – Ashburton 1640-53 Devon 1654 1656 1659 1660 Barnstaple 1667-76
2. Sir Henry Northcote 5 Bt – Exeter 1735-43
3. Henry Northcote – Heytesbury 1826-30
4. Stafford Northcote 1 Earl of Iddesleigh – Dudley 1855-57 Stamford 1858-66 N. Devon 1866-85
5. Henry Northcote 1 Baron Northcote – Exeter 1880-99

Seats: The Pynes, Devon (medieval, purch. later 17th c. by Stafford family, rebuilt early 18th c., passed by mar. to Northcotes mid-18th c., add. c. 1852, family departed 1980s, sold 2001); Hayne, Devon (acq. by mar. of 1585, add. c. 1810 and c. 1864, became a farm house, sold 20th c.)
Estates: Bateman 5663 (E) 6000. Worth £1,500 pa in 1660.
Titles: Baron Northcote 1900-11 UK; Baronet 1641- ; 1887-1911

Peers: 4 peers 1885-1945 1900-11
1 Ld Lt 19th
1 in Cabinet 1866-68 1874-80 1885-87
Notes: 1 Bt first cr. and 1 Baron and 1 Earl in ODNB.

NORTHEY

Origins: A barrister in the 17th century. His son was Attorney General and an MP 1710.

1. Sir Edward Northey – Tiverton 1710-22
2. William Northey – Calne 1713-15 Wootton Bassett 1715-22
3. William Northey – Calne 1747-61 Maidstone 1761-68 Great Bedwyn 1768-70
4. William Northey – Newport 1796-1826

Seats: Compton Bassett House, Wiltshire (medieval, remod. 1672, purch. 1715, sold 1758 and 1768, demolished c. 1930); Cheney Court, Wiltshire (medieval, rebuilt mid-17th c., purch. early 18th c., sold 1964, school); Hazelbury Manor (Box Hall), Wiltshire (medieval, purch. early 18th c., sold 1920); Woodcote House, Surrey (old house, purch. 1710, remod. 18th c., sold 1941, flats); Ivy House (The Ivy), Wiltshire (purch. and built 1758, sold 1791)
Estates: Bateman 2905 (E) 4835
Notes: One in ODNB.

NORTON I

Baron Grantley (1782- GB)

Origins: The Nortons were a gentry family that produced a politician under Henry VIII and High Sheriff of Yorkshire under Elizabeth I. However, the latter was later attainted as a rebel. The family's fortunes were restored by the career of an Attorney General and Speaker of the House of Commons raised to the peerage. **First MP 1640**.

1. Fletcher Norton 1 Baron Grantley – Appleby 1756-61 Wigan 1761-68
2. William Norton 2 Baron Grantley – Richmond 1768-74 Wigtown Burghs 1774-75 Richmond 1775-80 Guildford 1782-84 Surrey 1784-89
3. Fletcher Norton – Appleby 1773-74 Carlisle 1774-75
4. Edward Norton – Haslemere 1780-84 Carlisle 1784-86
5. Chapple Norton – Guildford 1784-90 1796-1806 1807-12
6. George Norton – Guildford 1826-30
7. Charles Norton – Guildford 1831-32

Seats: Grantley Hall, Yorkshire (built mid-18th c., add. 1760, remod. early 19th c., sold mid-19th c.); Markenfield Hall, Yorkshire (built 1310, add. 16th c., purch. c. 1770s, remod. 1850s, still own); Kettlethorpe Hall, Yorkshire (built 1727, acq. by mar. 1836, sold sec. half 19th c.)
Estates: Bateman 10721 (E) 14154
Peers: 6 peers 1782-1945
Notes: 1 Baron and three others in ODNB.

NORTON II

Origins: Began as Britsol merchants in the 14th century. Gentry by the 16th century. **First MP 1399 for Bristol. Two further MPs 1436-1653.** Thomas Norton MP 1436 served in the Agincourt campaign.

1. Edward Norton – Westbury 1680-81

Seats: Ashe, Dorset; Leigh Court (Abbot's Leigh), Somerset (medieval, purch. and rebuilt 1559, passed out of the family c. 1715, demolished c. 1811 and rebuilt, institutional use)
Notes: **Two MPs for Bristol in the later 14th century** from the Spelling family that left most of their property and manors to Thomas Norton MP 1436. Three in ODNB.

NOSWORTHY (Noseworthy)

Origins: Merchants in Devon in the 13th century. Acquired landed property in the mid-17th century. **First MP 1523.**

1. Edward Nosworthy – St. Ives 1660-61 1665-81
2. Edward Nosworthy – St. Ives 1679-81

Seat: Ince Castle, Cornwall (built c. 1640-42, purch. c. 1652, sold by 1722)
Notes: Last Nosworthy resident of Ince became a Jacobite exile d. in France 1701.

NUGENT [Craggs, Fitzgerald, Greville, Knight, Newsham, Vincent] *IRELAND & ENGLAND*

Marquess of Westmeath (1822-71 I)

Origins: The senior line of the Nugents claimed descent from Count de Perche living in the 7th century. Anglo-Normans who emigrated to Ireland in 1171 and acquired the Barony of Devlin c. 1172 (attended Irish Parliaments as hereditary barons). The 1 Baron (as an Irish peer and 10th feudal baron) was Lord Deputy of Ireland 1449 and the 5 Baron (14th feudal baron) acquired new grants of land c. 1560s. **First {MP 1559 for County Westmeath}. Five further {MPs 1585-1639, three for the county}.** The daughter and heiress of the 1 Marquess of Westmeath married the 1 Baron Greville, who in 1871 inherited Clonyn Castle and the Nugent estates (see Greville). The title of Earl of Westmeath passed to cousins at Pallas in Galway, whose estates are listed below.

1. Walter Nugent – {Fore 1727}
2. Richard Nugent Baron Devlin – {Fore 1759-60}
3. George Nugent 7 Earl of Westmeath – {Fore 1780-92}

Seats: Clonyn Castle, Westmeath (old castle, resident in 16th c., burned in mid-17th c., new house built 19th c., passed by mar. to Grevilles 1871); Pallas, Galway (castle built 15th/16th c., new house built c. 1797, remod. 19th c., sold 1934, demolished)
Estates: Bateman 15695 (I) 5486. Worth £3,000 pa in 1642 and between £11,000 and £14,000 pa in 1815.
Titles: Baron Devlin 1486- I; Earl of Westmeath 1621- I; Baron Nugent 1689-91 I
Peers: {4 peers 1660-72 1714-52 1755-1800} 3 Irish Rep peers 1800-15 1831-71 1901-33
2 Lds Lt 19th
1 KP 18th
Notes: Roman Catholic family. The 5 Earl went into exile with James II in 1691. The 6 Earl was the first title holder in the family to conform to the Established Church. 1, 3, and 5 Barons Devlin, 1 Baron Nugent, and 1, 2, 4, and 5 Earls, and two others in ODNB.

Earl Nugent (1776-1889 I)

Origins: Descended from a younger son of the 12 Baron Devlin (see above). The 1 Earl married the daughter and co-heiress of James Craggs. She had previously married John Knight of Gosfield Hall, an estate she inherited as well.

1. Robert Craggs-Nugent 1 Earl Nugent – St. Mawes 1741-54 Bristol 1754-74 St. Mawes 1774-84
2. Edmund Nugent – Liskeard 1754-59 St. Mawes 1761-70
3. Charles Nugent – Buckingham 1784-90
4. Sir George Nugent 1 Bt – Buckingham 1790-1802 {Charleville 1800} Aylesbury 1806-12 Buckingham 1818-32

Seats: Gosfield Hall, Essex (built c. 1545 and 1691, part rebuilt c. 1720, purch. by Knight 1714, passed by mar. to Nugents 1736, add. 1755, passed to Grenvilles (see) by mar. 1788); Cabinteely House (Clare Hill), Dublin (built 18th c., passed by inher. to O'Byrnes (see) in 1788); Westhorpe House, Buckinghamshire (built c. 1700, purch. 1810, sold 1862, offices)

Estates: Worth £14,000 pa in 1788.
Title: Viscount Clare 1767-88 I; Bt 1806-
Peer: {1 peer 1767-88}
1 in Cabinet 1766-68
Notes: The 1 Earl conformed to the Established Church c. 1730. On the death of the 1 Earl Nugent his estates and titles passed by marriage to the Dukes of Buckingham (see Grenville). 1 Bt and 1 Earl in ODNB.

Craggs

Origins: The first Craggs rose from humble origins to gain a large fortune as a financier. He began as Steward of the Duke of Norfolk in the 1680s and gained access to wealth through army contracting. His son was a Secretary of State in 1718. James Craggs left his fortune, worth £1,500,000 (ODNB), divided among three daughters and the illegitimate daughter of his son. Two of these married into the Eliot family of Port Eliot (see that family). The youngest daughter married John Newsham (see below), then John Knight, and finally the 1 Earl Nugent.

1. James Craggs – Grampound 1702-13
2. James Craggs – Tregony 1713-21

Seat: Kidbrook Manor (Charlton), Kent (purch. c. 1710, passed by mar. to Eliots 1765, became a farm house later 18th c.)
Estates: Worth £14,000 pa in 1721.
1 in Cabinet 1718-21
Notes: Two in ODNB.

Newsham

Origins: The Newshams entered the gentry in the 16th century. John Newsham married Anne Craggs (see above) and their son took the additional name Craggs and inherited a large property from the Craggs estate.

1. John Newsham – Lostwithiel 1720-22
2. James Craggs-Newsham – St. Germans 1741-47 St. Mawes 1754-61

Seat: Chadshunt Hall, Warwickshire (purch. 1552, rebuilt 1631, remod. 1714, sold 1764 for £19,300)

Knight

Origins: Anne Craggs married John Knight of Gosfield, whose estates she inherited and passed on to the Nugents. The first Knight MP was a Director of the Bank of England 1694.

1. John Knight – Weymouth & Melcombe Regis 1695-98
2. John Knight – St. Germans 1710-22 Sudbury 1722-33

Seat: Gosfield Hall, Essex (built c. 1540 and 1691, purch. 1715, part rebuilt c. 1720, passed to Nugents by mar. 1736)
Notes: John Knight MP 1695-98 was expelled from the House of Commons as a criminal.

Vincent

Origins: A family of lawyers. Commissioners of Victualling for several generations. One married the heiress to Battens 1581. Nicholas Vincent, the last of the family, left his estates to John Knight of Gosfield (see above).

1. Walter Vincent – Truro 1656 1659 1660 Mitchell 1679-80
2. Henry Vincent – Mitchell 1681 Truro 1685-87 1689-1713
3. Sir Matthias Vincent – Lostwithiel 1685-87
4. Shadrack Vincent – Fowey 1689-95
5. Walter Vincent – St. Ives 1689-90 Grampound 1690-92
6. Henry Vincent – Fowey 1708-19
7. Nicholas Vincent – Fowey 1719-26

Seats: Trelavan (Treleven), Cornwall (purch. 1669, passed to Knights 1726); Battens, Cornwall (acq. by mar. 1581, passed out of family by mar. 1664, became a farm house)
Note: Male line extinct 1726.

Nugent

Origins: Descended from the youngest son of the 10 Baron Devlin (see above). Percy Fitzgerald took the name Nugent in 1831 on the death of his grandfather Christian Nugent to whose estates he succeeded.

1. James Nugent – {Fore 1692-93}
2. Sir Percy Nugent 1 Bt – Westmeath 1847-52
3. Sir Walter Nugent 4 Bt – S. Westmeath 1907-18

Seat: Donore, Westmeath (acq. mid-15th c., rebuilt 18th c., still there 1930s, demolished)
Estates: Bateman 7955 (I) 5122
Title: Baronet 1763-97; 1831-

O'BRIEN (O'Bryen) [Hunt, Keightley, de Vere] *IRELAND & ENGLAND*

Marquess of Thomond (1800-55 I)

Origins: Descended from the Kings of Thomond and Brian Boru, High King of Ireland slain in 1014. The last King of Thomond died in 1528. The O'Brien's were created Earls of Thomond in 1551, attainted in 1741, and extinct 1774. A junior line, Earls of Inchiquin (Baron Inchiquin 1543) were created Marquesses of Thomond in 1800. The Barony of Inchiquin passed to a junior line of Baronets in 1855. **First {MP 1585 for County Clare}. Four additional {MPs 1613-39, three for the county}.**

1. Henry O'Brien Baron Ibrackan – {County Clare 1661-66} Northampton 1670-78
2. Sir Donagh O'Brien 1 Bt – {County Clare 1692-93 1695-99 1703-14}
3. Lucius O'Brien – {County Clare 1703-14}
4. Henry O'Brien 7 Earl of Thomond – Arundel 1710-14
5. William O'Brien 4 Earl of Thomond – New Windsor 1722-27 Tamworth 1727-34 Camelford 1740-47 Aylesbury 1747-54
6. James O'Brien – {Charleville 1725-27 Youghal 1727-60}
7. Sir Edward O'Brien 2 Bt – Peterborough 1727-28 {County Clare 1728-65}
8. Murrough O'Brien 1 Marquess of Thomond – {County Clare 1757-60 Harristown 1761-68} Richmond 1784-96
9. Sir Lucius O'Brien 3 Bt – {Ennis 1761-68 County Clare 1768-76 1778-83 Tuam 1783-90 Ennis 1790-95}
10. Edward O'Brien – {Ennis 1773-76}
11. Sir Edward O'Brien 4 Bt – {Ennis 1795-1800} County Clare 1802-26
12. Sir Lucius O'Brien 13 Baron Inchiquin – Clare 1826-30 1847-52
13. William Smith O'Brien – Ennis 1828-31 County Limerick 1835-49

Seats: Dromoland Castle, Clare (old castle, became principal seat c. 1670, new house early 18th c., demolished c. 1826, new house 1829-35, sold 1962, hotel, smaller house on 1,000 acre estate built for family 1960s); Cliveden, Buckinghamshire (acq. by mar. 1793, fire 1795, sold 1819); Moor Park, Shropshire (built c. 1720, add. 1874, acq. by mar. 1896, family departed 1939, most of estate sold by 1952, school); (Great) Billing Hall, Northamptonshire (purch. 1628, built 1629, sold 1776, demolished 1956); Cahirmoyle, Limerick (O'Brien mar. 1795 the Smith heiress to Cahirmoyle, new house built 1871, sold in 20th c., institutional use); Moyarta Castle, Clare (acq. 15th c., forfeited 1689); Carrigaholt Castle, Clare (built c. 1480, captured by O'Briens, forfeited 1689, rebuilt c. 1700 and passed to Burtons (see Conyingham), sold 1919, a ruin); Shortgrove Hall, Essex (rebuilt c. 1684, purch. 1712, add. 1712, passed to Wyndhams 1741 by mar. who took name O'Brien, passed to Earl of Egremont 1774, sold 1802, fire 1966); Rostellan Castle, Cork (Inchiquin seat) (built 13th c., acq. 1645, rebuilt before 1750, add. 1777, add. early 19th c., sold 1860, demolished 1944)

Estates: Bateman 25318 (I) 16997. Worth £16,000 pa in 1670s and £9,000 pa in 1777. Earls of Inchiquin held 60,000 acres in the 1670s.
Titles: Baron Inchiquin 1543- I; Earl of Thomond 1551-1741 I; Earl of Inchiquin 1654-1855 I; Baron Moyarta and Viscount Clare 1662-91 I; Viscount Tadcaster 1714-41 E; Earl of Thomond 1756-74 I; Baron Thomond 1801-08 UK; Baron Tadcaster 1826-46 UK; Baronet 1686-
Peers: {9 peers 1660-92 1661-91 1695-1719 1709-41 1721-77 1756-74 1777-1800} 5 Irish Rep peers 1816-26 1863-1945 3 peers 1714-41 1801-08 1826-46
4 Lds Lt 18th, 19th
3 KP 18th, 19th, 20th
Notes: The O'Briens settled in England in 1628 at Great Billing, although they continued to sit in the Irish Parliament. Some members of the family remained Roman Catholic and in exile in the 18th century. Percy Wyndham, brother of the 2 Earl of Egremont, inherited the Thomond estates; the last Earl of Thomond married his mother's sister. He took the name O'Brien (see Wyndham). The third son of the 2 Earl of Thomond was created Viscount Clare, outlawed 1691 and extinct 1774. William Smith (died 1809) was a rich lawyer (leaving Cahirmoyle and £120,000). He was the maternal grandfather of William Smith O'Brien, whose mother was the Smith heiress, and he took the additional name Smith. He was convicted of treason in 1848 and transported to Tasmania (pardoned 1856). The 15 Baron Inchiquin served in the Southern Irish Senate in the 1921-22. Three Kings of Thomond and 1, 3, 4, 6, and 9 Earls of Thomond, and 3 Marquess of Thomond, and 1 and 2 Earls of Inchiquin, and 1, 3, and 5 Viscounts Clare, 3 Bt and six others in ODNB.

O'Brien-Stafford

Origins: A cadet of the 1 Baron Inchiquin (see above) seated at Stonehall. Henry O'Brien married the Stafford heiress of Blatherwycke Park (Hall) 1699 and succeeded to that estate in the early 18th century. The Staffords were frequently **represented in Parliament from 1290-1547** (See Jerningham under Howard I)

1. Augustus O'Brien-Stafford – N. Northamptonshire 1841-57

Seats: Blatherwycke Park (Hall), Northamptonshire (Staffords acq. early 15th c. by mar., new house 1713-22, passed by mar. to O'Briens in 1720, rebuilt 1720-24, remod. 1811, demolished 1948); Stonehall (Stone Hall), Clare (acq. by mar. 1699, leased out from later 17th c., demolished); Cratloe Woods, Clare (acq. and built 17th c., remod. c. 1850, still own)
Estates: Bateman 27394 (E & I) 17472

Keightley

Origins: Yeomen 16th century. **First MP 1621** a substantial London merchant. Fortunate marriages. Thomas Keightley {MP} through royal favor (connected to the Hyde family) was appointed Commissioner of Revenue for Ireland 1702 and acquired estates there. His daughter and heiress married Lucius O'Brien MP 1703-14 (see above).

1. Thomas Keightley – {Innistiogue 1695-99 County Kildare 1703-14}

Seat: Hertingfordbury Park, Hertfordshire (purch. 1643, built 1685, sold 1681, demolished 1816)
Notes: One in ODNB.

Vere O'Brien

Origins: Curragh Chase was built in 1657 by Vere Hunt, a Cromwellian officer granted the estate in that year. His grandmother was Jane Vere, granddaughter of the 15 Earl of Oxford. The family dropped the name Hunt and used Vere in 1832. On the death of Sir Stephen de Vere 4 Bt in 1904 his estates passed to a great nephew of the 13 Baron Inchiquin, Robert O'Brien, who took the name Vere.

1. Sir Vere Hunt 1 Bt – {Askeaton 1798-1800}
2. Sir Stephen de Vere 4 Bt – County Limerick 1854-59

Seat: Curragh Chase, Limerick (acq. 1657 by Vere Hunt, built 1660, rebuilt mid-18th c., add. early 19th c. passed to O'Briens 1889, fire 1941, sold 1956 to forestry commission)
Estates: Bateman 4167 (E) 2123. Worth £800 pa mid-18th c. and £1,464 pa in 1800.
Title: Baronet 1784-1904
Notes: See: de Vere, *The Ruin Reconciled: A Memoir of Anglo-Ireland: 1913-1959*. 2 and 4 Bts and one other in ODNB.

O'CALLAGHAN *IRELAND*

Viscount Lismore (1806-98 I)

Origins: First MP emerged as a lawyer in late 17th century. He made a fortune foreclosing on mortgages. Roman Catholics, conformed early 18th century. Sheriff 1745.

1. Cornelius O'Callaghan – {Fethard 1713-14}
2. Cornelius O'Callaghan 1 Baron Lismore – {Fethard 1768-85}
3. Cornelius O'Callaghan – {Fethard 1761-68 Newtown 1775-76}
4. Sir Robert O'Callaghan – {Bandon 1797-1800}

5. Cornelius O'Callaghan 1 Viscount Lismore – Lostwithiel 1806-07
6. James O'Callaghan – Tregony 1806-12 1818-26
7. Cornelius O'Callaghan – Tipperary 1832-35 Dungarvon 1837-41
8. William O'Callaghan – Tipperary 1874-77

Seat: Shanbally Castle, Tipperary (purch. c. 1700 but part of ancestral lands, rebuilt 1806-12, passed to cousins Pole-Carew post 1898, sold 1954, demolished 1957)
Estates: Bateman 42206 (I) 16354. Worth £6,000 pa in 1775 and £15,000 pa in c. 1805.
Titles: Baron Lismore 1785-1898 I; Baron Lismore 1838-98 UK
Peers: {2 peers 1785-1800} 2 peers 1838-98
2 Lds Lt 19th
Notes: The first MP converted to the Established Church from Roman Catholicism. One in ODNB.

Callaghan

Origins: First MP a distant kinsman of Lord Lismore who remained Roman Catholic. The family endured confiscations, and their fortunes were revived by the MP's father, a merchant in Cork, who supplied the Royal Navy during the Napoleonic Wars.

1. Gerard Callaghan – Dundalk 1818-20 Cork 1829-30
2. Daniel Callaghan – Cork 1830-49

Seat: Lotabeg, Cork (built c. 1800, purch. 1837, sold late 19th c.)
Notes: One in ODNB.

O'CONNELL *IRELAND*

Origins: Old but minor Roman Catholic gentry. Hereditary Constables of Ballycarbery Castle of McCarthy More. Cromwell dismantled the castle 1650. Captain John O'Connell, who fought for James II at Limerick, settled at Derrynane in 1702. His son was a merchant and smuggler supplying Ascendancy gentry with goods. Traders throughout the 18th century. Daniel O'Connell, "The Liberator", a great lawyer and patriot, succeeded in 1825. (MacDonagh, *O'Connell*, 4-5) The family became a political machine in the 19th century.

1. Daniel O'Connell – County Clare 1828-30 County Waterford 1830-31 County Kerry 1831-32 Dublin 1832-36 Kilkenny 1836-37 Dublin 1837-41 County Cork 1842-47
2. Maurice O'Connell – Clare 1831-32 Tralee 1832-53
3. Morgan O'Connell – Meath 1832-40
4. Charles O'Connell – Kerry 1832-34

5. John O'Connell – Youghal 1832-37 Athlone 1837-41 Kilkenny 1841-47 Limerick 1847-51 Clonmell 1853-57
6. Morgan O'Connell – Kerry 1835-52
7. Daniel O'Connell – Dundalk 1846-47 Waterford 1847-48 Tralee 1853-63

Seats: Derrynane Abbey, Kerry (built c. 1702, add. 1745, add. c. 1825, museum 1958, still own part of estate); Lakeview, Kerry (built c. 1740, purch. mid-19th c., new house built 1870, still own)
Estates: Bateman 18752 (I) 3050 and 8057 (I) 4684
Title: Baronet 1869-
Notes: The Liberator's uncle was created a French Count in 1782. Daniel O'Connell's son-in-law is included here. He was born an O'Connell. Six in ODNB.

O'CONOR [Henchy] *IRELAND*

Origins: It is claimed that no family in Europe can trace its legitimate descent through as many generations as the O'Conor family. Kings of Connaught from a very early period (possibly the 4th century) to the 14th century. Descended from the last High King of Ireland Rory O'Conor. The head of the family is known as "O'Conor Don". A Roman Catholic family. {**MP late 16th century**}.

1. Owen O'Conor, O'Conor Don – Roscommon 1830-31
2. Denis O'Conor, O'Conor Don – County Roscommon 1831-47
3. Charles O'Conor, O'Conor Don – Roscommon 1860-80
4. Denis O'Conor – County Sligo 1868-83

Seats: Clonalis, Roscommon (owned estate for perhaps 1,000 years, old house, ruious by 18th c., new house built on new site 1878-80, still own); Belanagare (Bellanagare, Ballinagar) Castle, Roscommon (there by 17th c., ruin – Hermitage House built nearby c. 1760, now derelict, estate sold 1916); Ballintober Castle, Roscommon (medieval, acq. 1362, remod. 17th c., family abandoned 1701, ruin); Mount Druid, Roscommon (built 18th c., remod. 19th c., resident into 20th c., part demolished 20th c., sold)
Estates: Bateman 12650 (I) 5435 and 2776 (I) 2030 and 9003 (I) 2358. Still owned 700 acres in Roscommon in 1980s.
Notes: Two High Kings of Ireland and one King of Connaught and three O'Conor Dons and one other in ODNB.
2 Ld Lt 19th

<u>O'Conor-Henchy</u>

Origins: Cadet line. Married Henchy heiress in 1796. Henchy's gained estates in the 18th c.

1. David O'Conor-Henchy – Kildare 1852-59

Seats: Stonebrook, Kildare (acq. 19th c., still resident in 20th c.); Moyvilla Castle, Galway (acq. by mar. 1887)
Estates: 1090 (I) 1002 in 1878

O'FERRALL [More] *IRELAND*

Origins: The O'Ferral Bouy, Chief of the sept, fell at Clontarf in 1014. The O'Mores were Lords of Leix. Letitia More the daughter and heiress of James O'More of Ballyna married 1751 Richard O'Ferral (d. 1790), a Dublin banker and son of a brewer, who succeeded to Ballyna. **First O'Ferrall {MP 1585 for County Longford}. Five additional {MPs 1585-1639, all for the county}.**

1. Richard More-O'Ferrall – Kildare 1830-47 Longford 1851-52 Kildare 1859-65

Seats: Ballyna House (Balyna), Kildare (acq. by O'Mores later 16th c., new house built 1815, fire 1878, rebuilt 1880s, sold 1960, owned by a business); Kildangan Castle, Kildare (old castle, new house built 1784, acq. by mar. 1849, fire 1880, new house 1886, sold 1986)
Estates: Bateman 8747 (I) 5252
Notes: Roman Catholic family. The More-O'Ferralls inherited Kildangan from the Reillys by mar. 1849. The Reillys were merchants who purch. the Castle c. 1705. One in ODNB.

OGLETHORPE

Origins: Can be traced to the 14th century, but may date back to the Conquest. The first MP revived the family fortunes after the Civil War, although the family estates in Yorkshire had been sold, through a military career.

1. Sir Theophilus Oglethorpe – Morpeth 1685-87 Haslemere 1698-1702
2. Lewis Oglethorpe – Haslemere 1702-04
3. Theophilus Oglethorpe – Haslemere 1708-13
4. James Oglethorpe – Haslemere 1722-54

Seat: Westbrook Place, Surrey (purch. 1688, sold 1788)
Notes: A Jacobite Irish peerage: Countess Oglethorpe 1722-56. The last MP was the founder of the Colony of Georgia. Two in ODNB.

O'HAGAN *IRELAND*

Baron O'Hagan (1870- UK)

Origins: The 1 Baron, a barrister, was the son of a Roman Catholic merchant in Belfast. He became Lord Chancellor of Ireland 1868.

1. Thomas O'Hagan 1 Baron O'Hagan – Tralee 1863-65

Seat: Woodlands (formerly Clonshagh), Dublin (built c. 1735, acq. later 19th c., sold by 1920)
Estates: Bateman 5299 (E) 4884
Peers: 3 peers 1870-85 1899-1900 1903-45
1 KP 19th
Notes: 1 Baron was the first Roman Catholic to be Lord Chancellor since 1688. O'Hagans lived in England post 1920s. 1 Baron in ODNB.

O'HARA [Cooper] *IRELAND*

Origins: A medieval Gaelic and Roman Catholic family. Sheriff 1608. In the early 17th century sons who were minors inherited. They were put in charge of the Court of Wards to be raised as Protestants, which preserved the family estates. (Simms, Hayton, and O'Brien, *War and Politics in Ireland*, 308-09) **First {MP 1613 for County Sligo}. One further {MP 1639}**. Arthur Cooper, the son of a Cromwellian soldier acquired 2,832 acres in County Sligo in the 1650s and established his seat at Cooper's Hill. He married Jane O'Hara daughter and heiress of the O'Haras of Annaghmore and took the additional name O'Hara 1860 on inheriting the O'Hara estates.

1. Arthur Cooper – {Carrick 1695-99}
2. Charles O'Hara – {Ballinakill 1761-68 Armagh 1769-76}
3. Charles O'Hara – {Dungannon 1776-83 County Sligo 1783-1800} 1801-22
4. Charles Cooper O'Hara – County Sligo 1859-65

Seats: Annaghmore (aka Nymphsfield), Sligo (chief seat of O'Haras from medieval times until 1860, old house demolished by 1684 rebuilt c. 1750, remod. c. 1820, add. 1860-70, still own); Cooper's Hill (Coopershill), Sligo (acq. early 18th c., built 1755-74, remod. 19th c., still own, inn)
Estates: Bateman 21070 (I) 8324. Worth £4,000 to £5,000 pa in 1800 but indebted.
1 Ld Lt 19th-20th

OKEOVER

Origins: Held manorial land as early as 1113. **First MP 1331 for Derbyshire. Two further MPs 1382-1421, both for the county**.

1. Rowland Okeover – Stafford 1685-87

Seats: Okeover Hall, Staffordshire (acq. by 12th c., medieval, rebuilt later 16th-17th c., rebuilt 1745-48, add. 1953-60, passed to Walker Bts, who took the add. name Okeover, by mar. 1956, still own); Oldbury Hall, Warwickshire (acq. by mar. mid-18th c., rebuilt 1777, sold 1836, fire 1941)
Estates: Bateman 3927 (E) 6200. Owned 13,000 acres in Scotland in 1996.
Notes: The last male Okeover died in 1955, the 24th in a direct male line descended from Orm of Okeover who lived in the reign of William II. (*Country Life*, 134, p. 172)

OLIPHANT *SCOTLAND*

Baron Oliphant (1458-1633 S; 1633-1748 S)

Origins: Norman family, one became Justiciar of Scotland in the 12th century. One married a sister of Robert the Bruce. Baron 1458. **First [MP 1467]**.

1. Thomas Oliphant – [Perthshire 1703]
2. Charles Oliphant – Ayr Burghs 1710-19

Seats: Aberdalgie, Perthshire (acq. 13th c., forefeited 1746?, demolished); Gask House, Perthshire (forefieted 1746, repurch. later 18th c., rebuilt 1801-05, demolished 20th c.); Woodend House, Perthshire (built late 17th c., sold mid-18th c.)
Peers: [3 peers 1660-1707]
Notes: Attainted after 1745. Charles Oliphant MP above descended from the 3 Baron Oliphant. He was a doctor, the son of a lawyer. His brother voted in the election of Scottish representative peers as Lord Oliphant in 1750 but did not subsequently assume the title. Oliphant family has an entry and 3, 4, and 9 Barons and one other biography in ODNB.

OLIVER [Gascoigne, Silver] *IRELAND & ENGLAND*

Oliver

Origins: Robert Oliver, a Cromwellian army captain, was granted land in Ireland in 1666. Sheriff 1692.

1. Robert Oliver – {County Limerick 1661-66}
2. Charles Oliver – {Midleton 1695-99 County Limerick 1703-06}
3. Robert Oliver – {Kilmallock 1703-13 Castlemartyr 1713-14 County Limerick 1715-27 Kilmallock 1727-39}
4. Robert Oliver – {Kilmallock 1739-45}
5. Philip Oliver – {Kilmallock 1745-60}
6. Silver Oliver – {Kilmallock 1757-68 County Limerick 1768-83}
7. Richard Oliver-Gascoigne – {County Limerick 1788-90}
8. Silver Oliver – {Kilmallock 1797-99}
9. Charles Oliver – {Kilmallock 1798-99} County Limerick 1802-06

Seats: Castle Oliver (Cloghanodfoy), Limerick (old house, acq. 1660s, old house decayed by early 19th c., new house c. 1850, passed by mar. to Trench family, derelict but still own in 1980s); Inchera, Cork (acq. early 19th c., add. mid-19th c., sold later 19th c., burned post-1950)
Estates: Bateman 18198 (I) 9355. Held 13,770 acres worth £998 in 1668.

Silver

Origins: A soldier went to Ireland in the mid-17th century and acquired estates in 1668. The daughter and heiress of John Silver married 1734 Robert Oliver who succeeded to the Silver estates in 1745.

1. Oliver Silver – {Youghal 1661-66}
2. John Silver – {Rathcormack 1703-13}

Gascoigne

Origins: Medieval family at Gawthorpe, Yorkshire. The son of a lawyer became Chief Justice of the King's Bench. **First MP 1421 for Yorkshire. Seven additional MPs 1495-1559, one for Yorkshire and two for Bedfordshire**. The elder son of Silver Oliver, Richard, married in 1812 Mary Turner of the Kirkleatham family (see Vansittart). She was the heiress of Sir Thomas Gascoigne 8 Bt of Parlington Park, her stepfather, who died in 1810. Richard took the additional name Gascoigne. Their daughter inherited Parlington and married 1850 Frederick Trench, who took the additional name Gascoigne. Richard's younger brother was seated at Inchera, Cork. The family moved to Yorkshire and let Castle Oliver decay by 1830s.

1. Sir Thomas Gascoigne 8 Bt – Thirsk 1780-84 Malton 1784 Arundell 1795-96

Seats: Parlington Park (Hall), Yorkshire (acq. 1546, rebuilt 18th c., remod. 1811-12, abandoned early 20th c., ruin by 1952); Lotherton Hall, Yorkshire (built 18th c., purch.

1825, became principal seat later 19th c., add. 1896-1931, given to City of Leeds 1970) Craignish Castle, Argyllshire (medieval, rebuilt 16th c., purch. for £26,000 and rebuilt 1832, sold 20th c.)
Estates: Bateman 19355 (E, S, & I) 16339
Title: Baronet 1635-1810
Notes: The Gascoignes reverted to Roman Catholicism in 1604 and remained so to 1780. 2 and 8 Bts and five others in ODNB.

O'LOGHLEN *IRELAND*

Origins: Gaelic Princes of the Burren whose lands were confiscated in the mid-17th century. The family below emerged in the mid-18th century as minor gentry. The first MP was Attorney General of Ireland in 1835 and Master of the Rolls of Ireland in 1837, the first Roman Catholic raised to the Bench since 1688.

1. Sir Michael O'Loghlen 1 Bt – Dungarvon 1835-36
2. Sir Colman O'Loghlen 2 Bt – County Clare 1863-77
3. Sir Bryan O'Loghlen 3 Bt – County Clare 1877-79

Seat: Drumconora (Nutfield), Clare (built c. mid-18th c., purch. mid-19th c., sold 1930s, demolished)
Estates: Held c. 1200 acres worth c. £1,500 pa in thc 1870s
Title: Baronet 1838-
1 Ld Lt 20th
Notes: The 3 Bt went to Australia and became Premier of the State of Victoria. 1 and 2 Bts in ODNB.

O'MAHONY (Mahony) *IRELAND*

Origins: Lords of Ivagha in the 14th century. Assumed the title "The O'Mahony" later 19th century. The family was Protestant in the 19th century.

1. Pierce Mahony – Kinsale 1837
2. Pierce O'Mahony, The O'Mahony – N. Meath 1886-92
3. Dermot O'Mahony – {TD Wicklow 1927-38}

Seats: Kilmorna House, Kerry (purch. c. 1840, passed to female line 1912, burned 1921); Woodlawn, Kerry (purch. 18th c., sold); Grange Con, Wicklow (purch. 1830s, burned 1920, rebuilt, still resident 1950s)
Estates: 5761 (I) 2167

O'NEILL [Chichester] *IRELAND*

Earl of Tyrone (1542-1608 I) and Earl O'Neill (1800-41 I)

Origins: A Celtic family powerful in northern Ireland since the 5th century. Said to be the oldest traceable family in Europe (to 360 A.D.). Princes of Tyrone, High Kings of Ireland, and "The O'Neill". **First {MP 1585 for County Antrim}. Another {MP 1641}.** On the death of the 3 Viscount O'Neill in 1855 the estates passed via a cousin, Mary O'Neill, who married Arthur Chichester, a kinsman of the Marquess of Donegall (see Chichester). His great-grandson took the name O'Neill and was created Baron O'Neill. Captain Terence O'Neill was Prime Minister of Northern Ireland 1963-69, capping a unique record as leaders of a European region lasting over 1500 years.

1. Henry O'Neill – {Randalstown 1695-97}
2. Charles O'Neill – {Randalstown 1697-99 Bangor 1707-13 Randalstown 1713-14}
3. Charles O'Neill – {Randalstown 1727-71}
4. Clotworthy O'Neill – {Randalstown 1746-49}
5. John O'Neill 1 Viscount O'Neill – {Randalstown 1764-83 County Antrim 1783-93}
6. St. John O'Neill – {Randalstown 1771-76}
7. Charles O'Neill – {Clonakilty 1784-93}
8. John O'Neill 3 Viscount O'Neill – County Antrim 1802-41
9. Sir Arthur Chichester 1 Bt – Carrickfergus 1812-18 Belfast 1818-20 Carrickfergus 1820-30 Belfast 1830-32
10. Edward O'Neill 2 Baron O'Neill – County Antrim 1863-80
11. Arthur O'Neill – Mid-Antrim 1910-14
12. Sir Hugh O'Neill 1 Baron Rathcavan – Mid-Antrim 1915-22 Antrim 1922-50 N. Antrim 1950-52
13. Phelim O'Neill – Antrim North 1952-59

Seats: Shane's Castle, Antrim (medieval, rebuilt 17th c., add. 18th c., add. early 19th c., fire 1816, new house 1860, add. 1901, burned 1922, new house 1958, still own); Cleggan Lodge, Antrim (built 18th c., acq. 19th c., rebuilt 1820, remod. 1895, add. 1929, add. 1988, still own)
Estates: Bateman 65919 (I) 44000. Held 120,000 acres in 17th c. Owned 15,000 acres worth 65 million pounds in 2001.
Titles: Baron O'Neill 1793-1855 I; Viscount O'Neill 1793-1855 I; Baron O'Neill 1868- UK; Baron Rathcavan 1953- ; Baron O'Neill of the Maine 1970-90 UKLife; Baronet 1666-91 1929-
Peers: {1 peer 1793-98} 2 Irish Rep peers 1801-41 1843-55 3 peers 1868-1944
3 Lds Lt 19th, 20th
1 KP 19th

Notes: 1, 2, and 6 Earls of Tyrone and 1 and Viscounts and 1 Earl O'Neill and 1 Baron and 1 Baron of the Maine and 2 Bt and eleven others in ODNB.

O'Neill

Origins: Kinsmen of the O'Neills.

1. Robert O'Neill – Mid-Antrim 1885-1910

Seats: Derrynogd (Derrynoid), Londonderry (built mid-19th c., sold 20th c.); Tullymore (Tollymore) Lodge, Antrim (burned and demolished 20th c.)
Estates: Bateman 5648 (I) 2242

O'Neill

Origins: Descended from a younger son of the 1 Earl of Tyrone.

1. Daniel O'Neill – {Downpatrick 1661-64} St. Ives 1662-64

Seats: Belsize House, Middlesex (leased estate and built 1661, passed out of family 1667); Clandeboy, Down (held from an early period, sold c. 1664)
Estates: Worth about £12,000 pa in early 17th c.
Notes: The male line became extinct in 1664. Three in ODNB.

ONGLEY [Henley]

Baron Ongley (1776-1877 I)

Origins: First MP was a linen draper in London, financier, and a Director of the South Sea Company. Withdrew from business and purchased landed estates. High Sheriff 1703.

1. Sir Samuel Ongley – Maidstone 1713-15
2. Samuel Ongley – New Shoreham 1729034 Bedford 1734-47
3. Robert Henley-Ongley 1 Baron Ongley – Bedford 1754-61 Bedfordshire 1761-80 1784-85

Seat: Old Warden, Bedfordshire (purch. c. 1698, sold 1872 for £165,000)
Estates: Under 2000 acres in Bateman. First MP worth £5,000 to £10,000 pa. Rubinstein – 2 Baron left £100,000 in probate 1814. Estates worth about £4,000 pa in 1860s.
Notes: Heavily indebted mid-19th c. Male line extinct 1877.

ONSLOW

Earl of Onslow (1801- UK)

Origins: Gentry in Shropshire in the 13th century. Married an heiress to Surrey property. A lawyer became Speaker of the House of Commons 1566. A member of Cromwell's House of Lords. **First MP 1558. One further MP 1584.**

1. Sir Richard Onslow – Surrey 1628 1640-48 1654 1656-57 Guildford 1660-64
2. Sir Arthur Onslow 2 Bt – Bramber 1641-48 Surrey 1654 1656 1659 Guildford 1660-79 Surrey 1679-81
3. Richard Onslow 1 Baron Onslow – Guildford 1679-81 1685-87 Surrey 1689-1710 St. Mawes 1710-13 Surrey 1713-15
4. Denzil Onslow – Haslemere 1680-81 1689-95 Surrey 1695-98 Guildford 1701-13 1715-17 Surrey 1717-21
5. Foot Onslow – Guildford 1689-1700
6. Thomas Onslow 2 Baron Onslow – Gatton 1702-05 Chichester 1705-08 Bletchingley 1708-15 Surrey 1715-17
7. Arthur Onslow – Guildford 1720-27 Surrey 1727-61
8. Richard Onslow – Guildford 1727-60
9. Richard Onslow 3 Baron Onslow – Guildford 1734-40
10. Denzil Onslow – Guildford 1740-47
11. George Onslow 1 Earl of Onslow – Rye 1754-61 Surrey 1761-74
12. George Onslow – Guildford 1760-84
13. Middleton Onslow – Rye 1774-75
14. Thomas Onslow 2 Earl of Onslow – Rye 1775-84 Guildford 1784-1806
15. Edward Onslow – Aldborough 1780-81
16. Thomas Onslow – Guildford 1806-18
17. Arthur Onslow – Guildford 1812-30
18. Guildford Onslow – Guildford 1858-74
19. Denzil Onslow – Guildford 1874-85
20. Gwendolen Onslow Guinness Countess of Iveagh – Southend-on-Sea 1927-35
21. Cranley Onslow Baron Onslow of Woking – Woking 1964-97

Seats: Clandon Park, Surrey (built later 16th c., purch. 1641, rebuilt c. 1729-31, remod. 1870s, NT 1956, fire 2015, still own estate); Pyrford Court, Surrey (purch. 1677, sold 1906); Imber Court, Surrey (acq. by mar. 1720, sold 1784); Mickleham, Surrey (acq. by mar. 1660s, sold by 1765); Hengar House (Manor), Cornwall (built 1620, acq. by mar. 1847, fire 1904, rebuilt 1905, sold 1959, holiday park)
Estates: Bateman 41568 (E & S) 27328 (including Baronets at Hengar and lines at Risby Park, Yorkshire; Balkissock, Ayrshire; and Oxenhall, Gloucestershire). Owned 2,500 acres in 2001.

Titles: Baron Onslow 1716- GB; Baron Cranley 1776- GB; Baron Onslow of Woking 1997-2001 UKLife; Baronet 1660- ; 1674-; 1797-
Peers: 9 peers 1716-1827 1829-70 1874-1945
4 Lds Lt 18th, 19th
2 in Cabinet 1714-15 1903-05
Notes: 1 Baron and 1, 2, and 4 Earls and 1 Baron Onslow of Woking and eight others in ODNB.

ORD

Origins: A family of Newcastle attorneys married money and managed investments skillfully in the late 17th and early 18th centuries. Acquired coal mines and urban property as well as landed estates.

1. Robert Ord – Mitchell 1734-41 Morpeth 1741-55
2. John Ord – Mitchell 1741-45
3. William Ord – Bossiney 1747-54
4. John Ord – Midhurst 1774-80 Hastings 1780-84 Wendover 1784-90
5. William Ord – Morpeth 1802-32 Newcastle-upon-Tyne 1835-52
6. William Ord – Newport (IoW) 1832-37

Seats: Whitfield Hall, Northumberland (purch. 1748, built 1785, still own); Fenham Hall, Northumberland (purch. c. 1685, family departed 18th c., subsumed in urban sprawl of Newcastle 19th c., demolished)
Estates: Bateman 15868 (E) 14076
Notes: The Ord estates passed through the female line to the Blacketts of Halton Castle in 1855. Four in ODNB.

ORMSBY *IRELAND*

Origins: Settled in Ireland under Elizabeth I in a military capacity. Sheriff 1672. The relationships between some of these MPs is unclear (see also Gore).

1. Robert Ormsby – {Tuam 1661-64}
2. Gilbert Ormsby – {Tuam 1692-93 1695-99 1703-13}
3. Robert Ormsby – {Kilmallock 1692-93}
4. John Ormsby – {Kilmallock 1692-93 Charleville 1695-99 Kilmallock 1703-13}
5. Robert Ormsby – {Castlebar 1692-93 Galway 1695-99}
6. John Ormsby – {Athenry 1695-99 1703-21}
7. Edward Ormsby – {County Galway 1709-13 Carrick 1714 County Galway 1715-27}
8. William Ormsby – {County Sligo 1713-27}
9. Arthur Ormsby – {Athenry 1725-27}
10. Francis Ormsby – {Sligo 1727-51}

11. William Ormsby – {Sligo 1757-76}
12. Sir Charles Ormsby 1 Bt – {Dunleek 1790-1800} Carlow 1801-06
13. Arthur Ormsby – {Athy 1790-97}
14. Joseph Ormsby – {Gorey 1799-1800}

Seats: Tobervaddy (Toberavaddy), Roscommon (acq. c. 1667, resident 18th c., sold by mid-19th c., ruin); Shrulegrove, Mayo (Shrule Castle - medieval, now a ruin; Shrulegrove - extant 19th c., demolished); Gortner Abbey, Mayo (acq. and built 18th c., sold 20th c., institutional use); Willowbrook, Sligo (acq. later 17th c., passed to Gores by mar. 1815, see Gore); Ballinamore (Ballynemore) House, Mayo (acq. 1677, rebuilt late 18th c. sold 1938, institutional use); Cabinteely House (Clare Hill), Dublin (built 18th c., passed by inher. 1888 to Ormsby-Hamiltons, sold 20th c.); Red Hill, Sligo; Clog(h)ans Castle (House), Mayo (acq. 17th c., still resident 19th c.)
Estates: Worth £890 pa in 1688. Held 9,260 acres in the late 18th c. Held 3,186 acres worth £659 pa in 1878.
Title: Baronet 1812-33
Notes: An Ormsby mar. mid-19th c. the Hamilton of Hampton Hall heiress (see Hamilton I). Ormsbys of Tobervaddy and Shrule emigrated to Australia in 19th c. One in ODNB.

ORR-EWING *SCOTLAND*

Origins: The Ewings were from the lower professional class in the early 19th century. The 1 Bt was a chemical manufacturer in Glasgow from the 1850s. His father married in 1805 an Orr, a daughter of a Provost of Paisley. The Orr-Ewings purchased landed estates but were also possessed probably the largest non-landed fortune in Scotland in the 20th century. (Fraser and Morris, *People and Society in Scotland*, II, 116)

1. James Ewing – Glasgow 1832-35
2. Sir Archibald Orr-Ewing 1 Bt – Dumbartonshire 1868-92
3. Charles Orr-Ewing – Ayr Burgh 1895-1903
4. Sir Ian Orr-Ewing – Weston-super-Mare 1934-58
5. Ian Orr-Ewing 1 Baron Orr-Ewing – N. Hendon 1950-70

Seats: Cardross House, Perthshire (built 1598, remod. 18th c., add. 1790, add. 1820, purch. 1920, still own); Lennoxbank House, Dumbartonshire (built 1826, purch. mid-19th c., sold early 20th c.); Ballikinrain Castle, Stirlingshire (purch. and built 1862 by Ewings, fire 1913, part restored, family departed 1920, sold, school); Gollanfield, Inverness-shire (purch. c. 1870); Castle House, Dunoon, Argyllshire (purch. and built 1824, donated to town 1924, museum)
Estates: Bateman 6041 (S) 7385. Owned 5,400 acres in 1996.
Titles: Baron Orr-Ewing 1971-99 UKLife; Baronet 1886-1999; 1963-99
Notes: Owned valuable quarries.

OSBALDESTON

Osbaldeston

Origins: The first Osbaldeston was recorded in Lancashire in the reign of Richard I. Lords of Osbaldeston manor by 1295. A knight at Agincourt 1415. **First MP 1597. Another MP 1601**.

1. William Osbaldeston – Scarborough 1685-87
2. William Osbaldeston – Scarborough 1736-47 1754-66
3. Fountayne Osbaldeston – Scarborough 1766-70
4. George Wickens Osbaldeston – Scarborough 1784-90
5. George Osbaldeston – East Retford 1812-18

Seats: Hunmanby Hall, Yorkshire (purch. and built 1623, passed out of family 1835); Gateforth House, Yorkshire (built 1812, sold 1848); Hutton Bushel (Buscel), Yorkshire (purch. 1739, fire 1840, sold and demolished)
Estates: The last squire lost huge sums in gambling and the estates were sold. The landed property went for £200,000 in 1848. Two in ODNB.

Osbaldeston

Origins: Cadet settled in Oxfordshire in the 15th century.

1. Sir Littleton Osbaldeston 1 Bt – New Woodstock 1679-81 1685-87

Seat: Chadlington Manor House, Oxfordshire (acq. by mar. 15th c., rebuilt early/mid-17th c., passed out of family mid-18th c.)
Title: Baronet 1664-1749
Notes: Male line extinct 1749

OSBORN (Osborne)

Origins: First recorded in Essex in the 15th century. Rose higher as an official under Edward VI and High Commissioner of Ecclesiastical Affairs under Elizabeth I. **First MP 1559. Three further MPs 1572-1625**. Kt 1611.

1. Sir Danvers Osborn 3 Bt – Bedfordshire 1747-53
2. Henry Osborn – Bedfordshire 1758-61
3. Sir George Osborn 4 Bt – Northampton 1768-69 Bossiney 1769-74 Penryn 1774-80 Horsham 1780-84

4. Sir John Osborn 5 Bt – Bedfordshire 1794-1807 Cockermouth 1807-08 Queenborough 1812-18 Bedfordshire 1818-20 Wigtown Burghs 1821-24

Seats: Chicksands Priory, Bedfordshire (built 13th c. and 15th c., purch. 1538 by Snowe family passing to Osborns 1576, remod. 1740-53, add. 1814 and 1835, sold 1935, institutional use); Haynes Grange, Bedfordshire (purch. 1553, became a farm house, sold 1936)
Estates: Bateman 3049 (E) 4695. Worth £4,000 pa in mid-17th c.
Title: Baronet 1662-
Notes: Four in ODNB.

OSBORNE I [Conyers, Darcy, Godolphin]

Duke of Leeds (1694-1964 E)

Origins: The 1 Duke was the great-grandson of a London apprentice cloth worker who made a fortune as a Turkey merchant. He acquired estates in Yorkshire by marrying his master's daughter. Lord Mayor of London 1583. Kt 1583. Bt 1620. High Sheriff 1661. Viscount 1673. The 1 Duke was a politician. **First MP 1586, for London. Two further MPs 1621-28.**

1. Thomas Osborne 1 Duke of Leeds – York 1665-73
2. Peregrine Osborne 2 Duke of Leeds – Berwick-on-Tweed 1677-79 Corfe Castle 1679 York 1689-90
3. Edward Osborne Viscount Latimer – Corfe Castle 1677-79 Buckingham 167-81
4. Charles Osborne – East Looe 1677-79 Kingston-on-Hull 1690-1700
5. Thomas Conyers – Durham 1698-1727
6. Francis Osborne 5 Duke of Leeds – Eye 1774 Helston 1774-75
7. Francis Godolphin Osborne 1 Baron Godolphin – Helston 1799-1802 Lewes 1802-06 Cambridgeshire 1810-31
8. Francis Godolphin D'Arcy-Osborne 7 Duke of Leeds – Helston 1826-30
9. George Osborne 10 Duke of Leeds – Brixton Div. Lambeth 1887-95

Seats: Hornby Castle, Yorkshire (built 14th c., acq. by Conyers by mar. early 15th c., rebuilt c. 1506, passed to Darcys by mar. c. 1620s, passed by mar. to Osbornes 1778, remod. c. 1800, contents sold in 1920 and 1930 and house demolished 1930); Kiveton Hall (Park), Yorkshire (built 1694-1704, demolished 1812); Gog Magog House (Wandlebury), Cambridgeshire (built c. 1700, acq. by mar. 1766, demolished 1950s); Godolphin, Cornwall (acq. by mar. 1766, reduced in size 1850, sold 1921)
Estates: Bateman 24237 (E) 33381 and 7078 (S) 8809

Titles: Baron Osborne and Viscount Latimer 1673-1964 E; Earl of Danby 1674-1964 E; Marquess of Carmarthen 1689-1964 E; Baron Godolphin 1832-1964 UK; Baronet 1620-1964
Peers: 12 peers 1673-1731 1735-99 1798-1945 1832-72
5 Lds Lt 17th, 18th, 19th
2 in Cabinet 1673-79 1689-99 1783-91
4 KG 17th, 18th, 19th
Notes: Hornby Castle came to the Osbornes via the St. Quintins, owners in the 14th century, whose heiress married Sir John Conyers, whose son married the co-heiress of Sir Philip Darcy (see below). The Osbornes also were left estates via an heiress of the Earl of Danby (Danvers family, Baron Danvers 1605, Earl of Danby 1625, extinct 1644). **Four MPs 1571-1659**. The last Earl left his property to the Osbornes rather than his brother due to his horror at the latter's role as a regicide in the Civil War. (Williams, *The Parliamentary History of the City of Oxford 1313-1899*, 146) Notes: Conyers family has an entry and 1, 2, and 5 Dukes and two others in ODNB.

Earl of Holdernesse (1682-1778 E)

Origins: The Darcys held land in Lincolnshire from the 11th century and could trace back to a tenant in the Domesday Book. Philip Darcy was summoned to Parliament as Lord Darcy circa 1299. John Darcy was the 1 Baron Darcy de Knayth 1344. The Barony of Fauconberg was inherited through a marriage with the Nevilles. **First MP 1319 for Lincolnshire. Six further MPs 1319-1628, three of them kts of the shire**. The daughter and heiress of the 6 Baron Darcy de Knayth married John Conyers of Hornby Castle and the Barony fell into abeyance. Their grandchild was created 1 Baron Conyers in 1509. The Conyers were also a very old family, Kts in the 13th century. **First MP 1586**. The 4 Baron Conyers became 7 Baron Darcy. His son was created Earl of Holdernesse. The daughter and heiress of the 4 Earl (d. 1778) married the 5 Duke of Leeds. A cadet line was created, Baron Darcy of Navan (1721-33). The Conyers and Fauconberg baronies passed in 1892 and 1903 to the Countess of Yarborough (see Pelham). The Barony Darcy de Knayth went to the Countess of Powis (see Herbert).

1. James Darcy – Richmond 1660
2. Conyers Darcy 2 Earl of Holdernesse – Boroughbridge 1660 Yorkshire 1661-79
3. Marmaduke Darcy – Richmond 1665-79
4. John Darcy – Richmond 1681 1685-87 1689
5. Philip Darcy – Newark-upon-Trent 1685-87 Richmond 1689-90
6. James Darcy 1 Baron Darcy of Navan – Richmond 1698-1705
7. Sir Conyers Darcy – Yorkshire 1707-08 Newark 1715-22 Richmond 1722-27 1728-47 Yorkshire 1747-58

Seats: Hornby Castle, Yorkshire (built 14th c., acq. by Conyers by mar. early 15th c., rebuilt c. 1506, passed to Darcys by mar. c. 1620s, passed by mar. to Osbornes 1778, demolished 1930); Aske Hall, Yorkshire (medieval, purch. 1722 and remod. 1727, sold 1763 for £45,000)
Estates: Bateman for Lord Conyers 3460 (E) 8538. Worth £4,000 pa in 1650.
Titles: Baron Darcy de Knayth 1344- E; Baron Conyers 1509- E; Baron Darcy of Navan 1721-33 I
Peers: 4 peers 1661-89 1680-92 1702-22 1739-78
3 Lds Lt 18th
2 in Cabinet 1718-19 1751-61
Notes: Darcy family has several entries and 1 Baron Darcy of Dracy and 4 Earl and one other in ODNB.

Earl Godolphin (1706-66 E)

Origins: An old family that gained important property by marriage in the late 14th century. Became rich through tin mining. Sheriff 1504. **First MP 1539 for Cornwall. Seven additional MPs 1553-1648, three for the county.** The 4 Duke of Leeds married in 1740 Mary daughter and heiress of the 2 Earl Godolphin.

1. Sir Francis Godolphin – Helston 1626 St. Ives 1628 Cornwall 1640 Helston 1640-44 1660
2. Sir William Godolphin – Camelford 1665-79
3. Sir William Godolphin 1 Bt – Helston 1665-79
4. Sidney Godolphin 1 Earl Godolphin – Helston 1668-79 St. Mawes 1679 Helston 1679-81
5. Charles Godolphin – Helston 1681 1685-87 1689-1701
6. Sidney Godolphin – Helston 1685-87 Penryn 1690-95 Helston 1698-1713 1715-22 St. Mawes 1722-27 St. Germans 1727-32
7. Francis Godolphin 2 Earl Godolphin – Helston 1695-98 East Looe 1701 Helston 1701-08 Oxfordshire 1708-10 Tregony 1710-12
8. Francis Godolphin 2 Baron Godolphin – Helston 1741-66

Seats: Godolphin House, Cornwall (acq. by mar. late 14th c., built by 1475, expanded mid-16th c., add. 1630s, passed by mar. to Dukes of Leeds 1766, a large part demolished 1850, sold 1921); Baylis House, Buckinghamshire (built c. 1695, purch. 1708, add. 1725-26, add. 1733-35, passed to Osbornes 1785, leased out, sold 1908, hotel); Spargor, Cornwall (resident 17th c.); Coulston, Wiltshire (purch. c. 1650, built c. 1658, part sold 1678, remaining sold 1781); Broniarth, Montgomeryshire (resident 17th c.); Gog Magog House, Cambridgeshire (built c. 1700, passed to Osbornes by mar. 1766)
Estates: Worth £1,000 pa in 1660. Held at least 8,000 acres. Leased the Scilly Isles 1570-1831.

Title: Baron Godolphin 1684-1766 E; Viscount Rialton 1706-66 E; Baron Godolphin 1735-85 GB; Baronet 1661-1710
Peers: 3 peers 1684-1785
2 Lds Lt 18th
2 in Cabinet 1679-97 1700-10 1735-40
1 KG 18th
Notes: The Godolphin tin mines were the richest in Cornwall in the 17th c. (Thrush and Ferris, *The House of Commons 1604-1629*, IV, 402). 1 and 2 Earls and eight others in ODNB.

OSBORNE II [Bernal] *IRELAND & ENGLAND*

Osborne

Origins: Emigrated to Ireland from England in the later 16th century and acquired land. The grandson of the first settler was a lawyer who increased the size of the estate. Bt 1629. Sheriff 1672.

1. Sir Richard Osborne 1 Bt – {Dungarvon 1639 County Waterford 1639 1661-66}
2. John Osborne – {County Meath 1692}
3. Francis Osborne – {Navan 1692-93 1695-99}
4. Sir John Osborne 7 Bt {Lismore 1719-27 County Waterford 1727-43}
5. Sir William Osborne 8 Bt – {Carysfort 1761-68 Dungarvon 1768-83 Carysfort 1783}
6. Sir Thomas Osborne 9 Bt – {Carysfort 1776-97}
7. John Osborne – {Carysfort 1783-87}
8. Charles Osborne – {Carysfort 1790-1800}
9. Sir Henry Osborne 11 Bt – {Carysfort 1797-99 Enniskillen 1800}
10. George Osborne – Tatton 2001-

Seats: Beechwood Park, Tipperary (built 17th c.?, add. early to mid-18th c., acq. by mar. 1831, sold mid-20th c.); Newtown Anner, Tipperary (built c. 1820, purch. 1835, passed by inher. to 12 Duke of St. Albans 1880, sold c. 1959); Ballyntaylor (Ballytaylor, Ballintaylor), Waterford (acq. and built 1619, sold 18th c., demolished); Mount Osborne, Waterford (acq. 17th c., resident 18th c.)
Estates: Bateman 13184 (I) 5853. Worth £10,000 pa c. 1800 and £8,000 pa in 1870. 500 acres left 1918.
Title: Baronet 1629-
1 in Cabinet 2010-
Notes: The 10 Duke of St. Albans mar. 1874 the Osborne heiress and succeeded to Newtown Anner 1880. George Osborne MP 2001-, son of the current Baronet, was Chancellor of the Exchequer (2010-16). One in ODNB.

Earl of Norbury (1827- I)

Origins: The Tolers came over with Cromwell and were settled at Beechwood in the second half of the 17th century. The first Earl was a lawyer and Chief Justice of the Common Pleas in Ireland 1800-27. Beechwood passed 1796 by marriage of Daniel Toler's daughter and heiress to Sir Henry Osborne 11 Bt (see above).

1. John Toler 1 Earl of Norbury – {Tralee 1776-83 Philipstown 1783-90 Gorey 1790-1800}
2. Daniel Toler – {County Tipperary 1783-96}

Seats: Beechwood Park (Graige), Tipperary (acq. later 17th c., passed by mar. to Osbornes 1796); Durrow Abbey, King's County (built 18th c., acq. 19th c., rebuilt c. 1837, rebuilt 1924, sold 1950s); Cabra (Cabragh) House, Dublin (tenants only 19th c.); Carrigmore, Cork (built 1842, purch mid-19th c., sold 1860)
Estates: Bateman 12281 (I) 4409 and 16531 (I) 9911 (Graham-Toler). Estate worth £2,500 pa in the later 18th c. The 1 Earl left £138,000 in 1831. His estates were said to amount to more than 16,000 acres worth £8,000 pa.
Titles: Baron Norwood 1797-1832 I; Baron Norbury 1800- I
Notes: The 3 Earl was murderd in 1839. 1 Earl in ODNB.

Bernal

Origins: London merchants of Sephardic descent who had emigrated from Seville to Amsterdam and then to Britain. They acquired West Indian estates by foreclosing on mortgages in the 18th century. The daughter of the 9 Osborne Bt married 1844 Ralph Bernal. He took the name Osborne and succeeded to the Osborne estates but not the Baronetcy. Their daughter was the mother of the 12 Duke of St. Albans (see Beauclerk).

1. Ralph Bernal – Lincoln 1818-20 Rochester 1820-41 Weymouth & Melcombe Regis 1842-47 Rochester 1847-52
2. Ralph Bernal Osborne – Wycombe 1841-47 Middlesex 1847-57 Dover 1857-59 Liskeard 1859-65 Nottingham 1866-68 Waterford 1870-74

Seat: Newtown Anner, Tipperary (built c. 1820, passed via Osborne heiress to Bernals, who took name Osborne (see above. Later passed to grandson, the 12th Duke of St. Albans, sold c. 1959)
Estates: 13,000 acres worth £5,000 pa c. 1880. The art collection of the first MP was worth £71,000. He also spent £66,000 on elections. Three in ODNB.

OSWALD I *SCOTLAND*

Origins: The first MP was a wealthy merchant and skipper who purchased landed estates.

1. James Oswald – [Kirkcaldy 1703-07] Dysart Burghs 1710-15
2. James Oswald – Dysart Burghs 1741-47 Fifeshire 1747-54 Dysart Burghs 1754-68
3. James Oswald – Dysart Burghs 1768-74 Fife 1776-79

Seat: Dunnikier House, Fife (built 1692, purch. 1703, new house 1791-93, old house became a manse 1891, new house became a hotel 1971)
Notes: Two in ODNB.

OSWALD II *SCOTLAND*

Origins: Merchants in Glasgow (from the early 18th c.) and London. Exceedingly successful military contractor in the Seven Years War (made a profit of £125,000). Married a West Indian heiress 1750.

1. James Oswald – Glasgow 1832-37 1839-47
2. Richard Oswald – Ayrshire 1832-35
3. Alexander Oswald – Ayrshire 1843-52

Seats: Auchincruive House, Ayrshire (purch. 1764, built 1766-67, add. late 19th c., sold 1926); Cavens House, Kirkcudbrightshire (purch. 1759, held into 19th c.)
Estates: Bateman 36120 (S) 41874. Scottish estate reached 102,679 acres in 1782. Owned 50,000 acres in N. America c. 1784. Worth between £250,000 and £500,000 in 1778
Notes: See Hancock, *Citizens of the World: London Merchants and the Integration of the British Atlantic Community*, 1735-1785. Two in ODNB.

OWEN I [Barlow, Lort, Phillips] *WALES*

<u>Owen</u>

Origins: Medieval Anglesey family. **First MP 1545. Two further MPs 1553-72, both for Anglesey**. Married a Pembrokeshire heiress in the mid-16th century. The 6 Bt devised Orielton in 1809 to John Lord of Taynton, a cousin by marriage, who took the name Owen.

1. Sir Hugh Owen 1 Bt – Pembroke 1626 1628 Haverfordwest 1640 Pembroke 1640-48 1660
2. Arthur Owen – Pembrokeshire 1646-48 1654 1660-78

3. Sir Hugh Owen 2 Bt – Pembroke 1676-79 Pembrokeshire 1679-81 1689-95
4. John Owen – Pembrokeshire 1678-79
5. Arthur Owen – Pembroke 1679-81 1685-87 1689-95
6. Sir Arthur Owen 3 Bt – Pembrokeshire 1695-1705 Pembroke Boroughs 1708-12 Pembrokeshire 1715-27
7. Wyrriott Owen – Pembrokeshire 1705-10
8. Sir William Owen 4 Bt – Pembroke Boroughs 1722-47 Pembrokeshire 1747-61 Pembroke Boroughs 1761-74
9. John Owen – West Looe 1735-41
10. Sir Hugh Owen 5 Bt – Pembrokeshire 1770-86
11. Hugh Owen Barlow – Pembroke Boroughs 1774-1809
12. Sir Hugh Owen 6 Bt – Pembroke Boroughs 1809
13. Sir John Lord Owen 1 Bt – Pembroke Boroughs 1809-12 Pembrokeshire 1812-41 Pembroke Boroughs 1841-61
14. Sir Hugh Owen 2 Bt – Pembroke 1826-38 1861-68

Seats: Orielton, Pembrokeshire (acq. by mar. 1571 from the Wyrriotts who were there by 1188, new house built 1809, family departed c. 1850, sold 1857, institutional use); New Moat, Pembrokeshire (leased 17th c.); Landshipping House, Pembrokeshire (acq. 17th c., closed up 1790, demolished c. 1840)
Estates: Orielton estate 6,800 acres in the 1570s. Coal mines from the 17th century. 6,800 acres worth at least £1,000 pa in the 1640s. 3,800 acres worth £1,000 pa in the 1830s. Rubinstein – 6th Bt left £175,000 probate 1809 and Lady Owen left £100,000 in 1823.
Titles: Baronet 1641-1851; 1813-
4 Lds Lt 18th, 19th
Notes: The family remained Roman Catholic well into the 17th century. The Owens heavily overspent on elections, which led to sales of almost the entire estate and bankruptcy in the mid-19th century. They retreated to a rental property in Gloucestershire.

Barlow

Origins: The founder was a Bishop of St. Davids and later Chichester who acquired monastic property in Pembrokeshire in 1546. Sheriff 1562. The daughter of John Barlow MP was the mother of Hugh Owen, who took the additional name Barlow (see above).

1. William Barlow – Pembrokeshire 1685-87
2. John Barlow – Pembrokeshire 1710-15
3. Sir George Barlow 2 Bt – Cardigan Boroughs 1713-15 Haverfordwest 1715
4. John Barlow – Haverfordwest 1715-18
5. Lewis Barlow – Orford 1734-37

6. George Barlow – Haverfordwest 1743-47
7. Hugh Barlow – Pembroke Boroughs 1747-61

Seats: Slebech, Pembrokeshire (Barlows there by 16th c., passed by mar. to Symmons family 1773, sold 1780s); Lawrenny (Castle) Park, Pembrokeshire (acq. early 17th c., built 1680, passed by mar. to Owens 1788, demolished c. 1954); Cresswell, Pembrokeshire (purch. mid-16th c., abandoned later 18th c., ruin)
Estates: Worth £1,500 pa in the 1670s. 7,000 acres in 1792. When owned in the 19th c. by the Barons de Rutzen the estate consisted of 5573 (W) 4126 in Bateman.
Title: Baronet 1677-1760?
Notes: The last male Barlow died 1763. Seven in ODNB.

Phillips

Origins: Dorothy Barlow, daughter of John Barlow of Lawrenny, had a daughter Eliza Lort, who married George Phillips. Their son succeeded to Lawrenny in 1851.

1. George Lort Phillips – Pembrokeshire 1861-66

Seat: Lawrenny Park (Castle), Pembrokeshire (acq. by mar. 1st half 19th c., rebuilt mid-19th c., demolished 1950, still own estate)
Estates: Bateman 6522 (W) 5709
Notes: Two Lorts in ODNB.

OWEN II

Origins: Emerged in the 16th century. The first MP, son of a mercer, was a successful lawyer and judge (1594), the son of a merchant in Shrewsbury. **First MP 1584 for Shrewsbury. Three additional MPs 1597-1640, all for Shrewsbury.** Kt 1604.

1. Roger Owen – Shropshire 1702-05

Seat: Condover Hall, Shropshire (purch. and built 1586-1600, later passed to Corbets)
Notes: Two in ODNB.

OXENDEN [Chudleigh, Dixwell]

Oxenden

Origins: Held land in Kent in the 14th century. **First MP 1553.**

1. Sir Henry Oxenden 1 Bt – Winchelsea 1645-48 Kent 1654 Sandwich 1660

2. Sir James Oxenden 2 Bt – Sandwich 1679-81 1685-87 1689-90 Kent 1698-1700 Sandwich 1701-02
3. George Oxenden – University of Cambridge 1695-98
4. Sir Henry Oxenden 4 Bt – Sandwich 1713-20
5. Sir George Oxenden 5 Bt – Sandwich 1720-54

Seats: Deane (Dene) Court (Park), Kent (purch. 14th c., built late 16th c., leased out from 1775, demolished 19th c.); Broome Park, Kent (built 1635-39, inher. by mar. 1750, becomes main seat 1775, remod. 1778, sold 1920s); Great Maydeken, Kent (purch. 14th c., demolished c. 1830s)
Estates: Bateman 5266 (E) 5370
Title: Baronet 1678-1924
Notes: A younger son and his son were businessmen in the East India Company. This line inherited Deane and the Baronetcy. Five in ODNB.

Chudleigh

Origins: Emerge in the 14th century. **First MP 1346 for Devon. Five further MPs 1381-1628, three for the county**. The 5th Oxenden Baronet's son married the heiress of Sir George Chudleigh.

1. Thomas Chudleigh – New Romney 1685-87

Seats: Ashton, Devon (acq. c. 1320, sold 1745); Haldon House, Devon (built c. 1735-40 by Sir George Chudleigh, sold soon afterwards)
Title: Baronet 1622-1745
Notes: Nearly bankrupt late 16th c. and majority of estates sold. Five in ODNB.

Dixwell

Origins: Seated at Dixwell Hall, Warwickshire from the reign of Richard I. **First MP 1624. Another MP 1646**. Sir Basil Dixwell 2 Bt – left his estates to his great nephew, grandson of his sister and wife of George Oxenden. The estates then passed to the 6 Oxenden Bt.

1. Sir Basil Dixwell 2 Bt – Dover 1689-90 1695-1700

Seat: Broome Park, Kent (inher. by mar. c. 1630, built 1635-39, passed to Oxendens 1750)
Title: Baronet 1660-1750
Notes: The second MP was a regicide. Extinct 1750.

PAGET I [Bagenall, Bayly, Blackney, Irby, Wallis] *ENGLAND, WALES, & IRELAND*

Marquess of Anglesey (1815- UK)

Origins: Possibly descended from an old Staffordshire family with an **MP 1455-61**, the Paget origins were obscure. Their fortunes were made by the 1 Baron, the son of a City of London official of small fortune, who became Clerk of the Privy Council 1540, a diplomat, and Secretary of State under Henry VIII. Kt 1543. Baron 1549. **First MP 1529. Another MP 1555**. A younger son of the 5 Baron Paget went to Ireland. His granddaughter married Sir Nicholas Bayly 2 Bt of Plas Newydd. Their son succeeded to the Paget Barony and was created Earl of Uxbridge. A younger son succeeded to Ballyarthur, Wicklow.

1. Henry Paget 1 Earl of Uxbridge – Staffordshire 1695-1712
2. Thomas Paget – Staffordshire 1715-22
3. Thomas Paget – Ilchester 1722-27
4. Henry Paget 1 Marquess of Anglesey – Caernarvon 1790-96 Milborne Port 1796-1804 1806-10
5. William Paget – Anglesey 1790-94
6. Air Arthur Paget – Anglesey 1794-1807
7. Sir Edward Paget – Caernarvon 1796-1806 Milborne Port 1810-20
8. Sir Charles Paget – Milborne Port 1804-06 Caernarvon 1806-26 1831-34
9. Berkeley Paget – Anglesey 1807-20 Milborne Port 1820-26
10. Henry Paget 2 Marquess of Anglesey – Anglesey 1820-32
11. Lord William Paget – Caernarvon 1826-30 Andover 1841-47
12. Frederick Paget – Beaumaris 1832-47
13. Lord Alfred Paget – Lichfield 1837-65
14. Lord William Paget – Andover 1841-47
15. Lord Clarence Paget – Sandwich 1847-52 1857-76
16. Lord George Paget – Beaumaris 1847-57
17. Henry Paget 3 Marquess of Anglesey – S. Stafford 1854-57
18. Almeric Paget 1 Baron Queenborough – Cambridge 1910-17

Seats: Beaudesert Hall, Staffordshire (medieval, acq. 1546, built 1573-83, add. 1771-72, fire 1909, rebuilt 1909-12, family departed 1920, demolished 1930-35, estate sold 1932); Plas Newydd, Anglesey (Griffth family acq. c. 1470, passed to Baylys and then to Pagets 1737, built c. 1480, rebuilt 1793-99, remod. 1930s, NT); West Drayton, Middlesex (acq. and built 1537-47, demolished before 1774, sold 1786)
Estates: Bateman 33422 (E, W, & I) 112609; at Ballyarthur 3685 (I) 2011. Worth £1,500 pa in 1563. Rubinstein – the 1 Earl left £150,000 probate in 1812. Owned 8,000 acres in 2001.

Titles: Baron Paget 1548- E; Baron Burton 1712-69 GB; Earl of Uxbridge 1714-69 GB; Earl of Uxbridge 1784- GB; Baron Queenborough 1918-49 UK; Baronet 1730-
Peers: 12 peers 1660-1713 1712-1854 1833-1945 1918-45
6 Lds Lt 17th, 18th, 19th, 20th
1 in Cabinet 1827-33
1 KG 19th
Notes: The 6 Marquess died in 1904 leaving over half a million pounds of debt. 1, 4, 5, 6, and 7 Barons and 1 and 2 Earls first cr. and 1 Marquess and thirteen others in ODNB.

<u>Baron Boston</u> (1761- GB)

Origins: Came to Lincolnshire from Cumberland in the early 14th century and became prominent by the 16th century through the law. **First MP 1545, for Boston (1553). Another MP 1589-1621 also for Boston.** The 1 Baron Boston succeeded in 1743 to the unsettled estates of the 1 Earl of Uxbridge, his cousin in 1769.

1. Sir Anthony Irby – Boston 1628 1640-48 1656 1659 1660-81
2. Sir Edward Irby 1 Bt – Boston 1702-08
3. William Irby 1 Baron Boston – Launceston 1735-47 Bodmin 1747-61

Seats: Irby Hall, Lincolnshire (purch. 1552, became a farm house 18th c.); Llanidan House, Anglesey (built 1631, purch. by Pagets 1740, passed by inher. to Irbys 1769, leased out later 18th c., remod. 18th c., owned into 20th c.); Boyland Hall, Norfolk (purch. 1534 by Garney family, built 1571, passed by mar. to Irbys 1804, remod. soon after, contents sold 1938, demolished 1947); Hedsor House, Buckinghamshire (built 1583, fire 1775, purch. and built 1778, fire 1795, restored, rebuilt 1865-68, sold 1926); Lligwy, Anglesey (purch. by Pagets 1740, passed to Irbys by inher. 1769, held at least until 1945)
Estates: Bateman 14934 (E & W) 19091
Title: Baronet 1704-
Peers: 7 peers 1761-1877 1881-1945
Notes: See Hopkins for inherited property. Four in ODNB.

<u>Bayly</u> (Baily)

Origins: The 1 Bt was a grandson of a Bishop of Bangor (d. 1631) of obscure origin. The 2 Bt inherited Plas Newydd from the Griffith family by marriage (acq. c. 1470). His marriage to Caroline Paget brought the Paget Baronry to their son, the father of the 1 Marquess of Anglesey.

1. Nicholas Bayly – {Newry 1661-66}
2. Sir Edward Bayly 1 Bt – {Newry 1705-14}

3. Sir Nicholas Bayly 2 Bt – Anglesey 1734-41 1747-61 1770-74
4. Nicholas Bayly – Anglesey 1784-90
5. Lewis Bayly Wallis – Ilchester 1799-1802

Seats: Plas Newydd, Anglesey (see above); Mount Bagnel(l), Louth (acq. by mar. 1712, sold 19th c.)
Title: Title: Baronet 1730-
1 Ld Lt 18th
Notes: Succeeded to Stalbridge, Dorset by inher. 1754 (see Walter). Three in ODNB.

Bagenall (Bagenal)

Origins: John Bagenall was a tailor in Newcastle-under-Lyme and five times Mayor 1529-33. A son gained a place at court as a "gamester, dicer, and whoremoneger". (Bindoff, *The House of Commons*, I, 363) Metoric rise under Edward VI as a soldier and official. To Ireland c. 1540. Gained estates in Down 1552. The family became moneylenders. Foreclosed on the mortgage on Plas Newydd in the 1580s. **First MP 1547. One further MP 1555.** To Ireland as a soldier and official. **First {MP 1579}. Two additional {MPs 1585-1613}.** Marshall General of the Army in Ireland early 17th century. Nicholas Bagenall left his Welsh estates to his cousin Edward Bayly in 1712 (see above). An Irish branch continued in Carlow (see Burgh). The estates in northern Ireland went to the Needhams.

1. Nicholas Bagenall – Anglesey 1661-79
2. Beauchamp Bagenal – {Enniscorthy 1761-68 County Carlow 1768-76 1778-83}
3. Walter Bagenal – County Carlow 1802-12

Seats: Mount Bagenal(l), Louth (passed by mar. from Bagealls to Baylys 1712); Dunleckney Manor, Carlow (acq. 17th c., passes by inher. (mar. 1785) to Newtons early 19th c.); Killedmonde, Carlow; Bert House, Kildare (built 1725-30, add. early 19th c., passed by mar. to De Burghs of Dromkeen, Limerick, etc., 19th c.); Bagenalstown House (Moneybeg), Carlow (acq. early 17th c., built 18th c., sold 1760s)
Estates: Held 30,000 acres in 1760 worth £6,681 pa, but much sold. Down to a small estate by 1812.
Notes: Dudley Bagenall was {MP 1689} in James II's Parliament. Two in ODNB.

Blackney

Origins: Walter Blackney, of a Roman Catholic family, inherited in the 1680s Ballycormack, Carlow from his maternal grandfather Dudley Bagenall, son of George Bagenall **{MP 1613}** of Dunleckney. The latter estate also passed to the Blackneys.

1. Walter Blackney – County Carlow 1831-34

Seats: Ballyellin (Ballyellen) House, Carlow (purch. 1781, sold later 19th c.); Dunleckney Manor, Carlow (acq. and built by Bagenals c. 1610, passed to Newton family mid-19th c. by mar., rebuilt 1845-57, sold early 20th c.); Ballycormack, Carlow (acq. early 17th c. by Bagenals, inher. by mar. by Blackneys 1685)
Notes: The Blackneys ceased to live at Ballyellin in the later 19th century.

PAGET II

Baron Paget of Northampton (1974-90 UKLife)

Origins: Farmers in Leicestershire since the 15th century. The first MP the son of a banker, and he was also a banker until his death in 1861. High Sheriff 1869.

1. Thomas Paget – Leicestershire 1831-32
2. Charles Paget – Nottingham 1856-65
3. Thomas Paget – S. Leicestershire 1867-68 1880-86
4. Thomas Paget – Bosworth Div. Leicestershire 1922-23
5. Reginald Paget 1 Baron Paget of Northampton – Northampton 1945-74

Seats: Meadow House (Humberstone Hall), Leicestershire (acq. and built mid-19th c., family departed 1923, sold 1927 for £10,000); Ibstock, Leicestershire (acq. 1548, sold c. 1860); Sulby Hall, Northamptonshire (built 1792-94, add. 1824, purch. 1847, sold 1930, demolished 1952); Lubenham, Leicestershire (purch. 1843, sold 20th c.)
Estates: Bateman 4782 (E) 10884. 1 Baron left £2,300,000 in 1990.
Title: Baronet 1897-1936
Notes: 1 Baron and two others in ODNB.

PAKENHAM [Aungier, Conolly, Hanger, Hare, Mahon, Townsend] *IRELAND & ENGLAND*

Earl of Longford (1677-1704 I; 1785- I)

Origins: The Aungier family was granted Whitefriars, Middlesex by James I and created Barons in 1621. The father of the 1 Baron was a lawyer and landowner who went to Ireland c. 1600 as Master of the Rolls, and he acquired extensive estates there. **First MP 1589**. The Earls of Longford descended from the senior line of the family, while the brother of the 1 Baron Aungier (otherwise Hanger) established a cadet line, the Barons Coleraine. The sister of the 2 Earl married Sir James Cuffe. Their son, Michael, had a daughter and heiress who married Sir Thomas Pakenham. She was created Countess of Longford in her own right and her husband 1 Baron. The first prominent

Pakenham was a soldier who came to Ireland during the Civil War and his successor held the office of Keeper of the Great Seal of Ireland in 1693. **First {MP 1661}.**

1. Francis Aungier 1 Earl of Longford – {King's County, Longford, Westmeath 1659} Surrey 1660 Arundel 1661-79
2. Henry Pakenham – {Navan 1661-66}
3. Sir Thomas Pakenham – {Augher 1695-99}
4. Ambrose Aungier 2 Earl of Longford – {Longford 1697-99}
5. Edward Pakenham – {County Westmeath 1713-21}
6. Thomas Pakenham 1 Baron Longford – {Longford 1745-56}
7. Edward Pakenham 2 Baron Longford – {County Longford 1765-66}
8. Robert Pakenham – {County Longford 1768-75}
9. Sir Thomas Pakenham – {Longford 1783-90 Kells 1790-97 Longford 1797-1800}
10. Sir Edward Pakenham – {Longford 1799-1800}
11. Sir Hercules Pakenham – County Westmeath 1808-26
12. Edward Pakenham Conolly – County Donegal 1831-48
13. Thomas Pakenham Conolly – Donegal 1849-76

Seats: Pakenham Hall (Tullynally), Westmeath (acq. by Pakenhams 1655 and house built, add. 1738, add. 1780, remod. 1801-06, add. 1820, add. 1839-42, add. 1860, still own); Whitefriars, Middlesex (acq. early 17th c.); Cookesboro(ugh), Westmeath (acq. by Cookes 1641, built early 18th c., passed to Pakenhams by inher. 1876)
Estates: Bateman 24846 (I) 50080. Owned 900 acres in 2001.
Titles: Baron Aungier 1621-1704 I; Viscount Longford 1675-1704 I; Baron Longford 1756 I; Baron Silchester 1821- UK; Baron Pakenham 1945- UK; Baron Pakenham 1999-2001 UKLife
Peers: {5 peers 1660-1704 1756-92 1795-1800} 1 Irish Rep peer 1801-35 5 peers 1821-35 1838-1915 1923-45
3 Lds Lt 19th, 20th
1 in Cabinet 1964-68
2 KP 19th, 20th
1 KG 20th
Notes: Edward Pakenham inherited Castletown House via descent from the marriage of Thomas Pakenham with the great-granddaughter of William Conolly. (see below) 1 Earl of first cr. and one other Aungier and 7 Earl of sec. cr. and eight other Pakenhams in ODNB.

<u>Pakenham</u>

Origins: Langford Lodge passed to a younger son of the Earls of Longford through the marriage of Catherine, daughter of the 2 Viscountess Langford to the 2 Baron Longford.

1. Edward Pakenham – Antrim 1852-54
2. Thomas Pakenham – County Antrim 1854-65

Seat: Langford Lodge, Antrim (built 18th c., acq. by mar. from Langfords 1796, rebuilt c. 1825, sold 1940, demolished)
Estates: See Taylour (Rowley)

Baron Hartland (1800-1845 I)

Origins: A younger son of the 2 Baron Longford married a Mahon heiress. Their son inherited Strokestown. He married the heiress of the last Baron Hartland. Nicholas Mahon (d. 1680) fought in the Civil War and went to Ireland where he acquired estates. Sheriff 1686.

1. John Mahon – {Jamestown 1692-93 1695-99 1703-09}
2. Nicholas Mahon – {County Roscommon 1730-35}
3. Thomas Mahon – {Roscommon 1740-60 County Roscommon 1761-82}
4. Maurice Mahon 1 Baron Hartland – {County Roscommon 17682-83}
5. Thomas Mahon 2 Baron Hartland – {County Roscommon 1799-1800} 1801-02
6. Stephen Mahon – {Knocktopher 1800} County Roscommon 1806-26

Seat: Strokestown House (Park), Roscommon (acq. by 1670, built 1696, add. 1730, remod. 1819, passed by mar to Pakenhams 1847, sold 1979, museum)
Estates: Bateman 28123 (I) 15080. Worth £767 pa c. 1725, £3,178 pa in 1791, £4,000 pa. c. 1819, and £8,751 pa c. 1836. Rubinstein – the 2 Baron left £120,000 in probate in 1835.

Conolly

Origins: William Conolly was of Irish Roman Catholic ancestry. He was born in 1662 into a probably minor gentry family that conformed to the Established Church. Conolly made his fortune as an attorney, through an astute marriage, and in dealing in forfeited estates after the Battle of the Boyne 1690. No rise in modern Irish history was more meteoric than his (save perhaps the 1 Earl of Cork, but he started with a more "gentle" lineage). He came to hold land in ten Irish counties and in Wales, and controlled eight parliamentary boroughs. Speaker of the Irish House of Commons 1715-29. He married a Conyngham of Mount Charles and built the largest and most beautiful house in Ireland, dying as the richest man in the country. Castletown passed to the Pakenhams by marriage (see above).

1. William Conolly – {Donegal 1692-93 1695-99 County Londonderry 1703-29}
2. William Conolly – {Ballyshannon 1727-54} Aldeburgh 1734-47 Petersfield 1747-54

3. Thomas Conolly – Malmesbury 1759-68 {County Londonderry 1761-1800} Chichester 1768-80

Seats: Castletown, Kildare (purch. 1709, built 1722, add. 1758, remod. 1776, passed by mar. to Pakenhams and then Lord Carew, sold 1965 and preserved by IGS from 1979); Stretton Hall, Staffordshire (medieval, rebuilt c. 1720, purch. c. 1734, sold c. 1795)
Estates: Bateman 26853 (I) 12611. The first William Conolly left Irish estates worth at his death in 1729 £300,000. Income £17,000 pa in 1729, £15,275 pa in 1758, and £21,000 pa in 1773.
Notes: Two in ODNB.

<u>Baron Coleraine</u> (1625-1749 I; 1762-1824 I)

Origins: Descended from a younger brother of the 1 Baron Aungier (otherwise Hanger). Merchants in the Turkey trade 17th c. The 1 Baron Coleraine (Hanger) of the second creation succeeded to the estates of a cousin, Anne, widow of Henry Hare 3 Baron Coleraine of the first creation (Hare). The Hares emerged in Suffolk in the 15th century. (Shared descent with the Earls of Listowel, see Hare.) The first prominent one was a lawyer, Master of the Rolls, Lord Keeper, and Speaker of the House of Commons in the mid-16th century. **First MP 1529. Seven additional MPs 1539-1654**. The 1 Baron inherited a fortune made in the law by an uncle 1620.

1. Henry Hare 2 Baron Coleraine – Old Sarum 1679-81
2. Hugh Hare – Bletchingly 1698-1700
3. Henry Hare 3 Baron Coleraine – Boston 1730-34
4. Gabriel Hanger 1 Baron Coleraine – Maidstone 1753-61 Bridgwater 1763-68
5. William Hanger 3 Baron Coleraine – East Retford 1775-78 Aldborough 1778-80 Mitchell 1780-84

Seats: Cannon Place, Berkshire (resident 18th c.); Kempsford Hall, Gloucestershire (medieval, derelict 17th c., new house c. 1639, purch. 1767, demolished before 1784, sold c. 1810); Driffield Hall, Gloucestershire (medieval, purch. early 17th c., add. early 17th c., sold 1803); Bruce Castle, Middlesex (medieval, rebuilt c. 1570, purch. 1626, add. first half 18th c., passed by mar. to an illegitimate daughter of 3 Baron who mar. a Townsend, see below)
Estates: A younger line at Docking Hall, Norfolk 3778 (E) 3758. The Barons of the second creation were near ruin c. 1800.
Peers: 1 peer 1660-67
Notes: The Hanger family ran into serious financial trouble early 19th c. See also Legh. 1, 2, and 3 Barons first cr. and three other Hares and 4 Baron of the sec. cr. in ODNB.

Townsend

Origins: Henry Hare 3 Baron Coleraine had an illegitimate daughter who married James Townsend, and he inherited the Middlesex estates of the family. The Townsends were London brewers in the 18th century. James Townsend was Lord Mayor of London 1772.

1. Joseph Townsend – Wallingford 1740-41 Westbury 1741-47 Wallingford 1747-54
2. Chauncey Townsend – Westbury 1748-68 Wigtown Bughs 1768-70
3. James Townsend – West Looe 1767-74 Calne 1782-87
4. Frederick Townsend – Stratford-on-Avon Div. Warwickshire 1886-92

Seats: Honington Hall, Warwickshire (purch. 1737, remod. c. 1745, sold 1924); Bruce Castle, Middlesex (medieval, rebuilt c. 1570, purch. by Hares 1626, passed by mar. to husband of the illegitimate daughter of the 3 Baron Coleraine (see Hare above) 1749, he purch. 1763, remod. c. 1770s, sold 1792, museum)
Estates: Bateman 3716 (E) 4441
Notes: One in ODNB.

Hare

Origins: The 1 Baron Coleraine was a descendent of a younger son of the Stow Bardolph Hares. **First MP 1604**. On the death of the 5 Bt in 1764 the estates passed to Edward Leigh of Iver, Buckinghamshire. That family received a baronetcy and took the name Hare (see Legh).

1. Sir Ralph Hare 1 Bt – Norfolk 1654 1656 Kings Lynn 1660 Norfolk 1661-72
2. Sir Thomas Hare 2 Bt – Norfolk 1685-87
3. Thomas Hare – Truro 1713-15

Seat: Stow Bardolph Hall, Norfolk (purch. 1553, built 1589, rebuilt 1796, rebuilt 1873, institutional use from 1940-80, demolished 1994, still own estate)
Estates: Bateman 11310 (E) 12044
Title: Baronets 1641-1764; 1818-1941; 1905-41

PAKINGTON [Perrott, Russell] *ENGLAND & WALES*

Baron Hampton (1874- UK)

Origins: Acquired land in Worcestershire in the 15th century. Additional estates purchased at the Dissolution by a lawyer and judge. **First MP 1515 (1539 for Worcestershire). One additional MP 1624**. The 1 Baron Hampton was the son of

William Russell of Powick Court by the daughter of Sir Herbert Pakington 5 Bt. He took the name Pakington in 1830.

1. Sir John Pakington 2 Bt – Worcestershire 1640 Aylesbury 1640-42 Worcestershire 1661-79
2. Sir John Pakington 3 Bt – Worcestershire 1685-87
3. Sir John Pakington 4 Bt – Worcestershire 1690-95 1698-1727
4. Sir Herbert Pakington 5 Bt – Worcestershire 1727-41
5. John Russell Pakington 1 Baron Hampton – Droitwich 1837-74

Seat: Westwood Park (House), Worcestershire (medieval, acq. by Pakingtons 16th c., rebuilt c. 1598, add. 1660-70, sold c. 1900); Harvington Hall, Worcestershire (medieval, inher. by mar. 1529, remod. c. 1560-75, add. mid-17th c., part demolished and remod. 1701, passed to Throckmortons in the 18th c.)
Estates: Bateman 5500 (E & W) 8837
Title: Baronet 1620-1830; 1846-
Peers: 4 peers 1874-1945
1 in Cabinet 1852 1858-59 1866-68
Notes: The Baldwin family left their estates (14th century gentry in Buckinghamshire) to the Pakingtons. **Two MPs 1453-1529**. The Pakingtons were granted the right to keep their hat on in the King's presence in 1529. Pakingtons were Roman Catholic until mid-17th century. 2, 3, and 4 Bts and 1 Baron and four others in ODNB.

<u>Perrott</u> (Perrot)

Origins: Minor gentry in 13th century Pembrokeshire. Sir John Perrot was a courtier under Edward VI, a soldier in Ireland, and Lord Deputy of Ireland 1584 (but not, as is sometimes asserted, an illegitimate son of Henry VIII). **First MP 1547 for Carmarthenshire. Two further MPs 1572-1628, both kts of the shire**. Estates passed by marriage of 1700 to the Pakingtons.

1. Sir Herbert Perrott – Weobley 1659 1660 Haverfordwest 1677-79

Seats: Wellington, Herefordshire (purch. 1650s, passed by mar. 1700 to Pakingtons, sold 1752); Haroldston (House), St. Issels, Pemborkeshire (held by Harolds pre-1200, 13th c. and later buildings, passed by mar. to Perrots in 1442, passed by mar. 1700 to Pakingtons, sold 1763 and demolished, ruins remained) (a Haroldston Hall also existed on the estate, but was not the main residence. It survived into the 20th c.).
Estates: Worth over £1,000 pa c. 1700.
Notes: The Jones family of Haroldston, Pembrokeshire were close kin whose estates passed to the Perrotts. **Four MPs 1553-71**. Three in ODNB.

PALK

Baron Haldon (1880-1939 UK)

Origins: Founder a nabob, son of a farmer, Governor of Madras 1763.

1. Sir Robert Palk 1 Bt – Ashburton 1767-68 Wareham 1768-74 Ashburton 1774-87
2. Sir Lawrence Palk 2 Bt – Ashburton 1787-96 Devon 1796-1812
3. Walter Palk – Ashburton 1796-1811
4. Sir Lawrence Palk 3 Bt – Ashburton 1818-31
5. Lawrence Palk 1 Baron Haldon – S. Devon 1854-68 E. Devon 1868-80

Seats: Manor House, Torquay, Devon (purch c. 1768, rebuilt 1864, sold 1906, institutional use); Haldon House, Devon (built c. 1735-40, purch. mid-18th c., demolished c. 1925)
Estates: Bateman 10109 (E) large urban rentals in Torquay, hard to estimate. Worth £15,000 pa c. 1800.
Title: Baronet 1782-1939
Peers: 4 peers 1880-1939
Notes: 1 Bt in ODNB.

PALMER I

Baron Palmer (1933- UK)

Origins: The founder of Huntley & Palmer of Reading mid-19th century was the son of a farmer. He mechanized the production of biscuits. Annual turnover of company in 1857 was £125,000, rising to £1,250,000 in 1897.

1. George Palmer – Reading 1878-85
2. George Palmer – Reading 1892-95 1898-1904
3. Sir Walter Palmer 1 Bt – Salisbury 1900-06

Seat: Marlston House, Berkshire (built 16th c., purch. c. 1896, rebuilt c. 1899, sold 1945, school)
Estates: Bateman 2001 (E) 2446. Added 2,800 acres later. Founder left an estate of nearly £1,000,000 in 1897.
Title: Baronet 1904-10; 1916-
Peer: 1 peer 1933-48
Notes: Three in ODNB.

PALMER II

Earl of Selborne (1822- UK)

Origins: Kt reign of Charles I. Merchants and shipowners in London in the 18th and 19th centuries. Owned plantations in the West Indies. Director of the Bank of England c. 1810. The 1 Baron, son of a clergyman, was a lawyer and Lord Chancellor 1869-72.

1. Archdale Palmer – Leicester 1695-98
2. George Palmer – S. Essex 1836-47
3. Roundell Palmer 1 Earl of Selborne – Plymouth 1847-57 Richmond 1861-72
4. William Palmer 2 Earl of Selborne – Petersfield Div. Hampshire 1885-92 W. Edinburgh 1892-95
5. Roundell Palmer 3 Earl of Selborne – Newton Div. Lancashire 1910-18 Aldershot Div. Hampshire 1918-40

Seats: Blackmoor House, Hampshire (purch. 1865, built 1869-72 and 1882-86, sold c. 1976); Nazeing Park, Essex (purch. and built 1780-1820, sold c. 1936); Temple Manor, Hampshire (medieval, demolished, purch. 1865 and rebuilt, still own); Wanlip Hall, Leicestershire (medieval, purch. 1622, rebuilt c. 1750, family departed 1933, demolished 1938, still own estate)
Estates: A bit under 2,000 acres. 1 Baron purchased Blackmoor for £155,000 in 1865 (*Country Life*, 156, pp. 554, 556) and spent £25,000 on building the house (Pevsner and Lloyd, *Hampshire and the Isle of Wight*, 111).
Titles: Baron Selborne 1872- UK; Viscount Wolmer 1882- UK
Peers: 3 peers 1872-1942 1940-45
2 in Cabinet 1872-74 1880-85 1900-05 1915-16
Notes: 1, 2, and 3 Earls and five others in ODNB.

PALMER III

Origins: An eminent lawyer in the 15th century acquired Carlton by marriage. **First MP 1433 for Leicestershire**.

1. Geoffrey Palmer 1 Bt – Stamford 1640-42 Ludgershall 1661
2. Sir Lewis Palmer 2 Bt – Higham Ferrers 1661-79
3. Edward Palmer – Peterborough 1666-67
4. Sir Geoffrey Palmer 3 Bt – Leicestershire 1708-13 1714-22
5. Sir Thomas Palmer 4 Bt – Leicestershire 1754-65
6. Sir John Palmer 5 Bt – Leicestershire 1765-80

Seats: Carlton (East Carlton) Park (Hall), Northamptonshire (medieval, acq. by mar. before 1441, rebuilt 1776-81, add. 1817-20, remod. 1868, sold c. 1933); Carlton Curlieu Hall, Leicestershire (medieval, rebuilt 1630s, purch. 1664, leased as farm house 18th c., became principal seat after 1933, still own)
Estates: Bateman 4120 (E) 7529
Title: Baronet 1660-
Notes: 1 Bt in ODNB.

PALMES

Origins: Held manorial land from c. 1200. **First MP 1510. Three additional MPs 1586-1643.**

1. William Palmes – Malton 1668-81 1689-1713
2. Francis Palmes – West Looe 1707-08 {Youghal 1715-19}

Seats: Lindley Hall, Yorkshire (acq. by mar. later 16th c., passed to the Stricklands of Sizergh by mar. c. 1713); Ashwell, Rutland (purch. c. 1513, sold 1699); Naburn Hall, Yorkshire (acq. 1226, sold 1974)
Estates: The Naburn line held 1,100 acres in 1972.
Notes: A senior branch at Naburn Hall, Yorkshire remained Roman Catholic until 1874. Estates of the Lindley Hall/Ashwell line were sold to pay debts in the early 18th century. Two in ODNB.

PARKER I

Earl of Macclesfield (1721- GB)

Origins: A younger son of a gentry family in the 17th century was a lawyer; his son was Chief Justice of the Queen's Bench 1710 and Lord Chancellor 1718.

1. Thomas Parker 1 Earl of Macclesfield – Derby 1705-10
2. George Parker 2 Earl of Macclesfield – Wallingford 1722-27
3. Thomas Parker 3 Earl of Macclesfield – Newcastle-under-Lyme 1747-54 Oxfordshire 1755-61 Rochester 1761-64
4. George Parker – Yarmouth (IoW) 1769-79 Tregony 1774-80
5. George Parker 4 Earl of Macclesfield – New Woodstock 1777-84 Minehead 1790-95
6. Thomas Parker 6 Earl of Macclesfield – Oxfordshire 1837-41
7. Francis Parker – Henley Div. Oxfordshire 1886-95

Seats: Shirburn Castle, Oxfordshire (medieval castle, purch. 1716, add. 1716-25, remod. 1830 and 1873, still own); Eynsham Hall, Oxfordshire (built 18th c., purch. 1805, sold.

c. 1825, demolished 1904 and rebuilt, hotel); Woodbury Hall, Cambridgeshire (old house, acq. by mar. 1746, sold 1803, rebuilt)
Estates: Bateman 14553 (E) 17937. Worth £3,000 pa in 1725.
Title: Baron Parker 1716- GB
Peers: 7 peers 1716-1896 1909-45
1 Ld Lt 19th
1 in Cabinet 1718-25
Notes: 1, 2 and 4 Earls and four others in ODNB.

PARKER II [Long]

Parker

Origins: Established in Suffolk since the 15th century. Through heiresses held Erwarton Hall since the late 13th century. **First MP 1601 for Suffolk. One additional MP 1640-48 for the county**.

1. Henry Parker – Orford 1679-81
2. Sir Philip Parker 1 Bt – Harwich 1679-81 Sandwich 1685-87
3. Sir Philip Parker 3 Bt – Harwich 1715-34

Seat: Erwarton Hall, Suffolk (acq. 13th c., built c. 1549-75, sold 1775)
Title: Baronet 1661-1741

Long

Origins: Clothiers who held Whaddon since the mid-16th century. **First MP 1571. One other MP 1654**. On the death of Sir Walter Long his estates passed 1729 to his nephew, Sir Philip Parker 3 Bt, who took the additional name Long.

1. Sir Walter Long 2 Bt – Bath 1679-81

Seat: Whaddon, Wiltshire (acq. 1555, built 16th c., passed to Parkers by mar. 1729, passed to Longs of Wraxall 1748 – see Long I)
Estates: Worth £4,000 pa in 1710.
Title: Baronet 1661-1710
Notes: See Long I. 1 Bt in ODNB.

PARKER III [Holford]

Earl of Morley (1815- UK)

Origins: Descended from medieval barons. One was Standard Bearer for Richard III. **First MP 1539, Hertfordshire.**

1. George Parker – Plympton Erle 1690 Plymouth 1695-98
2. John Parker 1 Baron Boringdon – Bodmin 1761-62 Devon 1762-84
3. Montagu Parker – S. Devon 1835-41

Seats: Saltram, Devon (built 16th c., remod. late 17th c., purch. 1712, rebuilt 1743-49 and 1768-72, NT 1957); Boringdon Hall, Devon (old house, acq. by mar. 1582, remod. 1587, add. 1740, family moved to Saltram 1750, decayed, became a farm house, donated NT 1957, sold, hotel, fire 1989)
Estates: Bateman 4238 (E) 8209 and 12464 (I & E) 5199
Title: Baron Boringdon 1784- GB
Peers: 5 peers 1784-88 1793-1945
1 Ld Lt 20th
Notes: 10, 11, and 13 Barons of earlier creation and 1, 2 and 3 Earls and three others in ODNB.

Parker

Origins: The senior line of the family (broke off in the 16th century). Cadet of old Devon family who became merchants in London in the 16th and 17th centuries. A lawyer built up the estate in the 1660s. Then five generations of naval officers (four admirals).

1. Sir Henry Parker 2 Bt – Evesham 1679-81 1685-87 1689-90 1695-1700
2. Hugh Parker – Evesham 1701-08
3. Sir Hyde Parker 8 Bt – W. Suffolk 1832-35

Seats: Melford Hall, Suffolk (built 1550s-60s, purch. 1786, fire 1942, restored, NT 1960); Honington Hall, Warwickshire (purch. c. 1660-70, built c. 1685, sold 1737)
Estates: Bateman 3482 (E) 4880. Admiral Sir Hyde Parker was said to have made £200,000 in prize money.
Title: Baronet 1681-
Notes: 5 Bt and two others in ODNB.

Holford

Origins: A gentry family. An 18th century Master in Chancery. His son, the first MP, also a lawyer. Became millionaires due legal fees and to investment in the New River Company that supplied London's water. The 4 Earl of Morely succeeded to part of the Holford estates in 1926.

1. George Holford – Bossiney 1803-06 Lostwithiel 1807-12 Dungannon 1812-18
2. Robert Holford – E. Gloucestershire 1854-72

Seat: Westonbirt House, Gloucestershire (built late 16th c., acq. by mar. 1665 from the Crewe family (acq. 1632), demolished 1818, rebuilt 1823, rebuilt 1863-72, passed to 4 Earl of Morley in 1926 who sold it to a school)
Estates: Bateman 16319 (E) 21277. Worth a million pounds in 1838. (Girouard, *The Victorian Country House*, 423). The art collection alone at Westonbirt sold for over £400,000 in 1927.
Notes: Westonbirt cost £200,000 to build in the 1860s, a titanic sum. (Kingsley, *The Country Houses of Gloucestershire*, III, 256). Extinct in the male line 1924. Estates sold and wealth divided among a number of heirs. Two in ODNB.

PARKER IV

Origins: Wool merchants in Sussex in the 13th, 14th, and 15th centuries. **First MP 1371. Eight MPs 1417-1656, first for the county in 1597**.

1. George Parker – Seaford 1659 1660
2. Sir Robert Parker 1 Bt – Hastings 1679-81
3. Sir George Parker 2 Bt – Sussex 1705-08 1710-13

Seat: Ratton, Sussex (acq. by mar. mid-15th c., passed out of family by mar. first half 18th c., sold)
Title: Baronet 1674-1750
Notes: Represented Hastings five times between 1371 and 1681. Two in ODNB.

PARKER V [Stringer]

Parker

Origins: Minor gentry from 13th century leased land near Brownsholme by 1380 and purchased as a seat by the 15th century. Anthony Parker succeeded in 1706 to part of the estates of Sir Thomas Stringer of Durrants.

1. Anthony Parker – Clitheroe 1689-93
2. Christopher Parker – Clitheroe 1708-13
3. John Parker – Clitheroe 1780-82

Seats: Brownsholme Hall, Yorkshire (acq. in medieval period, built 1507, remod. 1604, add. early 18th c. and 1754, remod. 1805-08, sold from one branch of family to another 1820, still own); Bradick Hall, Lancashire (acq. early 17th c., sold 1723); Alkincoats Hall, Lancashire (acq. by ancestors 13th c., purch. c. 1700, built c. 1575, remod. 1720, sold 1921, demolished 1957)
Estates: Bateman 3106 (E) 3446
Notes: One in ODNB.

Stringer

Origins: First to emerge was a lawyer in the 17th century. Judge of King's Bench 1688. Kt 1669.

1. Sir Thomas Stringer – Clitheroe 1675-81
2. Thomas Stringer – Clitheroe 1698-1706
3. William Stringer – Bramber 1695-98

Seat: Durrants, Middlesex (purch. 1673 for £8,900, sold c. 1723, demolished 1910)

PARKHURST

Origins: The first MP was the grandson of a mercer, related to a Bishop of Durham, son of a Lord Mayor of London. The family fortune was enhanced by John Parkhurst MP 1678, a government official. **First MP 1625. Two further MPs 1625-59.**

1. John Parkhurst – Durham 1678-79 Northamptonshire 1679-81 Brackley 1689-90 Northamptonshire 1690-95 1698-1701

Seat: Catesby (Abbey, Priory) House, Northamptonshire (medieval, remod. mid-16th c., purch. 1664, add. later 17th c., passed to Baxters by mar., sold 1847, demolished 1863)
Estates: Worth £400 pa in the 1660s, £3,000 pa by the 1730s.
Notes: One in ODNB.

PARKYNS [James]

Baron Rancliffe (1795-1850 I)

Origins: The Parkyns rose through the law in the reign of Elizabeth I. **First MP 1584. Another MP 1597 and a probable kinsman 1597.** The 1 Baron Rancliffe married Elizabeth James, daughter and heiress of Sir Edward James 2 and last Bt of Park Farm Place, Eltham, Kent. The 1 James Bt was of humble birth, a soldier in the East India Company service. Chairman of the East India Company and a nabob.

1. Sir William James 1 Bt – West Looe 1774-83
2. Thomas Parkyns 1 Baron Rancliffe – Stockbridge 1784-90 Leicester 1790-1800
3. George Parkyns 2 Baron Rancliffe – Minehead 1806-07 Nottingham 1812-20 1826-30

Seats: Bunny Hall (Park), Nottinghamshire (acq. by mar. 1603 by Parkyns, rebuilt 1723, remod. 1826-35, sold 1910); Park Farm Place (Eltham), Kent (acq. by mar. 1792, sold 19th c.)
Estates: Worth £21,000 pa c. 1800. In Bateman under Forteath 3923 (E) 5949 – the 2 Baron left estates to his mistress. (Fisher, *History of Parliament*, VI, 642)
Peer: {1 peer 1795-1800}
Titles: Baronet 1681-1850 (Parkyns); 1778-92 (James)
Notes: 1 Bt and two others in ODNB.

PARNELL [Hayes] *IRELAND*

Baron Congleton (1841- UK)

Origins: Founder a mercer and draper in Cheshire in the mid-17th century. At Congleton c. 1620. Purchased Irish estates in the 1660s-70s. Judge in Ireland 1722. Sheriff 1753.

1. John Parnell – {Granard 1713-22}
2. Sir John Parnell 1 Bt – {Maryborough 1761-82}
3. Sir John Parnell 2 Bt – {Bangor 1767-68 Innistiogue 1777-82 Queen's County 1783-1800} 1801
4. Henry Parnell 1 Baron Congleton – {Maryborough 1797-1800} Portarlington 1802 Queen's County 1802 1806-32 Dundee 1833-41
5. William Parnell-Hayes – Wicklow 1817-21
6. Charles Stewart Parnell – County Meath 1875-80 Cork 1880-91
7. John Parnell – S. Meath 1895-1900

Seats: Rathleague House, Queen's County (acq. c. 1670-80, resident in 19th c.); Anneville House, Westmeath (built c. 1745, acq. 19th c.); Avondale, Wicklow (built 17th c., rebuilt 1779, passed by mar. to Parnells 1810, sold 20th c. to government)
Estates: Bateman 6247 (I) 4435 and 2900 (I) 2070
Title: Baronet 1766-
Peers: 1841-42 1852-1932
Notes: Charles Stewart Parnell was one of the great leaders of Irish nationalism of the 19th century despite being Protestant and Ascendancy bred. 2 Bt and 1 and 2 Barons and five others in ODNB.

Hayes

Origins: Emerged 18th century. Sheriff 1773.

1. Samuel Hayes – {Wicklow 1783-90 Maryborough 1790-95}

Seat: Avondale (Ballytrasna, Hayesville), Wicklow (acq. and built late 17th c., rebuilt 1779, passed by mar. to Parnells 1810)
Estates: 4,500 acres in 1795

PARSONS

Origins: London brewers in the 17th and 18th centuries. Lord Mayor of London 1730. The first MP was a successful victualling agent.

1. Sir John Parsons – Reigate 1685-87 1689-98 1701-17
2. John Parsons – Reigate 1690-98
3. Humphrey Parsons – Harwich 1722-27 London 1727-41
4. Henry Parsons – Lostwithiel 1724-27 Maldon 1727-39

Seat: The Priory, Reigate, Surrey (medieval, rebuilt as house 1541, purch. 1703, remod. c. 1704, sold 1766)
Notes: One in ODNB.

PARTHERICH (Partridge)

Origins: Kentish gentry in the 16th century, steward for large landowner. **First MP 1563. Another MP 1640.**

1. Edward Partherich – Cambridgeshire 1679

Seats: Bridge, Kent (acq. later 16th c., sold 1638); Littleport, Cambridgeshire
Estates: Worth £1,300 pa c. 1660.

PARTINGTON

Baron Doverdale (1917-49 UK)

Origins: 1 Baron was a paper manufacturer.

1. Oswald Partington 2 Baron Doverdale – High Peak Div. Derbyshire 1900-10 Shipley Div. W. R. Yorkshire 1915-18

Seat: Westwood Park, Worcestershire (built c. 1598, add. 1660-70, purch. c. 1900, sold c. 1950, flats)
Peers: 3 peers 1917-45

PASTON

Earl of Yarmouth (1679-1732 E)

Origins: A medieval judge (1378-1444), probably the son of a yeoman, was the founder of the family, and marriage to heiresses helped expand the estates. (Bennett, *The Pastons and Their England*, 1-2.) **First MP 1460 for Norfolk. Seven additional MPs 1467-1563, three for the county.**

1. Robert Paston 1 Earl of Yarmouth – Thetford 1660 Castle Rising 1661-73
2. William Paston 2 Earl of Yarmouth – Norwich 1678-81
3. Robert Paston – Norwich 1685-87
4. Charles Paston Lord Paston – Thetford 1699-1700

Seats: Oxnead Hall, Norfolk (purch. 1423, built later 16th c., add. 1678, sold 1757, demolished c. 1809); Paston Hall, Norfolk (acq. 15th c., sold 1757); Barningham Hall, Norfolk (built 1612, sold c. 1756); Horton Court, Gloucestershire (medieval house, rebuilt c. 1520, belonged to a Roman Catholic branch of the family, acq. 1550, sold c. 1800, NT 1946)
Estates: Worth £5,594 pa in the 1640s.
Titles: Baron Paston and Viscount Yarmouth 1673-1732; Baronet 1641-1732
Peers: 2 peers 1673-1732
1 Ld Lt 17th
Notes: The family was in dire financial straits in the years before the extinction of the title. (Cannon, *Aristocratic Century*, 69) Extinct in the male line 1732 after which all property was sold. The Paston family has an entry and the 1 and 2 Earls and nine other members of the family in the ODNB.

PAUL *IRELAND*

Origins: Went to Ireland as a soldier with Ireton and Cromwell in the 1640s and gained estates. Sheriff 1708.

1. Jeffrey Paul – {New Ross 1711-13 County Carlow 1713-14 Baltinglass 1715-21}
2. Jeffrey Paul – {County Carlow 1725-30}
3. Christmas Paul – {Waterford 1741-48}
4. Robert Paul – {Lismore 1791-96}

Seats: Ballyglan, Waterford (built late 18th c., sold 1963); Tinoran, Wicklow; Paulville, Carlow
Estates: Bateman 5246 (I) 3468. Worth £1,638 pa in 1712.
Title: Baronet 1794-1961
Notes: Extinct in male line 1961.

PAUNCEFORT (Pauncefoote, Pauncefote) [Smith]

<u>Baron Pauncefote</u> (1899-1902 UK)

Origins: Rose during the military campaigns in Wales under Edward I. Descent can be traced from 1199, when they were already at Hasfield. **First MP 1413 for Gloucestershire. One additional MP 1447 also for the county**. They fell on hard times but fortunes were revived by Edward Pauncefort MP (1698-1705), Paymaster of the Army. Baron Paunceforte (1899-1902) was the great-grandson of Abel Smith of East Stoke, Nottinghamshire (see Smith I). He changed his name to Pauncefote on inheriting Preston Court from his cousin Sir George Pauncefote-Bromley (previously Smith). The 1 Smith Bt married the daughter and heiress of William Howe by Elizabeth, daughter and heiress of William Pauncefote of Preston Court (d. 1710).

1. Edward Pauncefort – Malmesbury 1698-1705
2. Tracy Pauncefort – Great Bedwyn 1707

Seats: Hasfield, Gloucestershire (acq. by c.1200, sold 1598); Preston Court, Gloucestershire (built late 16th c., acq. c. 1700, sold 1820)
Peer: 1 peer 1899-1902
Notes: 1 Baron in ODNB.

PEACHEY [Knight, Lewknor, May]

Baron Selsey (1794-1838 GB)

Origins: Rose as London merchants. Purchased estates in Sussex 1672.

1. Sir Henry Peachey 1 Bt – Sussex 1701-02 1708-10 Midhurst 1736-37
2. Bulstrode Peachey Knight – Midhurst 1722-36
3. Sir John Peachey 2 Bt – Midhurst 1738-44
4. Sir John Peachey 3 Bt – Midhurst 1744-61
5. James Peachey 1 Baron Selsey – Seaford 1755-68
6. John Peachey 2 Baron Selsey – St. Germans 1776-80 New Shoreham 1780-90
7. William Peachey – Yarmouth (IoW) 1797-1802 Taunton 1826-30

Seats: Newgrove (New Grove), Sussex (acq. by mar. c. 1670 and then rebuilt, remod. 18th c., sold 19th c.); Burghope, Herefordshire (built early 17th c., purch. c. 1770, later passed out of the family 1872, demolished); West Dean, Sussex (acq. by mar. from the May/Knight family 1738, sold 1872); Ebernoe House, Sussex (acq. and built late 18th c., descendents owned at least until 1945)
Estates: Bateman 2760 (E) 2435 and see Knight.
Title: Baronet 1736-1838
Peers: 3 peers 1794-1838
Notes: The last Peachey died in 1872.

Knight

Origins: Yeomen at Chawton since the reign of Edward II. Purchased the manor 1551. **First MP 1593**. The descendents of Thomas Knight May succeeded to the Peachey estates by inheritance from his father's cousin, Elizabeth Knight, widow of William Woodward Knight and Bulstrode Peachey Knight.

1. Sir Richard Knight – Lymington 1678-79
2. Christopher Knight – Arundel 1698-1700
3. William Woodward Knight – Midhurst 1713-21
4. Thomas Knight May – Canterbury 1734-41
5. Thomas Knight – New Romney 1761-68 Kent 1774-80

Seats: Chawton House, Hampshire (old house, Knights purch. 1551, rebuilt late 16th c., add. c. 1630, still own estate but a long lease for the house sold to a trust 1993); West Dean, Sussex (acq. by mar. from Lewknors 1706, passed briefly to the Mays and then to the Peacheys by mar. 1738); Godmersham Park, Kent (owned by Broadnax family

since 16th c., inher. May estates 1726 and took name May, took the add. name Knight on inher. estates 1738, rebuilt 1732, passed to Austens by mar. 1794, sold early 20th c.)
Estates: Bateman 5044 (E) 4291. Estate stood at 3,000 acres in 1980s.
Notes: Thomas Brodnax owned Godmersham in the 16th century. In the early 18th century another Thomas Brodnax inherited estates from the Mays and the Knights, changing his name from Brodnax to May to Knight. In 1794 he left it to a distant cousin of his mother, Edward Austen, the brother of Jane Austen. (*Country Life*, 97, p. 376ff). For Austen family see entry under that name.

May

Origins: The first prominent May was a merchant tailor who purchased landed estates in the 1580s. Chancellor of the Duchy of Lancaster 1618, Stuart courtiers. **First MP 1640**. Thomas Knight succeeded to the estates of his mother's cousin Sir Thomas May in 1718 and took the additional name May. A May son established a line in Ireland at Mayfield, Waterford (see May).

1. Baptist May – Midhurst 1670-79 New Windsor 1690 Thetford 1690-95
2. Sir Richard May – Chichester 1673-79 1685-87
3. Sir Algernon May – New Windsor 1689-90
4. Sir Thomas May – Chichester 1689-95 1701

Seat: Rawmere, Sussex (purch. 1581, passed to Broadnax family 1718 by mar. who took name May, passed to Knights by mar. 1726 who took the name May and then in 1738 Knight, sold 1777)
Notes: Two in ODNB.

Lewknor

Origins: Sussex gentry since the 12th century. **First MP 1331. Twenty further MPs 1335-1644, nine kts of the shire**. William Wooodward Knight was the son of Edward Woodward and the daughter and heiress of Sir Charles Lewknor of West Dean. He succeeded to the Lewknor estates in 1707 (see above).

1. Sir John Lewknor – Midhurst 1661-69
2. John Lewknor – Sussex 1679 Midhurst 1679-81 1685-87 1689-1705

Seat: West Dean, Sussex (acq. 1558, passed by mar. to Knights 1706)
Notes: Sir John Lewknor MP succeeded to the Mynne estates by mar. **One MP 1621.** Two in ODNB.

PEARSON

Viscount Cowdray (1917- UK)

Origins: The 1 Viscount was an engineer, involved in the petroleum business, and a contractor on a global scale. His father was a building contractor, and he joined the family business. He made a great fortune.

1. Weetman Pearson 1 Viscount Cowdray – Colchester 1895-1910
2. Weetman Pearson 2 Viscount Cowdray – Eye Div. Suffolk 1906-18

Seats: Cowdray Park, Sussex (old house a ruin after 1793, new house built mid-19th c., purch. 1908, for sale 2011); Parham, Sussex (built 1577, purch. 1922, still own); Dunecht (Dun Echt), Aberdeenshire (add. c. 1866-71, purch. 1908, add. c. 1910, still own)
Estates: 1 Viscount left £4,000,000 plus landed property in 1927. Worth £352,000,000 in 1990 with 17,000 acres in Sussex and 60,000 in Scotland. The Scottish estate continued to grow larger. Viscount Cowdray owned 93,600 acres in 2001.
Titles: Baron Cowdray 1910- UK; Baronet 1894-
Peers: 3 peers 1910-45
Notes: 1 and 3 Viscounts and one other in ODNB.

PEASE [Aldam, Ward]

Baron Gainford (1917- UK)

Origins: The family began as yeomen farmers in the 18th century. They entered the Yorkshire woolen industry and established great coal and iron interests, entered banking, and became involved in railway development, financing Stephenson's locomotive works and the Stockton and Darlington railway in 1819. (Scott, *Who Rules Britain*, 74).

1. Joseph Pease – S. Durham 1832-41
2. Henry Pease – S. Durham 1857-65
3. Sir Joseph Pease 1 Bt – S. Durham 1865-85 Barnard Castle Div. Durham 1885-1903
4. Arthur Pease – Whitby 1880-85 Darlington 1895-98
5. Sir Alfred Pease 2 Bt – York 1885-92 Cleveland Div. N. R. Yorkshire 1897-1902
6. Henry Pease – Cleveland Div. N. R. Yorkshire 1885-96
7. Joseph Pease 1 Baron Gainford – Tyneside Div. Northumberland 1892-1900 Saffron Walden Div. Essex 1901-10 Rotherham Div. W. R. Yorkshire 1910-16
8. Herbert Pease 1 Baron Daryngton – Darlington 1898-1923

Seats: Southend, Durham (purch. 1st half 19th c., engulfed in Darlington urban growth); Hutton Hall, Yorkshire (built 1865-68, add. 1871, derelict 1980s); Stanhope Castle, Durham (medieval, add. 17th c., new house 1798, add. 1875, family departed 1939, school from 1940); Headlam Hall, Durham (built 16th c., rebuilt 19th c., purch. 1912, sold 1940s, hotel)
Estates: Bateman 4749 (E) 6113 and 2500 (E) 2075
Titles: Baron Daryngton 1923- UK; Baronet 1882- ; 1920-
Peers: 2 peers 1917-45 1923-45
1 in Cabinet 1910-15
Notes: Joseph Pease MP 1832 was the first Quaker elected to Parliament. The family bank collapsed in 1902 with severe consequences for some members of the family. 1 Baron Wardington and 1 Baron Gainford and eleven others in ODNB.

Baron Wardington (1936- UK)

Origins: A cadet line founded by an uncle of Joseph Pease MP.

1. William Pease – Darlington 1923-26

Seats: Manor House, Wardington, Oxfordshire (built 16th c., remod. 1905-14, purch. 1917, remod. 1917-30, fire 2004, restored, still own); Nether Grange, Northumberland (acq. later 19th c., sold before 1945, hotel); Pendower Hall, Northumberland (acq. and built 1867, sold 1920, institutional use)
Peer: 1 peer 1936-45

Aldam

Origins: Thomas Pease, a younger brother of Joseph Pease of Southend married Susannah Benson, granddaughter of Thomas Aldam of Warmsworth. His grandson took the name Aldam. The Aldams claimed ownership of Warmsworth since the medieval period, certainly by the 16th century.

1. William Pease Aldam – Leeds 1841-47

Seats: Warmsworth, Yorkshire (Aldams acq. by 16th c., acq. by mar. by Peases 1807); Healey Hall, Northumberland (old house, add. 17th c., acq. by mar. 1882, rebuilt 1834, still own); Frickley Hall, Yorkshire (built mid-18th c., purch. 1844, remod. 19th c., still own); Hooton Pagnell Hall, Yorkshire (acq. by mar. c. 1878 see below, remod. 1894-1904 and 1914-20, flats 1970, still own); Ederline, Argyllshire (built 18th c., add. 1869-70, purch. 1899, demolished 1966/1983, rebuilt 1964, still own)
Estates: Bateman 4944 (E) 7403

Notes: The Ormstons (18th-century bankers and estate stewards in Newcastle) purchased Healy Hall in 1716 for £22,000. They left it to their cousins the Aldams in 1882.

Ward (Warde)

Origins: The Wards were merchants, Lord Mayor of London 1681 and 1718, descended from Yorkshire gentry. Governor of the Bank of England 1701, Director of the East India Company 1703. William Pease Aldham of Frickley and Warmsworth married Sarah Ward 1878 and took the additional name Ward.

1. Sir Patience Warde – Pontefract 1679 1681 London 1689-90
2. Sir John Ward – Bletchingley 1701-08 London 1708-10 1715-22 Dunwich 1722-26

Seats: Tanshelf Court, Yorkshire (acq. 16th c., resident 17th c., engulfed by expansion of Pontefract 19th c.); Hooton Pagnell Hall, Yorkshire (medieval, add. 16th c., remod. 17th c., purch. 1704, add. 1787, passed by mar. to Aldams later 19th c. see above)
Estates: Bateman 2416 (E) 3767. Worth c. £1,600 pa in 1800.
Notes: Male line extinct 1868. Three in ODNB.

PEDLEY [Deverell]

Origins: Founded by a lawyer who rose into the gentry by marriage and office. High Sheriff 1620s.

1. Sir Nicholas Pedley – Huntingdonshire 1656 1659 Huntingdon 1660 Huntingdonshire 1673-79 Huntingdon 1679
2. John Pedley – Huntingdon 1706-08
3. John Pedley – Hindon 1802-06 Saltash 1808-08
4. Robert (Pedley) Deverell – Saltash 1802-06

Seats: Abbotsleigh, Huntingdonshire (acq. lease 1622); Tetworth Hall, Huntingdonshire (purch. 1705, built 1710, sold 1726, repurch. 1759, passed to Foleys by mar. 1827, sold soon afterwards)
Notes: Male line of Pedleys extinct 1727. One in ODNB.

PEEL (Peele)

Earl Peel (1929- UK)

Origins: The common ancestor of the family was Robert Peele, a dealer in linen and cotton cloth. He had five sons who established landed families. The most prominent of these was that of the third son, Sir Robert Peel 1 Bt of Drayton Manor, a great industrialist in the later 18th century who invested heavily in land. He had 15,000 employees. Members of the family remained active in the management of textile mills into the middle of the 19th century. The 1 Earl Peel married a linoleum heiress in Lancashire and inherited the business, which the family managed in the 20th century.

1. Sir Robert Peel 1 Bt – Tamworth 1790-1820
2. Sir Robert Peel 2 Bt – Cashel 1809-12 Chippenham 1812-17 University of Oxford 1817-29 Westbury 1829-30 Tamworth 1830-50
3. William Peel – Bossiney 1817-18 Tamworth 1818-30 Yarmouth (IoW) 1830-31 University of Cambridge 1831-32 Tamworth 1835-37 1847
4. Jonathan Peel – Norwich 1826-30 Huntingdon 1831-37
5. Lawrence Peel – Cockermouth 1827-30
6. Edmund Peel – Newcastle-under-Lyme 1831-32 1835-37
7. Sir Frederick Peel – Leominster 1849-52 Bury 1852-57 1859-65
8. Sir Robert Peel 3 Bt – Tamworth 1850-80 Huntingdon 1884-85 Blackburn 1885-86
9. John Peel – Tamworth 1863-68 1871-72
10. Arthur Peel 1 Viscount Peel – Warwick 1865-85 Warwick & Leamington 1885-95
11. William Peel 1 Earl Peel – S. Div. Manchester 1900-06 Taunton 1909-12
12. Robert Peel – Woodbridge Div. Suffolk 1910-20
13. George Peel – Spalding Div. Lincolnshire 1917-18
14. Sir Sidney Peel – Uxbridge Div. Middlesex 1918-22

Seats: Drayton Manor, Staffordshire (built 1824, contents sold for huge sums from 1899, sold 1926 and demolished – Worsley, *England's Lost Houses*, 45-47); Hyning Hall (The Hyning), Lancashire (built 19th c., acq. c. 1910?, house sold 1969, still own estate)
Estates: Worth £40,000 pa in 1850. Bateman 9923 (E) 24532 and at Trenant Park, Cornwall & Peelfold, Lancashire 2415 (E) 2468; at Taliarvis, Carmarthenshire 3197 (W) 3113; at Bryn-y-Pys, Flintshire (demolished 1956) & Llandrinio Hall, Montgomeryshire 5777 (W) 11187; at Knowlemere, Lancashire 3019 (E) 7086; at Denant, Pembrokeshire 2460 (W) 2159 (purch. 1844, sold 1894); Hampton Manor, Warwickshire (built 1855, sold 1919). Rubinstein – Lawrence Peel left £250,000 in probate 1827, the 1 Bt left above one million, perhaps 1.5 million pounds in 1830, and Jonathan Peel left £600,000 in 1834.
Titles: Viscount Peel 1895- UK; Baronet 1800- ; 1936-38
Peers: 3 peers 1895-1932 1937-45
4 in Cabinet 1812-18 1822-30 1834-35 1841-46 1858-59 1861-65 1866-67 1921-29 1931
Notes: 1, 2, and 3 Bts and 1 Viscount and 1 Earl and eight others in ODNB.

PELHAM [Anderson, Clinton, Cressett, Holles, Papillon]

Duke of Newcastle (1694-1711 E; 1715-56 GB; 1756-1988 GB)

Origins: The Pelhams rose from relatively humble origins (the first notable one was the son of a coroner in Sussex) in the 14th century. Became very rich in one generation due to royal favor. Sir John Pelham captured King Jean of France at the Battle of Poitiers in 1356. The various branches shared a common descent from Sir William Pelham, whose younger son was the ancestor of the Earls of Yarborough. His great-grandson, the 2 Bt of Laughton, Sussex, was the ancestor of the Pelhams of Crowhurst and Cound and grandfather of the 1 Baron Pelham and a younger brother of Henry Pelham of Stanmer, grandfather of the 1 Earl of Chichester. The 1 Baron Pelham married Lady Grace Holles, daughter of the 3 Earl of Clare and sister of the last Duke of Newcastle-upon-Tyne (1694-1711) of the second creation (the first creation for the Cavendishes was extinct in 1680). (The wife of the Earl of Clare, Margaret Cavendish, was co-heiress of the 2 Duke.) The son of the Holles-Pelham match was created Duke of Newcastle-upon-Tyne in 1715. He had no direct heir. His brother's daughter, Catherine Pelham, married the 7 Earl of Lincoln (Clinton), who succeeded by special remainder to a newly reconfigured Dukedom of Newcastle-under-Lyne in 1756 as 2 Duke. The Clintons rose from obscure origins in the 12th century and one became Lord Chamberlain and Treasurer to Henry I. Barons from 1299, but not consistently summoned to Parliament. **First MP 1301 for Warwickshire. Five further MPs 1397-1610, two kts of the shire.**

1. George Clinton – Saltash 1754-61
2. Sir Henry Clinton – Boroughbridge 1772-74 Newark 1774-84 Launceston 1790-94
3. Henry Pelham-Clinton Earl of Lincoln – Aldborough 1772-74 Nottinghamshire 1774-78
4. Thomas Pelham-Clinton 3 Duke of Newcastle – Westminster 1774-80 East Retford 1781-94
5. Lord John Pelham-Clinton – East Retford 1778-81
6. Sir William Clinton – East Retford 1794-96 Boroughbridge 1806-18 Newark 1818-29
7. Henry Fynes-Clinton – Aldborough 1806-26
8. Sir Henry Clinton – Boroughbridge 1808-18
9. Clinton Fynes-Clinton – Aldborough 1826-32
10. Henry Pelham-Clinton 5 Duke of Newcastle – S. Nottinghamshire 1832-46 Falkirk District 1846-51
11. Lord Charles Pelham-Clinton – Sandwich 1852-57
12. Lord Robert Pelham-Clinton – N. Nottinghamshire 1852-65
13. Henry Pelham-Clinton 6 Duke of Newcastle – Newark 1857-59
14. Lord Edward Pelham-Clinton – N. Nottinghamshire 1865-68
15. Lord Arthur Pelham-Clinton – Newark 1865-68

Seats: Clumber Park, Nottinghamshire (acq. 17th c., park enclosed and lodge built 1707, built 1760-67, add. 1829, fire 1879, rebuilt 1880s, fire 1912, demolished 1938, park sold to NT 1948); Nottingham Castle, Nottinghamshire (medieval, leased 1641, demolished 1651, purch. and new house built c. 1662-79, burned 1831, restored 1875 and leased as a museum); Ranby Hall, Nottinghamshire (built late 18th c., purch. 1828, sold later 19th c.); Claremont, Surrey (built 1708, purch. 1714, add. c. 1714, sold 1768, school 1931); Worksop Manor, Nottinghamshire (rebuilt 1767, purch. 1839 for £370,000, part demolished, sold 1890); Tattersall Castle, Lincolnshire (built 1231, new house c. 1433, acq. 1531 by Clintons, passed to Fortescues 1693, ruin, NT); Hope Castle (Blayney Castle), Monagahan (built 17th c., inher. from Hopes 1861, sold 1916, now a convent); Oatlands Park, Surrey (acq. 1716, sold 1788)
Estates: Bateman 40124 (E) 77815
Titles: Earl of Lincoln 1572- E; Baron Pelham 1706-68 E; Viscount Houghton 1714-68 GB; Earl of Clare 1715-68 GB
Peers: 14 peers 1660-93 1705-28 1706-12 1712-68 1741-95 1806-79 1885-1945
7 Lds Lt 18th, 19th
2 in Cabinet 1717-62 1765-66
5 KG 18th, 19th
Notes: The 6 Duke of Newcastle married the Hope heiress to The Deepdene (see Hope). 1 (Pelham – Lyme), 2, 4 and 5 Dukes and eight Clintons and six Pelhams in ODNB.

Marquess of Clare (Duke of Newcastle) (1694-1711 E)

Origins: William Holles was a baker in London in the 15th century. His son was a mercer who made a fortune, Lord Mayor of London 1539. He purchased estates in Nottinghamshire. **First MP 1553 for Nottinghamshire. Three additional MPs 1584-1626**. Several branches of the family are included in this entry. The 4 Earl of Clare married the daughter of the 2 Duke of Newcastle (see Cavendish) and succeeded to estates worth perhaps £40,000 pa in 1711. He was created Duke of Newcastle in his own right. His sister Grace was his heiress, and her marriage to the 1 Baron Pelham brought these great estates to that family (see above).

1. Denzil Holles 1 Baron Holles – Mitchell 1624 Dorchester 1628 1640-48 1660-61
2. Gervase Holles – Great Grimsby 1640-42 1661-72
3. Francis Holles 2 Baron Houghton – Lostwithiel 1647 Wiltshire 1654 Dorchester 1679-80
4. Gilbert Holles 3 Earl of Clare – Nottinghamshire 1660
5. Sir Frescheville Holles – Great Grimsby 1667-72
6. John Holles 1 Duke of Newcastle – Nottinghamshire 1689

Seats: Houghton (Haughton), Nottinghamshire (purch. 1537, family abandoned early 18th c., decayed into a ruin); Dorchester Priory (Friary), Dorset (acq. by mar. of 1626, sold 1787)
Estates: Worth £4,000 pa in 1637. 1 Duke spent £200,000 purchasing land in the 1690s gained through inheritances.
Titles: Baron Houghton 1624-1711 E; Earl of Clare 1624-1711 E; Baron Holles 1661-94 E; Duke of Newcastle-upon-Tyne 1694-1711 E
Peers: 5 peers 1661-90 1660-1711
1 Ld Lt 17th-18th
1 KG 17th-18th
Notes: Married Ashley heiress of Dorchester Priory (Friary), held since 1622 (of Ashley-Cooper family). Denzil Holles inherited an Ashley estate worth £1,200 pa. 1 Baron Holles, 1, 2, and 3 Earls of Clare and 1 Duke (Tyne - Holles) and four others in ODNB.

Earl of Chichester (1801- UK)

Origins: See above under Dukes of Newcastle. This branch was descended from a brother of the 1 Baron Pelham (cr. 1706). Involved in the iron industry in the 16th c. **First MP 1399 for Sussex. Seven additional MPs 1547-1654, four for the county.**

1. Sir John Pelham 3 Bt – Hastings 1645-48 Sussex 1654 1656 1660-79 1685-87 1689-98
2. Sir Nicholas Pelham – Seaford 1671-79 Sussex 1679-81 Seaford 1689-90 Lewes 1702-05 1726-27
3. Thomas Pelham 1 Baron Pelham – East Grinstead 1678-79 Lewes 1679-81 1685-87 1689-1702 Sussex 1702-05
4. Henry Pelham – Seaford 1690-95 Lewes 1695-1702
5. Thomas Pelham – Lewes 1705-41
6. Henry Pelham – Hastings 1715-22 Lewes 1722-25
7. Henry Pelham – Seaford 1717-22 Sussex 1722-54
8. Thomas Pelham – Lewes 1727-37
9. Thomas Pelham 1 Earl of Chichester – Rye 1749-54 Sussex 1754-68
10. Henry Pelham – Lewes 1780-96
11. Thomas Pelham 2 Earl of Chichester – Sussex 1780-1801 {Carrick 1783-90 Clogher 1795-97 Armagh 1797-99}
12. Walter Pelham 4 Earl of Chichester – Lewes 1865-74

Seats: Stanmer House, Sussex (purch. 1713, built 1722, remod. 1860, family depart 1942, sold 1946, institutional/business use); Laughton Place (and Halland House, in same vicinity), Sussex: (Laughton Place) medieval, purch. 1466, rebuilt 1534, abandoned and a ruin in 18th c., brick tower remains; (Halland House) purch. and built 1595, demolished c. 1770)

Estates: Bateman 16232 (E) 13650. Income from iron industry £4,000 pa while land brought in £2,700 in the 1630s.
Titles: Baron Pelham 1762- GB; Baronet 1611-
Peers: 8 peers 1768-1813 1801-1944
1 Ld Lt 19th
2 in Cabinet 1743-54 1783-84 1795-98 1801-04
Notes: 1 Baron and 1, 2, and 3 Earls and five others in ODNB.

Pelham

Origins: Descended from a younger son of the 2 Baronet. A younger son of this line married into the Cressett family of Cound Hall and inherited that property. The Cressetts were established in Shropshire since at least the 14th century. Royal officials 15th century. Sheriffs mid-16th century. They inherited Cound by marriage from the Townshends, judges from the reign of Edward IV. **Two MPs 15th century**. The senior line became extinct in 1838, when Crowhurst passed to the Papillons of Acrise Place. The Papillons were Huguenots who arrived in England in the early 17th century. They were builders, architects, and property developers. They married into minor Kentish gentry in 1651 and acquired Acrise. Became victuallers to the Royal Navy and East India merchants in the 18th century.

1. Thomas Papillon – Dover 1674-81 1689-95 London 1695-1700
2. Philip Papillon – Dover 1701-20
3. Edward Cressett – Shrewsbury 1710-15
4. James Pelham – Newark 1722-41 Hastings 1741-61
5. David Papillon – New Romney 1722-34 Dover 1734-41
6. Thomas Pelham – Hastings 1728-41 Lewes 1741-43
7. Henry Cressett-Pelham – Bramber 1751-54 Tiverton 1754-58
8. John Cressett-Pelham – Lewes 1796-1802 1822-32 Shrewsbury 1835-37
9. Philip Papillon – Colchester 1859-65

Seats: Crowhurst Park, Sussex (acq. by Pelhams 1412, built c. 1627, became main seat and add. 1740, later 18th c., early 19th c., passed by mar. from Cressett-Pelhams to Papillons 1838, sold 1942, holiday site); Catsfield Place, Sussex (acq. 1412 by Pelhams, built 16th c., add. 18th c., passed from Cressett-Pehams 1838 to Papillons, still owned 1940, hotel); Acrise Place, Kent (built 16th c., purch. 1666, remod. 18th c., sold 1861, repurch. 1950, sold 1986); Cound Hall, Shropshire (built 1704, passed by mar. to Pelhams later 1792, remod. 1840, sold c. 1878); Upton Cressett Hall, Shropshire (Cressetts acq. by mar. to Upton heiress 14th c., built c. 1431, remod. 1540, rebuilt 1580, passed to Pelhams 1792, sold 1926, derelict, restored, hotel)
Estates: Bateman 11028 (E) 11768
Notes: Three Papillons in ODNB.

Earl of Yarborough (1837- UK)

Origins: For the Pelham descent see the first entry. **First MP of this line 1597 for Lincolnshire. Another MP 1621.** The Andersons were a Lincolnshire family. Francis Anderson of Manby Hall married Mary, sister of Charles Pelham of Brocklesby. The wife of the 2 Baron Yarborough was heiress of the Worsley Baronets of Appuldurcombe, Isle of Wight to whose properties they succeeded in 1825 (see that family). Anderson cousins received a baronetcy in 1660 and were seated at Lea Hall and Kilnwick Percy, Lincolnshire. The first prominent Anderson was Lord Chief Justice of the Common Pleas 1582.

1. George Pelham – Great Grimsby 1679-81
2. Charles Pelham – Great Grimsby 1722-27 Beverley 1727-34 1738-54
3. Charles Anderson-Pelham 1 Baron Yarborough – Beverley 1768-74 Lincolnshire 1774-94
4. Francis Anderson – Great Grimsby 1774-80 Beverley 1780-84
5. Charles Anderson-Pelham 1 Earl of Yarborough – Great Grimsby 1803-07 Lincolnshire 1807-23
6. George Anderson-Pelham – Great Grimsby 1806-07 Newtown 1808-20
7. Charles Anderson-Pelham 2 Earl of Yarborough – Newtown 1830-31 Lincolnshire 1831-32 N. Lincolnshire 1832-46
8. Dudley Anderson-Pelham – Boston 1849-50
9. Charles Anderson-Pelham 3 Earl of Yarborough – Great Grimsby 1857-62

Seats: Brocklesby Park, Lincolnshire (purch. c. 1565-70, house built c. 1600, rebuilt c. 1710-30, add. 1772, 1807, 1827, and 1858, fire 1898, rebuilt, reduced in size 1957-58, still own); Manby Hall, Lincolnshire (Anderson house, medieval house, rebuilt 1770-73, remod. 1862, ruin by 1921, demolished 1933); Appledurcombe, Hampshire (acq. by mar. 1825, sold 1858)
Estates: Bateman 61986 (E) 91643. The 7 Earl left £68,000,000 at his death in 1991. (Leach, *Lincolnshire Country Houses, Part Two*, 134). Owned 28,000 acres in 2001.
Titles: Baron Yarborough 1794- GB; Baron Worsley 1837- UK
Peers: 6 peers 1794-1875 1880-1945
2 Lds Lt 19th, 20th
1 KG 20th
Notes: The 1 Baron Yarborough planted 12 million trees at Brocklesby. (Thorold, *Lincolnshire Houses*, 34.) One in ODNB.

PELLEW

Viscount Exmouth (1816- UK)

Origins: An old Cornish family that had seen better times. The 1 Viscount was the grandson of a ship owner and son of a mail packet captain. Three admirals in the early 19th century.

1. Edward Pellew 1 Viscount Exmouth – Barnstaple 1802-04
2. Pownoll Pellew 2 Viscount Exmouth – Launceston 1812-29

Seat: Canonteign House (Manor), Devon (built 16th c., purch. 1812, new house 1828, sold 1990s)
Estates: Bateman 2864 (E) 2755
Titles: Baron Exmouth 1814- UK; Baronet 1796-
Peers: 8 peers 1814-76 1882-92 1911-45
Notes: 1 Viscount and four others in ODNB.

PEMBERTON I [Leigh]

Baron Kingsdown (1858-67 UK; 1993-2013 UKLife)

Origins: The founder of the Pembertons was Chief Justice of the Common Pleas (d. 1697). Very successful barristers followed in succeeding generations. The first significant Leigh was an attorney in the 18th century who became Mayor of Wigan and purchased estates. The 1 Baron succeeded to the valuable property of his mother, heiress of Sir Robert Holt Leigh 1 Bt of Hindley Hall in 1843 (see Legh). (Succession was complicated, see Fisher, *The House of Commons*, V, 722-23).

1. Sir Robert Leigh 1 Bt – Wigan 1802-20
2. Thomas Pemberton-Leigh 1 Baron Kingsdown – Rye 1831-32 Ripon 1835-43
3. Sir Edward Leigh Pemberton – E. Kent 1868-85

Seats: Torry Hill, Kent (acq. and built c. 1840, rebuilt 1925, demolished c. 1938, rebuilt and demolished 1958, rebuilt 1960s, still owned 2013); Hindley Hall, Lancashire (Leighs acq. 1721, passed to 1 Bt and rebuilt 1811, passed to Pembertons 1843, leased out 1855, sold 1983); Trumpington Hall, Cambridgeshire (built later 16th c., Pembertons purch. 1675, remod. and add. early 18th c., still own)
Estates: Bateman 6280 (E) 6708
Title: Baronet 1814-43
Peer: 1 peer 1858-67
1 Ld Lt 20th

1 KG 20th
Notes: Robin Leigh-Pemberton, Lord Kingsdown, was Governor of the Bank of England 1983-93. 1 Baron and two others in ODNB.

PEMBERTON II [Rudd]

Pemberton

Origins: Medieval gentry. Court servant in the 15th century. Money lender to aristocracy 16th-17th century. **First MP 1477. Another MP 1601-04**. High Sheriff 1480. Kt 1603.

1. Thomas Pemberton – Higham Ferrers 1702-03

Seats: Rushden Hall, Northamptonshire (built 14th-15th c., purch. mid-16th c., add. early 17th c., sold mid-17th c.); Hertingfordbury, Hertfordshire (acq. Crown lease later 16th c. to 1619); Castle Yard, Higham Ferrers, Northamptonshire (property acq. 16th c., inher. "castle" 1701, sold c. 1703)
Notes: Male line extinct 1703.

Rudd

Origins: Yorkshire family. Bishop of St. Davids 1594, who purchased estates in Wales. Northamptonshire estates passed to Pembertons by marriage 1701.

1. Sir Rice Rudd 2 Bt – Higham Ferrers 1679-81
   Carmarthenshire 1689-1701

Seats: Aberglasney, Carmarthenshire (medieval, purch. c. 1600, rebuilt c. 1601, sold 1710, derelict 1990s); Castle Yard (Manor House), Higham Ferrers, Northamptonshire (medieval, acq. by mar. 1683, passed by mar. to Pembertons 1701)
Title: Baronet 1628-1739
Notes: 2 Bt heavily indebted.

PENDARVES [Wynne]

Origins: Settled at Pendarves in the reign of Elizabeth I.

1. William Pendarves – Penryn 1661-71
2. Alexander Pendarves – Penryn 1689-98 1699-1705 Saltash 1708-10 Penryn 1710-14 Helston 1714-15 Launceston 1721-25
3. Sir William Pendarves – St. Ives 1713-15
4. Edward Wynne-Pendarves – Cornwall 1826-32 W. Cornwall 1832-53

Seats: Pendarves, Cornwall (acq. and built later 16th c., remod. 1832 and 1841, demolished 1955); Roskrow (Roscrow), Cornwall (passed to Bassets by mar. 1724)
Estates: Bateman 3584 (E) 5330
Notes: Edward Wynne-Pendarves was born Stackhouse and assumed the name Wynne-Pendarves. One in ODNB.

PENDER [Denison]

Baron Pender (1937- UK)

Origins: Manchester businessmen, involved with textiles and the trans-Atlantic cable.

1. Sir John Pender – Totnes 1862-66 Wick District 1872-85 1892-96
2. Sir James Pender 1 Bt – Mid Northamptonshire 1895-1900
3. John Denison-Pender 1 Baron Pender – Newmarket Div. Cambridgeshire 1913-18 Balham & Tooting Div. Wandsworth 1918-22

Seats: Thornby Hall, Northamptonshire (built 17th c., purch. sec. half 19th c., remod., sold by 1923, institutional use); Footscray Place, Kent (built 1754, leased? 1890s, fire 1949, demolished); Middleton Hall, Linlithgowshire (built 1710, add. later 18th c., acq. later 19th c., sold 1899); Lower Hare Park, Cambridgeshire (acq. by mar. of 1906)
Estate: 1 Bt left £337,000 in 1897.
Title: Baronet 1897-1921
Peer: 1 peer 1937-45

PENN

Origins: The family owned a small estate acquired at the Dissolution. This was sold and the Penns became merchants in Bristol in the late 16th century. Sir William Penn MP became a naval commander. He acquired estates in Ireland by marriage. Further property there was granted by Cromwell and acquired through purchase. Great estates in North America followed.

1. Sir William Penn – Weymouth & Melcombe Regis 1660-70
2. Richard Penn – Appleby 1784-90 Haslemere 1790-91 Lancaster 1796-1802 Haslemere 1802-06
3. John Penn – Helston 1802-05

Seats: Laleham House, Middlesex (resident c. 1735-85); Stoke Poges Park (Stoke Park), Buckinghamshire (old house, purch. 1760, rebuilt 1790-1813, sold 1851, hotel)

Estates: 12,000 acres worth £1,500 pa in Ireland acq. 1661. In 1681 acquired 24 million acres in Pennsylvania by royal grant, lost with compensation of £130,000 in 1779 from the state of Pennsylvania and £4,000 pa annuity from the Crown.
Notes: Eight in ODNB.

PENNEFATHER *IRELAND*

Origins: To Ireland as a soldier in the 1650s. Acquired grants of land in the 1660s. Sheriff 1703.

1. Kingsmill Pennefather – {Cashel 1703-14 County Tipperary 1715-35}
2. Matthew Pennefather – {Cashel 1710-33}
3. Richard Pennefather – {Cashel 1734-77}
4. Kingsmill Pennefather – {Cashel 1753-71}
5. William Pennefather – {Cashel 1771-83}
6. William Pennefather – {Cashel 1783-97}
7. Richard Pennefather – {Cashel 1777-1800} 1818-19
8. Matthew Penenefather – Cashel 1830-31

Seat: Ballyowen (New Park), Tipperary (acq. 1702, built c. 1750, sold mid-19th c.)
Estates: "Extensive" (Fisher, *The House of Commons*, VI, 725). Sold after the Famine of the 1840s. Worth £1,500 pa in 1713 and £2,000 pa in 1775. 1,730 acres worth £1,450 pa in 1852. 721 acres worth £525 in 1878.
Notes: Six in ODNB.

PENNINGTON

Baron Muncaster (1783-1917 I; 1898-1917 UK)

Origins: Held Muncaster Castle from the 13th century. Sir John Pennington MP fought at Agincourt (Roskell, Clark, and Rawcliffe, *The House of Commons*, IV, 49). **First MP 1407 for Westmorland. Three further MPs 1432-1597, all for Cumberland**.

1. Sir Joseph Pennington 2 Bt – Cumberland 1734-44
2. Sir John Pennington 3 Bt – Cumberland 1745-68
3. John Pennington 1 Baron Muncaster – Milborne Port 1781-96 Colchester 1796-1802 Westmorland 1806-13
4. Josslyn Pennington 5 Baron Muncaster – W. Cumberland 1872-80 Egremont Div. Cumberland 1885-92

Seats: Muncaster Castle, Cumberland (acq. 1208, add. 1325, add. 15th c., add. 16th c. and 1780 and 1860-66, passed to Ramsdens by mar. 1917 who took the name Pennington,

still own); Warter Hall (Priory), Yorkshire (inher. from Stapletons by Penningtons later 17th c., built c. 1700, add. 1872, sold 1878, demolished 1972)
Estates: Bateman 5811 (E) 2629
Title: Baronet 1676-1917
Peers: {1 peer 1783-1800} 1 peer 1898-1917
2 Lds Lt 18th, 19th
Notes: Male line extinct 1917. Estates passed to the Ramsdens (see that family). 1 and 2 Barons and one other in ODNB.

PENRUDDOCKE (Penruddock, Penruddoke)

Origins: The family was from Penruddock, Cumberland by the 14th century. Married a Wiltshire heiress in the 16th century, and they elevated their status in that county. Granted arms 1548. Fought at St. Quentin 1557. **First MP 1553 (Wiltshire 1558). Five additional MPs 1572-1614, two for Cumberland.** The first MP rose by marriage, war, and court favor.

1. Thomas Penruddoke – Wilton 1679 1689-90
2. Charles Penruddocke – Wiltshire 1770-88
3. Wadham Penruddocke Wyndham – Salisbury 1818-33
4. John Penruddocke – Wilton 1821-37

Seat: Compton Park (House) (Compton Chamberlayne), Wiltshire (medieval, purch. and rebuilt 1558, rebuilt 17th c., rebuilt 18th c., sold 1930)
Estates: Bateman 3788 (E) 5390
Notes: One in ODNB.

PEPPER *IRELAND*

Origins: Acquired land in Ireland 1650s-60s. High Sheriff 1670. First MP a Major General.

1. John Pepper – {Gowran 1715-25} Steyning 1715-25
2. Thomas Pepper – {Kells 1761-76}
3. Thomas Pepper – {Longford 1794-97 Kells 1800}

Seat: Ballygarth Castle, Meath (tower built by 1372, acq. c. 1660, add. 18th c., remod. c. 1800, remod. 1860s, sold 1979)
Estate: 1884 (I) 2070 in 1878.

PEPYS

Earl of Cottenham (1850- UK)

Origins: Held land at Impington since 1579. Granted arms in the reign of Elizabeth I. Lord Chief Justice of Ireland 1654. Banker early 18th century. First Bt (1784) a physician. First Bt (1801) a Master in Chancery. 1 Earl Lord Chancellor. The father of the famous diarist, a naval administrator and a cousin of the Impington line, was a tailor. **First MP 1625. One other MP 1640.**

1. Roger Pepys – Cambridge 1661-79
2. Samuel Pepys – Castle Rising 1673-79 Harwich 1679 1685-87
3. John Pepys – Cambridge 1695-96
4. Charles Pepys 1 Earl of Cottenham – Higham Ferrers 1831 Malton 1831-36

Seats: Tandridge Court, Surrey (purch. 1834, sold 1896); Impington Hall (Manor), Cambridgeshire (purch. and built 1579, remod. c. 1725, passed out of family 1805, most demolished 1953); Cottenham, Cambridgeshire (acq. 1570, sold c. 1782)
Estates: Bateman 4556 (E) 5674. Rubinstein – 1 Bt left £120,000 in probate in 1830.
Titles: Baron Cottenham 1836- UK; Baronet 1784- ; 1801-
Peers: 7 peers 1836-81 1895-1919 1922 1924-45
1 in Cabinet 1836-41 1846-50
Notes: 1 Earl and three others in ODNB.

PERCEVAL *ENGLAND & IRELAND*

Earl of Egmont (1733-2011 I)

Origins: Originally medieval gentry in Somerset, but the modern family was founded in the second half of the 16th century by a confidential agent to Lord Burghley and Registrar of the Court of Wards in Ireland. Moved to Ireland c. 1600 and became an official and acquired estates there beginning in 1616. His son was a land speculator and by 1641 owned 100,000 acres in Cork. He sold his last English acres. A uniquely peripatetic family crossing and re-crossing the Irish Sea. The 2 Earl purchased an English estate in Somerset and built a new house. **First MP 1604.**

1. Sir John Perceval 1 Bt – {County Cork 1661-65}
2. John Perceval – {Granard 1692-93 1695-99 1703-13 Trim 1715-19}
3. John Perceval 1 Earl of Egmont – {County Cork 1703-14} Harwich 1727-34
4. Philip Perceval – {Askeaton 1713-14}
5. Robert Perceval – {Trim 1717-27 1761-68 Fore 1727-60}

6. John Perceval 2 Earl of Egmont – {Dingle 1731-48} Westminster 1741-47 Weobley 1747-54 Bridgwater 1754-62
7. John Perceval 3 Earl of Egmont – Bridgwater 1762-69
8. Charles Perceval 2 Baron Arden – Launceston 1780-90 Warwick 1790-96 Totnes 1796-1802
9. Spencer Perceval – Northampton 1796-1812
10. Spencer Perceval – Ennis 1818-20 Newport (IoW) 1827-31 Tiverton 1831-32
11. Henry Perceval 5 Earl of Egmont – East Looe 1826
12. George Perceval 6 Earl of Egmont – W. Surrey 1837-40
13. Charles Perceval 7 Earl of Egmont – Midhurst 1874

Seats: Burton Park (House), Cork (acq. 1636, built c. 1665—86, burned 1689, rebuilt later 18th c., leased out 1814, sold later 19th c.); Nork House, Surrey (built 1740, purch. 1847 and sold 1890, demolished 1939); Liscarroll Castle, Cork (built 13th c., acq. 1625, ruin from mid-17th c., passed to care of the state 1936); Lohort Castle, Cork (medieval, acq. c. 1641, ruined in Civil War, rebuilt 1740-50, remod. 1876, sold 1890, burned 1921, partly restored); Cowdray Park, Sussex (old house a ruin after 1793, purch. 1843, new house built mid-19th c., sold 1908); Enmore Castle, Somerset (medieval, purch. 1751, new house built 1751-55, sold 1833); Kanturk Castle, Cork (built 1601, acq. c. 1632, never completed, given to NT 1900, now owned by Irish state); Charlton, Kent (leased)
Estates: Bateman 34972 (E & I) 35510. Rubinstein – Edward Perceval left £120,000 in probate in 1829.
Titles: Baron Perceval 1715-2011 I; Viscount Perceval 1723-2011 I; Baron Lovel and Holland 1762-2011 GB; Baron Arden 1770- I; Baron Arden 1802- UK; Baronet 1661-2001
Peers: {3 peers 1715-1800} 10 peers 1762-1841 1802-1929 1939-45
2 Lds Lt 18th, 19th
2 in Cabinet 1763-66 1807-12
Notes: The 2 Earl lost £12,000 in an ill-conceived settlement on Amelia Island, East Florida c. 1770. (Hancock, *Citizens of the World*, 159) The finances of the 4 and 5 Earls were rocky with debts of £300,000, much trouble being created by lawsuits. Both fled into exile. The 4 Earl was improvident and the Somerset estate of over 7,000 acres was sold for £134,000. Spencer Perceval was the only British Prime Minister to be assassinated. The 8 Earl was a fireman (Girouard, "Enmore Castle", 39-46; Fisher, *The House of Commons*, VI, 734.). 2 Baron Arden and 1 and 2 Earls and four others in ODNB.

Perceval

Origins: Kinsmen of the Earls of Egmont. Settled in Ireland mid-17th century and acquired Temple house by marriage. Sheriff 1728.

1. Thomas Perceval – {Dundalk 1692-93 1695-99}
2. Alexander Perceval – County Sligo 1831-41

Seat: Temple House, Sligo (old castle, acq. by mar. mid-17th c., new house c. 1820, add. 1860, still own)
Estates: Bateman 7821 (I) 4612
Notes: One in ODNB.

PERCY [Greatheed, Heber, Smithson]

Duke of Northumberland (1766- GB)

Origins: One of the great and ancient dynasties of the English aristocracy. A Norman family that participated in the Conquest of 1066. In the Domesday Book listed as owners of 80 lordships in Yorkshire. Summoned to the Council of William I by 1086. At Runneymeade and Crecy. Earls of Northumberland in 1377. **First MP 1297 for Yorkshire. Six additional MPs 1379-1654, five of them kts of the shire**. Lady Elizabeth Percy, heiress of the last Earl, married the 6 Duke of Somerset, who succeeded to the Percy estates in 1722. The 7 Duke of Somerset was created Earl of Northumberland (see Seymour). His daughter and heiress married Sir Hugh Smithson, who was created Duke of Northumberland and took the name Percy. The Smithsons began as yeomen and tenant farmers in Yorkshire. The 1 Baronet was a haberdasher in London in the first half of the 17th century, who purchased estates and was granted arms 1660. **First MP 1654**.

1. Hugh Smithson – Middlesex 1701 1702-05 1710-22
2. Hugh Smithson 1 Duke of Northumberland – Middlesex 1740-50
3. Hugh Percy 2 Duke of Northumberland – Westminster 1763-76
4. Algernon Percy 1 Earl of Beverley – Northumberland 1774-86
5. George Percy 5 Duke of Northumberland – Bere Alston 1799-1830
6. Hugh Percy 3 Duke of Northumberland – Buckingham 1806 Westminster 1806 Launceston 1806-07 Northumberland 1807-12
7. Lord Josceline Percy – Bere Alston 1806-20
8. Lord William Percy – Stamford 1818-26
9. Lord Henry Percy – Bere Alston 1820-25
10. Charles Greatheed-Bertie-Percy – Newport 1826-29
11. Algernon Percy 6 Duke of Northumberland – Bere Alston 1831-32 N. Northumberland 1852-65
12. Josceline Percy – Launceston 1852-59
13. Lord Henry Percy – N. Northumberland 1865-68
14. Henry Percy 7 Duke of Northumberland – N. Northumberland 1868-85
15. Lord Algernon Percy – Westminster 1882-85 St. George's Hanover Square 1885-87
16. Henry Percy 8 Duke of Northumberland – S. Kensington 1895-1909
17. Lord Eustace Percy – Hastings 1921-37

Seats: Alnwick Castle, Northumberland (built 11th c. and 12th c., purch. 1309, rebuilt 1314-52, restored 1752-78 and 1854-65, still own); Syon House, Middlesex (built 15th c., rebuilt c. 1547-50, acq. 1594, remod. 1762-83 and 1854-65, still own); Kielder Castle, Northumberland (built 1772-75, add. 19th c., sold 20th c.); Albury Park, Surrey (medieval, rebuilt mid-later 17th c and 1697, remod. c. 1800 and c. 1815, purch. 1819, remod. soon after, passed to Percies by mar. from the Drummonds 1860, house sold 1965, the Duke still owns the estate); Stanwick Park, Yorkshire (Smithsons purch. 1638, built mid-17th c., rebuilt c. 1740, sold c. 1921, demolished 1923); Petworth, Sussex (acq. 1150, built 1260s and 1309-15, passed via the mar. of Lady Elizabeth Percy to the Duke of Somerset 1670 and then the Wyndhams in 1750); Cockermouth Castle, Cumberland (mid-13th c. castle, add. c. 1360-70, passed via the mar. of Lady Elizabeth Percy to the Dukes of Somerset and then in 1750 to the Wyndhams); Wressle Castle, Yorkshire (acq. early 14th c., built late 14th c., remod. c. 1500, decayed by 1577, partly demolished 1650, fire 1796, ruin, passed to Earls of Egremont)
Estates: Bateman 192080 (E) 184368. Worth £50,000 pa in 1780s. Rubinstein – 2 Duke left £660,000 in probate 1817. James Lewis Smithson left £120,000 in probate 1829 – part used to found the Smithsonian Institution in Washington, DC. Spent £250,000 remod. Alnwick 1854-65. Owned 132,000 acres worth 800 million pounds in 2001.
Titles: Earl of Northumberland 1557-1670; Baron Warkworth and Earl of Northumberland 1749- GB; Earl Percy 1766- GB; Baron Lovaine 1784- GB; Earl of Beverley 1790- GB; Baron Prudoe 1816-65 UK; Baronet 1660-
Peers: 12 peers 1660-70 1750-1865 1786-1899 1887-1945
10 Lds Lt 17th, 18th, 19th, 20th
5 in Cabinet 1763-65 1829-30 1852 1878-80 1924-29 1935-39
8 KG 17th, 18th, 19th, 20th
1 KP 19th
Notes: 1, 2, and 3 Barons and 1, 2, 3, 4, 5, 6, 7, 8, 9, and 10 Earls and 1, 2, 3, 4, 6, and 8 Dukes and one Smithson and twenty-six Percys in ODNB.

Heber

Origins: An old gentry family established in the mid-16th century, settled at Marton Hall in 1601. They inherited Hodnet Hall form a Vernon heiress in the 18th century. The Vernons had inherited it from the Ludlows who had held the estate from the reign of Henry I. (see Vernon I) The son of the 1 Earl of Beverley (see above) married the heiress of Richard Heber of Hodnet in 1839 and took the name Heber-Percy.

1. Richard Heber – University of Oxford 1821-26

Seats: Hodnet Hall, Shropshire (acq. by mar. from Vernons 1752, rebuilt 1870, still own); Aimyn Hall, Yorkshire (built later 17th c., purch. 1865, sold 1920); (West) Marton Hall, Yorkshire (medieval, purch. 1601, sold 1786, demolished 1960)

Estates: Bateman 7447 (E) 14524. Richard Heber MP was worth £200,000 in 1833.
Notes: Richard Heber MP spent £100,000 on book collecting. Two in ODNB.

Greatheed

Origins: The first notable Greatheed was a wealthy West Indian planter who settled in Warwickshire in the 18th century. A brother of the 5 Duke of Northumberland married in 1822 the heiress of Bertie Bertie-Greatheed of Guyscliff and took the name Greatheed-Bertie-Percy.

1. Samuel Greatheed – Coventry 1747-61

Seat: Guyscliff (Guy's Cliff), Warwickshire (medieval, new house built c. 1720s, purch. 1751, add. 1750s and early 19th c., passed to Percies later 19th c., remod. 1872, sold 1946, ruin from 1950s)
Notes: One in ODNB.

PERY *IRELAND*

Earl of Limerick (1803- I)

Origins: Emerged as gentry in Ireland in the later 17th century. Acquired Stackpole Court by marriage to a Stackpole heiress. The Stackpoles came from Pembrokeshire to Ireland in the 12th century. The son of that marriage also married an heiress. His son was Speaker of the Irish House of Commons 1771.

1. Edmond Pery 1 Viscount Pery – {Wicklow 1751-60 Limerick 1761-85}
2. Edmond Pery 1 Earl of Limerick – {Limerick 1786-94}

Seats: Dromore Castle, Limerick (old castle, acq. 18th c., built 1866-73, sold 1939, dismantled c. 1954, ruin); Stackpole Court (Stacpoles Court, Enagh), Clare (built 17th c., acq. by mar. from Stackpoles c. 1700, ruin by mid-19th c.); Tewin Water, Hertfordshire (built 1689, remod. 1798, purch. 1892, sold 1896, school)
Estates: Bateman 5709 (I) 14986. Worth £8,000 pa in 1806.
Titles: Viscount Pery 1785-1806 I; Baron Glentworth 1790- I; Viscount Limerick 1800- I; Baron Foxford 1815- UK
Peers: {3 peers 1786-1800 1791-1800} 1 Irish Rep peer 1801-15 5 peers 1815-1945
1 KP 19th
Notes: 1 Viscount and 1 Earl in ODNB.

PETO

Origins: The 1 Bt was a bricklayer's apprentice as a boy. He inherited his uncle's building business and became a huge contractor and engineer involved in railway development.

1. Sir Morton Peto 1 Bt – Norwich 1847-54 Finsbury 1859-65 Bristol 1865-81
2. Sir Basil Peto 1 Bt – Devizes Div. Wiltshire 1910-18 Barnstaple Div. Devon 1922-23 1924-35
3. Geoffrey Peto – Frome Div. Somerset 1924-29 Bilston Div. Wolverhampton 1931-35
4. Basil Peto – Kings Norton Div. Birmingham 1941-45
5. Sir Christopher Peto 3 Bt – Barnstaple N. Devon 1945-55

Seats: Cheddington (Chedington) Court, Somerset (medieval, rebuilt c. 1840, purch. 1893, remod. c. 1900, sold 1938, hotel); Sandford Park, Oxfordshire (built c. 1700, add. later 18th c., purch. 1930, still own); Somerleyton Hall, Suffolk (built c. 1610, purch. 1843, rebuilt 1844-51, sold 1863)
Estates: Purchased 4,500 acres in 1843. Rubinstein – Henry Peto left £120,000 in probate in 1830.
Titles: Baronet 1855- ; 1927-
Notes: The 1 Bt went bankrupt 1866. 1 Bt and three others in ODNB.

PETRE

Baron Petre (1603- E)

Origins: Began as Devon yeomen and local officials. A rich tanner in Exeter in the early Tudor period had a son who became a lawyer and Secretary of State under Henry VIII 1543-66. Gained land at the Dissolution of the Monasteries. Kt 1544. High Sheriff 1575. **First MP 1536 (for Essex 1547-63). Five further MPs 1554-97, two for the county**. The 1 Baron Petre gave allegiance to the Roman Catholic Church, which ended the family's participation in the Commons until after Catholic Emancipation.

1. Edward Petre – Ilchester 1831-32 York 1832-34

Seats: Thorndon Hall, Essex (purch. 1573, principal seat from c. 1575, remod. c. 1731, new house built 1764-70, burned 1878, ruin, flats, still own estate); Ingatestone Hall, Essex (purch. 1539, built 1548-60, remod. c. 1790, restored after 1918, still own); Dunkenhalgh Hall, Lancashire (medieval, purch. by Walmesleys 1571, new house 1580, passed by mar. to Petres 1712, rebuilt 1799, engulfed by industrialization); Writtle Park, Essex (acq. 1550s, still own); Buckenham Tofts Hall, Norfolk (built later 17th c.,

purch. c. 1736 by Howards from whom it passed by mar. to Petres 1803, rebuilt later 18th c., remod. 1803, sold c. 1830, demolished 1946)
Estates: Bateman 19085 (E) 22595 (cadet line 5754 (E) 10995). Owned 15,000 acres worth 95 million pounds in 2001.
Title: Baronet 1642-1722
Peers: 1660-78 1829-1908 1911-15 1935-45
1 Ld Lt 17th
Notes: One of the leading Roman Catholic families in England. The Petre family have an entry plus the 4, 8, and 9 Barons and eight others biography in ODNB.

PEYTON

Origins: Built up estates in Suffolk and Cambridgeshire by marriage to heiresses in the 14th and 15th centuries. A younger son established a branch in Kent in the 16th century. **First MP 1299 for Suffolk. Eight further MPs 1529-1626, four for Cambridgeshire**. Two lines are combined here.

1. Sir Thomas Peyton 2 Bt – Sandwich 1640-44 Kent 1661-79
2. Sir Robert Peyton – Middlesex 1679-80
3. Craven Peyton – Boroughbridge 1705-13

Seat: Knowlton Court, Kent (acq. r. Henry VIII, sold 1680s)
Estates: The Kentish estates were worth £1,000 pa in the 1620s, but much indebted.
Title: Baronet 1611-84
Notes: On the death of the last Baronet 1684 four daughters divided up the estates and sold the property. Much of the Cambridgeshire estate sold in 1630s due to a financial crisis. 2 Bt and three others in ODNB.

PHELIPS [Lockyer]

<u>Phelips</u>

Origins: The first Phelips and his son rose from yeoman status to gentry through the profits of lucartive local offices and royal service in the later 15th and 16th centuries. The great house at Montacute was built by a Master of the Rolls 1611. **First MP 1512 (Dorset 1554). Five further MPs 1545-1628, two kts of the shire**.

1. Edward Phelips – Ilchester 1640-44 Somerset 1661-79
2. Robert Phelips – Stockbridge 1661-79 Andover 1685-87
3. Sir Edward Phelips – Ilchester 1661-79 1685-87 Somerset 1690-95 1698-99
4. John Phelips – Ilchester 1698-1700
5. Edward Phelips – Ilchester 1708-15 Somerset 1722-27

6. Edward Phelips – Somerset 1774-80
7. Edward Phelips – Somerset 1784-92

Seats: Montacute, Somerset (acq. by 1480 and built, rebuilt 1588-1601, remod. 1786, leased out from 1911, estate sold by 1918, 1931 to NT); Court House, Dorset (purch. 1538, built c. 1540, passed out of family 1747, most demolished 1850)
Estates: Bateman 2926 (E) 5238
Title: Baronet 1620-90
1 in Cabinet 1687-89
Notes: A gentry family that owned a great house they could not afford properly to maintain. Became virtually insolvent by c. 1900. Began to sell off farms one by one c. 1900-18. Two in ODNB.

Lockyer

Origins: A leading Dissenting family in Ilchester. Chief Accountant of the South Sea Company, financiers and bankers. Edward Phelips married Elizabeth, daughter and heiress of Thomas Lockyer of Mapperton. Purchased landed estates 1746 and 1755.

1. Charles Lockyer – Ilchester 1727-47
2. Thomas Lockyer – Ilchester 1747-61
3. Joseph Lockyer – Ilchester 1756-65

Seat: Mapperton (Maperton), Somerset (old house, purch. 1746, sold 1800) (not to be confused with Mapperton, Dorset)

PHILIPPS [Laugharne, Scourfield] *WALES*

Baron Milford (1776-1823 I; 1847-57 UK; 1939- UK)

Origins: Descended from the 12th-century lords of Cilsant in Carmarthenshire. **First MP 1555. Three further MPs 1559-1659, three for Pembrokeshire**.

1. William Philipps – Haverfordwest 1660
2. Sir John Philipps 4 Bt – Pembroke Boroughs 1695-1702 Haverfordwest 1718-22
3. Sir Erasmus Philipps 5 Bt – Haverfordwest 1726-43
4. Sir John Philipps 6 Bt – Carmarthen 1741-47 Petersfield 1754-61 Pembrokeshire 1761-64
5. Richard Philipps 1 Baron Milford – Pembrokeshire 1765-70 Plympton Erle 1774-79 Haverfordwest 1784-86 Pembrokeshire 1786-1812
6. Richard Grant Philipps 1 Baron Milford – Haverfordwest 1826-35

Seats: Picton Castle, Pembrokeshire (built 13th c., acq. by mar. 1490s, additions 18th c., still own); Haythog, Pembrokeshire (medieval, acq. early 17th c., passed to junior line, leased to farmers after 1834); Dalham Hall, Suffolk (built 1704-05, purch. and add. 1928, fire 1954, remod. c. 1955, sold 2009)
Estates: Bateman 23105 (W) 25206. Owned 3,000 acres in 2001.
Titles: Baronet 1621- ; 1887-
Peers: {1 peer 1776-1800} 1 peer 1847-57
5 Lds Lt 18th, 19th, 20th
Notes: The Philippses inherited Picton from the 12th c. owners the de Pictons, through the Wogans by marriage. The Milford title was recreated in 1939 for Sir Laurence Philipps Bt, a kinsman of the main family. He was a softdrink maker in the 1920s and 1930s and shipowner. 4, 5, 6, and 12 Bts and 2 Baron of the 2nd cr. and one other in ODNB.

Viscount St. Davids (1918- UK)

Origins: Descended from a younger son of the 1 Baronet of Picton Castle (see above). On the death of the 1 Baron Milford of the first creation, the 1621 Baronetcy passed to this line. 1 Viscount married an heiress. 1 Baron Kyslant was a shipowner.

1. John Philipps 1 Viscount St. Davids – Mid-Lanarkshire 1884-94 Pembrokeshire 1898-1908
2. Sir Ivor Philipps – Southampton 1906-22
3. Owen Philipps 1 Baron Kylsant – Pembroke and Haverfordwest Boroughs 1906-10 Chester 1916-18

Seats: Landwade Hall, Suffolk (medieval, add. 17th c., derelict 19th c., restored 19th c., purch. 1912, sold c. 1945); Amroth Castle (Earwere), Pembrokeshire (built early 12th c., add. 14th c., remod. 18th c., purch. 1897, family departed 1930s, hotel); Cosheston Hall (Woodfield), Pembrokeshire (built by 16th c., rebuilt mid-19th c., acq. c. 1890s, still own)
Titles: Baron St. Davids 1908- UK; Baron Kyslant 1914-37 UK; Baronet 1919-
Peers: 3 peers 1908-45 1923-37
2 Lds Lt 20th
Notes: 1 Baron Kyslant and 1 Viscount in ODNB.

Laugharne

Origins: Charles Philipps married Phillippa Laugharne and their son took the additional name Laugharne. He also married a Laugharne. The Laugharnes were merchants in Haverfordwest in the 16th century. Sheriff 1568.

1. Rowland Laugharne – Pembroke Boroughs 1661-75
2. John Laugharne – Haverfordwest 1702-15

Seat: St. Brides, Pembrokeshire (medieval building, acq. by mar. 16th c., passed to Philipps family in the 17th c., new house 1st half of the 18th c., passed via heiress to the Allens c. 1800)
Notes: The male line failed in 1715. One in ODNB.

Scourfield

Origins: Medieval origins. Gentry by the reign of Elizabeth I. Five Sheriffs in the 17th century. Owen Philipps married the daughter and heiress of Henry Scourfield of the Mote and in 1862 took the name Scourfield.

1. William Scourfield – Haverfordwest 1818-26 1835-37
2. Sir John Philipps Scourfield 1 Bt – Haverfordwest 1852-68 Pembrokeshire 1868-76

Seats: Williamston, Pembrokeshire (built 16th c., passed by mar. through various families to the Scourfields, sold 1921); The Mote (New Moat), Pembrokeshire (acq. 14th c., abandoned as main seat late 18th c., became a ruin by 1811, rebuilt c. 1830, passed to Philipps 1843, demolished 1926); Robertson (Robeston) Hall, Pembrokeshire (built by 17th c., purch. c. 1783, adopted as main seat later 18th c., sold 1812); Lochmeilir (Lochmeyler), Pembrokeshire (acq. by mar. 1600, sold 1875)
Estates: Bateman 13439 (E) 10087
Title: Baronet 1876-1921
1 Ld Lt 19th
Notes: Last male Scourfield died 1843. Last Phillips Scourfield died 1921.

PHILIPS I

Philips

Origins: A family of yeomen in the 16th century. They raised themselves over two centuries (1550s-1750s) to squires "by slowly building up their lands and choosing their wives with care." (John Cornforth, *Country Life*, 133, pp. 18-19) Younger sons went into trade. One developed a power loom in the 1740s and built a mill attached to the manor house at The Heath. The J. and N. Philips Company became a great textile firm in Manchester. The heads of the family tended to stay aloof from the business but took income from it in the 19th century while other family members were directly engaged.

1. Mark Philips – Manchester 1832-47
2. Robert Philips – Bury 1857-59 1865-85

Seats: Welcombe House (Lodge), Warwickshire ("Lodge" built 16th c., purch. 1845, new house built 1866-8, passed to Trevelyans by mar. 1890, hotel); Snitterfield Hall

(Park), Warwickshire (purch. 1816, sold 1929); The Heath House, Staffordshire (acq. c. 1600, built orig. house, new house built 1836-40, sold c. 2010)
Estates: Bateman 4048 (E) 8535. The new house at Welcombe cost £100,000 in 1866. (Tyack, *Warwickshire Country Houses*, 215.)
Notes: One in ODNB.

Philips

Origins: A younger brother in the 18th century established a family at Weston Park. They also became engaged in textile manufacturing and banking in Manchester and became "cotton lords". In 1816 the 2 Baronet achieved social acceptance as a member of Brooks's Club, the citadel of the Whig aristocracy.

1. Sir George Philips 1 Bt – Ilchester 1812-18 Steyning 1818-20 Wootton Bassett 1820-30 S. Warwickshire 1832-34
2. Sir George Philips 2 Bt – Horsham 1818-20 Steyning 1820-32 Kidderminster 1835-37 Poole 1837-52

Seat: Weston Park, Warwickshire (purch. 1819, rebuilt 1827-30, passed by mar. to Earl of Camperdown 1883, passed by mar. to the Warriners 1918, demolished 1934, still own estate)
Estates: Bateman 6693 (E) 10655. New house in 1827 cost £40,000 (Tyack, *Warwickshire Country Houses*, 218). 1 Bt withdrew £250,000 from his business 1807-31.
Title: Baronet 1828-74
Notes: See Brown, "'Cotton Lord' to Landed Aristocrat: the Rise of Sir George Philips," 62-82. On the death of the last Baronet the estates passed to the Earl of Camperdown (see Haldane). 1 Bt and one other in ODNB.

PHILIPS II *IRELAND*

Origins: In 1612 Sir Thomas Philips, a revenue farmer, was granted the manor of Castle Dawson and Limavady. George Philips MP was a burgess of Londonderry and Registrar of the Court of Claims 1668. **First {MP 1639}.**

1. George Philips – {Newtown Limavady 1661-66 County Londonderry 1692-93 1695-96}
2. Thomas Philips – {Clonmines 1692-93}
3. William Philips – {Doneraile 1703-13}

Seat: Castle Dawson, Londonderry (acq. 1612, destroyed 1689)
Notes: The finances of the family were severely affected by the war in 1689. Estates sold by 1700. Two in ODNB.

PHILLIMORE

Baron Phillimore (1918- UK)

Origins: Came to London from Gloucestershire in the late 17th century. First merchants and then a legal dynasty. The first MP was Regius Professor of Civil Law at Oxford and a judge. All three MPs were judges.

1. Joseph Phillimore – St. Mawes 1817-26 Yarmouth (IoW) 1826-30
2. John Phillimore – Leominster 1852-57
3. Sir Robert Phillimore 1 Bt – Tavistock 1853-57

Seats: Coppid Hall (The Coppice), Oxfordshire (purch. mid-19th c., still own); Shiplake House, Oxfordshire (purch. and built early 19th c., add. mid-19th c., sold 20th c.); Shedfield House, Hampshire (medieval, rebuilt 17th c., purch. 1866, still own)
Estate: Acquired by marriage 64 acres in Kensington in the 18th century, a substantial part of which they still own.
Title: Baronet 1881-
Peers: 2 peers 1918-45
Notes: 1 Baron and eight others in ODNB.

PHILLIPPS [Wallwyn, Watson]

Origins: Held some land in the 16th c. Mayor of Hereford 1646. Barrister in the early 18th century. High Sheriff 1838. The heiress of James Watson married into the Phillipps family and brought Berwick House. James Watson MP was the son of a Presbyterian minister in London. He became a barrister and judge.

1. Robert Phillipps – Hereford 1784-85
2. James Watson – Bridport 1790-95
3. William Phillipps – Shrewsbury 1885-92

Seats: Berwick House, Shropshire (built 1731, remod. 1780, acq. c. 1800, sold 19th c.); Longworth (Longford) Hall, Herefordshire (purch. 1805, sold 1864)
Estates: Bateman 2754 (E) 9484

Wallwyn (Walwyn)

Origins: An old Marcher family held Walwyns Castle, Pembroke under William II. Gentry in 14th century Herefordshire. **First MP 1327 for Herefordshire. Five additional MPs 1395-1554, four for the county.**

1. James Wallwyn – Hereford 1723-27
2. James Wallwyn – Hereford 1785-1800

Seat: Longworth Hall, Herefordshire (medieval, acq. c. 1400, sold 1685, repurch. 1691, new house built early 18th c., rebuilt later 18th c., sold 1805)
Estate: Valued at £38,000 in 1859, but it had been enlarged since 1805.
Notes: The main male line died out in 1686 and the family seat was sold. However, it was bought back a few years later by a cousin who made money as a sugar planter in the West Indies. This line ended the connection with Longworth in 1805, but the purchaser was a maternal uncle of the last Wallwyn of Longworth.

PHILLIPPS DE L'ISLE [Gordon, Lisle]

<u>Phillipps de L'Isle</u>

Origins: The founder of the family was a successful lawyer who purchased Garendon in 1683. His son was a merchant and grandson the first MP.

1. Ambrose Phillipps – Leicestershire 1734-37
2. Charles March Phillipps – Leicestershire 1818-20 1831-32
3. Edwin de Lisle – Loughborough Div. Leicestershire 1886-92

Seats: Garendon Park (Hall, House), Leicestershire (built c. 1540, purch. 1683 for £28,000, remod. 1730s, remod. early-mid 19th c., demolished and sold 1964); Grace Dieu Manor, Leicestershire (medieval monastic building, rebuilt 1833-35, leased out from 1898, sold 1972, now a school)
Estates: Bateman 7358 (E) 15334
Notes: Three in ODNB.

<u>Gordon</u>

Origins: The widow of Samuel Phillipps of Garendon married the diplomat Sir William Gordon who held the estates during his lifetime. His father was a merchant and planter in Jamiaca.

1. Sir William Gordon – Portsmouth 1777-83

Seat: Garendon Park, Leicestershire (see above)
Estates: Worth £7,000 pa in 1776.

Lisle

Origins: Held land on the Isle of Wight from the 12th century. First summoned as barons in 1299. **First MP 1314. Four further MPs 1401-1542, all for Hampshire**. Member of Cromwell's House of Lords. They married into the Phillipps family, who took their name in 1863.

1. Edward Lisle – Marlborough 1727-34 Hampshire 1734-41

Seat: Moyles Court, Hampshire (medieval, acq. by mar. 1638, rebuilt mid-17th c., became a farm house in early 19th c., sold by descendents 1845, school)
Notes: Male line extinct 1818. Lisle family has an entry in ODNB plus two others.

PHIPPS I

Origins: Settled in north Wiltshire by 1450. By the late 16th century they were prominent linen drapers, mill owners, and London merchants. In the 18th century the family produced several colonial governors.

1. Thomas Phipps – Wilton 1701 Westbury 1702
2. J. L. Phipps – Westbury 1868-69
3. Charles Phipps – Westbury 1869-74
4. Charles Phipps – Westbury 1880-85

Seats: Leighton House, Wiltshire (old house possibly 16th c., leased by Phipps from early 17th c., purch. 1791, rebuilt c. 1800, sold 1888, institutional use); Chalcot House, Wiltshire (medieval, purch. 1585, sold 1640, rebuilt c. 1680 and early 18th c., repurch. 1842, add. later 19th c., part demolished c. 1970, sold c. 1971); Dilton Court, Wiltshire (purch. 1689, built 18th c., became a farm house 19th c., still own); Heywood Place (House), Wiltshire (purch. 1700, sold 1789)
Estates: Bateman 2129 (E) 5338

PHIPPS II [Gamon, Grace, Sheffield] *ENGLAND & IRELAND*

Marquess of Normanby (1838- UK)

Origins: Rose by law, politics, and marriage in the later 17th and 18th centuries. The founder, Lord Chancellor of Ireland 1710, was the son of a yeoman.

1. Constantine Phipps 2 Baron Mulgrave – Lincoln 1768-74 Huntingdon 1776-84 Newark 1784-90
2. Charles Phipps – Scarborough 1779-84 Minehead 1784-86

3. Henry Phipps 1 Earl of Mulgrave – Totnes 1784-90 Scarborough 1790-94
4. James Phipps – Peterborough 1780-86
5. Edmund Phipps – Scarborough 1794-1818 Queenborough 1818-20 Scarborough 1820-32
6. Constantine Phipps 1 Marquess of Normanby – Scarborough 1818-20 Higham Ferrers 1822-26 Malton 1826-30
7. George Phipps 2 Marquess of Normanby – Scarborough 1847-51 1852-57

Seat: Mulgrave Castle, Yorkshire (built c. 1220, add. 14th c. and 16th c., dismantled 1647, ruin, new house later 17th c., acq. by mar. 1743, still own)
Estates: Bateman 6834 (E) 7037. Worth £33,000,000 in 1990 with 50,000 acres.
Titles: Baron Mulgrave 1767- I; Baron Mulgrave 1790-92 GB; Baron Mulgrave 1794- GB; Earl of Mulgrave 1812- UK
Peers: {2 peers 1765-92 1767-75} 6 peers 1790-92 1794-1945
2 Lds Lt 18th, 19th
2 in Cabinet 1804-20 1834-41
2 KG 19th, 20th
Notes: The 4 Marquess married a Guinness heiress, which may explain the increase in acreage in the 20th c. 2 Baron and 1 Earl and 1 and 2 Marquesses and five others in ODNB.

<u>Duke of Buckingham and Normanby</u> (1703-35 GB)

Origins: The Sheffields rose through the law and legal office in the 15th century. Speaker of the House of Commons 1510. Baron 1547. **First MP 1442, for Lincolnshire. Six additional MPs 1467-1640 , two for the county**. The widow of the 2 and last Duke married William Phipps. Their son was 1 Baron Mulgrave (see above). The Phipps family succeeded to Mulgrave Castle in 1743.

No post-1660 MPs

Seats: Mulgrave Castle, Yorkshire (built c. 1220, add. 14th c. and 16th c., acq. 1591, dismantled 1647, ruin, passed by mar. to Phipps 1743, see above); Normanby Park, Lincolnshire (acq. 1589 and house built, rebuilt late 17th c., passed by inheritance to Phipps 1743, rebuilt 1820-30, add. 1905-07, sold 1963)
Estates: Worth £4,230 pa in 1721.
Titles: Baron Sheffield 1547-1735; Earl of Mulgrave 1626-1735 E; Marquess of Normanby 1694-1735 E
Peer: 1 peer 1669-1721
1 Ld Lt 17th, 18th
1 in Cabinet 1702-05 1711-14
1 KG 17th-18th

Notes: Normanby Park passed to an illegitimate son. 1 Baron and 1 and 2 Earls and 1 Duke and two others in ODNB.

Sheffield

Origins: A great part of the estates of the Dukes of Buckingham and Normanby passed to an illegitimate brother of the 2 Duke. This family gained a Baronetcy in 1755.

1. Sir Berkeley Sheffield 6 Bt – Brigg Div. Lincolnshire 1907-10 1922-29

Seats: Normanby Park, Lincolnshire (inher. 1735, house rebuilt 1825-30, add. 1906, family depart 1963, still own but leased to Scunthorpe Borough Council); Sutton Park, Yorkshire (built sec. half 16th c., rebuilt 1730, purch. and became principal residence 1963, still own)
Estates: Bateman 9370 (E) 13480
Title: Baronet 1755-
1 Ld Lt 18th
Notes: The family sold Buckingham House (now Palace) in London to the Crown in 1762. They gained new prosperity in the late 19th c. through ownership of urban property in expanding Scunthorpe.

Grace

Origins: The daughter of the 1 Duke of Buckingham and Normanby married Walter Walsh. Their daughter, Ursula, married John Bryan. Their daughter married Oliver Grace. Their son, Michael Grace of Gracefield, was heir to the undevised estates of the Sheffield family in Suffolk, Middlesex, and Yorkshire. His eldest son was seated at Mantua House, and a younger son established the Grace Baronets at Castle Grace. The Graces were among the earliest Anglo-Norman families to settle in Ireland. Sheriff of Tipperary 1279. **First {MP 1559 for County Tipperary}. Two further {MPs 1568 and 1613 for County Kilkenny}. Three Graces sat in James II's Parliament of 1689.**

1. Richard Grace – {Baltimore 1790-97}
2. Oliver Dowell Grace – County Roscommon 1847-59

Seats: Mantua House, Roscommon (acq. by mar. and built c. 1747, passes to Bowens by mar. 1897, derelict later 20th c., ruin); Gracefield (Shanganagh), Queen's County (resident 17th c., rebuilt c. 1817, passed by mar. 1886 to White family of Suffolk)
Estates: 2085 (I) 1446 and 2131 (I) 1066 in the 1870s. Owned 32,807 acres before 1689. Much land confiscated.
Title: Baronet 1795-

Notes: The family was a Roman Catholic one, and hence elected few MPs after 1689. One in ODNB.

Gamon

Origins: The younger brother of Oliver Grace (see above) had a daughter, Elizabeth, who married Sir Richard Gamon 1 Bt of Michenden House. His estates and Baronetcy passed in 1818 to Sir William Grace 2 Bt of Castle Grace. Gamon was a government official.

1. Sir Richard Gamon 1 Bt – Winchester 1784-1812

Seat: Minchendon House, Middlesex
Title: Baronet 1795- (see above)

PICKERING I

Origins: Tudor gentry. The 1 Baronet, son of a clergyman, was a Colonel under Cromwell. The family became planters in Barbados. **First MP 1626 for Northamptonshire. Another MP 1654 for Cambridgeshire**.

1. Sir Henry Pickering 2 Bt – Morpeth 1685-87 Cambridge 1698-1705

Seat: Whaddon, Cambridgeshire (purch. 1648, sold 1705)
Estates: Worth £1,400 pa c. 1668 in England. Plantation in Barbados.
Title: Baronet 1661-1705

PICKERING II

Origins: Acquired estates second half of the 16th century. The 1 Baronet was Cromwell's Chamberlain and sat in the House of Lords during the Protectorate. **First MP 1626. One additional MP 1640 also for Northamptonshire**.

1. Sir Gilbert Pickering 3 Bt – Leicestershire 1708-10
2. Sir Edward Pickering 4 Bt – St. Michael 1745-47

Seats: Titchmarsh, Northamptonshire (acq. c. 1553, sold 1766); (West) Langton Hall, Leicestershire (built 1660-69 acq. by mar. later 17th c., sold by descendents mid-19th c.)
Title: Baronet 1638-1749
Notes: Descent of the title is uncertain after 1749. Lord Pickering and three others in ODNB.

PIERREPONT [Hall, Meadows]

Duke of Kingston (1715-73 GB)

Origins: Large landowners in Nottinghamshire since the 13th century. Came from Picardy in France and originally settled in Sussex soon after the Conquest. Rose to great fortune by estate management. (Stone, *The Crisis of the Aristocracy*, 190) Married the daughter and heiress of Sir Michael Manvers (d. 1255) of Holme. The 1 Earl also married an heiress in 1601. (Payling, *Political Society in Lancastrian England*, 21) **First MP 1417 for Nottinghamshire. Five further MPs 1472-1640, three of them for the county. Possibly three further MPs 1399-1461.**

1. William Pierrepont – Shropshire 1640 Much Wenlock 1640-48 Nottinghamshire 1654 1660
2. Robert Pierrepont – Nottingham 1660-81
3. Francis Pierrepont – Nottingham 1689-90
4. Evelyn Pierrepont 1 Duke of Kingston – East Retford 1689-90
5. William Pierrepont – Nottingham 1695-1706
6. Gervase Pierrepont 1 Baron Pierrepont – Appleby 1698-1705
7. Charles Meadows Pierrepont 1 Earl Manvers – Nottinghamshire 1778-96
8. Evelyn Pierrepont – Bossiney 1796 Nottinghamshire 1796-1801
9. Charles Pierrepont 2 Earl Manvers – Nottinghamshire 1801-16
10. Charles Pierrepont Viscount Newark – East Retford 1830-34
11. Sydney Pierrepont 3 Earl Manvers – S. Nottinghamshire 1852-60
12. Charles Pierrepont 4 Earl Manvers – Newark Div. Nottinghamshire 1885-95 1898-1900

Seats: Thoresby Park, Nottinghamshire (acq. first half 17th c., house built 1680s, rebuilt 1760s, rebuilt 1864-75 at a cost of £171,000 – Franklin, *The Gentleman's Country House*, 268 – sold 1980, hotel); Holme Pierrepont, Nottinghamshire (acq. by mar. 1288 from the Manvers, built c. 1499, add. 1628, main seat moved to Thoresby 1680, much of it demolished 1730s, add. 1870s, still own); Oldcotes, Derbyshire (medieval, rebuilt 1592-3, purch. 1608, remod. 1690, demolished 1711)
Estates: Bateman 38036 (E) 51649. Worth £7,000 pa in 1640 and £21,000 pa in 1773. Largest landowners in Nottinghamshire 17th c.
Titles: Baron Pierrepont and Viscount Newark 1627-1773 E; Earl of Kingston 1628-1773 E; Marquess of Dorchester 1645-80 E; Baron Pierrepont 1703-15 I; Marquess of Dorchester 1706-73 GB; Baron Pierrpont 1714-15 GB; Earl Manvers 1806-1955 UK
Peers: 11 Peers 1660-1726 {1 peer 1703-15} 1714-15 1732-73 1796-1945
2 Lds Lt 17th, 18th
1 in Cabinet 1716-26
2 KG 18th

Notes: 1 Earl of Kingston and 1 Earl Manvers and 1 Marquess and 1 and 2 Duke and two others in ODNB.

Meadows (Meadowes, Medows)

Origins: The founder of the family was Latin Secretary to Cromwell and Ambassador to Portugal in the 1650s. Kt 1658. The sister and heiress of the 2 and last Duke of Kingston had a son, Charles Meadows, who took the name Pierrpont and was created Earl Manvers in 1806 (see above).

1. Sir Philip Meadows – Truro 1698-1700 1702-08 Tregony 1705-08
2. Sir Sidney Meadows – Penryn 1722-27 Tavistock 1727-41

Seat: Conholt House (Park), Hampshire (acq. by mar. and built later 17th c., rebuilt c. 1795, passed by inher. 1826 to Pierreponts and later Nories who took name Meadows, remod. 1826, sold 1897)
Notes: Three in ODNB.

Hall

Origins: The heiress of John Hall, the last of his line, married the heir of the 1 Duke of Kingston. The Halls resided in Bradford from the mid-13th century. **First MP 1425 for Wells. One further MP 1431.**

1. John Hall – Wells 1673-81

Seat: The Hall, Bradford-on-Avon (aka Kingston House), Wiltshire (medieval, property acq. 14th c., rebuilt c. 1580, passed to Pierreponts by inher. after 1711, sold 1802)
Estates: Worth £900 pa in 1660.
Notes: Extinct in male line 1711.

PIGOT

Baron Pigot (1766-77 I)

Origins: 1 Baron was Governor of Fort St. George, Madras 1755, son of a royal stables manager. Returned to England a nabob 1763 and purchased estates.

1. George Pigot 1 Baron Pigot – Wallingford 1765-68 Bridgnorth 1768-77
2. Sir Robert Pigot 2 Bt – Wallingford 1768-72
3. Hugh Pigot – Penryn 1768-74 Bridgnorth 1778-84
4. Sir Robert Pigot 4 Bt – Bridgnorth 1832-37 1838-53

Seats: Patshull Hall, Staffordshire (built 1720s, purch. 1765, sold 1848); Branches Park, Cambridgeshire (Suffolk) (demolished 1957)
Estates: Purchased Patshull for £80,000 to £100,000.
Title: Baronet 1764-
Peer: 1 peer 1766-77
Notes: 1 Baron and four others in ODNB.

PIGOTT [Pershall] *IRELAND & ENGLAND*

Pigott

Origins: Established in Shropshire soon after the Conquest (Fisher, *The House of Commons*, VI, 777). Branches were established at Chetwynd Park, Doddershall, Knapton, Brockley Court, and Capard, combined here. The estates of several lines, though remotely separated, eventually passed from one branch to another. For example the Doddershall estates passed to the Chetwynd Pigotts in 1704. **First MP 1589. Another MP 1604-07**. The Irish branch began with an official who acquired estates in Queen's County 1562. **First {MP 1613}. Another {MP 1634}.**

1. Thomas Pigott – {Queen's County 1661-66}
2. Alexander Pigott – {Maryborough 1661-66}
3. Robert Pigott – {Maryborough 1703-30}
4. John Pigott – Somerset 1705-07
5. Robert Pigott – Huntingdonshire 1713-2 1730-41
6. Emanuel Pigott – {Cork 1735-60}
7. John Pigott – {Banagher 1761-63}
8. Thomas Pigott – {Taghmon 1776-83 Midleton 1783-93}
9. George Pigott – St. Mawes 1830-32

Seats: Brockley Hall (Court), Somerset (purch. and built mid-17th c., remod. 18th and 1825, sold 20th c., institutional use); Chetwynd Park, Shropshire (orig. Chetwynd seat, acq. 15th c., rebuilt 17th c., sold 1774, demolished c. 1970); Chesterton, Huntingdonshire (acq. 1708-10, sold late 18th c.); Doddershall House (Park), Buckinghamshire (medieval, Pigotts began to purch land 15th c., rebuilt 1520s, remod. c. 1600, c., add. 1689, add. 19th c., still owned 1927, passed to descendents who still own); Knapton, Queen's County (built 16th c., acq. 18th c., rebuilt c. 1773, sold later 19th c.); Capard, Queen's County (acq. and built 1622, add. late 18th c., resident 20th c.)
Estates: Bateman 14409 (E & I) 15663. Chetwynd Park sold for £70,000 in 1774. Rubinstein – Wadham Pigott left £140,000 in probate 1823.
Title: Baronet 1808-
Notes: Lords of the manor of Weston-super-Mare. Lived exclusively in England in 20th c. Four in ODNB.

Pershall (Peshale, Peshall)

Origins: Emerged as gentry in the mid-14th century. **First MP 1341 for Staffordshire. Four further MPs 1373-1529, three kts of the shire.** Chetwynd Park passed from the Chetwynd heiress to Sir Richard de Peshale (living c. 1330s). It passed by marriage in the 15th century from the Peshales to Robert Pigot via an heiress. The Pigots held it for 12 generations until they sold it in 1774.

1. John Pershall – Stafford 1701-02

Seats: Horsley, Staffordshire (purch. 14th c., sold 1712); Great Sugnall House, Staffordshire (acq. 17th c., passed 1761 to Earls of Breadalbane by mar. to Pershall heiress)
Estates: Worth £1,500 pa in 1696.

PINKERTON *SCOTLAND*

Origins: Merchants 17th century. **First [MP 1612 for Rutherglen]. Another [MP 1649]. One further possible [1621].** First two [MPs] Provosts of Rutherglen.

1. Andrew Pinkerton – [Rutherglen 1667]

Notes: Andrew Pinkerton above was forced to leave Rutherglen for a period to avoid creditors.

PITT [Beckford, Darcy, Freke, Nassau de Zuylenstein, Pynsent, Ridgeway, Savage] *ENGLAND & IRELAND*

Baron Rivers (1776-1828 GB; 1802-80 UK)

Origins: The Pitts were a Dorset family that rose over three generations in the service of James I. Sir William Pitt, the King's Comptroller of the Household, purchased Stratfield Saye. **First MP 1604. Three further MPs 1621-25**. A Pitt of Stratfield Saye married the daughter and heiress of the 2 Earl Rivers of St. Osyth's, Essex (purch. by 1539 by D'Arcys and passed by mar. to Savages) also heiress of the 6 Baron Chandos of Sudeley Castle. Their son was created the 1 Baron Rivers. His daughter married Peter Beckford of Stepleton House (see below). Their son took the name Pitt-Rivers in 1828 and succeeded to the Rivers Barony of Sudeley Castle by special remainder. The heiress of the Barons Rivers married a younger son of James Lane Fox of Bramham (see that family). Her grandson, Augustus Lane Fox, took the additional name Pitt-Rivers on succeeding to the estates in 1880. He resided at Rushmore.

1. George Pitt – Wareham 1660-79
2. George Pitt – Stockbridge 1694-95 Wareham 1698-1702 Hampshire 1702-05 Wareham 1705-10 Hampshire 1710-13 Wareham 1713-15 Hampshire 1715-22 Old Sarum 1725-27
3. John Pitt – Stockbridge 1698-1701 St. Ives 1702-05
4. George Pitt – Wareham 1715-22 Dorset 1727
5. George Pitt – Old Sarum 1722-24 Pontefract 1741-54
6. John Pitt – Wareham 1734-47 1748-50 Dorchester 1751-61 Wareham 1761-68
7. George Pitt 1 Baron Rivers – Shaftesbury 1742-47 Dorset 1747-74
8. William Pitt – Wareham 1754-61
9. George Pitt 2 Baron Rivers – Dorset 1774-90
10. William Pitt – Poole 1780-90 Dorset 1790-1826

Seats: Stratfield Saye, Hampshire (purch. 1629 for £4,800, built 1630, add. 18th c., sold 1817); Kingston Maurward, Dorset (medieval, rebuilt 1590s, acq. by mar. early 18th c., rebuilt 1717-20, remod. 1794, sold early 19th c.?); Heckfield Park (changed to Highfield Park 1818), Hampshire (purch. before 1778, sold 1817); Shroton, Dorset (built later 16th c., acq. by mar. 1714, house sold 1789, demolished 1790s, estate held by Pitt-Rivers, sold 1918); Sudeley Castle, Gloucestershire (medieval, rebuilt mid 15th c., acq. c. 1554, remod. 1572 and 1614, slighted 1648-50, acq. by mar. 1789, sold 1810); Rushmore House, Dorset (built 15th c., rebuilt early 17th c., acq. by mar. 1714, rebuilt 1817, passed to Lane Fox family 1880 who took name Pitt-Rivers, family departed 1927, sold 1963, house is a school); Stepleton House, Dorset (built later 16th c., acq. 1623, rebuilt 1670s, purch. by Beckfords 1745, add. 1758, passed by mar. to Pitt-Rivers 1811, sold 1917); Encombe, Dorset (purch. 1734, rebuilt c. 1730s, 1770, sold 1807)
Estates: Bateman 27704 (E) 35396. Estates worth £10,000 to 12,000 pa in 1694. Estate stood at 7,500 acres in the 1960s (Legg, *Dorset Families*, 117).
Peers: 5 peers 1776-1880
1 Ld Lt 18th-19th
Notes: 1 Baron 1st cr. and three others in ODNB.

<u>Earl Rivers</u> (1626-1737 E)

Origins: The Savage family was established in Cheshire in the early 14th century. They succeeded to the Darcy estates in Essex by marriage (see below). **First MP 1491 for Staffordshire. Seven further MPs 1491-1628, three kts of the shire. First {MP 1613}**. On the death of the last Earl his estates were divided between the 4 Earl's daughter and the 2 Earl's daughter, who married into the Pitt family. The former, Lady Elizabeth Savage, married the 4 Earl of Barrymore (see Barry). Their daughter Penelope married James Cholmondeley. His illegitimate child married 1714 the 3 Earl of Rochford (see below), whose son succeeded to St. Osyth's. The descendents of

Cholomondeley's brother, the Marquesses of Cholomondeley, succeeded to the Rivers estates in Cheshire in the mid-18th century (see Cholomondeley).

1. Richard Savage 4 Earl Rivers – Wigan 1681 Liverpool 1689-94

Seats: Rock Savage (Rocksavage), Cheshire (medieval, rebuilt 1565-8, passed to Cholmondeleys mid-18th c. and left to fall into ruin); St. Osyth's Priory, Essex (built 13th c. and 1527, acq. by Darcys c. 1540, passed by mar. to Savages and then to Earls of Rochford 1737); Wardley Hall, Lancashire (medieval, acq. by mar. of 1679, passed to an heiress 1712)
Estates: Northern estates worth £1,919 pa in the 1660s.
Titles: Baron Darcy 1613-1737 E; Viscount Colchester 1621-1737 E; Viscount Savage 1626-1737 E; Baronet 1611-1737
Peers: 2 peers 1660-1712
1 Ld Lt 17th-18th
Notes: A Roman Catholic family. The last Earl was a priest. Savage family and the 4 Earl and two others have entries in the ODNB.

Earl of Rochford (1695-1830 E)

Origins: The Darcys rose through business and law in the 14th and 15th centuries. They were London vintners, Lord Mayor of London 1337. Barons 1551. **First MP 1401 (for Essex 1416). Two further MPs 1450-1547, both for the county.** The Darcys acquired St. Osyth's at the Dissolution. The 3 Baron Darcy was created Earl Rivers (see above), which passed by special remainder through the female line, and St. Osyth's passed to the Savage family and then to the Earls of Rochford. The latter family of Nassau descended from an uncle of King William III, an illegitimate son of Frederick Henry Prince of Orange, who came to England in 1688.

1. Sir Thomas Darcy 1 Bt – Malden 1679-81 1685-87 1689-93
2. William Nassau de Zuylenstein 2 Earl of Rochford – {Kilkenny 1705-09} Steyning 1708
3. Richard Nassau – Colchester 1747-54 Maldon 1774-80

Seats: St. Osyth's Priory, Essex (built 13th c. and 1527, acq. by Darcys c. 1540, passed to Earls of Rochford, 1737, add. mid-18th c., passed to illegitimate branch of Nassaus (Johnson) 1830, remod. 1865, sold 1924); Easton Park, Suffolk (built early 17th c., purch. c. 1700, passed by inher. to the Duke of Hamilton 1830, demolished 1923); Braxted Lodge, Essex (purch. early 17th c., built mid 17th c., sold 1692)
Estates: The 1 Earl of Rochford was granted 30,000 acres in Ireland, later given up. Illegitimate descendents of the 4 Earl of Rochford inherited St. Osyth's 1830 – 3940 (E) 4500. Worth £2,000 pa in 1781.

Titles: Baron Enfield and Viscount Tunbridge 1695-1830 E
Peers: 5 peers 1696-1830
1 Ld Lt 18th
1 in Cabinet 1768-75
1 KG 18th
Notes: 1 Baron Darcy of 1551 cr. and one other Darcy and 1, 2, 3, and 4 Earls of Rochford and two other Nassaus in ODNB.

Freke

Origins: The Frekes were Tudor yeomen who gradually built up an estate in service to the Crown (Teller of the Exchequer 1571-92). Sheriff 1597. Kt 1603. **First MP 1584 (Dorset 1604). One additional MP 1614.**

1. Thomas Freke – Dorset 1679-81 1685-87 1689-1701
2. Thomas Freke – Cricklade 1685 1689-90 Weymouth & Melcombe Regis 1691-1700 Lyme Regis 1705-10

Seats: Shroton, Dorset (acq. 1564 and 1577, passed by mar. to Pitts 1714 see above); Abbey House, Cerne Abbey, Dorset (medieval monastic buildings, fire c. 1750, new house built mid-18th c., passed to Pitts 1714, passed to Lane Fox family 1880 who took name Pitt-Rivers, sold 1919)
Estates: Estates worth £100,000 in the 16th century. Worth £4,000 pa in 1657.
Notes: The family became extinct and the estates passed to the Pitts of Stratfield Saye (see above) 1714. For the Irish branch of the family see Evans-Freke. Two in ODNB.

Hussey-Freke

Origins: The Husseys were burgesses of Salisbury in the 18th century, Mayor 1737. The Mayor was a clothier. He inherited considerable landed property in Dorset. Ambrose Hussey MP married in 1862 Florence Freke of the Frekes of Shroton and took the additional name Freke.

1. William Hussey – St. Germans 1765-68 Hindon 1768-74 Salisbury 1774-1813
2. Ambrose Hussey-Freke – Salisbury 1843-47

Seat: The Hall, Salisbury, Wiltshire (built mid-18th c. still resident later 19th c.)
Estates: Bateman 3911 (E) 5925. Rubinstein – William Hussey left £125,000 probate in 1813.

Beckford

Origins: Gentry in the 17th century. Emigrated to Jamaica in the early 17th century and became sugar planters. Speaker of the Jamaican Assembly. Returned and settled in London in 1735, Lord Mayor of London 1762. The daughter of the 1 Baron Rivers married Peter Beckford (see above), whose son took the name Pitt-Rivers in 1828 on succeeding his mother in the Pitt barony.

1. William Beckford – Shaftesbury 1747-54 London 1754-70
2. Julines Beckford – Salisbury 1754-64
3. Richard Beckford – Bristol 1754-56
4. Peter Beckford – Morpeth 1768-74
5. Richard Beckford – Bridport 1780-84 Arundel 1784-90 Leominster 1791-96
6. William Beckford – Wells 1784-90 Hindon 1790-94 1806-20

Seats: Stepleton House (Steepleton Iwerne), Dorset (built. later 16th c., rebuilt 1670s, purch. 1745, add. 1750s, passed by mar. to Pitt-Rivers 1811, see above); Fonthill Abbey, Wiltshire (house built 16th c., purch. 1745, fire 1755, rebuilt (House) 1755-57, new house (Abbey) built 1794-1807, sold 1823, collapsed 1825 – see Morrison and Grosvenor for development of the two houses); Witham Hall, Somerset (purch. 1761, built 1762-70, incomplete, sold early 19th c., demolished, farm house)
Estates: Peter Beckford (d. 1710) held twenty estates, 1,200 slaves and, it is said, £1,500,000 in funds. His son Peter was worth £300,000. William Beckford, the 18th century MP, left an estate worth £27,000 pa. The Fonthill estate consisted of 4,000 to 5,000 acres.
Notes: Extinct in male line 1844. Five in ODNB.

Earl of Chatham (1766-1835 GB)

Origins: A younger brother of Sir William Pitt (d. 1636) established the branch seated at Boconnoc. They were tradesmen and professional men for five generations. Robert Pitt MP and Thomas Pitt MP went to India in 1698 as merchants. The latter returned to England as "Diamond" Pitt (the diamond sold for £125,000), one of the most celebrated nabobs. The family produced two prime ministers.

1. Thomas Pitt – Old Sarum 1689 Salisbury 1689-95 Old Sarum 1695-98 1710-16 Thirsk 1717-22 Old Sarum 1722-26
2. Robert Pitt – Old Sarum 1705-10 Salisbury 1710-13 Old Sarum 1713-22 Okehampton 1722-27
3. John Pitt – Hindon 1720-22 Old Sarum 1724-27 Camelford 1727-34
4. Thomas Pitt – Okehampton 1727-54 Old Sarum 1754-55 1761

5. William Pitt 1 Earl of Chatham – Old Sarum 1735-47 Seaford 1747-54 Aldeburgh 1754-56 Buckingham 1756 Okehampton 1756-57 Bath 1757-66
6. Thomas Pitt 1 Baron Camelford – Old Sarum 1761-68 1774-84 Okehampton 1768-74
7. William Pitt – Appleby 1781-84 University of Cambridge 1784-1806

Seats: Boconnoc, Cornwall (purch. 1718, remod. mid-18th c., passed by mar. through the Grenvilles to the Fortescues 1864); Marwarden Court, Wiltshire (built c. 1600, purch. 1690, occupied first half 18th c.); Hayes Place, Kent (purch. 1757, sold 1785, demolished 1933); Burton Pynsent, Somerset (inher. 1765, rebuilt 1760s, sold 1805 and most of the house demolished); Swallowfield Park, Berkshire (built 1680s, purch. 1719, sold later 18th c.)
Estates: Bateman 22985 (E) 18093. Worth £300,000 in 1710 and £500,000 in 1804. Descendents still held 8,000 acres in 1968.
Titles: Baron Pitt 1761-1835 GB; Baron Camelford 1784-1804 GB
Peers: 4 peers 1766-1835 1784-93 1796-1804
3 in Cabinet 1756-61 1766-68 1782-1801 1788-1806 1803-06 1807-10
1 KG 18th-19th
Notes: On the extinction of the Camelford peerage the estates passed to the sister of the last Lord, the wife of Lord Grenville, who left the property to her husband's nephew the second son of the 1 Earl Fortescue (see Fortescue). 1 and 2 Barons Camelford and and 1 and 2 Earls and Pitt the Younger and two others in ODNB.

Pynsent

Origins: Yeomen and then merchants. Gained estates in the 1670s. High Sheriff 1693. The 1 Baronet was a barrister. Sir William Pynsent 2 Bt left his estates to the 1 Earl of Chatham in the spirit of patriotism.

1. Sir William Pynsent 1 Bt – Devizes 1689-90
2. Sir William Pynsent 2 Bt – Taunton 1715-22

Seats: Burton Pynsent, Somerset (purch. and built by the Jennings mid-16th century, passed by heiress to Pynsents 1679, passed to the Earl of Chatham by bequest 1765 see above); Urchfont, Wiltshire (built 15th c., purch. and rebuilt c. 1680, remod. 1700, passed to Chatham 1765, sold 1767)
Title: Baronet 1687-1765

Earl of Londonderry (1622-1714 I; 1726-65 I)

Origins: A younger son "Diamond" Pitt (see above, Chatham) married the heiress of Robert Ridgeway 4 Earl of Londonderry of the first creation. He was created Earl of Londonderry after the extinction of the Ridgeway title in 1714. The 1 Earl of

Londonderry of the first creation rose as a soldier in Ireland under Elizabeth I. **First MP 1539. Another MP for Devon 1604 and {MP 1613 for County Tyrone}. Another {MP 1613}.**

1. Thomas Pitt 1 Earl of Londonderry – Wilton 1713-27 Old Sarum 1727-28
2. Ridgeway Pitt 3 Earl of Londonderry – Camelford 1747-54

Seats: Soldon (Souldon), Devon (built mid-16th c., add. mid-17th c., purch. 1713, passed by inher. to Earl Stanhope 1734); Tor Mohum (Torwood, Torre Abbey), Devon (purch. 1599); The Down House (Blandford), Dorset (Pitts purch. and built early 18th c., sold 1804, fire 1941, demolished 1954)
Titles: Baron Ridgeway 1616-1714 I; Baron Londonderry 1719-65 I; Baronet 1611-1714
Notes: On the extinction of the Pitts, the estates passed by marriage to the Meyricks of Bodorgan, Anglesey (see that family). The Ridgeways owned estates in Ulster acquired in the early 17th c. Held official positions. **{MP 1613}.** 1 Earl 2nd cr. in ODNB.

PLEYDELL-BOUVERIE [Morton, Pusey]

Earl of Radnor (1765- GB)

Origins: The Bouveries were Huguenot silk weavers who moved from Lille to Canterbury in 1568. The founder of the aristocratic family was a Turkey merchant in the City in the 17th century. William Bouverie 1 Earl of Radnor married Harriet Pleydell, daughter and heiress of Sir Mark Pleydell 1 Bt of Coleshill. The 2 Earl succeeded to the Pleydell estates and took the additional name Pleydell (see below).

1. Jacob des Bouverie – Hythe 1695-1700 1713-22
2. Sir Edward Bouverie 2 Bt – Shaftesbury 1719-34
3. Jacob Bouverie 1 Viscount Folkestone – Salisbury 1741-47
4. William Bouverie 1 Earl of Radnor – Salisbury 1747-61
5. Edward Bouverie – Salisbury 1761-71 Northampton 1790-1810
6. Jacob Pleydell-Bouverie 2 Earl of Radnor – Salisbury 1771-76
7. William Bouverie – Salisbury 1776-1802
8. Bartholomew Bouverie – Downton 1779-80 1790-96 1806-12 1819-30
9. Edward Bouverie – Downton 1796-1803
10. William Pleydell-Bouverie 3 Earl of Radnor – Downton 1801-02 Salisbury 1802-28
11. Duncombe Pleydell-Bouverie – Downton 1806-07 Salisbury 1828-32 1833-34
12. Charles Bouverie – Dorchester 1811-12 Downton 1812-13
13. Philip Pleydell-Bouverie – Cockermouth 1830-31 Downton 1831-32 Berkshire 1857-65
14. Edward Pleydell-Bouverie – Kilmarnock 1844-74

15. William Pleydell-Bouverie 5 Earl of Radnor – S. Wiltshire 1874-85 Enfield Div. Middlesex 1885-89
16. Jacob Pleydell-Bouverie 6 Earl of Radnor – S. Wiltshire 1892-1900

Seats: Longford Castle, Wiltshire (built 1576-91, purch. 1717, remod. 1870, still own); Coleshill, Berkshire (built 1649-62, sold 1945, fire 1952); Delapre Abbey, Northamptonshire (medieval, add. early 17th and early 18th c., purch. 1764, add. 1820-40, sold 1946, institutional use)
Estates: Bateman 24870 (E) 42900+. Worth £75,000,000 in 1990. Owned 11,000 acres in 2001. A younger son at Brymore, Somerset 4082 (E) 4091; younger son at East Lavington Manor, Wiltshire 3349 (E) 4811; younger son's line at Delapre Abbey, Northamptonshire 3188 (E) 8676
Titles: Viscount Folkestone 1747- GB; Baronet 1714-
Peers: 8 peers 1747-1945
3 Lds Lt 18th, 19th, 20th
Notes: The 2 Earl of Radnor married the daughter of the 1 Baron Feversham, and she brought with her Downton and the Wiltshire estates of that family (see Duncombe). 1 Viscount and 3 Earl and three others in ODNB.

<u>Pusey</u>

Origins: The earliest certain reference to the Puseys dates to 1086. (Fisher, *The House of Commons*, VI, 908) The family tradition was that the estates were granted by King Canute. (*Victoria County History, Berkshire*, ed. Wm. Page and P. H. Ditchfield, 1924, IV, 472) The last male Pusey died in 1710. He left his estates to a nephew, John Allen, who took the name Pusey. He married Jane Bouverie. The estates passed to Allen's sisters. The last of these left the property to her sister-in-law's nephew, Philip Bouverie, a younger son of the 1 Viscount Folkestone (see above). He succeeded in 1789 and changed his name to Pusey in 1784.

1. Philip Pusey – Rye 1830 Chippenham 1830-31 Cashel 1831-32 Berkshire 1835-52

Seat: Pusey House, Berkshire (acq. 11th century, sold 1935)
Estates: Rubinstein – Philip Pusey left £140,000 in probate in 1828.
Notes: Two in ODNB.

<u>Pleydell</u>

Origins: The Pleydells were monastic tenants, who acquired estates after the Dissolution. Two lawyers in the 17th century raised the family higher. **First MP 1563. Two further MPs 1593-1644**. The Coleshill estates passed by marriage to the Bouveries (see above).

1. John Pleydell – Wootton Bassett 1660-79 Cricklade 1680-81 Wootton Bassett 1681 1685-87
2. Edward Pleydell – Cricklade 1698-1700
3. John Pleydell – Wootton Bassett 1705-06
4. Edmund Pleydell – Wootton Bassett 1710-15
5. Edmund Pleydell – Dorchester 1722-23 Dorset 1727-47

Seats: Coleshill, Berkshire (see above); Whatcombe House, Dorset (acq. by mar. c. 1700, rebuilt 1750, owned into 2nd half 20th c., leased to institutional use 1989); Midgehall (Midge Hall), Wiltshire (medieval, leased 1534, family departed c. 1726, farm house)
Estates: Bateman (Mansel-Pleydell) 8699 (E) 7435

Morton

Origins: The family could trace its origins to the 14th century when it inherited lands by marriage from a family with early medieval lineage. Master of the Rolls 1475. Cardinal Morton, Archbishop of Canterbury, was an official in Henry VII's government. **First MP 1437. Two other MPs 1572-1625.** The daughter and heiress of Sir John Morton 2 Bt married Edmund Pleydell (see above).

1. Sir John Morton 2 Bt – Poole 1661-79 Weymouth & Melcombe Regis 1679-81 1685-87 1689-95

Seats: Milborne St. Andrew, Dorset (acq. early 15th c., family abandoned mid-18th c., no longer standing); Whatcombe House, Dorset (became principal seat of Morton Pleydells c. 1750, rebuilt c. 1752, add. 1802, passed to descendents until family departed 1939, sold 1960s)
Title: Baronet 1619-99
Notes: Financially troubled 17th c. Two in ODNB.

PLUMER [Ward]

Origins: The Plumers were London merchants seated at Blakesware from 1685. A junior line gained a Baronetcy (1661-97). A descendent of the senior line, William Plumer of Gilston Park, married as her first husband James Hamilton, granddaughter of the 7 Earl of Abercorn by Anne Plumer of Blakesware. Her second husband was Robert Ward, who took the additional name Plumer and succeeded to Gilston. The Wards were successful London merchants. The Plumers and Wards are merged in this entry.

1. Walter Plumer – Aldeburgh 1719-27 Appleby 1730-41
2. William Plumer – Yarmouth (IoW) 1721-22 Hertfordshire 1734-41 1755-61

3. Richard Plumer – Lichfield 1722-34 St. Mawes 1734-41 Aldeburgh 1741-47 Weymouth & Melcombe Regis 1747-50
4. William Plumer – Lewes 1763-68 Hertfordshire 1768-1807 Higham Ferrers 1812-22
5. Robert Plumer Ward – Cockermouth 1802-06 Haslemere 1807-23
6. William Ward – London 1826-31
7. Sir Henry Ward – St. Albans 1832-37 Sheffield 1837-49

Seats: Blakesware, Hertfordshire (Plumer purch. 1685, sold mid-19th c.); Gilston Park, Hertfordshire (Plumer purch. 1701, sold by 1852); Chediston Hall, Suffolk (built 16th c., purch. 1722, sold 1833, demolished 1955); Hyde House, Buckinghamshire (built early 18th c., purch. 1804, remod. early 19th c., sold 1832); Northwood Park, Hampshire (IoW) (purch. and built 1793, donated 1929 to local council)
Estates: Bateman 10,000 (E) 11,000. Rubinstein – George Ward left £200,000 in probate in 1829.
Notes: Two in ODNB.

PLUMMER

Origins: The first MP was a West Indian merchant dealing in rum. The next two MPs were West Indian merchants also involved with insurance.

1. Thomas Plummer – Ilchester 1802-03
2. Thomas Plummer – Yarmouth (IoW) 1806-07
3. John Plummer – Hindon 1820-26

Notes: On the death of the last MP in 1839 the family property was divided among six heirs.

PLUMPTRE [Bridges]

Baron Fitzwalter (1295- E)

Origins: The Plumptres were an old Nottinghamshire family dating from the 12th century. The first MP was a clothier and Mayor of Nottingham. **First MP 1388 for Nottingham. One further MP 1430 for the city.** On the death of the 1 Earl of Fitzwalter (see St. John) the medieval Barony of Fitzwalter went into abeyance. It was revived for Henry Plumptre in 1924. He was the grandson of Eleanor Bridges, granddaughter of Fanny Fowler, who was the granddaughter of Frances Mildmay, a descendent of the 11 Baron.

1. John Plumptre – Nottingham 1706-13 1715-27 Bishop's Castle 1727-34 Nottingham 1734-61 St. Ives 1747-51

2. John Plumptre – Penryn 1758-61 Nottingham 1761-74
3. John Plumptre – E. Kent 1832-52

Seats: Plumptre House, Nottinghamshire (original house 13th c., rebuilt on a different site 1707, remod. c. 1723, sold c. 1791, demolished 1853); Fredville Park, Kent (acq. by mar. 1750, add. 1750s, add. 1880, abandoned in favor of a smaller house in the park 1921, big house fire c. 1940, demolished 1945, still own estate)
Estates: Bateman 2420 (E) 3660
Peers: 1 peer 1924-32
Notes: Nine in ODNB.

Baron Fitzwalter (1868-75 UK)

Origins: The first significant Bridges was Auditor of the Exchequer 1672. The 3 Bt married the co-heiress of the medieval Barons Fitzwalter (see above).

1. William Bridges – Liskeard 1695-1714
2. Sir Brook Bridges 3 Bt – Kent 1763-74
3. Brook Bridges 1 Baron Fitzwalter – E. Kent 1852 1857-68

Seat: Goodnestone Park, Kent (purch. 1700, built 1704, add. 1780, c. 1820-30, and 1838-44, fire 1959, restored, for sale 2015)
Estates: Bateman 5971 (E) 9742. Still owned 2,500 acres in the 1980s.
Title: Baronet 1718-1899
Peers: 1 peer 1868-75

PLUNKET *IRELAND*

Baron Plunket (1827- UK)

Origins: Poor Presbyterian clergymen in the 18th century. Barrister, Attorney General of Ireland, Lord Chancellor of Ireland 1830.

1. William Plunket 1 Baron Plunket – {Charlemont 1798-1800} Midhurst 1807 Dublin University 1812-27
2. David Plunket 1 Baron Rathmore – Dublin University 1870-95

Seat: Old Connaught House, Wicklow (built early 19th c., resident in 20th c.)
Estates: Bateman 3567 (I) 3254
Title: Baron Rathmore 1895-1919 UK
Peers: 8 peers 1827-1938 1895-1919 1944-45
Notes: 1 and 4 Barons in ODNB.

PLUNKETT *IRELAND*

Earl of Fingall (1628-1974 I)

Origins: Supposedly of Danish origin settled in Louth by the 12th century. In Meath in the 15th century. Deputy to the Lord Lieutenant 1432. Baron 1449 or earlier. **First {MP 1310}. Five other {MPs 1559-1639}**. Remained loyal to the Roman Catholic Church.

1. Arthur Plunkett 9 Earl of Fingall – Meath 1830-32

Seat: Killeen Castle, Meath (acq. by Norman Cusack family c. 1175, built 1181-1200, passed by mar. to Plunkets 1403, remod. 1780-81, add. c. 1804, remod. 1841, sold 1952, fire 1981, ruin, restored, hotel)
Estates: Bateman 9594 (I) 8727
Titles: Baron Killeen c. 1449- I; Baron Fingall 1831- UK
Peers: {1 peer 1795-1800} 5 peers 1831-1945
1 Ld Lt 19th
2 KP 19th
Notes: Estates squandered by 4 Earl. 2 Earl and two others in in ODNB.

Baron Dunsany (1462- I)

Origins: Descended from an uncle of the 1 Baron Killeen. Exiled in 1689 and the title was outlawed in 1691, restored 1791. The family recovered Dunsany in the early 18th century after the heir conformed to the Established Church.

1. Randall Plunkett 15 Baron Dunsany – Drogheda 1835-37
2. Randall Plunkett – W. Gloucestershire 1874-80
3. John Plunkett 17 Baron Dunsany – S. Gloucestershire 1886-92
4. Horace Plunkett – S. Dublin 1892-1900

Seat: Dunsany Castle, Meath (built c. 1200, acq. by mar. 1403, remod. 1780s, remod. 1840s, add. 1910, still own)
Estates: Bateman 8400 (I & W) 9680. Owned 900 acres in 2001.
Peers: {3 peers 1660-66 1689-90 1785-1800} 3 Irish Rep peers 1850-52 1864-89 1893-99
1 Ld Lt 19th
Notes: 9 and 18 Barons and one other (Ernle-Erle-Drax) and one other in ODNB.

Baron Louth (1541- I)

Origins: Descended from John Plunkett, from whose younger son Richard are descended the Earls of Fingall and Barons Dunsany. The Barons Louth were outlawed in 1642, declared not eligible to sit in the House of Lords in 1698, and readmitted in 1798.

1. Charles Plunkett – {Banagher 1711-29}

Seat: Louth Hall (Tallanstown), Louth (medieval castle, enlarged later 16th c., add. 1760 and 1805, sold 1941, ruin)
Estates: Bateman 4099 (I & E) 4604. Worth £3,000 pa in 1714. Blocks of land sold 1679 and 1720. Most of estate sold by 1909.
Peers: {2 peers 1689 1798-1800}

Plunkett

Origins: Kinsmen of the Earls of Fingall. **First {MP 1639}.**

1. Sir Walter Plunkett – {Gorey 1661 Granard 1692-93 1695-99}
2. William Plunkett – {Swords 1713-27}

Seats: Rathbe(a)le Hall (House) (aka St. Catherine's Grove), Dublin (built late 1680s, sold 1748); The Manor, Ratoath, Meath (resident 18th c., sold 1813)

POLEY

Origins: Gentry in Suffolk by the end of the 14th century. Several of the MPs were lawyers. **First MP 1545. Four additional MPs 1559-1628**. Sir John Poley MP was a distant cousin seated at Boxted.

1. Sir Edmund Poley – Bury St. Edmunds 1661-71
2. Henry Poley – Eye 1689-95 West Looe 1703-05 Ipswich 1705-07
3. Sir John Poley – Sudbury 1689-90

Seats: Badley Hall, Suffolk (medieval, acq. by mar. and built late 15th c., part collapsed 1703, passed by mar. to Gipps family 1715, sold c. 1720s, two-thirds demolished 1759, became farm houses); Boxted Hall, Suffolk (medieval house, acq. 14th c., rebuilt 16th c., passed to Weller family by mar. 1773 took name Poley, still own)
Estates: Bateman 5061 (E) 5794
Notes: Male line at Badley extinct 1707. One in ODNB.

POLHILL [Turner]

Origins: Settled with some land in Sussex since the 17th century. First eminent Polhill was a tobacco merchant in London and banker mid-18th century. Purchased estates 1770s. High Sheriff 1805.

1. Nathaniel Polhill – Southwark 1774-82
2. Frederick Polhill – Bedford 1830-32 1835-47
3. Frederick Polhill-Turner – Bedford 1874-80

Seats: Howbury Hall, Bedfordshire (built 18th c., purch. 1781 for £17,500, fire 1847 and rebuilt 1852, still own); Burwash, Sussex (purch. 1657, held into the 19th c.)
Estates: Bateman 2625 (E) 3593
Notes: Serious financial difficulties 1840s. One in ODNB.

POLLARD

Origins: Established in Devon in the 13th century. Judge 1515. **First MP 1536. Another MP 1553.** Originally at Forde Abbey, Devon (now Dorset) (leased from Crown after Dissolution 1539 for some years).

1. Sir Hugh Pollard 2 Bt – Berealston 1640-41 Callington 1660 Devon 1661-66

Seats: Eggesford, Devon (acq. by mar. 17th c., sold 1701); King's Nympton, Devon (purch. and built c. 1490, sold c. 1660)
Title: Baronet 1627-1701
Notes: Heavily indebted by 1665. Family extinct and estates sold 1701. Four in ODNB.

POLLEN

Origins: Merchants in London in the 17th century. Involved with the East India trade. High Sheriff 1669. Judge 1742.

1. John Pollen – Andover 1689-95
2. John Pollen – Andover 1734-54
3. George Pollen – Leominster 1796-1802
4. Sir John Pollen 2 Bt – Andover 1820-31 1835-41

Seats: Rodbourne House, Wiltshire (built c. 1700, inher. by mar. 1816, add. 1859, for sale 2014); The Priory, Andover, Hampshire (medieval, leased 17th-18th c.); Redenham House, Hampshire (old house, perhaps 16th c., acq. by mar. of 1778, rebuilt 1784, sold 1908)

Estates: Bateman 4502 (E) 5444
Title: Baronet 1795-
Notes: Second MP was a lawyer and 2 Bt a barrister. Three in ODNB.

POLLOCK

Viscount Hanworth (1936- UK)

Origins: The founder was a barrister and Chief Justice of Bombay (d. 1847), son of a saddler. The family produced a number of other judges.

1. Sir Frederick Pollock 1 Bt – Huntingdon 1831-44
2. Henry Pollock – Spalding Div. Lincolnshire 1895-1900
3. Ernest Pollock 1 Viscount Hanworth – Warwick & Leamington Div. Warwickshire 1910-23

Seat: Hanworth Park, Middlesex (medieval, fire 1797, rebuilt 1802, purch. 1834, part sold and part donated c. 1936, now a park)
Estates: The 1 Baronet earned £18,000 pa in 1844 as a lawyer but had 12 children.
Titles: Baron Hanworth 1926- UK; Baronet 1866- ; 1922-
Peers: 2 peers 1926-45
Notes: 1 Viscount and seven others in ODNB.

POMEROY *IRELAND & ENGLAND*

Viscount Harberton (1791- I)

Origins: The Pomeroys were one of the few Norman families who actually came over at the Conquest (Roskell, Clark, and Rawcliffe, *The House of Commons*, IV, 107, 108). They were established at Berry Pomeroy. Listed in the Domesday Book with 59 manors. They ran into hard times in the 16th century, and one son, a cleric, went to Ireland in 1672.

1. John Pomeroy – {Carrick 1755-60 Trim 1761-90}
2. Arthur Pomeroy 1 Viscount Harberton – {County Kildare 1761-83}
3. Henry Pomeroy 2 Viscount Harberton – {Strabane 1776-97}

Seats: Lyston Court, Hereford (built 19th c., sold by 20th c.); Newberry Hall, Kildare (old castle, ruin by c. 1760s, new house built c. 1760 on Castle Carbury estate to replace castle after acq. by mar. from Colley [see Wellesley] heiress 1747, sold c. 1840); Aghamarta Castle, Cork (13th c. castle, acq. 1696, sold 1824)
Estates: Bateman 5223 (E) 3799

Title: Baron Harberton 1783- I
Peers: {2 peers 1783-1800}
Notes: Family resident in England post 1920s.

Pomeroy

Origins: A remnant of the great and ancient family. **First MP 1377 for Devon. Four additional MPs 1407-1611, two for the county.**

1. Roger Pomeroy – Dartmouth 1685-87

Seat: Sandridge, Devon (acq. by mar. 14th c., sold first half 18th c.)
Notes: Male line extinct 1719.

PONSONBY *IRELAND & ENGLAND*

Earl of Bessborough (1739- I; 1937- UK)

Origins: Seated at Haile Hall, Cumberland from the 14th century. Major of the Horse under Cromwell in Ireland 1649. Sheriff 1654. Partly by grants from the state and partly by shrewd speculation he acquired a large estate and married into the peerage. (Beckett, *The Anglo-Irish Tradition*, 39) Became, however, more an English than an Irish family, rarely residing at Bessborough. Purchased Stansted in Sussex in the 1920s and continued to be active in British politics.

1. Sir John Ponsonby – {County Kilkenny 1661-62}
2. William Ponsonby 1 Viscount Duncannon – {County Kilkenny 1692-93 1695-99 1703-21}
3. Brabazon Ponsonby 1 Earl of Bessborough – {Newton 1705-14 County Kildare 1715-24}
4. Henry Ponsonby – {Fethard 1715-27 Innistiogue 1727-45}
5. William Ponsonby 2 Earl of Bessborough – {Newton 1725-27 County Kilkenny 1727-59} Derby 1741-54 Saltash 1754-56 Harwich 1756-58
6. Richard Ponsonby – {Kinsale 1731-60}
7. John Ponsonby – {Newton 1739-60 County Kilkenny 1761-83 Newton 1783-87}
8. Richard Ponsonby – {Knocktopher 1747-60 Newton 1761-68}
9. Chambre Ponsonby – {Newton 1750-60}
10. William Ponsonby 1 Baron Ponsonby of Imokilly – {Cork 1764-76 Bandon 1776-83 County Kilkenny 1783-1800} County Kilkenny 1801-06
11. James Ponsonby – {Tulske 1776-83 Tralee 1783-90}

12. George Ponsonby – {Wicklow 1778-83 Innistoigue 1783-97 Galway 1797-1800} County Wicklow 1801-06 Tavistock 1808-12 Peterborough 1812-16 County Wicklow 1816-17
13. Frederick Ponsonby 3 Earl of Bessborough – Knaresborough 1780-93
14. Chambre Ponsonby – {Dungarvon 1790-97}
15. John Ponsonby 1 Viscount Ponsonby – {Tallow 1793-97 Dungarvon 1797-1800}
16. Sir William Ponsonby – {Bandon 1796-97 Fethard 1797-1800} County Londonderry 1812-15
17. George Ponsonby – {Lismore 1796-98} County Kilkenny 1806 County Cork 1806-12 Youghal 1826-32
18. John Ponsonby 4 Earl of Bessborough – Knaresborough 1805-06 Higham Ferres 1810-12 Malton 1812-26 County Kilkenny 1826-32 Nottingham 1832-34
19. Sir Frederick Ponsonby – County Kilkenny 1806-26 Higham Ferrers 1826-30
20. Frederick Ponsonby – Galway 1811-13
21. William Ponsonby 1 Baron de Mauley – Poole 1826-31 Knaresborough 1832 Dorset 1832-37
22. John Ponsonby 5 Earl of Bessborough – Bletchingley 1831-34 Derby 1835-37 1841-47
23. Charles Ponsonby 2 Baron de Mauley – Poole 1837-47 Dungarvon 1851-52
24. Ashley Ponsonby – Cirencester 1852-57 1859-65
25. Arthur Ponsonby 1 Baron Ponsonby of Shulbrede – Stirling Burghs 1908-18 Brightside Div. Sheffield 1922-30
26. Vere Ponsonby 9 Earl of Bessborough – Cheltenham 1910 Dover 1913-18 Dover Div. Kent 1918-20
27. Sir Edwin Ponsonby 1 Bt – Sevenoaks Div. Kent 1935-50

Seats: Bessborough (Kildalton), Kilkenny (acq. later 17th c., built 1745, burned 1923, rebuilt but never lived in, sold 1944, religious institution); Garryhill (Garahill) Castle, Carlow (medieval castle, ruin, acq. 17th c., possible bawn 1696, house built 1740, sold later 1930s); Stansted Park, Sussex (medieval, remod. mid. 16th c., new house built 1688, destroyed by fire 1900, rebuilt 1900-04, purch. 1924, still own); Hatherop Castle (House), Gloucestershire (de Mauley seat) (built 16th c., Ponsonbys inher. 1797 by mar. from a family descended from the original owners acq. in 1553, fire 1848, rebuilt 1856, sold c. 1871); Parkstead, Roehampton, Surrey (purch. 1760, built 1761, sold 1861, institutional use); Haile Hall, Cumberland (acq. 14th c., rebuilt 1591, remod. early 18th c., still own); Bishop's Court, Kildare (Imokilly seat, acq. by mar. early 18th c., built 1780-90, sold 1838); Canford Manor, Dorset (De Mauley seat, medieval, most demolished 1765 rebuilt 1826-36, sold 1846)
Estates: Bateman 35440 (I & E) 22384 Worth £1,500 pa in 1715, £11,660 pa in 1793; Viscount Ponsonby of Imokilly 10367 (I) 6768; Lord de Mauley 3712 (E) 9334. Inherited £100,000 in 1810 from Henry Cavendish.
Titles: Baron Bessborough 1721- I; Viscount Duncannon 1723- I; Baron Ponsonby of Sysonby 1749- GB; Baron Ponsonby of Imokilly 1806-66 I; Baron Duncannon 1834-

UK; Baron de Mauley 1838- UK; Viscount Ponsonby of Imokilly 1839-55 UK; Baron Ponsonby of Shulbrede 1930- UK; Baron Sysonby 1935- UK; Baronet 1956-
Peers: {2 peers 1721-49} 21 peers 1750-1844 1834-1945 1838-1918 1839-45 1930-45 1935-45
2 Lds Lt 19th
3 in Cabinet 1741-44 1835-41 1931
Notes: The 9 Earl was Governor General of Canada in 1931 and the 10 Earl was Vice President of the European Parliament and an EMP in the 1970s. The estates of the Viscount Ponsonby of Imokilly passed in 1866 through the sister of the 3 Baron Ponsonby to the Talbots. 1 Baron Ponsonby and 1 Baron Ponsonby of Shulbrede and 1 Baron Sysonby and the 2, 3, 4, 6, and 9 Earls and twelve others in ODNB.

POOLE

Origins: Emerged in Wiltshire in the 15th century. **First MP 1442. Nine other MPs 1478-1648, four of them kts of the shire. Four further MPs possible 1461-1584**.

1. Sir Edward Poole – Wootton Bassett 1640-48 Cricklade 1659 Chippenham 1660 Malmesbury 1668-73

Seats: Kemble House, Gloucestershire (acq. by mar. 1564, built late 17th c., sold 1732); Oaksey (Oxsey) House, Wiltshire (acq. 1612-14, built early 17th c., sold 1716-26, demolished c. 1956)
Estates: Worth £1,000 pa in the 1670s.
Notes: Family in decline in the late 17th century. Male line of Kemble extinct 1726.

POPE

Origins: Shrewsbury draper acquired Woolstaston c. 1540. **First MP 1647**.

1. Roger Pope – Bridgnorth 1685-87
2. Roger Pope – Bridgnorth 1699-1702

Seats: Woolstaston Hall, Shropshire (acq. c. 1540, built c. 1675, add. late 17th c., family departed 1754, demolished c. 1784); Diamond Hall, Shropshire (built mid-17th c., passed out of the family by mar. 1754)
Notes: Male line of Woolstaston extinct between 1722 and 1754.

PORTER

Origins: Held Newent, Gloucestershire from the 15th century. Noble servants in Spain and courtiers in England in the 16th and 17th century. **First MP 1515. Three further MPs 1554-1643, two for Gloucestershire**.

1. Aubrey Porter – Bury St. Edmunds 1705-17

Notes: Endymion Porter (MP 1640-43) was a courtier who mortgaged most of his estates in 1640 and then went into exile. All was lost. Three in ODNB.

PORTERFIELD *SCOTLAND*

Origins: Landed by the 15th century. **First [MP 1645]. One further [MP for Renfrewshire 1648]**.

1. Alexander Porterfield – [Renfrewshire 1700-12]

Seats: Porterfield, Renfrewshire (original medieval seat, declined to farm house later 17th c., demolished 19th c.); Duchal House, Renfrewshire (medieval castle, acq. 1544, rebuilt c. 1710, add. 1768, sold mid-19th c.)
Notes: Male line extinct 1815.

POTTER I

Origins: Manchester textile merchants in the 19th century. Sir Thomas Potter was the first Lord Mayor of Manchester.

1. Richard Potter – Wigan 1832-39
2. Sir John Potter – Manchester 1857-58
3. Edmund Potter – Carlisle 1861-74
4. Thomas Potter – Rochdale 1865-95

Seats: Buile Hill, Lancashire (acq. and built 1826-28, sold 1870s, now museum); Broughton House, Lancashire (sold 1916)
Notes: Two in ODNB.

POTTER II [MacQueen]

Potter

Origins: The first MP was son of an Archbishop of Canterbury (1737-47). The second MP married the heiress to Ridgmont.

1. Thomas Potter – St. Germans 1747-54 Aylesbury 1754-57 Okehampton 1757-59
2. Thomas Potter – Lostwithiel 1776-80

Seat: Ridgmont House, Bedfordshire (acq. by mar. 1747, passed by mar. to MacQueens 1759)
Estates: The Archbishop left between £70,000 and £100,000 in 1747.
Notes: Two in ODNB.

MacQueen

Origins: The MP below was the son of a physician (Scottish gentry) and the daughter and heiress of Thomas Potter MP 1776-80 above.

1. Thomas Potter MacQueen – East Looe 1816-26 Bedfordshire 1826-30

Seat: Ridgmont House, Bedfordshire (acq. by mar. 1759, sold 1833)
Notes: MacQueen was ruined by election expenses.

POWELL *WALES*

Origins: Claimed ancient descent but the first notable Powell was a lawyer in the later 17th century. Acquired Nanteos through marriage in the 1730s.

1. Thomas Powell – Cardigan Boroughs 1725-27 Cardiganshire 1742-47
2. William Powell – Cardiganshire 1816-54
3. William Powell – Cardiganshire 1859-65

Seat: Nanteos, Cardiganshire (acq. by mar. to Jones family – who acq. in 1640s – c. 1735, new house built 1738-57, sold 1951, hotel)
Estates: Bateman 33675 (W) 9597
Notes: The family was deeply indebted in the 19th century. Extinct 1930.

POWLE [Ireton]

Powle

Origins: Settled in Berkshire in the Tudor period. High Sheriff 1633. The family continued to rise higher in the 17th century through the political career of the first MP. The second MP was Master of the Rolls.

1. Sir Richard Powle – Berkshire 1660-78
2. Henry Powle – Cirencester 1660 1671-81 East Grinstead 1681 New Windsor 1689 Cirencester 1690

Seats: Williamstrip Park, Gloucestershire (built c. 1600, purch. c. 1610, sold 1751); Quenington, Gloucestershire (purch. 1648, sold 1751); Shottesbrooke Park, Berkshire (acq. and built late 16th c., sold later 17th c.)
Notes: The family became extinct 1751. One in ODNB.

Ireton

Origins: Henry Ireton (MP 1645-51), a great figure of the Civil War period, was the son of a gentleman. His brother was Lord Mayor of London 1658. **First MP 1645. One other MP 1654**. Ireton was a regicide and his estates were confiscated in 1660. Henry Ireton MP 1698-1711 married the daughter and heiress of Henry Powle MP above and succeeded to the Powle estates.

1. Henry Ireton – Cirencester 1698-1700 1705-08 Tewkesbury 1710-11

Seat: Attenborough, Nottinghamshire (acq. c. 1605, passed out of family later in 17th c.)
Notes: Two in ODNB.

POWLETT (Paulet, Poulett) [Norton, Orde]

Duke of Bolton (1689-1794 E)

Origins: Migrated from France to the West Country in the reign of Henry II. Acquired Basing by marriage in 1428. Rose high under the Tudors through a close connection with Henry VIII. **First MP 1385 for Devon. Ten further MPs 1529-1628.** Baron 1539 and Marquess 1551. The Dukes of Bolton were descended from a younger son. The senior line of the Marquesses of Winchester spelled their name Paulet.

1. Charles Powlett 1 Duke of Bolton – Winchester 1660 Hampshire 1661-75
2. Francis Powlett – Andover 1679-81 1689-95
3. Charles Powlett 2 Duke of Bolton – Hampshire 1681 1685-87 1689-98
4. Lord William Powlett – Winchester 1689-1710 Lymington 1710-15 Winchester 1715-29
5. Charles Powlett 3 Duke of Bolton – Lymington 1705-08 Hampshire 1708-10 Carmarthenshire 1715-17
6. Norton Powlett – Petersfeld 1705-34
7. Harry Powlett 4 Duke of Bolton – St. Ives 1715-22 Hampshire 1722-54
8. Lord Nassau Powlett – Hampshire 1720-27 Lymington 1727-34 1741
9. William Powlett – Lymington 1729-34 Winchester 1741-47 Whitchurch 1754-57
10. Charles Powlett – Newton (IoW) 1729-34 Christchurch 1740-51
11. Norton Powlett – Winchester 1730-34
12. Charles Powlett 5 Duke of Bolton – Lymington 1741-59

13. Harry Powlett 6 Duke of Bolton – Christchurch 1751-54 Lymington 1755-61 Winchester 1761-65
14. George Paulet 12 Marquess of Winchester – Winchester 1765-74
15. William Powlett-Powlett – Totnes 1790-96
16. Charles Burroughs Paulet 13 Marquess of Winchester – Truro 1792-96

Seats: Amport House, Hampshire (acq. an interest in the manor by mar. 1429, old house, gained control of the house and park 1660s, rebuilt 1857, sold 1919, institutional use); Rotherfield Park, Hampshire (acq. by mar. from Nortons 1687, remod. early 18th c., sold 1808); Hackwood Park, Hampshire (owned by 16th c., built lodge 16th c., built 1683-87, passed to Orde-Powletts 1794, see below); Bolton Hall, Yorkshire (built 15th-16th c., acq. by mar. mid-17th c., rebuilt 1678, passed to Orde-Powletts 1794, see below); Basing House, Hampshire (medieval castle, acq. by mar. 1428, add. c. 1531-71, destroyed 1645, new house c. 1660s, fire c.1740, ruin); Hooke Court, Dorset (medieval, descended via heiresses from the family in possession in 1281, Paulets acq. 1609, house nearly destroyed 1647, restored 1747, passed early 19th c. to Earls of Sandwich, see Montagu I)
Estates: Bateman 4797 (E) 4635, see also Baron Bolton. Rubinstein – the last Duchess of Bolton left £150,000 probate 1809.
Titles: Baron St. John 1538- E; Earl of Wiltshire 1549- E; Marquess of Winchester 1551- E
Peers: 12 peers 1660-1722 1717-1945
9 Lds Lt 17th, 18th, 19th, 20th
2 in Cabinet 1697 1697 1717-20
2 KG 18th
Notes: On the extinction of the Dukedom some of the estates passed to the Winchester line. Others went to an illegitimate daughter of the 5 Duke (see Baron Bolton), and some to the 1 Duke of Cleveland, whose mother was a daughter of the last Duke of Bolton (see Vane). 1, 3, and 5 Marquesses of Winchester and 1, 2, 3, and 6 Dukes of Bolton and three others in ODNB.

<u>Baron Bolton</u> (1797- GB)

Origins: Descended from an illegitimate daughter and part heiress of the 5 Duke of Bolton. Thomas Orde married in 1778 this heiress. He took the additional name Powlett and inherited the greater part of the Bolton estates in 1794. The Ordes purchased ex-monastic land in the mid-16th century. Lease holders of land in the 1570s. Alderman and Mayor of Berwick in the 1590s. Rising gentry by 1600. Purchased main estates in 1619. High Sheriff of Northumberland 1638.

1. William Orde – Berwick-on-Tweed 1713-15
2. Thomas Orde-Powlett 1 Baron Bolton – Aylesbury 1780-84 Harwich 1784-96 {Rathcormick 1784-90}
3. William Orde-Powlett 2 Baron Bolton – Yarmouth (IoW) 1807

4. Sir John Orde 1 Bt – Yarmouth (IoW) 1807-12

Seats: Bolton Hall, Yorkshire (inher. 1794, remod. c. 1823-24, fire 1902, rebuilt, still own); Hackwood Park, Hampshire (inher. 1794, remod. c. 1800-13, sold 1936); Nunnykirk, Northumberland (acq. by mar. 18th c., leased out 1980s); Auchnaba House, Argyll (acq. by mar. 1828 to a Campbell heiress); Kilmory Castle, Argyll (Campbell's acq. 1575, remod. 1816-20 and 1826, acq. by mar. to Campbell heiress 1828, rebuilt 1828-36, add. 1860-63, sold 1938)
Estates: Bateman 128632 (E & S) 41828. Rubinstein – 1st Bt left £180,000 in probate 1824. Worth £50,000,000 in 1990 with 17,000 acres.
Title: Baronet 1790-
Peers: 6 peers 1794-1945
2 Lds Lt 19th, 20th
1 in Cabinet 1784-87
Notes: Sir John Powlett Orde 2 Bt inherited Auchnaba, Argyll and estates in Jamaica from his wife, a Campbell heiress in 1828. The baronet family of 1790 took the name Campbell-Orde in 1880. 1 Baron and one other in ODNB.

Norton

Origins: Francis Powlett married the daughter and heiress of Sir Richard Norton 2 Bt of Rotherfield. His grandson succeeded as 12 Marquess of Winchester and inherited Rotherfield. The Nortons held the manor of Tisted in 1308. **First MP 1306 for Hampshire. Seven additional Norton MPs 1339-1628, four for the county.**

1. Richard Norton – Hampshire 1645-48 1651-53 1654 1656 1658 1660 Portsmouth 1661-79 Hampshire 1679 Portsmouth 1679-81 1689-90 Hampshire 1690-91
2. Sir John Norton 3 Bt – Hampshire 1661-79 Petersfield 1679-81 1685-87
3. Richard Norton – Hampshire 1693-1700 1702-05
4. Thomas Norton – Bury St. Edmunds 1727-47

Seats: Rotherfield Park, Hampshire (original owners acq. 1308, passed by mar. to Nortons 1495, new house 16th c., passed by mar. heiress to Powletts 1687, see above); Southwick, Hampshire (medieval buildings, converted to house c. 1538, acq. by mar. mid-17th c., passed to Thistlethwaytes 1733, see that family)
Estates: Worth £1,000 pa in 1660.
Title: Baronet 1622-87
Notes: Richard Norton MP 1693-1705 died in 1732, leaving his estates to help paupers and appointed Parliament as his executor. The will was set aside on the grounds of insanity – see Thistlethwayte (Hayton, *The House of Commons*, IV, 1052). One in ODNB.

Earl Poulett (1706-1973 E)

Origins: This family shared a common descent from Sir John Paulet of Basing House, ancestor of the Marquesses of Winchester (see above). The family served the Tudors in various offices. **First MP 1495 for Somerset. Four additional MPs 1529-1642, all for the county**. Baron 1627.

1. John Poulett 3 Baron Poulett – Somerset 1662-65
2. Peregrin Poulett – Bossiney 1737-41 Bridgwater 1747-52
3. Vere Poulett 3 Earl Poulett – Bridgwater 1741-47
4. Anne Poulett – Bridgwater 1769-85
5. Vere Poulett – Bridgwater 1790-96 1806-07

Seats: Hinton House, Somerset (acq. by mar. 1429, rebuilt c. 1500, remod. mid-17th c., further remod. 18th c., sold 1968-73, now flats); Court de Wick (Wick, Wyck, Wyke Court), Somerset (medieval, remod. 15th and 16th c., acq. by mar. and rebuilt 17th c., passed out of family or leased); Walcot Hall, Northamptonshire (acq. by mar. 1662, sold by 1700)
Estates: Bateman 22129 (E) 21998. Rubinstein – Dowager Countess left £100,000 in probate in 1838.
Title: Baron Poulett 1627-1973 E
Peers: 10 peers 1660-79 1696-1743 1734-1899 1903-18 1930-45
5 Lds Lt 17th, 18th, 19th
1 in Cabinet 1710-11
1 KG 18th
1 KT 18th-19th
Notes: 1 and 2 Barons and 1 Earl and three others in ODNB.

POWNEY (Povey)

Origins: Yeomen in Berkshire in the 16th century. The father of the first MP married the heiress of a large landowner. Treasurer of the Navy first half of the 17th century.

1. John Powney – New Windsor 1679-80
2. Peniston Powney – Berkshire 1739-57
3. Peniston Powney – New Windsor 1780-94

Seat: Ives Place, Berkshire (acq. by mar. later 17th c., sold by early 19th c.)

POWYS

Baron Lilford (1797- GB)

Origins: An old Welsh family. A number of lawyers in the 17th century, including a Chief Justice of the King's Bench 1692 and a judge of the Queen's Bench in 1713. English estates were purchased in the early 18th century.

1. Sir Thomas Powys – Ludlow 1701-13
2. Richard Powys – Orford 1734-41
3. Thomas Powys 1 Baron Lilford – Northamptonshire 1774-97

Seats: Lilford Hall (Park), Northamptonshire (built 1675, purch. 1711, add. c. 1740s, requisitioned 1940, sold post 1945, repurch. 1971, sold 1990); Bank Hall (Bretherton), Lancashire (built 1608, add. 1832-33, passed to Powys family by mar. 1860, empty since 1945, derelict, still own); Stoughton Grange, Leicestershire (acq. by mar. 1860 from the Kecks – see Legh -, demolished 1926); Hintlesham Hall, Suffolk (built later 16th c., purch. 1720, remod. 1724, sold 1747)
Estates: Bateman 15554 (E) 26398 with Fox-Powys 2896 (E) 5881
Peers: 6 peers 1797-1945
Notes: 4 Baron and five others in ODNB.

PRATT

Marquess Camden (1812- UK)

Origins: The Pratts emerged in Devonshire late 15th century. They lost estates in the Civil War. A Chief Justice 1714 and his son, a Lord Chancellor, restored the family fortunes. The 1 Earl married a Jeffreys heiress (see that family).

1. Sir John Pratt – Midhurst 1711-14
2. John Pratt – Sandwich 1741-47
3. Charles Pratt 1 Earl Camden – Downton 1757-62
4. Robert Pratt – Horsham 1763-74
5. John Pratt 1 Marquess Camden – Bath 1780-94
6. George Pratt 2 Marquess Camden – Ludgershall 1821-26 Bath 1826-30 Dunwich 1831-32
7. John Pratt 3 Marquess Camden – Brecon Boroughs 1866

Seats: Bayham Abbey, Kent (medieval abbey buildings, now ruin, house purch. 1714, house rebuilt 1869-72, abbey ruins donated to state 1961, house sold c. 1975); Wildernesse Park (House) (The Wildernesse), Kent (medieval, built 1669, purch. 1705,

add. c. 1750, add. c. 1800, sold 1885, housing estate, institutional use); The Priory, Brecon (Brecknock Priory), Breconshire (built 1530s, acq. by mar. of 1749, still owned c. 1900); Camden Place, Kent (built early 17th c., rebuilt 1717, purch. c. 1760, add. 1780s, sold c. 1806, golf club)
Estates: Bateman 17399 (E & W) 16379
Titles: Baron Camden 1765- GB; Viscount Bayham and Earl Camden 1786- GB; Earl of Brecknock 1812- UK
Peers: 5 peers 1765-1872 1893-1945
3 Lds Lt 19th, 20th
3 in Cabinet 1721 1766-70 1782-94 1795-1801 1804-12
2 KG 18th, 19th
Notes: 1 Earl and 1 Marquess and one other in ODNB.

PRENDERGAST [Smyth, Vereker] *IRELAND*

Viscount Gort (1816- I)

Origins: An Irish Roman Catholic family (conformed c. 1690s) that lost their property in the Civil War and owed its modern rise to a general under William III and Anne granted estates in the 1690s. Other estates purchased with loans. The daughter and heiress of Sir Thomas Prendergast 1 Bt married Charles Smyth, son of the Bishop of Limerick. Their eldest son was Charles Smyth. Their second son took the name Prendergast and was created Viscount Gort. The title passed via his sister, who married 1759 Thomas Vereker, to her son Charles Vereker 2 Viscount Gort. The Verekers, of Flemish extraction long settled in Limerick, were soldiers in the Civil War and gained estates in 1660.

1. Sir Thomas Prendergast 1 Bt – {Monaghan 1703-09}
2. Sir Thomas Prendergast 2 Bt – Chichester 1733-34 {Clonmell 1733-60}
3. Charles Smyth – {Limerick 1731-76}
4. George Smyth – {Blessington 1759-68}
5. Thomas Smyth – {Ballyshannon 1775-76 Limerick 1776-85}
6. John Prendergast 1 Viscount Gort – {Carlow 1776-83 Limerick 1785-97}
7. Charles Vereker 2 Viscount Gort – {Limerick 1794-1800} 1802-17
8. John Prendergast-Vereker 3 Viscount Gort – Limerick 1817-20

Seats: Lough Cutra Castle, Galway (acq. 1697, passed by mar. 1760 to Smyth family, passed by mar. to Verekers, rebuilt 1811-17, sold 1851, add. 1856, add. 1900, repurch. 1950s, sold late 1960s); Gort, Galway (acq. 1697, burned 1740)
Estates: Worth £18,000 pa in the 1 Viscount's lifetime. Gort estate originally worth £500 pa in 1697.
Titles: Baron Kiltarton 1810- I; Viscount Gort 1946-46 UK; Baronet 1699-1760

Peers: 2 Irish Rep peers 1823-42 1865
Notes: The 2 Bt died while a patent for his elevation as Viscount Gort was being prepared. His nephew and heir was raised to the title in 1816. The 3 Viscount inherited debts of £50,000 and was ruined financially by the Famine. He sold most of the Irish estates and was reduced to near penury. The 6th Viscount was Chief of the Imperial General Staff and later Commander-in-Chief of the British Army in France in 1940. 1 and 2 Bts and 2 and 6 Viscounts in ODNB.

PRESTON I *IRELAND*

Baron Tara (1800-21 I)

Origins: Emigrated to Ireland mid-17th century. A merchant in Dublin (Lord Mayor 1653) acquired estates 1650s. Sheriff 1676.

1. John Preston – {Navan 1661-66}
2. John Preston – {County Meath 1709-32}
3. John Preston – {Navan 1713-60}
4. John Preston – {Navan 1732-53}
5. Nathaniel Preston – {Navan 1713-60}
6. Joseph Preston – {Navan 1761-1800}
7. John Preston – {Navan 1761-81}
8. John Preston 1 Baron Tara – {Navan 1783-1800}

Seats: Bellinter (Ballinter) House, Meath (acq. mid-18th c., built c. 1750-56, remod. c. 1800, passed to Briscoe family by mar. 1892, sold 1957, hotel); Swainstown House, Meath (acq. early 18th c., still own); Ardsallagh Castle, Meath (acq. by mar. 1666, became a ruin, estate left by Prestons by mar. to Ludlows 1710, passed by inher. to Lord John Russell 1842); Balsoon House, Meath (acq. 1716, built 18th c., sold later 19th or early 20th c.)
Estates: Bateman 7415 (I) 6839. Worth £600 pa in 1713 and £7,000 pa. c. 1800. Estates sold from the 1870s onwards.

PRESTON II *IRELAND*

Viscount Gormanston (1478- I)

Origins: To Ireland in the 14th century. Justice of the King's Bench in Ireland 1331. Kt 1361. Lord Chancellor of Ireland 1391. Baron 1370. Outlawed 1691. Restored 1800. Roman Catholic family.

No MPs

Seats: Gormanston (Gormanstown) Castle, Meath (acq. 1363, built 14th c., add. 1687, rebuilt early 19th c., sold 1947, school); Whitewood House (Lodge), Meath (on part of original estate, house built c. 1735, sold 1947)
Estates: Bateman 10957 (I) 9364. Still owned large estate in 1935.
Titles: Baron Gormanston 1370- I; Baron Gormanston 1868- UK; Viscount Tara 1650-74 I
Peers {1 peer 1661-91} 4 peers 1868-1925 1935-40
Notes: 1 Viscount Tara in ODNB.

PRETYMAN [Tomline]

Tomline

Origins: The Pretymans descended from a Suffolk family that held land since 1361. They succeeded to the Tomline estates in 1803 and took the name Tomline. The families were not related, and it is not known why the will of Marmaduke Tomline was drawn up in this way. A Pretyman-Tomline Bishop of London and Winchester accumulated a fortune of £200,000 by his death in 1827. His son William (Pretyman) Tomline MP below left £400,000 in 1836.

1. William Tomline – Christchurch 1812-18 Truro 1818-20 1826-29 Minehead 1830-31
2. George Tomline – Sudbury 1840-41 Shrewsbury 1841-47 1852-68 Great Grimsby 1868-74
3. Ernest Pretyman – Woodbridge Div. Suffolk 1895-1906 Chelmsford Div. Essex 1908-23

Seats: Orwell Park, Suffolk (built mid-Georgian period, add. 1851-53 and 1873, sold house 1930s, still own estate); The Manor House, Bacton, Suffolk (built c. 1720, became a farm house in the 19th c., Pretymans still own the estate); Riby Grove, Lincolnshire (Tomline seat, purch. 1680, built 18th c., add. 19th c., sold and demolished 1930s)
Estates: Bateman 26914 (E) 35542. Rubinstein – 5 Bt left £200,000 in probate in 1827 and William Tomline £400,000 in 1836.
Notes: The Pretyman-Tomline Bishop of Winchester claimed a dormant Pretyman baronetcy (see below) in 1823 and held it until his death in 1827, but none of his successors claimed it. He, the 5 Bt, appears in the ODNB.

Pretyman

Origins: Kinsmen of the Pretymans above.

1. Sir John Pretyman 1 Bt – Leicester 1661-76

Seats: Loddington Hall, Leicestershire (built late 16th c., acq. mid-17th c., sold 1670); Horninghold, Leicestershire (acq. by mar. 1633, sold 1676)
Title: Baronet 1660-1749

PRICE I [Green] *WALES*

Origins: Claimed medieval princely descent. Emerged in the 18th century, a barrister. Made money office-holding. The sister of Richard Price MP married George Green. Their child took the name Green-Price in 1861.

1. Chase Price – Leominster 1759-67 Radnorshire 1768-77
2. Richard Price – New Radnor 1799-1847
3. Sir Richard Green-Price 1 Bt – New Radnor 1863-69 Radnorshire 1880-85

Seat: Norton Manor (Hall), Radnorshire (Price purch. estate 18th c., built 1858, Greens acq. by mar to Price heiress 1861, sold 1891, hotel)
Estates: Bateman 8774 (W) 7638
Title: Baronet 1874-
Notes: One in ODNB.

PRICE II [Savage] *IRELAND*

Price

Origins: Emigrated to Ireland in the later 16th century. Emerged in the mid 17th century as a general in the Civil War. High Sheriff 1704.

1. Nicholas Price – {Downpatrick 1692-93 County Down 1695-99 Downpatrick 1703-14}
2. Cromwell Price – {Downpatrick 1727-60}
3. Nicholas Price – {Lisburn 1736-42}
4. Francis Price – {Lisburn 1759-76}
5. Cromwell Price – {Kinsale 1783-90 Monaghan 1791-97 Fore 1798}

Seats: Saintfield House, Down (purch. 1709, new house c. 1750, add. c. 1800, still own); Hollymount, Down (acq. 1695, built c. 1700, rebuilt 1781, passed by mar. to Savages c. 1820)
Estates: Bateman 6807 (I) 7641. Worth £1,003 pa in 1741.

Savage

Origins: Anglo-Norman family settled in County Down in the 13th century, probably a soldier. Francis Savage succeeded to Hollymount on his marriage to the daughter and heiress of Cromwell Price.

1. Francis Savage – {County Down 1794-1800} 1801-12

Seats: Ardkeen (Castle) House, Down (acq. and built castle in 13th c., passed to Bayly family by mar. and sold 1837 for £85,000); Hollymount House, Down (built 1781, acq. by mar from Price family c. 1820, passed to Baylys and then Meredith Bts by mar. 1837, no longer standing); Portaferry Castle (House), Down (acq. 13th c., rebuilt 16th c., castle a ruin, house built 1821, family departed 1977)
Estates: Bateman 6775 (I) 9345
Titles: Baronet 1961-62
1 Ld Lt 20th c.
Notes: The Savages of Portaferry House took the name Nugent on mar. to heiress 1812. Speaker of N I Senate 1937-61. The Bayly's of Norelands, Kilkenny who inherited Ardkeen and Hollymount in 1837, took the name Savage.

PRICE III

Origins: Landowners since the 16th century. **First MP 1558, for Herefordshire**. The next MP 1685 was a successful lawyer and judge.

1. Robert Price – Weobley 1685-87 1690-1702
2. Thomas Price – Weobley 1701-05
3. Uvedale Price – Weobley 1713-15 1727-34
4. Sir Robert Price 2 Bt – Herefordshire 1818-41 Hereford 1845-57

Seat: Foxley, Herefordshire (acq. by mar. from Rodd family 1681, built 1717, sold 1856, demolished 1948)
Estates: Bateman 4756 (E) 6691 (sold to Davenports 1856). Worth £2,461 pa in 1775.
Title: Baronet 1828-57
Notes: The Rodd family of Foxley held land in Herefordshire from the 13th c., **two MPs both 1621**. Finances of the family in disarray in the 1830s and 1840s. Excessive speculation in railways led to virtual bankruptcy. Related to the Price family of the Priory, Brecon (see Jeffreys). 1 Bt and two others in ODNB.

PRICE IV [Thelwall] *WALES*

Origins: Rose through royal patronage of Henry VII. The great-grandfather of the first MP fought at Bosworth. The family acquired a large estate after the Dissolution of the Monasteries. **First MP 1555 for Merioneth. Three further MPs 1558-84, two for the county**. Richard Price MP 1754-68 married the daughter and heiress of Edward Thewall of Bathavan (Bathavern, Bathafarn) Park, Plas y Ward (acq. c. 1380), Denbighshire and Plas Coch, Denbighshire and took the name Thelwall. That family entered the gentry before 1380 and produced **five MPs 1553-1655, four for Denbighshire**. Their estates passed by inheritance to the Williams Wynns in 1719 (see that family).

1. William Price – Merioneth 1640-44 1673-79
2. Richard Price Thelwall – Beaumaris 1754-68

Seats: Rhiwlas (Rulacc House), Merionethshire (acq. medieval period, old house, passed to an illegitimate son 1775, rebuilt 19th c., demolished 1955, new house built c. 1960, still own); Bathafarn (Bathavan, Bathavern) Park (Hall), Denbighshire (Thewell seat since 16th c., rebuilt c. 1700, passed to Price family by mar. mid-18th c., passed to an illegitimate son 1775 who took name Price, sold 1811, flats)
Estates: Bateman 41264 (W) 11091. Worth £1,500 pa c. 1660. Owned 17,000 acres in 2015.
Notes: One Thelwall in ODNB.

PRICE V

Origins: A timber merchant in Gloucester in the late 18th century founded the family fortune. Chairman of the Midland Railway mid-19th c. High Sheriff 1849.

1. William Price – Gloucester 1852-59 1865-73
2. William Price – Tewkesbury 1868-80
3. Morgan Price – Whitehaven Div. Cumberland 1929-31 Forest of Dean Div. Gloucestershire 1935-50 W. Gloucestershire 1950-59

Seat: Tibberton Court, Gloucestershire (built c. 1790, purch. 1837, add. 1853 and 1860s, part demolished 1938, house converted into flats after 1945, still own estate)
Estate: The Tibberton estate was relatively small when purchased by the Price family, but they kept adding until it reached maximum size in the early 20th c. (Kingsley, *The Country Houses of Gloucestershire*, III, 237-38)

PRICE VI (Pryce) *WALES*

Origins: Gentry from the 14th century. Several lines of MPs were produced. **First MP 1555 for Radnorshire. Eight additional MPs 1563-1655, five of them kts of the shire.** The senior line at Newtown and Vaynor, Montgomeryshire were Baronets 1628-1791, ended in destitution in the 18th century.

1. Matthew Pryce – Montgomery Boroughs 1679-81

Seat: Park Penprice, Montgomeryshire (acq. by mar. 17th c., estate divided among heiresses 1700)
Notes: Extinct in male line 1700.

PRIDEAUX [Gwyn] *ENGLAND & WALES*

Prideaux

Origins: The Prideaux family of Prideaux Castle can be traced in Cornwall to the time of the Conqueror. (Thrush and Ferris, *House of Commons 1604-29*, V, 763.) Several lawyers of this family in the Tudor period did well out of the Dissolution of the Monasteries. In the mid-17th century another successful lawyer, Sir Edmund Prideaux, established a national postal delivery system that yielded £15,000 pa in the 1650s. **First MP 1298. Nine additional MPs 1331-1658, three for Devon.**

1. Sir Peter Prideaux 3 Bt – Honiton 1661-79 St. Mawes 1685-87
2. Edmund Prideaux – Taunton 1680-81
3. John Prideaux – Newport 1701
4. Sir Edmund Prideaux 4 Bt – Tregony 1713-20

Seats: Netherton Hall (House), Devon (purch. and built 1607, restored and rebuilt 1836-44, sold after 1875); Forde Abbey, Dorset (in Devon until 1844) (medieval, remod. 16th c., purch. 1649, remod. 1650s, passed to Gwyns 1702); Souldon (Soldon), Devon (purch. and built mid-16th c., add. mid-17th c., sold c. 1713)
Estates: Bateman 2261 (E) 3154.
Title: Baronet 1622-1875; Cromwellian Baronet 1658
Notes: Male line extinct 1875. Two in ODNB.

Prideaux

Origins: Cadet line. **First MP 1625. One other MP 1640.**

1. Jonathan Prideaux – Callington 1689-95

Seats: Theuborough (Thuborough), Devon (purch. c. 1500, declined into a farm house 18th c.); Trecarne, Cornwall (acq. by mar. early 17th c., sold after 1710, now guest house)
Notes: Land being sold in the 17th c. Male line extinct 1710. Remaining estates dispersed among six heiresses.

Gwyn

Origins: An old family but did not lay claim to joining the Quarter Session Bench until the later 16th century. (Williams, *Glamorgan County History*, IV, 172) Margaret Prideaux, daughter and heiress of the Prideaux of Forde Abbey (cadet of the Netherton line), married in 1690 Francis Gwyn, and he succeeded to Forde Abbey in 1702. He was a lawyer, Secretary of War 1713.

1. Francis Gwyn – Chippenham 1673-79 Cardiff Borough 1685-87 Christchurch 1689-95 Callington 1695-98 Totnes 1699-1701 Christchurch 1701-10 Totnes 1710-15 Christchurch 1717-22 Wells 1722-27
2. Edward Prideaux Gwyn – Christchurch 1724-27 Wells 1727-29
3. Francis Gwyn – Wells 1741-54

Seats: Llansannor (Llansanwyr) Court, Glamorganshire (acq. by mar. and built mid-16th c. add. 17th c., add. 19th c., sold 1846); Forde Abbey, Dorset (Devon until 1844) (see above, acq. by mar. 1702, sold 1846)
1 in Cabinet 1713-14
Notes: The last Gwyn died in 1846. Forde was sold for £54,650. One in ODNB.

PRIESTLEY

Origins: Worsted manufacuturers in Leeds. Mayor of Bradford 1904.

1. Briggs Priestley – Pudsey Div. W. R. Yorkshire 1885-1900
2. Sir Arthur Priestley – Grantham 1900-18
3. Sir William Priestley – E. Bradford 1906-18

Seats: Hungerton Hall, Lincolnshire (built c. 1782, purch. later 19th c., resident 1930, sold); Littledale Hall, Lancashire (built c. 1849, purch. later 19th c., sold 20th c., institutional use)

PRIMROSE *SCOTLAND*

Earl of Rosebery (1703- S)

Origins: Clerk of Privy Council 1599. The **first MP [1628]** was a merchant in Culross. A number of lawyers and officials connected with the Revenue Department in the 17th century. Baronet 1651. Lord Clerk Register 1660, Lord of Session 1661. The latter's son was a courtier and created a viscount in 1700. The family almost doubled its income by marriage to a Rothschild heiress in the 19th century.

1. Archibald Primrose 1 Earl of Rosebery – [Edinburghshire 1696-1700]
2. James Primrose 1 Viscount Rosebery – [Edinburghshire 1703]
3. Archibald Primrose 4 Earl of Rosebery – Helston 1805-06 Cashel 1806-07
4. Francis Primrose – Stirling Burghs 1819-20
5. Archibald Primrose Lord Dalmeny – Stirling Burghs 1832-47
6. Albert Primrose 6 Earl of Rosebery – Edinburghshire 1906-10
7. Neil Primrose – Wisbech Div. Cambridgeshire 1910-17

Seats: Dalmeny Park (House), Linlithgowshire (purch. 1662, built 1814-20, still own); Mentmore Towers, Buckinghamshire (built 1850-55, acq. by Primrose family by mar. 1878, sold 1978, institutional use); Rosebery House, Edinburghshire (old house, purch. 1695, rebuilt late 17th c., sold 1712 or 1749, demolished 1805-12, repurch. 1821, owned into 20th c., still own?); Barnbougle Castle, Linlithgowshire (built 13th c., add. 17th c., purch. 1662, remod. 1881, still own)
Estates: Bateman 32411 (S & E) 36479. 6 Earl died worth £10,000,000 in 1974 plus landed property. Owned 20,000 acres in 1996.
Titles: Viscount Rosebery 1700- S; Viscount Primrose 1703-41 S; Baron Rosebery 1828- UK; Earl of Midlothian 1911- UK; Baronet 1651-
Peers: [2 peers 1700-07 1704-06] 3 Scottish Rep peers 1707-15 1768-84 1818-28 3 peers 1828-1945
3 Lds Lt 19th, 20th
2 in Cabinet 1885-86 1892-95 1945
1 KG 19th-20th
3 KT 18th, 19th, 20th
Notes: 1 Bt and 1, 4, 5, and 6 Earls and five others in ODNB.

PRINGLE *SCOTLAND*

Pringle

Origins: The Pringles claimed distinction from the 14th century and had a charter of lands by 1485. The senior line was seated at Whytbank. **First [MP 1628 for Selkirkshire].**

1. Alexander Pringle – Selkirkshire 1830-32 1835-46

Seats: Whytbank, Selkirkshire (acq. and built c. 1510, family abandoned 1790, roofless by 1823, restored 1992); Yair House, Selkirkshire (purch. 1510, sold 1759 due to debts, repurch. with East India profits of a son of the laird and rebuilt 1788, became principal seat after Whytbank abandoned, sold 1924)

Pringle

Origins: Descended from a younger son (d. 1513). **First [MP 1617, for Selkirkshire]. One additional [MP 1641, for the county].**

1. George Pringle – [Selkirkshire 1689]
2. James Pringle – [Selkirkshire 1693-1702]

Seat: Torwoodlee House, Selkirkshire (medieval, acq. 1501-10, sacked 1568, rebuilt 1601, ruin, rebuilt 1784, add. 1864, still own)
Estates: Bateman 7901 (S) 4080
Notes: Attainted 1686, reversed 1690. One in ODNB.

Pringle

Origins: Kinsmen. **First [MP 1621]. One other [MP 1639, for Roxburghshire].**

1. Robert Pringle – [Roxburghshire 1678 1681]
2. Sir James Pringle 4 Bt – Berwickshire 1761-79

Seats: Newhall (Craiglieth), Selkirkshire (acq. from 1492, sold 1920); Stichill House, Roxburghshire (purch. 1628, built 1866, demolished 1938, still own estate); Langton House, Berwickshire (leased 18th c.)
Estates: Bateman 8133 (S) 8785
Title: Baronet 1683-; 1766-82
Notes: 1 Bt and three others in ODNB.

Pringle

Origins: Kinsmen. Judge 1703.

1. John Pringle – [Selkirkshire 1703-07] Scotland 1707-08 Selkirkshire 1708-29
2. John Pringl – Selkirkshire 1765-86
3. Mark Pringle – Selkirkshire 1786-1802
4. John Pringle – Linlithgow Burghs 1819-20
5. Robert Pringle – Selkirkshire 1832-35

Seat: The Haining, Selkirkshire (purch. 1701, built c. 1703, add. 1794, remod. 1819-20, part burned 1944, flats 1983, institutional use)
Notes: One in ODNB.

PRITTIE *IRELAND*

Baron Dunalley (1800- I)

Origins: Cromwellian officer in Ireland c. 1650. Gained estates c. 1660.

1. Henry Prittie – {County Tipperary 1761-68}
2. Henry Prittie 1 Baron Dunalley – {Banagher 1767-68 Gowran 1769-76 County Tipperary 1776-90}
3. Henry Prittie 2 Baron Dunalley – {Carlow 1797-1800} Carlow 1801 Okehampton 1819-24
4. Francis Prittie – {Doneraile 1800} Carlow 1801 County Tipperary 1806-18 1819-31

Seats: Dunalley Castle (Kilboy), Tipperary (acq. 1650s, rebuilt c. 1780, burned 1922, rebuilt, demolished c. 1955); Corville, Tipperary (built 18th c., purch. c. 1818, sold later 19th c.)
Estates: Bateman 21081 (I) 7162. Worth £6,000 pa in 1775.
Peers: 2 Irish Rep peers 1828-54 1891-1927
1 Ld Lt 19th-20th
Notes: Two in ODNB.

PROBY *ENGLAND & IRELAND*

Earl of Carysfort (1789-1909 I)

Origins: A grocer shifted to serve as an official late in the reign of Elizabeth. Lord Mayor of London 1622. **First MP 1593**. Two infusions of wealth: first a younger son in the East India Company, Governor of Fort St. George at Madras, ultimately inherited and brought his nabob wealth into the family. The second came when 1 Lord Carysfort married 1750 the sister and heiress of the 3 Viscount Allen (see Allen).

1. Sir Thomas Proby 1 Bt – Amersham 1660-79 Huntingdonshire 1679-81
2. John Proby – Huntingdonshire 1693-95 1698-1702 1708-10
3. John Proby – Huntingdonshire 1722-27 Stamford 1734-47
4. John Proby 1 Baron Carysfort – Stamford 1747-54 Huntingdonshire 1754-68
5. John Proby 1 Earl of Carysfort – East Looe 1790 Stamford 1790-1801
6. William Proby Lord Proby – Buckingham 1802-04
7. John Proby 2 Earl of Carysfort – Buckingham 1805-06 Huntingdonshire 1806-07 1814-18
8. Granvile Proby 3 Earl of Carysfort – County Wicklow 1816-29
9. Granville Proby 4 Earl of Carsyfort – County Wicklow 1858-68

Seats: Elton Hall, Huntingdonshire (built 15th c., purch. 1617, ruin, rebuilt 1663-66, remod. 1790s and 1812-14 and 1856-60, add. 1868-78, still own); Glenart Castle (Kilcarra Castle), Wicklow (hunting lodge built c. 1700, add. early 19th c., add. 1869, partly burned c. 1920, family still resided there, sold early 1940s, institution); Stillorgan House, Dublin (built 1695, acq. by mar. with Allens (see) 1745, demolished 1860)
Estates: Bateman 25914 (E & I) 31075. Irish estates sold 1890s.
Titles: Baron Carysfort 1752-1909 I; Baron Carysfort 1801-1909 UK; Baronet 1662-89; 1952-
Peers: {2 peers 1755-1800} 4 peers 1801-28 1855-1909
1 Ld Lt 19th-20th
3 KP 18th, 19th, 20th
Notes: On the extinction of the Earldom in 1909 the estates passed to the Hamiltons by the marriage of Lady Elizabeth Proby, daughter of the 3 Earl, to Lord Claude Hamilton, son of the 1 Marquuess of Abercorn. Their son took the name Proby (see Hamilton). 1 Baron and 1 and 3 Earls in ODNB.

PRYSE (Price) [Loveden, Philipps] *WALES*

Pryse

Origins: Genuine descent from the 11th century. (Colyear, "Decline of a Great Estate", 418). Owned mines discovered in the time of the 4 Bt, which led the estate to be called "the Welsh Potosi". (Burke and Burke, *The Extinct and Dormant Baronetcies of England,* 431). **First MP 1553 for Cardiganshire. Three further MPs 1584-1648, all for the county.** Margaret Pryse, heiress of Gogerddan, married 1773 Edward Loveden of Buscot Park. Their son, Pryse Loveden took the name Pryse 1798. His heir, Pryse Pryse, took the name Loveden.

1. Sir Richard Pryse 2 Bt – Cardiganshire 1660
2. Sir Carbery Pryse 4 Bt – Cardiganshire 1690-94
3. Lewis Pryse – Cardiganshire 1701-02 Cardigan Boroughs 1705-08 Cardiganshire 1708-10 1715-16
4. Thomas Pryse – Cardigan Boroughs 1741-45
5. John Pryse – Cardiganshire 1761-68 Merioneth 1768-74
6. Pryse Loveden – Cardigan 1849-55
7. Edward Pryse – Cardigan 1857-68

Seats: Plas Gogerddan, Cardiganshire (acq. 14th c., built c. 1500, passed to Lovedens by mar. 1776, sold c. 1962); Glanfraed, Cardiganshire (acq. by mar. mid-16th c., passed to Campbells by mar. later 18th c., sold 1802); Noyadd (Neuadd, Neyadd) Trefawr, Cardiganshire (built early 17th c., remod. 18th c. and 19th c., acq. by mar. 1891, sold 20th c.); Lodge Park (Parc Bodvage), Cardiganshire (acq. 1637, sold 1962); (Ystrad) Peithyll (Stradpeithyll, Strath Peithell), Cardiganshire (medieval castle, ruin, house built 1844, sold 1962, offices); The Priory, Cardigan, Cardiganshire (acq. by mar. 1693, see below, sold 1774, demolished and rebuilt later 18th c.)
Estates: Bateman 32357 (W) 11324. Worth £1,,000 in 1637 and £3,000 pa in c. 1720.
Title: Baronet 1641-94; 1866-1962
1 Ld Lt 19th
Notes: 4 Bt in ODNB.

Loveden

Origins: Rose by land speculation in the 16th century. See above.

1. Edward Loveden – Abingdon 1783-96 Shaftesbury 1802-12
2. Pryse Pryse – Cardigan 1818-49

Seat: Buscot Park, Berkshire (purch. 1557, new house built 1780, sold 1887)

Philipps

Origins: Emerged in the 16th century. On the death of Hector Philipps MP in 1693 Cardigan Priory passed to the Pryses of Gogerddan.

1. James Philipps – Wales 1653 Cardiganshire 1654 Pembrokeshire 1656 Cardiganshire 1659 Cardigan Boroughs 1660-62
2. Hector Philipps – Cardigan Boroughs 1679-81 1685-87 1689-93

Seat: The Priory, Cardigan, Cardiganshire (acq. 1616, passed to Pryses by mar. 1693)
Notes: Male line extinct 1693.

PUCKERING

Origins: Rose from humble origins through the law in the reign of Elizabeth I. Speaker of the House of Commons 1584. **First MP 1584. One other MP 1621.** The daughter and heiress of Sir John Puckering 2 Bt (Lord Keeper of the Privy Seal) married 1605 Adam Newton 1 Bt (tutor of Charles I) and succeeded to the Puckering estates and took the name Puckering.

1. Sir Henry Puckering 2 Bt – Warwickshire 1661-79 Warwick 1679
2. Henry Puckering – Warwick 1661-64

Seats: The Priory, Warwick, (Warwick Priory), Warwickshire (built 16th c., purch. 1582 by Puckerings, add. 1620, inherited by Newtons 1736, sold 1709, demolished 1925); Charlton, Kent (medieval house, purch. by Newtons 1607, rebuilt 1607-16, sold 1660)
Estates: Worth £2,000 to £3,000 pa c. 1596.
Title: Baronet 1611-36; 1620-1700
Notes: The family became extinct in 1700 and the estates were sold to creditors. Three in ODNB.

PUGH *WALES*

Origins: Owned land at Mathanfarn since the 13th century. **First MP 1572. Another MP 1624.**

1. John Pugh – Cardiganshire 1705-08 Montgomery Boroughs 1708-27

Seat: Mathafarn (Mathavarn), Montgomeryshire (acq. 13th c., sold 1752)
Estates: Worth £1,000 pa in 1660.
Notes: Extinct 1737.

PULESTON *WALES*

Origins: The family was at Emral by the 13th century. Fought at Bosworth. Royal officials under the Tudors. Cromwellian judge. **First MP 1542. Three additional MPs 1547-1604.**

1. Sir Roger Puleston – Flintshire 1689-95 Flint boroughs 1695-97

Seat: Emral Hall, Flintshire (acq. 1283 and built, rebuilt early 17th c., add. 1724-27, sold and demolished 1936)
Estates: 3,500 to 4,000 acres in 1587. Worth £3,000 pa in the 1660s.
Title: Baronet 1813-96
Notes: Last MP died in debt and a large part of the estates were sold. Senior line extinct 1732 and remaining estates passed to several collateral branches. Two in ODNB.

PULTENEY [Guy]

Earl of Bath (1742-64 GB)

Origins: Owned the manor of Pulteney by 1308. A younger son was a merchant and Lord Mayor of London 1331. His seat was at Penshurst Place in Kent. He owned land in eight counties by his death in 1349. Significant property was also acquired in London 1575. Rose high pimping for Charles II. **First MP 1404 for Hertfordshire. Two additional MPs 1563-1611.**

1. Sir William Pulteney – Westminster 1679-81 1689-91
2. John Pulteney – {Wexford 1692-93} Hastings 1695-1710
3. William Pulteney 1 Earl of Bath – Hedon 1705-34 Middlesex 1734-42
4. Daniel Pulteney – Tregony 1721 Hedon 1721-22 Preston 1722-31
5. Harry Pulteney – Hedon 1722-34 1739-41 Kingston-on-Hull 1744-47
6. William Pulteney Viscount Pulteney – Old Sarum 1754-61 Westminster 1761-63

Seats: Misterton Hall, Leicestershire (acq. 1335, passed to Crewes by mar. c. 1640, acq. again mid-18th c., passed out of family again later 18th c.); Harefield, Middlesex (leased 18th c.?)
Estates: Worth £1,100 pa c. 1620. The estates of the 1 Earl were said to be worth £30,000 pa with anywhere from £400,000 to over a million pounds in cash. Held a large London estate in the West End.
Peer: 1 peer 1742-64
1 Ld Lt 18th
1 in Cabinet 1714-17
Notes: The estates of the 1 Earl of Bath passed to his cousin Frances Pulteney, who married Sir William Johnstone 5 Bt (see Hope). Ultimately, the Pulteney estates went to the 1 Duke of Cleveland (under Vane) and the Sutton Baronets (under Manners). 1 Earl and two others in ODNB.

Guy

Origins: Henry Guy was a successful lawyer. He left his estates to his grandson, the 1 Earl of Bath (see above).

1. Henry Guy – Hedon 1670-81 1685-87 1689-95 1702-05

Seat: Tring, Hertfordshire (purch. 1669, built 1670s, sold 1702)
Estates: Estates worth £100,000 in 1711.
Notes: One in ODNB.

PUREFOY [Lumm] *IRELAND*

Purefoy

Origins: Gentry in England by 16th c. **First MP 1621. Another MP 1628-59**. A cadet line emigrated from Warwickshire. Acquired estates in Ireland 1678.

1. William Purefoy – {Ennis 1661-66}
2. Arthur Purefoy – {Kells 1661-66}
3. Peter Purefoy – {Philipstown 1692-93}
4. William Purefoy – {King's County 1707-13 Philipstown 1713-14 King's County 1715-27}

Seats: Purefoy's Place, King's County (Clonbully, Clonbogle, Clonbulloge) (acq. 1678, passed by mar. to Lumms mid-18th c., depart late 18th c.); Ballybracken, King's County (acq. mid-17th c., resident 18th c.); Ballylikin (Ballyleaken?), King's County
Note: Purefoy estates pass to Lumms in mid-18th c. One in ODNB.

Lumm (Lum)

Origins: To Ireland in the later 17th century. Banker in Dublin 1680's and 1690's. Sheriff 1755. Elnatham Lumm of Lummville married Dorothea Purefoy, heiress of her brother William Purefoy and succeeded to Purefoy estates mid-18th c.

1. Elnatham Lum – {Carlingford 1692-93 1695-99}

Seat: Lum(m)ville, King's County (acq. later 17th c., resident 18th c.)
Title: Baronet 1775-97

PYE

Origins: Minor Herefordshire gentry since the 15th century. Rose to profitable high office under the patronage of the Duke of Buckingham in the 1620s. Kt 1621. **First MP 1597. Two further MPs 1621-58**. Several branches are combined here.

1. Sir Robert Pye – Berkshire 1654 1659 1660
2. Richard Pye – Wallingford 1698-1700
3. Sir Charles Pye 2 Bt – Derby 1701
4. Sir Richard Pye 3 Bt – Derby 1710
5. Henry Pye – Berkshire 1746-66
6. Thomas Pye – Rochester 1771-74
7. Henry Pye – Berkshire 1784-90

Seats: Faringdon House, Berkshire; (built 16th c., purch. 1623, demolished 1642-46, rebuilt, fire 1780, rebuilt 1770-85, sold 1780s); Clifton (Campville) Hall, Staffordshire (purch. and built 1700, passed through the female line after 1734, reverted to Faringdon line 1833, still owned 1895, derelict 1960s, restored by 2003)
Estates: Faringdon line worth £2,000 pa in 1662. The Clifton branch in Bateman 3251 (E) 5626
Title: Baronet 1607-73; 1665-1734
Notes: One Pye became a Jacobite peer. The Faringdon branch got into financial difficulties (£50,000 in debts in 1776) 1780s. Six in ODNB.

PYM

Origins: Merchants with interests in Holland and India who married heiresses and acquired landed estates in the later 17th century and entered the gentry. **First MP 1614.**

1. Francis Pym – Bedfordshire 1806-18 1820-26
2. Charles Pym – Bedford 1895-1906
3. Leslie Pym – Monmouth 1939-45
4. Francis Pym Baron Pym – Cambridgeshire 1961-83 Cambridge S. E. 1983-87

Seats: The Hasells (Hazells Hall), Bedfordshire (built before 1634, rebuilt c. 1698, purch. by Kingsleys 1721, add. 1721-36, inherited by mar. by Pyms 1761, add. 1789-90, remod. c. 1885, institutional use from 1940, sold 1981, flats); Tetworth Hall, Huntingdonshire (built 1710, purch. 1930s, sold c. 1939)
Estates: Bateman 3630 (E) 7587. Lord Pym left two and a half million pounds in 2008.
1 in Cabinet 1973-74 1981-83
Title: Baron Pym 1987-2008 UK Life
Notes: Members of the family remained active in business. Charles Pym MP was chairman of an Insurance company. Lord Pym in ODNB.

RADCLIFFE (Radclyffe, Ratcliffe) [Alcock, Delmé, Farnaby]

Earl of Derwentwater (1688-1716 E)

Origins: Perhaps the most powerful family in Lancashire during the Middle Ages. High Sheriff 1194. Fought at Crécy. The Radcliffes inherited the estates of the Derwentwater family of Cumberland and Westmorland (**two MPs 1295-1388**) in the late 14th century. Sir John Radcliffe MP fought at Agincourt. The family broke into a number of branches. **First MP 1334 for Lancashire. Twenty-four further MPs 1339-1628, ten for Lancashire and for other counties**. Created Earls of Sussex 1529-1643 and other titles. The family remained Roman Catholic (with some exceptions) and lived for a time in France at the court of James II after 1688 but returned to Dilston in 1709.

The 3 Earl of Derwentwater was executed for his part in the rebellion of 1715 and the Earldom was attainted in 1716. The Radclyffe estates passed to Greenwich Hospital. The Jacobite "5" Earl was also executed for treason in 1746.

No post-1660 MPs

Seat: Dilston, Northumberland (built 13th c., acq. by mar. 1521, enlarged 1622, 1710-14, confiscated 1731, much of it demolished 1765)
Estates: Worth £9,000 pa in the mid-18th c.
Titles: Baron Tyndale and Viscount Radclyffe and Langley 1688-1716 E; Baronet 1620-1716
Peers: 3 peers 1688-1705 1710-16
Notes: 6 Baron Fitzwalter and 3 and 5 Earls of Derwentwater and 1, 2, 3, 4 and 5 Earls of Sussex and five others in ODNB.

Ratcliffe

Origins: A younger son of the Lancashire family became a brewer and the family became established in Chester. **First MP for Chester 1621.**

1. John Ratcliffe – Chester 1646-48 1660 1661-73

Seat: Chester, Cheshire

Radcliffe

Origins: These Radcliffes were a cadet line from the 16th century when they acquired Hitchin, which was first operated as a school. The son of the schoolmaster was a successful lawyer and his brother physician to James I. A younger son who was a Turkey merchant inherited Hitchin in the 18th century.

1. John Radcliffe – St. Albans 1768-83

Seat: Hitchin Priory, Hertfordshire (medieval, purch. 1553, new house 1770-71, passed via an heiress 1783 to the Farnabys, who took the name Radcliffe, then passed to Delmé Radcliffes, see below, sold 1963, hotel)

Delmé

Origins: Anne Radcliffe, sister and heiress of John Radcliffe MP (see above), had a daughter Anne who married in 1802 Emilius Delmé, whose descendents took the additional name Radcliffe.

1. Peter Delmé – Ludgershall 1734-41 Southampton 1741-54
2. Peter Delmé – Morpeth 1774-89

Seats: Titchfield Place (Place House), Hampshire (medieval, remod. 1542, purch. 1741, abandoned and partly demolished 1781); Erle Stoke Park (Erlestoke, Stoke Park), Wiltshire (old house, purch. 1737, sold and house demolished 1780, rebuilt 1786, fire 1950, prison); Cams Hall, Hampshire (built 17th c., rebuilt 1771, purch. 1776, sold 1895, derelict 1960s, restored 1990s)
Estates: Bateman 6258 (E) 6986

Farnaby-Radcliffe

Origins: Sir Charles Farnaby of Kippington married Penelope, a Radcliffe heiress in 1762. They succeeded to Hitchin Priory in 1783 and took the additional name Radcliffe.

1. Sir Charles Farnaby Radcliffe 3 Bt – East Grinstead 1765-68 Kent 1769-74 Hythe 1774-98

Seats: Kippington House (Park), Kent (old house, purch. 1636, rebuilt early 18th c., sold 1796); (West) Wicken Court, Kent (medieval, acq. by mar. late 18th c., passed out of family 1861)
Title: Baronet 1726-1859

Alcock

Origins: The daughter and heiress of Lawrence Alcock MP carried his property to John Radcliffe of Hitchin. The Radcliffe heiress married Sir Charles Farnaby 3 Bt.

1. Lawrence Alcock – Midhurst 1701-13

Seat: Trotton Place, Sussex (purch. 1679, passed to Radcliffes 1723, sold 1779)
Notes: Male line extinct 1723.

RALEIGH

Origins: An old Devon family in decline by the 16th century. Several branches produced MPs. **First MP 1295 for Somerset. Ten further MPs 1297-1621, eight of them kts of the shire.**

1. Gilbert Raleigh – Downton 1661-75
2. Sir Charles Raleigh – Downton 1685-87 1689-98
3. Carew Raleigh – Downton 1698-1702

Seat: (The) Rectory House, Downton, Wiltshire (built 14th c., leased 1590s, remod. 17th c., lease given up and estate sold 1720)
Estates: Worth £400 pa in 1675.
Notes: Two in ODNB.

RAM *IRELAND*

Origins: The first Ram to emigrate to Ireland in 1599 was a clergyman, Dean of Cork and Bishop of Ferns and Leighlin 1605. Gained further land 1615. High Sheriff 1673. Lord Mayor of Dublin 1684.

1. Andrew Ram – {Dunleek 1692-93 1695-98}
2. Abel Ram – {Gorey 1692-93 1695-99 1703-13 1715-40}
3. George Ram – {Gorey 1713-25}
4. Stephan Ram – {Dunleek 1728-46 Gorey 1741-60}
5. Abel Ram – {Gorey 1727-76}
6. Humphreys Ram – {Gorey 1741-60 1776-81}
7. Andrew Ram – {County Wexford 1755-60 Dunleek 1761-90}
8. Stephan Ram – {Gorey 1764-90}
9. Abel Ram – {Dunleek 1783-90 County Wexford 1797-1800} 1801-12

Seats: Ramsfort, Wexford (acq. c. 1615, rebuilt 1751, burned 1798, rebuilt early 19th c., add. 19th c., sold 1870); Clonattin, Wexford (acq. 17th c., fire 1798, rebuilt, sold 1944)
Estates: 4227 (I) 3700 in 1870. Worth £5,000 pa c. 1800.
Notes: The Rams began selling land 1815. Three in ODNB.

RAMSAY I [Maule] *SCOTLAND*

Marquis of Dalhousie (1849-60 UK)

Origins: Emerged in the 12th century. Member of the Council of Magnates 1255. **First [MP 1617].** Baron 1618. Earl 1633. Lord Ramsay, father of the 8 Earl of Dalhousie, married the sister of the 1 Earl of Panmure (who was attainted in 1716). The brother of the 9 Earl of Dalhousie was created Baron Panmure in 1831 and took the name of Maule. His son succeeded as 11 Earl of Dalhousie.

1. William Ramsay Maule 1 Baron Panmure – Forfarshire 1796 1805-31
2. John Ramsay – Aberdeen Burghs 1806-07
3. William Ramsay – Stirlingshire 1831-32 Edinburghshire 1841-45
4. Fox Ramsay-Maule 11 Earl of Dalhousie – Perthshire 1835-37 Elgin District Burghs 1838-41 Perth 1841-52
5. James Ramsay 1 Marquis of Dalhousie – Haddington 1837-38

6. Lauderdale Maule – Forfarshire 1852-54
7. John Ramsay 13 Earl of Dalhousie – Liverpool 1880
8. Charles Maule Ramsay – Forfarshire 1894-95
9. Archibald Ramsay – Peebles & S. Div. Midlothian & Peebles 1931-45
10. Simon Ramsay 16 Earl of Dalhousie – Forfarshire 1945-50

Seats: Dalhousie Castle, Edinburghshire (acq. 12th c., built 15th c., remod. 1633, remod. 1780s, remod. 1825, post WWII a school and then hotel, sold 2003); Panmure House, Forfarshire (acq. 1224 by Maules, medieval, castle abandoned and new house built 1666, acq. by mar. by Ramsays 1782, remod. 1852-55, demolished 1955/60); Brechin Castle, Forfarshire (passed from Maules to Ramsays 1782 by mar., still own)
Estates: Bateman 138021 (S) 58603 and 6992 (S) 3639 and 2702 (S) 4843. Sold 11,070 acres 1951. Sold 18,000 acres for £2,500,000 in 1987. Held 150,000 acres at greatest extent. Held 47,200 acres in 1996. Estate at 55,000 in 2016.
Titles: Baron Ramsay 1618- S; Earl of Dalhousie 1633- S; Baron Dalhousie 1815-60 UK; Baron Panmure 1831-74 UK; Baron Ramsay 1875- UK
Peers: [4 peers 1660-1707] 2 Scots Rep peers 1774-87 1796-1806 1807-18 7 peers 1815-60 1831-52 1875-1945
1 Ld Lt 19th
2 in Cabinet 1845-46 1846-52 1848-56 1855-58
3 KT 19th
Notes: The Earls of Dalhousie produced major political figures in the 19th and 20th centuries including the last colonial governor of importance in the 1960s in Rhodesia. The Ramsay family has an entry as well as the 1 Baron Panmure and 1, 9, 11, 12, and 13 Earls and 1 Marquis and four others in ODNB.

Earl of Panmure (1646-1716 S; 1743-82 GB)

Origins: The first Earl rose after a career in trade and court service. **First [MP 1560]. Two other [MPs 1596-1651].**

1. James Maule – [Forfarshire 1667]
2. Henry Maule – [Brechin Burgh 1689-93]
3. William Maule 1 Earl of Panmure – Forfarshire 1735-82
4. John Maule – Aberdeen 1739-48

Seats: Panmure, Forfarshire (acq. 1224, medieval, castle abandoned and new house built 1660s, passed to Ramsays by mar., see above); Kellie Castle, Forfarshire (built 14th c., rebuilt late 15th c., ruin, purch. by Maules 1679, new house built 18th c., still own); Brechin Castle, Forfarshire (acq. 12th c., Maule seat, rebuilt 1696-1709, passed to Ramsays by mar. 1782, see above)
Estates: Worth £3,456 pa in 1716. Estates forfeited 1716, repurchased 1764 for £50,000.

Peers: [4 peers 1660-71 1673-87 1689]
Notes: 4 Earl an attainted Jacobite exile. 1, 4, and 5 Earls and one other in ODNB.

RAMSAY II [Burnett] *SCOTLAND*

Ramsay

Origins: Prominent from c. 1320. Lord of Parliament 1433. **First [MP 1609]. Two further [MPs 1612-21].**

1. Sir Gilbert Ramsay 1 Bt – [Kincardineshire 1639-41 1645-46 1661-63]
2. Sir David Ramsay 4 Bt – [Kincardineshire 1705-07] Scotland 1707-08 Kincardineshire 1708-10
3. Sir Alexander Ramsay 5 Bt – Kincardineshire 1710-13
4. Sir Alexander Ramsay-Irvine 6 Bt – Kincardineshire 1765-68
5. Sir Alexander Ramsay 2 Bt – Kincardineshire 1820-26
6. Sir Alexander Ramsay 3 Bt – Rochdale 1857-59

Seats: Balmain, Kincardineshire (acq. medieval period, passed by mar. to Sir Thomas Burnett 6 Bt. of the Leys by mar to Ramsay heiress 1754, he took the name Ramsay); Fasque, Kincardineshire (old house, rebuilt 1809 for £30,000, sold 1833)
Estates: Bateman 4028 (S) 3760
Titles: Baronet 1625-1806; 1806-
Notes: 5 Bt emigrated to Australia late 19th c. Six in ODNB.

Burnett

Origins: Ancient lineage (*Country Life*, 33, p. 598). Came to Scotland from Huntingdonshire in the train of King David I. Granted "the Leys" by Robert I in 1323. **First [MP 1605]. One additional [MP 1621]**. Sir Thomas Burnett 6 Bt married the Ramsay heiress. The eldest son succeeded to the Burnett estates. The younger son, who took the name Ramsay, succeeded to Balmain and was created a Bt 1806.

1. Sir Thomas Burnett 3 Bt – [Kincardineshire 1689-1702 1703-07] Scotland 1707-08

Seats: Crathes Castle, Kincardineshire (acq. 1323, also called "the Leys" from the 15th century, built 1553-96, add. 18th c., remod. 1877, add. 1894, NT 1956, fire 1966, rebuilt); Muchalls Castle (House), Kincardineshire (built 1619-27, sold 1705)
Estates: Bateman 12109 (S) 5114. 6,700 acres in 1996.
Title: Baronet 1626-
3 Lds Lt 19th, 20th
Notes: The 12th Bt was the 24th laird at "the Leys". One in ODNB.

RAMSDEN

Origins: The Ramsdens were yeomen clothiers who became modest gentry in the mid-16th century through monastic land purchases. They achieved great wealth through agricultural improvements, land speculation, and management of woodlands, collieries, iron forges, and fulling mills. With their profits they purchased more acreage. They also embezzled royal funds through office-holding (Smith, *Land and Politics in the England of Henry VIII*, 232-35) and made advantageous marriages. Kt 1619. Cousins seated at Norton, Yorkshire, who also elected MPs listed here, were Hull merchants. The Ramsdens acquired half the manor of Huddersfield in 1599, and the other half later (sold 1920). (Roebuck, *Yorkshire Baronets 1640-1760*, 37) They built the first cloth hall there in 1766. Their wealth expanded exponentially as Huddersfield emerged as an important industrial city in the 19th century. **First MP 1628.**

1. John Ramsden – Hull 1659 1660
2. William Ramsden – Hull 1678-79
3. John Ramsden – Hull 1685-87 1689-96
4. Sir John Ramsden 3 Bt – Appleby 1727-54
5. Sir John Ramsden 4 Bt – Grampound 1780-84
6. John Ramsden – Malton 1812-31 Yorkshire 1831-32 Malton 1833-36
7. Sir John Ramsden 5 Bt – Taunton 1853-57 Hythe 1857-59 W. R. Yorkshire 1859-65 Monmouth District 1868-74 E. Div. W. R. Yorkshire 1880-85 Osgoldcross Div. Yorkshire 1885-86

Seats: Byram Park, Yorkshire (purch. 1612, enlarged 1770s, sold 1922, demolished 1930s and 1955); Longley Hall, Yorkshire (medieval, acq. by mar. 1540, new house 1576, restored 1885, sold 1975); Ardverikie, Inverness-shire (purch. long lease 1867, fire 1871, rebuilt 1873-77, still own); Norton Hall, Yorkshire (purch. and built sec. half 17th c., donated to St. Catherine's College, Cambridge 1745, demolished c. 1756); Bulstrode Park, Buckinghamshire (built 1865-70, acq. inher. by Ramsdens 1885, estate sold 1932, house sold c. 1958, institutional use); Muncaster Castle, Cumberland (medieval onwards, inher. by mar. 1917, still own)
Estates: Bateman 150,000 (E & S) very large income – an inaccurate figure given in Bateman.
Title: Baronet 1689-
Notes: One of the very few families of exceptional wealth not to receive a peerage in modern English history. The Ramsdens moved their principal seat from Byram to Bulstrode Park, Buckinghamsghire in the late 19th century, then to Muncaster after 1932.

RASHLEIGH

Rashleigh

Origins: Leading merchants and ship owners in Fowey from 1520 into the 18th century. Involved in overseas trade. Purchased estates at the Dissolution. **First MP 1589 for Fowey**.

1. Jonathan Rashleigh – Fowey 1614 1621 1625 1640-44 1661-75
2. Jonathan Rashleigh – Fowey 1675-81 1689-95
3. Philip Rashleigh – Liskeard 1710-22
4. Jonathan Rashleigh – Fowey 1727-64
5. Philip Rashleigh – Fowey 1765-1802
6. William Rashleigh – Fowey 1812-18
7. William Rashleigh – E. Cornwall 1841-47

Seat: Menabilly, Cornwall (acq. 1545, built early 17th c., rebuilt 18th c., still own)
Estates: Bateman 36896 (E & I) 11291. Owned 15,000 acres worth 52 million pounds in 2001.
Notes: One in ODNB.

Rashleigh

Origins: Kinsmen. **First MP 1628 for Fowey**.

1. John Rashleigh – Fowey 1661-79

Seat: Coombe, Cornwall (acq. 16th c., sold 1699)
Notes: Extinct in male line c. 1700.

Rashleigh

Origins: Cadet founded by a younger son of the Menabilly family.

1. Sir Colman Rashleigh 2 Bt – E. Div. Cornwall 1874-80

Seat: Prideaux House, Cornwall (medieval, purch. 1806, rebuilt 1808, succ. to Menabilly in 1961 and moved there as the main seat 1969)
Title: Baronet 1831-

RATHBONE

Origins: Eminent Quaker merchants and shipowners in Liverpool from 1730 into the 20th century.

1. William Rathbone – Liverpool 1868-80 Caernarvonshire 1880-85 N. Div. Caernarvonshire 1885-95
2. Hugh Rathbone – Wavetree Div. Liverpool 1923-24
3. Eleanor Rathbone – Combined English Universities 1929-46
4. John Rathbone – Bodmin Div. Cornwall 1935-40
5. Beatrice Wright (wife) – Bodmin Div. Cornwall 1941-45
6. John Rathbone – Lewes 1974-97

Seats: Greenbank House, Lancashire (built early 18th c., leased 1788, purch. 1808, remod. mid-19th c., donated to U. Liverpool 1939-48); Bassenfell Manor, Cumberland (purch. and built 1842, sold c. 1910, institutional use)
Estates: The profits alone from their trade in cotton brought in £53,000 in the decade of the 1850s. (S. Beckert, *Empire of Cotton*, 214).
Notes: Three in ODNB.

RAWDON-HASTINGS [Abney, Clifton] *ENGLAND & IRELAND*

Marquess of Hastings (1816-68 UK)

Origins: The Hastings family came over with the Conqueror. They were feudal barons and claimants to the Scottish throne 1290. Called by writ as Barons 1295, Earl of Pembroke 1389, Earl of Huntingdon 1529. At Agincourt. (Acheson, *A Gentry Community: Leicestershire in the Fifteenth Century*, 234). **First MP 1455 for Leicestershire. Eleven additional MPs 1472-1628, seven for Leicestershire**. The Hastings Earldom of Huntingdon became separated from its patrimony in 1789. On the death of the 10 Earl his estates passed to an illegitimate son and thence to the descendents of his sister, who had married the 1 Earl of Moira (Rawdon family). The Rawdons were gentry in the 16th century. The 1 Bt was a diplomat and courtier. He went to Ireland in 1630 and acquired estates soon thereafter. **First MP 1628**. Sheriff 1692. The son of the 1 Earl of Moira became the 1 Marquess of Hastings. He married the Countess of Loudon in her own right (see Campbell I). The 2 Marquess of Hastings and 7 Earl of Loudon married Baroness Grey de Ruthin in her own right (see Grey II). On the death of the 4 Marquess of Hastings the title became extinct. The Earldom of Loudon went to one sister and the Barony of Grey to another, whose descendents bear these titles. The Earldom of Huntingdon passed in 1789 to a remote cousin seated in Ireland.

1. Sir George Rawdon 1 Bt – {Belfast 1639 Carlingford 1661-66}
2. Sir Arthur Rawdon 2 Bt – {County Down 1692-93 1695}
3. Sir John Rawdon 3 Bt – {County Down 1717-24}
4. Francis Rawdon-Hastings 1 Marquess of Hastings – {Randalstown 1781-83}
5. John Rawdon – Appleby 1791-96 Launceston 1796-1802
6. George Rawdon – Lincoln 1796-1800

Seats: Donington (Donnington) Park (Hall), Leicestershire (acq. c. 1648, new house later 17th c., new house 1790-93, sale of contents 1869, sold 1902, now offices); The Manor House, Ashby-de-la-Zouche, (Ashby Place) Leicestershire (built 12th c., acq. 1464, part demolished 1648, new house 1720s, new house 1830, castle ruins given to state 1932, remaining house leased out since 1950); Moira Park, Down (acq. mid-17th c., built 18th c., demolished early 19th c., sold); Rawdon Hall, Yorkshire (Rawdons owned property at Rawdon from 14th c., house rebuilt 17th c., declined to a farm house in 19th c.); Clashmore House, Waterford (old house, acq. by mar. by Earl of Huntingdon 1838, rebuilt but never completed in 1830s, ruin by 1940); Willesley Hall, Derbyshire (built late 17th c., inher. by Earl of Loudon mid to later 19th c., sold 1919, demolished 1953)
Estates: Bateman 13523 (I) 6765 (Earl of Huntingdon); 14272 (E) 24691 (Earl of Loudon – English estates of Hastings family); the Earl of Moira's Irish estates were worth £3,500 pa in 1741. £18,000 pa in 1793. The estates were heavily mortgaged in the second half of the 19th c.
Titles: Baron Botreaux 1368- E; Baron Stanley 1456- E; Baron Hastings 1461- E; Earl of Huntingdon 1529- E; Baron Loughborough 1643-67 E; Baron Rawdon 1750-1868 I; Earl of Moira 1762-1868 I; Baron Rawdon 1783-1868 GB; Baron Donington 1880-1927 UK; Baronet 1665-1868
Peers: 1660-67 1673-92 1701-05 1717-46 1750-1804 {1 peer 1750-93} 1783-1826 1819-85 1829-44 1863-68 1889-1945
4 Lds Lt 17th, 18th, 19th
1 in Cabinet 1806-07
1 KG 19th
Notes: The 3rd Earl of Huntingdon accumulated large debts that began the slow decline of the family. 4 Marquess, who died age 26, ruined the family fortune through gambling and dissolute activities. 1 Marquess and three others in ODNB.

Abney-Hastings

Origins: The Abney's acquired Willesley via an heiress 1424 from a family that had held it from c. 1270. Sir Thomas Abney was Lord Mayor of London 1701 and Director of the Bank of England. Sir Thomas Abney was Chief Justice of the Common Pleas 1743. Sir Charles Hastings 1 Bt was the illegitimate son of the 10 Earl of Huntingdon. He succeeded to the Huntingdon estates and inherited by marriage the Abney estates. His son took the additional name Abney. The 2 Bt died without children, when the estates passed to the Countess of Loudon and the 4 Marquess of Hastings (see above).

1. Sir Edward Abney – Leicester 1690-98
2. Sir Thomas Abney – London 1701-02
3. Sir Charles Abney-Hastings 2 Bt – Leicester 1826-31

Seats: Willesley Hall, Derbyshire (acq. c. 1270, built early 17th c., remod. late 17th c., add. 1820, rebuilt 1840-45, passed by inher. to Earls of Loudon 1858, sold 1919, golf club, house demolished 1953); Measham Hall, Derbyshire (purch. and built 1767, sold 1924, demolished 1959)
Title: Bt 1806-58
Notes: Two in ODNB.

Clifton

Origins: Emerged in the 11th century. **First MP 1302 for Lancashire. One additional MP 1382, also for the county**. Charles Clifton married Maude, Countess of Loudon in her own right, daughter of the 2 Marquess of Hastings and sister and heiress of the 4 Marquess. He was created Baron Donington in 1880. Their son succeeded as Earl of Loudon and Baron Donington (see Campbell I). Charles's brother, Augustus, married the Countess of Loudon's sister, Baroness Grey de Ruthin, and their son succeeded as 23 Baron Grey de Ruthin.

1. John Clifton – N. Lancashire 1844-52
2. Thomas Clifton – N. Lancashire 1874-80

Seats: Lytham Hall, Lancashire (old house built mid-16th c., purch. 1606, new house built 1757-62, demolished old house 1759, sold 1963); Clifton Hall, Lancashire (original seat destroyed by fire 1745, rebuilt 1833, sold by 1850)
Estates: Bateman 15802 (E) 41965
Title: Baronet 1660-94
Peers: 1880-95 1886-1934
Notes: A Roman Catholic family until 1831 (reverted late 19th century), which accounts for the paucity of MPs before Emancipation. Acquired great wealth developing Lythan St. Anne's as a holiday resort after the arrival of the railway in 1844. Sold 16,000 acres of their estate between 1937 and 1963.

RAWLINSON

Baron Rawlinson (1919-25 UK)

Origins: Quaker merchants in the 18th century. Lord Mayor of London 1753.

1. Sir Walter Rawlinson – Queenborough 1774-84 Huntingdon 1784-90
2. Abraham Rawlinson – Lancaster 1780-90
3. Henry Rawlinson – Liverpool 1780-84
4. Sir Henry Rawlinson 1 Bt – Reigate 1858 Frome 1865-68

Seats: Grassyard Hall (aka Gresgarth Hall), Lancashire (c. 15th c., purch. 1780, sold 1806); Ellel(l) Hall, Lancashire (leased 18th c.); Stowlangtoft Hall, Suffolk (old house, purch. 1760, rebuilt 1792, passed to an heiress 1805, sold 1825, rebuilt 1859)
Estates: Parliamentary grant of £30,000 in 1919.
Title: Baronet 1891-
Peer: 1 peer 1919-25
Notes: The 1 Bt was a diplomat and the 1 Baron a general. 1 Baron and one other in ODNB.

READE (Rede)

Origins: Purchased manorial land 1545 and married well. High Sheriff 1581. Granted arms 1597. **First MP 1529 for Cricklade. Two further MPs 1553-54.**

1. Sir Thomas Reade 4 Bt – Cricklade 1713-41
2. George Reade – Tewkesbury 1722-34

Seats: Shipton Court, Oxfordshire (built 1603, purch. 1663, left to a footman 1868 who took the name Reade, sold 1900); Barton Court, Berkshire (purch. 1547, sold 1787); Oddington House, Gloucestershire (built c. 1600, acq. 18th c., rebuilt c. 1810, passed by inher. to Talbot Rice family 1868, part demolished soon after, sold 1948)
Estates: Worth £3,000 pa c. 1700; cadet line in Wales Bateman 3764 (W) 3273.
Titles: Baronet 1642-1712; 1661-1982
Notes: The 7 Bt, who died in 1868, left part of his estate to his servant Joseph Wakefield, upheld in court. (Cockayne, *The Complete Baronetage*, III, 1741) A cadet line succeeded in 1650 to the estates of the Brockets of Brocket, Hertfordshire through an heiress of John Brocket 3 Bt, a Jacobite in 1715. **Three Brocket MPs 1542-72.**

READING *IRELAND*

Origins: The first MP was a lawyer.

1. Daniel Reading – {Newcastle 1692-93 1703-07}
2. John Reading – {Swords 1692-93 1695-99}
3. Daniel Reading – {Newcastle 1707-26}

Seat: Rathfarnham, Dublin
Notes: Extinct 1726?

REDMOND *IRELAND*

Origins: Old Catholic gentry dispossessed during the Civil War and after the Boyne. Merchants in Wexford in the 18th century. Founded a bank in 1780 and regained wealth. (Gwynn, *The Life of John Redmond*, 34-5.)

1. John Redmond – Wexford 1859-65
2. William Redmond – Wexford 1872-80
3. John Redmond – New Ross 1881-85 Wexford 1885-91 Waterford 1891-1918
4. William Redmond – Wexford 1883-85 N. Fermanagh 1885-92 E. Clare 1892-1917
5. William Redmond – E. Tyrone 1910-18 Waterford 1918-22 {TD Waterford 1923-33}
6. Bridget Redmond (wife) – {TD Waterford 1933-52}

Seats: Aughavanagh, Wicklow (purch. later 19th c.); Glenbrook House, Wicklow (built c. 1800, purch. later 19th c., sold 20th c.); Ballytrent House, Wexford (built 18th c., purch. 1799, passed out of family by mar. mid-19th c.)
Notes: Four in ODNB.

REYNELL [Taylor] *ENGLAND & IRELAND*

Reynell

Origins: In Devon since at least the later part of the 12th century. Increased gradually in landed wealth. Walter Reynell at Agincourt. (Adams, "Some Notes on the Churches at the Manors of East and West Ogwell", 229-48.) **First MP 1404 for Devon. Six additional MPs 1447-1628, three for Devon.** First Bt was Justice of the King's Bench in Ireland. Kt 1673.

1. Thomas Reynell – Devon 1654 1656 Ashburton 1659 1679-81 1689-90
2. Sir Richard Reynell 1 Bt – {Athboy 1661-66} Ashburton 1690-95
3. Sir Richard Reynell 2 Bt – {Wicklow 1692-93}
4. Richard Reynell – Ashburton 1702-08 1711-34

Seats: (East and West) Ogwell Houses, Devon (East acq. by mar. 14th c., became a ruin; West purch. 16th c., built c. 1588, passed by mar. to Taylors 1735); Denbury, Devon (acq. and built mid-16th c., passed to Taylors 1735, house sold but manor retained into 19th c.)
Title: Baronet 1678-1848
Notes: Reynell family has an entry and four others in the ODNB.

Taylor

Origins: The first MP was the son of a Captain in the Royal Navy under Queen Anne. Joseph Taylor MP succeeded to the estates of his uncle Richard Reynell MP in 1735.

1. Joseph Taylor – Ashburton 1739-41

Seat: (West) Ogwell House, Devon (acq. by mar. 1735, passed to Carews 1837, sold 1869, institutional use)
Notes: One in ODNB.

REYNOLDS (Reynell) *IRELAND*

Origins: Native Irish chiefs Mac Rannall or Mac Raghnaill, anglicized to Reynolds. Sheriff 1620. **First {MP County Leitrim 1613}. One additional {MP 1639 also for the county}.** Fought for James II.

1. John Reynolds – {County Leitrim 1692-93 1695-99}
2. Edmund Reynolds – {Jamestown 1695-98}

Seat: Loughscur Castle, Leitrim (acq. 1667, resident 18th c., ruin 19th c.)
Estate: 6,600 acres c. 1660. 2,500 acres in the 19th c. (Peyton).
Notes: Estates passed to Peyton family by mar. 18th c.

RICARDO

Origins: Sephardic Jews, founder a broker in Amsterdam naturalized in GB in 1771. The first MP was a broker on the stock exchange and contractor for government stock and economist. High Sheriff 1818.

1. David Ricardo – Portarlington 1819-23
2. David Ricardo – Stroud 1832-33
3. John Ricardo – Stoke-on-Trent 1841-62
4. Osman Ricardo – Worcester 1847-65
5. Samson Ricardo – Windsor 1855-57

Seats: Gatcombe Park, Gloucestershire (built 1771, purch. 1814, add. 1820, sold 1937); Brinsop Court, Herefordshire (built 14th c., add. 16th c., c. 1700, and 18th c., purch. 1820, sold 1909); Bromsberrow Place, Gloucestershire (built 1768-72, purch. 1818, remod. c. 1825, sold 1897); Bramley Park, Surrey (built 1837, demolished 1951); Kiddington Hall, Oxfordshire (built 1673, purch. 1840, rebuilt c. 1850, sold 1855)
Estates: Bateman 5107 (E) 7117. Rubinstein – David Ricardo left £500,000 in probate in 1823.
Notes: David Ricardo (first MP) divided his estates among three sons and a number of daughters, who received large settlements or dowries. The total value of his estate must have been between £625,000 and £775,000 (Fisher, *The House of Commons*, VI, 940). Four in ODNB.

RICH I

Origins: Merchants in Gloucester in the 16th century. The first MP was a Turkey merchant in London.

1. Sir Thomas Rich 1 Bt – Reading 1660
2. Sir William Rich 2 Bt – Reading 1689-98 Gloucester 1698-1700 Reading 1705-08
3. Sir Thomas Rich 5 Bt – Great Marlow 1784-90

Seat: Sonning, Berkshire (medieval, demolished c. 1574, new house late 17th c., demolished 1760)
Estates: Worth £2,000 pa in 1667.
Title: Baronet 1661-1803

RICH II [Edwardes] *ENGLAND & WALES*

<u>Earl of Warwick and Holland</u> (1618-1759 E and 1624-1759 E)

Origins: The Rich family probably descended from a leading London mercer who died in 1469. The founder of the family was a lawyer, Speaker of the House of Commons 1536, and Lord Chancellor 1548. **First MP 1529 (Essex 1536). Five additional MPs 1572-1641, four for Essex.** The 3rd Baron Rich was created Earl of Warwick. His younger son was created Earl of Holland, and the two titles later merged.

No post-1660 MPs

Seats: Leez Priory, Essex (acq. 1530s, rebuilt 1540s, demolished 1753, 1768 passed to Earls of Manchester, sold); Rochford Hall, Essex (built 1216, rebuilt c. 1545 and later in c., purch. c. 1552, sold 1712, golf club); Holland House, Middlesex (acq. and built

1605-06 by Cope family, passed by mar. to 1 Earl 1614, add. 1638-40, part demolished 1704, leased to Fox family 1746 who purch. 1768)
Estates: Worth £5,000 pa later 16th c. and £6,000 pa in c. 1635.
Titles: Baron Rich 1547-1759 E; Baron Kensington 1623-1759 E
Peers: 5 peers 1660-75 1660-73 1694-1701 1719-59
Notes: 1 Baron and 1 Earl of Holland and 1 and 2 Earls of Warwick and five others in ODNB.

Rich

Origins: Senior line of the family founded by the London mercer, Sheriff of London 1441. **First MP 1624**. Continued as merchants in the 17th century.

1. Sir Peter Rich – Southwark 1679-81 London 1685-87 Southwark 1689-90

Seat: Marblethorpe, Lincolnshire (purch. mid-17th c., sold c. 1692)
Notes: Male line of this branch of the family extinct 1692.

Rich

Origins: Descended from a younger son of the 2 Baron Rich. The daughter and heiress of the 1 Baronet married Sir Robert Rich of Roos Hall, a distant relation, who succeeded to the Baronetcy by special remainder. **First MP Nathaniel Rich mid-17th century**.

1. Sir Robert Rich 2 Bt – Dunwich 1689-99
2. Sir Robert Rich 4 Bt – Dunwich 1715-20 Bere Alston 1724-27 St. Ives 1727-41

Seat: Roos Hall, Suffolk (built 1583, sold 1613)
Title: Baronet 1675-1799
Notes: 4 and 5 Bts in ODNB.

Baron Kensington (1776- I; 1886- UK)

Origins: Claimed descent from medieval Welsh lords. Emerged in the early 17th century in the modern line. Francis Edwardes MP inherited from his wife, a Rich heiress of the 7 Earl of Warwick, considerable estates including London property that became valuable.

1. Francis Edwardes – Haverfordwest 1722-25
2. William Edwardes 1 Baron Kensington – Haverfordwest 1747-84 1786-1801
3. William Edwardes 2 Baron Kensington – Haverfordwest 1802-18
4. Edward Edwardes – Bletchingley 1820-26
5. William Edwardes 4 Baron Kensington – Haverfordwest 1868-85

Seats: Johnston Hall, Pembrokeshire (occupied since the 15th c., purch. 1703, sold 1835); St. Brides, Pembrokeshire (built 18th c., purch. 1880, sold 1920)
Estates: 7471 (W) 5379. Their London estate was sold in 1902 for £565,000.
Peers: {1 peer 1776-1800} 5 peers 1886-1945
2 Lds Lt 19th

RICHARDSON *IRELAND*

Origins: Major Edward Richardson MP married the Sacheverell heiress to Rich Hill (acq. 1611). Sheriff 1665.

1. Edward Richardson – {County Armagh 1661-66}
2. William Richardson – {County Armagh 1692-93 Hillsborough 1703-13 County Armagh 1715-27}
3. William Richardson – {County Armagh 1739-58}
4. John Richardson – {Newton Limavady 1780-97}
5. William Richardson – {County Armagh 1783-97} 1807-20

Seat: Rich Hill (Richill and aka Legacorry), Armagh (old house, acq. 1611, rebuilt 1664-90, remod. 18th c., sold 1881)
Estates: Bateman 6878 (I) 7600. Worth £2,000 pa in 1759 and £5,990 pa in 1823.
Notes: The Richardson heiress mar. 1832 the eldest son of the 10th Bacon Bt of Reveningham Hall, Norfolk. He died without a son in 1852 and his widow died in 1881.

RIDDELL *SCOTLAND*

Origins: Lairds from the 14th century. **First [MP 1617 for Roxburghshire]. Two further [MPs 1639-50, both for county seats]**. Bt 1628.

1. John Riddell – [Selkirkshire 1665 1678]
2. Sir John Riddell 3 Bt – [Roxburghshire 1690-98]
3. Sir John Buchanan Riddell 9 Bt – Linlithgow Burghs 1812-19

Seats: Riddell, Roxburghshire (acq. 14th c., medieval, 17th c., burned 1943); The Haining, Selkirkshire (medieval, acq. 1625, sold 1701)
Estates: Bateman under 2000
Title: Baronet 1628-
Notes: One in ODNB.

RIDER [Barnham]

Origins: The Riders were merchants in Tudor London. Thomas Rider married the heiress of the first Barnham Bt and succeeded to the Barnham estates in 1685. The Barnhams were drapers in London in the mid-16th century. **First MP 1589. Two further MPs 1601-46.**

1. Sir Robert Barnham 1 Bt – Maidstone 1660-79
2. Thomas Rider – Maidstone 1690-98
3. Sir Barnham Rider – Maidstone 1716-22 1723-27
4. Thomas Rider – Kent 1831-32 W. Kent 1832-34

Seat: Boughton Monchelsea Place, Kent (medieval, built 1567-75, acq. by Barnhams by inher. 1613, passed to Riders 1685, part demolished c. 1740, remod. c. 1790, remod. 1818-19, sold 1888)
Title: Baronet 1663-85
Notes: Robert Rudston, a draper, Lord Mayor of London 1528, purchased Boughton Monchelsea in 1551. **One MP 1547**. Sir Martin Barnham married the Rudston heiress in 1572. The house then passed to the Riders by inheritance 1685. One Barnham and one Rider in ODNB.

RIDLEY [Colborne]

<u>Viscount Ridley</u> (1900- UK)

Origins: The Ridleys began as merchants in Newcastle-upon-Tyne in the 17th c., Mayor 1713, 1733. They assembled landed estates, purchasing property confiscated from Jacobite rebels after 1715. Remained engaged in banking in the 19th century and also owned ships and coal mines (McCord, *British History 1815-1906*, 98)

1. Matthew Ridley – Newcastle-upon-Tyne 1747-74
2. Sir Matthew Ridley 2 Bt – Morpeth 1768-74 Newcastle-upon-Tyne 1774-1812
3. Sir Matthew Ridley 3 Bt – Newcastle-upon-Tyne 1812-36
4. George Ridley – Newcastle-upon-Tyne 1856-60
5. Sir Matthew Ridley 4 Bt – N. Northumberland 1868-85 Blackpool Div. Lancashire 1886-1900
6. Sir Edward Ridley – S. Northumberland 1878-80
7. Matthew Ridley 2 Viscount Ridley – Stalybridge 1900-04
8. Nicholas Ridley Baron Ridley – Cirencester and Tewkesbury 1959-92

Seats: Blagdon Hall, Northumberland (White seat: acq. 1700, rebuilt 1st half 18th c., inher. by Ridleys 1763, still own); Heaton Hall, Northumberland (Ridley seat: medieval castle, demolished, rebuilt by Ridleys 1713-15, sold 19th c., demolished 1933)
Estates: Bateman 10152 (E) 12189 exclusive of mines
Title: Baron Ridley 1992-93 UKLife; Baronet 1756-
Peers: 3 peers 1900-16 1923-45
2 in Cabinet 1895-1900 1983-90
1 KG 20th
Notes: The Ridleys and Whites were both early industrial entrepreneurs in Newcastle. Matthew Ridley married the White heiress. Baron Ridley and 1 Viscount and three others in ODNB.

Baron Colborne (1839-54 UK)

Origins: Nicholas Ridley, brother of the 2 Bt succeeded to the estates of his uncle, William Colborne, and was created Baron Colborne. His heiress married Sir George Nugent 2 Bt to whom West Harling passed in 1854.

1. Nicholas Ridley Colborne 1 Baron Colborne – Bletchingley 1805-06 Malmesbury 1806-07 Appleby 1807-12 Thetford 1818-26 Horsham 1827-32 Wells 1834-37
2. William Ridley Colborne – Richmond 1841-46

Seat: West Harling Hall, Norfolk (built 1725, acq. by Colbornes by 1820 and passed to Nugents, sold 1929, demolished 1931)
Estates: Bateman 4350 (E) 2342
Peers: 1 peer 1839-54

RIGBY

Origins: The family rose through the law in the late 16th and early 17th centuries. The first MP was Baron of the Exchequer and was active politically in the Civil War. **First MP 1640.**

1. Alexander Rigby – Lancashire 1659 Preston 1660
2. Edward Rigby – Preston 1660-81
3. Edward Rigby – Preston 1701-02 1705-06
4. Sir Alexander Rigby – Wigan 1701-02

Seats: Middleton Hall (in Goosnargh), Lancashire (purch. c. 1600, sold 1720); Layton Hall, Lancashire (acq. 1592, sold 1720)
Notes: Sir Alexander Rigby MP was imprisoned for debt in 1714 and died there. The estates were sold 1720. Three in ODNB.

RIGGS [Miller] *IRELAND*

Riggs

Origins: To Ireland in the mid-17th c. Merchants in Cork.

1. Edward Riggs – {Bandon 1692-93 1695-99}
2. Edward Riggs – {Baltimore 1707-13 Bangor 1716-27 Newtown Limavady 1739-41}

Seat: Riggsdale (Rigsdale) House, Cork (acq. c. 1651, passed by mar. 1765 to Millers)
Estates: Worth £800 pa in 1689. Purchased 2,859 additional acres in 1702. Worth £1,200 pa in 1706. One in ODNB.

Miller

Origins: To Ireland from Scotland later 17th century. Sir John Miller 1 Bt of Ballycaseymore House married 1762 the Riggs heiress and succeeded to the family fortune and property.

1. Sir John Riggs-Miller 1 Bt – Newport 1784-90

Seats: Ballycaseymore (Ballicasey) House, Clare (built 18th c., passed by mar. to Ryans 1889, sold 1913); Drumlin, Clare (acq. late 17th c.); Bath Easton, Somerset (purch. and built 1760s, sold 1801)
Estates: small estate by 1880s.
Title: Baronet 1778-1825
Notes: A Ryan of Tyrone House, Tipperary mar. 1889 the Riggs-Miller heiress and succeeded to the estates taking the name Riggs-Miller. One in ODNB.

RIVERS

Origins: The family is recorded in the 15th century, but their fortunes were made by a businessman, Lord Mayor of London 1572. **First MP 1597. One further MP 1640-41.**

1. Nizel Rivers – Lewes 1660

Seat: Chafford Park (Place), Kent (acq. r. Henry VIII, demolished 1743)
Estates: 155 (I) 107 in 1878
Title: Baronet 1621-1870

RIVETT (Revett, Ryvett) [Carnac]

Rivett

Origins: A medieval family. Kt 16th century. **First MP 1597. Two further MPs 1624-59**. Mayor of Derby 18th century. The 1 Bt was the son of a younger son who went to India in the early 19th century. Director of the East India Company 1827, Chairman 1836. A number of Rivetts joined the Indian Civil Service.

1. Thomas Rivett – Derby 1748-54
2. Sir James Rivett-Carnac – Sandwich 1837-38
3. Sir John Rivett-Carnac – Lymington 1852-60

Seat: Mapleton Hall, Derbyshire (purch. 1757, sold c. 1763)
Title: Baronet 1836-
Notes: A peripatetic family. 1 Bt in ODNB.

Carnac

Origins: The Carnacs were of Huguenot extraction and settled in Dublin. One served with Clive in India in the 18th century and returned a nabob. James Rivett, father of the 1 Bt, married the sister and heiress of John Carnac and took the additional name Carnac in 1801.

1. John Carnac – Leominster 1768-74

Seat: Cams Hall, Hampshire (medieval, purch. and rebuilt c. 1770, sold 1776, offices and golf club)
Notes: Worth £80,000 in 1765. One in ODNB.

ROBARTS

Origins: Began as a West Indian factor and then Director of the East India Company. Bankers in the 19th century.

1. Abraham Robarts – Worcester 1796-1816
2. Abraham Robarts – Maidstone 1818-37
3. William Robarts – St. Albans 1818-20
4. George James Robarts – Wallingford 1820-26

Estates: An extremely rare example of a parliamentary family that never put down landed roots. Abraham Robarts MP 1818-37 (a Writer for the East India Company in

Canton and then a banker) inherited a fortune of hundreds of thousands of pounds. He divided this wealth between his two sons, who were also bankers in the later 19th century. Although the family did not aspire to landed status, they were accepted as members of Brooks's and friends of the Whig aristocracy. Rubinstein – Abraham Robarts left £350,000 in probate in 1815 and William Robarts left £120,000 in 1820 and James Robarts left £120,000 in 1830. Abraham Robarts left an estate of £300,000 in 1858.
Notes: Robarts family has an entry in ODNB.

ROBERTS

Origins: Lived in Sheffield from the 17th century. Manufacturers and businessmen. Lord Mayor of Sheffield 1900. Master Cutler 1935.

1. Sir Samuel Roberts 1 Bt – Eccleshall Div. Sheffield 1902-23
2. Sir Samuel Roberts 2 Bt – Herefordshire 1921-29 Eccleshall Div. Sheffield 1929-35
3. Sir Peter Roberts 3 Bt – Eccleshall Div. Sheffield 1945-50 Heeley Div. Sheffield 1950-66

Seats: Queen's Tower, Yorkshire (purch. and built c. 1839, add. 1860s, resident until recently, flats 2004); Cockley Cley Hall, Norfolk (built c. 1698, rebuilt 1870-71, purch. 1926, still own)
Title: Baronet 1919-
Notes: One in ODNB.

ROBINSON I

Origins: Local merchants. Alderman of Helston 1620.

1. John Robinson – Liskeard 1660
2. Thomas Robinson – Helston 1660-65
3. George Robinson – Tregony 1710-13

Seats: Treveneage, Cornwall (leased?); Cadgwith, Cornwall (resident late 17th and early 18th c.)
Notes: George Robinson MP, last of the line, left his estate to a non-family member 1728.

ROBINSON II

Origins: Began with a wealthy Reading clothier. His son was a half brother of Archbishop Laud. His son was a merchant. Lord Mayor of London 1662. High Sheriff 1737.

1. Sir John Robinson 1 Bt – London 1660 Rye 1661-79
2. Sir George Robinson 5 Bt – Northampton 1774-80
3. Sir George Robinson 6 Bt – Northampton 1820-32

Seats: Cranford Hall, Northamptonshire (old house, acq. and rebuilt c. 1699, house became flats 1950, still own estate); Stretton Hall, Leicestershire
Estates: Bateman 2087 (E) 4737
Title: Baronet 1660-
Notes: 1 Bt in ODNB.

ROCHE I *IRELAND*

Origins: The Roches arrived in Ireland with the Norman invasion c. 1167. By the end of the 14th century numerous lines had been established. (Donnelly, "The Roches, Lords of Fermoy", 86-91 and ff.) Viscount Roche (1448 I). Estates confiscated 1652. The 9 Viscount was killed at Aughrim fighting for James II in 1691. The Roche Baronets 1782-1801 descended from Jordan Roche, Mayor of Limerick 1639 (created Viscount Cahervahalla in the Jacobite peerage 1694). Owned flour mills.

1. George Roche – {Limerick 1713-27}
2. Sir Boyle Roche 1 Bt – {Tralee 1775-76 Gowran 1777-83 Portarlington 1784-90 Tralee 1790-97 Old Leighlin 1797-1800}

Seat: Carrass (Carrgh, Carass, Caherass) House, Limerick (acq. early 19th c., fire before 1940)
Estates: 3951 (I) 3457 and 1497 (I) 1602
Title: Baronet 1782-1801; 1838-
Notes: Several 19th-century Roche MPs may also have descended from the medieval Viscounts Fermoy. 1 Bt in ODNB.

ROCHE II *IRELAND*

Baron Fermoy (1856- I)

Origins: No proven connection to the medieval Viscounts Fermoy. Began with Philip Roche, a merchant in Cork who purchased estates in 1554. High Sheriff 1641.

1. Edmund Roche 1 Baron Fermoy – County Cork 1837-55 Marylebone 1855-69
2. James Roche 3 Baron Fermoy – E. Kerry 1896-1900
3. Edmund Roche 4 Baron Fermoy – King's Lynn Div. Norfolk 1924-35 1943-45

Seats: Trabolgan, Cork (acq. first half 17th c., built early 19th c., add. 19th c., sold 1880, demolished c. 1980); Kilshannig, Cork (built 1765, purch. mid-19th c., sold early 20th c.)
Estates: Bateman 21314 (I) 11071
1 Ld Lt 19th
Notes: The Roches were living in Norfolk by the 1930s.

ROCHFORT [Marlay] *IRELAND*

<u>Earl of Belvedere</u> (Belvidere) (1756-1814 I)

Origins: The Rochforts were an "Old English" family settled in County Kildare as early as 1243. Lord Deputy 1302. However, the modern rise of the family was thanks to a lt. colonel under Cromwell whose son was Speaker of the House of Commons 1695 and Chief Baron of the Exchequer in 1707. He made a fortune as a lawyer and land speculator. **First {MP 1639}**.

1. Robert Rochfort – {County Westmeath 1692-93 1695-99 1703-07}
2. George Rochfort – {County Westmeath 1707-13 1713-14 1727-30}
3. John Rochfort – {Ballyshannon 1713-27 Mullingar 1727-60}
4. Arthur Rochfort – {County Westmeath 1738-60}
5. Robert Rochfort 1 Earl of Belvedere – {County Westmeath 1731-38}
6. George Rochfort 2 Earl of Belvedere – {Philipstown 1759-60 County Westmeath 1761-74}
7. Richard Rochfort – {County Westmeath 1761-68 Philipstown 1768-76}
8. Robert Rochfort – {Philipstown 1761-68 Augher 1768-76 County Westmeath 1776-97}
9. George Rochfort – {County Westmeath 1775-76}
10. John Rochfort – {Coleraine 1796-97 Fore 1798-1800}
11. Gustavus Rochfort-Hume – {County Westmeath 1798-1800} 1801-24
12. Gustavus Rochfort – County Westmeath 1826-32

Seats: Belvedere (Belvidere), Westmeath (built 1740, passed to Marlays 1867); Gaulston Park, Westmeath (original seat built late 17th c., resident 17th-18th c., rebuilt 1770s, sold 1784, burned 1920); Rochfort House (Bridge) (Tudenham), Westmeath (built 1742, sold 1836); Clogrenane Castle (House), Carlow, (castle, became ruinous, acq. early 18th c., rebuilt early 19th c., ruin 20th c.)
Estates: Bateman 14285 (I) 10282 (under Marlay) 16397 (I) 9730 under Rochfort-Boyd. Worth £443 pa in 1689 and £3,500 pa in 1713.
Titles: Baron Belfield (Bellfield) 1737-1814 I; Viscount Belfield 1751-1814 I

Peers: {2 peers 1738-74 1776-1800}
Notes: The Rochfort property was split in 1814. The unsettled estates of the last Earl went to his wife, who married Abraham Boyd 1815, whose descendents took the name Rochfort (seated at Middleton Park, Westmeath). The settled estates and Belvedere went to the sister of the last Earl, the Countess of Lanesborough. In 1828 and 1867 her great-grandson Charles Marlay inherited. One in ODNB.

Marlay

Origins: Tradesmen in Newcastle-upon-Tyne in the 16th century. Sir John Marlay MP, started as a coal-fitter and alehouse keeper and became rich. Kt 1639. His grandson emigrated to Ireland in the late 17th century. Lord Chief Justice of Ireland 1753 and Bishop 1745. The Marlays inherited part of the Rochfort estates in 1867 (see above).

1. Sir John Marlay – Newcastle-upon-Tyne 1661-73
2. Thomas Marlay – {Newtown Limavady 1717-27 Lanesborough 1727-30}
3. Anthony Marlay – {Lanesborough 1731-60}

Seat: Belvedere (Belvidere), Westmeath (built 1740, acquired by Marlays 1867, remod. 19th c., passed to Howard-Burys and then Beaumonts, sold 1982)
Estates: See above.
Notes: On the extinction of the Marlays, the Rochfort estates passed to cousins, the Howard-Bury family.

RODNEY

Baron Rodney (1782- GB)

Origins: An old gentry family from Somerset established by the end of the 11th century. **First MP 1351 for Somerset. Six further MPs 1352-1644, five of them for the county.** The modern family descended from a younger son and rose thanks to the career of a celebrated admiral, the 1 Baron.

1. George Brydges Rodney 1 Baron Rodney – Saltash 1751-54 Okehampton 1759-61 Penryn 1761-68 Northampton 1768-74 Westminster 1780-82
2. George Rodney 2 Baron Rodney – Northampton 1780-84
3. John Rodney – Launceston 1790-96

Seats: Alresford House, Hampshire (purch. 1740s, built c. 1752, sold 1870); Berrington Hall, Herefordshire (built 1778, acq. 1804 by mar. from a younger son of the 3 Earl of Oxford (Harley), sold 1900)
Estates: Bateman 6269 (E) 7540

Title: Baronet 1764-
Peers: 8 peers 1782-1864 1878-1909 1912-45
1 Ld Lt 19th
Notes: Berrington (purch. c. 1775) was built by a younger son of the 3 Earl of Oxford (see Harley) who made a fortune in the City as a government contractor, Lord Mayor of London 1767. His only daughter married 1 Baron Rodney, and the estate passed to that family. 1 Baron and one other in ODNB.

ROGERS

Baron Blachford (1871-89 UK)

Origins: Descended from the Reverend John Rogers, a martyr under Mary I. A merchant in Plymouth purchased estates in the 1690s. High Sheriff 1701.

1. Sir John Rogers 1 Bt – Plymouth 1698-1700
2. Sir John Rogers 2 Bt – Plymouth 1713-22
3. Sir John Rogers 3 Bt – Plymouth 1739-40
4. Sir Frederick Rogers 5 Bt – Plymouth 1780-84 1790-97
5. Sir John Rogers 6 Bt – Callington 1812-13

Seats: Blachford (Blackford) Park (House), Devon (purch. 1694, sold c. 1895, hotel); Wisdome (Wiscombe), Devon (purch. 1690s, sold c. 1895)
Estates: Bateman 2919 (E) 2575
Title: Baronet 1699-1895
Peer: 1 peer 1871-89
Notes: 1 Baron and one other in ODNB.

ROGERSON [Matthews] *IRELAND*

Rogerson

Origins: **The first MP 1604** was a draper in Coventry. Moved to Ireland 1674 where Sir John Rogerson was a businessman and Lord Mayor of Dublin 1693. He purchased substantial landed property in and around Dublin. His eldest son became Chief Justice of the King's Bench 1727.

1. Sir John Rogerson – {Clogher 1692-93 Dublin 1695-99}
2. John Rogerson – {Granard 1713-14 Dublin 1715-27}

Seat: Glasnevin (The Glen) House, Dublin (acq. and built c. 1703, poss. rebuilt later 1720s, estates dispersed among heiresses 1741, institutional use)

Matthews

Origins: Joseph Matthews MP was the son of a Mayor of Kilkenny by a daughter and heiress of William Rogerson, son of Sir John Rogerson MP.

1. Joseph Matthews – {Innistoige 1768-76}

Seat: Bonnettstown Hall, Kilkenny (built 1737, passed to Blundens 19th c.)

ROLLE [Trefusis, Walter]

Baron Rolle (1748-50 GB; 1796-1842 GB)

Origins: Began as London merchants. A successful lawyer purchased Stephenstone in 1524. Lord Chief Justice 1649-55. In the 18th century one of the wealthiest gentry families in England. **First MP 1542. Five further MPs 1601-56.**

1. Robert Rolle – Devon 1654 1659 Callington 1660
2. Sir Francis Rolle – Somerset 1656 Bridgwater 1660 1669 Hampshire 1675-81
3. Sir John Rolle – Barnstaple 1660 Devon 1661-79
4. Samuel Rolle – Callington 1665-79 Devon 1680-81 1689-1701 Callington 1701-19
5. Samuel Rolle – Devon 1679-81
6. Samuel Rolle – Barnstaple 1705-08
7. Robert Rolle – Callington 1701-02 Devon 1702-10
8. John Rolle – Saltash 1703-05 Devon 1710-13 Exeter 1713-15 Barnstaple 1715-22 Exeter 1722-27 Devon 1727-30
9. John Rolle – Bridgwater 1713-15
10. Henry Rolle 1 Baron Rolle – Devon 1730-41 Barnstaple 1741-48
11. Henry Rolle Walter – Exeter 1754-76 Devon 1776-79
12. Denys Rolle – Barnstaple 1761-74
13. John Rolle 1 Baron Rolle – Devon 1780-96

Seats: Stephenstone (Stevenstone) House, Devon (purch. 1524, built mid-16th c., remod. 18th c., passed to Trefusis family by mar. 1842, remod. 1869-73, house sold and reduced in size 1912, from 1932 derelict and mostly demolished, ruin); Heanton Satchville, Devon (acq. by mar. c. 1600, passed by heiress 1717 to 15 Baroness Clinton - born Rolle, mar. a Walpole - and then passed by inher. to a Trefusis 17 Baron Clinton 1791, see below); Bicton House, Devon (acq. by mar. 1552, Tudor house, remod. 1730, rebuilt c. 1800, passed to Trefusis family by mar. 1842); Marrais (Marhayes, Marrays), Cornwall (acq. by mar. later 16th c., sold 1770s); Shapwick, Somerset (purch. and rebuilt 1630, sold 1786); East Tytherley, Hampshire (built 16th c., purch. 1654, remod. c. 1660s, sold 1801)

Estates: Bateman 55592 (E) 47170. Worth £10,000 pa c. 1710. Still owned 25,000 acres 1968.
Peers: 2 peers 1748-50 1796-1842
Notes: Estates passed to Trefusis family by mar., who took the name Rolle, 1842. Land sales after WWI. Lord Rolle literally "rolled" down the steps of the throne at Queen Victoria's coronation. 1 Baron sec. cr. and two others in ODNB.

Walter

Origins: The Walters' rise was due to a Welsh judge under Elizabteh I. Another was Lord Chief Baron of the Exchequer under James I. **First MP 1589. Three additional MPs 1614-28.** Bt 1641. John Rolle, brother of the 1 Baron Rolle, succeeded to the estates of the Walter Baronets in 1731 and took the additional name Walter.

1. Sir John Walter 3 Bt – Appleby 1694-95 1697-1700 Oxford 1706-22

Seat: Sarsden House, Oxfordshire (purch. c. 1613, rebuilt 1689, sold by heirs 1791)
Title: Baronet 1641-1731
Notes: Family died out in 1731. One in ODNB.

Baron Clinton (1298- E)

Origins: The 4 Earl of Lincoln was also 12 Baron Clinton. His daughter Margaret had a daughter who married Hugh Fortescue, from whom descended the Earls Fortescue. Their eldest son succeeded as 14 Baron Clinton and was created Earl of Clinton. He died without heirs in 1751 (see Fortescue). The Clinton Barony then passed to the descendents of the eldest son of the Earl of Lincoln's other daughter. This line became extinct in 1791, when the Barony passed to the Trefusis family. They had inherited Heanton Satchville and other estates from the Rolles, after Lord Lincoln's daughter Arabella married Robert Rolle. His daughter and heiress married Francis Trefusis, who represented an ancient Cornish line. It is possible that the Trefusis family were of pre-Conquest origins (Hasler, *The House of Commons*, III, 524). Seated at Trefusis by the reign of Edward I. **First MP 1584. Two further MPs 1621-46.**

1. Francis Trefusis – Penryn 1679
2. Samuel Trefusis – Penryn 1698-1713 1714-22
3. Robert Trefusis – Truro 1734-41
4. Thomas Trefusis – Grampound 1739-41
5. Charles Trefusis 19 Baron Clinton – Callington 1813-18
6. Charles Rolle Hepburn-Stuart-Forbes-Trefusis 20 Baron Clinton – N. Devon 1857-66

Seats: Heanton Satchville, Devon (inher. 1791, see above, fire 1795, purch. nearby estate 1812 and name transferred to it, fire 1935, rebuilt 1938, still own); Bicton House, Devon (acq. by mar. 1842, add. 1898, sold 1957, institutional use); Trefusis, Cornwall (acq. by 13th c., medieval, became a manorial farm house, still own)
Estates: Bateman 18121 (E) 18385. Worth £52,000,000 in 1990 with 26,000 acres.
Peers: 5 peers 1794-97 1808-1945
1 Ld Lt 19th-20th

ROLLESTON (Rolston)

Origins: Old gentry at Rolleston "time out of mind." (Bindoff, *The House of Commons*, III, 211) **First MP 1547**.

1. Lancelot Rolleston – Nottinghamshire 1837-49
2. Sir John Rolleston – Leicester 1900-06 E. Hertfordshire 1910-16

Seats: Watnall Hall, Nottinghamshire (acq. by mar. early 17th c., built c. 1690, school from 1945, demolished 1954); Rolleston, Staffordshire (acq. by 13th c., sold 1617)

ROLLO *SCOTLAND*

Baron Rollo (1651- S)

Origins: Duncrub was acquired in 1380 by a secretary of Robert III. Burgess in Edinburgh 1410. At Flodden 1513. Kt reign of James I. **First [MP 1466]. Two further [MPs 1481-1651, with possible other ones]**.

No post-1660 MPs.

Seat: Duncrub Castle (House), Perthshire (acq. 1380, add. 1799, add. 1836-37, rebuilt 1861-63, demolished 1950)
Estates: Bateman 17368 (S) 11462
Title: Baron Dunning 1869- UK
Peers: [3 peers 1661-1701 1703-07] 3 Scottish Rep peers 1841-46 1847-52 1860-68 3 peers 1869-1945
Notes: 5 Baron and one other in ODNB.

ROMILLY *ENGLAND & WALES*

Baron Romilly (1866- UK)

Origins: Huguenot refugee came to England c. 1701. One became a jeweler in London. His son was a lawyer, Solicitor General 1806, and MP. His son was Attorney General and Master of the Rolls 1851.

1. Sir Samuel Romilly – Queenborough 1806-07 Horsham 1807-08 Wareham 1808-12 Arundel 1812-18 Westminster 1818
2. Edward Romilly – Ludlow 1832-35
3. John Romilly 1 Baron Romilly – Bridport 1832-35 1846-47 Devonport 1847-52
4. Frederick Romilly – Canterbury 1850-52

Seat: Porthkerry Park (Porth Kerry), Glamorganshire (acq. and built 1812, sold 1929, public park)
Estates: Bateman 2771 (W) 3535
Peers: 4 peers 1866-1905 1920-45
Notes: 1 Baron and four others in ODNB.

ROSCARROCK

Origins: Landowners in the 12th century. **First MP 1347 for Cornwall. Five additional MPs 1545-54, one for Cornwall.**

1. Charles Roscarrock – Camelford 1661-65

Seats: Trevenna (Trevena), Cornwall (acq. by mar. mid-17th c., became a farm house); Roscarrock, Cornwall (built 16th c., sold 1673, became a farm house)
Notes: The family remained Roman Catholic and became impoverished. One in ODNB.

ROSE I *SCOTLAND*

Origins: Ancient Scottish family. Settled in Nairnshire by 1230. No other family in Scotland can show a longer or more direct descent. (Rampini, *A History of Moray and Nairn*, 256) Cadet lines descended from the 11th laird of Kilravock at Clavag and Broadley are combined here. **First [MP 1646].**

1. John Rose – [Nairn 1648 1661]
2. Hugh Rose – [Nairn 1649 1665]
3. William Rose – [Nairn 1665]
4. William Rose – [Nairn 1667]

5. Harry Rose – [Forres 1667]
6. Alexander Rose – [Nairn 1669-72]
7. David Rose – [Nairn 1678]
8. Hugh Rose – [Nairn 1681]
9. Hugh Rose – [Nairnshire 1685-86]
10. John Rose – [Nairn 1689-1707]
11. Hugh Rose – [Nairnshire 1700-01 1703-07] Scotland 1707-08
12. Hugh Rose – Nairnshire and Ross-shire 1708-10 Nairnshire 1710 1734-41
13. Hugh Rose – Nairnshire 1812-13

Seats: Kilravock Castle, Nairnshire (acq. 1293, built 15th c., add. 1553, add. 17th c., still own); Clavalg (Clava) House, Nairnshire (acq. c. 1610, sold 1758); Broadley (Braidley), Nairnshire (acq. 15th c., became a farm house 19th c., still own)
Estates: Bateman 4395 (S) 2345
2 Lds Lt 18th, 19th, 20th
Notes: One in ODNB.

ROSE II

Baron Strathnairn (1866-88 UK)

Origins: The first MP was the son of a clergyman. He made his way as a placeman and aide to William Pitt. He became rich through holding places and sinecures. Claimed descent from the Roses of Kilravock.

1. George Rose – Launceston 1784-88 Lymington 1788-90 Christchurch 1790-1818
2. Sir George Rose – Southampton 1794-1818 Christchurch 1818-32 1837-44
3. William Rose – Chirstchurch 1796-1800
4. George Pitt Rose – Christchurch 1826-32

Seat: Cuffnells, Hampshire (purch. later 18th c., built 1794-95, demolished c. WWII)
Peer: 1 peer 1866-88
Notes: The 1 Baron was a field marshal. 1 Baron and three others in ODNB.

ROSS I *IRELAND*

Origins: Sir David Ross was a Commissioner in Ulster under James I. His sons and grandsons had military careers. High Sheriff 1709.

1. Robert Ross – {Killyleagh 1715-27 Newry 1727-50}
2. Robert Ross – {Carlingford 1723-68}
3. Robert Ross – {Carlingford 1768-76 Newry 1776-99}

4. David Ross – Belfast 1842-47

Seat: Rostrevor House (formerly Topsy-Turvey, formerly Carrickbawn, Rosetrevor, Rosstrevor), Down (purch. by the 1st MP's father-in-law, Robert King, as a present c. 1700, add. 1836, resident into 20th c.)
Estates: Held 3,746 acres in 1770. Worth £947 pa in 1790s.
Title: Granted the hereditary right to bear the honorific "of Bladensburg" by the Crown in 1815 in reference to a battle.
Notes: Much of the estate around the house sold under Encumbered Estates Act 1850. One in ODNB.

ROSS II [Boyle, Farquharson, Lockhart] *SCOTLAND*

Baron Ross (1499-1754 S)

Origins: Claimed Norman descent. Medieval Earls, a title that passed to another family through marriage. Lord of Parliament 1489. The 2 Baron fell at Flodden 1513.

1. Sir David Ross – [Ross-shire 1669-74]
2. Charles Ross – Ross-shire 1710-22 1727-32
3. Charles Ross – Ross-shire 1741-45

Seats: Halkhead (Hawkhead) House (Castle), Renfrewshire (acq. 1367, medieval, rebuilt 1634, remod. 1750-80, passed by mar. to Boyles 1791, see below); Balnagown Castle, Ross-shire (built 1375, passed to Lockharts 1760)
Peers: [2 peers 1661-1707] 1 Scottish Rep peer 1715-22
Notes: Ross family and 12 Baron in ODNB.

Lockhart-Ross

Origins: The Lockharts were of medieval descent. Sir James Lockhart of Lee was knighted by James VI (see Lockhart). The 2 Bt married the daughter and heiress of the 12 Baron Ross, taking the additional name Ross and succeeding to some of the Ross estates in 1760.

1. Sir John Lockhart-Ross 6 Bt – Linlithgow Burghs 1761-68 Lanarkshire 1768-74
2. Sir Charles Lockhart-Ross 7 Bt – Tain Burghs 1786-96 Ross-shire 1796-1806 Linlithgow Burghs 1806-07

Seats: Blanagown Castle, Ross-shire (acq. by mar. 1760, add. c. 1820, sold 1978); Carstairs House, Lanarkshire (Lockharts early 17th c., sold 1783? or late 18th or early 19th c.)

Estates: Bateman 356500 (S) 17264
Title: Baronet 1672-
Notes: 6 Bt and one other in ODNB.

Earl of Glasgow (1703- S)

Origins: Lairds holding Kelburn from 1140. The sister of the last Baron Ross married the 3 Earl of Glasgow, who succeeded to Ross estates.

1. John Boyle – [Bute 1678 1681 1685]
2. James Boyle – [Irvine 1681 1685-86]
3. David Boyle 1 Earl of Glasgow – [Buteshire 1689-98]
4. David Boyle – Ayrshire 1807-11
5. James Carr-Boyle 5 Earl of Glasgow – Ayrshire 1839-43
6. George Boyle 6 Earl of Glasgow – Buteshire 1865-69

Seats: Kelburn(e) House (Castle), Ayrshire (acq. 1140, rebuilt 1581 and 1692-1722, add. 1879-80, still own); The Garrison (Garrison House), (Arran) Buteshire (built c. 1745, add. 1819, sold c. 1900); Crawfurd (Crawford) Priory, Fife (built c. 1758, add. 1809-13, sold later 19th c., derelict from 1968); Halkhead House, Renfrewshire (acq. by mar. from Ross family 1791, sold 1886, demolished 1953); The Craig (Fairlie Castle), Ayrshire (medieval, purch. c. 1650s, ruin in 19th c., sold 20th c.)
Estates: Bateman 37825 (S) 41088. Owned 3,200 acres in 1996.
Titles: Baron Boyle 1699- S; Baron Ross 1815-90 UK; Baron Fairlie 1897- UK
Peers: 2 Scottish Rep peers 1707-10 1790-1815 5 peers 1815-90 1897-1945
3 Lds Lt 18th, 19th
Notes: The 1 Earl of Glasgow married the daughter of the Hon. P. Lindsay Crawford of Kilbirney Castle, Ayrshire, sister of Viscount Garnock and granddaughter of the 17 Earl of Crawford. In right of his ancestress, the first Countess of Glasgow, the 4 Earl succeeded in 1833 to the great estates of the house of Lindsay and Crawford in Fife and Ayr on the death of Lady Mary Lindsay Crawford (see Crawford), sister of the Earl of Crawford and Lindsay (d. 1808). The 4 Earl also acquired Etal Castle (sold 1886) in Northumberland by marriage to the daughter of the Earl of Erroll and heiress of the Carr family (see Carr). 6 Earl went bankrupt and most of the family estates were sold. 6 Earl and two others in ODNB.

Farquharson

Origins: At Invercauld in the 16th century. The daughter and heiress of James Farquharson of Invercauld married James Lockhart-Ross, a younger son of the 6 Bt in 1799, and he changed his name to Farquharson.

1. Archibald Farquharson – Elgin Burghs 1820-26
2. Robert Farquharson – W. Aberdeenshire 1880-1906

Seats: Finzean House, Aberdeenshire (purch. and built c. 1683, remod. late 19th c., fire 1950s, rebuilt, still own); Invercauld Castle (House), Aberdeenshire (built 16th c., add. 1750, add. 1820, remod. 1847 and 1870-75, still own)
Estates: Bateman 16809 (S) 6166.
Notes: The Invercauld, Aberdeenshire line held 109562 (S) 12974 in Bateman – worth £87,000,000 in 1990 with over 100,000 acres. Two in ODNB.

ROTHSCHILD

Baron Rothschild (1885- UK)

Origins: A German banking family that established a branch in London in 1798. Bt 1847. Remained active in the bank into the 21st century.

1. Baron Lionel de Rothschild – London 1847-74
2. Baron Mayer Amschel de Rothschild – Hythe 1859-74
3. Nathaniel Rothschild 1 Baron Rothschild – Aylesbury 1865-85
4. Baron Ferdinand de Rothschild – Aylesbury Div. Buckinghamshire 1885-98
5. Lionel Rothschild 2 Baron Rothschild – Aylesbury Div. Buckinghamshire 1899-1910
6. Lionel Rothschild – Aylesbury Div. Buckinghamshire 1910-23
7. James de Rothschild – Isle of Ely Div. Cambridgeshire 1929-45

Seats: Tring Park, Hertfordshire (built 1682, purch. 1873, remod. 1870s, family departed 1935, much of estate sold 1970s, house a school from 1945); Mentmore Towers, Buckinghamshire (built 1850-55, passed by mar. to Earls of Rosebery 1878, see Primrose); Exbury House, Hampshire (purch. and rebuilt 1919, remod. 1927, rebuilt 1964-65, still own); Waddesdon Park (Manor), Buckinghamshire (purch. 1874, built 1874-89 purch. of land and building cost at least £400,000 - Franklin, *The Gentleman's Country House*, 268-9 - NT 1957, still own estate); Gunnersbury Park, Middlesex (built 1658-63, new house 1800-02, purch. 1834, add. 1835, sold 1925); Ascott House, Buckinghamshire (built 17th c., purch. 1874, rebuilt 1874-75 and 1878-80, add. late 1930s, NT 1950); Halton House, Buckinghamshire (purch. 1851, rebuilt 1882-88, sold 1919, now RAF); Aston Clinton House, Buckinghamshire (purch. 1851, add. 1853, sold 1930s, demolished 1958)
Estates: Bateman 15378 (E) 28901. Most of the male Rothschilds in the 19th century left over one million pounds each, often over 2 million, aside from landed property. Rubinstein – cites Naill Ferguson saying Nathan Mayer Rothschild died worth £3.5 million in 1836 excluding landed property. Worth £400,000,000 in 1990. Owned 12,000 acres in 2001.

Title: Baronet 1847-
Peers: 3 peers 1885-1945
1 Ld Lt 19th-20th
Notes: Austrian Barons 1822. 1, 2, and 3 Barons and twelve others in ODNB.

ROUND

Origins: Barrister in the 18th century. Bankers in Colchester in the 19th century. High Sheriff 1834.

1. John Round – Ipswich 1812-18 Maldon 1837-47
2. Charles Round – N. Oxfordshire 1837-47
3. James Round – E. Essex 1868-85 Harwich Div. Essex 1885-1906

Seat: Birch Hall, Essex (purch. 1726, built 1727, demolished and new house 1843-47, demolished 1954, still own estate)
Estates: Bateman 5418 (E) 7621
Notes: One in ODNB.

ROUS I [Wilson] *ENGLAND & IRELAND*

<u>Earl of Stradbroke</u> (Stradbrooke) (1821- UK)

Origins: Held manorial property in Suffolk since 1305 (ODNB says lived in Suffolk since the 10th century). The **First MP 1437** was a lawyer and noble servant. **Six further MPs 1449-1626 one for the county**.

1. Sir John Rous 1 Bt – Dunwich 1661-70
2. Sir John Rous 2 Bt – Eye 1685-87 Suffolk 1689-90
3. Sir John Rous 3 Bt – Dunwich 1705-08
4. Sir John Rous 5 Bt – Suffolk 1768-71
5. John Rous 1 Earl of Stradbroke – Suffolk 1780-96
6. Henry Rous – Westminster 1841-46

Seats: Henham Hall, Suffolk (medieval, acq. 1545, rebuilt later 16th c., fire 1773, rebuilt 1792-1800, remod. 1858, demolished 1953, still own estate); Worstead House, Norfolk (built 1791-97, purch. by Rous by 1845, demolished 1939); Caherconlish, Limerick (passed by mar. from Wilsons 1788, resident in 19th c., sold)
Estates: Bateman 12203 (E) 15434. Owned 3,750 acres in 2001.
Titles: Baron Rous 1796- GB; Baronet 1660-
Peers: 3 peers 1796-1945
3 Lds Lt 19th, 20th
Notes: Three in ODNB.

Wilson

Origins: Acquired estates by 1681. Sheriff 1721. Estates passed by marriage in 1788 to Earls of Stradbroke.

1. William Wilson – {Limerick 1739-41}

Seat: Caherconlish, Limerick (built later 17th c., passed to Rous family 1788, see above)
Estates: Held 14,000 acres in 1800. In 1840 the Caherconlish estate was valued at £63,618 and urban property at another £3,000.

ROUS II (Rowse)

Rous

Origins: Claimed to have come over with the Conqueror. Seated in Devon by the reign of Henry III. **First MP 1312. Five further MPs 1584-1656, two for Cornwall.** (Lawrence, *Parliamentary Representation of Cornwall*, 34-52)

1. Richard Rous – Bossiney 1661-73

Seat: Halton, Cornwall (acq. 16th c., sold later 17th c.)
Estates: 10,000 acres c. 1620.
Notes: Richard Rous MP 1661-73 died in debt, the last of his family. Halton was sold by his wife's brother. One in ODNB.

Rous

Origins: Cadet line. **First MP 1653**.

1. Anthony Rous – Helston 1660

Seat: Wotton, Cornwall
Notes: One in ODNB.

RUDGE

Origins: Chandlers in Evesham in the 16th century. London Alderman in the early 17th century. The first MP was an apprentice to a London haberdasher and made a fortune as a merchant. He purchased the manor of Evesham in 1664.

1. Edward Rudge – Evesham 1681 1690-95

2. John Rudge – Evesham 1698-1701 1702-34
3. Edward Rudge – Aylesbury 1728-34 Evesham 1741-54 1756-61

Seat: Abbey Manor House, Evesham, Worcestershire (medieval, purch. 1664, rebuilt c. 1817 or 1840, owned well into 20th c., flats and hotel)
Estates: Bateman 2234 (E) 6037

RUMBOLD

Origins: Gentry by the early 17th century. Minor civil servant 1629. Merchant and consul in Spain c. 1660. Nabob with the East India Company (Governor of Bengal) 1750s and 1760s.

1. Sir Thomas Rumbold 1 Bt – New Shorham 1770-74 Shaftesbury 1774-75 1780-81 Yarmouth (IoW) 1781-84 Weymouth & Melcomb Regis 1784-90
2. William Rumbold – Weymouth & Melcombe Regis 1781-84
3. Charles Rumbold – Great Yarmouth 1818-34 1837-57

Seat: Woodhall Park, Hertfordshire (purch. 1774 for £87,000 (Hussey, *English Country Houses: Mid Georgian 1760-1800*, 177) built 1778-82, sold 1794)
Title: Baronet 1779-
Estates: 1 Bt said to be worth £200,000 to £300,000 on his return from India in 1769 but wealth declined later in his life.
Notes: 1, 2, 5, 8, and 9 Bts and three others in ODNB.

RUNCIMAN

Viscount Runciman (1937- UK)

Origins: The son of a coast guard employee became a shipping magnate in the second half of the 19th century. The family continued in the shipping business well into the 20th century.

1. Walter Runciman 1 Viscount Runciman – Oldham 1899-1900 Dewsbury 1902-18 Swansea W. 1924-29 St. Ives Div. Cornwall 1931-37
2. Walter Runciman 1 Baron Runciman – Hartlepool 1914-18
3. Hilda Runciman Viscountess Runciman – St. Ives Div. Cornwall 1928-29

Seats: Fernwood House, Northumberland (purch. early 20th c., owned mid-20th c.); Doxford Hall, Northumberland (built 1818, purch. and remod. early 20th c., sold 1953); Shoreston Hall, Northumberland (purch. early 20th c., rebuilt c. 1913)
Estates: Worth £20,000,000 in 1990.

Title: Baron Runciman 1933- UK; Baronet 1906-
Peers: 2 peers 1933-45
1 in Cabinet 1908-16 1931-39
Notes: The family has produced a number of distinguished academics. 1 Baron and 1 and 2 Viscounts and four others in ODNB.

RUSHOUT [Bowles, Cockerell]

Baron Northwick (1797-1887 GB)

Origins: A Flemish weaver and merchant was naturalized in 1634. His son was a fishmonger who purchased an estate near Evesham in the 1660s.

1. Sir James Rushout 1 Bt – Evesham 1670-81 Worcestershire 1689-90 Evesham 1690-98
2. Sir James Rushout 2 Bt – Evesham 1701-02
3. Sir John Rushout 4 Bt – Malmesbury 1713-22 Evesham 1722-68
4. John Rushout 1 Baron Northwick – Evesham 1761-96
5. George Rushout-Bowles 3 Baron Northwick – Evesham 1837-41 E. Worcestershire 1847-59

Seats: Northwick Park, Worcestershire (became part of Gloucestershire in 1931) (medieval, rebuilt early 17th c., purch. 1683, remod. 1686, 1728-30, later 18th c., 1828-30, add. 1832, passed by inher. to Spencer-Churchill family 1912, sold 1964); Burford House, Worcestershire (built 1728, acq. by mar. 1749, sold later 19th c.)
Estates: Bateman 9895 (E) 17725
Title: Baronet 1661-1887
Peers: 3 peers 1799-1887
Notes: 2 Baron and one other in ODNB.

Cockerell

Origins: Founded by a nabob who returned from the East in 1801. He became a London banker. High Sheriff 1814. Sir Charles Cockerell 1 Bt was heir to the Rushout estates and took the name Rushout.

1. Sir Charles Cockerell 1 Bt – Tregony 1802-06 Lostwithiel 1807 Bletchingley 1809-12 Seaford 1816-18 Evesham 1819-30 1831-37

Seat: Sezincote, Gloucestershire (purch. 1795, rebuilt c. 1805, sold 1888)
Estates: Bateman 3993 (E) 4864. The 1 Bt was worth £140,000.
Title: Baronet 1809-1931

Notes: A drafting error in the last Lord Northwick's will led to the Rushout estates going to the Spencer-Churchills, and the legal suit that followed wiped out the Cockerell fortune.

Bowles

Origins: The first MP was a Turkey merchant who founded the Vauxhall glassworks. The Bowles estates passed to the Rushouts by marriage.

1. William Bowles – Bridport 1727-41 Bewdley 1741-48
2. Phineas Bowles – Bewdley 1735-41

Seat: Burford House, Worcestershire (purch. 1720, passed to Rushouts 1749)
Estates: Phineas Bowles MP left £200,000 in 1749.
Notes: Three in ODNB.

RUSSELL I *ENGLAND & IRELAND*

Duke of Bedford (1694- E)

Origins: Merchants and ship owners in medieval Dorset. Engaged in the French wine trade in the 14th century. Gradually acquired landed estates. Rose dramatically in the service of the early Tudors, purchased monastic property, married an heiress, and gained a peerage. **First MP 1340 for Melcombe. Thirteen further MPs 1384-1644, five kts of the shire**. (For de Clifford title, see Southwell).

1. William Russell Lord Russell – Tavistock 1640-41 1660-79 Bedfordshire 1679-81
2. Lord Edward Russell – Tavistock 1679-81 Bedfordshire 1689-1705 1708-13
3. Lord Robert Russell – Camelford 1679-81 1689-1703
4. Lord James Russell – Whitchurch 1685-87 1689-1701 Tavistock 1702-03
5. Edward Russell 1 Earl of Orford – Launceston 1689-90 Portsmouth 1690-95 Cambridgeshire 1695-97
6. Francis Russell Marquess of Tavistock – {Armagh 1759-60} Bedfordshire 1761-67
7. John Russell 6 Duke of Bedford – Tavistock 1788-1802
8. Lord William Russell – Surrey 1789-1807 Tavistock 1807-19 1826-30
9. Francis Russell 7 Duke of Bedford – Peterborough 1809-12 Bedfordshire 1812-32
10. Lord George Russell – Bedford 1812-30
11. John Russell 1 Earl Russell – Tavistock 1813 Huntingdonshire 1820-26 Bandon Bridge 1826-30 Tavistock 1830-31 Devonshire 1831-32 S. Devonshire 1832-35 Stroud 1835-41 London 1841-61
12. John Russell – Kinsale 1826-32
13. William Russell 8 Duke of Bedford – Tavistock 1830-31 1832-41

14. Francis Russell – Tavistock 1831-32
15. Lord Charles Russell – Bedfordshire 1832-41 1847
16. Lord Edward Russell – Tavistock 1841-47
17. Francis Russell 9 Duke of Bedford – Bedfordshire 1847-72
18. Edward Southwell Russell 23 Baron de Clifford – Tavistock 1847-52
19. Lord Arthur Russell – Tavistock 1857-85
20. John Russell Viscount Amberley – Nottingham 1866-68
21. George Russell 10 Duke of Bedford – Bedfordshire 1875-85
22. George Russell – Aylesbury 1880-85 N. Bedfordshire 1892-95

Seats: Woburn Abbey, Bedfordshire (medieval, granted Woburn in Henry VIII's will 1548, rebuilt 1619, became principal seat c. 1627, add. 1747-61, remod. 1788-89, part demolished 1950, still own); Endsleigh, Devonshire (acq. c. 1530s, built 1810-11, fishing club from 1930s); Ampthill Park, Bedfordshire (built c. 1525-50, rebuilt late 1680s, add. 1704-07, remod. 1769-71, purch. 1840, sold c. 1945, flats); Chenies Manor, Buckinghamshire (acq. by Chenies 13th c., add. 15th and 1520s, passed to Russells 1525, add. 1550s reduced in size and became a farm house by mid-18th c., sold 1957); Oakley House, Bedfordshire (built late 17th c., purch. 1737, new house built 1748-50, remod. 1787-92, sold 1935); Houghton Park (House) (built 1615-21, purch. 1738, remod. 1764-65, gutted 1794, ruin, sold 1804, repurch. 1842, sold 1918); Chippenham Hall (Park), Cambridgeshire (seat of Earl of Orford, purch. 1688, built late 17th c., sold soon after 1727, demolished mid-18th c.); Orford House, Essex (Earl of Orford acq. and built c. 1700, sold c. 1727, institutional use)
Estates: Bateman 86335 (E) 141793 income exclusive of large urban estate in London; Earl Russell 4184 (I) 4527; Baron de Clifford 13000 (I) 5691. Duke's income c. £20,000 pa in 1700. London estate worth £339,458 pa in 1890. Worth £200,000,000 in 1990. Owned 23,000 acres in 2001.
Titles: Baron Russell 1538- E; Earl of Bedford 1549- E; Baron Russell 1603- E; Marquess of Tavistock 1694- E; Baron Howland 1695- E; Earl of Orford 1697-1727 E; Earl Russell 1861- UK; Baron Ampthill 1881- UK
Peers: 19 peers 1660-1711 1697-1727 1729-71 1787-1839 1833-1945 1861-78 1886-1945 1881-1945
8 Lds Lt 17th, 18th, 19th, 20th
5 in Cabinet 1694-99 1709-10 1714-17 1744-48 1748-51 1757-61 1761-63 1763-65 1806-07 1831-34 1835-41 1846-55 1859-66
8 KG 17th, 18th, 19th, 20th
Notes: The cadet line spawned by Lord John Russell (1 Earl Russell) produced a prime minister, a renowned philosopher, and an eminent historian. 1 Baron Russell of Thornhaugh and 1, 2, and 3 Barons Ampthill and 1 Earl of Orford and 1, 2 and 4 Earls of Bedford and 1 and 3 Earls Russell and 1, 4, 5, 6, 9, 11, and 12 Dukes and twelve others in ODNB.

Earl Ludlow (1760-1842 I)

Origins: The family was founded by a Lancastrian official of the Royal Household. Acquired estates in Wiltshire in the mid-15th century. **First MP 1432. Four additional MPs 1571-1659, one kt of the shire**. A younger son went to Ireland 1660. Sheriff 1714. The 3 Earl devised his estates to the Duke of Bedford and a younger son, Lord John Russell (Earl Russell) 1842.

1. Edmund Ludlow – Wiltshire 1646 Hindon 1659 1660
2. Stephen Ludlow – {Boyle 1692-93 Charlemont 1695-99 Dunleer 1703-13 1715-22 County Louth 1713-14}
3. Peter Ludlow – {Dunleer 1713-14 County Meath 1719-50}
4. Peter Ludlow 1 Earl Ludlow – Huntingdonshire 1768-96

Seats: South Court (Maiden Bradley), Wiltshire (acq. first half 16th c., confiscated 1660); Cople Hall (House), Bedfordshire (purch. by Duke of Bedford 1774, leased to Earl Ludlow 1803-42, demolished and rebuilt 1820s, sold later 19th c., fire 1971, demolished); Great Staughton, Huntingdonshire (purch. 1730s-1768, sold 1803-06); Ardsallagh Castle, Meath (old castle, acq. by mar. 1710, ruin by 1840s, estate passed to Earl Russell 1842, built 1844, sold 20th c.)
Estates: Worth £2,000 pa in 1713 and £5,278 pa in 1802.
Titles: Baron Ludlow and Viscount Preston 1755-1842 I; Baron Ludlow 1831-42 UK
Peers: {1 peer 1776-1800} 1 peer 1831-42
Notes: Edmund Ludlow of South Court was a regicide and fled into exile at the Restoration. 3 Earl and one other in ODNB.

RUSSELL II

Russell

Origins: At Strensham by 1283. **First MP 1365 for Worcestershire. Three further MPs, all for the county 1529-1625.**

1. Sir Francis Russell 2 Bt – Tewkesbury 1673-81 1685-87 1689-90

Seat: Strensham Court (Castle), Worcestershire (purch. 1298, built 1388, rebuilt c. 1660s, sold 1817, burned 1974)
Estates: Worth £2,000 pa in 1660.
Title: Baronet 1627-1706
Notes: One in ODNB.

Russell

Origins: A cadet of the Russells of Worcestershire. The 1 Bt was a lawyer and Chief Justce of Bengal. Purchased estates on return from India in 1820.

1. Charles Russell – Reading 1830-37 1841-47
2. Sir Charles Russell 3 Bt – Berkshire 1865-68 Westminster 1874-87
3. Sir George Russell 4 Bt – Wokingham Div. Berkshire 1885-98

Seat: Swallowfield Park, Berkshire (built 1690, purch. and remod. 1820, sold 1965, flats)
Estates: Bateman 2381 (E) 3224
Title: Baronet 1812-1964

RUSSELL III

Origins: **First MP 1626** was an entrepreneur and Treasurer of the Navy 1618-42. Kt 1618. **Another MP 1640-58**.

1. Gerard Russell – Cambridgeshire 1679

Seat: Chippenham Hall, Cambridgeshire (purch. c. 1600, sold 1688)
Title: Baronet 1629-1804
Notes: The 2 Bt was a member of Cromwell's House of Lords.

RUTHERFURD (Rutherford) *SCOTLAND*

Earl of Teviot (1663-64 S)

Origins: Emerged in the 17th century. The 1 Earl was a soldier in France in the 1650s. **First [MP 1630 for Roxburghshire]**.

1. John Rutherford – Roxburghshire 1734-42
2. John Rutherford – Selkirkshire 1802-06 Roxburghshire 1806-12

Seats: Hunthill House, Roxburghshire (medieval, acq. 15th c., rebuilt 19th c.); Edgerston, Roxburghshire (built c. 1720, add. 1834-35, sold 1915)
Estates: Bateman 8479 (S & E) 4266
Title: Baron Rutherfurd 1661-1724 S
Peers: [4 peers 1661-1707]
Notes: 1 Earl in ODNB.

RUXTON *IRELAND*

Ruxton

Origins: To Ireland in the 16th century. Sheriff 1659. Acquired estates in Louth 1667.

1. John Ruxton – {Ardee 1661-63}
2. William Ruxton – {Ardee 1748-51}
3. John Ruxton – {Ardee 1751-76 1783-85}
4. Charles Ruxton – {Ardee 1761-68 1783-90 1797-99}
5. William Ruxton – {Ardee 1785-90 1797-1800}
6. William Ruxton – {Ardee 1790-97 1799-1800}

Seats: Ardee House, Louth (acq. and built 1667, new house mid-18th c., sold 20th c., hospital); Red House, Louth (built early 18th c., inher. by mar. c. 1760, left to nephew 1 Baron Carlingford (see Fortescue) early/mid-19th c.)
Estates: Bateman 2262 (I) 2279

Parkinson

Origins: Small landowners. Robert Parkinson MP was a lawyer.

1. Robert Parkinson – {Ardee 1727-60}

Seat: Red House, Louth (acq. 18th c., passed by mar. to Ruxtons c. 1760)

RYDER

Earl of Harrowby (1809- UK)

Origins: Founder a mercer in London late 17th century. His son was a linen draper. His son was Lord Chief Justice of the King's Bench 1754. He was granted a peerage in 1754 but died before kissing hands (Cannon, *Aristocratic Century*, 24). His son was made a Baron 1776.

1. Martin Ryder – Plympton Erle 1698-1701
2. Dudley Ryder – St. Germans 1733-34 Tiverton 1734-54
3. Thomas Ryder – Tiverton 1755-56
4. Nathaniel Ryder 1 Baron Harrowby – Tiverton 1756-76
5. Dudley Ryder 1 Earl of Harrowby – Tiverton 1784-1803
6. Richard Ryder – Tiverton 1795-1830
7. Dudley Ryder 2 Earl of Harrowby – Tiverton 1819-31 Liverpool 1831-47

8. Granville Ryder – Tiverton 1830-32 Hertfordshire 1841-47
9. Dudley Ryder 3 Earl of Harrowby – Lichfield 1856-59 Liverpool 1868-82
10. Granville Ryder – Salisbury 1869-80
11. John Ryder 5 Earl of Harrowby – Gravesend 1898-1900
12. Dudley Ryder 6 Earl of Harrowby – Shrewsbury Div. Shropshire 1922-29
13. Robert Ryder – Merton and Morden 1950-55

Seats: Sandon Hall, Staffordshire (purch. 1776, fire 1848, rebuilt 1852, add. 1854, still own); Burnt Norton, Gloucestershire (built 1620s, fire 1741, purch. 1753 for £19,400, partly restored house soon after, remod. 1901-02 and restored 1998-99, still own)
Estates: Bateman 12625 (E) 20291. Sir Dudley Ryder, Chief Justice died 1756 with £3,000 pa in landed estates and £110,000 in securities and cash. Rubinstein - Richard Ryder MP left £140,000 in probate in 1832.
Title: Baron Harrowby 1776- GB
Peers: 6 peers 1776-1945
1 Ld Lt 20th
4 in Cabinet 1804-06 1809-27 1809-12 185-59 1878-80 1885-86
1 KG 19th
Notes: 1 Baron and 1, 2, and 3 Earls and six others in ODNB.

SACKVILLE [Cornwallis, Germain, Stopford, West] *ENGLAND & WALES*

Duke of Dorset (1720-1843 GB)

Origins: One of the most ancient English families of direct Norman descent (Saul, *Knights and Esquires: The Gloucestershire Gentry in the Fourteenth Century,* 7-13). Held Fawley, Buckinghamshire from the time of the Conquest (Roskell, Clark, and Rawcliffe, *The House of Commons*, IV, 271-2). Acquired Buckhurst by marriage c. 1200. Made a great fortune under the Tudors by shrewd purchase of monastic and other land, office holding, and marriage. **First MP 1324. 17 further MPs 1361-1644, eight kts of the shire.**

1. Charles Sackville 1 Earl of Middlesex – East Grinstead 1661-75
2. Edward Sackville – East Grinstead 1675-78
3. Edward Sackville – East Grinstead 1679
4. Thomas Sackville – East Grinstead 1689-93
5. Charles Sackville 2 Duke of Dorset – East Grinstead 1734-42 Sussex 1742-47 Old Sarum 1747-54 East Grinstead 1761-65
6. Lord John Sackville – Tamworth 1734-47
7. Lord George Sackville Germain 1 Viscount Sackville – Dover 1741-61
8. John Sackville 3 Duke of Dorset – Kent 1768-69

Seat: Knole, Kent (built 12th c., add. mid-15th c. and mid-16th c., acq. 1566, remod. 1603-08, NT 1946, still own estate)
Estates: Bateman 8551 (E) 11250. Worth £2,180 pa in 1646. Owned 2,000 acres in 2001.
Titles: Baron Buckhurst 1567-1843 E; Earl of Dorset 1603-1843 E; Earl of Middlesex 1675-1843 E; Baron Bolebroke and Viscount Sackville 1782-1843 GB; Baron Sackville 1876- UK
Peers: 12 peers 1660-77 1675-1706 1709-99 1782-85 1815-43 1876-1945
6 Lds Lt 17th, 18th
2 in Cabinet 1730-37 1745-55 1750-55 1775-82
4 KG 17th, 18th, 19th
Notes: The Cranfields (very rich in business in London, raised to Earldom of Middlesex 1622), whose estates the Sackvilles inherited, elected **MPs 1614 and 1640**. Knole is one of the most remarkable country houses in England, evoked well both by V. Sackville-West's history of the building and her novel, *The Edwardians*. The Sackville family has an entry as well as the 2 and 5 Barons Sackville and 1 Viscount and 1, 2, 4, 5, and 6 Earls of Dorset and 1, 2, and 3 Dukes and three others in ODNB.

Germain/Stopford

Origins: The 1 Baronet was a Dutch gamester of "mean extraction" who came to England with William III. He married in 1701 the *suro jure* Baroness Mordaunt, who brought him Drayton House (see Mordaunt). He predeceased her. She left her estates to Lord George Sackville, created 1 Viscount Sackville. His son was the last Duke of Dorset. The niece of the last Duke married 1837 William Stopford and her descendents inherited Drayton taking the name Stopford-Sackville (see Stopford).

1. Sir John Germain 1 Bt – Morpeth 1713-15 Totnes 1717-18
2. Sackville Stopford Sackville – N. Northamptonshire 1867-80 1900-06

Seats: Drayton House, Northamptonshire (built 1328, add. late 14th c., inher. 1515 by Mordaunts, rebuilt late 16th c. and c. 1670s, passed 1697 by mar. to the Sackvilles 1769, remod. 1702-04 and 1771-74, still own); Stoneland Lodge, Sussex (part of the Buckhurst estate, which was originally called Stonelands, acq. 12th c., see below)
Estates: Bateman 4667 (E) 8723
Title: Baronet 1698-1718
Notes: 1 Bt in ODNB.

Earl De La Warr (1761- GB)

Origins: The le Warres were of Norman ancestry. Summoned as a Baron 1298. Their estates passed by marriage to the Wests, a landed family by the 14th century. Barons 1402. **First MP 1554. Four further MPs 1571-97**. The sister of the 4 Duke of Dorset married Earl De La Warr. On the death of the 5 Duke, Knole descended to the second son of this marriage while the eldest son was seated at Buckhurst as Earl De La Warr. The family took the name Sackville-West.

1. Charles West – Andover 1678-79 1681
2. John West 1 Earl De La Warr – Grampound 1715-22
3. Frederick West – Denbigh Boroughs 1802-06
4. George Sackville-West Viscount Cantilupe – Helston 1837-40 Lewes 1840-41
5. Tom Sackville - Bolton West 1983-97

Seats: Buckhurst Park, Sussex (acq. by Sackvilles by mar. 12th c., medieval, rebuilt 1603, still own); Bourn Hall, Cambridgeshire (built c. 1602, acq. by mar. late 18th c., sold mid-20th c.); Wherwell Abbey (Priory), Hampshire (medieval, acq. c. 1540, sold 1695, old buildings demolished and replaced with a new house 1820)
Estates: Bateman 23366 (E) 21606. Owned 6,500 acres in 2001.
Titles: Baron De La Warr 1298 E; Baron Delaware 1569 E; Baron Buckhurst 1864- E
Peers: 11 peers 1660-1795 1812-1915 1921-45
1 in Cabinet 1937-40 1951-55
Notes: Members of the Sackville-West family held high positions in North America in three successive centuries (Governor of Jamestown Colony 17th, Governor of New York Colony 18th, and British Minister in Washington 19th c.) as well as lending their name to the state of Delaware. The 9 Earl was the first hereditary peer to join the Labour Party and became a government minister in 1924, aged 23. Tom Sackville MP, brother of the 11 Earl, was a junior Minister in John Major's government in the 1990s. 3 and 9 Barons and 1, 5, 6, and 9 Earls and four others in ODNB.

West

Origins: A younger son of the 8 Baron De La Warr married an heiress and purchased Alscot Park. The family had been cloth merchants in Banbury. They added the name Roberts in 1808 on marriage to another heiress. A junior line was established at Elmdon Hall by marriage to yet another heiress named Alston.

1. James West – St. Albans 1741-68 Boroughbridge 1768-72
2. James West – Boroughbridge 1767-68

Seats: Alscot Park, Warwickshire (built early 17th c., altered 1720s, purch. 1747, 1750-2, 1762-4, still own); Priors Marston, Warwickshire (resident 17th and 18th c.); Elmdon Hall, Warwickshire (built 1785, Alstons purch. c. 1835, passed to Wests by mar. later 19th c., sold 1920, demolished 1948)
Estates: Bateman 11128 (E) 15584

Cornwallis-West

Origins: Frederick West MP was the son of the 2 Earl De La Warr and Marie, daughter and co-heiress of Richard Myddelton of Chirk Castle (see Myddelton). They inherited Ruthin Castle. Frederick West married 1827 Theresa Cornwallis, daughter of the 5 Earl Cornwallis (see Wykeham). On the latter's death in 1862 he left his Welsh estates to Frederick West's eldest son and Hampshire estates to a younger son, William Cornwallis-West MP.

1. Frederick West – Denbigh Borough 1827-30 East Grinstead 1830-32 Denbigh District 1847-57
2. William Cornwallis-West – Denbighshire 1885-92

Seats: Ruthin Castle, Denbighshire (built c. 1280, dismantled 1648, ruin, purch. and new house built by Myddeltons 1826, passed by mar. to Wests mid-19th c., sold 1923); Newlands Manor, Hampshire (purch. late 18th c., built early 19th c., sold 1920)
Estates: Bateman 7861 (E & W) 13244
1 Ld Lt 19th-20th

ST. GEORGE [Lee, Ussher] *IRELAND*

Baron St. George (1715-35 I)

Origins: Members of the family were heralds in the 17th and 18th centuries including two Garter Kings of Arms and one Ulster King of Arms. Fees, bribes, and payments for providing fraudulent ancestries brought the family considerable wealth. Moved to Ireland in the early 17th century. Sir Henry St. George, Garter King of Arms, built a house at Hatley St. George, Cambridgeshire c. 1635-41. The senior line of the family descended from Sir Richard St. George, common ancestor of the family. Sheriff 1702.

1. George St. George – {Carrick 1639 County Leitrim 1661-66}
2. Sir Oliver St. George 1 Bt – {County Galway 1661-66 1692-93}
3. George St. George 1 Baron St. George – {Roscommon 1692-93 1695-99 1703-14}
4. Sir George St. George – {County Galway 1695-99 Carrick 1703-13}
5. Oliver St. George – {Carrick 1703-13 Dungannon 1713-31}

Seat: Carrickdrumrusk, Leitrim (acq. sec. half 17th c., passed by mar. to Usshers 1775)
Estates: Worth £1,600 pa in 1713.
Title: Baronet 1660-1735
Peer: {1 peer 1715-35}
Notes: On the death of the 1 Baron, his estates passed via an heiress to her husband John Ussher (see below). Four in ODNB.

<u>St. George</u>

Origins: Descended from the son of a younger son of Sir Richard St. George.

1. Arthur St. George – {Athlone 1661-66 1692-93 1695-99}
2. Richard St. George – {Galway 1695-99 Carrick 1715-55}
3. Richard St. George – {Clogher 1703-26}
4. Richard St. George – {Charleville 1783-90}

Seats: Kilrush House, Kilkenny (16th c. castle, new house built early 19th c., still own); Hatley (Manor) St. George, Leitrim (resident in 18th c., rebuilt c. 1830, passed to Whytes by mar. 1876)
Estates: 2,873 acres worth £1,710 pa in the 1870s. Held 7,021 acres worth £6,000 pa in 1768.
Notes: Hatley St. George passed by mar. to the Hallbergs and then in 1876 to the Whytes.

<u>St. George</u>

Origins: Descended from a brother of the head of the Kilrush line.

1. Thomas St. George – {Clogher 1776-85}

Seat: Wood Park, Armagh (acq. 19th c., resident 20th c.)
Estates: Held 1,008 acres and £428 pa in 1878.

<u>St. George</u>

Origins: Descended from the youngest brother of the head of the Kilrush line.

1. Henry St. George – {Clogher 1703-13 Athlone 1715-23}
2. George St. George – {Athlone 1723-60}
3. Henry St. George – {Athlone 1761-63}
4. Sir Richard St. George 1 Bt – {Athlone 1763-89}
5. Sir Richard St. George 2 Bt – {Athlone 1789-1800}

Seat: Woodsgift, Kilkenny (acq. 1666, built later 18th c., add. 19th c., burned before 1914, demolished)
Estates: 1694 (I) 775 (in GEC); held 1,913 acres worth £1,136 pa in 1878. 2,864 acres in 1699.
Title: Baronet 1766-

Baron St. George (1763-75 I)

Origins: The daughter of the last Baron St. George of the first creation married John Ussher MP. Their son took the name St. George and was created a Baron.

1. John Ussher – {Carrick 1715-41}
2. St. George Ussher St. George 1 Baron St. George – {Carrick 1741-63}

Seat: Carrickdrumrusk, Leitrim (acq. by mar. with St. George heiress 1775, passed by mar. Dukes of Leinster, sold late 18th c.)
Peer: {1 peer 1763-75}
Notes: The daughter of the 1 Baron married the 2 Duke of Leinster. Much property passed to the Leinsters (see Fitzgerald I) through this marriage amounting to a value of £60,000 in 1775 when sold.

St. George

Origins: The daughter of John Ussher and Mary St. George married Arthur French, who took the name St. George 1774. Their son was seated at Tyrone House.

1. Christopher St. George – County Galway 1847-52

Seat: Tyrone House, Galway (acq. by mar. 1774, built 1779, abandoned 1905, burned 1920)
Estates: Bateman 15777 (I) 4453
Notes: The French family conformed to the Established Church 1704.

Ussher

Origins: The first known Ussher emigrated from England and was Constable of Dublin Castle 1302. Merchants in Dublin before 1439. Mayor of Dublin 1467-71. Several Archbishops in the 16th and 17th centuries. **First {MP 1613}. Three additional {MPs 1613-39}.**

1. Sir William Ussher – {County Wicklow 1639 County Dublin 1661-66}
2. William Ussher – {Newton Limavady 1714}
3. Charles Ussher – {Blessington 1745-70}
4. John Ussher – {Innistiogue 1783-90}

Seats: Mount Ussher, Wicklow (acq. 17th c., resident 18th c.); Eastwell, Galway (acq. 1796, held into 20th c., demolished c. 1990s); Castle of Grange (Castlegrange), Wicklow (acq. later 16th, resident 17th and 18th c.)

Estates: 3666 (I) 1781
Notes: John Ussher {MP} above, died without male heirs. The senior line of Usshers remained Roman Catholic, and their estates were eventually confiscated. For lineages see Wright, *The Ussher Memoirs*. Six in ODNB.

Ussher

Origins: Descended from a younger son of Arthur Ussher of Mount Ussher. A younger son was the John Ussher, father of Baron St. George (see above).

1. Beverley Ussher – {County Waterford 1735-57}
2. John Ussher – {Dungarvon 1747-49}

Seat: Kilmeadon, Waterford (acq. later 18th or early 19th c.)
Estates: 1,543 acres worth £1,033 pa in 1870s

Lee

Origins: The daughter and heiress of Beverley Ussher of Kilmeadon married Edward Lee of Tramore Park. The Lees were bankers in the 18th century. Purchased landed estates. Sheriff 1804.

1. Edward Lee – {Dungarvon 1798-1800} 1801-02 County Waterford 1802-06

Seat: Tramore Park, Waterford (acq. later 18th c., resident 19th c.)

ST. JOHN [Fitzwalter, Mildmay]

Earl of Bolingbroke (1624-1711 E)

Origins: Norman feudal barons. They claimed with some probability descent from the largest lay tenant-in-chief in Hampshire in the Domesday Book. Engaged in the Norman conquest of Glamorgan in the 11th century. The senior line descended from a St. John who married a Beauchamp heiress to Bletso in the 15th century. Baron 1559. **First MP 1410 for Northamptonshire. Twelve additional MPs 1529-1648, eight for Bedfordshire.**

1. Francis St. John – Tewkesbury 1654-55 Peterborough 1656-58 1660 1679-81 1698-1700
2. Paulet St. John 3 Earl of Bolingbroke – Bedford 1663-81
3. St. Andrew St. John 14 Baron St. John – Bedfordshire 1780-84 1785-1805
4. Ambrose St. John – Callington 1803-06

Seats: Bletso (Castle), Bedfordshire (built 1327, acq. by mar. 1482, add. 16th and 17th c., family abandoned late 18th c. in favor of Melcbourne, much reduced in size 19th c., became a farm house, sold 1972); Melchbourne Park (House), Bedfordshire (purch. 1604, built c.1610, rebuilt 1741, family departed 1939, post-war divided into flats); Woodford House, Northamptonshire (purch. 1621, sold early 19th c.); Thorpe Hall, Northamptonshire (old manor house, purch. and built new house 1650s, passed to an heiress 1756, sold 1791, institutional use)
Estates: Bateman 8438 (E) 11900. Owned 4,000 acres in 2001.
Titles: Baron St. John of Bletso 1559- E; Baronet 1660-
Peers: 11 peers 1660-1711 1722-67 1779-1817 1832-1934 1938-45
2 Lds Lt 17th, 20th
Notes: 5 Baron and 1 Earl and three others in ODNB.

<u>Viscount Bolingbroke</u> (1712-15 GB and 1725- GB)

Origins: Cadet of Bletso line. Created Viscount Grandison (I) in 1621. The title passed to the Villiers family by special remainder in 1630 (see Villiers). A younger brother of the 1 Viscount succeeded to Lydiard Tregoze and this line also gained a viscountcy. The title was attainted in 1715 and revived in 1725. **First MP 1529. Five further MPs 1553-1625, one kt of the shire.**

1. Sir Walter St. John 3 Bt – Wootton Basset 1656 1659 1661-79 Wiltshire 1679-81 1690-95
2. Henry St. John 1 Viscount St. John – Wootton Bassett 1701-08 Berkshire 1710-12
3. Sir St. Andrew St. John 2 Bt – Northamptonshire 1690-98
4. Henry St. John 1 Viscount Bolingbroke – Wootton Bassett 1701-08 Berkshire 1710-12
5. John St. John 2 Viscount St. John – Wootton Bassett 1727-34
6. Henry St. John – Wootton Bassett 1761-84 1802
7. John St. John – Newport (IoW) 1773-74 Eye 1774-80 Newport 1780-84
8. George St. John 3 Viscount Bolingbroke – Cricklade 1782-84
9. Frederick St. John – Oxford 1818-20

Seat: Lydiard Tregoze (Park), Wiltshire (medieval, acq. by mar. 1482, rebuilt 1743-49, sold 1943, museum)
Estates: Bateman 3382 (E) 5556
Titles: Viscount Grandison (1621- I) Baron Tregoze 1626-30 Viscount St. John 1716- GB; Baronet 1611-
Peers: 8 peers 1712-15 1716-49 1725-51 1754-1899 1917-45
1 Ld Lt 18th
1 in Cabinet 1704-08 1710-14
Notes: 1 Viscount Grandison and 1 Viscount Bolingbroke first cr. and two others in ODNB.

St. John Mildmay

Origins: The uncle of the 1 Viscount Grandison (see above) was the ancestor of Sir Henry St. John 3 Bt, who married Jane Mildmay, heiress to the estates of the last Earl of Fitzwalter and to the Mildmay estates of Hazelgrove, Somerset and Marks, Essex. The eldest son of this marriage headed the line of Baronets at Dogmersfield Park. The second son received Hazelgrove and the descendents of the third son became Barons Mildmay of Flete. **First St. John MP of this line MP 1604. Two further MPs 1563-1614 and one Irish {MP 1613}.**

1. Oliver St. John – Stockbridge 1679-81 1689
2. Sir Paulet St. John 1 Bt – Winchester 1734-41 Hampshire 1741-47 Winchester 1751-54
3. Sir Henry St. John 2 Bt – Hampshire 1772-80
4. Sir Henry St. John Mildmay 3 Bt – Westbury 1796-1802 Winchester 1802-07 Hampshire 1807-08
5. Sir Henry St. John Mildmay 4 Bt – Winchester 1807-18
6. Paulet St. John Mildmay – Winchester 1818-34 1837-41
7. Humphrey St. John Mildmay – Southampton 1842-47

Seats: Dogmersfield Park (House), Hampshire (medieval, acq. by mar. 1702, rebuilt 1570s, new house 1728, sold 1933, hotel); Farley Chamberlayne Manor, Hampshire (medieval, acq. by mar. 1525, abandoned by family mid-18th c., demolished later 18th c., sold 1830); Mildmay Park, Middlesex (acq. by mar. 1650s, engulfed by London and sold 1850s); Hazelgrove House, Somerset (purch. and built c. 1556, remod. 1730-35, leased after 1882, sold 1920, institutional use); Moulsham Hall, Essex (acq. 1540, built 1540?, rebuilt 1729-41, demolished 1816)
Estates: Bateman 10883 (E) 15031 and 2500 (E) 5000 at Hazelgrove. Humphrey St. John Mildmay MP left £300,000.
Title: Baronet 1772-

Baron Mildmay of Flete (1922- UK)

Origins: See previous entry. Henry Mildmay, who purchased Flete in 1876, was a partner in Barings Bank.

1. Humphrey Mildmay – Herefordshire 1859-65
2. Francis Mildmay 1 Baron Mildmay – Totnes Div. Devon 1885-1922

Seats: Flete House, Devon (built late 16th c., purch. 1876, rebuilt 1878-83, institutional use during WWII and from 1961); Shoreham Place, Kent (acq. 1830s, family departed 1939, demolished c. 1961)
Estates: Bateman 2564 (E) 3563

Peer: 1 peer 1922-45
1 Ld Lt 20th
Notes: 2 Baron in ODNB.

Earl of Fitzwalter (1735-56 GB)

Origins: The Earl of Fitzwalter was descended from the eldest son of Sir Thomas Mildmay of Moulsham, Essex. The Barony of Fitzwalter was inherited from the Radcliffe Earls of Sussex by marriage (see Radcliffe). The Fitzwalters were Norman lords. (**One MP for Norfolk 1478-84**). On the death of the 1 Earl of Fitzwalter the estates passed to cousins and then to an heiress who married into the St. John family (see above). The Mildmays began as small tradesmen in Chelmsford and rose high as legal officials and speculators in monastic land in the 16th century. **First MP 1545 (Northamptonshire 1558-89). Seven further MPs 1547-1653.**

1. Henry Mildmay – Essex 1654 1658 Maldon 1659 1660 Essex 1679-81 1689-92
2. Carew Mildmay – Harwich 1714-15

Seats: Moulsham Hall, Essex (purch. 1540, see above); Apethorpe Hall, Northamptonshire (acq. 1552, passed to the Earl of Westmorland by mar. c. 1600); Hazelgrove House, Somerset (acq. and built mid-16th c., see above)
Titles: Baron Fitzwalter 1295-1756 E; Baronet 1611-1756 1765-96
Peers: 3 peers 1670-79 1691-1756
1 Ld Lt 18th
1 in Cabinet 1735-37
Notes: Three in ODNB.

ST. LAWRENCE *IRELAND*

Earl of Howth (1767-1909 I)

Origins: The family acquired Howth soon after the Norman Conquest of Ireland. Lord Chancellor of Ireland 1489. More than 30 generations have been seated at the Castle and the family still owns it.

1. William St. Lawrence 14 Baron Howth – {Ratoath 1716-27}
2. William St. Lawrence 4 Earl of Howth – Galway 1868-74

Seats: Howth Castle, Dublin (acq. c. 1176, medieval keep, add. 15th c., add. 16th c., add. 1738, add. 1840s, add. 1910, still own); Baldongan Castle, Dublin (built 13th c., damaged 1642, ruin)
Estates: Bateman 9438 (I) 18936

Titles: Baron Howth poss. 1440 or 1489-1909 I; Baron Howth 1881-1909 UK
Peers: {4 peers 1661-71 1680-1748 1751-1800} 1 peer 1881-1909
1 Ld Lt 19th
2 KP 19th, 20th
Notes: Howth Castle is the oldest inhabited house in Ireland. The St. Lawrence heiress married a Gainsford in 1859, who took the additional name St. Lawrence. 2, 3, 7, 8, and 9 Barons in ODNB.

ST. LEGER [Aldworth, Hayes] *IRELAND & ENGLAND*

Viscount Doneraile (1703-67 and 1785 I)

Origins: Began as Kentish gentry. To Ireland 1537. One was appointed Lord Deputy of Ireland 1540, KG and PC. His son and grandson were Presidents of Munster. The family gained large grants of land in 1619. **First MP 1346 for Kent. Five additional MPs 1367-1572, three kts of the shire. First Irish {MP 1585 for Queen's County}. One additional {MP 1634 for County Cork}**. On the extinction of the Viscountcy of the first creation the St. Leger estates passed to St. Leger Aldworth, son of the sister of the 2 Viscount and Richard Aldworth of Newmarket, Cork. He took the name St. Leger and was created Viscount Doneraile. The Aldworths were minor gentry in Berkshire. To Ireland later 16th c. One gained office there in 1610, Kt 1612. Established in Newmarket by 1620.

1. Mayward St. Leger – {Mallow 1661-66}
2. John St. Leger – {Fethard 1665-66}
3. John St. Leger – {County Cork 1665-66 Doneraile 1692-93 Tralee 1695-96}
4. Arthur St. Leger 1 Viscount Doneraile – {Doneraile 1692-93}
5. Richard Aldworth – {Dublin University 1695-99}
6. Sir John St. Leger – {Doneraile 1713-14}
7. Arthur St. Leger 2 Viscount Doneraile – {Doneraile 1715-27}
8. Hayes St. Leger 4 Viscount Doneraile – {Doneraile 1728-51}
9. Richard Aldworth – {Lismore 1728-60}
10. Arthur St. Leger 3 Viscount Doneraile – Winchelsea 1741-47 Old Sarum 1747-50
11. St. Leger Aldworth St. Leger 1 Viscount Doneraile – {Doneraile 1761-76}
12. Richard Aldworth – {Doneraile 1768-76}
13. Hayes St. Leger 2 Viscount Doneraile – {Doneraile 1776-88}
14. Richard St. Leger – {Doneraile 1777-83}
15. Barry Boyle St. Leger – {Doneraile 1798-99}

Seats: Doneraile Court, Cork (old castle, purch. 1627, burned 1645, rebuilt 1666, new house 1703, add. c. 1730, remod. late 18th c., fire 1805, rebuilt, add. 1869, sold 1969, restored, owned by government); Grangemellon, Kildare (medieval castle, remod.

early 17th c., purch. 1716, restored c. 1720, demolished c. 1800 and sold); Newmarket Court, Cork (Aldworths acq. c. 1621, rebuilt c. 1725, sold 1926, institutional use)
Estates: Bateman 28700 (I) 15000; Aldworths at Newmarket 8739 (I) 2648
Titles: Baron St. Leger 1776- I
Peers: {3 peers 1739-67 1789-1800} 2 Irish Rep peers 1830-54 1855-87
Notes: The daughter and heiress of the last Potyn of Kent (originally a merchant family) married a St. Leger. **Six MPs 1295-1397, the last a kt of the shire for Kent.** Seven in ODNB.

St. Leger

Origins: Descended from a younger son of John St. Leger, father of the 1 Viscount Doneraile. Seated firstly at Grangemellon and then Park Hill.

1. John St. Leger – {Doneraile 1761-68 Athy 1768-69} Okehampton 1791-96
2. Anthony St. Leger – Great Grimsby 1768-74

Seat: Park Hill, Yorkshire (purch. 1765-67, leased out as a school c. 1900, sold and demolished 1934-35)
Estates: Bateman 5179 (E & I) 5052
Notes: The family gave their name to a celebrated horse race at Doncaster. On the extinction of this line John Chester succeeded to the estates, which he sold (see Bagot).
Notes: One in ODNB.

Hayes

Origins: Minor gentry in the 17th century. John Hayes {MP} was Vice Treasurer of Ireland. Founder of the Hudson's Bay Company. Kt 1670. He had a daughter and heiress who married Arthur St. Leger 1 Viscount Doneraile. **First MP 1658.**

1. John Hayes – {Thomastown 1692-93 Donerale 1695-99} Winchelsea 1698-1700 1701-02
2. James Hayes – Winchelsea 1702-08

Seat: Bedgebury Park (Manor), Kent (medieval, purch. 1682, built new house 1688, sold c. 1740, school)
Notes: James Hayes MP died without issue in 1731. He left his property to his wife.

ST. LOE

Origins: Old family settled at St. Loe in Somerset in the 13th century. Sir John St. Loe served at Acre with Edward I in 1271. Soldiers and royal servants. **First MP 1447 for Wiltshire. Three further MPs 1545-72, two kts of the shire.**

1. George St. Loe – Weymouth & Melcombe Regis 1701-05

Seats: Knighton House, Wiltshire (acq. mid-16th c., resident through 1682, passed out of family); Little Fontmell (Fontmell Parva) House, Dorset (built 1665, passed to Malets by mar. 18th c. who took name St. Loe, sold 1864)

ST. QUINTIN (St. Quentin)

Origins: A Norman family established in the East Riding of Yorkshire by the end of the 11th century. This line eventually became merchants in Hull. Large blocks of land were accumulated due to an official career of the 3 Bt (d. 1723), and his successor married an heiress (daughter of a Lord Mayor of London). The 5 Bt also married an heiress. **First MP 1306 (for the county). One other MP 1382.**

1. Sir William St. Quintin 3 Bt – Kingston-upon-Hull 1695-1723
2. Sir William St. Quintin 4 Bt – Thirsk 1722-27
3. Matthew St. Quintin – Old Sarum 1728-34

Seats: Scampston Hall, Yorkshire (acq. c. 1720s, built c. 1730, rebuilt 1801-03, descendents still own); Harpham, Yorkshire (acq. by 1250, medieval manor house, family ceased use early 18th c., derelict and demolished, still own estate)
Estates: Bateman 7033 (E) 10244
Title: Baronet 1642-1797
Notes: The last Bt died in 1797, and the estates passed to a nephew, William Griffith (see Griffth II), who changed his name to St. Quintin. The family remained among the largest landowners in the East Riding until the early 19th century, after which they dropped out of the top ten. (English, *The Great Landowners of East Yorkshire*, 27) Last of the male line died in 1933, but estates continued to pass through the female line. 3 Bt in ODNB.

SASSOON

Baron Sassoon (UKLife 2010-)

Origins: Jewish merchant and banking family. Emerged in Iraq in the 18th century and moved to India in the 19th. Also became established in Shanghai and London in the later 19th century.

1. Sir Edward Sassoon 2 Bt – Hythe 1899-1912
2. Sir Philip Sassoon 3 Bt – Hythe 1912-39

Seats: Trent Park, Hertfordshire (built 1770s, rebuilt 1890s, purch. 1909, family departed 1939, sold c. 1992, institutional use); Port Lympne, Kent (medieval, restored 1906-10, new house built 1911-13, add. 1920s, family departed 1939, sold 1973, hotel); Ashley Park, Surrey (built c. 1500, remod. c. 1800, purch. c. 1890s, sold and demolished c. 1920); Heytesbury House, Wiltshire (built 1782, remod. 1820, purch. 1933, sold 1994, now flats)
Estates: The 3 Bt left nearly 2 million pounds and landed property in 1939.
Titles: Baronets 1890-1939; 1909-61
Notes: The poet Siegfried Sassoon wrote one of the iconic accounts of modern gentry life in the countryside (*Memoirs of a Fox-Hunting Man*, 1928). Sir Philip Sassoon 3 Bt and Lord Sassoon served in senior government positions in the 20th century. Rachel Sassoon, inherited the Beer banking fortune by mar. and owned and edited *The Observer* and the *Sunday Times*, which she had purchased in 1893. The Sassoon family and three others have entries in ODNB.

SAVILE [Fullarton] *ENGLAND & SCOTLAND*

Marquess of Halifax (1687-1700 E)

Origins: One of the oldest families in Yorkshire (Cliffe, *The Yorkshire Gentry from the Reformation to the Civil War*, 30). They established themselves in the West Riding by the mid-12th century, if not before. (Roskell, Clark, and Rawcliffe, *The House of Commons*, IV, 313). Major landowners by the late 14th century. **First MP 1376 for the county. Eleven further MPs 1442-1642, eight for the county**. On the death of the 2 Marquess of Halifax in 1700 the family estates passed to a cadet, George Savile 6 Bt.

1. George Savile 1 Marquess of Halifax – Pontefract 1660
2. Henry Savile – Newark 1677-79 1685-87
3. William Savile 2 Marquess of Halifax – Newark 1689-96
4. Sir George Savile 7 Bt – Yorkshire 1728-34
5. Sir George Savile 8 Bt – Yorkshire 1759-83

Seats: Rufford Abbey, Nottinghamshire (medieval monastic buildings, remod, later 16th c., acq. 1625 by mar. to a Talbot heiress by 1 Bt, add. 1677, add. 18th c., passed by mar. to Lumleys 1784, sold 1938, partially demolished 1950s, county council owns); Thornhill, Yorkshire (acq. by mar. c. 1400, destroyed 1640s); Barrabie (Barrowby), Lincolnshire (acq. 1362, passed out of family by mar. 1700); Rishworth Lodge, Yorkshire (medieval, acq. by mar. by 1337, Hall demolished and farm house built 18th c., passed to Lumleys 1784, Lodge built late 19th c., sold 1990s, flats); Walshaw (Moor)

Lodge, Yorkshire (purch. and built 1850s, became principal seat 1939, sold 2002-09, hotel)
Estates: Bateman 33820 (E) 52213. Held between 50,000 and 70,000 acres worth £7,000 pa in 1644. Still owned 6,000 acres 2016.
Titles: Baron Savile 1628-71 E; Baron Savile and Viscount Halifax 1668-1700 E; Earl of Halifax 1679-1700 E; Baron Savile 1888- UK; Baronet 1611-1784
Peers: 5 peers 1668-1700 1888-1931 1940-45
1 in Cabinet 1682-85 1689-90
Notes: After the Btcy became extinct in 1784 the estates were divided between a niece (Savile-Foljambe, see Jenkinson) and a nephew, son of the Marquess's sister, the Countess of Scarborough. This heir, John Lumley, succeeded as 7 Earl of Scarborough and took the name Savile-Lumley (see Lumley). The Savile estates passed to an illegitimate son who was created Lord Savile. A junior line of the original Savile family gained the titles Baron Savile in 1628 and Earl of Sussex in 1644 (extinct 1671). Savile family and 1 Baron 1 cr. and 1 Baron 2 cr. and 1 Earl of Sussex and 1 and 2 Marquesses and four others have entries in the ODNB.

<u>Earl of Mexborough</u> (1776- I)

Origins: Descended from a younger son of Henry Savile (fl. 14th c.) whose eldest son established the line at Rufford (see above). The cadet line was established by a late Tudor judge. They held Methley Park and Thrybergh. His eldest son, John, had a daughter who married into the Finch family to whom Thrybergh passed. The Earls of Mexborough retained Methley. **First MP 1572. One additional MP 1604, sitting for Yorkshire 1629**.

1. John Savile 1 Earl of Mexborough – Hedon 1747-54 New Shoreham 1761-68
2. John Savile 3 Earl of Mexborough – Pontefract 1807-26 1831-32
3. John Savile 2 Earl of Mexborough – Lincoln 1808-12
4. John Savile 4 Earl of Mexborough – Gatton 1831-32 Pontefract 1835-37 1841-47

Seat: Methley Park, Yorkshire (purch. and rebuilt c. 1588, rebuilt 1778, 1830s, abandoned by mid-20th c., demolished 1963); Howley Hall, Yorkshire (purch. 1578, built c. 1590, demolished 1730)
Estates: Bateman 9534 (E) 34565
Titles: Baron Pollington 1753- I; Baronet 1611-32
Peers: {2 peers 1753-1800}
Notes: The 3 Earl ran into serious financial difficulties. The 4 Earl became a Roman Catholic. Methley became surrounded by mining and industrial workings by the early 20th c. Three in ODNB.

Fullarton

Origins: The Fullarton's claimed Saxon descent. (Burke, *A Visitation of Seats and Arms of the Noblemen and Gentlemen of Great Britain and Ireland*, I, 249) Granted lands by Robert I of Scotland. **First [MP 1572] and a further [MP 1643].** John Finch (see Finch under Earl of Aylesford) married Elizabeth Savile, heiress of Thrybergh. Their son, Savile Finch MP married Judith Fullarton (d. 1803). She inherited Thrybergh. The MP listed below was from the senior line of the Fullartons of Fullarton, Ayrshire. Judith Fullarton left her husband's estate to her own family.

1. William Fullarton – Plympton Erle 1779-80 Haddington Burghs 1787-90 Horsham 1793-96 Ayrshire 1796-1803

Seats: Fullarton House, Ayrshire (built 1745, remod. 1790s, sold 1805, demolished 1966); Skeldon House, Ayrshire (built 1780-99, sold 1867); Thrybergh, Yorkshire (purch. by the Saviles c. 1705 from the Reresbys, passed through heiresses 1803 to Fullertons, rebuilt early 19th c., leased to golf club from 1903, sold later in 20th c.)
Estates: Bateman 3331 (E) 13000
Notes: Two in ODNB.

SAMBROOKE [Vanacker]

Origins: Rose as merchants in the 17th century in London. The 1 Bt was a Turkey merchant (as was John Sambrooke MP below). Sir Samuel Sambrooke 3 Bt succeeded to his baronetcy by special remainder from Sir John Vanacker 2 Bt.

1. Sir Samuel Sambrooke 3 Bt – Bramber 1704-05 Great Bedwyn 1708-10
2. John Sambrooke – Dunwich 1726-27 Wenlock 1727-34
3. Sir Jeremy Vanacker-Sambrooke 4 Bt – Bedford 1731-40

Seat: Bush Hill Park, Middlesex (built early 17th c., purch. 1682, sold 1745, demolished 1929)
Estates: Worth £12,000 pa in the 18th century.
Title: Baronet 1701-54

SAMUELSON

Origins: The first MP, son of a merchant in Hull, founded a business for manufacturing agricultural implements, exploited a new process in large iron ore deposits in Yorkshire (his blast furnaces produced 300,000 tons of pig iron annually in 1905), and was a pioneer of technical education. High Sheriff 1917.

1. Sir Bernhard Samuelson 1 Bt – Banbury 1859 1865-85 Banbury Div. Oxfordshire 1885-95
2. Sir Henry Samuelson 2 Bt – Cheltenham 1868-74 Frome 1876-85
3. Godfrey Samuelson – Forest of Dean Div. Gloucestershire 1887-92

Seats: Hatchford Park, Surrey (built 17th c., rebuilt 1850s, remod. c. 1890, purch. c. 1900, sold c. 1930, fire 1990s); Bodicote Grange, Oxfordshire (purch. c. 1860s, still own)
Estates: 1 Bt died worth three-quarters of a million pounds in 1905.
Title: Baronet 1884-
Notes: 1 Bt in ODNB.

SANDES *IRELAND*

Origins: Went to Ireland with Cromwell in 1640s as a soldier. Acquired O'Conor estates. Sheriff 1666.

1. Lancelot Sandes – {Dingle 1661-66}
2. William Sandes – {County Kerry 1697-99}
3. Lancelot Sandes – {Portarlington 1723-27}

Seats: Carrigafoyle Castle (House), Kerry (built c. 1500, damaged in war, acq. 1652, ruin part restored, placed in care of Public Works 1937, still own); Sallow Glen (Sallowglen), Kerry (acq. later 17th c., rebuilt mid-18th c., add. later 18th c., sold c. 1929, demolished 1942); Oak Park (Killeen), Kerry (built late 17th c., rebuilt 1820, purch. 1849, rebuilt 1857-60, sold 1922, institutional use)
Estates: Bateman 7143 (I) 2783 and 11172 (I) 3297
Notes: The rebuilder of Oak Park in 1857 made a fortune in India.

SANDFORD *IRELAND*

Baron Mount Sandford (1800-46 I)

Origins: Founded by a soldier in Ireland during the Civil War. Sheriff 1694.

1. Henry Sandford – {Roscommon 1692-93 1695-99 1703-33}
2. Robert Sandford – {Boyle 1715-27 Newcastle 1727-60}
3. Edward Sandford – {Roscommon 1733 1759-60 Harristown 1761-68}
4. William Sandford – {Roscommon 1733-59}
5. Henry Sandford – {County Roscommon 1741-60 Kildare 1761-68 Carrick 1768-76}
6. Robert Sandford – {Athy 1753-68 Roscommon 1768-83}
7. George Sandford 3 Baron Mount Sandford – {Roscommon 1783-99}
8. Henry Sandford 1 Baron Mount Sandford – {Roscommon 1776-83 1791-1800}

Seat: Castlerea House, Roscommon (acq. 1667, built 18th c., remod. 19th c., sold and demolished early 20th c., public park)
Estates: Bateman 24410 (I) 10194. The last Lord Mount Sandford left £100,000 in 1846 plus property.
Notes: Part of estates passed 1846 to the Wills family via mar. of 1816 to the heiress of the last Lord Mount Sandford including Castlerea House. They adopted the additional name Sandford. The Wills arrived in Ireland in a military role later 17th c. Sheriff 1708. Seat at Willsgrove, Roscommon built later 17th c.

SANDILANDS *SCOTLAND*

Baron Torphichen (1564- S)

Origins: The family emerged in the 14th century. One married a daughter of the Regent of Scotland 1346. **First [MP 1560]. Two further [MPs 1596-1649, one for Linlithgowshire].**

No post-1660 MPs

Seat: Calder House (Hall), Edinburghshire (acq. 1348, built mid-16th c., add. early and late 17th c., remod. c. 1820, still own)
Estates: Under 2000 acres in Bateman.
Peers: [2 peers 1661-96 1704-07] 2 Scottish Rep peers 1790-1802 1894-1915
Notes: 1 and 7 Barons in ODNB.

SANKEY *IRELAND*

Origins: A younger son of old gentry in Shropshire went to Ireland as a Cromwellian officer in 1646 and acquired estates. **First MP 1659. First Irish {MP 1654}.**

1. Richard Sankey – {Fethard 1692-93}
2. William Sankey – {Philipstown 1790-97}

Seat: Coolmore, Tipperary (acq. 1723, sold 1920, business use)
Estates: 1250 (I) 944 in 1878. Originally granted 12,700 acres in Kerry in 17th c.

SAUNDERS *IRELAND*

Origins: The founder went to Ireland with Cromwell and was later appointed Governor of Kinsale. Acquired estates 1679. Sheriff 1707. The estates later passed to the Pendreds, who came to Ireland with William III and changed their name to Saunders.

1. Anderson Saunders – {Taghmon 1692-93 1695-99 1703-18}
2. Robert Saunders – {Cavan 1692-93 1695-99 1703-08}
3. Morley Saunders – {Enniscorthy 1703-14}
4. Anderson Saunders – {Ennicorthy 1740-60}

Seat: Saunders Grove, Wicklow (purch. early 18th c., built 1716, remod. c. 1740, burned 1923, rebuilt 1925, sold)
Estates: Bateman 3143 (I) 2059. Worth £1,200 pa in 1713.

SAUNDERSON (Sanderson) *IRELAND*

Origins: The son of an Edinburgh merchant emigrated to Ireland in 1613 and acquired 1,000 acres by 1619. Sheriff 1622. Acquired much larger estate during the aftermath of the Civil War. (Jackson, *Colonel Edward Saunderson*, 11)

1. Robert Sanderson – {County Cavan 1692-93 1695-99 1713-14}
2. James Saunderson – {Enniskillen 1727-60}
3. Francis Saunderson – {County Cavan 1788-1800} 1801-06
4. Alexander Saunderson – Cavan 1826-31
5. Edward Saunderson – County Cavan 1865-74 N. Armagh 1885-1906

Seat: Castle Saunderson, Cavan (built mid-17th c., burned 1689 and rebuilt 18th c., major alterations 1840s, looted in the early 1920s, abandoned by family 1927, sold 1977, burned later)
Estates: Bateman 12361 (I) 7370. More than 10,000 acres sold to tenants c. 1908. (Blake, *Abandoned Mansions of Ireland II*, 13)
1 Ld Lt 19th
Note: Changed name from Sanderson to Saunderson 1750s. Cadet line at Dromkeen, Cavan 4160 (I) 2664. One in ODNB.

SAYER

Origins: Originated as cloth makers in Essex in the 16th century. Purchased land worth £540 pa in the 1540s. Courtiers in the 17th century. Kt 1649. **First MP 1554. Another MP 1645.**

1. George Sayer – Canterbury 1695-1705

Seats: Pett Place, Kent (built 16th c., acq. by mar. 1685, rebuilt early 18th c., add. 19th c., sold by 1945); Bourchiers Hall, Essex (built 15th and 16th c., purch. c. 1566, sold 1724)
Estates: Bateman 2075 (E) 2712
Notes: Still in BLG in 20th c.

SCARLETT *ENGLAND & SCOTLAND*

Baron Abinger (1835- UK)

Origins: The first MP was a younger son of a planter family in Jamaica founded by the captain of a merchantman in the later 17th century. The 1 Baron returned to England in 1785 and became a barrister. Attorney General 1825.

1. James Scarlett 1 Baron Abinger – Peterborough 1819-30 Malton 1830-31 Cockermouth 1831-32 Norwich 1832-34
2. Robert Scarlett 2 Baron Abinger – Norwich 1835-38 Horsham 1841-44
3. James Scarlett – Guildford 1837-41

Seats: Abinger Hall, Surrey (purch. 1814, sold 1867); Inverlochie (Inverlochy) Castle, Inverness-shire (medieval castle, now ruin, purch. and new house built 1863, add. 1889-92, requisitioned WWII, sold 1944, hotel)
Estates: Bateman 40419 (S & E) 5035
Peers: 8 peers 1835-1945
Notes: 1 Baron and three others in ODNB.

SCAWEN

Origins: A Cornish family known in the reign of Edward I. Robert Scawen was a successful London attorney who purchased estates in Buckinghamshire in the mid-17th century. His son was a clothing contractor and successful financier, who added to the family properties c. 1700. His son was an eminent merchant and Director of the Bank of England in the early 18th century. **First MP 1640.**

1. Robert Scawen – Berwick 1640-53 Grampound 1659 Cockermouth 1662-70
2. Sir William Scawen – New Windsor 1693-98 Grampound 1698-1702 Surrey 1705-10 1721-22
3. Sir Thomas Scawen – Grampound 1708-10 London 1715-22
4. Thomas Scawen – Surrey 1727-41
5. James Scawen – Mitchell 1761-74 Surrey 1774-80

Seats: Carshalton Park (not House), Surrey (purch. c. 1700, demolished c. 1890); Horton, Buckinghamshire (purch. 1658, sold 1779); Maidwell Hall, Northamptonshire (built 1637, acq. by mar. mid-18th c., sold by 1781, fire 1895, school)
Estates: Worth perhaps £200,000 in 1730. Bankrupted by last MP and estates sold by 1781.
Notes: Two in ODNB.

SCHOMBERG

Duke of Schomberg (1689-1719 E)

Origins: The 1 Duke was a professional soldier from the Palatinate. He fought first for Louis XIV and then William III. Master General of the Ordnance 1689.

No MPs

Seat: Hillingdon House, Middlesex (old house, purch. 1698, rebuilt 1717, sold soon after 1719, fire c. 1840, rebuilt 1844, institutional and business use)
Estates: Granted £100,000 by Parliament 1688.
Title: Duke of Leinster 1691-1719 E
Peers: 3 peers 1689-1719
2 KG 17th, 18th
Notes: 1, 2, and 3 Dukes in ODNB.

SCOTT I *IRELAND*

Earl of Clonmell (1793-1935 I)

Origins: The founder of the family was a Captain in William III's army killed in the Irish war, who gained a modest estate. His son was a clergyman. His grandson, the 1 Earl, was a barrister and Chief Justice of the King's Bench in Ireland 1784. He earned £15,000 pa in the 1780s and purchased estates, but even so the extent of his wealth is somewhat mysterious. (Malcolmson, *John Foster: the Politics of the Anglo-Irish Ascendancy*, 5)

1. John Scott 1 Earl of Clonmell – {Mullingar 1769-83 Portarlington 1783-84}
2. Thomas Scott 2 Earl of Clonmell – New Romney 1807-12

Seats: Bishopscourt (Bishop's Court), Kildare (built 1780-90, purch. 1838, sold c. 1896); Eathorpe Hall, Warwickshire (built 1759, purch. 1858, sold 1930s)
Estates: Bateman 27646 (I) 17140. Worth £15,000 pa in the 1780s, £20,000-25,000 pa in 1799.
Titles: Baron Earlsfort 1784-1935 I; Viscount Clonmell 1789-1935 I
Peers: {1 peer 1784-98} 1 Irish Rep peer 1874-91
Notes: The 1 Earl was seen by other aristocrats as a self-made man and upstart, a "novus homo". (*DNB*, XVII, 983) Estates were sold on the death of the 5 Earl in 1896. 1 Earl in ODNB.

SCOTT II

Origins: The first MP made a fortune as a brick maker in the mid-18th century.

1. Thomas Scott – Bridport 1780-90
2. James Scott – Bridport 1820-26
3. James Scott – N. Hampshire 1832-37

Seat: Rotherfield Park, Hampshire (purch. 1808, rebuilt 1815-21, remod. 1860s and 1893, still own)
Estates: Bateman 3164 (E) 2933

SCOTT III

Origins: The 1 Baronet's father is unknown. The son was a self-made entrepreneur: government grain contractor, corn merchant, and banker. The 2 Baronet continued in the business.

1. Sir Claude Scott 1 Bt – Malmesbury 1802-06 Dungannon 1809-1812
2. Sir Samuel Scott 2 Bt – Malmesbury 1802-06 Camelford 1812-18 Whitchurch 1818-32
3. Sir Samuel Scott 6 Bt – West Marylebone 1898-1918 St. Marylebone 1918-22

Seats: Lytchet Minster (South Lytchett House), Dorset (purch. c. 1810, sold later 19th c.); Sundridge Park, Kent (old house, rebuilt in 18th c., purch. 1796, rebuilt later 1790s, add. 1870s, house sold 1920, estate sold 1976)
Estates: Bateman 59923 (S & E) 5752. The 2 Bt was worth £300,000 in 1813 and died worth over £700,000 in 1849.
Notes: Owned an estate on North Harris in the Outer Hebrides.

SCOTT IV *SCOTLAND*

Scott

Origins: This family shared descent with the Dukes of Buccleuch (see Montagu I) back to the 12th century. Three separate lines emerged in the mid-16th century descended from Sir William Scott of Balwearie. **First [MP 1593]. One additional [MP 1640].**

1. James Scott – [Forfarshire 1693-1702]
2. James Scott – [Forfarshire 1698-1702 Montrose Burgh 1703-07] Scotland 1707-08 Aberdeen Burghs 1710-11 Forfarshire 1716-36

Seats: Logie House, Forfarshire (purch. sec. half 16th c., passed out of family via an heiress late 18th c., demolished 1910); Castlested, Forfarshire; Brotherton Castle, Kincardineshire (purch. 1560, house built, demolished 1862, new house 1868, school 1949); Benholm Castle, Kincardineshire (built 15th c., purch. 1659, add. 18th c. and 19th c., derelict after 1945, part ruin 1990s)
Estates: 3912 (S) 5388
Notes: Three in ODNB.

Scott

Origins: Cadet of the Logie family. Robert Scott MP, Director of the East India Company, purchased Dunninald.

1. James Scott – Kincardineshire 1713-34
2. Robert Scott – Forfarshire 1733-34
3. David Scott – Forfarshire 1790-96 Perth Burghs 1796-1805
4. Sir David Scott 2 Bt – Yarmouth (IoW) 1806
5. Montagu Scott – E. Sussex 1874-85

Seats: Dunninald, Forfarshire (purch. late 17th c, sold 1811); Commieston, Kincardineshire; Sillwood (Silwood) Park, Berkshire (built 1769, demolished 1875, new house 1876, demolished)
Title: Baronet 1806-
Notes: One in ODNB.

Scott

Origins: Cadet line.

1. Sir John Scott 1 Bt – [Roxburghshire 1665]
2. Sir Patrick Scott 2 Bt – [Roxburghshire 1685-86 1689-90]
3. Sir William Scott 6 Bt – Carlisle 1829-30 Roxburghshire 1859-70

Seat: Ancrum House, Roxburghshire (acq. from the Ker family early 16th c., built 1558, destroyed by fire 1873, rebuilt and burned again 1885, rebuilt again, demolished 1970)
Estates: 2516 (S) 4753
Title: Baronet 1671-1902

SCOTT V

Earl of Eldon (1821- UK)

Origins: The 1 Earl was the grandson of a yeoman and son of a successful coal merchant in Newcastle, who left his two sons c. £25,000. The elder eloped with a banker's heiress and became Lord Chancellor, while the younger was also a leading judge. (Cannon, *Aristocratic Century*, 22) One became an Earl and the other a Baron.

1. John Scott 1 Earl of Eldon – Weobley 1783-96 Boroughbridge 1796-99
2. William Scott 1 Baron Stowell – Downton 1790-1801 University of Oxford 1801-21
3. John Scott – Boroughbridge 1799-1804
4. William Scott – Heytesbury 1818-20 Hastings 1820-26 Newport (IoW) 1826-30
5. William Scott – Gatton 1826-30
6. John Scott 2 Earl of Eldon – Truro 1829-32

Seats: Encombe House, Dorset (built c. 1730s, purch. 1807 for £56,000, remod. 1870s, sold 2003, retained part of the estate); Stowell Park, Gloucestershire (built early 17th c., purch. 1811, perhaps for £165,000, enlarged 1885-98 and 1918-20, sold 1923); Erleigh Court, Berkshire (built 16th c., acq. by mar. 1828, passed out of family via an heiress 1836, demolished 1935)
Estates: Bateman 35761 (E) 28457. Rubinstein - the 1 Baron Stowell left £250,000 in probate and land worth £12,000 pa, and the 1 Earl of Eldon £700,000 in 1838. The Stowell Park estate stood at about 5,000 acres in 1973.
Titles: Baron Eldon 1799- GB; Baron Stowell 1821-1835 UK
Peers: 5 peers 1799-1854 1821-36 1866-1945
1 in Cabinet 1801-06 1807-27
Notes: 1 Baron Stowell and 1 Earl of Eldon and one other in ODNB.

SCROPE (Scroop) [Lister, Poulett, Thomsen]

Scrope

Origins: The Scropes held land in Lincolnshire since the 12th century. One was Lord Chancellor another Chief Justice of the King's Bench, yet another Archbishop of York in the 14th century. Summoned as a Baron 1309, and regularly from 1350. (Denholm-Young, *The Country Gentry in the Fourteenth Century*, 132-33). Earl of Wiltshire (attainted). Earl of Sunderland (1627 – extinct) **First MP 1364 for Yorkshire. Six additional MPs 1365-1601, four kts of the shire**. The main line of the family died out in 1630. A cadet line was established at Cockerington in the 16th century.

1. Sir Adrian Scrope – Great Grimsby 1661-66

2. John Scrope – Ripon 1722-27 Bristol 1727-34 Lyme Regis 1734-52
3. Thomas Scrope – Lincoln 1768-74

Seats: Cockerington Hall, Lincolnshire (purch. 1565, rebuilt 18th c., passed to Thomson Scropes 1821, and then inher. by Scropes of Danby 1866, sold and demolished 1921); Wormsley Hall (House), Oxfordshire (acq. c. 1600, passed to Fanes by mar.); Coleby Hall, Lincolnshire (acq. by mar. from Listers 1731, passed to Tempests of Broughton 1792); Danby Hall, Yorkshire (built 14th c., acq. later 16th c. through mar. to a Conyers heiress, add. 1570, remod. 1855, still own)
Estates: John Scrope MP above died 1752 worth £2,000 pa and with £100,000 in money. The Danby Hall estate was 1,500 acres in 2012.
Title: Baronet 1667-80
Notes: Most Scropes were Roman Catholic. 1 of Masham and 1 of Bolton, 3, 5, and 9 Barons Scrope and Earl of Wiltshire and Earl of Sunderland and eight others in ODNB.

Lister

Origins: The Listers were settled at Wakefield in Yorkshire since the 15th century. Sir Richard Lister was Chief Justice of the King's Bench. Thomas Scrope married the daughter and heiress of Thomas Lister of Coleby Hall (see above). **First MP 1647.**

1. Thomas Lister – Lincoln 1705-15

Seat: Coleby Hall, Lincolnshire (acq. 1625, built c. 1628, add. 18th c., passed by mar. to Scropes 1731)
Estates: Worth c. £3,000 pa in 1730s. (Leach, *Lincolnshire Country Houses, Part Two*, 154)
Notes: One in ODNB.

Baron Sydenham (1840-41 UK) (Thomson)

Origins: George Poulett Thomson married in 1821 Emma, the heiress of William Scrope of Cockerington, and took the additional name Scrope in 1852. His brother was created Baron Sydenham. The Thomsons were bankers in Edinburgh in the mid-18th century and London in the 19th century. The 1 Baron was the son of a Russia merchant.

1. Charles Poulett Thomson 1 Baron Sydenham – Dover 1826-32 Manchester 1832-39
2. George Poulett Thomson Scrope – Stroud 1833-67

Seats: Manor House, Castle Combe, Wiltshire (passed by heiresses through several families from c. 1315 to the Scropes and eventually to the Thomsons by mar. in 1821, sold 1866); Cockerington Hall, Lincolnshire (inher. from Scropes – see above – 1821, later passed to Scropes of Danby 1866)

Estates: George Poulett Thomson Scrope of Castle Combe, inherited the Scrope landed estate and left £180,000 in personality in 1876. His brother Lord Sydenham also inherited business wealth and made some as well.
Peer: 1 peer 1840-41
1 in Cabinet 1834-39
Notes: 1 Baron and two others in ODNB.

Angerstein

Origins: John Julius Angerstein was probably the illegitimate son of the 1 Baron Sydenham's father (the mother may have been Empress Anna of Russia). He came to London from St. Petersburg c. 1750 and began a brilliant financial career at the Poulett Thomson's business premises. Sheriff 1831.

1. John Angerstein – Camelford 1796-1802 Greenwich 1835-37
2. William Angerstein – Greenwich 1859-65

Seats: Weeting Hall, Norfolk (purch. 1808, built early 19th c., sold 1901, demolished 1952); Woodlands House, Kent (purch. and built 1774-76, add. c. 1800 and 1818, sold 1876, now derelict)
Estates: Bateman 19731 (E) 17512. Also held urban property in London. Purch. 6,000 acres in Norfolk/Suffolk 1810. 38 paintings from the great collection of the founder were sold to the government for £57,000 in 1824 and became the core of the National Gallery. John Julius Angerstein left an estate of £500,000 plus landed property in 1823 (Rubinstein).
Notes: One in ODNB.

SCUDAMORE (Skydmore)

Viscount Scudamore (1628-1716 I)

Origins: Claim to have been in England before the Conquest (Skidmore, *The Scudamores of Upton Scudamore*, 1). Norman tenants in the Domesday Book. **First MP 1397 for Herefordshire. Four additional MPs 1529-1654, all for the county.**

1. James Scudamore – Hereford 1642-44 Herefordshire 1661-68
2. John Scudamore 2 Viscount Scudamore – Hereford 1673-79 Herefordshire 1679-81
3. James Scudamore 3 Viscount Scudamore – Herefordshire 1705-15 Hereford 1715-16

Seat: Holme Lacy, Herefordshire (acq. by mar. mid-14th c., rebuilt 1540s. rebuilt 1672, remod. 1828-31, sold by 10 Earl of Chesterfield 1909); Caradoc Court, Herefordshire (built 16th c. and c. 1620, passed to the Digbys in 1716); Ballingham Hall, Herefordshire

(built 1602 by Scudamore cadet line (Bts 1644-1727), remod. c. 1660-70, last Bt sold house to cousin the 3 Viscount in 1704, sold 1909)
Estates: Bateman 5192 (E) 6480. 1 Viscount died worth £4,000 pa in 1671. Holme Lacy estate estimated to be worth £30,000 pa in 18th c.
Peers: {3 peers 1660-97 1705-16}
Notes: On the death of the 3 Viscount in 1716 the family estates passed to Charles Fitzroy (Dukes of Grafton – see Hervey), whose daughter Frances married the Duke of Norfolk. On her death in 1820 they passed to a descendent of the 1 Viscount, sister of the 9 Earl of Chesterfield, whose multiple descendents sold them (see Stanhope). Scudamore family has an entry along with 1 Viscount and two others in the ODNB.

Scudamore

Origins: Cousins of the Viscount Scudamore (separated in the 14th century). **First MP 1414 for Herefordshire.**

1. John Scudamore – Hereford 1764-96
2. John Scudamore – Hereford 1796-1805
3. Richard Scudamore – Hereford 1805-18 1819-26

Seats: Kentchurch Court, Herefordshire (acq. and built 14th c., remod. c. 1700, rebuilt. 1795-1825, still own); Pontrilas Court, Herefordshire (built c. 1630, purch. 1840, became an inn by 1870s, sold)
Estates: Bateman 6510 (E & W) 5349. Owned 5,000 acres in 2001.
Notes: The finances of the last MP were in disarray in the 1820s.

SEBRIGHT

Origins: Landowners in Essex from at least the reign of Edward I. **First MP 1572.** Sheriff 1621. Baronet 1626.

1. Sir Thomas Sebright 4 Bt – Hertfordshire 1715-36
2. Sir John Sebright 6 Bt – Bath 1763-74 1775-80
3. Sir John Sebright 7 Bt – Hertfordshire 1807-34

Seats: Besford Court, Worcestershire (built c. 1500, remod. c. 1600, purch. 1606, sold 1885, institutional use); Beechwood Park, Hertfordshire (purch. by Thomas Saunders 1628 and passed by heiress to the 3rd Sebright Bt 1693, add. c. 1702, add. mid-18th c., remod. c. 1804, remod. 1859, sold 1954, school)
Estates: 7210 (E) 13567
Title: Baronet 1626-
Notes: 7 Bt in ODNB.

SEELY

Baron Sherwood (1941-70 UK)

Origins: Colliery owners in Nottinghamshire in the 19th century. Sheriff 1860.

1. Charles Seely – Lincoln 1847-48 1861-85
2. Sir Charles Seely 1 Bt – Nottingham 1869-74 1880-85 W. Nottingham 1885-86 1892-95
3. Sir Charles Seely 2 Bt – Lincoln 1895-1906 Mansfield Div. Nottinghamshire 1916-18
4. John Seely 1 Baron Mottistone – Isle of Wight 1900-06 Abercromby Div. Liverpool 1906-10 Illkeston Div. Derbyshire 1910-22 Isle of Wight 1923-24
5. Hugh Seely 1 Baron Sherwood – E. Div. Norfolk 1923-24 Berwick-on-Tweed 1935-41

Seats: Brooke House, Hampshire (IoW) (medieval, rebuilt 18th c., purch. 1856, requisitioned WWII, sold c. 1941); Sherwood Lodge, Nottinghamshire (purch. mid-19th c., add. c. 1860s, sold and demolished 1930s); Furzedown Park (House), Middlesex (built 1794, acq. mid-19th c.?, add. 1860s, sold c. 1900, institutional use); Gatcombe House, Hampshire (IoW) (old house, rebuilt 1750-51, purch. 1873, sold 1926); Mottistone Manor, Hampshire (IoW) (built 15th c., add. 1567, purch. 1861, restored 1926, NT 1963)
Estates: Bateman 9720 (E) 14666
Titles: Baron Mottistone 1933- UK; Baronet 1896-
Peers: 2 peers 1933-45 1941-45
1 Ld Lt 20th
1 in Cabinet 1912
Notes: 1 Baron Mottistone in ODNB.

SELWYN

Origins: Began as clothiers near Stroud. A London lawyer purchased estates 1597-1614. A lieutenant general and Governor of Jamaica in the 17th century.

1. William Selwyn – Gloucester 1698-1701
2. John Selwyn – Truro 1715-21 Whitchurch 1727-34 Gloucester 1734-51
3. Charles Selwyn – Mitchell 1722-27 Gloucester 1728-34 Ludgershall 1741-47
4. John Selwyn – Whitchurch 1734-51
5. George Selwyn – Ludgershall 1747-54 Gloucestershire 1754-80 Ludgershall 1780-91
6. William Selwyn – Whitchurch 1783-90
7. Sir Charles Selwyn – University of Cambridge 1859-68
8. Charles Selwyn – Wisbech Div. Cambridgeshire 1886-91

Seat: Matson House, Gloucestershire (built 1575-76, purch. 1598, remod. c. 1720, passed by mar. 1791 to 1 Viscount Sydney)

Notes: The Selwyn estates passed by marriage to Thomas Townshend 1 Viscount Sydney (see Townshend). Six in ODNB.

SEVERNE [Wodhull]

Origins: John Severne succeeded by marriage to Thenford from Michael Wodhull (Woodhull) (d. 1816). He was the heir male of the medieval Barons of Wahull or Wodhull, a Norman family granted land in Bedfordshire in 1068, **summoned to Parliament by writ 1283 and 1297**.

1. John Severne – Ludlow 1865-68 S. Shropshire 1876-85

Seats: Thenford House (Hall), Northamptonshire (medieval, acq. and remod. by Wodhulls in the 16th c., new house 1761-65, acq. by mar. by Severnes 1816, sold 1977); Wallop Hall, Shropshire (acq. and built mid-late 17th c., rebuilt 1870, demolished 1953)
Estates: Bateman 5546 (E & W) 7294
Notes: One Wodhull in ODNB.

SEYMOUR (St. Maur) [Conway, Ingram, Machell, Wallace] *ENGLAND, WALES & IRELAND*

Duke of Somerset (1547- E)

Origins: Established in Monmouthshire by 1128. Acquired Somerset estates by marriage to an heiress in the 14th century. Rose high in politics and war with royal favor under the Tudors. **First MP 1353 for Wiltshire. Seventeen further MPs 1388-1641, seven kts of the shire**. The Dukedom peregrinated through the family on a somewhat erratic course. The 1 Duke was attainted in 1552. The title was restored for his great-great-grandson in 1660 (created Marquess of Hertford in 1641). On the death of the 4 Duke the title passed to near cousins, the Barons Seymour of Trowbridge. The 6 Duke married the heiress of the last Earl of Northumberland (see Percy). On the death of the 7 Duke the estates were split between his daughter (whose husband took the name Percy and was created Duke of Northumberland) and his sister's son, Charles Wyndham, who became 2 Earl of Egremont (see Wyndham). The Dukedom passed to distant cousins seated at Berry Pomeroy in Devon. Since this was a distinct family, the Seymours below are divided between the pre-Percy Dukes (A) and the Berry Pomeroy Dukes (B).

Somerset A

1. Charles Seymour 2 Baron Seymour – Great Bedwyn 1640 Wiltshire 1661-64
2. John Seymour 4 Duke of Somerset – Marlborough 1661-72

3. William Seymour – Cockermouth 1698-1702 Totnes 1702-05 Newport (IoW) 1710-13
4. Algernon Seymour 7 Duke of Somerset – Marlborough 1705-08 Northumberland 1708-22
5. Lord Percy Seymour – Cockermouth 1718-21

Seats: Allington House, Wiltshire (built early 17th c., acq. by mar. c. 1635, allowed to decline into a farm house); Marlborough Castle, Wiltshire (ceased to be inhabited 1370, ruin by 1403, acq. c. 1550, new house early 16th c., rebuilt 1683-84, family departed and it declined to a coaching inn mid-18th c., now school); Petworth, Sussex (acq. 1150, built 1260s and 1309-15, passed via the mar. of Lady Elizabeth Percy to the Dukes of Somerset 1670, rebuilt 1688-96, passed to Wyndhams 1750); Cockermouth Castle, Cumberland (built mid-13th c. and c. 1360-70, passed from the Percys by mar. to Seymours, passed by mar. 1750 to the Wyndhams); Isel Hall, Cumberland (leased? see Lawson); Alnwick Castle, Northumberland (see Percy)
Estates: see Duke of Northumberland and Seymour B below.
Titles: Baron Seymour of Trowbridge 1641-1750 E; Earl of Egremont 1749-50 GB
Peers: 6 peers 1660 1660-65 1671-75 1683-1748 1723-50
3 Lds Lt 17th, 18th
2 in Cabinet 1660-64 1702
2 KG 17th, 18th
Notes: 1, 2, 6, and 7 Dukes and eight others in ODNB.

Somerset B

1. Sir Edward Seymour 3 Bt – Devon 1640-43 1660 Totnes 1661-81 1685-87
2. Sir Edward Seymour 4 Bt – Hindon 1661-79 Devon 1679 Totnes 1679-81 Exeter 1685-87 1689-95 Totnes 1695-98 Exeter 1698-1708
3. Sir Edward Seymour 5 Bt – West Looe 1690-95 Totnes 1708-10 Great Bedwyn 1711-15
4. Charles Seymour – West Looe 1703-05
5. Edward Seymour – Shaftesbury 1710-11
6. Edward Seymour 8 Duke of Somerset – Salisbury 1741-47
7. Edward Seymour 12 Duke of Somerset – Okehampton 1830-31 Totnes 1834-55
8. Richard St. Maur – Exeter 1910

Seats: Berry Pomeroy, Devon (built 11th c., add. c. 1485-95, purch. 1548, add. c. 1560, add. c. 1600-10, family departed for Maiden Bradley 1690s and Berry Pomeroy became a ruin, the 18 Duke placed it in care of the state 1970s); Maiden Bradley House (Bradley House), Wiltshire (acq. c. 1540, rebuilt c. 1690-1710, remod. early 19th c., still own); Bulstrode Park, Buckinghamshire (built 1676-85, remod. 1806-09, purch. 1810, rebuilt 1861-70, passed by mar. to Ramsdens 1885, estate sold 1932, house sold c. 1958, institutional use)
Estates: Bateman 25387 (E) 37577. Owned 2,000 aces in 2001.

Titles: Viscount Beauchamp 1536- E; Earl of Hertford 1537- E; Baron Seymour 1546- E; Earl St. Maur 1863-85 UK; Baronet 1611-
Peers: 11 peers 1750-93 1796-1945 1863-69
3 Lds Lt 19th, 20th
1 in Cabinet 1851-52 1859-66
2 KG 19th
Notes: Victorian Dukes of Somerset took up the "old" spelling of Seymour – St. Maur. The 3 Bt of Berry Pomeroy married the daughter of the 1st Portman Bt of Orchard Portman. A younger daughter of the 4 Bt inherited the Portman estates and her husband, William Berkeley of Pylle took the name Portman. Their descendents were created Viscounts Portman (see Berkeley). 11 and 12 Dukes and four others in ODNB.

Seymour

Origins: Descended from a younger son of the 2 Bt of Berry Pomeroy. The estates passed to Sir Edward Seymour 5 Bt above on the extinction of the line in 1714.

1. Henry Seymour – East Looe 1660-81
2. Sir Henry Seymour 1 Bt – East Looe 1699-1713

Seat: Langley Park (Langley Marish), Buckinghamshire (purch. 1674, sold 1714)
Title: Baronet 1681-1714

Marquess of Hertford (1793- GB)

Origins: The estates of the Earl of Conway passed by marriage to the younger sons of the 4 Bt of Berry Pomeroy. The heir took the name Conway. The Conways descended from William the Conqueror's High Constable. For a history of this family see under Taylour. This was a cadet line that rose as officials under the Tudors and early Stuarts and acquired estates in the later 16th century and early 17th century. Kt c. 1500, Baron 1625. **First MP 1558 for Flintshire. Four further MPs 1610-28. In addition three Irish {MPs 1613-39}.** The 4 Marquess of Hertford left his large Irish estates to his illegitimate son, Sir Richard Wallace 1 Bt, who also purchased the family's Suffolk estate from the 5 Marquess.

1. Popham Conway – {Lisburn 1697-99}
2. Francis Seymour Conway 1 Baron Conway – Bramber 1701-03
3. Henry Seymour Conway – {County Antrim 1741-69} Higham Ferrers 1741-47 Penryn 1747-54 St. Mawes 1754-61 Thetford 1761-74 Bury St. Edmunds 1775-84
4. Francis Ingram-Seymour Conway 2 Marquess of Hertford – {Lisburn 1761-68} Lostwithiel 1766-68 {County Antrim 1768-76} Orford 1768-94

5. Henry Seymour Conway – {County Down 1766-68} Coventry 1766-74 Midhurst 1774-80 {County Antrim 1776-83} Downton 1780-84
6. Lord Robert Seymour Conway – {Lisburn 1771-76} Orford 1771-84 Wootton Bassett 1784-90 Orford 1794-1807 Carmarthenshire 1807-20
7. Lord William Seymour Conway – Coventry 1783-84 Downton 1785-90 Orford 1790-96
8. Lord Hugh Seymour Conway – Newport (IoW) 1784-86 Tregony 1788-90 Wendover 1790-96 Portsmouth 1796-1801
9. Lord George Seymour Conway – Orford 1784-90 Totnes 1796-1801
10. Francis Seymour Conway 3 Marquess of Hertford – Orford 1797-1802 Lisburn 1802-12 Antrim 1812-18 Camelford 1820-22
11. Henry Seymour Conway – County Antrim 1818-21
12. Sir Horace Seymour Conway – Lisburn 1819-26 Bodmin 1826-32 Midhurst 1841-45 County Antrim 1845-47 Lisburn 1847-51
13. Richard Seymour Conway 4 Marquess of Hertford – Antrim 1822-26
14. Henry Conway Seymour – County Antrim 1865-69
15. George Seymour – Antrim 1865-69
16. Hugh Conway Seymour 6 Marquess of Hertford – County Antrim 1869-74 S. Warwickshire 1874-80
17. Sir Richard Wallace 1 Bt – Lisburn 1873-85 (illegitimate son)

Seats: Ragley Hall, Warwickshire (medieval castle, purch. Ragley Castle 1591, new house begun 1680-90, resumed 1749-60, 1780s, still own); Sudbourne Hall, Suffolk (built early 17th c., purch. 1743, rebuilt 1784, purch. by Sir Richard Wallace 1871, sold 1884, demolished 1951); Park Place, Berkshire (built c. 1720, purch 1752 by Conways, remod. 1780s, sold 1797); Lisburn Castle, Antrim (built 16th c.?, acq. by Conway 1611, house built 1622, fire 1707, new house aka "Castle House" 1870s, donated to town 1903)
Estates: Bateman 84596 (E & I) 104129. Worth about £70,000 pa c. 1700. 70,000 acres worth £43,000 pa in 1817. Rubinstein – 2 Marquess left £300,000 in probate in 1822 and the Dowager Marchioness £180,000 in 1834.
Titles: Baron Conway 1625-83 E; Viscount Conway 1627-83 E; Viscount Kiltulagh 1627-83 I; Earl of Conway 1679-83 E; Baron Conway 1703- E; Baron Conway 1712- I; Viscount Beauchamp and Earl of Hertford 1750- GB; Earl of Yarmouth 1793- GB; Baron Alcester 1882-95 UK; Baronet 1871-90
Peers: {4 peers 1660-83 1712-32 1739-1800} 9 peers 1660-83 1703-32 1739-1940
5 Lds Lt 17th, 18th, 19th, 20th
3 in Cabinet 1681-83 1755-57 1765-68 1765-66 1782
4 KG 18th, 19th
Notes: Sir Richard Wallace donated the Wallace Collection housed in Hertford House, London. 1 Baron Alcester and 1 and 2 Viscounts Conway and 1 Earl and 1, 2, 3, and 4 Marquesses and ten others in ODNB.

Viscount Irvine (1661-1778 S)

Origins: A London linen draper, son of a tallow chandler, built a fortune as a revenue farmer and invested in land. His son was also at first a userer and merchant. **MP 1609-42**, Kt 1613, Viscount 1661. The family rose to the top of the Yorkshire gentry by 1640 (Cliffe, *The Yorkshire Gentry from the Reformation to the Civil War,* 30). The daughter and heiress of the 9 Viscount married the 2 Marquess of Hertford, who took the name Ingram on inheriting the Irvine estates.

1. Sir Thomas Ingram – Thirsk 1640-42 1661-72
2. Arthur Ingram 3 Viscount Irvine – Scarborough 1693-1701 Yorkshire 1701-02
3. Arthur Ingram 6 Viscount Irvine – Horsham 1715-21
4. Arthur Ingram – Horsham 1715-22
5. Henry Ingram 7 Viscount Irvine – Horsham 1722-36
6. Charles Ingram – Horsham 1737-48
7. Charles Ingram 9 Viscount Irvine – Horsham 1747-63

Seats: Temple Newsham (Newsam), Yorkshire (built early 16th c., purch. for £12,000 and rebuilt house c. 1622-37, remod. 1738-45 and 1796, passed to Woods (Earl of Halifax) by mar. 1904, sold to Leeds Corporation 1922, museum); Hills Place, Sussex
Estates: Worth £9,000 to £12,000 pa in 1642.
Peer: 1 Scottish Rep peer 1768-78
4 Lds Lt 17th, 18th
Notes: Last private owner of Temple Newsham was Edward Wood, Lord Halifax (see Wood I), nephew of the Hon. Emily Ingram. One in ODNB.

Machell

Origins: The founder was a London cloth worker, Alderman 1553. The 3 Viscount Irvine inherited the Machell family estates by marriage.

1. John Machell – Horsham 1681 1685-87 1689-1700

Seat: Hills Place, Sussex (old house, rebuilt early 17th c., purch. 1654, passed by mar. to 3 Viscount Ingram 1704, passed by mar. 1776 to 2 Marquess of Hertford, sold 1811, demolished soon afterwards)

Seymour

Origins: Francis Seymour MP was a younger brother of the 8 Duke of Somerset (see above).

1. Francis Seymour – Great Bedwyn 1732-34 Marlborough 1734-41

2. Henry Seymour – Totnes 1763-68 Huntingdon 1768-74 Evesham 1774-80
3. Henry Seymour – Taunton 1826-30
4. Henry Seymour – Poole 1850-68
5. Alfred Seymour – Totnes 1853-68 Salisbury 1869-74

Seats: Sherborne House, Dorset (built c. 1570, part demolished and rebuilt 1720, inher. 1728, sold 1799, institutional use); Knoyle House, Wiltshire (acq. 1740, remod. 1880, sold 1948, demolished 1954); Northbrooke House (Lodge), Devon
Estates: Bateman 10360 (E) 15882

SHAFTO [Duncombe]

Shafto

Origins: One early Shafto served as Mayor of Newcastle in 1548. Several generations of successful lawyers in the mid-17th century led to the purchase of landed estates. Kt 1661, High Sheriff 1705.

1. Robert Shafto – Durham 1712-13 1727-29
2. John Shafto – Durham 1730-42
3. Robert Shafto – County Durham 1760-68 Downton 1780-90
4. Robert Duncombe Shafto – Durham 1804-06
5. Robert Duncombe Shafto – N. Durham 1847-68

Seats: Whitworth Park, Durham (purch. 1652, rebuilt c. 1820, burned 1876, part rebuilt, sold 1981, hotel); Beamish Hall (Park), Durham (medieval, rebuilt early 17th c., purch. 1693 by Davisons, passed to Edens by mar. of 1739, rebuilt c. 1813, Shaftos inher. from Edens by mar. of 1803, sold 1949, golf club and hotel)
Estates: Bateman 4160 (E) 10509
Notes: Married a Duncombe heiress in the 18th century. One in ODNB.

Shafto

Origins: Cousins.

1. Jenison Shafto – Leominster 1761-68 Castle Rising 1768-71

Seats: Benwell Tower, Northumberland (built 16th c., purch. by 1608, sold mid and late-18th c., demolished 1831); Wratting Park, Cambridgeshire (built early 18th c., purch. mid-18th c., sold 1789)
Note: Jenison Shafto MP shot himself in 1771 over gambling losses and his heiress sold his estates.

SHAKERLEY

Origins: Emerged as gentry in the 13th century. Kinsman an **MP 1553**.

1. Sir Geoffrey Shakerley – Wigan 1661-79
2. Peter Shakerley – Wigan 1690-98 Chester 1698-1715

Seats: Hulme Hall, Cheshire (medieval, acq. mid and later 16th c., rebuilt 17th c., family left 1720s, became a farm house); (Lower) Gwersyllt (Guersylt) Hall (Park), Denbighshire (purch. c. 1660, fire 1738, abandoned by family); Somerford Park, Cheshire (acq. r. Henry III, built 1720s as main seat, add. late 18th c. and 1859-60, demolished 1926)
Estates: Bateman 5978 (E) 11109
Title: Baronet 1838-
Notes: In 1726 the estates passed to the half brother of the last MP, who was a Jacobite.

SHARMAN [Crawford] *IRELAND*

Sharman

Origins: Scots who were granted land in the early 17th c. The first MP was a merchant in Belfast; his father was unknown. William Sharman married in 1805 the heiress of John Crawford, whose name he added to his own in 1827.

1. William Sharman – {Randalstown 1749-60}
2. William Sharman – {Lisburn 1783-90}
3. William Sharman Crawford – Dundalk 1834-37 Rochdale 1841-52
4. James Sharman Crawford – County Down 1874-78
5. Robert Sharman-Crawford – E. Belfast 1914-18 Mid Down 1921-22

Seats: Crawfordsburn, Down (acq. by mar. of 1805, add. 19th c., rebuilt 1906 for £20,000, family departed 1935, sold 1948, hospital); Moira Castle, Down (leased late 18th c. and early 19th c.); Rademan (Rademon) House, Down (acq. and built by Johnsons c. 1667, built c. 1740, passed by mar. to Crawfords later 18th c., add. mid-19th c., fire 1950s, rebuilt, sold); Florida, Down (acq. 1ater 17th c., passed to Gordons by mar. during early 18th c.)
Estates: Bateman 5749 (I) 5990
Notes: One in ODNB.

Crawford

Origins: A Scottish family who purchased land in County Down from 1670 onwards.

1. Arthur Crawford – Old Sarum 1818-20

Seats: Crawfordsburn, Down (purch. c. 1670, built c. 1780, passed by mar. of 1805 to Sharmans, see above); Rademan House, Down (see above)

SHAW LEFEVRE

Viscount Eversley (1857-88 UK)

Origins: The barrister, Charles Shaw, son of a clergyman and grandson of a grocer, married 1789 a Lefevre heiress. The latter family were Huguenot refugees of the diaspora after the revocation of the Edict of Nantes and made a fortune in distilling and banking in the mid-18th century.

1. Charles Shaw Lefevre – Newton (IoW) 1796-1802 Reading 1802-20
2. Charles Shaw Lefevre 1 Viscount Eversley – Downton 1830-31 Hampshire 1831-32 N. Hampshire 1832-57
3. John Shaw Lefevre – Petersfield 1832-34
4. George Shaw Lefevre 1 Baron Eversley – Reading 1863-85 Central Bradford 1885-95

Seat: Heckfield Place, Hampshire (purch. 1784 by the Lefevres, built 1780s, passed to Shaws by mar. 1790, add. 1818, sold 1895, business use)
Estates: Bateman 2388 (E) 3008
Title: Baron Eversley 1906-28 UK
Peers: 2 peers 1857-88 1906-28
1 in Cabinet 1884-85 1892-95
Notes: See Willson, *A Strong Supporting Cast: the Shaw Lefevres 1789-1936*. 1 Baron and 1 Viscount and two others in ODNB.

SHAW STEWART (Schaw) [Houston, Nicolson] *SCOTLAND*

Shaw Stewart

Origins: The Stewarts descended from an illegitimate son of Robert III. Granted large estates from 1390. Sir John Stewart 4 Bt succeeded his great uncle in 1752 and took the additional name Shaw. The Shaws acquired the port of Greenoch by marriage in the 14th century and became one of the most influential families in late medieval Scotland. They later acquired plantations in Trinidad. **First Shaw [MP 1467]. One additional [MP 1639 for Clackmannanshire].**

1. Sir Archibald Stewart – [Renfrewshire 1628-33 1661-63]
2. Sir John Shaw – [Renfrewshire 1643-44 1649 1667]
3. Sir Archibald Stewart 1 Bt – [Renfrewshire 1667]
4. Sir John Shaw 1 Bt – [Renfrewshire 1669-74 1678 1681]

5. Sir John Stewart 2 Bt – [Renfrewshire 1700-01]
6. John Stewart – [Renfrewshire 1700-01 1703-07]
7. Sir John Shaw 3 Bt – Renfrewshire 1708-10 Clackmannanshire 1722-27 Renfrewshire 1727-34
8. Sir John Shaw Stewart 4 Bt – Renfrewshire 1780-83 1786-96
9. Sir Michael Shaw Stewart 4 Bt – Renfrewshire 1780-83 1786-96
10. Patrick Shaw Stewart – Lancaster 1831-37 Renfrewshire 1841-46
11. Sir Houston Shaw Stewart – Greenwich 1852
12. Sir Michael Shaw Stewart 7 Bt – Renfrewshire 1855-65
13. Sir Hugh Shaw Stewart 8 Bt – E. Div. Renfrewshire 1886-1906

Seats: Ardgowan Castle and House, Renfrewshire (acq. 1404, built 15th c., old castle a ruin, new house 1797-1801, add. 1825, still own); Carnock Castle, Stirlingshire (built 1548, add. 1634, acq. early 18th c., add. 19th c., demolished c. 1941); Blackhall, Renfrewshire (acq. 1396, built 16th c., family departed mid-18th c., in late 18th c. became a farm house, donated to local government 1940); Sauchie Tower, Clackmannanshire (acq. by mar. 1431, rebuilt c. 1431, add. 1631-33, abandoned by family c. 1700, passed by mar. to Cathcarts 1752, sold 1930s, partly demolished 1961); Schawpark House, Clackmannanshire (acq. 1431, built and became Schaw principal seat c. 1700, passed to Cathcarts 1752, demolished 1961)
Estates: Bateman 26468 (S) 17851. Owned 9,200 acres in 1996.
Titles: Baronet 1667-; 1687-1732
4 Lds Lt 19th, 20th
Notes: Main male line of Schaws died out 1690. Estates passed to Cathcarts by mar. 1752. One in ODNB.

Stewart

Origins: Descended from a younger son of Sir Archibald Stewart, grandfather of the 1 Bt.

1. Walter Stewart – [Linlithgow Burgh 1700-07]

Seat: Pardovan, Linlithgowshire (acq. 1655)

Houston

Origins: One of the oldest families in Renfrewshire. Documented to 1150. Sir Peter Houston fell at Flodden. Sir John Houston 3 Bt married Margaret Shaw, daughter of Sir John Shaw 2 Bt and Eleanor, daughter and heiress of Sir Thomas Nicolson of Carnock. Their eldest son died in 1751. His sister and heiress married Sir Michael Stewart 3 Bt (see above). **First [MP 1560 for Renfrewshire]. Two further [MPs 1609-48, one for the county].**

1. Sir Patrick Houston 1 Bt – [Renfrewshire 1661-63 Dumbartonshire 1678 1681]
2. Sir John Houston 2 Bt – [Renfrewshire 1685-86 Stirlingshire 1689-1701 Renfrewshire 1703-07]
3. Patrick Houston – [Renfrew Burgh 1698]
4. Sir John Houston 3 Bt – Linlithgowshire 1708-15

Seat: Houston House (Castle), Linlithgowshire (medieval castle, ruin, new house built 17th c., sold 1722)
Title: Baronet 1668-1795

Houston

Origins: Descended from a younger brother of the 1 Baronet.

1. George Houston – Renfrewshire 1837-41

Seat: Johnstone Castle, Renfrewshire (built 1560, add. 1771, acq. 1773, remod. 1812, add. 19th c., family departed early 20th c., sold and much of the house demolished 1950)

Baron Carnock (1916- UK)

Origins: Lawyers in Edinburgh c. 1600. Lord Provost in the 17th century. Purchased estates in this period. **First [MP 1644 for Stirlingshire].** Bt 1637. For a brief period the 4 Bt held the peerage Baron Napier and Ettrick before it passed out of the family through the female line. The Carnock estate passed to the Shaws in 1751 (see above). The Baronetcy went to a cadet line, who produced soldiers, admirals, diplomats, and politicians.

1. Sir Harold Nicolson – Leicester West 1935-45
2. Nigel Nicolson – Bournemouth East and Christchurch 1952-59

Seats: Carnock House (Castle), Stirlingshire (built 1548, acq. and add. 1634, sold early 18th c., demolished); Plean Tower (Mengie Castle), Stirlingshire (built c. 1449, acq. 1650); Sissinghurst, Kent (built c. 1490, add. 1558, purch. 1930, NT 1967)
Notes: Nigel Nicolson left one and a half million pounds in 2004.
Title: Baronet 1637-
Peers: [1 peer 1683-86] 2 peers 1916-45
Notes: 1 Baron and three others in ODNB.

SHEE *IRELAND*

Shee

Origins: Kilkenny merchants in 16th century. The 1 Baronet (a Protestant) was Surveyor General of Ireland. Most members of the family were Roman Catholic. **First {MP 1559 for Kilkenny}. Four further {MPs 1585-1634}**.

1. Sir George Shee 1 Bt – {Knocktopher 1797-1800}

Seat: Dunmore House, Galway (purch. 1791, passed out of family 1870, ruin)
Title: Baronet 1794-1870
Shee

Origins: Cadet line from the 16th century.

1. Sir William Shee – County Kilkenny 1852-57

Seats: Upper Court (Uppercourt, Upperwood), Kilkenny (medieval, acq. mid-16th c., sold 1653); Cloran, Tipperary (acq. in the 16th c., sold c. 1750)

SHELDON

Origins: Acquired estates by marriage in the 15th and 16th centuries. **First MP 1542 for Worcestershire. Two further MPs 1542-63, one for the county.** Remained recusants. Conformed to the Established Church c. 1770s.

1. Ralph Sheldon – Wilton 1804-22
2. Edward Sheldon – S. Warwickshire 1835-36

Seats: Braile's House, Warwickshire (acq. 1547 only secure 1630, rebuilt 1822, passed to heiress 1901, sold after 1949); Weston House, Warwickshire (purch. 1534, built 1588-89, became principal seat 17th and 18th c., sold 1819, demolished 1934); Beoley Hall, Worcestershire (purch. r. Edward IV, built c. 1700, sold 1788); Skilts, Warwickshire (purch. and built 1561, ceased to be main seat c. 1600, reduced in size and became farm house in 18th c., sold 1783)
Estates: Bateman 2370 (E) 4231. Worth £2,000 pa in 1660s. Weston estate was sold for £75,000 in 1819. (Tyack, *Warwickshire Country Houses*, 218)
Notes: The Sheldons were a leading family in Worcestershire in the 16th century, but they suffered serious financial reverses due to their Roman Catholicism and their fortunes declined in the 18th and 19th centuries. Male line extinct 1901. Six in ODNB.

SHELLEY [Reeve, Rolls, Sidney (Sydney)] *ENGLAND & WALES*

Shelley

Origins: A medieval burgess in Kentish coastal towns founded the family in the later 14th century. One married an heiress c. 1411. By the mid 15th century they were mercers and aldermen in London. A judge in the Court of Common Pleas 1527. Kt 1529, Bt 1611. **First MP 1410 for Rye. Five further MPs 1491-1654.**

1. Sir John Shelley 4 Bt – Arundel 1727-41 Lewes 1743-47
2. Sir John Shelley 5 Bt – East Retford 1751-68 Newark 1768-74 Shoreham 1774-80
3. Sir John Shelley 6 Bt – Helston 1806 Lewes 1816-31
4. Sir John Shelley 7 Bt – Gatton 1830-31 Great Grimsby 1831 Westminster 1852-65

Seats: Michelgrove (Mitchelgrove) (House), Sussex (acq. by mar. of 1474, rebuilt c. 1540, add. 18th c., sold 1801, demolished c. 1830); Maresfield Park, Sussex (medieval, acq. by mar. 1814, sold later 19th c., demolished c. 1924); Shobrooke House (Park), Devon (built 16th c., rebuilt 1815, remod. 1850, acq. by mar. 1880, fire 1945, rebuilt 1975, still own)
Estates: Bateman 6500 (E) 7300 and 5052 (E) 6023
Title: Baronet 1611-
Notes: The poet was a member of the family. Five in ODNB.

Shelley

Origins: Cadet descended from John Shelly (c. 1500).

1. Sir Timothy Shelley 2 Bt – Horsham 1790-92 New Shoreham 1802-18

Seats: Castle Goring, Sussex (acq. and built 1797-98, sold 1845); Avington Park, Hampshire (built 16th c., add. 1670s, remod. 18th c., purch. 1848, sold 1952)
Estates: Bateman 5627 (E) 5101

Shelley

Origins: The junior line also descended from John Shelley (see above).

1. Henry Shelley – Lewes 1802-11

Baron Llangattock (1892-1916 UK)

Origins: The 6th Shelley Bt of Castle Goring married the daughter and heiress of Lord Llangattock. The Rolls family emerged in the 18th century as London property owners.

1. John Rolls 1 Baron Llangattock – Monmouthshire 1880-85

Seats: The Hendre, Monmouthshire (original family acq. from 1639-48, passed via heiresses to Rolls family 1801, rebuilt 1830-41, add. 1858, 1872, sold 1984, golf club); Llangattock Manor, Monmouthshire (built 17th c., acq. by mar. 1801, rebuilt 1877, sold 1984)
Estates: The car family. Bateman 4082 (W) 3710
Peers: 2 peers 1892-1916
Notes: Male line extinct 1916. One in ODNB.

Earl of Leicester (1618-1743 E)

Origins: Landowners in the 14th century. Rose high in service of the Tudors as soldiers and officials. Lord Deputy in Ireland under Elizabeth I. **First MP 1439 for Surrey. Six additional MPs 1547-1646, three kts of the shire**. The niece of the 7th and last Earl of Leicester married William Perry. Their daughter, Elizabeth Perry, heiress of the Sidneys, married the 1 Shelley Bt, and his son was the 1 Baron De L'Isle.

1. Henry Sydney 1 Earl of Romney – Bramber 1679-81 Tamworth 1689
2. Philip Sydney 5 Earl of Leicester – Kent 1695-98
3. John Sidney 6 Earl of Leicester – Brackley 1705
4. Philip Sidney 1 Baron De L'Isle – Eye 1829-31
5. William Sidney 1 Viscount De L'Isle – Chelsea 1944-45

Seats: Penshurst Place, Kent (medieval, rebuilt 14th c. and 15th c., acq. 1552, add. later 16th c., still own); Ingleby Manor, Yorkshire (built early 16th c., Foulis family purch. 1608, passed via heiress to Sidneys 1850, sold 1950)
Estate: Bateman 9252 (E) 10232. Worth about £4,000 pa in 1630s. 1 Viscount De L'Isle left £4,678,000 in 1992. Owned 2,500 acres in 2001.
Titles: Baron Sidney 1603-1743 E; Viscount Sidney 1603-1704 E; Viscount L'Isle 1605-1743 E; Baron Milton 1689-1704 E; Earl of Romney 1694-1704 E; Baron De L'Isle and Dudley 1835- UK; Viscount De L'Isle 1956-
Peers: 12 peers 1660-98 1689-1743 1689-1704 1835-1945
2 Lds Lt 17th, 18th
2 in Cabinet 1690-93 1951-55
1 KG 20th
Notes: 1 Earl of Romney and 1, 2, and 3 Earls of Leicester and 1 Viscount De L'Isle and four others in ODNB.

Reeve

Origins: The niece of the 7 Earl of Leicester who married William Perry also succeeded to the Reeve estates through her mother. The Reeves held estates from the reign of Edward VI.

1. Sir George Reeve 1 Bt – Eye 1660-78
2. Sir Robert Reeve 2 Bt – Eye 1675-81

Seat: Thwaite (Thwayte) Hall, Suffolk (acq. mid-16th c., passed to 5 Earl of Leicester by mar. 1688, and then out of the family 1705, demolished)
Title: Baronet 1663-88
Notes: Male line extinct 1688.

SHEPHEARD [Chamberlayne]

Origins: London merchants in the later 17th and early 18th century. One was a Director of the East India Company and another a very rich ship owner involved in the wine trade and a founder of the South Sea Company.

1. Francis Shepheard – Andover 1701-08
2. Samuel Shepheard – Malmesbury 1701 Cambridge 1708-22 Cambridgeshire 1724-47 Cambridge 1747-48
3. Samuel Shepheard – Newport (IoW) 1701 London 1705-08

Seat: Exning, Suffolk (purch. and built 1734, sold c. 1758, demolished)
Estates: Samuel Shepheard MP 1701-08 died worth £800,000.
Notes: Samuel Shepheard's illegitimate daughter married the last Viscount Irvine (see Seymour). They had five daughters among who the inheritance was split up 1758. (Habakkuk, *Marriage, Debt and the Estates System: English Landownership 1650-1950*, 198; Hayton, *The House of Commons*, V, 465). Three in ODNB.

Chamberlayne

Origins: Francis Chamberlayne MP inherited an estate in Warwickshire from his uncle Samuel Shepheard, who purchased Stoneythorpe as an investment. Chamberlayne was also connected with overseas trade. The family did not assume a gentry style of life until later in the century.

1. Francis Chamberlayne – New Shoreham 1713-15 1720-28

Seat: Stoneythorpe (Stoney Thorpe) Hall, Warwickshire (built c. 1600, purch. 1671, sold after 1951)

SHERARD

Earl of Harborough (1719-1859 GB)

Origins: Prosperous gentry in the Middle Ages. In France with Henry V in 1415. **First MP 1407 for Leicestershire. Two other MPs 1491-1558 both for the county**. Kt 1622. Baron 1627.

1. Philip Sherard – Rutland 1660-81
2. Bennet Sherard 2 Baron Sherard – Leicestershire 1679-81 1685-87 1689-95
3. Bennet Sherard – Rutland 1689-98
4. Bennet Sherard 1 Earl of Harborough – Leicestershire 1701-02 Rutland 1713-14
5. Philip Sherard 2 Earl of Harborough – Rutland 1708-10
6. Philip Sherard 5 Earl of Harborough – Rutland 1795-96

Seats: Whissendine, Rutland (estate acq. mid-15th c., 16th and 17th c., estate broken up and sold 1861, declined to a farm house); Stapleford Park, Leicestershire (acq. by mar. 1402, built c. 1500, remod. 1633, add. 1670-80, sold 1894); Glatton Hall, Huntingdonshire (acq. by mar. 1658, sold c. 1910)
Estates: Bateman 5123 (E) 7655
Titles: Baron Sherard 1627-1931 I; Baron Harborough 1714-1859 GB; Viscount Sherard 1718-32 GB
Peers: {2 peers 1660-1732} 1714-1807 1818-1859
3 Lds Lt 17th, 18th
Notes: In 1859 the barony passed to a distant cousin and the estates were sold by the widow of the last Earl.

SHIRLEY [Browne, Bourchier, Devereux, Ferrers, Martin, Norborne, Withypoll]
ENGLAND, WALES, & IRELAND

Earl Ferrers (1711- GB)

Origins: The founder was Master of the Horse to William the Conqueror and present at the Battle of Hastings. (Elton et. al., *Researching the Country House: a Guide for Local Historians*, 32) Held great estates in Warwickshire at the time of the Domesday Book (Carpenter, *Locality and Polity: a Study of Warwickshire Landed Society 1401-1499*, 149), and they still retain the Domesday manor of Shirley at which they were domiciled in the 1080s. (Wedgwood, *Staffordshire Parliamentary History*, 766) One of the wealthiest families in Leicestershire in the 15th c. (Acheson, *A Gentry Community: Leicestershire in the Fifteenth Century, c. 1422-1485*, 249) Sir Robert Shirley MP 1420 served in the Agincourt campaign. **First MP 1295 for Warwickshire. Nine further**

MPs 1393-1625, six kts of the shire. Sir Henry Shirley 2 Bt married the heiress of the 2 Earl of Essex (see Devereux below). Her family had inherited Tamworth Castle and the Barony of Ferrers in 1446 from a Ferrers heiress, The de Ferrers family accumulated estates from 1066 onwards, had been created Earls of Derby in 1138, and later Marquess of Dorset 1475 and Duke of Suffolk 1554 (attainted). **First MP 1300 for Devon. Thirteen additional MPs 1302-1621, seven kts of the shire**. The Ferrers had inherited the estates of the Brownes of Badesley Clinton by virtue of a marriage in 1497. The Brownes rose via the law. **First MP 1366. Three additional MPs 1392-1554**.

1. John Ferrers – Derbyshire 1660 Tamworth 1669-70
2. Washington Shirley 2 Earl Ferrers – {Fore 1713-14}
3. Robert Shirley Viscount Tamworth – Leicestershire 1713-14
4. Robert Shirley – Stamford 1727-34
5. Sewallis Shirley – Brackley 1742-54 Callington 1754-61

Seats: Staunton Harold Hall, Leicestershire (medieval house, acq. by mar. from Stauntons 1423, became main residence c. 1440, add. 15th c., remod. and add. late 17th early 18th c., remod. 1762, sold 1954, institutional use); Tamworth Castle, Staffordshire (medieval, acq. by Ferrers by mar. 1423, c. 1600, passed by mar. 1714 to the Marquesses of Northampton – see Compton, then to Townshends 1751, became an industrial site, sold 1897 to Tamworth Corporation, museum); Chartley Castle (Hall), Staffordshire (medieval castle, acq. by mar. by Ferrers 1232, passed to Devereux by mar. 15th c., new house passed to Shirleys by mar. 1646, fire 1781, rebuilt 1787, fire and rebuilt 1847, sold early 20th c.); Baddesley Clinton, Warwickshire (medieval, acq. by mar. of 1517, sold 1940, NT 1980); Shirley Hall, Derbyshire (built 11th c., abandoned c. 1440, remains demolished c. 1770, family still own land at Shirley); Astwell Castle (Manor), Northamptonshire (built 1492, inher. by mar. 1586 from a family who possessed it in the 15th c., add. 1606-07, abandoned by family early 18th c., sold 1763, most demolished soon after)
Estates: Bateman 8665 (E) 12707. Ferrers worth £666 pa in 1436.
Titles: Earl of Derby 1138-1266; Baron Ferrers of Groby 1299- E; Baron Ferrers of Chartley 1677- E; Baronet 1611-
Peers: 12 peers 1677-1745 1754-1859 1868-1945
2 Lds Lt 17th, 18th
1 in Cabinet 1746
Notes: The line established at Baddesley Clinton in the 16th c. remained Roman Catholic and impecunious with no MPs post 1660. Ferrers family has an entry and 1 Earl Ferrers of the 1st creation, 6 Earl of Derby and 4 and 5 Earls Ferrers of the second cr. and seven Shirleys and five Ferrers in ODNB.

Shirley

Origins: On the death of the 1 Earl Ferrers in 1717 the estates were divided. The Warwickshire properties, including Ettington went to a younger son of a second marriage. The Shirleys held Ettington from the Conquest (Roskell, Clark, and Rawcliffe, *The House of Commons*, IV, 364).

1. Evelyn Shirley – County Monaghan 1826-31 S. Warwickshire 1836-49
2. Evelyn Shirley – County Monaghan 1841-47 S. Warwickshire 1853-65
3. Sewallis Shirley – County Monaghan 1868-80

Seats: Ettington (Eatington) Park, Warwickshire (acq. before 1100, medieval house, rebuilt 16th c., add. early 19th c., remod. 1858-63, family departed 1904, contents sold 1946, leased out for business use after that); Lough Fea, Monaghan (Earl of Essex acq. 1576, built castle at Carrickmacross, later demolished, c. 1630, Shirleys acq. by mar. 1646, built c. 1750, new house 1827-47, main seat 1904-77, fire 1966, still own)
Estates: Bateman 32957 (I & E) 26573. Most of the Irish estates sold before WWI. Irish estate of c. 1,000 acres in 2015.
Notes: The family largely abandoned Ettington c. in 20th c. They had built a house on their Irish estates in 1827 and lived there increasingly from that time forward. They had acq. land in Ireland by mar. from one of the heiresses of Robert Devereux last Earl of Essex in 1646 who had held 47,000 acres in Ireland. Four in ODNB.

Viscount Hereford (1550- E)

Origins: An old family that had held manorial land since at least the reign of Henry II. The family rose high through an exceptional series of marriages to heiresses and via a Chief Justice of S. Wales, who acquired much forfeited land in 1531. Walter Devereux of Chartley was created Viscount Hereford in 1550, and his son Earl of Essex in 1572. The Essex title became extinct in 1646. **First MP 1340 for Shropshire. Ten additional MPs 1378-1647, seven kts of the shire.** The Barony of Ferrers and Tamworth passed through the family to the Shirleys (see above).

1. Walter Devereux – Orford 1660 1661-79
2. Price Devereux 9 Viscount Hereford – Montgomery 1691-1700
3. Price Devereux 10 Viscount Hereford – Montgomeryshire 1719-40

Seats: Tregoyd House (Park), Breconshire (built 16th c., family departed 1939, adventure center); Vanyor Park, Montgomeryshire (built mid-15th c., purch. c. 1570s by Price family, passed by mar. of 1633 to Devereux, passed out of family 1740); Hampton Court, Herefordshire (built 1435, purch. 1924, sold 1972); Chartley Castle (Hall), Staffordshire (medieval castle, Devereux acq. by mar. 1453, new manor house built c.

1485, passed to Shirleys by mar. 1646, see above); Christchurch, Suffolk (acq. by mar. with Withypolls 1642 – **4 MPs 1529-1625**, passed to Martins, reacquire by mar with Martin heiress (see below) early 18th c., sold 1732)
Estates: Bateman 2100 (E & W) 2241. Worth £1,000 pa in 1558.
Titles: Baron Ferrers 1461-1646 E; Earl of Essex 1572-1646 E; Baronet 1611-
Peers: 12 peers 1660-83 1696-1855 1864-1945
1 Ld Lt 18th
Notes: Among the estates the Devereux inherited were those of the Bourchiers. The founder was Chief Justice of the King's Bench 1337 and Lord Chancellor 1340. Barons 1348, and Earls of Essex 1461. The heiress of the 6 Baron married William Parr, created Earl of Essex 1543. The 8 Baron was Walter Devereux Viscount Hereford, grandson of a Bourchier heiress, created Earl of Essex 1572. **Four MPs 1329-1597, three kts of the shire.** A Withypoll heiress married 1642 Leicester Devereux 6 Viscount Hereford, bringing with her Christchurch, Suffolk, sold 1732. The Withypolls made a fortune in London in the export wool trade under Henry VII and Henry VIII, though they were prominent as Bristol merchants from the reign of Edward IV. Kt 1600. **Four MPs 1529-1625.** 1 Baron Ferrers of Chartley and 1 Viscount Hereford and 1 and 2 Earls of Essex and thee others in ODNB.

Norborne

Origins: Held property in Calne since the mid-16th century. The heiress of Walter Norborne MP married the 8 Viscount Hereford. **First MP 1640 for Calne.**

1. Walter Norborne – Calne 1679-81

Seat: Castle House, Wiltshire (acq. mid-16th c., built early 17th c., passed to Devereux by mar. 1684, flats, fire 1967)
Estates: Worth £35,000 in the later 17th century.

Martin

Origins: Leicester Martin MP married the daughter of the 6 Viscount Hereford and inherited Christchurch (originally a Withypoll seat inherited by the Devereux, see above). His only daughter and heiress married the 10 Viscount Hereford and brought Christchurch back to the Devereux.

1. Leicester Martin – Suffolk 1707-08

Seat: Christchurch Park (Mansion), Suffolk (medieval, demolished, new house built 1550, acq. by mar. by Devereux mid-17th c., passed by mar. of 1700 to Martins, passed back by mar. to Devereux 1732, sold 1734)

SHUTTLEWORTH [Kay]

Baron Shuttleworth (1902- UK)

Origins: At Shuttleworth Hall in the 12th century and at Gawthorpe since the 14th century. The family rose in status under Elizabeth I when a successful lawyer served as Chief Justice of Chester. **First MP 1640. One further MP 1640-59.** In 1842 a Shuttleworth heiress married Sir James Kay, the first Secretary of Education.

1. Richard Shuttleworth – Lancashire 1705-49
2. James Shuttleworth – Preston 1741-54 Lancashire 1761-68
3. Ughtred Kay-Shuttleworth – Hastings 1869-80 Clitheroe Div. N. E. Lancashire 1885-1900

Seats: Gawthorpe Hall, Lancashire (acq. 14th c. and built, rebuilt 1599-1605, passed to Kays by mar. 1842, restored 1849-50, family departed 1953, donated to NT 1972); Forcett Park, Yorkshire; Barbon Manor, Westmorland (acq. late 16th c., built 1863, add. 1893, still own); Barton Lodge, Lancashire (purch. 16th c., rebuilt late Georgian period, sold 1834, demolished c. 1991); Smithills Hall, Lancashire (built 15th c., remod. 16th c., acq. 16 or 17th c., sold 1801)
Estates: Bateman 4142 (E) 5290; junior line at Old Warden, Bedfordshire 3800 (E) 7923; junior line at Hathersage Hall, Derbyshire 2303 (E) 2006
Title: Baronet 1850-
Peers: 4 peers 1902-45
Notes: 1 Bt in ODNB.

SIBTHORP (Sibthorpe) [Waldo]

Origins: Emerged in Nottinghamshire in the early 16th century. Moved to Lincolnshire in the mid-17th century. Fortunate marriages lifted the family into the gentry. Sir Christopher Sibthorpe was Justice of the King's Bench and Irish **{MP 1613}** d. 1631.

1. John Sibthorpe – Lincoln 1713-15
2. Coningsby Sibthorp – Lincoln 1734-41 1747-54 1761-68
3. Humphrey Waldo-Sibthorp – Boston 1777-84 Lincoln 1800-06
4. Coningsby Waldo-Sibthorp – Lincoln 1814-22
5. Charles Waldo-Sibthorp – Lincoln 1826-32 1835-55
6. Gervaise Waldo-Sibthorp – Lincoln 1856-61

Seats: Canwick Hall, Lincolnshire (old house, purch. and rebuilt c. 1720, rebuilt 1810, sold 1939, flats); Potterells, Hertfordshire
Estates: Bateman 7700 (E) 10300. Worth £8,536 pa in 1826.
Notes: One in ODNB.

SIDEBOTTOM

Origins: Founded by an artisan who became a mill owner in the early 19th c.

1. James Sidebottom – Stalybridge 1868-71
2. Tom H. Sidebottom – Stalybridge 1874-80 1885-1900
3. William Sidebottom – High Peak Div. Derbyshire 1885-1900
4. Joseph Sidebottom – Hyde Div. Cheshire 1886-1900

Seats: Etherow House (Lodge), Cheshire (acq. c. 1800, sold c. 1910, park); Acres Bank, Cheshire; Merle Bank, Cheshire
Estates: Bateman 2600 (E) 11182
Notes: Mill firm was liquidated in 1896.

SINCLAIR I *SCOTLAND*

Origins: Medieval family. Stevenson line founded by a younger son of Longformacus, merchant in Edinburgh and Lord Provost. The 1 Bt succeeded as 10th laird at Longformacus. **First [MP 1633].**

1. Sir Robert Sinclair 1 Bt – [Berwickshire 1665-67 1669-74]
2. Sir Robert Sinclair 3 Bt – [Haddington Constabulary 1689-1702]
3. Sir Archibald Sinclair – [Wick 1690-1702]
4. Sir Robert Sinclair 3 Bt – [Berwickshire 1703-07]
5. Sir John Sinclair 4 Bt – [Lanarkshire 1703-07]

Seats: Stevenson House, Haddingtonshire (medieval, damaged 1544, rebuilt 1560, purch. 1624, sold 1931); Longformacus House, Berwickshire (acq. later 14th c., built early 18th c., add. late 19th c.)
Estates: Bateman 19347 (S) 6326 and 4422 (S) 5250
Titles: Baronet 1636- ; 1664-1843
Notes: The daughter and heiress of Sir John Lockhart of Castlehill married the son of Sir John Sinclair 4 Bt. One in ODNB.

SINCLAIR II (St. Clair) *SCOTLAND*

Earl of Caithness (1455- S)

Origins: Great Scandinavian lords. Invested by Haakon VI of Norway as Earl of Orkney 1379 (*Country Life*, 182, p. 74). Lord of Parliament 1449. Chancellor of Scotland 1455. **First [MP 1641 for Caithness-shire]. One additional [MP 1649, also for the county]. Two cadets of Roslin [MPs 1560-80].**

1. James Sinclair – Caithness-shire 1826-30

Seats: Barrogill Castle (Castle of Mey), Caithness-shire (built 1566-72, remod. 1819, sold early 20th c.); Braelangwell, Ross-shire (built late 18th c., remod. 1839-45); Girnigoe Castle, Caithness-shire (built late 15th c., add. 1606, abandoned to decay after 1690); Thurso Castle, Caithness-shire (owned from an early time, rebuilt c. 1600, passed to cadet line of Ulbster, see below) Stagenhoe Park, Hertfordshire (rebuilt c. 1740, acq. 1881 for £37,700, family departed 1889, sold 1923, institutional use)
Estates: Bateman 15073 (S & E) 5451
Peers: [4 peers 1660-76 1681-98 1704-07] 3 Scottish Rep peers 1807-18 1848-66 1918-29 1 peer 1866-81
4 Lds Lt 18th, 19th
Notes: Many of the Earls succeeded to the title when they were young, and hence not many were elected as MPs. Sinclair family has an entry in ODNB. 4, 5, and 14 Earls of Caithness and three others in ODNB. Four of Roslin in ODNB.

Sinclair

Origins: Cadet of the Caithness family in the 17th century.

1. James Sinclair – [Caithness-shire 1689-93]

Seat: Freswick Castle (Tower, House), Caithness-shire (built 13th c., purch. 1661, new house built c. 1662, rebuilt late 18th c., sold 1948)
Notes: One in ODNB.

Baron Sinclair (1449- and 1487- S)

Origins: Descended from the eldest son of the 1 Earl of Caithness. **First [MP 1644 for Haddingtonshire].** The Barons Sinclair were attainted 1716-82.

1. John St. Clair Master of Sinclair (11 Baron but for the attainder) – Dysart Burghs 1708
2. James St. Clair Master of Sinclair (12 Baron but for the attainder) – Dysart Burghs 1722-34 Sutherland 1736-47 Dysart Burghs 1747-54 Fifeshire 1754-62

Seats: Sinclair, Fife (resident 18th c.); Herdmanston (Hermiston) House (Castle), Haddingtonshire (medieval, acq. c. 1401, built 17th c., demolished by Sinclairs due to war damage c. 1950); Nisbet House, Berwickshire (medieval, rebuilt 1630, purch. by Kers 1652, passed by mar. to Sinclairs, add. 1774, sold 1950s)
Estates: Bateman 4346 (S) 6600
Peers: [2 peers 1660-76 1682-1707] 3 Scottish Rep peers 1807-59 1868-80 1885-1922
Notes: 9 and (11 and 12 Barons) and one other in ODNB.

Viscount Thurso (1952- UK)

Origins: Descended from a younger son of the 4 Earl of Caithness.

1. John Sinclair – [Caithness-shire 1678]
2. Sir George Sinclair – [Caithness-shire 1681 1685-86 1703-05]
3. Sir John Sinclair 1 Bt – Caithness 1780-84 Lostwithiel 1784-90 Caithness 1790-96 Petersfield 1797-1802 Caithness 1802-06 1807-11
4. Sir George Sinclair 2 Bt – Caithness 1811-12 1818-20 1831-41
5. Sir John Sinclair 3 Bt – Caithness-shire 1869-85
6. Archibald Sinclair 1 Viscount Thurso – Caithness & Sutherland 1922-45
7. John Sinclair, 3 Viscount Thurso – Caithness, Sutherland, and Easter Ross 2001-15

Seats: Ulbster, Caithness-shire (an estate name and denominator of this branch of the Sinclairs but no modern residence); Thurso Castle, Caithness-shire (acq. from Earls of Caithness, see above, demolished and rebuilt 1872-78, fire and demolished 1952, ruin, still own Thurso estate); Lochdhu Lodge, Caithness-shire (built 1895, still own?)
Estates: Bateman 12700 (S) 5117 and 78053 (S) 12833 + 1378. Owned 36,800 acres in 1996.
Title: Baronet 1786-
1 Ld Lt 20th
1 in Cabinet 1931-32 1940-45
Notes: The 3 Viscount assumed his seat in the House of Lords in 1995 until the presence of most hereditary peers was abolished in 1999. He then became the first titled peer to be elected to the Commons in 2001. 1 Viscount and four others in ODNB.

Baron Pentland (1909-84 UK)

Origins: Descended from a younger son of the 4 Earl of Caithness.

1. William Sinclair – [Caithness-shire 1661-63]
2. Sir James Sinclair 1 Bt – [Caithness-shire 1704-07]
3. John Sinclair 1 Baron Pentland – Dumbartonshire 1892-95 Forfarshire 1897-1909

Seats: Barrock House, Caithness-shire (acq. and built 1631, rebuilt 18th c., rebuilt mid-19th c., descendents still own); Dunbeath Castle, Caithness-shire (built 14th c., rebuilt c. 1624, sold 1752 to another branch of the family, add. mid-19th c., remod. 1881, sold 1945); Keiss Castle (House), Caithness-shire (built 16th c., ruin by 18th c., purch. by Dunbeath Sinclairs from another branch of the family c. 1710, new house built 1755, sold mid-19th c.)
Estates: Bateman 6900 (S) 2354 and 57757 (S) 6377
Title: Baronet 1704-

Peers: 2 peers 1909-25 1938-45
Notes: 1 Baron in ODNB.

SINGLETON [Fowke] *IRELAND*

Origins: The Singletons were merchants in Drogheda in the 17th and 18th centuries. Became a legal family first half of the 18th century. Purchased estates from 1702. A Fowke came to Ireland c. 1700 and married the Singleton daughter of the Lord Chief Justice of Ireland and took the name Singleton 1759.

1. Edward Singleton – {Drogheda 1692-93 1695-99 1703-10}
2. Henry Singleton – {Drogheda 1713-40}
3. Edward Singleton – {Drogheda 1717-26}
4. Sydenham Fowke Singleton – {Drogheda 1776-83}
5. Mark Singleton – {Eye 1796-99 Carysfort 1800} Eye 1807-20

Seat: Mell, Louth (acq. 19th c., resident into 20th c.); Piers Court, Cavan
Estates: Bateman 8879 (I & E) 6715
Notes: One in ODNB.

SITWELL [Sacheverell]

Sitwell

Origins: Small gentry in the Middle Ages. One went on a Crusade (d. 1301). Inherited the Reresby estates from a "Conquest" family. Profited from enclosures in the later 16th century and through iron founding and the manufacture of nails in the 17th century. Later coal was discovered on the Renishaw estate.

1. Sir Sitwell Sitwell 1 Bt – West Looe 1796-1802
2. Francis Sitwell – Berwick 1803-06
3. Sir George Sitwell 4 Bt – Scarborough 1885-86 1892-95

Seat: Renishaw, Derbyshire (purch. and rebuilt 1619, rebuilt after 1793-1808, still own)
Estates: Bateman 5582 (E) 13326. William Sitwell died in 1776 leaving £400,000. Estate has continued to grow in size the 20th century. (Craven and Stanley, *The Derbyshire Country House*, 171)
Title: Baronet 1808-
Notes: The Wilmot-Sitwells were seated at Stainsby House, Derbyshire (acq. c. 1800, add. 1837, sold 20th c., demolished 1972) and inherited most of the Morely estates (see below). In Bateman 4087 (E) 6297. Five in ODNB.

Sacheverell

Origins: Leading landowners in Derbyshire since the 12th century. **First MP 1449 for Derbyshire. One further MP 1523 (?) or 1529 for Leicestershire. Two Irish {MPs 1634-46}.** The Sacheverell estates passed to the Sitwells by marriage in the 18th century.

1. William Sacheverell – Derbyshire 1670-81 Heytesbury 1689-90 Nottinghamshire 1690-91
2. Robert Sacheverell – Nottingham 1699-1702 1705-08 1710-14

Seats: Morely Hall, Derbyshire (medieval, acq. by mar. with the de Morleys c. 1480 and rebuilt, passed to Batemans by mar. 1st half 18th c., demolished 1757); Barton, Nottinghamshire (sold to Robert Clifton 5 Bt c. 1714); New Hall, Warwickshire (medieval, rebuilt 16th c., purch. 1586, passed by mar. to the Chadwicks 1715)
Estates: Worth £1,300 pa in the 1660s.
Notes: Male line extinct 1715. Two in ODNB.

SKEFFINGTON [Foster] *IRELAND*

Earl of Massereene (1756-1816 I)

Origins: Small gentry in Leicestershire in the Middle Ages (Acheson, *A Gentry Community: Leicestershire in the Fifteenth Century, c. 1422-1485*, 249). Emerged as significant under the Tudors as officials and soldiers. Sir William Skeffington went to Ireland as Lord Deputy 1535. A branch was also established by a younger son in London as merchants of staple, Sheriff. **First MP 1529 for Leicestershire. Five additional MPs 1555-1659, three kts of the shire**. The 2 Viscount Massereene married 1654 Mary, daughter and heiress to the large Irish estates of Sir John Clotworthy 1 Viscount Massereene, to which they succeeded in 1665. **One Irish {MP 1634}.** The daughter of the 4 Earl of Massereene succeeded as 9 Viscountess Massereene in her own right. She married 1810 Thomas Foster 2 Viscount Ferrard, and their son succeeded as Viscount Massereene and Ferrard (see below).

1. John Skeffington 2 Viscount Massereene – {County Antrim 1661-65}
2. Clotworthy Skeffington 3 Viscount Massereene – {County Antrim 1692-93}
3. Clotworthy Skeffington 4 Viscount Massereene – {County Antrim 1703-14}
4. John Skeffington – {Antrim 1717-41}
5. Arthur Skeffington – {County Antrim 1741-47}
6. Hungerford Skeffington – {Antrim 1749-68}
7. Hugh Skeffington – {County Antrim 1747-68 Antrim 1769-76}
8. Henry Skeffington 3 Earl of Massereene – {Belfast 1768-97 Antrim 1797-1800}

9. Chichester Skeffington 4 Earl of Massereene – {Antrim 1776-97}
10. William Skeffington – {Antrim 1768-1800}

Seats: Antrim Castle, Antrim (built 1613 by Clotworthys, add. 1662, acq. by mar. 1665, rebuilt 1813, remod. 1887, burned 1922, family lived in converted stables until 1956, sold, institutional use); Oriel Temple, Louth (built 1780, add. c. 1812, sold 20th c., institutional use); Skeffington Hall (House), Leicestershire (acq. 13th c., built c. 1450, rebuilt c. 1530, remod. early-mid-17th c., sold 1786); Fisherwick Park, Staffordshire (purch. 1520, built late 16th c., sold 1755)
Estates: Bateman 21024 (I) 15013. Worth £4,340 pa in 1689. Owned 16,600 acres in Scotland in 1996.
Titles: Baron Loughneagh and Viscount Massereene 1660- I; Baronet 1627-1816
Peers: {5 peers 1660-1757} 3 peers 1843-1945
2 Lds Lt 19th, 20th
1 KP 19th
Notes: 2 and 10 Viscount and 2 Earl and two others in ODNB.

Viscount Ferrard (1797- I)

Origins: See previous entry. The Foster family was of humble origin, and came to Ireland in the 1660s as mowers of hay. They acquired a farm and eventually the control over a parliamentary seat at Dunleer c. 1715 due to the inattention of the existing patrons, the Tenisons. The father of the first {MP} was a country attorney of modest means. The first {MP} was a successful barrister, appointed Lord Chief Baron of the Exchequer in 1767. His son was a politician, created 1 Baron Oriel. (Malcolmson, *John Foster: the Politics of the Anglo-Irish Ascendancy*, 2, 6-7)

1. Anthony Foster – {Dunleer 1738-60 County Louth 1761-66}
2. John Foster 1 Baron Oriel – {Dunleer 1761-68 County Louth 1768-1800} 1801-21
3. John Foster – {Dunleer 1776-83 Ennis 1783-90}
4. John Foster – {Dunleer 1783-90}
5. John Foster – {Dunleer 1790-92}
6. Thomas Foster 2 Viscount Ferrard – {Dunleer 1792-1800} Drogheda 1807-12 County Louth 1821-24
7. John Foster – University of Dublin 1807-12 Yarmouth (IoW) 1816-18 Armagh 1818-20 County Louth 1824-30
8. Frederick Foster – Bury St. Edmunds 1812-18

Seat: Oriel Temple (Collon House), Louth (see above)
Estates: (See above) Held 6,000 acres by 1750. Worth £5,000 pa by 1778 and £10,000 pa by 1800 (but heavily indebted).
Titles: Baron Oriel 1790- I; Baron Oriel 1821- UK

Peers: {1 peer 1790-1800} 2 peers 1821-43
Notes: 1 Baron in ODNB.

<u>Foster</u>

Origins: Descended from a younger son of the uncle of the 1 Baron Oriel.

1. John Foster – {Dunleer 1776-83 Ennis 1783-90}
2. Sir Augustus Foster 1 Bt – Cockermouth 1812-16

Seat: Glyde Court, Louth (acq. and built later 18th c., remod. 1868, still resident 1st half 20th c., ruin later 20th c.)
Estates: Bateman 3506 (I & E) 3363
Title: Baronet 1831-1947
Notes: Two in ODNB.

SKIPPON

Origins: In Norfolk in the 13th century. **First MP 1646.**

1. Sir Philip Skippon – Dunwich 1679-81 1689-91
2. Philip Skippon – Sudbury 1705-10

Seat: Foulsham Old Hall, Norfolk (built 1556, acq. by mar. 1634, sold 1715)
Notes: Cromwellian peer 1657. Philip Skippon MP 1705-10 sold off the bulk of the family estates. The male line was extinct 1716.

SKIPWITH

<u>Skipwith</u>

Origins: Originated in Yorkshire in the early medieval period. Already "ancient" in 1400. (Roskell, Clark, and Rawcliffe, *The House of Commons*, IV, 388) Chief Justice of Ireland 1370. **First MP in 1348. Eight additional MPs 1406-1610, five kts of the shire. One Irish {MP 1634}**. Several branches of the family included here.

1. Sir Fulwar Skipwith 2 Bt – Coventry 1713-15
2. Sir Thomas Skipwith 4 Bt – Warwickshire 1769-80 Steyning 1780-84
3. Sir Grey Skipwith 8 Bt – Warwickshire 1831-32 S. Warwickshire 1832-34

Seat: Newbold Revel, Warwickshire (medieval, inherited 1640 via an heiress from Sir Simon Clarke, new house c. 1716, sold c. 1852, today a prison service college)

Estates: Worth £300 pa c. 1398.
Title: Baronet 1622- ; 1670-1790
Note: The 3 Bt sold much of his English property and settled in Virginia. The 8 Bt was raised in Virginia and was descended from Pocahantas. Estates encumbered by debt mid -19th c and sold. Two in ODNB.

Skipwith

Origins: An illegitmate line descended (in the 16th century) from Sir William Skipwith.

1. Sir Thomas Skipwith 1 Bt – Grantham 1659 1660
2. Sir Thomas Skipwith 2 Bt – Malmesbury 1696-98

Seat: Metheringham, Lincolnshire (acq. 16th c., passed out of family 18th c.)
Title: Baronet 1678-1756
Notes: Male line extinct 1756.

SLANNING

Origins: A steward of the Inner Temple made a fortune buying monastic property after the Reformation. **First MP 1558. One additional MP 1640.**

1. Sir Nicholas Slanning 1 Bt – Plympton Erle 1667-79 Penryn 1679-81 1685-87

Seat: Maristow, Devon (medieval, purch. 1550, rebuilt c. 1560, passed to Heywoods by mar. c. 1700)
Title: Baronet 1663-1700
Notes: One in ODNB.

SLINGSBY

Slingsby

Origins: At Scriven by the mid-14th c. Married a sister of the Earl of Northumberland 1550s. The **first MP 1572 for Knaresborough** was a soldier and local official. He consolidated his estates around Scriven from the 1550s onwards. **Three additional MPs 1597-1642, all for Knaresborough**.

1. Sir Thomas Slingsby 2 Bt – Yorkshire 1670-79 Knaresborough 1679-81
2. Henry Slingsby – Portsmouth 1685-87 1689-90
3. Sir Henry Slingsby 3 Bt – Knaresborough 1685-87
4. Sir Henry Slingsby 5 Bt – Knaresborough 1714-15 1722-63

Seats: Scriven Park (Hall), Yorkshire (acq. by mar. 1333, rebuilt c. 1707, destroyed by fire 1952); Red House, Yorkshire (medieval, acq. 1560, new house 1620, remod. 1860s, family departed 1899, sold 1916, flats); Loftus Hill, Yorkshire (acq. c. 1300, medieval, remod. 1840s, sold 1842)
Estates: Bateman 6407 (E) 10485. Worth £1,800 pa in 1640.
Title: Baronet 1638-1869
Notes: Extinct in the male line 1869. The estates passed to heiress, whose heirs assumed the Slingsby name. Two in ODNB.

Slingsby

Origins: A younger son of the Scriven line was Comptroller of the Navy under James I. His son was secretary to the Earl of Strafford in Ireland and established an estate there. **First {MP 1634}. One additional {MP 1639}.**

No post-1660 MPs

Seat: Bellaughcaple (Ballycapple) House, Tipperary (acq. first half 17th c., sold after 1661?)
Title: Baronet 1657-1700; 1661-61
Notes: Two in ODNB.

SLOPER

Origins: The family emerged in the 18th century. Kt 1788. (Probably business origins.)

1. William Sloper – Great Bedwyn 1715-22 Camelford 1722-27 Great Bedwyn 1729-41 Whitchurch 1742-43
2. William Sloper – Great Bedwyn 1747-56
3. William Sloper – St. Albans 1780-90

Seat: West Woodhay House, Berkshire (built 1635, purch. c. 1714, sold 1880)

SMITH I [Bromley, Carington, Holt, Wilson]

Marquess of Lincolnshire (1912-28 UK)

Origins: Yeomen in the first half of the 17th century. Opened a bank in Nottingham after 1660, which became immensely lucrative in the 18th century. Moved to London. Granted arms and High Sheriff 1718. Bt 1757. The most senior line was seated at East Stoke (see Bromley-Wilson below). The line here was founded by a younger son who gained a peerage as Baron Carrington in 1796. The 2 Baron married Charlotte, daughter of Lord Willoughby de Eresby, and took the name Carington. Their son succeeded to the Gwydir estates (see Bertie) and became Marquess of Lincolnshire in 1912. The title died with him, and he was succeeded as Baron Carrington by his brother.

1. Abel Smith – Aldborough 1774-78 St. Ives 1780-84 St. Germans 1784-88
2. Abel Smith – Nottingham 1778-79
3. Robert Smith 1 Baron Carrington – Nottingham 1779-97
4. Samuel Smith – Ilchester 1780-84 Worcester 1784-90 Ludgershall 1791-93
5. Samuel Smith – St. Germans 1788-90 Leicester 1790-1818 Midhurst 1818-20 Wendover 1820-32
6. Robert Carington 2 Baron Carrington – Wendover 1818-20 Buckinghamshire 1820-31 High Wycombe 1831-38
7. Charles Carington 1 Marquess of Lincolnshire – Wycombe 1865-68
8. William Carington – Wycombe 1868-83
9. Robert Carington 4 Baron Carrington – Buckinghamshire 1880-85

Seats: Wycombe Abbey (Loakes House), Buckinghamshire (purch. 1799, sold by 1 Marquess c. 1896, school); Gwydir Castle, Caernarvonshire (medieval, remod. 16th c., 1 Marquess acq. by inher. from his mother dau. Of 22 Baron Willoughby 1895 – see Bertie, sold 1921)
Estates: Bateman 25809 (E) 42254. Rubinstein – 1 Baron left £120,000 in probate in 1838. Owned 4,500 acres in 2001.
Titles: Baron Carrington 1796- I; Baron Carrington 1797- GB; Viscount Wendover and Earl Carrington 1895-1928 UK; Baron Carington of Upton 1999-
Peers: 6 peers 1797-1938 1940-45
2 Lds Lt 19th, 20th
2 in Cabinet 1905-12 1963-64 1970-74 1979-82
1 KG 20th
Notes: 1 Baron was one of the first bankers and businessmen to gain a peerage and stay active in trade. The 6 Baron was one of the most important politicians in the Cabinet in the 1970s and 1980s, a great rarity having never served in the House of Commons. 1 Marquess and 1 Baron and two Smiths in ODNB.

Smith

Origins: Descended from the eldest son of Abel Smith, third son of Able Smith of East Stoke. The first MP was a younger brother of the 1 Baron Carrington see above. He was a Director of the East India Company for 38 years.

1. George Smith – Lostwithiel 1791-96 Midhurst 1800-06 Wendover 1806-30 Midhurst 1830-31
2. George Smith – Midhurst 1831-32 High Wycombe 1838-41

Seat: Selsdon House (Park), Surrey (built 1809, purch. c. 1810, sold 1890, hotel)
Estates: Rubinstein – George Smith MP left £200,000 in probate in 1836.

Smith

Origins: Descended from a younger brother of 1 Baron Carrington.

1. Abel Smith – Malmesbury 1810-12 Wendover 1812-18 Midhurst 1820-30 Wendover 1830-32 Hertfordshire 1835-47
2. Abel Smith – Hertfordshire 1854-57 1859-65 1866-85 E. Hertfordshire 1885-98
3. Samuel Smith – Aylesbury 1859-80
4. Rowland Smith – S. Derbyshire 1868-74
5. Frederick Smith – N. Nottinghamshire 1868-80
6. Abel Smith – Christchurch 1892-1900 Hertford Div. Hertfordshire 1900-10

Seats: Woodhall Park, Hertfordshire (built 1778-82, purch. 1801 for £180,000, remod. mid-19th c., family abandoned house pre 1939, became a school, live in converted stables and still own estate); Sacombe Park, Hertfordshire (built c. 1800, purch. 1825, still own); Duffield Hall, Derbyshire (medieval, rebuilt 1630, purch. 1860, rebuilt 1870-71, sold 1919, now offices)
Estates: Bateman 11212 (E) 14617; Abel Smith, first MP of this line, inherited Woodhall and £400,000 in 1834.

Smith

Origins: Descended from a younger brother of the 1 Baron Carrington. John Smith, the first MP, was Chairman of the East India Company and involved in banking and insurance. Other MPs were also Directors of the East India Company and bankers.

1. John Smith – Wendover 1802-06 Nottingham 1806-18 Midhurst 1818-30 Chichester 1830-31 Buckinghamshire 1831-34
2. John Abel Smith – Midhurst 1830-31 Chichester 1831-59 1863-68
3. Martin Smith – Midhurst 1831-32 High Wycombe 1847-65
4. Jervoise Smith – Falmouth 1866-68
5. Sir Gerard Smith – High Wycombe 1883-85

Seats: Dale Park, Sussex (built 1784, purch. 1825, sold 1848, demolished c. 1960); Blendon Hall, Kent (old house, rebuilt 1763, purch. and remod. c. 1810, sold later 19th c.)
Estates: Martin Smith left around £400,000 in personality mid-19th c.
Notes: Two in ODNB.

Bromley-Wilson

Origins: The son of Sir George Smith 1 Bt of East Stoke, Nottinghamshire took the name Bromley in 1778 at the direction of the first cousin of his mother, Robert Bromley of Abberley, Worcestershire. His son, the 3 Bt married Ann, daughter and heiress of Daniel Wilson of Dallam Tower, Westmorland. The brother of the 6 Bt succeeded to the Dallam Tower estates in 1822 and took the name Bromley-Wilson. The Wilsons began as businessmen in Kendal in the early 17th century and purchased land.

1. Daniel Wilson – Westmorland 1708-22 1727-47
2. Edward Wilson – Westmorland 1747-54
3. Robert Bromley – S. Nottinghamshire 1849-50

Seats: Dallam Tower, Westmorland (medieval, rebuilt 16th c., Wilsons purch. later 17th c., new house 1720-22, Bromleys succ. 1822, add. 1826, still own); Stoke Hall, Nottinghamshire (Smiths purch. mid-18th c., took name Bromley in 1778, add. 1812, sold 1923, part demolished 1920s); Parkhouse, Lancashire; Casterton Hall, Westmorland (Wilsons acq. by mar. 1793 and rebuilt 1811, sold c. 1952)
Estates: Bateman 9897 (E) 11401
Title: Baronet 1757-

Holt

Origins: A younger brother of Edward Wilson of Dallam Tower married in 1754 Lucinda eldest daughter of Rowland Holt of Redgrave Hall, Suffolk, acquired by Sir John Holt, Lord Chief Justice of the King's Bench in 1702. Their son, George Holt-Wilson, succeeded to Redgrave.

1. Sir John Holt – Bere Alston 1689
2. Rowland Holt – Suffolk 1759-68 1771-80

Seat: Redgrave Hall, Suffolk (medieval and 1545-60, purch. 1702, remod. 1765, passed to Wilsons 1786, contents sold 1936, sold 1946, fire 1946, demolished 1947 and 1970)
Estates: Bateman 6249 (E) 7997
Notes: One in ODNB.

Carus-Wilson

Origins: Cousins of the Wilsons of Dallam. **First Carus MP for Lancashire 1553**. Judge 1567.

1. Wilson Carus-Wilson – Cockermouth 1821-27

Seats: Casterton Hall, Westmorland (succ. aunt, Anne Place, to Casterton and took the name Wilson 1793); Halton Hall, Lancashire (purch. 1553, sold 1743, demolished 1930s)
Estates: Bateman 2700 (E) 4300
Notes: Carus family Roman Catholic until the 18th century. Two in ODNB.

SMITH II

Origins: Founded by a successful Chester (Mayor 1558) goldsmith and Alderman. He purchased land in the reign of Henry VIII and entered the gentry, High Sheriff 1553, and knighted, sitting as MP for the city and the county (B. E. Harris, ed., *Victoria County History of the County of Cheshire*, 1979, II, 102). **First MP 1545 for Cheshire. One additional MP 1640 for Chester**.

1. Sir Thomas Smith 1 Bt – Chester 1661-75

Seats: Hatherton Hall (House), Cheshire (purch. later 16th c., sold c. 1700, later demolished); Hough, Cheshire (purch. early 16th c., rebuilt 17th c., sold by 1706)
Estates: Worth £900 pa in the 1650s.
Title: Baronet 1660-1706
Notes: Bankrupt and extinct early 18th century.

SMITH III

<u>Viscount Hambleden</u> (1891- UK)

Origins: The Smiths began with a small newspaper delivery business in the 1780s that built up to a national chain of newsstands and bookshops of the mid-19th century and beyond, W. H. Smith.

1. William Smith – Westminster 1868-85 Strand Div. Westminster 1885-91
2. William Smith 2 Viscount Hambleden – Strand Div. Westminster 1891-1910

Seats: Greenlands, Buckinghamshire (old house, new house built early 19th c., add. c. 1855, purch. 1871, family departed 1945, sold 1952, institutional use); Manor House, Hambleden Manor, Buckinghamshire (built 1603, purch. estate 1871, remod. 19th c., purch. house 1923, family departed after WWII, part sold 2008); Hampton Court, Herefordshire (built 1435, purch. 1972, sold 1975)
Estates: Bateman 6777 (E) 10485. W. H. Smith left £1,773,000 in 1892. Worth £200,000,000 in 1990.
Peers: 2 peers 1913-45
1 in Cabinet 1877-80 1885-91

Note: W. H. Smith remained in the Commons, his wife being created Viscountess Hambleden in 1891 with special remainder to the future male line. 2 Viscount and one other in ODNB.

SMITH IV [Howard, Stephen] *ENGLAND & SCOTLAND*

Baron Strathcona and Mount Royal (1897-1914 1900- UK)

Origins: The 1 Baron Strathcona (Smith) was the son of a village tradesman. He became a clerk in the Hudson's Bay Company in Canada and was co-founder of the Canadian Pacific Railroad Company with his cousin the 1 Baron Mount Stephen (Stephen). The 1 Baron Strathcona was a Canadian MP before returning to the UK.

1. Donald Howard 3 Baron Strathcona – N. Cumberland 1922-26

Seats: Colonsay House (Kiloran), Argyllshire (built 1722, add. early 19th c., purch. 1904, add. c. 1910, still own); Debden Hall, Essex (old house with add. 1795, purch. c. 1910, demolished 1936)
Estate: A large highland property. The 1 Baron Strathcona left £4,000,000 in estates and £500,000 in cash in 1914.
Peers: 3 peers 1897-1914 1926-45
Note: The 4 Baron was a Minister of State in the 1970s. See McPhee, *The Crofter and the Laird.* 1 Baron in ODNB.

Baron Mount Stephen (1891-1921 UK)

Origins: The 1 Baron Mount Stephen, the son of a carpenter (last name Stephen), started as a draper and manufacturer of woolen goods in Canada. Later he became the President of the Bank of Montreal 1876. He returned to England in the 1890s and purchased Brocket.

No MPs

Seat: Brocket Hall, Hertfordshire (old house, new house built 1760, leased 1893, lease expired 1921)
Estates: The 1 Baron left a million and a half pounds in 1921.
Titles: Baronet 1886-1921
Peer: 1 peer 1891-1921
Notes: 1 Baron in ODNB.

SMITH V (Smyth, Smythe)

Origins: Merchants in Bristol in the 16th century (Mayor) who set up as gentry. **First MP 1554. Two further MPs 1558-1642.** On the extinction of the male line in 1741, the sister of the 3 Bt married Jarrit Smith (Smyth) MP, who was created a Baronet and succeeded to Ashton Court.

1. Sir Hugh Smith 1 Bt – Somerset 1660 1679
2. Sir John Smith 2 Bt – Somerset 1685-87 1695-98
3. Sir Jarrit Smith 1 Bt – Bristol 1756-68

Seats: Ashton Court, Somerset (purch. and built 1545, remod. 18th c., sold 1946, owned by local govt.)
Estates: Bateman 14974 (E) 35465
Titles: Baronet 1661-1741; 1763-1849; 1859-1901
Notes: Smyth family and one other have an entry in ODNB.

SMITH VI (Smijth, Smyth) [Bowyer]

Origins: Mercers in London mid-16th century. The Smiths acquired Hill Hall by marriage in 1554. The first MP was a Secretary of State under Edward VI and Elizabeth I. **First MP 1547 (Essex 1571-72). One other MP 1589.**

1. Sir William Bowyer-Smijth 11 Bt – S. Essex 1852-57

Seats: Hill Hall, Essex (acq. by mar. 1554, built 1556-75, leased from 1900, sold 1925, fire c. 1969, flats 2003); Mounthall (Mount Hall), Essex (medieval, acq. by mar. and purch. 1553-56, remod. 16th c., declined into a farm house, sold 1925)
Estates: Bateman 7237 (E) 9100
Title: Baronet 1661-
Note: The 10 Bt assumed the name Bowyer in 1839

SMITH VII [Assheton] *ENGLAND & WALES*

Origins: A prosperous London merchant acquired some landed property in the mid-17th century. His grandson became Chancellor of the Exchequer and Speaker of the House of Commons 1705. He acquired the Vaynol estate in the reign of Queen Anne, where great quarries made the family rich. The son of the first MP left Vaynol to his nephew Thomas Assheton, who took the name Smith. The Asshetons were gentry by the 15th century, Sheriff 1473, Kt 1482, Bt 1620.

1. John Smith – Ludgershall 1679 1689-90 Bere Alston 1691-95 Andover 1695-1713 East Looe 1715-23
2. Thomas Smith – Milborne Port 1709 10 East Looe 1710-13 Eye 1715-22 Tregony 1727-28
3. Thomas Assheton Smith – Caenarvonshire 1774-80 Andover 1797-1821
4. Thomas Assheton Smith – Andover 1821-31 Caernarvonshire 1832-37

Seats: Vaynol (Vaenol) Park, Caenarvonshire (built c. 1550, acq. 1696, sold 1980 - part passed to Duffs c. 1800 and new house built for them); Ashley Hall, Cheshire (acq. by 17th c., sold 1860, partly demolished 1972) (Assheton seat); Tidworth House, Hampshire (purch. 1650, built c. 1825-30, remod. c. 1860, sold 1877)
Estates: Bateman 34482 (W) 43022. Rubinstein – Thomas Assheton Smith left £180,000 in probate in 1828. (Personal wealth over £800,000 in 1904.)
Titles: Baronet 1620- ; 1911-
1 Ld Lt 19th
1 in Cabinet 1699-1701 1708-10
Notes: In 1859 Vaynol was left to the grandson of the last MP's sister, who took the name Assheton Smith. Tidworth went to a nephew of his wife who sold it. Bateman 3580 (E) 2666. Three in ODNB.

SMOLLETT *SCOTLAND*

Origins: The founder of the family was a merchant and Baillie of Dumbarton in the early 16th century. The family rose into the gentry in the lifetime of Sir James Smollett MP below, who gained estates through the law and business acumen and purchased Bonhill. Kt 1698.

1. Sir James Smollett – [Dumbartonshire 1685-86 1689-1702 1703-07] Scotland 1707-08
2. Alexander Smollett – Dumbartonshire 1797-99
3. Alexander Smollett – Dumbartonshire 1841-59
4. Patrick Smollett – Dumbartonshire 1859-69 Cambridge 1874-80

Seats: Bonhill House, Dumbartonshire (purch. 1684, ceased to be main seat after 1763, passed to the female line, who took the name Smollett 1775, continued as part of the Cameron House estate); Cameron House, Dumbartonshire (medieval, acq. 1763, built c. 1830 and 1865, sold 1983); Stainflett (Dalquhurn House), Dumbartonshire (purch. 1692, ceased to be a residence later 18th c. when it became an industrial site, demolished 19th c.)
Estates: Worth c. £1,600 pa in later 18th c.
Notes: Two in ODNB.

SMYTH I (Smythe) [Meade-Ogle] *IRELAND*

Smyth

Origins: Emigrated from Yorkshire to Ireland in the 17th century. The first {MP} was the son of a Mayor of Waterford. His brother was Bishop of Kilmore and Ardagh, who left him landed estates. Sheriff 1691.

1. Thomas Smyth – {Killybegs 1692-93 Fore 1695-99 1703-12}
2. William Smyth – {County Westmeath 1784-1800} 1801-08
3. Robert Smyth – County Westmeath 1824-26

Seat: Drumcree House, Westmeath (acq. 17th c., built mid-18th c., resident into 20th c., now derelict)
Estates: Bateman 4432 (I) 3195; and another branch at Ballynegall, Westmeath 11056 (I) 7768

Meade-Ogle

Origins: Wealthy merchants in Drogheda. The Meade-Ogle estates passed by marriage to William Meade Smythe MP 1822-26.

1. William Meade-Ogle – {Drogheda 1768-83 1790-97}
2. Henry Meade-Ogle – {Drogheda 1783-90} 1806-07 1812-20
3. William Meade Smythe – Drogheda 1822-26

Seats: Barba Villa House, Westmeath (Smythes acq. 1670, built c. 1730, sold 1955, now offices); Deer Park (Deerpark), Devon (built 1755, resident 19th c., hotel)
Estates: Bateman: 5035 (I) 2320 and 2108 (I) 1653

SMYTH II (Smith)

Origins: Businessman dealing in tin, invested in overseas voyages, Mayor of Exeter 1567 and **first MP 1604**, Kt. **Another MP 1614**. High Sheriff 1616.

1. Sir James Smyth – Exeter 1661 Camelford 1679-81

Seats: Trehenick, Cornwall (purch. 1609, sold by 1681); Larkbeare House, Devon (medieval, acq. c. 1617, sold by 1681)
Notes: Sir George Smyth MP left £20,000 in 1619. Heavily indebted, extinct 1681.

SMYTH III

Origins: Became rich as wool merchants in Wakefield c. 1700. Gradually built up a landed estate over the 18th century. A great house built by Carr of York in the 1760s-70s.

1. John Smyth – Pontefract 1783-1807
2. John Smyth – University of Cambridge 1812-22
3. John Smyth – York 1847-65

Seat: Heath Hall, Yorkshire (built c. 1584-98, acq. 1709, rebuilt 1754-80, family departed 1882, sold c. 1935, repurch. 1938, sold 1958 – Old Hall purch. 1809)

SMYTH IV

Origins: The father of the 1 Bt was a London draper. Kt 1660. Lord Mayor of London 1684. 1 Bt was a silk merchant and purchased Upton. The 5 Bt was a banker in Paris.

1. Sir Robert Smyth 3 Bt – Andover 1695-98
2. Sir Robert Smyth 5 Bt – Cardigan 1774-75 Colchester 1780-90
3. Sir George Smyth 6 Bt – Colchester 1826-29 1835-50

Seats: Upton House, Essex (purch. 1666, sold 1782); Berechurch Hall, Essex (built early 18th c., add. c. 1772, sold 1860s, demolished 1952)
Titles: Baronet 1665-1852; 1714-1811
Notes: On the extinction of the title on the death of the 6 Bt in 1852 the estates passed to the children of an illegitimate daughter Charlotte, wife of Thomas White of Wetherfield, Essex and were sold. One in ODNB.

SMYTH V

<u>Viscount Carrington</u> (1643-1706 I)

Origins: Claimed falsely descent from the standard bearer of Richard II. Rose by the law in the first half of the 16th century and married the heiress to Wootton Wawen (d. 1606). Baron of the Exchequer 1539, Kt. His son married the heiress of Ashby Folville. Estates passed to Wright family 1758, who were distantly related and took the name Smyth.

No MPs

Seats: Ashby Folville, Leicestershire (acq. by mar. 1540, descendents still own); Wootton Hall, Warwickshire (medieval, acq. mar. 1531 and 1559, rebuilt 1687, passed to relatives 1706, sold 1904)

Title: Baron Carrington 1643-1706 E
Peers: 3 peers 1660-1706
1 Ld Lt 17th
Notes: A Roman Catholic family. Not related to the Smith Barons Carrington above (Smith I). One in ODNB.

SMYTH VI *IRELAND*

Origins: In Waterford in the later 16th century. Connected by marriage to the Earl of Cork. **First {MP 1634},** Kt.

1. Boyle Smyth – {Tallagh 1661-62}
2. Boyle Smyth – {Youghal 1713-14}

Seat: Ballynatray (Ballynetra) House, Waterford (acq. later 16th c., passed out of family mid-19th c.)

SMYTHE

Viscount Strangford (1628-1869 I)

Origins: The original Smythe was a yeoman, son of a clothier and small landowner (d. 1538). His son was a haberdasher and then a government official. Farmer of Customs under Elizabeth I. The grandson of the yeoman was first Governor of the East India Company. JP 1587. Sheriff 1600. Kt 1603. **First MP 1553. Four additional MPs 1583-1626. One additional MPs possible 1604.**

1. Philip Smythe 1 Viscount Strangford – Hythe 1660
2. Charles Smythe – Lostwithiel 1668-79 Penryn 1679-81
3. George Smythe 7 Viscount Strangford – Canterbury 1841-52

Seat: Westenhanger (Ostenhanger) House (Castle), Kent (medieval, remod. c. 1505-25, acq. 1585, add. 17th c., sold c. 1685, most of old house demolished and new house c. 1701, business venue)
Estates: Worth £4,000 pa in the 1630s, later much less. The 2 Viscount was already in financial trouble in the 1660s. Several Viscounts were granted royal pensions to maintain the dignity of the title. The 7 Viscount left c. £7,000 in personality 1858 and the 8 and last Viscount under £3,000 in 1869.
Title: Baron Penshurst 1825-69 UK
Peers: {3 peers 1715-24 1736-1800} 3 peers 1825-69
Notes: John Fyneux (**MP 1571**) of Hearne, Kent left his estates to his daughter who married Sir John Smyth (MP 1584-1604) see above. The 6 Viscount left most of whatever

money he had to his illegitimate children. 6, 7, and 8 Viscounts and three others in ODNB.

SNEYD

Origins: Small gentry by the 14th century, but rose high under the Tudors through law and trade. Mayor of Chester under Henry VIII. His son was a soldier at Pinkie, Kt. Purchased more land at the Dissolution (*Country Life*, 23, p. 306). **First MP 1547. Two additional MPs 1640-43.**

1. William Sneyd – Staffordshire 1660
2. William Sneyd – Newcastle-under-Lyme 1685-87
3. Ralph Sneyd – Staffordshire 1713-15
4. William Sneyd – Lichfield 1718
5. Walter Sneyd – Castle Rising 1784-90

Seat: Keele Hall, Staffordshire (built later 16th c., add. 1830-33, rebuilt 1855-61 at a cost of £62,000 – Franklin, *The Gentleman's Country House*, 263 – leased out from 1900 and war use, sold 1948, now university use)
Estates: Bateman 9232 (E) 18329
Note: Two 18th c. Irish MPs may have been relatives.

SOAME [Buckworth]

Origins: Grocers in London in the 15th century. Entered the gentry in Norfolk but also stayed in business. A very rich Lord Mayor of London 1598. **First MP 1601. One additional MP 1640-48**. The 6 Buckworth Bt succeeded to the Soame estates and took the additional name Soame 1806, even though he was not a relative of the Soames. The 1 Bt was a fishmonger.

1. Edmund Soame – Thetford 1702-05
2. Sir John Buckworth 2 Bt – Weobley 1734-61

Seats: Dereham Grange, Norfolk (purch. 1702-06, sold 1806); (Little) Thurlow Hall, Suffolk (purch. 1613, house built soon after, fire 1809, rebuilt 1849, sold 1885); Heydon (Haydon), Essex (purch. before 1517, rebuilt 18th c., sold 1840s)
Title: Baronet 1684-1798

SOMERSET *ENGLAND & WALES*

Duke of Beaufort (1682- E)

Origins: The illegitimate son of Henry Beaufort Duke of Somerset (descended from an illegitimate son of John of Gaunt, cr. Earl of Somerset 1397, Duke 1443), married a Welsh heiress, a cousin of Henry VII, and was granted many forfeited estates post-1485. The family also did very well out of the Reformation. **First MP 1553 for Monmouthshire. Three additional MPs 1558-1614, all for the county**.

1. Henry Somerset 1 Duke of Beaufort – Breconshire 1654 Monmouthshire 1660-67
2. Charles Somerset Marquess of Worcester – Monmouth 1677-80 Monmouthshire 1679
3. Charles Somerset 4 Duke of Beaufort – Monmouthshire 1731-34 Monmouth 1734-45
4. Henry Somerset 6 Duke of Beaufort – Monmouth 1788-90 Bristol 1790-96 Gloucestershire 1796-1803
5. Lord Charles Somerset – Scarborough 1796-1802 Monmouth 1802-13
6. Lord Robert Somerset – Monmouth 1799-1802 Gloucestershire 1803-31 Cirencester 1834-37
7. Lord Arthur Somerset – Monmouthshire 1805-16
8. Henry Somerset 7 Duke of Beaufort – Monmouth 1813-32 W. Gloucestershire 1835
9. Lord Granville Somerset – Monmouthshire 1816-48
10. Fitzroy Somerset 1 Baron Raglan – Truro 1818-20 1826-29
11. Henry Somerset 8 Duke of Beaufort – E. Gloucestershire 1846-53
12. Poulett Somerset – Monmouthshire 1859-71
13. Edward Somerset – W. Gloucestershire 1867-68
14. Lord Henry Somerset – Monmouthshire 1871-80

Seats: Badminton House, Gloucestershire (medieval and 16th c., purch. 1612, rebuilt c. 1620, rebuilt 1665-1700, remod. c. 1740, still own); Troy House, Monmouthshire (built 16th c., add. early 17th c., rebuilt 1681-84, add. 18th and 19th c., sold 1900, institutional use, abandoned); Llangattock Park, Breconshire (built c. 1838, add. 1906, still own); Cefntilla Court, Monmouthshire (built 1616 by Herberts, acq. by Lord Raglan 1856, add. 1860s and late 19th c., for sale 2014); Raglan Castle, Montgomeryshire (medieval, rebuilt 15th c., acq. and add. 16th c., slighted 1646, ruin)
Estates: Bateman 51085 (E & W) 56226. Worth £850 pa in 1526 and possibly £30,000 pa in 1714. Worth £107,000,000 with 52,000 acres in 1990. Lord Raglan owned 2,500 acres in 2001.
Titles: Baron Botetourt 1305- E (see Berkeley); Baron Herbert 1461- E; Earl of Worcester 1514- E; Marquess of Worcester 1642- E; Baron Raglan 1852- UK
Peers: 15 peers 1660-1700 1705-14 1728-56 1765-1945 1852-1945
6 Lds Lt 17th, 18th, 19th, 20th

1 in Cabinet 1841-46
7 KG 17th, 18th, 19th, 20th
Notes: The family remained Roman Catholic until the 3 Marquess of Worcester conformed in 1667. 1, 3, and 4 Barons Raglan and 1, 3, and 4 Earls and 2 Marquess and 1, 2, 4, 7, and 10 Dukes and seven others in ODNB.

SOMERVILLE I *IRELAND*

Baron Athlumney (1863-1929 I)

Origins: Scots to Ireland in the 17th c. The father of the 1 Bt was a wine merchant and userer in Dublin in the late 17th and early 18th centuries. The 1 Bt was Lord Mayor of the city.

1. James Somerville – {Dundalk 1703-05}
2. Sir James Somerville 1 Bt – {Dublin 1729-48}
3. James Somerville – {Carlow 1769-76 Newtown 1776-83}
4. Sir Marcus Somerville 4 Bt – {County Meath 1800} 1801-31
5. William Somerville 1 Baron Athlumney – Drogheda 1837-52 Canterbury 1854-65

Seats: Somerville House, Meath (purch. 1702, built soon after, add. c. 1830, passed by mar. to Agnews 1929, later sold); Dollardstown, Meath (built late 17th c., acq. mid-18th c., neglected by family 19th c., demolished 1986)
Estates: Bateman 10487 (I) 11364. Worth £5,000 pa in 1810.
Titles: Baron Meredyth 1866-1929 UK; Baronet 1748-
Peers: 2 peers 1866-1929
1 in Cabinet 1847-52
Notes: The Agnews inherited the estates in 1929 and took the name Somerville. 1 Baron in ODNB.

SOMERVILLE II *SCOTLAND*

Baron Somerville (1445?-1868 S)

Origins: The family was prominent in Scotland from 1350 onwards. An English branch was established in Warwickshire, which became extinct in the 18th century, when the estates of the two families were unified. **First MP 1295 for Warwickshire**.

No post-1660 MPs

Seats: The Drum (Drum House, Somerville House), Edinburghshire (acq. medieval period, built 1584, fire 1629, rebuilt 1726-34, sold 1817-20); Carnwarth, Lanarkshire (original seat, sold 1602, demolished 1970); Edstone Hall, Warwickshire (acq. by mar.

c. 1460, sold 1745, demolished c. 1929); Aston Somerville, Gloucestershire (inher. 1742, sold 1871 for £47,600); The Pavillion, Roxburghshire (purch. c. 1805, built c. 1806, add. c. 1836, passed to an heiress 1870, flats)
Estates: Worth £800 Scots in 1542. The Drum estate was worth £2,500 pa in 1796. The Aston estate was worth £1,000 pa in 1796. The Edstone estate was 2,015 acres in 1920.
Peers: 3 Scottish Rep peers 1741-47 1793-96 1796-1807
Notes: 1, 2, 4, 5, and 15 Barons and one other in ODNB.

SOUTHBY [Hayward]

Origins: Purchased estates in the late 16th century. **First MP 1654 for Berkshire.**

1. Richard Southby – Cirencester 1659 Berkshire 1679-81 1685-87
2. John Southby – Abingdon 1689-90

Seats: Carswell (Manor), Berkshire (purch. 1584, rebuilt early 17th c., passed to Haywards 1797 via heiress and that family resumed name Southby, see below); Somerford Keynes, Wiltshire (built 15th c., purch. by Straunge family 1554, acq. from them by Southbys mar. 1653, owned – Hayward line – into 19th c.)
Estates: Straunge estates worth £500 pa in 1630. Southbys worth £1,000 pa in 1667.
Notes: Thomas Strange and Robert Straunge of Somerford Keynes family were **MPs Cirencester 1572 and 1614**. The latter was a lawyer.

<u>Hayward</u>

Origins: Lawyers and officials in the 18th century. Inherited Southby estates by marriage 1797.

1. Thomas Hayward – Ludgershall 1741-47 1754-56

Seat: Woolstrop House (aka Quedgeley House), Gloucestershire (purch. 1670, rebuilt 1820, sold 1939, demolished 1980s); Carswell (Manor), Berkshire (inher. by mar. 1797, sold 1892, school)
Notes: Three in ODNB.

SOUTHCOTE

Origins: The first to rise above peasant status was a lawyer, Clerk of the Peace 1525. Judge 1563. **First MP 1547. Five further MPs 1553-93.**

1. Thomas Southcote – Dartmouth 1661-64

Seat: Buckland Tout Saints, Devon (acq. by mar. late 16th c., sold 1793, hotel)
Notes: Remained Roman Catholic into the 18th century. Two in ODNB.

SOUTHWELL [Coussmaker] *IRELAND & ENGLAND*

Viscount Southwell (1776- I)

Origins: Acquired land by marriage to an heiress in the late 15th century. Several members of the family were courtiers and officials under Henry VII and Henry VIII. Master of the Rolls 1540s. Acquired monastic land. Three brothers went to Ireland to seek their fortunes under James I as undertakers in the Munster plantation and as officials. Sheriff 1660. **First MP 1449. Six additional MPs 1455-1597, three kts of the shire.**

1. Richard Southwell – {Askeaton 1661-66}
2. Thomas Southwell 1 Baron Southwell – {County Limerick 1695-99 1703-13 1715-17}
3. William Southwell – {Kinsale 1703-13 Castlemartyr 1713-14 Baltimore 1715-20}
4. Thomas Southwell 2 Baron Southwell – {County Limerick 1717-20}
5. Richard Southwell – {County Limerick 1727-29}
6. Henry Southwell – {County Limerick 1729-58}
7. Thomas Southwell 1 Viscount Southwell – {Enniscorthy 1747-60 County Limerick 1761-66}
8. Bowen Southwell – {Downpatrick 1755-60}
9. Thomas Southwell 2 Viscount Southwell – {County Limerick 1767-68}
10. Robert Southwell – {Downpatrick 1776-83}

Seat: Castle Mattress (Matrix), Limerick (built 15th c., acq. by mar. c. 1610, passed to Browns by mar. to a Southwell heiress 1751, remod. 1837, sold 1928, institutional use)
Estates: Bateman 11781 (I) 7276. Held 23,195 acres worth £7,540 pa in 1832.
Titles: Baron Southwell 1717- I; Baronet 1662-
Peers: {5 peers 1717-96 1798-1800}
1 Ld Lt 19th
2 KP 19th
Notes: Resident in England post 1930. 1 Baron and six others in ODNB.

Baron de Clifford (1299- E)

Origins: A cadet line. Sir Robert Southwell MP (below) was a diplomat and politician in England. Edward Southwell married in 1729 Katherine, heiress of Thomas 6 Earl of Thanet and 18 Baron de Clifford. (The Cliffords were great feudal barons in the Middle Ages, see Clifford.) Their son succeeded as 20 Baron de Clifford in 1776. His daughter married George Coussmaker. On the death of the son, George Coussmaker MP in 1824, the estates and title passed to a daughter, 22 Baroness de Clifford, who married a nephew of the Duke of Bedford (see Russell). The Coussmakers came from Flanders in the 17th century and were seated at Dane Court, Kent.

1. Sir Robert Southwell – Penryn 1673-79 Lostwithiel 1685-87
2. Edward Southwell – {Kinsale 1692-93 1695-99} Rye 1702-08 {Dublin University 1703-13 Kinsale 1713-30} Tregony 1713 Preston 1713-15
3. Edward Southwell – {Downpatrick 1727-55} Bristol 1739-54
4. Edward Southwell 20 Baron de Clifford – {Kinsale 1761-68} Bridgwater 1761-63 Gloucestershire 1763-76
5. George Coussmaker – Kinsale 1818-21

Seats: Kings Weston, Gloucestershire (built 1580s, purch. 1679, remod. 1680s, rebuilt 1707-19, remod. 1763-73, sold 1833); Henbury, Gloucestershire (leased)
Estates: Irish estates worth £1,000 in later 17th c. English and Irish estates worth £2,000 pa in 1702, increased by marriage, etc. to £6,000 pa by 1730.
Peers: 2 peers 1776-77 1789-1832
1 in Cabinet 1703 1710-13
Notes: Two in ODNB.

SPECCOT

Speccot (Specote, Spekote)

Origins: Medieval Cornish and Devon family. **First MP 1341 for Cornwall. Four additional MPs 1558-1640.**

1. John Speccot – Newport 1661-78
2. John Speccot – Newport 1685-87 1689-95 Cornwall 1695-1701

Seat: Penheale, Cornwall (medieval, purch. 1620, rebuilt 1620-30s, passed to Sparks 1705)
Notes: Family extinct 1705 and Penheale passed by mar. to John Spark MP.

Sparke (Spark)

Origins: Settled in Plymouth and elected **first MP 1554**. Merchants and owned town property. **One additional MP 1628.**

1. John Sparke – Plymouth 1677-80
2. John Spark – Newport 1701-07

Seats: The Friary, Plymouth, Devon (purch. 1580s, passed out of family c. 1680); Penheale, Cornwall (acq. by mar. 1705, divided into three dwellings late 18th c., sold 1920)

SPEIRS *SCOTLAND*

Origins: Edinburgh merchants dealing in tobacco and sugar from the mid-18th century. The father of the first MP purchased a landed estate. The first MP also owned a cotton mill.

1. Archibald Speirs – Renfrewshire 1810-18
2. Alexander Speirs – Richmond 1835-41
3. Alexander Speirs – Paisley 1835-36
4. Archibald Speirs – Renfrewshire 1865-68

Seats: Elderslie House, Renfrewshire (purch. 1767, passed by inher. to Maitlands 1959, still own); Houston House, Renfrewshire (built 1625, demolished 1780, purch. 1782, new house 1872, passed by inher. to Maitlands 1959, flats from 1995)
Estates: Bateman 11493 (S) 17844
2 Lds Lt 19th, 20th

SPEKE

Speke

Origins: Settled in Somerset since the reign of Henry III. Acquired considerable estates in the 15th century by marriages. Added further property at the Dissolution and became one of the wealthiest and most influential families in the county by the 18th century. **First MP 1332 for Devon. Four additional MPs 1427-1572, all kts of the shire**.

1. George Speke – Somerset 1679-81
2. John Speke – Ilchester 1679-81 Taunton 1690-98
3. George Speke – Milbourne Port 1722-27 Taunton 1727-34 Wells 1735-47

Seats: White Lackington, Somerset (acq, mid-15th c., sold 1795); Jordans, Somerset (built 17th c., rebuilt 1796, demolished 1964, still own estate); Dillington, Somerset (purch. 1719, rebuilt first half 18th c., sold 1795)
Estates: Bateman 2536 (E) 4570. Estates worth £83,000 sold 1795.
Notes: The Spekes inherited Cornish estates from John Beauchamp **MP Cornwall 1545** in the later 16th century. The last Speke (George, MP below) left property worth £4,000 pa to his daughter Anne, who married Lord North (see North). Five in ODNB.

Speke

Origins: A cadet line early 17th century.

1. Sir Hugh Speke 1 Bt – Chippenham 1660-61
2. Sir George Speke 2 Bt – Bath 1675-81 Chippenham 1681

Seat: Hazelbury (Haxelbury), Wiltshire (acq. 1602, sold early 18th c.)
Title: Baronet 1660-83
Notes: Some members of the family remained Roman Catholic.

SPELMAN

Origins: Landed by the 14th century. Judge 1531. **First MP 1593. One further MP 1626.** These MPs were kinsmen.

1. John Spelman – Castle Rising 1645 1660

Seats: Narborough, Norfolk (acq. by mar. from the Narboroughs 1514, built early 16th c., rebuilt c. 1770, sold 1773); Congham House, Norfolk (purch. c. 1600, sold 18th c., burned 1938)
Estates: 3,396 acres in 1773
Notes: Male line extinct 1810. Four in ODNB.

SPENCE (Spens) *SCOTLAND*

Origins: Merchants and baillies in Rutherglen. **First [MP 1587 for Rutherglen].**

1. David Spence – [Rutherglen 1639-41 1643 1645-47 1648 1661 1665 1672-74 1678]
2. George Spence – [Rutherglen 1703-07]

Seat: Stonelaw Tower, Lanarkshire (medieval, acq. 16th c., passed out of family 1821, demolished 20th c.)

SPENCER I [Churchill, Jenyns, Ley]

Duke of Marlborough (1702- GB)

Origins: The Spencer family has two major branches, seated at Blenheim Palace and Althorp. Althorp was the original seat, but after the marriage of the 3 Earl of Sunderland with Lady Anne Churchill, the heiress of the 1 Duke of Marlborough, the senior line moved to Blenheim and eventually took the name Churchill. The Churchill family were merchants in Dorchester in the 16th century. (A number of kinsmen seated at Colliton House, Dorset and Churchill, Somerset are included here.) The grandfather of the 1 Duke achieved success as a lawyer and purchased a small estate. High Sheriff 1639. His son was also a lawyer. His son was a great soldier and politician, the 1 Duke, rewarded liberally by a grateful Quen and Parliament. The dukedom passed by special remainder via Lady Anne Churchill to the Spencers.

1. Sir John Churchill – Dorchester 1661-79
2. Sir Winston Churchill – Weymouth and Melcombe Regis 1661-79 Lyme Regis 1685-87
3. John Churchill 1 Duke of Marlborough – Newton (IoW) 1679
4. William Churchill – Dorchester 1685-87
5. Sir John Churchill – Bristol 1685
6. George Churchill – St. Albans 1685-87 1689-1708 Portsmouth 1708-10
7. Charles Churchill – Weymouth and Melcombe Regis 1701-10
8. Awnsham Churchill – Dorchester 1705-10
9. John Churchill – Dorchester 1708-09
10. William Churchill – Ipswich 1707-17
11. Charles Churchill – Castle Rising 1715-45
12. Joshua Churchill – Corfe Castle 1719-21
13. William Godolphin Marquess of Blandford – Penryn 1720-22 New Woodstock 1727-31
14. Charles Churchill – Stockbridge 1741-47 Milborne Port 1747-54 Great Marlow 1754-61
15. Lord Charles Spencer – Oxfordshire 1761-1801
16. Lord Robert Spencer – New Woodstock 1768-71 Oxford 1771-90 Wareham 1790-91 Tavistock 1802-07 1817-18 New Woodstock 1818-20
17. George Spencer-Churchill 5 Duke of Marlborough – Oxfordshire 1790-96 Tregony 1802-04
18. Lord Henry Spencer – Woodstock 1790-95
19. Horatio Churchill – Castle Rising 1796-1802
20. John Spencer – Wilton 1801-04
21. Lord Charles Spencer Churchill – St. Albans 1818-20 Woodstock 1830-32 1835-37
22. George Churchill 6 Duke of Marlborough – Chippenham 1818-20 Woodstock 1826-31 1832-34 1838
23. Lord Alfred Churchill – Woodstock 1845-47 1857-65
24. John Churchill 7 Duke of Marlborough – Woodstock 1847-57
25. Lord Randolph Churchill – Woodstock 1874-85 South Paddington 1885-95
26. Sir Winston Churchill – Oldham 1900-06 N. W. Manchester 1906-08 Dundee 1908-22 Epping Div. Essex 1924-45 Woodford 1945-64
27. Randolph Churchill – Preston 1940-45
28. Winston Churchill – Stratford 1970-83 Davyhulme 1983-97

Seats: Blenheim Palace, Oxfordshire (acq. 1704, built 1705-32, still own); Fen Ditton Hall, Cambridgeshire (built 15th c., add c. 1630, purch. post WWI, sold c. WWII); Minterne Magna, Dorset (leased 1660, ended occupation 1768); Colliton House, Dorset (acq. 16th c., built 1630s, sold 1933, club); Muston Manor, Dorset (purch. 1609, leased out from late 17th c., sold 1901, repurch. 1915, sold 1976, hotel); Langley Park, Buckinghamshire (purch. 1738, sold 1788)
Estates: Bateman 23511 (E) 36557. 1 Duke died worth c. one million pounds in 1722. Rubinstein – 4 Duke left £200,000 in probate 1817. Worth £38,000,000 with 11,500 acres in 1990.
Titles: Baron Spencer 1603- E; Earl of Sunderland 1643- E; Baron Churchill 1682-1722 S; Baron Churchill 1685- E; Earl of Marlborough 1689- E
Peers: 12 peers 1660-1729 1685-1722 1729-58 1760-1817 1806-1945
6 Lds Lt 18th, 19th, 20th
6 in Cabinet 1701-11 1714-21 1755 1763-65 1794 1867-68 1876-80 1885-87 1908-15 1917-22 1924-29 1939-45 1951-55
5 KG 18th, 19th, 20th
Notes: Blenheim cost a fantastic £300,000 to build (Lees-Milne, *English Country Houses: Baroque 1685-1715*, 183). See Rowse, *The Early Churchills*. The great Sir Winston Churchill was born at Blenheim and is buried at Bladon nearby. 1, 3, 4, 5, 6, and 7 Dukes and fifteen others in ODNB.

Viscount Churchill (1902- UK)

Origins: A cadet line established by the second son of the 4 Duke of Marlborough.

1. Francis Spencer 1 Baron Churchill – Oxfordshire 1801-15

Seats: Cornbury Park, Oxfordshire (purch. 1751, owned until 1894); West Lavington House, Wiltshire (purch. 1766, sold 1905)
Estates: Bateman 9112 (E) 11543
Title: Baron Churchill 1815- UK
Peers: 4 peers 1815-1945
Notes: 1 Viscount was Chairman of the Great Western Railway 1908-34. 1 Baron and one other in ODNB.

Earl Spencer (1765- GB)

Origins: Began as farmers in Warwickshire and became sheep breeders and graziers: agricultural entrepreneurs on a grand scale. Leased Althorp in the late 15th century and later purchased the estate. (Carpenter, *Locality and Polity: a Study of Warwickshire Landed Society 1401-1499*, 76; Finch, *The Wealth of Five Northamptonshire Families 1540-1640*, 38). Granted arms 1504. Kt and Sheriff 1551. Married a great heiress 1566.

First MP 1554 for Northamptonshire. Five additional MPs 1572-1648, one for the county. The senior line (Earls of Sunderland) inherited the Dukedom of Marlborough and Blenheim through marriage to a daughter of the great general, and a younger brother kept the Althorp and the Warwickshire estates. This line gained an earldom in its own right.

1. Richard Spencer – Northampton 1621 1624 1625 1626 1628 1661
2. Robert Spencer 1 Viscount Teviot – Great Bedwyn 1660 Brackley 1661-79
3. William Spencer – Lancaster 1679-81
4. Charles Spencer 3 Earl of Sunderland – Tiverton 1695-1702
5. John Spencer – New Woodstock 1732-46
6. John Spencer 1 Earl Spencer – Warwick 1756-61
7. George John Spencer 2 Earl Spencer – Northampton 1780-82 Surrey 1782-83
8. John Charles Spencer 3 Earl Spencer – Okehampton 1804-06 Northamptonshire 1806-32 S. Northamptonshire 1832-34
9. Frederick Spencer 4 Earl Spencer – Worcestershire 1831-32 Midhurst 1832-34 1837-41
10. John Poyntz Spencer 5 Earl Spencer – S. Northamptonshire 1857
11. Charles Robert Spencer 6 Earl Spencer – N. Northamptonshire 1880-85 Mid Northamptonshire 1885-95 1900-05

Seats: Althorp Park, Northamptonshire (purch. 1506, built c. 1508, add. 1570s, remod. 1666-68, remod. 1787-90, add. 1877, still own); Wimbledon Park (House), Surrey (built c. 1585-88, remod. 1639-42, demolished 1717, purch. by Ds. of Marlborough 1723 new house 1732-33 cost £70,000 with a park of 1,200 acres – Knight, *London's Country Houses*, 332-33 – fire 1785, service buildings converted to a house, new house 1800, sold 1843, demolished 1949); North Creake, Norfolk (purch. c. 1794, still own); Wormleighton Manor, Warwickshire (purch. 1506, built 1516-7, ceased to be a principal seat 1650s, still own); Ashton Hall, Lancashire (leased?); Dallington Hall, Northamptonshire (built c. 1720, purch. c. 1818, sold early 20th c., flats)
Estates: Bateman 27185 (E) 46764. Worth £6,500 to £8,000 pa in 1627 and £20,000 pa in 1783. Rubinstein – 2 Earl left £160,000 in probate in 1834. Worth £42,000,000 with 15,000 acres in 1990. ODNB says £89,000,000 in 1992.
Titles: Viscount Teviot 1685-94 S; Viscount Spencer 1761- E; Viscount Althorp 1905 – UK
Peers: [1 peer 1685-94] 7 peers 1761-1910 1905-1945
4 Lds Lt 17th, 19th, 20th
6 KG 17th, 18th, 19th, 20th
6 in Cabinet 1679-81 1683-89 1706-10 1714-19 1715-16 1718-21 1794-1801 1806-07 1830-34 1880-83 1886 1892-95
Notes: A large and valuable south London estate sold in the late 1830s to pay off debts. 1 Baron and 1, 2, and 3 Earls of Sunderland and 1, 2, 3, 4, 5, and 8 Earls Spencer and seven others in ODNB.

Spencer

Origins: Kinsmen descended from a younger son in the 16th century. **First MP 1584. One other MP 1604.**

1. Sir Thomas Spencer 3 Bt – Woodstock 1660-79
2. William Spencer – Bedford 1698-1705

Seats: Yarnton, Oxfordshire (old house, acq. 1580 rebuilt 1611, remod. 1670, sold 1695-1712, institutional use); Cople Hall, Bedfordshire (acq. 1531 or earlier, sold 1720)
Title: Baronet 1611-c.1771

Spencer

Origins: Cadet line descended from a younger son of Sir John Spencer of Althorp. He married the co-heiress of Brocket Hall, Hertfordshire.

1. Sir John Spencer 4 Bt – Hertfordshire 1705-08

Seat: Offley Place, Hertfordshire (purch. 1554, divided up among heiresses 1712)
Estates: Worth £1,500 pa in 1700.
Titles: Baronet 1627-33; 1642-1712
Notes: The male line became extinct in 1712 and the estates were divided among four sisters.

Jenyns (Jennyns, Jennings)

Origins: Master of the Skinners' Company in the 1550s. Purchased landed estates in the 1570s. Made a fortune as Manager of the Fen Company in the 17th century. Sarah Jenyns, wife of the 1 Duke of Marlborough, became the sole heiress of Richard Jenyns. **First MP 1628.**

1. Richard Jennings – St. Albans 1642 1659 1660-68
2. John Jenyns – Cambridgeshire 1710-17
3. Soame Jenyns – Cambridgeshire 1741-54 Dunwich 1754-58 Cambridge 1758-80

Seats: Bottisham Hall, Cambridgeshire (built later 16th c., acq. late 17th c., remod. c. 1700, built 1797, add. c. 1840, successors still own); Sandridge, Hertfordshire (acq. by mar. 1571, passed by inher. 1609 to Spencers and later by purch. to Duke of Marlborough, passed back to Spencers 1744 and held by the Earls Spencer into 20th c.); Hayes, Middlesex (purch. 1677); Holywell (Halywell), Hertfordshire (acq. by mar. 1571, passed to Spencers 1744, demolished and sold 1837)

Estates: Sarah Jenyns, Duchess of Marlborough died worth £17,000 pa in landed property and £250,000 in money.
Notes: The estates of Sir Ralph Rowlett (**MP 1547 for Hertfordshire**) in passed to the Jenyns in 1571. Two in ODNB.

Earl of Marlborough (1626-79 E)

Origins: The 1 Earl of Marlborough (Ley) married the sister of the 1 Baron Boteler. His daughter's daughter married the father of the 1 Duke of Marlborough (see above). The 1 Earl, who came from a gentry family, was Lord Chief Justice 1604. **First MP 1597. Two further MPs 1597-1626, one for Wiltshire**.

No post-1660 MPs

Seats: Teffont-Ewyes (Evias), Wiltshire (acq. 1545, sold 1652); Heywood, Wiltshire (acq. c. 1595, built early 16th c., sold by 1700, offices)
Titles: Baron Ley 1624-79 E; Baronet 1619-79
Peers: 2 peers 1660-65 1670-79
Notes: Weak finances in last years of the earldom. 1 and 3 Earls and two others in ODNB.

SPENCER II *IRELAND*

Origins: The first MP, whose father is unknown, was agent for the Marquess of Hertford. Sheriff 1704. His son was a barrister.

1. Brent Spencer – {Lisburne 1709-36}
2. Joshua Spencer – Sligo 1813-15
3. Sir Brent Spencer – Sligo 1815-18

Seat: Tremary (Trumery), Antrim (acq. c. 1700)
Estates: Worth £500 pa in 1714.
Notes: One in ODNB.

SPRING

Origins: Descended from a successful clothier in the 15th century. Acquired monastic property after the Dissolution. Kt 1547. **First MP 1624 for Suffolk. One additional MP 1646, also for the county.**

1. Sir William Spring 2 Bt – Suffolk 1679-81

Seat: Pakenham Hall, Suffolk (medieval, acq. 1545, rebuilt mid-16th c., estates divided between two heiresses 1735, sold 1779, demolished 1900 and rebuilt)
Estates: Worth £1,500 pa in 1735.
Title: Baronet 1641-1769
Notes: Estates remaining after 1735 passed to an heiress in 1811. Spring family has an entry in ODNB.

SPRING RICE *IRELAND*

<u>Baron Monteagle of Brandon</u> (1839- UK)

Origins: The Rice family came from Wales and settled in Ireland by the 14th century. They lost their land under Cromwell and built up new estates in the late 17th century. Chief Baron of the Exchequer (d. 1715). His son married a daughter of the Knight of Kerry. His grandson married 1785 Catherine Spring and took her name in addition to his own. Their son was a politician and 1 Baron. **First Spring {MP 1585 for County Kerry}. One possible additional {MP 1703}. First Rice {MP 1613 for County Kerry}. Three additional {MPs 1613-35}.**

1. Thomas Spring Rice 1 Baron Monteagle – Limerick 1820-30 Cambridge 1832-39

Seat: Mount Trenchard (Cappa), Limerick (built early 17th c., purch. and rebuilt 1770s by Thomas Rice, add. mid-19th c., sold 1947, institutional use)
Estates: Bateman 8755 (I) 6137
Peers: 5 peers 1839-66 1870-1945
1 in Cabinet 1834-39
1 KP 19th-20th
Notes: 1 Baron and one other in ODNB.

STANDISH [Stephenson]

<u>Standish</u>

Origins: The family was established in the parish from which it took its name by the reign of Richard I. **First MP 1626.**

1. Richard Standish – Lancashire 1654 1656 1659 1660
2. Sir Richard Standish 1 Bt – Wigan 1690-93
3. Sir Frank Standish 3 Bt – Preston 1768
4. Charles Standish – Wigan 1837-47

Seats: Standish Hall, Lancashire (acq. c. 1206, built 15th c., add. 1574, add. 1748, passed to Towneleys by mar. 1752 who took name Standish, passed to Stricklands later 18th c. who took the name Standish, add. 1822, sold 1920, most demolished 1930); Duxbury Hall (Park), Lancashire (acq. early 14th c., built 1632, rebuilt 1823-28, passed by mar. to Carrs 1840 who took name Standish, fire 1859, rebuilt 1861, sold 1891, demolished 1956); Borwick Hall, Lancashire (medieval, add. 1595, acq. by mar. 1688, sold 1854, institutional use)
Estates: Bateman 3080 (E) 6962
Title: Baronet 1677-1812
Notes: The main line at Standish remained Roman Catholic while a cadet at Duxbury became Protestant in the 17th century. The main line died out in the 18th c. A younger son of the Stricklands whose mother was a Standish took that name. The Biggs estates (Bt 1620-21) passed to the Standishes by marriage 1621. The Bindloss (Baronets – **2 MPS 1628-60 for Lancashire**) estates at Borwick Hall also came to the Standishes by mar. 1688. **First MP 1604. One additional MP 1614.** Five in ODNB.

<u>Stephenson</u>

Origins: Edward Stephenson of Farley Hill married the heiress Mary Standish in 1785 and took the name Standish. The Stephensons were London bankers in the mid 18th century.

1. Rowland Stephenson – Carlisle 1787-90
2. Rowland Stephenson Standish – Leominster 1827-30

Seats: Farley Hill Place, Berkshire (built c. 1730, purch. mid-18th c., still owned later 19th c.); Scaleby Castle, Cumberland (medieval, add. 16th c., rebuilt 1597-1606, restored early 17th c., purch. 1741, ruin by 1770s, sold most of estate c. 1800)
Estates: Bateman 3549 (E) 3866
Notes: The last MP was a bankrupt and fled to the USA to avoid prosecution for embezzlement. Family retained some estates. One in ODNB.

STANHOPE [Banks, Collingwood, Dormer, Hodgkinson, Spencer]

<u>Earl of Chesterfield</u> (1628-1967 E)

Origins: Began as merchants in Newcastle-upon-Tyne, a cadet line of an old gentry family, engaged in the Flanders wool trade. Collector of Customs 1364, Mayor 1364. His son married an heiress, acquired an estate in Nottinghamshire and reentered the gentry. (Payling, *Political Society in Lancastrian England: the Greater Gentry of Nottinghamshire*, 47-49) An official under Henry VIII acquired large estates during the Dissolution. **First MP 1360, for Newcastle. Fourteen additional MPs 1377-1628, eight of them kts of the shire and one {1634} Irish.**

1. Arthur Stanhope – Nottingham 1660-79
2. Philip Stanhope 4 Earl of Chesterfield – St. Germans 1715-22 Lostwithiel 1722-23
3. John Stanhope – Nottingham 1727-34 Derby 1736-48
4. Sir William Stanhope – Lostwithiel 1727 Buckinghamshire 1727-41 1747-68
5. Charles Stanhope – Derby 1730-36
6. Philip Stanhope – Liskeard 1754-61 St. Germans 1761-65
7. Lovell Stanhope – Winchester 1774-83
8. George Stanhope 7 Earl of Chesterfield – S. Nottinghamshire 1860-66

Seats: Bretby Park, Derbyshire (14th c. castle, purch. c. 1600, new house 1620s-30s, add. 1670, castle a ruin by 1712, demolished 1777-81, rebuilt 1812-13, passed to Carnarvons mid-19th c., sold 1915, hospital); Stanhope House (Chesterfield House), Mansfield Woodhouse, Nottinghamshire (purch. and built c. 1736, sold 1812); Eythrope House, Buckinghamshire (acq. by mar. from Dormers 1709, remod. mid-18th c., demolished c. 1810-11, sold 1875); Shelford Manor, Nottinghamshire (medieval, purch. 1537-40, rebuilt c. 1600, destroyed 1645, rebuilt c. 1678, declined into a farm); Holme Lacy, Herefordshire (built 1672, inher. by mar. 1820, remod. 1828-31, sold 1909); Beningborough Hall, Yorkshire (built c. 1714-16, purch. 1917, NT 1957)
Estates: 18494 (E) 34685 (includes estates that passed to the Earl of Carnarvon). The estate was 50,207 acres before 1850. (Craven and Stanley, *The Derbyshire Country House*, 45)
Titles: Baron Stanhope 1616-1967 E; Baronet 1807-
Peers: 11 peers 1660-1815 1826-71 1873-1945
1 Ld Lt 18th
1 in Cabinet 1745-48
3 KG 18th, 19th, 20th
Notes: The 2 Earl married Lady Elizabeth Dormer and became coheir to the estates of the Earl of Carnarvon (see below). The sister of the 7 Earl married the 4 Earl of Carnarvon (see Herbert), who inherited Bretby and the Nottinghamshire estates of the Earls of Chesterfield in 1871. 1 Baron and 1, 2, 4, and 5 Earls and four others in ODNB.

<u>Earl of Carnarvon</u> (1628-1709 E)

Origins: See above. The Dormers were established in Buckinghamshire since the 13th century. Became prosperous wool merchants in the 16th century. Sir Robert Dormer, **first MP 1529**, Lord Mayor of London 1541, purchased landed estates from which this line is descended. **Four additional MPs 1542-1646, two for Buckinghamshire**. The family was Roman Catholic through most of the 18th and into the 19th century. The 10 Baron Dormer conformed to the Established Church and took his seat in the House of Lords in 1823.

1. John Dormer – Buckingham 1646 1660
2. Fleetwood Dormer – Chipping Wycombe 1696-98 1701-10 Malmesbury 1719-22

3. Philip Dormer – Aylesbury 1698-1700
4. Robert Dormer – Aylesbury 1699-1700 Buckinghamshire 1701-02 Northallerton 1702-05 Buckinghamshire 1705-06

Seats: Lee Grange, Buckinghamshire; Idsworth, Hampshire (sold 1789); Peterley Manor, Buckinghamshire (sold c. 1785 and demolished); Grove Park, Warwickshire (medieval, remod. 16th c., acq. 1615, rebuilt early 19th c., remod. 1833-38, principal seat in the 19th c., family departed post-1945, demolished 1976, still own estate); Eythrope House, Buckinghamshire (acq. and built 16th c., add. c. 1610, passed by mar. to Stanhopes 1709, see above)
Estates: What remained after the Stanhopes inherited most of the property - Bateman 3435 (E) 6020. The family had an income of £6,000 pa in 1616.
Titles: Baron Dormer 1615- E; Viscount Ascott 1618-1709 E
Peers: 7 peers 1660-1709 1823-1922 1924-45
Notes: 1 Earl and three others in ODNB.

<u>Earl Stanhope</u> (1718-1967 GB)

Origins: Descended from the third son of the 1 Earl of Chesterfield.

1. James Stanhope 1 Earl Stanhope – Newport (IoW) 1702 Cockermouth 1702-13 Wendover 1714-15 Cockermouth 1715-17 Newport 1717
2. Charles Stanhope 3 Earl Stanhope – Chipping Wycombe 1780-86
3. Philip Stanhope 4 Earl Stanhope – Wendover 1806-07 Hull 1807-12 Midhurst 1812-16
4. James Stanhope – Buckingham 1817-18 Fowey 1818-19 Dartmouth 1822-25
5. Philip Stanhope 5 Earl Stanhope – Wootton Bassett 1830-32 Hertford 1832-33 1835-52
6. Arthur Stanhope 6 Earl Stanhope – Leominster 1868 E. Suffolk 1870-75
7. Philip Stanhope 1 Baron Weardale – Wednesbury 1886-92 Burnley 1893-1900 Market Harborough Div. Leicestershire 1904-05

Seats: Chevening, Kent (built 16th c., rebuilt 1616-30, purch. 1717, remod. 1718, remod. 1786-96, donated to the government 1967); Soldon Manor, Devon (built mid-16th and mid-17th c., inher. by mar. 1734, remod. 18th c., sold 1932)
Estates: Bateman 14341 (E & I) 13982
Titles: Viscount Mahon 1717- GB; Baron Weardale 1906-23 UK
Peers: 8 peers 1717-21 1735-1945 1906-23
1 Ld Lt 19th-20th
2 in Cabinet 1714-21 1936-40
1 KG 20th
Notes: 1, 3, 4, and 5 Earls and three others in ODNB.

Banks Stanhope

Origins: The founder was a country attorney who made a fortune as the agent of the Dukes of Leeds, Newcastle, and Norfolk. He purchased landed estates in Lincolnshire and Nottinghamshire. A younger grandson of the 3 Earl Stanhope succeeded to the Banks estates 1820. Later these passed to a younger son of the 5 Earl. The Hodgkinson estates passed to the Banks family by marriage in 1743.

1. Joseph Banks – Great Grimsby 1715-22 Totnes 1722-27
2. Joseph Banks – Peterborough 1728-34
3. William Banks – Grampound 1741-47
4. Robert Banks Hodgkinson – Wareham 1748-54
5. James Banks Stanhope – Lincolnshire 1852-68
6. Edward Stanhope – Mid Lincolnshire 1874-85 Horncastle Div. Lincolnshire 1885-93

Seats: Revesby Abbey, Lincolnshire (medieval, new house, 16th c., purch. 1714, rebuilt 18th c., passed by mar. to Stanhopes 1820, rebuilt 1843-44, sold 1990, now derelict); Overton Hall, Derbyshire (built mid-late 17th c., add. 1702, Banks acq. from the Hodgkinsons in 1743, add. 1788, passed to Stanhopes 1820, sold by 1873, institutional use)
Estates: Bateman 7847 (E) 13015
Title: Baronet 1781-1820
1 in Cabinet 1885-92
Notes: Two in ODNB.

Earl of Harrington (1742- GB)

Origins: Descended from a younger brother of the 1 Earl of Chesterfield. **First MP 1624. One additional MP 1640.**

1. Sir William Stanhope – Nottingham 1685-87
2. Thomas Stanhope – Derby 1702-05
3. William Stanhope 1 Earl of Harrington – Derby 1715-22 Steyning 1727 Derby 1727-30
4. Charles Stanhope – Milbourne Port 1717-22 Aldborough 1722-34 Harwich 1734-41
5. William Stanhope 2 Earl of Harrington – Aylesbury 1741-47 Bury St. Edmunds 1747-56
6. Charles Stanhope 3 Earl of Harrington – Thetford 1774 Westminster 1776-79
7. Henry Stanhope – Bramber 1782-84
8. Robert Stanhope – Dover 1831-32

Seats: Elvaston Castle, Derbyshire (medieval house, purch. 1550s, new house 1633, remod. 1670, c. 1700, c. 1750, rebuilt 1815-29 and 1836, family abandoned before WWII,

sold 1964 to County Council); Gawsworth New Hall, Cheshire (medieval, rebuilt 16th c., part demolished 1701, rebuilt 1707-12, purch. 1727, remod. 1914, sold 1935)
Estates: Bateman 12994 (E) 24528. Worth £45,000,000 in 1990. Owned 29 acres in London said to be worth 290 million pounds in 2001. Also owned 900 acres in County Limerick where the 11 Earl lives.
Title: Baron Harrington 1730- GB
Peers: 11 peers 1730-1929 1943-45
1 in Cabinet 1730-51
Notes: 1, 2, 3, 4, and 5 Earls and one other in ODNB.

Spencer Stanhope

Origins: Descended from a younger son of Thomas Stanhope (later 15th c.). Walter Stanhope of Horsforth (his father was a woolen merchant whose estates were inherited from his uncles, a lawyer and an ironmaster, [Ward and Wilson, *Land and Industry: The Landed Estates and the Industrial Revolution*, 12]) married the daughter and heiress of William Spencer of Cannon Hall (originally from Montgomeryshire), also involved in the iron industry. The latter family dominated the iron industry in Yorkshire from the mid-17th to mid-18th century. Walter's two younger sons succeeded to estates of their own. For the elder, see below, while the younger inherited Roddam Hall.

1. Walter Stanhope – Carlisle 1775-80 1802-12 Haselmere 1780-84 Kingston upon Hull 1784-90 Cockermouth 1800-02
2. Sir Walter Spencer Stanhope – S. Div. W. R. Yorkshire 1872-80

Seats: Cannon Hall, Yorkshire (built c. 1690-1710, add. 1764-68, add. 1890-91, sold 1951); Horsforth Hall, Yorkshire (built by Stanhopes 1699-1707, sold 1930, demolished early 1950s); Roddam Hall, Northumberland (built early 18th c., add. 1768-83, acq. by mar. 1808 by Spencer Stanhopes, who took name Roddam, sold c. 1970)
Estates: Bateman 16613 (E) 14659
Notes: Spencer family has an entry in and one other in the ODNB.

Collingwood

Origins: Edward Stanhope, son of Walter Spencer Stanhope, succeeded in the mid-19th century to the Collingwood estates. The Collingwoods rose from the status of famers in the late 15th and early 16th centuries. **First MP 1478**, Sheriff 1538. **A second MP 1529, both for Northumberland.** A junior line produced a lawyer, Recorder and Mayor of Newcastle 1740. The son of the Mayor left the Dissington estate to his niece, who married Walter Spencer Stanhope. The property passed to a younger son who took the name Collingwood. Another estate was left to a kinsman, Admiral Lord Collingwood of Trafalgar fame.

1. Daniel Collingwood – Berwick-on-Tweed 1665-79 Morpeth 1679-81

Seats: Dissington Hall, Northumberland (purch. 1673, rebuilt 1790s, passed by mar. to Spencer Stanhopes, who took the name Collingwood, 1806, passed to the Caltrops by mar. who changed name to Collingwood 1868, family departed 1920, sold 1955); Chirton House, Northumberland (built 1693 by Milbournes, passed to Collingwoods in the 18th c., sold 1876, demolished 1899)
Estates: Bateman 5704 (E) 5848. The 1 Baron left £163,000 in 1810.
Notes: Family departed for New Zealand 1934. 1 Baron Collingwood and one other in ODNB.

STANLEY [Baker-Holroyd, Massey, Morley, Smith] *ENGLAND & WALES*

Earl of Derby (1485- E)

Origins: One of the most ancient and powerful dynasties in the English aristocracy. The family became gentry under Kings Stephen and Henry II in the mid-12th century. Lord Deputy in Ireland under Richard II. Married a great heiress c. 1380s. KG 1405. Lords of the Isle of Man (170,000 acres) from 1406 to 1736 (when it passed to the Duke of Atholl). A celebrated soldier at Potiers. (Coward, *The Stanleys, Lord Stanley, and Earls of Derby, 1385-1672*, 2-7) **First MP 1407. Twelve further MPs 1413-1626, 11 kts of the shire**. Baron 1456. Earl 1485. Continued to hold high political office through the Second World War.

1. William Stanley – Liverpool 1661-70
2. Edward Stanley – Lancashire 1661-64
3. James Stanley 10 Earl of Derby – Clitheroe 1685-87 Preston 1689-90 Lancashire 1690-1702
4. Sir Thomas Stanley 4 Bt – Preston 1695-98
5. Charles Stanley – Preston 1702-05 Lancashire 1705-13 Clitheroe 1713-14
6. Edward Stanley 11 Earl of Derby – Lancashire 1727-36
7. James Smith Stanley Lord Strange – Lancashire 1741-71
8. Edward Smith Stanley 12 Earl of Derby – Lancashire 1774-76
9. Thomas Stanley – Lancashire 1776-79
10. Edward Smith Stanley 13 Earl of Derby – Preston 1796-1812 Lancashire 1812-32
11. Edward Stanley 14 Earl of Derby – Stockbridge 1822-26 Preston 1826-30 Windsor 1831-32 N. Lancashire 1832-44
12. Henry Stanley – Preston 1832-37
13. Edward Stanley 15 Earl of Derby – Kings Lynn 1848-69
14. Frederick Stanley 16 Earl of Derby – Preston 1865-68 N. Div. Lancashire 1868-85 Blackpool Div. Lancashire 1885-86
15. Edward Stanley 17 Earl of Derby – Westhoughton Div. S. E. Lancashire 1892-1906

16. Arthur Stanley – Ormskirk Div. S. Lancashire 1898-1918
17. George Stanley – Preston 1910-22 E. Willesden 1924-29
18. Edward Stanley 18 Earl of Derby – Abercromby Div. Liverpool 1917-18 Flyde Div. Lancashire 1922-38
19. Oliver Stanley – Westmorland 1924-45 Bristol W. 1945-50
20. Edward Stanley – N. Fylde Div. Lancashire 1950-66

Seats: Knowsley, Lancashire (Lathoms acq. 12th c., Stanleys acq. 1380s by mar. to Lathom heiress, add. early 16th c. and late 17th c., became principal seat after the destruction of Lathom in the Civil War, add. 1722-37, add. 1820 and 1836-39, remod. 1890 and 1912, partially demolished and family departed for a new house in the park 1954, restored and resumed residence 1990s, still own); Lathom Hall, Lancashire (medieval house, acq. by mar. to a great Lathom heiress 1385, ruined 1644, sold 1714); Coworth Park, Berkshire (built 1776, purch. 1899, sold 1957, hotel); Witherslack Hall, Lancashire (acq. 1743, built 1874, sold 1973, school); Leasowe Castle, Cheshire (built 1593, passed by mar. to the Egertons of Oulton, sold c. 1800?); Crag Hall, Cheshire, (built 1795-1815, purch. late 19th c., still own); The Oaks, Surrey (built c. 1770, demolished c. 1956); Holwood House, Kent (built c. 1823, purch. 1852, sold 1953)
Estates: Bateman 68942 (E) 163273. Worth £5,688 pa in 1651. Worth £100,000,000 with 30,000 acres in 1990.
Titles: Baron Stanley 1456- E; Baron Strange 1482- E; Baron Stanley 1886- UK; Baronet 1628-
Peers: 10 peers 1660-72 1676-1834 1832-51 1844-1908 1915-45
9 Lds Lt 17th, 18th, 19th, 20th
9 in Cabinet 1706-10 1762-71 1783 1806-07 1830-34 1841-45 1852 1858-59 1858-59 1866-68 1866-68 1874-78 1878-80 1882-85 1885-88 1903-05 1916-18 1922-24 1934-37 1937-40 1938 1942-45
5 KG 19th, 20th
Notes: The Earls of Derby inherited the Bickerstaffe estates by mar. in the 16th c., **two MPs for Lancashire 1313-38.** 1 Baron Monteagle and 1 Baron Stanley and 1, 3, 4, 5, 6, 7, 9, 10, 12, 13, 14, 15, 16, and 17 Earls and twelve others in ODNB.

Massey Stanley

Origins: Descended from Sir William Stanley, common ancestor of the Earls of Derby and the Stanley's of Hooton (created Baronets in 1661). The 6 Baronet succeeded to the Massey estates of Puddington and took the additional name Massey 1715. The 9 Baronet married Mary Haggerston, heiress to the Errington estates of Sandhoe (collieries and smelting mills) (Rubinstein - Henry Errington left £140,000 in probate 1819). The 11 Baronet took the name Errington. The Masseys acquired estates in the reign of Henry VI or earlier. The family remained Roman Catholic after the Reformation. **First Stanley MP of this line 1553.**

1. Sir William Stanley-Massey-Stanley 10 Bt – Pontefract 1837-41

Seats: Hooton Hall, Cheshire (acq. and built 1486, rebuilt 1770-88, sold c. 1848, demolished c. 1935); Puddington College (Old Hall), Cheshire (built 15th c., New Hall built on a different site 1760, fire 1867, rebuilt c. 1870, demolished 1904, rebuilt c. 1910); Sandhoe Hall, Northumberland (Errington seat) (old house, passed from Erringtons by mar. to Stanleys who changed name to Errington 1819, rebuilt 1850, family departed c. 2000, flats); Chorlton Hall (House), Cheshire (acq. and built 1666, rebuilt mid-18th c., sold 1811)
Estates: Bateman 13710 (E) 13381
Title: Baronet 1661-1893
Notes: Two in ODNB.

Stanley

Origins: Cousins of the Earls of Derby connected in the 14th century.

1. Edward Stanley – W. Cumberland 1832-52

Seat: Ponsonby Hall (Pelham Hall), Cumberland (medieval, purch. 1388, rebuilt c. 1700, rebuilt 1774, sold 1951, still own estate)

Stanley

Origins: Descended from a younger brother of the 2 Earl of Derby. The 5 Baronet succeeded as 11 Earl, when Cross Hall passed to an uncle.

1. Thomas Stanley – Lancashire 1780-1812
2. Edward Stanley – W. Somerset 1882-85 Bridgwater Div. Somerset 1885-1906

Seats: Cross Hall, Lancashire (medieval, acq. by mar. 1516, new house, c. 1700, demolished early 20th c.); Quantock Lodge, Somerset (built 1857-68, acq. by mar. 1872, sold 1919)
Estates: Bateman 7156 (E) 8260

Morley

Origins: The Morleys started with an Exchequer official who purchased estates in the later 16th century. They were iron masters on the side (see Hill I). Sir William Morley of Halnaker left his estates to his daughter, who married the Earl of Derby in 1705. **First MP 1584. Three further MPs 1601-42.**

1. Sir William Morley – Sussex 1667-79 Midhurst 1679 1685-87 1689-1700

2. William Morley – Arundel 1689-94

Seat: Halnaker House, Sussex (medieval, purch. r. Elizabeth I, passed by mar. to Earls of Derby 1705, sold 1765, ruin)
Notes: One in ODNB.

Baron Stanley of Alderley (1839- UK)

Origins: Descended from the third son of the 1 Baron Stanley. **First MP this line 1491 for Lancashire. Another MP for Cheshire 1571.**

1. John Stanley 1 Baron Stanley of Alderley – Wootton Bassett 1790-96
2. Edward Stanley 2 Baron Stanley of Alderley – Hendon 1831-32 N. Cheshire 1832-41 1847-48
3. William Stanley – Anglesey 1837-47 Chester 1850-57 Beaumaris 1857-74
4. Edward Stanley 4 Baron Stanley of Alderley – Oldham 1880-85
5. Arthur Stanley 5 Baron Stanley of Alderley and 5 Baron Sheffield – Eddisbury Div. Cheshire 1906-10

Seats: Alderley Park, Cheshire (acq. by mar. mid-15th c., built early 17th c., burned 1779, rebuilt on new site 1817, burned 1931, sold 1938); Penrhos, Anglesey (acq. by mar. 1763, family departed 1939, sold c. 1945, demolished in the years afterwards); Winnington Hall, Cheshire (built 1660, 1775, purch. 1809, sold 1872); Weaver Hall, Cheshire (acq. mid-15th c., built c. 1556, rebuilt early 17th c., sold c. 1700)
Estates: Bateman 16779 (E & W) 21406
Titles: Baron Eddisbury 1848- UK; Baronet 1660-; succeeded to the Barony of Sheffield (see below)
Peers: 6 peers 1839-50 1848-1945
1 Ld Lt 19th
1 in Cabinet 1860-66
Notes: Kings of the Isle of Man 1405-1736. 2, 3, and 4 Barons and seven others in ODNB.

Earl of Sheffield (1816-1909 I)

Origins: The Holroyds were an old West Riding family that migrated to Ireland after 1660 and acquired estates there. A barrister was Sheriff of Dublin 1686. His son succeeded to the Baker estates in England and took the additional name Baker. Entered politics in London in the later 18th century and gained a peerage. On the death of the 3 Earl in 1909 the Irish Barony of Sheffield passed to descendents of the 1 Earl, one of whom had married the 1 Baron Stanley of Alderley (see above).

1. John Baker-Holroyd 1 Earl of Sheffield – Coventry 1780 1781-84 Bristol 1790-1802

2. Henry Baker-Holroyd 3 Earl of Sheffield – E. Sussex 1857-65

Seats: Sheffield Park (Place), Sussex (medieval, rebuilt 16th c., purch. 1769, rebuilt 1775-78, add. 1780-90, sold c. 1910); Grave Hall, Yorkshire
Estates: Bateman 6468 (E & I) 5633. Worth £4,000 pa in 1807.
Titles: Baron Sheffield 1781-1909 and 1783- I; Baron Sheffield 1802-1909 GB
Peers: 3 peers 1802-21 1823-1909
Notes: Family extinct 1909. 1 Earl and one other in ODNB.

STANNUS *IRELAND*

Origins: Emigrated from Scotland to Ireland as part of the plantations under James I 1611. Acquired estates 1618. Sheriff 1704.

1. James Stannus – {Carlingford 1713-21}
2. William Stannus – {Carlingford 1721-27 Portarlington 1730-33}
3. Thomas Stannus – {Portarlington 1798-1800}

Seat: The Elms, Queen's County (old house, acq. c. 1700, built 1789, sold 1908-12)
Estates: 530 acres worth £556 pa in 1878.
Notes: Two in ODNB.

STANTON

Origins: Woolen manufacturers in the 18th and 19th centuries.

1. William Stanton – Stroud 1841-52
2. Walter Stanton – Stroud 1874 1880-85
3. Alfred Stanton – Stroud 1874-80

Seat: The Thrupp, Gloucestershire

STAPLES *IRELAND*

Origins: The family emigrated to Ireland c. 1610. Bt. 1628, Sheriff of Tyrone 1640.

1. Sir Alexander Staples 3 Bt – {Strabane 1661-65}
2. Sir Robert Staples 4 Bt – {Dungannon 1692-93 Clogher 1695-99}
3. John Staples – {Newtown Limavady 1765-68 Clogher 1768-76 Ballyshannon 1776-83 Newtown Limavady 1783-96 County Antrim 1796-1800} 1801-02
4. Sir Thomas Staples 9 Bt – {Knocktopher 1800}

Seat: Lissan(e) (House), Tyrone (acq. and built c. 1620, remod. 18th c., established a trust 1997, business use)
Estates: Bateman 5525 (I) 4018
Title: Baronet 1628-
Notes: Two in ODNB.

STAPLEY [Springlet, Thomas]

Origins: The Springlets were merchants in Lewes in the mid-16th century. They entered the gentry by the early 1600s, Baronet 1660. Sir Herbert Springlet 1 Bt of Broyle left his property to two daughters. One married Sir William Thomas 1 Bt of Folkington and the other Sir John Stapley of Patcham. The Thomas family was granted arms in 1608. The Stapleys were established gentry by the 15th century. **First MP 1624 for Shoreham, and also sat for Lewes and Sussex.** Baronet 1660. The heirs to the property are listed here.

1. Sir Herbert Springlet 1 Bt – New Shoreham 1646-48 Sussex 1654 New Shoreham 1660-62
2. Sir John Stapley – Sussex 1654 Lewes 1656 1660-79
3. Sir William Thomas 1 Bt – Seaford 1661-81 Sussex 1681 Seaford 1685-87 Sussex 1689-1702 Seaford 1702-06
4. Herbert Stapley – Seaford 1679-81

Seats: Broyle Place, Sussex (medieval, acq. by Springlets and rebuilt early 17th c., estate broken up among heirs in 18th c., demolished and became a farm house); Patcham Place, Sussex (built 1558, purch. by Stapleys c. 1620, sold 1700); Folkington, Sussex (purch. 1652 by Thomases, passed to Dobells 1707)
Titles: Baronet 1660-1706 1660-1701 1661-62
Notes: In 1706 the Stapley estates passed to the Dobell family of Wivelsfield, Sussex. Two in ODNB.

STARKIE

Origins: Huntroyde has descended in the male line since the 15th century. It came to the Starkies by marriage to a Simmondstone heiress. Hall-i'th'-Wood was inherited from the Morris family, founded by a successful Bolton clothier whose son acquired forfeited estates during the Civil War.

1. Edmund Starkie – Preston 1754-68
2. Le Gendre Starkie – Pontefract 1826-30
3. Le Gendre Starkie – Clitheroe 1853-57
4. John Starkie – N. E. Lancashire 1868-80

Seats: Huntroyde, Lancashire (acq. by mar. 1464, built 1576, add. 1777, add. 1850 and 1879-88, partially demolished 1963, remains sold 1983, family still own estate); Lovely (Loveley) Hall, Lancashire (built c. 1600, remod. 1735, purch. 1757, add. 1874, sold mid-20th c.); Ashton Hall, Lancashire (built 14th c., add. early 17th c., purch. 1853, add. 1856, sold 1884, part demolished 1961); Hall-i'th'-Wood, Lancashire (built c. 1500, add. 1591, purch. by Morris family c. 1600, add. 1648, acq. by mar. to Morris heiress, became a farm house, sold 1899, museum)
Estates: Bateman 8564 (E) 19544

STAUNTON [Lambert, Lynch] *ENGLAND & IRELAND*

Staunton

Origins: Buckinghamshire gentry. A soldier went to Ireland in 1634 and acquired estates. The 1 Bt was a diplomat, and established an English seat.

1. Sir George Staunton 2 Bt – Mitchell 1818-26 Heytesbury 1830-32 Hampshire 1832-34 Portsmouth 1838-52

Seats: Clydah (Clydagh) House, Galway (acq. later 17th c., built early 1820s, passed in the 19th c. to Lynch family in 1859 who took the name Staunton, burned 1922, sold 1947); Waterdale, Galway (acq. later 17th c., passed by mar. to Lamberts 1859); Leigh Park, Hampshire (purch. 1820, passed to Lamberts 1859 and demolished 1859, public park)
Estates: Bateman 8895 (I) 3311 (under Lynch)
Title: Baronet 1785-1859
Notes: The Staunton estates passed in 1859 to cousins by mar., the Lynch family of Duras Park, Galway (emerge early 18th c.).
Notes: Two in ODNB.

Staunton

Origins: Probable descendents of George Staunton, settler in Ireland in 1634.

1. John Staunton – {Galway 1703-14 1727-35}
2. Thomas Staunton – {Galway 1732-60} Ipswich 1757-84
3. Thomas Staunton – {Galway 1727-32}

Seat: Holbrook Hall, Suffolk (acq. by inher. c. 1764, sold late 18th c.)

Lambert

Origins: The Lamberts originated from Yorkshire and came to Ireland in a military capacity 1669. Successful merchants in Dublin in 18th century. They settled in Galway in the early 18th century and intermarried with the Stauntons, inheriting Staunton estates in the mid-19th century.

1. James Staunton Lambert – County Galway 1827-32

Seats: Creg Clare (Cregaclare), Galway (acq. 1726, built 1802, sold c. 1855, became a ruin); Castle Lambert, Galway (acq. 1756, demolished old house and new house 1756 onwards, sold 1855); Castle Ellen House, Galway (old tower, acq. 1785, new house 1875 resident into the 20th c.); Aggard, Galway (acq. and built late 18th c., some land sold 1857, still resident 1894); Waterdale, Galway (inher. mid-19th c. from Stauntons, sold mid-19th c. and then repurchased, sold 1903, demolished)
Estates: Bateman 14546 (I) 4878 and 3829 (I) 1442
Notes: Forced sales of a near bankrupt estate by the Encumbered Estates Commission in the 1850s. A number of members of the family emigrated to the USA and Australia.

STEPHENS I

Origins: Successful sheep farmers and wool merchants in the 16th century. Became a dynasty of attorneys. Lawyers to the royal family in the 17th century. **First MP 1593. Three additional MPs 1593-1658, one for Gloucestershire.**

1. Edward Stephens – Tewkesbury 1643-48 Gloucestershire 1660
2. John Stephens – Tewkesbury 1645-48 Gloucestershire 1659 Bristol 1660
3. Thomas Stephens – Gloucestershire 1695-98
4. Thomas Stephens – Gloucestershire 1713-20

Seats: Lypiatt Park, Gloucestershire (medieval house, rebuilt early 16th c., purch. 1610, burned 1645, repaired, sold c. 1800); Chavenage House, Gloucestershire (built 14th c., purch. c. 1562-64, remod. c. 1576, c. 1670s, and early 19th c., sold 1871); Eastington Manor, Gloucestershire (medieval, purch. 1569, rebuilt 1578, demolished 1778, estate sold 1871)
Notes: The male line died out in the 18th century and the de la Beres succeeded to the estates some of which were later sold. Chavenage and Eastington passed by mar. to the Townsends of Castle Townsend, Cork, who sold the estate.
Notes: Three in ODNB.

STEPHENS II

Origins: Hampshire yeomen in the late 16th century. They acquired a farm on the Isle of Wight by marriage in 1633. One served as Governor of the Isle of Wight in the 1640s and acquired gentry scale estates during the Civil War. **First MP 1640.**

1. Sir William Stephens – Newport (IoW) 1685-87 1689-95
2. William Stephens – Newport (IoW) 1702-22 Newtown (IoW) 1722-27

Seats: Bowcombe, Hampshire (purch. 1671, sold 1728); Barton, Hampshire (leased)
Estates: Worth £1,200 pa c. 1660.
Notes: The family was seriously indebted from the late 17th century. The last MP died in poverty in 1753. One in ODNB.

STERN

Baron Michelham (1905-84 UK)

Origins: German Jewish merchant bankers in the 19th century. Created Barons in Portugal in 1864, later Viscounts. Established a bank in London.

No MPs

Seat: Highdown, Sussex (purch. 1909, donated to Worthing Borough 1967)
Title: Baronet 1905-84
Peers: 2 peers 1905-45
Estates: 1 Baron left two million pounds in 1919.
Notes: Stern family has an entry plus two others in ODNB.

Baron Wandsworth (1895-1912 UK)

Origins: The 1 Baron was the eldest son of the 1 Viscount de Stern.

1. Sydney Stern 1 Baron Wandsworth – Stowmarket Div. Suffolk 1891-95

Seats: Hengrave Hall, Suffolk (medieval, rebuilt 16th c., remod. 18th c., purch. later 19th c., add. 1890s, sold 1896, institutional use); Bolney House, Sussex (purch. 1877, sold c. 1912)
Estates: Bolney estate 601 acres worth £709 pa. The 1 Baron died in 1912 worth £1,500,000, most of it left to charities.
Peers: 1 peer 1895-1912
Notes: Viscounts de Stern in Portugal.

STEUART (Stewart) [Denholm (Denham)] *SCOTLAND*

Steuart

Origins: Acquired estates in the late 16th century. **First [MP 1649 for Edinburgh]** was a merchant and moneylender, Kt and Lord Provost of Edinburgh 1649 and 1659. Became a legal dynasty, Lord Advocate 1692, in the 18th century.

1. Sir Thomas Steuart 1 Bt – [North Berwick Burgh 1689-96]
2. Sir James Stewart 1 Bt – [Queensferry 1705-07] Edinburgh 1713-15
3. Sir James Steuart Denham 8 Bt – Lanarkshire 1784-1802

Seats: Coltness House, Lanarkshire (purch. 1653, sold 1840, demolished c. 1980); Goodtrees, Edinburghshire (acq. by mar. 17th c.); Westshiels (Westshield), Lanarkshire (acq. by mar. from Denhams 1776, sold mid-19th c.)
Titles: Baronet 1698-1851; 1705-1851
Notes: The son of Sir James Stewart 1 Bt [MP] was a Jacobite. The 7 Bt took additional name Denham on inheriting their estates in 1776. The 8 Bt squandered the family fortune and the estates were sold before his death in 1839 while the Baronetcy passed to cousins. Four in ODNB.

Stewart

Origins: A younger son of the Coltness Baronets became a wine merchant in Edinburgh and sired this line.

1. Sir Robert Stewart 1 Bt – [N. Berwick 1698-1702]
2. Archibald Stewart – Edinburgh 1741-47
3. John Stewart – Arundel 1771-74

Seat: Allanbank House, Berwickshire (purch. 1687, rebuilt 1848, demolished 1968)
Title: Baronet 1687-1849

Denholm (Denham)

Origins: The Denholms were maternal cousins of the 6 Baronet of Coltness. The Steuarts succeeded to the Denholm estates and took the additional name Denham.

1. Sir William Denham 1 Bt – [Lanarkshire 1690-1702]

Seat: Westshiels (Westshield), Lanarkshire (purch. 1680, passed to Steuarts 1776)
Title: Baronet 1693-1776

STEWARD I [Tucker]

Steward

Origins: London bankers in the 18th century.

1. Gabriel Steward – Weymouth & Melcombe Regis 1778-86 1788-90
2. Gabriel Tucker Steward – Weymouth 1794-1810
3. Richard T. Steward – Weymouth 1806-12

Seat: Nottingham, Weymouth, Dorset (built 1830, sold 1853)

Tucker

Origins: Founded by a Quaker Weymouth merchant who also owned quarries. John Tucker MP left his property to the husband of his niece Gabriel Steward.

1. Edward Tucker – Weymouth 1727-37
2. John Tucker – Weymouth 1735-47 1754-78

STEWARD II (Stewart, Stuart) [Wendy]

Steward

Origins: **The first MP 1472** was a lawyer**. Three additional MPs 1589-1628.**

1. Robert Steward – Thetford 1659 Castle Rising 1661-72
2. John Steward – Midhurst 1660-79
3. Sir Nicholas Steward 1 Bt – Lymington 1663-79
4. Sir Simeon Stuart 2 Bt – Southampton 1708-10 Hampshire 1710-14
5. Sir Simeon Stuart 3 Bt – Hampshire 1761-79

Seats: Hartley Mauditt, Hampshire (purch. 1614, sold c. 1779, house demolished c. 1800); Pylewell Park, Hampshire (leased ? 17th c.); Milland, Sussex (purch. 1638, sold 1719)
Title: Baronet 1660-
Notes: The family spelled their name Steward in the early 17th century. It was later changed to Stewart or Stuart in the later 17th century. Finances deteriorated in 18th c.

Wendy

Origins: The founder, from Suffolk yeoman stock, was a physician to Henry VIII and Elizabeth I. **First MP 1554 (1555 for Cambridgeshire).** Thomas Wendy MP left his estate to his nephew, the older brother of Robert Steward MP (above).

1. Thomas Wendy – Cambridgeshire 1660-73

Seat: Haslingfield Hall, Cambridgeshire (medieval, purch. 1541, built c. 1555, remod. mid-17th c., sold 1728, largely demolished 1814-19)
Notes: One in ODNB.

STEWART I [Mackenzie] *SCOTLAND*

Earl of Galloway (1623- S)

Origins: Connected with the royal house in the 13th century through descent from the fourth Chief Steward of Scotland. Held high offices in the 15th century. **First [MP 1560]. Six further [MPs 1560-1644, three for shires].** Also closely connected with the Earls of Seaforth (Mackenzie).

1. Sir Archibald Stewart 2 Bt – [Orkney & Shetland 1702-07]
2. John Stewart – [Wigtownshire 1702-07] Scotland 1707-08 Wigtownshire 1708-10 1711-27
3. John Stewart – Kirkcudbrightshire Stewartry 1708-15 (parentage obscure)
4. James Stewart – Wigtown Burghs 1734-41 Wigtownshire 1741-47 Wigtown Burghs 1747-54 Wigtownshire 1754-61
5. William Stewart – Wigtown Burghs 1741-47
6. John Stewart 7 Earl of Galloway – Morpeth 1761-68 Ludgersall 1768-73
7. Keith Stewart – Wigtown Burghs 1762 Wigtownshire 1768-84
8. George Stewart 8 Earl of Galloway – Saltash 1790-95 Cockermouth 1805-06 Haslemere 1806
9. Sir William Stewart – Saltash 1795-96 Wigtownshire 1796-1802 Wigtown Burghs 1803-05 Wigtownshire 1812-16
10. Montgomery Stewart – Kirkcudbright Stewartry 1803-12
11. Edward Stewart – Wigtown Burghs 1806-09
12. James Stewart – Wigtown Burghs 1812-21
13. Randolph Stewart 9 Earl of Galloway – Cockermouth 1826-31
14. Edward Stewart – Wigtown Burghs 1831-34
15. J. A. Stewart Mackenzie – Ross-shire 1831-32 Ross & Cromarty 1832-37
16. Alan Stewart 10 Earl of Galloway – Wigtownshire 1868-73

Seats: Galloway House, Kirkcudbrightshire (built 1740-50, add. 1841, sold 1908); Cumloden House, Kirkcudbrightshire (built c. 1820, still own); Sorbie Castle, Wigtownshire (built 16th and 17th c., family departed 1748, ruin)
Estates: Bateman 79184 (S) 32197
Titles: Baron Garlies 1607- S; Baron Stewart 1796- GB; Baron Seaforth 1921-23 UK; Baronet 1627- ; 1687-1746
Peers: [3 peers 1660-90 1690-1707] 1 Scottish Rep peer 1774-90 6 peers 1796-1945
5 Lds Lt 18th, 19th, 20th
3 KT 18th, 19th, 20th
Notes: Stewart family has an entry in ODNB. Two other Stewarts in ODNB.

Stewart

Origins: Descended from a younger son of the 2 Earl of Galloway. **First [MP 1650 for Wigtownshire].**

1. William Stewart – [Wigtownshire 1685 1700-02 1703-07]
2. John Stewart – Wigtownshire 1747-54
3. William Stewart – Wigtown Burghs 1770-74 Kirkcudbrightshire Stewartry 1774-80
4. Alexander Stewart – Kirkcudbrightshire Stewartry 1786-94

Seats: Castle Stewart, Wigtownshire (purch. and built 17th c., sold 1777, repurch. 1826, ruin); Afton Lodge, Ayrshire (acq. by mar. 1770, built c. 1800, divided among heiresses 1818); Cairnsmore House, Wigtownshire (built 1740, still resident into 20th c., part demolished 1955)

STEWART II *IRELAND*

Stewart

Origins: Founder a Scottish soldier settled in Ireland in 1620.

1. Sir John Stewart 1 Bt – {Augher 1794-97 Bangor 1797-1800} County Tyrone 1802-06 1812-25
2. Sir Hugh Stewart 2 Bt – County Tyrone 1830-34

Seats: Athenree, Tyrone; Ballygawley Park, Tyrone (purch. 1811, built 1825-33, accidental fire 1920s, family departed, estate sold, ruin)
Estates: Bateman 28534 (I) 6752
Title: Baronet 1803-
Notes: Family now live in England.

Stewart

Origins: Cadet line.

1. William Stewart – {Charlemont 1692-93}
2. William Stewart – {County Tyrone 1748-68}
3. James Stewart – {County Tyrone 1768-1800} 1801-12
4. William Stewart – County Tyrone 1818-30

Seats: Killymoon Castle, Tyrone (purch. 1634, built early 18th c., fire 1800, rebuilt c. 1803-07, sold 1869); Ballymenagh, Tyrone (acq. early 17th c., sold mid-19th c.)
Estates: Worth £3,371 pa in 1764.
Notes: James Stewart MP of Killymoon married 1772 the heiress (1794) of the 3 Viscount Molesworth (see that family) including substantial urban property in Dublin. However, by the 1820s their children were obliged to go into exile in France to escape creditors. The Stewart estates were sold mid-19th c. The male line became extinct 1850.

STEWART III (Stuart) *IRELAND*

Origins: First MP a lawyer. Sheriff 1701.

1. Charles Stuart – {Tuam 1713-14}
2. William Stewart – {County Cavan 1766-68 Newcastle 1768-76}
3. Charles Stewart – {County Cavan 1783-93}

Seats: Bailieborough Castle, Cavan (acq. 18th c., passed by mar. to Corrys 1793, sold 1814); Mount Stewart, Armagh
Estates: Worth £4,000 pa in 1819.
Notes: Male line extinct 1793. Estates passed by mar. to Corry of Rockcorry, Monaghan.

STOCKDALE [Walters]

Origins: Landowners since the reign of Henry VI. **First MP (possible relative) 1553. Second MP 1641, for Knaresborough**.

1. William Stockdale – Knaresborough 1660-81 1685-87 1689-93
2. Christopher Walters (Stockdale) – Knaresborough 1693-1713

Seat: Bilton Park, Yorkshire (purch. 1630, sold 1742)
Notes: Bilton passed by marriage to a nephew of William Stockdale MP.

STONOR

Baron Camoys (1383-1426 1839- E)

Origins: The family claimed to have been at Stonor before the Conquest. In fact they rose through the law in the 14th century. Chief Justice of the Common Pleas 1315. They have been in continuous residence at Stonor for six centuries (Roskell, Clark, and Rawcliffe, *The House of Commons*, IV, 483). **First MP 1380 for Oxfordshire. Five further MPs 1416-1585, three for Oxfordshire.**

1. Thomas Stonor 3 Baron Comoys – Oxford 1832-33

Seats: Stonor Park, Oxfordshire (acq. late 12th c. or earlier, built c. 1280-1300, add. 1331, add. 1416-17, add. 1530s, add. and remod. 1757 and 1790, still own); Anderton Hall, Lancashire (acq. by mar. 1810, sold 1897); Watlington Park, Oxfordshire (purch. 1632, built 1650-75, sold 1758)
Estates: Bateman 6740 (E) 8829 and 2757 (E) 4864. Worth £243 pa in early 15th c. Owned 1,000 acres in 2001.
Peers: 3 peers 1839-97 1905-45
Notes: A Roman Catholic family debarred from participation in Parliament until Emancipation in the 19th century. The Stonor family has an entry plus one other in the ODNB.

STOPFORD *IRELAND*

Earl of Courtown (1762- I)

Origins: In the household of the Earl of Derby mid-16th century. Purchased property in Lancashire 1543. **First MP 1558**. Emigrated to Ireland as a Parliamentary officer during the Civil War and obtained land in many counties.

1. Robert Stopford – {Innistioge 1692-93 1695-99}
2. James Stopford – {Wexford 1703-13 County Wexford 1713-21}
3. James Stopford 1 Earl of Courtown – {County Wexford 1721-27 Fethard 1727-58}
4. James Stopford 2 Earl of Courtown – {Taghmon 1761-68} Great Bedwyn 1774 Marlborough 1780-93
5. Edward Stopford – {Duleek 1776-83}
6. James Stopford 3 Earl of Courtown – Great Bedwyn 1790-96 Linlithgow Burghs 1796-1802 Dumfries Burghs 1803-06 Great Bedwyn 1806-07 Marlborough 1807-10
7. Sir Robert Stopford – Ipswich 1806-07
8. Edward Stopford – Marlborough 1810-18
9. Thomas Stopford 4 Earl of Courtown – County Wexford 1820-30

Seats: Courtown House, Wexford (acq. 1762, sacked 1798, add. 1865-67, sold 1947, demolished 1948); Marlfield, Wexford (built 1852, became principal seat 1945, sold 1979, hotel)
Estates: Bateman 23314 (I & E) 12092
Titles: Baron Courtown and Viscount Stopford 1758- I; Baron Saltersford 1796- GB
Peers: {2 peers 1758-1800} 6 peers 1796-1945
1 Ld Lt 20th
2 KP 18th, 18th
Notes: Five in ODNB.

STOURTON [Langdale]

Baron Mowbray & Stourton (1283- & 1448- E)

Origins: The Stourtons have held Stourton since at least 1166 (Roskell, Clarke, and Rawcliffe, *The House of Commons*, III, 194). Rose high by law and office from the late 14th century. Speaker of the Commons 1413. **Baron 1283. First MP 1401 for Somerset. Eight further MPs 1419-1555, sitting three times for Somerset and three for Dorset**. They remained Roman Catholic after the Reformation and were excluded from participation in Parliament until after Emancipation in the 19th century.

1. Charles Stourton Langdale – Beverley 1832-34 Knaresborough 1837-41
2. Joseph Stourton – S. Div. Salford 1931-45

Seats: Stourton Towers (Allerton Park), Yorkshire (medieval, rebuilt 1740s, rebuilt 1780s, purch. 1805, demolished 1843, rebuilt 1844-56, family departed 1965, sold 1983, fire 2005); Hazelwood (Hazlewood) Castle, Yorkshire (Vavasour seat acq. and built 1290, new house c. 1770, passed by mar. to Stourtons 1828, sold 1908); Stourton, Wiltshire (acq. by 1166, sold 1714)
Estates: Bateman 5097 (E) 9347; Vavasour property 8480 (E) 10280. Stourtons worth £195 pa in 1413 and £600 pa in 1436.
Titles: Baronet 1628-1826; 1828-
Peers: 7 peers 1660-78 1829-1945
Notes: The Barony of Mowbray was called out of abeyance for the Stourtons in 1878. In 1828, after the male line failed, the Vavasour estates passed to the Stourtons, maternal cousins. The Vavsours had inherited Hazlewood Castle from the Domesday tenant in 1290. Summoned as Barons 1299 (not summoned after 1315). **First MP 1449. Three further MPs 1472-1611, one for Yorkshire**. A Roman Catholic family in the 17th and 18th centuries. Reduced to poverty during the Civil War, but reacquired some prosperity in the 18th century. Stourton family has an entry and one other in ODNB.

Baron Langdale (1658-1778 E)

Origins: The Langdales acquired manorial land by the 14th century. Mary Langdale, daughter of the 5 Baron Langdale, married the 17 Baron Stourton. Their son succeeded to the Langdale estates. A Roman Catholic family.

No MPs

Seats: Holme Hall, Yorkshire (purch. c. 1530, built c. 1720-30, add. 1766, passed to Stourtons by inher. 1778, sold 1920, institutional use); Houghton Hall, Yorkshire (acq. early Middle Ages by the Langdales, rebuilt 18th c., partially demolished 1959, still owned by descendents); Celbridge Abbey, Kildare (acq. mid-19th c., later passed to another family)
Estates: Bateman 6296 (E & I) 6126 and 3151 (E) 3777
Peers: 2 peers 1660-1703
1 Ld Lt 17th
Notes: 1 Baron in ODNB.

STOYTE *IRELAND*

Origins: Merchants. **First {MP 1634}.**

1. Francis Stoyte – {Hillsborough 1727-33}
2. John Stoyte – {Dublin 1728-29}

STRACHEY

Baron Strachie (1911-73 UK)

Origins: The first recorded Strachey was a yeoman who died in 1460. A merchant adventurer died 1621. Entered the gentry in the 17th century. Officials in the 18th and 19th centuries.

1. Sir Henry Strachey 1 Bt – Pontefract 1768-74 Bishop's Castle 1774-78 1780-1802
2. Edward Strachey 1 Baron Strachie – S. Somerset 1892-1911
3. John Strachey – Aston Div. Birmingham 1929-31 Dundee 1945-50 W. Dundee 1950-63

Seat: Sutton Court, Somerset (medieval, rebuilt 15-16th, purch. 1660s, remod. 1858, passed to Lord O'Hagan by mar. 1936, sold 1987, flats)
Title: Baronet 1801-
Peers: 2 peers 1911-45
Notes: 1 Baron and sixteen others in ODNB.

STRAHAN [Spottiswoode] *ENGLAND & SCOTLAND*

Origins: The father of William Strahan was an Edinburgh lawyer. The son started as a printer in London and became a rich publisher (King's Printer). The Strahan heiress married John Spottiswoode in 1779, and the latter's nephews inherited a great business fortune. The Spottiswoodes included in their ancestry a 16th-century Archbishop of St. Andrews, a 17th-century Lord Chancellor of Scotland, and a lawyer and the King's Printer in the 18th century.

1. William Strahan – Malmesbury 1774-80 Wootton Bassett 1780-84
2. Andrew Strahan – Newport (I o W) 1796-1802 Wareham 1802-07 Carlow 1807-12 Aldeburgh 1812-18 New Romney 1818-20
3. Andrew Spottiswoode – Saltash 1826-30 Colchester 1830-31

Seats: Spottiswoode House, Berwickshire (medieval tower, demolished 1730, built 1832-34, demolished c. 1928); Broome Hall, Surrey (acq. and built c. 1831, sold by 1848)
Estates: Bateman 11412 (S) 5425. Rubinstein – Andrew Strahan left £800,000 in probate in 1831.
Notes: Three in ODNB.

STRATFORD *IRELAND*

Earl of Aldborough (1777-1875 I)

Origins: The first Stratford emigrated to Ireland before 1660, possibly from Warwickshire. His son purchased Belan in the early 18th century. Sheriff 1719.

1. Robert Stratford – {County Wicklow 1692-93}
2. Edward Stratford – {Carysfort 1695-99 Baltinglass 1703-27 Harristown 1727-40}
3. John Stratford 1 Earl of Aldborough – {Baltinglass 1721-63}
4. Edward Stratford 2 Earl of Aldborough – {Baltinglass 1759-68} Taunton 1774-75 {Baltinglass 1775-77}
5. John Stratford 3 Earl of Aldborough – {Baltinglass 1763-76 County Wicklow 1776-90 Baltinglass 1790-1800}
6. Benjamin Stratford 4 Earl of Aldborough – {Baltinglass 1777-83 1790-1800}

Seats: Belan House, Kildare (purch. and built c. 1700, enlarged 1743, family departed 1837, dismantled 1840s, sold 1879, ruin); Mount Neale, Carlow (acq. by mar. early 18th c., sold mid-19th c.); Great Glemham House, Suffolk (acq. by mar. mid-18th c., passed out of family by inher. 1789); Stratford Lodge, Wicklow (built late 18th c., burned 1850s)
Estates: 2291 (I) 1695 in the 1870s. Worth £12,846 pa in 1792. In deep financial difficulties by 1830s. Big sales 1851. 7,392 acres worth £2,128 pa in 1854.

Title: Baron Baltinglass 1763-1875 I
Peers: {2 peers 1763-1800}
Notes: The 2 Earl alienated much property in a dispute with his heir, and the 5 Earl was a spendthrift. 2 Earl in ODNB.

STRATON (Straiton) *SCOTLAND*

Origins: An old landed family. **First [MP 1560]. One further [MP 1604]**.

1. Alexander Straton – [Kincardineshire 1661-63]

Seats: Lauriston Castle, Kincardineshire (acq. and built 14th c., add. 17th c., sold 1695, much demolished after 1945); Kirkside House, Kincardineshire (acq. 1582, rebuilt early 17th c., remod. c. 1764, add. c. 1805, sold 1872)
Estates: Lauriston estate was about 3,500 acres.

STRICKLAND

Baron Strickland (1928-40 UK)

Origins: Major landowners in Westmorland since the 12th century. Sir Thomas Strickland carried the banner of St. George at Agincourt (Roskell, Clarke, and Rawcliffe, *The House of Commons*, IV, 515; Bence-Jones, *The Catholic Families*, 34). **First MP 1258 for Westmorland. At least thirteen additional MPs, ten of them for Westmorland through to 1643.** Because they remained Roman Catholic no family members sat in Parliament in the 18th or early 19th centuries.

1. Walter Strickland – Yorkshire 1654 1656 Thirsk 1661-71
2. Sir Thomas Strickland – Westmorland 1661-77
3. Sir Roger Strickland – Aldborough 1685-87
4. Gerald Strickland 1 Baron Strickland – Lancaster Div. Lancashire 1924-28

Seats: Sizergh Castle, Westmorland (acq. by mar. to a Deincourt heiress in 1239 whose family had been granted it by Henry II, medieval, rebuilt c. 1350, add. 15th c., add. c. 1565, remod. c. 1777, family still resident, NT 1950); Thornton Briggs (Bridge), Yorkshire (acq. c. 1522 by mar., forfeited 1689)
Peer: 1 peer 1928-40
Notes: In financial difficulties in the 17th c. Counts della Catena in Malta. 1 Baron and two others in ODNB.

Strickland

Origins: This family was not directly related to the Stricklands of Sizergh, although one may have married a female descendent. The marriage probably took place in the 1540s and from that point forward they acted as if they were related. Granted arms 1550. **Two members of the family sat in Cromwell's House of Lords. First MP 1559. Three further MPs 1640-58.**

1. Sir William Strickland 3 Bt – Malton 1689-98 1701-08 Yorkshire 1708-10 Old Sarum 1716-22 Malton 1722-24
2. Sir William Strickland 4 Bt – Malton 1708-15 Carlisle 1715-22 Scarborough 1722-35
3. William Strickland – Beverley 1741-47
4. Sir George Cholmley-Strickland 7 Bt – Yorkshire 1831-32 W. R. Yorkshire 1832-41 Preston 1841-57

Seats: Hildenley Hall, Yorkshire (acq. 1565, rebuilt 1620, sold c. 1909, demolished 1927-31); Boynton, Yorkshire (purch. 1549, sold 1954); Wassand Hall, Yorkshire (acq. by Constables 1529, passed to Stricklands 19th c., still own)
Estates: Bateman 16000 (E) 17000. Worth £2,000 pa in c. 1670. The family succeeded to the Constable estates at Wassand Hall in the 19th c. 6271 (E) 10500 and 2975 (E) 4681 (Walcot Hall, Lincolnshire acq. by Goultons 17th c. into 20th c. Goulton-Constable). Worth £35,000 pa in 1874.
Title: Baronet 1641-
1 in Cabinet 1730-39
Notes: Inherited the Bamburgh family lands through the Wentworths and the Cholmondeleys (English, *The Great Landowners of East Yorkshire*, 16). Four in ODNB.

STRODE [Fitzjames, Oglander]

Strode

Origins: The Strodes held property in Dorset from the reign of Henry III. The line in Kent descended from a younger son who became a merchant. **First MP 1295 for Dorset.** Married an heiress 1522. **Four additional MPs 1572-1626, one for Dorset.**

1. Sir John Strode – Dorset 1661-79
2. John Strode – Sandwich 1665-79 1685-86
3. William Strode – Ilchester 1679-81
4. Sir George Strode – Lyme Regis 1679
5. Essex Strode – Stockbridge 1681 1685-87
6. Edward Strode – Ilchester 1705-08

Seats: Barrington Court, Somerset (medieval house, rebuilt 16th c., purch. 1625, sold 1755, later ruinous, NT purch. 1907, restored 1921-25); Squerryes (Squerries) Court, Kent (purch. by 1636, sold and new house built c. 1700); Leweston House, Dorset (acq. by mar. from Fitzjames family later 17th c., sold c. 1764, school); Parnham House, Dorset (built c. 1400, acq. by mar. r. Henry VI, rebuilt c. 1520s, passed to Oglanders 1764); Lydlinch, Dorset (held from medieval period, sold mid-18th c.); Chantmarle, Dorset (purch. 1606, built c. 1612, passed to Oglanders 1764 and became a farm house, sold 1910)
Notes: Male line extinct 1764. Five in ODNB.

Fitzjames

Origins: The Fitzjames family was established in Somerset in the 15th century. **First MP 1421. Six additional MPs 1467-1659, one for Dorset.** Sir George Strode married the daughter and heiress of John Fitzjames of Leweston.

1. John Fitzjames – Dorset 1654 1656 Poole 1659 Dorset 1660 Poole 1661-70
2. Thomas Fitzjames – Downton 1659 1660

Seat: Leweston House, Dorset (passed to Strodes later 17th c.)
Notes: Three in ODNB.

Oglander

Origins: The Oglanders claimed to have come over with the Conqueror. (Winter, *The Manor Houses of the Isle of Wight*, 119) It is possible that they held Nunwell by 1100. From c. 1135 an unbroken succession of the family held the estate until the death in 1874 of the 7 Baronet. **First MP 1625.** In 1764 the last male Strode of Parnham (with 16,000 acres) died, and the house and estate passed via an heiress to the Oglanders who held it until 1896.

1. Sir William Oglander 1 Bt – Newport (IoW) 1660-70
2. Sir William Oglander 6 Bt – Bodmin 1807-12

Seats: Nunwell House, Hampshire (IoW) (acq. c. 1100, medieval building, remod. 1609, rebuilt 1716, remod. 1760, passed to Glynns 1874, add. 1897 and 1905, sold 1982); Parnham House, Dorset (acq. by mar. 1764 from the Strodes, remod. 1807-11, sold 1896, now institution)
Estates: Bateman 7513 (E) 9966. Owned 24,000 acres c. 1800.
Title: Baronet 1665-1874
Notes: In 1874 the estates passed to a cousin, John Oglander Glynn, who took the name Oglander. One in ODNB.

STRUTT I

Baron Belper (1856- UK)

Origins: Began as small farmers. Jedediah Strutt was a cotton spinner and inventor of a stocking frame in 1756. He became a partner with Arkwright in 1771 (see Arkwright). The family accumulated a great fortune. High Sheriff 1850. Lord Lieutenant 1864.

1. Edward Strutt 1 Baron Belper – Derby 1830-48 Arundel 1851-52 Nottingham 1852-56
2. Henry Strutt 2 Baron Belper – E. Derbyshire 1868-74 Berwick-on-Tweed 1880

Seats: Kingston Hall, Nottinghamshire (acq. c. 1845, still own); St. Helen's House, Derbyshire (leased later 18th c.); Bridge Hill House, Derbyshire (built 1793-94, add. c. 1804, sold and demolished 1938)
Estates: Bateman 5226 (E) 11302. The sons of Jedediah Strutt were worth £1,000,000 in 1810 (£40,000 pa). Owned 5000 acres in 2001.
Peers: 3 peers 1856-1945
1 Ld Lt 19th
1 in Cabinet 1852-54
Notes: 1 Baron and five others in ODNB.

STRUTT II

Baron Rayleigh (1821- UK)

Origins: The first MP was a son of a successful miller. Then they became cotton manufacturers in the 18th century. Held 5,000 acres by 1781.

1. John Strutt – Maldon 1774-90
2. Joseph Strutt – Maldon 1790-1826 Okehampton 1826-30
3. Charles Strutt – E. Essex 1883-85 1895-1906

Seat: Terling Place, Essex (purch. 1761 for £18,000, built house 1772-78 for £6,000, add. 1818-21, still own)
Estates: Bateman 8632 (E) 12800. Worth £3,500 pa in 1781. Owned 4,000 acres in 2001.
Peers: 3 peers 1836-1945
1 Ld Lt 19th-20th
Notes: The 3 Baron discovered Argon in 1894. 3 and 4 Barons and two others in ODNB.

STUART (Stewart) [Cox, Crichton, Gray, Mackenzie, Villiers, Wortley]
SCOTLAND, IRELAND, WALES, & ENGLAND

Marquis of Bute (1796- GB)

Origins: The Stewarts claimed descent from the ruling family of Brittany. They rose to be Stewards of Scotland in 1124 and gained the crown in 1371. The Marquises of Bute were descended from an illegitimate son of King Robert II who became Sheriff of Bute 1385. The Stewart family had acquired Bute 14th c. (Stringer, *Essays on the Nobility of Medieval Scotland*, 167) **First [MP 1621 for Buteshire]. Three additional [MPs 1628-51, all for the county].** The mother of the 2 Marquis of Bute was the daughter of the Earl of Dumfries (Crichton family). The 2 Marquis succeeded as 7 Earl of Dumfries. The Crichtons were Lords of Parliament from the 14th century and held several earldoms in the 15th century. **First [1560]. One additional [MP 1625 for Aberdeenshire].**

1. Sir James Stuart 1 Bt – [Buteshire 1644-45 1661-62]
2. James Crichton – [Dumfriesshire 1661-63]
3. Sir Dugald Stuart 2 Bt – [Buteshire 1665 1669-70]
4. John Stuart – [Rothesay Burgh 1669-74]
5. James Stuart 1 Earl of Bute – [Buteshire 1685-86 1689 1703]
6. William Crichton – [Dumfriesshire 1693-1701]
7. Dugald Stuart – [Rothesay Burgh 1703-07] Buteshire 1708-09
8. John Stuart – [Buteshire 1704-07]
9. James Stuart Mackenzie – Argyllshire 1742-47 Buteshire 1747-54 Ayr Burghs 1754-61 Ross-shire 1761-80
10. John Stuart 1 Marquis of Bute – Bossiney 1766-76
11. James Stuart Wortley – Ayr Burghs 1768-74 Buteshire 1774-80 Plympton Erle 1780-84 Buteshire 1784-90 Bossiney 1790-96 1797-1802 Buteshire 1806-07
12. Sir Charles Stuart – Bossiney 1776-90 Ayr Burghs 1790-94 Poole 1794-1801
13. Frederick Stuart – Ayr Burghs 1776-80 Buteshire 1796-1802
14. John Stuart Lord Mount Stuart – Cardiff Boroughs 1790-94
15. Lord Evelyn Stuart – Cardiff Boroughs 1794-1802 1814-18
16. Lord William Stuart – Cardiff Boroughs 1802-14
17. Lord Patrick Crichton-Stuart – Cardiff Boroughs 1818-20 Buteshire 1820-26 Cardiff 1826-32 Ayr Burghs 1834-52 Ayrshire 1857-59
18. William Stuart – Armagh 1820-26 Bedfordshire 1830-34
19. Lord Dudley Stuart – Arundel 1830-37 Marylebone 1847-54
20. Henry Stuart – Bedford 1837-38 1841-54
21. William Stuart – Bedford 1854-57 1859-68
22. James Crichton-Stuart – Cardiff 1857-80
23. Lord Ninian Crichton-Stuart – Cardiff 1910-15
24. Lord Colum Crichton-Stuart – Northwich 1922-45

Seats: Mount Stuart, Buteshire (built 1718-22, remod. c. 1740, fire 1877, rebuilt 1879-1902, still own); Cardiff Castle, Glamorganshire (built 1080, 12th c, 14th c., 16th c., acq. by mar. 1766, remod. 1777-78, rebuilt 1867-85, given to Cardiff 1947); Kames Castle, Buteshire (medieval, built 18th c., purch. 1863, restored 1912, family departed 1956, sold 1984); Luton Hoo, Bedfordshire (medieval, purch. 1762, rebuilt 1769-74, remod. c. 1800, add. c. 1825, fire 1843, sold 1848); Dumfries House, Ayrshire (built 1754-59, add. 1895-99, family departed 1993, sold 2007, museum); Old Place of Mochrum, Wigtownshire (built 15th and 16th c., acq. 1694 by Earl of Dumfries, ruinous by 1780, passed to Marquis of Bute c. 1870, rebuilt 1873 onwards and 1903-08, still own); Highcliffe Castle, Dorset (built 1773 by 3 Earl of Bute, sold by a younger son of Lord Bute and then repurch. by Baron Stuart de Rothesay, a great-grandson and rebuilt 1830-34, passed to cousins the Stuart Wortleys – see Montagu I – in 1894)
Estates: Bateman 116668 (W & S) 151135. Rubinstein – William Stuart, Archbishop of Armagh, left £250,000 in probate 1822. Total income was near £300,000 pa in 1868 (Girouard, *The Victorian Country House*, 274). 3 Marquis left over 1 million pounds in personal wealth in 1900. Worth £60,000,000 in 1990. Owned 56,400 acres in 1996. Owned 49,700 acres in Scotland and 25,000 acres in Spain in 2001.
Titles: Baron Crichton 1488- S; Viscount Ayr 1622- S; Earl of Dumfries 1633- S; Earl of Bute 1703- S; Baron Mount Stuart 1761- GB; Baron Cardiff 1776- GB; Baron Stuart de Rothesay 1828-45; Baronet 1627-
Peers: [2 peers 1660-91 1703-07] 3 Scottish Rep peers 1715-23 1737-41 1761-80 1790-1803
5 peers 1766-1859 1828-45 1868-1900 1902-45
8 Lds Lt 18th, 19th, 20th
1 in Cabinet 1761-63
1 KG 18th 2 KT 19th, 20th
Notes: The Stuarts inherited large Welsh estates through a marriage to the heiress of Viscount Windsor. These originally were granted by Henry VIII and Edward VI to the Earl of Pembroke. (Cannadine, ed., *Patricians, Power and Politics*, 20) Eleven Crichtons in ODNB. One Mackenize in ODNB. 3 Earl and 1, 2, 3, 4, and 6 Marquises of Bute and two other Stuarts in ODNB. 1 Baron Stuart de Rothesay in ODNB.

Baron Stuart de Decies (1839-74 UK)

Origins: Lord Henry Stuart, son of the 1 Marquis of Bute, married in 1802 Lady Gertrude Mason-Villiers, daughter and heiress of the 2 Earl of Grandison (see Villiers). Their son was created Baron Stuart de Decies.

1. Henry Villiers Stuart 1 Baron de Decies – County Waterford 1826-29 Banbury 1830-31
2. William Villiers-Stuart – County Waterford 1835-47
3. Henry Villiers-Stuart – County Waterford 1873-74 1880-85

Seats: Dromana, Waterford (old castle, rebuilt 1780s, acq. by mar. 1802, remod. 1840s, house sold 1957, part demolished 1966, still own estate); Bramfield, Hertfordshire (acq. 1732, sold 1828)
Estates: Bateman 30953 (I) 11573
Peer: 1 peer 1839-74
2 Lds Lt 19th, 20th
Notes: No record of the marriage of the 1 Baron could be found and so his son, Henry Villiers-Stuart MP 1873-85, could not succeed to the peerage. Dromana has passed by descent for 800 years (as of 2015). One in ODNB.

Cox

Origins: A military captain of modest origins killed in 1651 had a son, the 1 Baronet, who became a lawyer in London and returned to Ireland. He served at the Battle of the Boyne and became Lord Chief Justice in the 1690s, Lord Chancellor of Ireland 1703. Sheriff 1711. On the death of Sir Richard Cox 8 Bt in 1846 the Castletown estates passed to his sister Catherine, who married 1833 Henry Villiers Stuart (see above).

1. Richard Cox – {Tallow 1703-14 Clonakilty 1717-25}
2. Sir Richard Cox 2 Bt – {Clonakilty 1727-66}
3. Richard Cox – {Charleville 1776-83}
4. Henry Cox – {Castlemartyr 1787-90}

Seat: Castletown (Cox), Kilkenny (old house, purch. 1703, rebuilt 1767-71, passed by mar. to Villiers Stuarts 1846, sold 1909)
Estates: Worth £400 pa in 1714 and held 6,891 acres worth £2,979 pa in 1858.
Title: Baronet 1706-1873
Notes: Two in ODNB.

Stuart

Origins: Cadet of the Bute Stuarts 16th century.

1. William Stuart – [Bute 1693-1702]

Seat: Ambrismore, Buteshire (acq. 1529, declined to a farm house, acq. by Marquis of Bute again, still owns)

Stuart

Origins: Cousins of the Earls of Bute.

1. Sir Robert Stuart 1 Bt – [Rothesay 1678 1689-93]
2. James Stuart – Buteshire 1761-62

Seat: Tilli(e)coultry House, Clackmannanshire (purch. 1703, sold 1724, unroofed 1938, demolished 1960)
Title: Baronet 1707-67

Earl of Erne (1789- I)

Origins: A cadet of the Crichtons (see above) sold their Scottish estates in 1590 and migrated to Fermanagh in 1613. Soldiers. Sheriff 1672.

1. Abraham Creichton – {County Fermanagh 1692-93 Enniskillen 1695-99}
2. David Creichton – {Augher 1695-99 Lifford 1703-28}
3. Abraham Creichton 1 Baron Erne – {Lifford 1727-68}
4. John Crichton 1 Earl of Erne - {Lifford 1761-72}
5. Abraham Crichton – {Lifford 1768-1800}
6. Abraham Crichton 2 Earl of Erne – {Lifford 1790-97}
7. John Crichton – {Lifford 1797-1800}
8. John Crichton 4 Earl of Erne – Enniskillen 1868-80 County Fermanagh 1880-85

Seat: Crom Castle, Fermanagh (built 1611, acq. by mar. to Spottiswoode heiress (Spottiswoodes acq. 1624) 1655, destroyed by fire 1764, new house 1830-39, still own)
Estates: Bateman 40365 (I) 23860. Owned 15,000 acres worth 55 million pounds in 2001.
Titles: Baron Erne 1768- I; Viscount Erne 1781- I; Baron Fermanagh 1876- UK
Peers: {2 peers 1768-1800} 2 Irish Rep peers 1801-28 1845-85 2 peers 1885-1914 1928-40
2 Lds Lt 19th, 20th
2 KP 19th, 20th
Notes: The Earls of Erne were still purchasing estates in the early 19th c. 6,274 acres in 1810 and 2,426 more in 1820s.

Stuart (Stewart)

Origins: Descended from Alexander Stewart Lord High Steward of Scotland 1283 (see above). **First [MP 1617 for Renfrewshire].**

1. Sir Archibald Stewart – [Renfrewshire 1669-74]
2. Sir William Stewart 2 Bt – [Lanarkshire 1696-1702]
3. James Stuart – Ayr Burghs 1734-41
4. Patrick Stuart – Lanarkshire 1750-54
5. Andrew Stuart – Lanarkshire 1774-84 Weymouth & Melcombe Regis 1790-1801

Seats: Torrance Castle, Lanarkshire (medieval, burned, rebuilt 1605, acq. 1652, add. late 18th c., remod. 1879, sold 1947); Castle Milk (Castlemilk), Lanarkshire (medieval castle, acq. c. 1460, rebuilt 1796, sold c. 1865, demolished 1969)
Estates: Bateman 2971 (S) 2949 and 2137 (S) 3260
Title: Baronet 1668-1797
Notes: One in ODNB.

Earl of Castle Stewart (1800- I)

Origins: Descended from King Robert II. His younger son, the Duke of Albany, was the ancestor of Lord Avandale (1500 S). His eldest son was created Lord Stewart of Ochiltree (1543 S), ancestor of the Earls of Castle Stewart. **First [MP 1586]. Another [MP 1617 for Ayrshire].** To Ireland early-mid-17th c. Sheriff 1665.

1. Arthur Stuart 7 Earl of Castle Stewart – Harborough Div. Leicestershire 1929-33

Seats: Stuart (Stewart) Hall, Tyrone (old house, add. 18th c., add. 19th c., demolished c. 1974); Drum Manor (Oaklands), Tyrone (built 18th c., rebuilt 1829, acq. by mar. 1866, sold 1964, part demolished 1975)
Estates: Bateman 34875 (I) 13113. Owned 5,500 acres in 2001.
Titles: Baron Castle Stewart 1619- I (dormant 1685-1774); Viscount Castle Stewart 1793- I; Baronet 1628-
Peers: {3 peers 1660-85 1775-1800}

Earl of Moray (1561- S)

Origins: The 1 Earl was an illegitimate son of King James V by Margaret Erskine (daughter of the Earl of Mar) and was a half brother of Mary Queen of Scots. The family also descended, probably legitimately, from Robert Duke of Albany, son of King Robert II. **First MP 1626 for Liskeard.**

1. John Stewart – Anstruther Easter Burghs 1741-47
2. John Stuart Lord Doune – Great Bedwyn 1790-91
3. John Stuart 12 Earl of Moray – Newport (IoW) 1825-26
4. James Stuart 1 Viscount Stuart of Findhorn – Moray & Nairn 1923-59

Seats: Darnaway Castle, Elginshire (built c. 1450, rebuilt 1802-10, still own); Doune Lodge, Perthshire (acq. and castle built 1401, ruin by mid-18th c., restored 1883 but not inhabited, lodge built 1805, still own); Castle Stuart, Inverness-shire (acq. mid-16th c., built 1625, uninhabited 17th-20th c., now a hotel); Donibristle House (Park), Fife (medieval, acq. 1540, add. c. 1700, rebuilt 1719-23, rebuilt 1740, fire 1858, military use from 1917, central block demolished)

Estates: Bateman 77612 (S) 36078. Owned 29,400 acres in 1996.
Titles: Baron Doune 1581- S; Baron Abernathy & Strathern 1611- S; Baron Stuart 1796- GB; Viscount Stuart of Findhorn 1959- UK; Baronet 1681-1735
Peers: [2 peers 1660-1707]; 2 Scottish Rep peers 1741-67 1784-96; 11 peers 1796-1945
3 Lds Lt 18th, 19th, 20th
2 in Cabinet 1680-88 1951-57
4 KT 17th, 18th, 19th
Notes: James Stuart, a younger son of the 17 Earl of Moray, was a major figure in post-WWII Conservative politics serving as Chief Whip and a Cabinet member. 1 and 2 Earls and 1 Viscount of Findhorn and one other in ODNB.

Baron Gray (1444- S)

Origins: The Grays were prominent from c. 1350. The 1 Baron was Ambassador to England. A younger daughter of the 11 Baron Gray married in 1763 the 9 Earl of Moray. The 14 Earl succeeded in 1878 as 18 Baron Gray. The title later passed to a nephew, son of his sister, seated at Brownswood, Wexford.

No MPs

Seats: Fowlis Castle, Forfarshire (built 1640, abandoned by family early 18th c., reduced in size); Broughty Castle, Forfarshire (built c. 1490, still intact 1716 but family ceased to occupy after 17th c., by 19th c. a ruin, repaired 1861 for government use); House of Gray, Forfarshire (built 1716, sold early 20th c., derelict, restored c. 1995, hotel); Castle Huntly, Forfarshire (built 1452, sold 1615); Kinfauns Castle, Perthshire (medieval, acq. by Grays mar. 1741, rebuilt 1820-26, passed to Stuarts (Earl of Moray) by mar. 1878, sold 1930); Brownswood, Wexford (built early 19th c., Morays acq. mid-19th c., rebuilt 1894-96, sold 1933, now hospital)
Estates: Bateman 4017 (S) 10785
Peers: [1 peer 1707] 2 Scottish Rep peers 1812-41 1847-67
Notes: Much of property confiscated 1629 due to being recusants. 1, 4, 6, and 7 Barons and one other in ODNB.

STUCLEY [Buck, Orchard]

Stucley (Stukeley)

Origins: The Stucley family acquired manorial land in 1434. Kt 16th c. George Buck of Moreton in the early 19th c. married the daughter and heiress of Lewis Stucley of Afferton and took the name Stucley. The Bucks were originally from Ireland and settled in Devon in the 17th century. They became tobacco merchants in Bideford in the 18th century (a father and son were mayors of the town). They acquired estates by marriage and inheritance and changed their name to Stucley in 1858. They also owned plantations in Virginia and Maryland.

1. Sir Thomas Stucley – Tiverton 1661-64
2. John Buck – Taunton 1741-45
3. Lewis Buck Stucley – Exeter 1826-32 N. Devon 1839-57
4. Sir George Stucley 1 Bt – Barnstaple 1855-59 1865-68

Seats: Moreton House (Daddon House), Devon (purch. by Bucks c. 1750, rebuilt c. 1760, sold 1956); Afferton (Affeton) Castle, Devon (built 15th c., acq. by mar. to Afferton heiress 1734, remod. 19th c., still own, principal seat); Hartland Abbey, Devon (medieval and 18th c., inher. by mar. of 1754 (from holders since 1539) early in 19th c., remod. c. 1845 and 1862, still own)
Estates: Bateman 19807 (E) 16677. Owned 15,000 acres worth 52 million pounds in 2001.
Title: Baronet 1859-
Notes: Two in ODNB.

<u>Orchard</u>

Origins: George Buck, who succeeded to the Stucley estates in 1755, married the daughter and heiress of Paul Orchard of Hartland Abbey. The Orchards gained wealth through holding Customs and Excise positions in the West Country in the 17th and 18th centuries.

1. Paul Orchard – Camelford 1711-13 Bossiney 1714-15
2. Paul Orchard – Callington 1784-1806

Seats: Hartland Abbey, Devon (medieval, acq. 1539 by the Abbott family and passed by heiresses to the Orchards, 1702, remod. 1779, passed by mar. to Stucleys early 19th c.); Aldercombe, Cornwall (acq. early 18th c., passed out of family by mar. early 19th c.)

STYLE

Origins: A London Alderman purchased estates at the end of 15th century. Also became brewers. **First MP 1656**.

1. Sir Thomas Style 4 Bt – Bramber 1715
2. Sir Thomas Style 8 Bt – Scarborough 1837-41

Seats: Wateringbury Place, Kent (old house, purch. c. 1600, rebuilt 1707, sold early 19th c.); Glenmore Lodge, Donegal (built 18th c., purch. by 1835, remod. early 20th c.,

demolished 1990s); Langley Park (Beckenham), Kent (purch. c. 1510, sold c. 1727, fire 1913, demolished)
Estates: Bateman 39564 (I) 4000
Titles: Baronet 1627-59 1627-
Notes: One in ODNB.

SUCKLING

Origins: Founded by a baker and Alderman in Norwich. The first MP was a mercer and merchant. **First MP 1571 for Norwich. Two further MPs 1601-59.**

1. Maurice Suckling – Portsmouth 1776-78

Seats: Woodton Hall, Norfolk (acq. 14th c., built late 16th c., rebuilt 1694, sold 1839, demolished); Barsham Hall, Suffolk (built 15th c., purch. 1613, part demolished 1802-12, farm house from 1846, land sales 1844-1912, more demolition 1948)
Estates: 2,000 acres at Barsham in 1613.
Notes: Four in ODNB.

SUGDEN

<u>Baron St. Leonards</u> (1852- UK)

Origins: The 1 Baron was the son of a hairdresser in London, and he married a kitchen maid. The 1 Baron was a lawyer earning £15,000 pa at the bar. He became Lord Chancellor of Ireland 1835 and of England 1852.

1. Edward Sugden 1 Baron St. Leonards – Weymouth 1828-31 St. Mawes 1831-32 Ripon 1837-41

Seat: Boyle Farm, Surrey (purch. 1839, sold 1890)
Estates: Bateman 4569 (E) 5128
Peers: 3 peers 1852-1908 1911-45
1 in Cabinet 1852
Notes: 1 Baron and one other in ODNB.

SULLIVAN (Sulivan)

Origins: Of obscure and modest Irish lineage. Discontinued the name "O'Sullivan" in 1755. The first MP was a nabob who returned to England in 1753 and purchased an estate. Chairman of the East India Company 1758. High Sheriff of Buckinghamshire 1797. Judge and Kt in 1801.

1. Laurence Sulivan – Taunton 1762-68 Ashburton 1768-74
2. Sir Richard Sullivan 1 Bt – New Romney 1787-96 Seaford 1802-06
3. John Sullivan – Old Sarum 1790-96 Aldborough 1802-06 Ashburton 1811-18
4. Sir Henry Sullivan 2 Bt – Lincoln 1812-14

Seats: Imber Court (Thames Ditton), Surrey (acq. by mar. 1823, sold 1861); Punsborne (Ponsborne) Park, Hertfordshire (purch. 1753 or 1761 for £13,000, sold c. 1811); Riching's Park, Buckinghamshire (purch 1786, fire 1788, new house built c. 1790, sold 1855, demolished c. 1946)
Title: Baronet 1804-
Notes: Laurence Sulivan was probably a kinsman and used his influence to help Richard MP. First MP had a fortune but seems to have lost most of it due to a crash and bad debts. Three in ODNB.

SURTEES

Origins: Medieval origins. Seneschal of Durham 1341. **First MP 1361 for Northumberland.** Banking and mercantile fortune in the 18th and 19th centuries.

1. Henry Surtees – Hertfordshire 1864-68
2. Charles Surtees – S. Durham 1865-68
3. Sir Herbert Surtees – Gateshead 1918-22

Seats: Redworth Hall (House), Durham (built 1693, acq. 1744, sold 1955, hotel); Mainsforth Hall, Durham (built c. 1625, purch. 1708, rebuilt c. 1725, empty 1952, demolished 1962); Dane End, Hertfordshire (acq. by mar. 1866, sold c. 1895)
Estates: Bateman 9456 (E) 7102. Rubinstein – William Surtees left £120,000 in probate in 1832.
Notes: Two in ODNB.

SWANTON

Origins: Lawyers in the 17th century.

1. Francis Swanton – Wilton 1660 Salisbury 1661
2. William Swanton – Salisbury 1673-79
3. Francis Swanton – Salisbury 1715-21

SWINBURNE

Origins: Gentry by the 13th century. At Capheaton by the late 13th century. **First MP 1295 for Northumberland. Three additional MPs 1313-1554, all for the county. Three additional MPs** from a cadet line at Swinburne, Northumberland **1377-1414, all for Essex**.

1. Sir John Swinburne 6 Bt – Launceston 1788-90
2. Sir John Swinburne 7 Bt – Lichfield 1885-92

Seat: Capheaton, Northumberland (purch. and built c. 1270, demolished and rebuilt 1668, add. c. 1800, still own)
Estates: Bateman 28902 (E) 13131
Title: Baronet 1660-
Notes: A Roman Catholic family. The 6 Bt conformed to the Established Church. Three in ODNB.

SWINTON *SCOTLAND*

Origins: Old family, perhaps originating in the early Middle Ages. **First [MP 1560]. Three additional [MPs 1612-58, all for Berwickshire].** Sir John Swinton MP below was the 25th laird.

1. Sir John Swinton – [Berwickshire 1690-1702 1703-07] Scotland 1707-08

Seats: Swinton House, Berwickshire (acq. c. 1140, medieval house, fire 1797, rebuilt 1800, passed out of the family mid-19th c., fire 2008); Kimmerghame House, Berwickshire (purch. later 18th c., rebuilt 1851, fire 1938, rebuilt, still own)
1 Ld Lt 21st
Notes: Family fortunes revived by an East India fortune in the later 18th century that paid for Kimmerghame. Seven in ODNB.

SYDENHAM [St. Barbe]

<u>Sydenham</u>

Origins: The family held manorial land from the reign of King John. **First MP 1298. Five additional MPs 1377-1654, three kts of the shire.** The 3 Bt sold his estates in 1723-24 to his cousin Humphrey Sydenham MP of Combe and Nutcombe.

1. Sir John Sydenham 2 Bt – Somerset 1669-79
2. Sir Philip Sydenham 3 Bt – Ilchester 1701 Somerset 1701-05

3. Humphrey Sydenham – Exeter 1741-54

Seats: Brympton d'Evercy (Brimpton), Somerset (medieval house, acq. by mar. 15th c., built c. 1520s, rebuilt 1650s c., add. 1722-23, house sold for financial reasons 1731); Combe Sydenham Hall, Somerset (built 15th c., remod. end of 16th c., sold 1693)
Estates: Worth about £4,000 pa c. 1700, but heavily in debt.
Title: Baronet 1641-1739
Notes: Cromwellian peer 1657. Six in ODNB.

St. Barbe

Origins: At Ashington in the 14th century. **First MP 1654, for Hampshire**. Sir John St. Barbe 1 Bt devised his estates in 1723 to Edward Sydenham of Brimpton, his great-grand-nephew.

1. Sir John St. Barbe 1 Bt – Ilchester 1681

Seats: Broadlands, Hampshire (built c. 1540, acq. by mar. second half 16th c., sold 1736); Ashington, Somerset (acq. 14th c., passed to Sydenhams by inher. 1723 and then to Tregonwells)
Title: Baronet 1663-1723
Notes: Extinct 1723.

SYKES

Sykes

Origins: Began as yeomen in Cumberland. Then they were rich clothiers in Leeds for centuries. They moved to Hull in the 17th century (Mayor 1660s and again mid-18th century) and became importers of iron ore from Germany and Sweden. One married an heiress to Sledmere in 1703. Another married the Tatton heiress worth £60,000 in 1770. They began to invest heavily in land (over £200,000) and built up a great estate by the 1780s. They increased their fortune through farming and foreclosing on mortgages via a family bank. (English, *The Great Landowners of East Yorkshire*, 29)

1. Sir Christopher Sykes 2 Bt – Beverley 1784-90
2. Sir Mark Masterman-Sykes 3 Bt – York 1807-20
3. Daniel Sykes – Hull 1820-30 Beverley 1830-31
4. Christopher Sykes – Beverley 1865-68 E. Riding Yorkshire 1868-85 Buckrose Div. E. Riding Yorkshire 1885-92
5. Sir Mark Sykes 6 Bt – Central Hull 1911-19

Seats: Sledmere House, Yorkshire (medieval, purch. by Kirkby family mid-17th c., passed in 1718 by mar. of 1703 to the Sykes family, rebuilt 1751, add. 1786-90, fire 1911 and rebuilt 1912-17, still own); Brantinghamthorpe (Brantingham Thorpe) Hall, Yorkshire (old house, purch. 1867, remod. 1868-82, sold 1899)
Estates: Bateman 34010 (E) 35870 and 3032 (E) 4541. Worth £30,000,000 with 30,000 acres in 1990; 13,000 acres in 2001.
Title: Baronet 1783-
Notes: Six in ODNB.

<u>Sykes</u>

Origins: Cadet line of the 17th century raised to wealth by a nabob in the mid-18th century.

1. Sir Francis Sykes 1 Bt – Shaftesbury 1771-75 1780-84 Wallingford 1784-1804
2. Sir Francis Sykes 2 Bt – Wallingford 1794-96

Seats: Basildon Park, Berkshire (purch. 1771 and rebuilt house 1776-83, sold 1838 for £97,000, NT - *Country Life*, 161, p. 1230); Ackworth Park, Yorkshire (purch. 1763, sold 1771, later demolished)
Estates: The nabob returned to England in 1768 with a fortune of possibly £250,000 (*Country Life*, 161 p. 1160).
Title: Baronet 1781-
Notes: One in ODNB.

TALBOT I [Bond, Carpenter, Chetwynd, Fletcher, Fox, Hopkins, Mansel, Phillips, Rice (Rhys)] *ENGLAND, WALES, IRELAND, & SCOTLAND*

<u>Duke of Shrewsbury</u> (1694-1718 E)

Origins: The family claimed Saxon descent. They held land in the Welsh marches from at least the reign of Henry III. Officials and courtiers under Henry III and Edward I. Baron 1332. KG 15th century. Hereditary Lord Stewards of Ireland. Sir Gilbert Talbot MP commanded a wing of Henry VII's army at Bosworth. The genealogy of the family became very complicated (only twice between 1618 and 1856 did the Shrewsbury Earldom pass from father to son - *Country Life*, 122, p. 924). The 7 Earl of Shrewsbury preferred his three daughters to his brother, and at his death in 1616 willed the bulk of his estate to them and only a relatively small part to the male line. Later the title passed to a distant cousin, a Catholic priest, who was the 9 Earl. The 1 Duke was a Protestant, but the family reverted to Catholicism, until 1856 when the Earls again became Protestants via inheritance by another remote cousin. **First MP 1386 for Berkshire. Nine further MPs 1442-1586, all kts of the shire**. The senior male line became extinct with the death of the 17 Earl of Shrewsbury in 1856. The Earldom passed to a cadet line headed by Earl Talbot of Hensol. The two lines have been combined here. The 17 Earl left his personal property to the third son of the 14 Duke of Norfolk, who initially took the name Talbot but later assumed the surname Fitzalan-Howard (see Howard I).

1. Charles Talbot 1 Baron Talbot – Tregony 1720-22 Durham 1722-33
2. John Talbot – Brecon 1734-54 Ilchester 1754-56
3. William Talbot 1 Earl Talbot (1st cr.) – Glamorgan 1734-37
4. John Chetwynd-Talbot 1 Earl Talbot (2nd cr.) – Castle Rising 1777-82
5. Sir Charles Talbot 2 Bt – Weobley 1800-02 Rye 1803-06 Bletchingley 1812
6. Henry Chetwynd-Talbot 18 Earl of Shrewsbury – Hertford 1830-31 Armagh 1831 Dublin City 1831-32 S. Staffordshire 1837-49
7. Charles Chetwynd-Talbot 19 Earl of Shrewsbury – Stafford 1857-59 N. Staffordshire 1859-65 Stamford 1868
8. Walter Chetwynd-Talbot Carpenter – County Waterford 1859-65
9. John Chetwynd-Talbot – W. Kent 1868-78 University of Oxford 1878-1910
10. Reginald Chetwynd-Talbot – Stafford 1869-74
11. Gustavus Chetwynd-Talbot – Hemel Hempstead Div. Hertfordshire 1918-29

Seats: Heythrop House (Park), Oxfordshire (built 1706-16, burned down 1831, sold c. 1870, now hotel); Hensol (Castle), Glamorganshire (built late 17th/early 18th c., acq. by mar. 1721, add. c. 1735, sold c. 1790); Ingestre Hall, Staffordshire (acq. from Chetwynds 1767, fire 1882, rebuilt, sold 1960, institutional use); Alton Towers (and Castle), Staffordshire (built c. 1170, add. c. 1300, acq. by mar. 1406, damaged 1640s, lodge built later 17th c., remod. 1811-27, transferred seat there 1831, built 1832-52, sold 1918-21, abandoned, ruin, theme park); Pontefract New Hall, Yorkshire (built c. 1591, abandoned by early 18th c.)
Estates: Bateman 40081 (E) 72512. Worth £1,735 pa in 1538 and £12,000 pa in 1616. The 1 Duke was worth £8,000 pa. Rubinstein – 15 Earl left £500,000 in probate in 1827.
Titles: Baron Talbot 1332-1616 E; Earl of Shrewsbury 1442- E; Earl of Waterford 1446- I; Baron Talbot 1733- GB; Earl Talbot 1761-82 GB; Baron Dynevor 1780- GB; Earl Talbot 1784- GB
Peers: 12 peers 1660-68 1680-1718 1733-82 1784-93 1798-1849 1829-56 1849-77 1881-1921 1935-45
2 Lds Lt 17th, 18th, 19th
3 in Cabinet 1689-90 1694-98 1713-14 1733-37 1817-21
2 KG 17th, 18th, 19th
1 KP 19th
Notes: 1 and 2 Barons Talbot, 2 Viscount Lisle, and and 1 Baron Talbot of Hensol and 2 Earl Talbot of Hensol and 1, 2, 4, 5, 6, 7, and 16 Earls of Shrewsbury and 1 Duke and fourteen others in ODNB.

Baron Dynevor (1780- GB)

Origins: The Rhys (Anglicized to Rice and in the modern era returned to Rhys) family was an ancient Welsh dynasty. One head of the family married in the 15th century a descendent of the Princes of South Wales. Fought at Bosworth for Henry VII and was rewarded with offices and estates. KG 1506. **First MP 1584 for Carmarthenshire**. The daughter and heiress of the 1 Earl Talbot of the first creation married George Rice of Newton Castle. She succeeded by special remainder as 2 Baroness Dynevor. The 4 Baron inherited the estates of the Trevors of Glynde and took the additional name Trevor (see Hill I).

1. Griffith Rice – Carmarthenshire 1701-10
2. Edward Rice – Carmarthenshire 1722-24
3. George Rice – Carmarthenshire 1754-79
4. George Talbot Rice 3 Baron Dynevor – Carmarthenshire 1790-93
5. George Rice-Rice-Talbot 4 Baron Dynevor – Carmarthenshire 1820-52
6. Walter Rhys 7 Baron Dynevor – Brighton 1910-11
7. Charles Rhys 8 Baron Dynevor – Romford Div. Essex 1923-29 Guildford Div. Surrey 1931-35

Seats: Dynevor (Dinefwr) Castle (also called Newton), Carmarthenshire (owned and built in medieval period, confiscated and repurch. 1439, built c. 1490, 1987 NT); Newton Castle (House), Carmarthenshire (in the park of Dynevor Castle) (medieval, rebuilt c. 1520, remod. 1595-1603, house built 1660, fire 18th c., sold 1974, NT 1990); Barrington Park, Gloucestershire (built 16th c., purch. 1735, fire 1736, rebuilt c. 1737, held until 1869, when it passed to the Wingfield's via an heiress, see Wingfield)
Estates: Bateman 10728 (E & W) 12562. Worth £1,500 pa in 1509.
Peers: 6 peers 1780-82 1793-1945
3 Lds Lt 18th, 19th, 20th
Notes: Rice family and 4 Baron and two others in ODNB.

Earl of Tyrconnel (1761-1853 I)

Origins: An old gentry family seated in Herefordshire since the 13th century. The 1 Baron rose by military prowess. He went to Ireland as a soldier in 1690 and later served in Spain and elsewhere. The wife of the 4 and last Earl Tyrconnel, was Sarah Crowe, heiress of Kiplin Park. She left Kiplin in 1868 to the second son of the 18 Earl of Shrewsbury, who took the name Carpenter.

1. George Carpenter 1 Baron Carpenter – {Newton 1703-05} Whitchurch 1715-22 Westminster 1722-27
2. George Carpenter 2 Baron Carpenter – Morpeth 1717-27 Weobley 1741-47
3. George Carpenter 1 Earl Tyrconnel – Taunton 1754-62

4. George Carpenter 2 Earl Tyrconnel – Scarborough 1772-96 Berwick-on-Tweed 1796-1802
5. Charles Carpenter – Berwick-on-Tweed 1790-96

Seats: Kiplin Park, Yorkshire (built 1622-25, acq. by mar. 1817, add. 1818, donated to a foundation 1973); (The) Homme (Holme) House, (Dilwyn), Herefordshire (acq. 13th c., sold 1787); Longwood House (Park) (Rosehill), Hampshire (acq. early 18th c., sold 1731, demolished)
Titles: Baron Carpenter 1719-1853 I; Viscount Carlingford 1761-1853 I
Peers: {4 peers 1719-62 1771-1800}
Notes: The last Talbot of Kiplin died in 1973. 1 Baron in ODNB.

Viscount Chetwynd (1717- I)

Origins: An early medieval family established by the 12th century. Inherited Ingestre either 1263 or 1285 from a family that held it from 1166. John Chetwynd MP fought at Agincourt (Roskell, Clark, and Rawcliffe, *The House of Commons*, II, 543-44). **First MP 1377 for Shropshire. Three additional MPs 1421-1614, two kts of the shire.** The 2 Viscount settled 10,500 acres and the house at Ingestre on his daughter Catherine, who married John Talbot. Their great-grandson succeeded as 18 Earl of Shrewsbury. The Irish Viscountcy descended to a cadet line without significant estates.

1. Walter Chetwynd – Stafford 1674-79 1685-87 Staffordshire 1690-93
2. John Chetwynd – Stafford 1689-95 Tamworth 1698-99 Stafford 1701-02
3. Walter Chetwynd 1 Viscount Chetwynd – Stafford 1702-22 1725-34
4. John Chetwynd 2 Viscount Chetwynd – St. Mawes 1715-22 Stockbridge 1722-34 Stafford 1738-47
5. William Chetwynd 3 Viscount Chetwynd – Stafford 1715-22 Plymouth 1722-27 Stafford 1734-70
6. William Chetwynd – Wootton Bassett 1722-27
7. William Chetwynd 4 Viscount Chetwynd – Stockbridge 1747-54
8. William Chetwynd – Stafford 1754-65

Seats: Ingestre Hall, Staffordshire (acq. by mar. 1263 or 1285, rebuilt 1613, passed by mar. 1767 to the Talbots, see above); (Little) Heywood (Haywood) Park, Staffordshire (acq. 17th c., passed by mar. to Talbots 1767, declined to a farm, demolished); Chetwynd House, Staffordshire; Rudge Hall, Staffordshire (acq. early 16th c., sold later 18th c.); Grendon Hall, Warwickshire (acq. by mar. by 1348, built c. 1600, remod. 1725, house passed to Brocton line in 1755) (see Brockton line below)
Estates: Bateman under 2000 acres. Worth £2,600 pa in the 1660s.
Title: Baron Rathbone 1717- I
Peers: {5 peers 1717-70 1773-1800}
Notes: 3 Viscount and three others in ODNB.

Chetwynd

Origins: An uncle of the 1 Viscount Chetwynd established a cadet line in the 17th century financed by wealth from the iron industry and the activity of a merchant and ship owner.

1. William Chetwynd – Stafford 1661-79
2. Walter Chetwynd – Lichfield 1715-31
3. William Chetwynd – Wootton Bassett 1722-27
4. Sir George Chetwynd 2 Bt – Stafford 1820-26
5. William Chetwynd – Stafford 1832-41

Seats: Grendon Hall, Warwickshire (acq. by mar. by 1348, built c. 1600, remod. 1725, house passed to Brocton line in 1755, rebuilt 1825, sold 1911, demolished 1933); Brocton Hall, Staffordshire (built 1801, sold 1922, golf club)
Estates: Bateman 6626 (E & W) 12445
Title: Baronet 1795-

Talbot

Origins: Sir Gilbert Talbot, brother of the 3 Earl of Shrewsbury had a grandson who married in the 16th century the Sharington heiress of Lacock Abbey. The Sharingtons rose via government office and purchased Lacock at the Dissolution. **First MP 1545 (sat for Wiltshire 1547). Two further MPs 1559-97**. Eventually, the Earldom of Shrewsbury descended to this family on the death of the 17 Earl. Lacock then passed to Ann Talbot, who married Sir John Ivory. Their son, John Ivory Talbot, married Mary Mansel of Margram Abbey, daughter of the 1 Baron Mansel. Their eldest son succeeded to Margram in 1750 on the death of his cousin the 4 Baron Mansel. The Mansel-Talbots of Margram descend from his younger brother. Their sister, Martha Talbot, had a son who took the name Talbot and inherited Lacock. His marriage to Elizabeth Fox-Strangeways added the name Fox to the family surname.

1. Sir John Talbot – Worcestershire 1660 Knaresborough 1661-79 Chippenham 1679 Devizes 1685-87
2. Sir Gilbert Talbot – Plymouth 1666-79
3. Sharington Talbot – Chippenham 1685-87
4. John Ivory-Talbot – Ludgershall 1715-22 Wiltshire 1727-41
5. John Talbot – Marlborough 1747-54
6. William Fox Talbot – Chippenham 1832-35

Seat: Lacock Abbey, Wiltshire (medieval monastic buildings, purch. by Sharringtons 1539, remod. 1540-50, passed by mar. to Talbots, remod. 1754-55 and 1827-30, NT 1944)

Estates: Under 2000 acres in the 1870s.
Notes: William Henry Fox Talbot was a pioneer of photography. One in ODNB.

Baron Mansel (1712-50 GB)

Origins: Traced their ancestry back to the Conquest. An English family that settled in the Gower Peninsula in the 13th century. Fought at Bosworth for Henry VII and became great lords and acquired additional land at the Dissolution. **First MP 1553 for Glamorganshire. Four additional MPs 1554-1628, three sat for Glamorganshire**. Involved in industrial activity in Wales and elsewhere for centuries. For the Talbot connection, see above.

1. Bussy Mansel – Wales 1653 Cardiff Boroughs 1660 Glamorganshire 1679-81 Cardiff 1681 Glamorganshire 1689-99
2. Sir Edward Mansel 4 Bt – Glamorganshire 1660 1670-79 1681 1685-87
3. Thomas Mansel – Brecon 1678-79
4. Thomas Mansel 1 Baron Mansel – Cardiff 1689-98 Glamorganshire 1701-12
5. Thomas Mansel – Glamorganshire 1699-1701 Cardiff 1701-06
6. Robert Mansel – Minehead 1721-23
7. Bussy Mansel 4 Baron Mansel – Cardiff 1727-34 Glamorgan 1737-44
8. Richard Mansel-Phillips – Stafford 1806-12
9. Christopher Mansel-Talbot – Glamorganshire 1830-85 Mid. Div. Glamorganshire 1885-90

Seats: Margram Abbey (Castle, Park), Glamorganshire (medieval monastic buildings, purch. 1540 and converted into a house 1552, remod. late 16th c., add. 17th c., orangery built, 1787-90, house dismantled 1789-93, house rebuilt 1830-40 and late Victorian period, sold 1941, fire 1977, restored, public ownership); Briton Ferry, Glamorganshire (built by Leyson (Leisian) Price in 16th c., descended to Mansels later 17th c., passed to the Lords Vernon in 1760 and to the Earl of Jersey 1813, sold 1821) (Lloyd, *The Lost Houses of Wales*, 79); Penrice Castle, Glamorganshire (built c. 1100, acq. by mar. to Penrice heiress 1410, rebuilt 1773-77, add. 1893-96, passed to Lady Blythswood 1918, much land sold 1950s, part demolished 1967-68, descendents still own); Oxwich Castle, Glamorganshire (built 14th-15th c., acq. by mar. by mid-15th c. from a family that owned it in the 13th c., rebuilt 16th c., much decayed, sold 1949, now in official guardianship)
Estates: Bateman 33920 (W) 44057. Owned over 23,000 acres in the 1580s. Worth £1,100 pa in 1645. In the 19th c. the family held millions of pounds in stocks and bonds and other forms of non-settled, non-agricultural wealth.
Title: Baronet 1611-1750
Peers: 4 peers 1712-23 1740-50
1 Ld Lt 19th

Notes: The Mansel estates included much land that became valuable in the industrial revolution due to mining and smelting. Leyson (Leisian) Price of Briton Ferry was **MP 1558**. Rose by the law. **One other MP 1614-26 for Glamorganshire**. The male line became extinct in 1890 and the estates passed to a nephew, Andrew Fletcher in 1918 (see below). 1 Baron and five others in ODNB.

Mansel

Origins: A younger brother of the 1 Baronet of Margram established a cadet line at Iscoed.

1. Sir William Mansel 9 Bt – Carmathenshire 1784-90
2. Sir Courteney Mansel 13 Bt – Penryn & Falmouth Div. Cornwall 1923-24

Seats: Iscoed, Carmarthenshire (acq. by mar. c. 1615, built 1772, sold 1812, ruin); The Manor, Maes-y-Crugiav (Maesycrugiau), Carmarthenshire (built later 16th c., acq. by mar. 1878, fire, rebuilt c. 1900, sold 1933?)
Title: Baronet 1621-

Hopkins

Origins: The family fortune was made by "Vulture" Hopkins, an early 18th-century merchant. Benjamin Bond succeeded to the estates of his grandmother's cousin, John Hopkins, and took the name Hopkins in 1772. He left his estate to Richard Mansel Phillips, MP 1806-12 (see above).

1. John Hopkins – St. Ives 1710-15 Ilchester 1715-22
2. Benjamin Bond Hopkins – Ilchester 1784-90 Malmesbury 1790-94

Seat: Painshill, Surrey (built mid-18th c., purch. 1773, rebuilt 1778, sold c. 1794, public ownership)

Fletcher

Origins: A Yorkshire family established in Scotland as gentry by 17th century. Christopher Mansel Talbot, MP 1830-90 (see above), bequeathed an estimated £1,000,000 worth of shares in the Great Western Railway Company and his landed estate to his unmarried daughter Emily, who died in 1918. He left his shares in the London and South West Railway Company and Margram to his daughter Bertha, who married in 1866 John Fletcher of Saltoun. Their grandson, John Mansel Talbot Fletcher (d. 1951) of Saltoun Hall, succeeded to Margram and to Emily's estate in 1918.

1. Andrew Fletcher – [Haddington Constabulary 1678 Haddingtonshire 1681 1703-07]
2. Andrew Fletcher – Haddington Burghs 1747-61 Haddingtonshire 1761-68

Seats: Saltoun Hall, Haddingtonshire (medieval, purch. 1643, add. 1769, remod. 1803, rebuilt 1817, house sold 1970, still own estate and live in former stables); Margram Abbey, Glamorganshire (acq. by mar. 1918, see above)
Estates: Bateman 3928 (S) 6456 (before the Mansel-Talbot inheritances)
Notes: One Fletcher was a Lord of Session mid-18th century. Three in ODNB.

Earl of Tyrconnel (Tyrconnell) (1685-1752 I)

Origins: The Talbots descended from a common ancestor with the Earls of Shrewsbury. They were one of the first Anglo-Norman families to establish themselves within the Pale in Ireland. Summoned to Parliaments by Henry I and Edward III as barons. Sheriff of Dublin in the 14th century. Remained Roman Catholics. Created Jacobite Dukes by James II in 1689 in exile (extinct 1691). **First {MP 1613}. Two additional {MPs 163-39}.** The 2 Baron Talbot converted to the Protestant Church of Ireland in 1779, and enjoyed a career in the army, banking, and as a cotton manufacturer while he was an eldest son (Fisher, *The House of Commons*, VII, 366).

1. Richard Talbot 2 Baron Talbot – County Dublin 1807-30
2. James Talbot 4 Baron Talbot – Athlone 1832-35

Seats: Malahide Castle, Dublin (acq. and built 1185, add. 16th and 17th c., rebuilt c. 1770, add. early 19th c., sold 1976); Liscarton Castle, Meath (built 15-16th c., acq. early 17th c., passed to Cadogans late 17th c.); Auchinleck House, Ayrshire (acq. by Boswells 1504, built 17th c., ruin, new house built 1759-61, inher. by mar. 1873, now owned by Scottish Historic Buildings Trust)
Estates: Bateman 20740 (E, S, & W) 24435
Titles: Baron Talbot of Malahide 1831- I; Baron Furnival 1839-49 UK; Baron Talbot of Malahide 1856- UK; Baronet 1623-1752
Peers: {1 peer 1685-90} 4 peers 1839-49 1856-1945
1 in Cabinet 1687-89
Notes: The Talbots inherited the estates (and celebrated manuscripts) of the Boswells of Auchinleck in 1873. Malahide was probably in continuous occupation by the same family for longer than any other house in Ireland (1185-1976). 1 Earl of Tyrconnell and 4 Baron Talbot of Malahide and five others in ODNB.

Talbot-Crosbie

Origins: The Talbots of Mount Talbot, a cadet of the Talbots of Malahide, Judge in Ireland 1557, inherited the estates of the 1 Earl of Glandore via marriage to a Crosbie heiress and assumed the additional name Crosbie. A junior line remained at Mount Talbot. Only those estates are listed here (see Crosbie for the Glandore estates).

1. William Talbot – {Kilkenny 1799-1800} 1801
2. William Talbot Crosbie – {Ardfert 1800}

Seats: Mount Talbot (House), Roscommon (acq. by 1690, new house built c. 1750, remod. c. 1820, burned 1922, sold 1923, ruin); Ardfert Abbey (House), Kerry (Crosbies acq. 17th c., built late 17th c., remod. 1720, passed to Talbots by mar. 1775, remod. c. 1830, burned 1922-23, estate sold)
Estates: Bateman 6374 (I) 2946

TALBOT II

Origins: Held landed estates by the reign of Henry III.
First MP 1658.

1. Roger Talbot – Northallerton 1661-79
2. Roger Talbot – Thirsk 1754-61

Seat: Old Hall, Thornton-le-Street (Wood End), Yorkshire (settled here and built 1549, sold 1793)
Estates: Worth £300 pa in c. 1646.
Notes: Male line extinct 1778.

TALBOT III *IRELAND*

Origins: William Talbot, Clerk of the Crown for County Wexford was mentioned in a lawsuit 1586. Sheriff 1649. **First {MP 1559 for Wexford}. Two other {MPs for Wexford 1585-1613}.** Another summoned to the Parliament of James II in 1689.

1. John Talbot – New Ross 1832-41 1847-52

Seats: Talbot Hall (Mount Corbett), Wexford (built mid-18th c., remod. 19th c., passed by mar. to Redingtons 1842, sold 1912); Castle Talbot (Ballynamony), Wexford (old castle, acq. 1617, new house 1753, remod. 1850s, sold c. 1924)
Estates: 2,954 acres in 1878 (Redington).
Notes: Roman Catholic family.

TAVERNER [Harris]

Origins: Owned some land in Norfolk early 16th century. Acquired more after the Dissolution. Tudor officials. **First MP 1545. Three additional MPs 1547-1628**. Estates passed 1637 to a great nephew, Taverner Harris MP below.

1. Taverner Harris – Wallingford 1681

Seat: Soundness House, Oxfordshire (purch. mid-16th c., Harris acq. by inher. 1637, sold 1685)
Notes: Three in ODNB.

TAYLOR I

Origins: The first MP was the son of a grocer. He was a silversmith but became a civil servant. Made a fortune through corruption. Sheriff 1765.

1. Peter Taylor – Wells 1765-66 Portsmouth 1774-77
2. Robert Taylor – Berwick-on-Tweed 1768-74
3. Sir Charles Taylor 1 Bt – Wells 1796-1830

Seats: Burcott (Briddicott) House, Somerset (built c. 1600, acq. and remod. mid-18th c., sold mid-19th c.); Purbrook Park, Hampshire (purch. 1764, built 1769, old house demolished 1829, sold 1839, school); Hollycombe, Sussex (built 1803, sold 1865)
Estates: The 1 Bt left £120,000 in personality at his death in 1857. Held 2,000 acres in Sussex estate 1850s.
Title: Baronet 1828-76

TAYLOR II *IRELAND*

Origins: The family emigrated to Ireland in the 1640s. High Sheriff 1670.

1. Robert Taylor – {Askeaton 1692-93 1695-96}
2. Robert Taylor – {Askeaton 1703-14 Tralee 1715-23}
3. Berkeley Taylor – {Askeaton 1723-36}
4. Edward Taylor – {Askeaton 1727-60}
5. William Taylor – {Askeaton 1737-46}

Seats: Ballynort, Limerick (acq. sec. half 17th c., passed to heiresses 1760, demolished); Moyallow, Limerick (acq. later 17th c., passed out of family 1760)
Notes: Male line extinct 1760.

TAYLOR III

Origins: The **first MP 1653** was a radical Puritan and lawyer. His son was a merchant, married to the daughter of a Baronet, who purchased Bifrons.

1. John Taylor – Sandwich 1695-98 1701
2. Edward Taylor – Canterbury 1807-12
3. Sir Herbert Taylor – Windsor 1820-23

Seat: Bifrons, Kent (purch. 1694, sold early 19th c. – probably 1830s, demolished 1948)
Notes: Three in ODNB.

TAYLOUR [Conway, Langford, Rowley, Shipley, Thompson] *IRELAND, ENGLAND, & WALES*

Marquess of Headfort (1800- I)

Origins: Originally from Sussex. Founder to Ireland as a surveyor 1653. Purchased property around Kells in 1660, an estate that amounted to 22,000 acres by 1661. Sheriff 1701. Bt. 1704.

1. Sir Thomas Taylour 1 Bt – {Kells 1692-93 1695-99 Belturbet 1703-13 Kells 1713-36}
2. Sir Thomas Taylour 2 Bt – {Kells 1713-57}
3. James Taylour – {Kells 1737-47}
4. Thomas Taylour 1 Earl of Bective – {Kells 1747-60}
5. Thomas Taylour 1 Marquess of Headfort – {Kells 1776-90 Longford 1790-94 County Meath 1794-95}
6. Hercules Taylour – {Kells 1781-90}
7. Robert Taylour – {Kells 1791-1800}
8. Clotworthy Taylour 1 Baron Langford – {Trim 1791-95 County Meath 1795-1800}
9. Thomas Taylour 2 Marquess of Headfort – County Meath 1812-29
10. Thomas Taylour – County Dublin 1841-83
11. Thomas Taylour 3 Marquess of Headfort – Westmorland 1854-70
12. Thomas Taylour Earl of Bective – Westmorland 1871-85 Kendal Div. Westmorland 1885-92

Seats: Headfort House, Meath (acq. c. 1660, built c. 1680, new house built 1760-70, leased to school 1949, sold 1981); Underley Hall, Westmorland (acq. by mar. to the Headforts 1854, add. 1873, hall sold 1939 but estate passed to relatives); Barnacre Lodge, Lancashire (acq. by Thompson 1854, passed to Taylours by mar. 1870, built 1876-77, sold 1899); Ardfillan (Ardgillan) Castle (Prospect House), Dublin (acq. 1737, built c. 1730, remod. c. 1790-1810, sold 1962)

Estates: 59832 (I & E) 50441 (includes Quin and Taylour of Ardfillan). Rubinstein – 1 Marquess left £250,000 in probate in 1830. Still own 3,000 acres in England 1971.
Titles: Baron Headfort 1760- I; Viscount Headfort 1762- I; Earl of Bective 1766- I; Baron Kenlis 1831- UK
Peers: {2 peers 1761-1800} 1 Irish Rep peer 1801-29 4 peers 1831-94 1899-1945
2 Lds Lt 19th
1 in Cabinet 1874-80
4 KP 18th, 19th
Notes: 4 Marquess was a Senator of the Irish Free State 1922-28. One in ODNB.

Thompson

Origins: William Thompson MP, the nephew of a silk merchant, was Lord Mayor of London 1828, Director of the Bank of England, and an iron master and ship owner. His daughter and heiress married the 3 Marquess of Headfort.

1. William Thompson – Callington 1820-26 London 1826-32 Sunderland 1833-41 Westmorland 1841-54

Seats: Perydarran House, Glamorganshire; Underley Hall, Lancashire (rebuilt 1825, purch. by Thompsons mid-19th c., passed by mar. to the Headforts in 1854, remod. 1871-78, passed by mar. to Cavendish Bentincks 1893, house sold 1940, still own estate)
Estates: William Thompson left £976,000 at his death in 1854 aside from land. (Thompson, "Life after Death: How Successful Nineteenth-Century Businessmen Disposed of Their Fortunes", 59)
Estates: Held 25,000 acres at Underley in 1901
Notes: One in ODNB.

Viscount Langford (1766-96 I)

Origins: An agent for the English Land Company settled in Ireland in the early 17th century. He was dismissed for corruption. (Bardon, *A History of Ulster*, 129) **First {MP 1613 for County Londonderry}. One further {MP 1634 and 1639 for the county}.** Sheriff 1690. A younger son of the 1 Earl of Bective married Frances Rowley. His mother was Jane Rowley, the aunt of his wife. He took the name Rowley and was created 1 Baron Langford. The father of Frances Rowley was the great-grandson of Sir John Rowley and Mary, daughter and heiress of Sir Hercules Langford 1 Bt of Summerhill. The Rowleys went to Ireland in the early 17th century.

1. Sir John Rowley – {County Londonderry 1661-66}
2. Hugh Rowley – {Newtown Limavady 1692-93}

3. Sir Arthur Langford 2 Bt – {Duleek 1692-93 Coleraine 1695-99 1703-13 County Antrim 1715-16}
4. Sir Henry Langford 3 Bt – {St. Johnstown 1695-99}
5. Hercules Rowley – {County Londonderry 1703-42}
6. Hercules Langford Rowley – {County Londonderry 1743-60 County Meath 1761-94}
7. Clotworthy Rowley – {Downpatrick 1771-1800} 1801
8. Hercules Langford Rowley 2 Viscount Langford – {County Antrim 1783-91}
9. Richard Rowley – Harwich 1860-65

Seat: Summerhill, Meath (acq. and built mid-17th c., inher. by Rowleys and rebuilt 1731-34, two fires in 19th c., burned 1921, ruin, demolished 1962); Langford Lodge, Antrim (built 18th c., passed by mar. to Pakenhams c. 1820)
Estates: Bateman 24374 (I) 24882 (includes Pakenham of Langford Lodge, Antrim). Rowleys held 10,259 acres worth £5,814 pa in the later 18th c.
Titles: Baron Somerhill 1766-96 I; Baron Langford 1800- I
Peers: {1 peer 1792-96} 1 Irish Rep peer 1884-1919
Notes: The Barony of Langford passed to the Conways at Bodrhyddan (see below).

Rowley

Origins: A cadet line in England. Sir William Rowley MP 1750-61 was an Admiral of the Fleet who purchased Tendring. The 1 Bt (1786) was also an admiral. Sir Josias Rowley 1 Bt married 1766 the heiress to Mount Campbell.

1. Sir William Rowley – Taunton 1750-54 Portsmouth 1754-61
2. William Rowley – {Kinsale 1790-1800} 1801-02
3. Samuel Rowley – {Kinsale 1797-1800} Downpatrick 1801-02 Kinsale 1802-06
4. Sir Josias Rowley 1 Bt – {Downpatrick 1797-1800} Kinsale 1821-26
5. Sir William Rowley 2 Bt – Suffolk 1812-30

Seats: Tendring Hall, Suffolk (medieval and 16th c., purch. 1750, rebuilt 1784-88, add. 19th c., sold and demolished 1960); Holbecks House, Suffolk (purch. 1788, became main seat early 20th c., still own); Mount Campbell (Mountcampbell), Leitrim (acq. by mar. 1766, resident early 20th c., demolished)
Estates: Bateman 8616 (E) 11608 and 2374 (I) 1295
Titles: Baronet 1786- ; 1813-42; 1836-
Notes: Five in ODNB.

Conway

Origins: The Conways descended from William the Conqueror's High Constable and probably came to Wales with Edward I in 1277. An established territorial family by the 14th century. Fought with the Black Prince in France c. late 14th century. The Lords Langford inherited the High Constableship of Ruddlan Castle (granted 1390, held into the 20th c.). Served in office under Edward IV and Henry VII. **First MP 1558**. A junior line created Barons Conway 1625 (see Seymour). Stayed Roman Catholic and were in exile with Charles II. Returned 1660. On the death of the last Bt in 1721 his sister married James Russell Stapleton (see Boscawen). Their daughter married Ellis Yonge of Flintshire. Their daughter married the Rev. William Shipley, Dean of St. Asaph. The Shipley-Conways inherited the medieval seat of the Conways at Bodrhyddan. Charlotte Conway, sister and heiress of William Shipley-Conway, married the second son of the 1 Baron Langford, and they inherited Bodrhyddan. This line succeeded as Lords Langford in 1953.

1. Sir Henry Conway 1 Bt – Flintshire 1661-69
2. Sir John Conway 2 Bt – Flintshire 1685-87 1695-1701 Flint Boroughs 1702-05 Flintshire 1705-08 Flint Boroughs 1708-13 Flintshire 1713-15 Flint Boroughs 1715-21
3. William Shipley – St. Mawes 1807 Flint Boroughs 1807-12 St. Mawes 1812-13

Seat: Bodrhyddan Hall, Flintshire (acq. 13th c., remod. later 16th c., remod. 1696, rebuilt 1872-74, still own)
Estates: Bateman 5526 (W) 6995. The 9 Baron Langford owned 2,000 acres in 2001.
Title: Baronet 1660-1721
1 Ld Lt 20th
Notes: Five Shipleys in ODNB.

TENNANT *SCOTLAND & ENGLAND*

<u>Baron Glenconner</u> (1911- UK)

Origins: A Glasgow chemist, son of a Ayrshire hill farmer and apprenticed as a hand-loom weaver, at the end of the 18th century invested in a new formula for bleach (tied to linen manufacture), patented 1798, and founded what became the greatest British chemical works of the 19th century.

1. Sir Charles Tennant 1 Bt – Glasgow 1879-80 Peebles & Selkirk 1880-86
2. Harold Tennant – Berwickshire 1894-1918
3. Edward Tennant 1 Baron Glenconner – Salisbury 1906-10

Seats: The Glen, Peeblesshire (purch. 1853, built 1854-58, add. 1874, fire and restored 1905, flats, still own estate); Wilsford Manor, Wiltshire (purch. 1900 and built 1900-06, sold 1987); Lympne Castle, Kent (medieval, purch. 1905 and rebuilt 1906-12, sold 1917); Great Maytham Hall, Kent (built 1721, fire 1893, purch. 1909, rebuilt 1909-10, sold 1936, flats); Innes House, Elginshire (built 1640-53, purch. c. 1900, still own)

Estates: Bateman 3616 (S) 7035. The founder died worth £76,000 in 1838. The 1 Baronet died the richest Scotsman of the 19th century leaving £3,146,000 (Rubinstein, *Men of Property*, 79,81 – not counting the Duke of Sutherland as a Scotsman?). Worth £20,000,000 with 9,000 acres in 1990.
Title: Baronet 1885-
Peers: 2 peers 1911-45
1 Ld Lt 20th
1 in Cabinet 1916
Notes: The 1 Baron purchased 2,000 acres in Wiltshire in 1900 and built a country house (Dakers, *Clouds*, 167). Eight in ODNB.

TENNYSON [D'Eyncourt]

Baron Tennyson (1884- UK)

Origins: Yeomen farmers and professional men moved from Yorkshire to Lincolnshire in the 18th century. A surgeon early in the 18th century married an heiress whose family owned much of Grimsby and was co-heiress of the Earls of Scarsdale and of the medieval family d'Eyncourt. His son was a very successful solicitor. Purchased Bayons Manor in the late 18th century.

1. George Tennyson – Bletchingley 1818-19
2. Charles Tennyson-d'Eyncourt – Great Grimsby 1818-26 Bletchingley 1826-31 Stamford 1831-32 Lambeth 1832-52

Seats: Bayons Manor, Lincolnshire (purch. late 18th c., built 1836-40, became a ruin although some of it was built deliberately as such, sold 1944, demolished 1964); Usselby Hall (House), Lincolnshire (built mid-18th c., remod. 19th c., sold 1911); Farringford House (IoW), Hampshire (built 1806, add. 1830s, purch. 1853, sold 1945, museum)
Estates: Bateman 3504 (E) 6200
Title: Baronet 1930-
Peers: 3 peers 1884-1945
Notes: Charles Tennyson MP took the bogus name of d'Eynecourt. The poet was the 1 Baron. 1 and 2 Barons and three others in ODNB.

THELLUSSON

Baron Rendlesham (1806- I)

Origins: Huguenots who fled to Geneva after the Revocation of the Edict of Nantes. They returned later to Paris and became merchants and bankers and moved to England in 1762.

1. Peter Thellusson 1 Baron Rendlesham – Midhurst 1795-96
2. George Thellusson – Soutwark 1796 Tregony 1804-06 Barnstaple 1807-11
3. Charles Thellusson – Evesham 1796-1806
4. Frederick Thellusson 4 Baron Rendlesham – E. Suffolk 1843-52
5. Frederick Thellusson 5 Baron Rendlesham – E. Suffolk 1874-85

Seats: Rendlesham Hall, Suffolk (built early 17th c., purch. 1796 for £51,000, add. c. 1801, fire 1830, rebuilt 1868-71, fire 1898 and rebuilt, sold 1923, demolished 1949); Brodsworth Hall, Yorkshire (old house, purch. c. 1790, new house 1861-63, donated to English Heritage 1990); Plaistow Lodge, Kent (purch. 1777 built soon after, sold 1810)
Estates: Bateman 24028 (E) 25024 and 8981 (E) 14064 (Brodsworth). Peter Thellusson MP left £100,000 to his family and £700,000 to trustees to compound for two generations. The overturning of his will became a celebrated legal case.
Notes: Coal mines were operated on the Brodsworth estate. Sales of land began in 1914 soon after the death of the 5 Baron to raise funds to meet family charges and tax liabilities. 6,000 acres in Suffolk sold for £48,000. Further sales delayed by the War until 1920-25 (Roberts, *Lost Country Houses of Suffolk*, 113). One in ODNB.

THESIGER

Viscount Chelmsford (1921- UK)

Origins: The family came originally from Dresden in Germany arriving in England in the mid-18th century. The first immigrant ended up as an official in a noble household and the father of the 1 Baron was a customs official in the West Indies. The 1 Baron was Lord Chancellor.

1. Frederick Thesiger 1 Baron Chelmsford – Woodstock 1840-44 Abingdon 1844-52 Stamford 1852-58

Seat: Ash Platts, Sussex
Estates: 1 Baron died worth £60,000 and the 1 Viscount £26,000.
Title: Baron Chelmsford 1858- UK
Peers: 4 peers 1858-1945
2 in Cabinet 1858-59 1866-68 1924
Notes: The noted explorer and travel writer was a family member. 1 and 2 Barons and 1 Viscount and four others in ODNB.

THISTLETHWAYTE [Whithed]

Thistlethwayte

Origins: The family claimed Saxon origins (*Burke's Landed Gentry*, 1871, II, 1370). Emerged as gentry in the reign of Henry VIII. **First MP 1654 for Wiltshire**. Alexander Thistlethwayte married in 1717 the daughter of Richard Whithed of Norman Court by his wife the daughter and heiress of Richard Norton of Southwick. Francis Thistlethwayte succeeded by a marriage of 1719 to his uncle Richard Whithed's estates of Norman Court and Southwick in 1733 and took the additional name Whithed.

1. Alexander Thistlethwayte – Salisbury 1679-81
2. Francis Thistlethwayte Whithed – Hampshire 1747-51
3. Alexander Thistlethwayte – Hampshire 1751-61
4. Robert Thistlethwayte – Hampshire 1780-90
5. Thomas Thistlethwayte – Hampshire 1806-07

Seats: Southwick Park (House, Priory), Hampshire (medieval, converted to house c. 1538, acq. by mar. 1733, fire 1750, rebuilt c. 1812, burned and rebuilt c. 1841, taken over by RN c. 1940 continuing after WWII); Compton Valence, Dorset (built 17th c., acq. by mar. 1717); Winterslow (House), Wiltshire (original seat of the Thistlethwaytes, acq. r. Henry VIII, sold by mid-18th c., burned 1774); Norman Court, Hampshire (acq. by mar. 1733, sold c. 1807)
Estates: Bateman 8084 (E) 9929. Worth £23,000,000 in 1990. The family inherited a large property in Paddington in London in the 18th century (Habakkuk, *Marriage, Debt and the Estates System: English Landownership 1650-1950*, 347).
Notes: Southwick Park was purchased at the Dissolution c. 1538 by John White. It passed via an heiress to the Nortons in the mid-17th century. Richard Norton left Southwick to Parliament in trust for the use of the poor, hungry, thirsty, naked, sick, etc. The will was set aside on the plea of insanity and the estate passed to Francis Thistlethwayte (see above and Powlett) (Burke, *A Visitation of Seats and Arms of the Noblemen and Gentlemen of Great Britain and Ireland*, sec. series, 1854, I, 209). One in ODNB.

Whithed

Origins: Gentry by the mid 15th century. High Sheriff 1479. **First MP 1625 for Hampshire. Two further MPs 1628-48, one for the county**.

1. Richard Whithed – Stockbridge 1659 1660
2. Henry Whithed – Portsmouth 1660 Stockbridge 1679-80
3. Richard Whithed – Stockbridge 1689-93.

Seat: Norman Court, Hampshire (acq. 1433, passed by mar. 1733 to Thistlethwaytes above)
Notes: The last male Whithed died in 1733.

THOMAS *WALES*

Origins: The grandfather of the 1 Baronet was a cooper, his father a lawyer. Gained a landed estate by marriage and shrewd land purchase late 16th early 17th c. High Sheriff 1612. Edmond Thomas **MP 1656** sat in Cromwell's House of Lords.

1. Sir Robert Thomas 2 Bt – Cardiff Boroughs 1661-81
2. Sir Edmond Thomas 3 Bt – Chippenham 1741-54 Glamorgan 1761-67

Seat: Wenvoe Castle, Glamorganshire (acq. and built early 17th c., sold 1765)
Titles: Baronet 1641-90; 1694-
Notes: Finances embarrassed 1760s, and some estates sold. One in ODNB.

THOMPSON I [Lawley, Meysey]

Thompson

Origins: The family was founded by a successful merchant and **MP for Scarborough in 1625**. Businessmen in Hull. The common ancestor of the family was Richard Thompson, whose eldest son, William of Humbleton, married the heiress of Scorborough Castle. The younger son Richard of Kilham spawned four cadet lines. His son, Sir Henry, was ancestor of the Barons Wenlock. Another son, Sir Stephen of Kirby Hall, was ancestor of the Barons Knaresborough. Two younger brothers established lines at Sheriff Hutton and Hartsbourn. Francis Thompson MP kidnapped an heiress worth £1,200 pa and married her in 1669.

1. William Thompson – Scarborough 1660-81 1689-92
2. Francis Thompson – Scarborough 1679-81 1689-93
3. William Thompson – Scarborough 1701-22 1730-44

Seat: Humbleton Manor, Yorkshire (medieval, acq. 1614, passed by mar. to a Hotham 1674, who took name Thompson, passed to Hothams outright 1794)
Notes: The daughter and heiress of Stephen Thompson, the last of this line, married Sir Beaumont Hotham 7 Bt to whom the Thompson estates passed (see Hotham).

Thompson

Origins: As a cadet line early members of the family were merchants, Lord Mayor of York 1663. Purchased landed estates in the 1660s, and more in the 18th and 19th centuries.

1. Sir Henry Thompson – York 1673-81
2. Henry Thompson – York 1690-95
3. Edward Thompson – York 1722-42
4. Beilby Thompson – Hedon 1768-80 Thirsk 1780-84 Hedon 1790-96

Seats: Long Marston Hall, Yorkshire (built late 17th c., purch. 1683, remod. 1723, add. mid-late 18th c., part demolished late 18th c.); Escrick Hall (Park), Yorkshire (medieval, purch. 1668, rebuilt house c. 1680s, remod. mid-18th c., add. 1763-75, passed to Lawleys by mar. 1820, see below); Wetherby Grange, Yorkshire (built c. 1784, sold 1856, demolished 1964)
Estates: Worth £8,000 pa in c. 1768. Estates passed to the Barons Wenlock below.

Baron Wenlock (1461-71 E; 1831-34 UK; 1839-1932 UK)

Origins: The 1 Baron Wenlock of the first creation descended from a 13th-century gentry family. William Wenlock was Joint Usher of the Exchequer in 1349. He acquired the manor of Luton, Befordshire 1377. One family member was Prior of Wenlock Abbey under Richard II. The Wenlock estate was acquired in the reign of Edward III. **The first MP 1404 sat for Bedfordshire. Sir Thomas Wenlock MP 1422-26** served at Agincourt. The 1 Baron was an **MP for Bedfordshire 1433-56**, Speaker of the House of Commons 1455, KG 1460, Baron 1461 and was killed at the Battle of Tewkesbury 1471. He died without male heirs and the estates passed to cousins, the Lawleys. **The first Lawley MP 1429** was a lawyer. **Nine other Lawley MPs 1447-1628, eight of them for Much Wenlock beginning in 1545, compiling a record of almost three centuries representing the borough**. Jane Thompson, daughter and heiress of Beilby Thompson of Escrick Park (see above) married 1764 Sir Robert Lawley 5 Bt. Their eldest son was created 1 Baron Wenlock of the second creation in 1831. His younger brother took the name Thompson and succeeded to Escrick. On the death of the elder brother in 1834 the younger brother resumed the name Lawley and the Wenlock title was revived for him in 1839.

1. Sir Francis Lawley 2 Bt – Much Wenlock 1659 1660 Shropshire 1661-79
2. Sir Thomas Lawley 3 Bt – Much Wenlock 1685-87
3. Sir Robert Lawley 5 Bt – Warwickshire 1780-93
4. Robert Lawley 1 Baron Wenlock – Newcastle-under-Lyme 1802-06
5. Sir Francis Lawley 7 Bt – Warwickshire 1820-32
6. Paul Lawley-Thompson 1 Baron Wenlock – Much Wenlock 1826-32 E. R. Yorkshire 1832-37

7. Beilby Lawley 2 Baron Wenlock – Pontefract 1851-52
8. Francis Lawley – Beverley 1852-54
9. Beilby Lawley – Chester 1880

Seats: Escrick Hall (Park), Yorkshire (inher. by mar. 1820, add. 1846-51, passed by mar. to Forbes Adam family 1920, house a school, still own estate); Canwell Priory (Hall), Staffordshire (medieval, purch. and new house c. 1660, rebuilt later 18th c., moved seat to Escrick 1820s, sold 1871 with the estate for £207,000, demolished 1957); Spoonhill House, Shropshire (acq. and built mid-16th c., ceased to reside in 18th c., sold 1901); Bourton Manor, Shropshire (acq. mid-16th c., add. 1874, sold 1901)
Estates: Bateman 26080 (E) 27590. The family income was £16,000 in 1813. The 7 Bt inherited £200,000 and a town house in Grosvenor Square from his uncle Richard Thompson in 1820 (Rubinstein – Richard Thompson left £250,000 in probate in 1820).
Title: Baronet 1641-1932
Peers: 6 peers 1831-34 1839-1932
2 Lds Lt 19th
Notes: 1 Baron Wenlock of 1st cr. and two others in ODNB.

Baron Knaresborough (1905-29 UK)

Origins: Thompson cadet family (see above). Richard Thompson of Kirby Hall married in 1803 Elizabeth Turton, whose mother was the heiress of Richard Meysey of Shakenhurst Hall, Worcesterhire. The son of this union was created a Baronet and the family took the additional name Meysey.

1. Sir Harry Thompson 1 Bt – Whitby 1859-65
2. Sir Henry Meysey-Thompson 1 Baron Knaresborough – Knaresborough 1880 Brigg Div. Lincolnshire 1885-86 Handsworth Div. Staffordshire 1892-1905
3. Ernest Meysey-Thompson – Handsworth Div. Staffordshire 1906-22

Seats: Kirby Hall, Yorkshire (old house, estate assembled from mid-17th c., new house built 1746-56, add. 1800 and 1860 most of the land sold 1912, demolished 1920); Shakenhurst Hall, Worcestershire (Meyseys acq. by mar. 1384, built 17th c., remod. 1798, Thompsons inher. by mar. 1803, passed via heiresses and even a godson to Severnes, sold 2014 for £16 million)
Estates: Bateman 5623 (E) 10600. Rubinstein – Henry Thompson left £175,000 in probate 1814.
Title: Baronet 1874-
Peer: 1 peer 1905-29
Notes: Shakenhurst was not bought or sold between 1384 and 2014. The 1 Baron made a fortune in railways. One in ODNB.

Thompson

Origins: Descended from the fourth son of Richard Thompson of Kilham. The first MP made a fortune as a wine merchant, Lord Mayor of York 1685.

1. Edward Thompson – York 1689-90 1695-98 1701
2. George Thompson – Haslemere 1823-30 Yarmouth (IoW) 1830-31

Seat: Sheriff Hutton Park (Castle), Yorkshire (medieval castle, ruin c. 1600, purch. c. 1676, sold 1880)
Estates: George Thompson MP 1823-31 left £104,000 in addition to real estate when he died in 1841.

Thompson

Origins: Descended from the fifth son of Richard Thompson of Kilham. The 1 Baronet was an admiral.

1. Sir Thomas Thompson 1 Bt – Rochester 1807-16

Seat: Hartsbourne Manor Place, Hampshire (acq. early 19th c., sold later 19th c., golf club)
Title: Baronet 1806-

THOMPSON II

Baron Haversham (1696-1745 E)

Origins: The Thompsons began as successful merchants in London in the 17th century. Father of the 1 Baron was an East India merchant. The purchaser of Haversham was considered a "person of mean extraction." (*Victoria County History, A History of the County of Buckingham: Volume 4*, London, 1927, 366-72). Alderman 1653. Kt 1660. High Sheriff 1669.

1. Sir William Thompson – London 1659 1661-79
2. John Thompson 1 Baron Haversham – Gatton 1685-87 1689-96
3. Maurice Thompson 2 Baron Haversham – Bletchingley 1695-98 Gatton 1698-1705

Seats: Manor House, Haversham, Buckinghamshire (medieval, purch. and rebuilt c. 1664, sold 1729 for £24,500, much demolished 1792); Upper Gatton Park, Surrey (acq. by inher. 1679, sold 1704); Elsham Hall, Lincolnshire (acq. by inher. 1679, rebuilt 1760, passed by mar. 1788 to Corbets, see)
Estates: Worth £1,800 pa in the 1660s.

Title: Baronet 1673-1745
Peers: 2 peers 1696-1745
Notes: The Thompsons inherited Gatton from the Owfields (Oldfields) 1679. 1 Baron in ODNB.

Owfield (Oldfield)

Origins: Successful fishmonger in London in the later 16th c. purchased estates. His son, a lawyer, was the **first MP 1624-43**. Kt 1641.

1. William Oldfield – Gatton 1645 1661-64

Seats: Upper Gatton Park, Surrey (purch. 1620s-30s, passed to Thompsons by mar. 1679); Elsham Hall, Lincolnshire (acq. and built 17th c., passed to Thompsons 1679)
Estates: Worth £22,000 in 1611.
Notes: Male line extinct by 1679.

THORNHILL

Thornhill

Origins: Emerged in the 14th century. **First MP 1355 for Yorkshire**. The common ancestor of the Thornhills was George Thornhill of Diddington. His eldest son was seated at Fixby, Yorkshire and Riddlesworth Hall, Norfolk. The junior branch succeeded to Diddington.

1. Sir Thomas Thornhill 1 Bt – W. Suffolk 1875-85

Seat: Riddlesworth Hall, Norfolk (built 16th c., rebuilt 1792, purch. early 19th c., sold 1893)
Estates: Bateman 6263 (E) 6247
Title: Baronet 1885-1900

Thornhill

Origins: Cadet line.

1. George Thornhill – Huntingdonshire 1837-52
2. Arthur Thornhill – Cambridgeshire 1884-85

Seat: Diddington Hall, Huntingdonshire (acq. and built c. 1730, sold c. 1957, demolished 1962)

Estates: Bateman 4830 (E) 10422
Notes: Male line extinct 1956.

THORNTON [Astell]

Thornton

Origins: The Thorntons, originally from Hull, then Russia merchants and bankers in London in the 18th century. Governor of the Bank of England 1799. **Two possible MPs for Hull in the 16th century**.

1. Henry Thornton – Southwark 1782-1815
2. Samuel Thornton – Kingston upon Hull 1784-1806 Surrey 1807-12 1813-18
3. Robert Thornton – Bridgwater 1785-90 Colchester 1790-1817
4. Percy Thornton – Clapham Div. Battersea and Clapham 1892-1910

Seat: Albury Park, Surrey (medieval, rebuilt mid-later 17th c., rebuilt 1697, purch. 18th c., remod. c. 1800 and c. 1815, sold 1819)
Estates: John Thornton died 1790 worth £600,000.
Notes: Six in ODNB.

Thornton Astell

Origins: William Thornton took the name Astell in 1807 on inheriting the estates of his great uncle Richard Astell. William was a Director of the East India Company. The Astells were merchants in London in the 18th century.

1. William Thornton Astell – Bridgwater 1807-32 Bedfordshire 1841-47
2. John Astell – Cambridge 1852-53 Ashburton 1859-65

Seats: Woodbury Hall, Cambridgeshire (built 1803-06, purch. 1858, remod. 1931, fire 1944, rebuilt 1950s, still own); Everton House, Huntingdonshire (purch. 1713-14, still resident 1908, demolished after 1908)
Estates: Estate worth £600,000 in 1790. Income £7,000 pa in 1796. Land sales 1880s.
Notes: One in ODNB.

THOROLD

Origins: The family enjoyed a long, slow rise from the 14th century. Emerged as important county gentry in the 16th century when they added to their estates through wealth accumulated by a successful merchant and became large-scale sheep masters. In the 1660s, they were called "a very spreading family in this county." (*Country Life*,

138, p. 688) **First MP 1558 for Grantham. Another MP 1584 also for Grantham, a borough they represented for over 300 years.** Sheriff 1571. Kt 1585. Harmston line of Bts descended from a younger son who was a merchant and Lord Mayor of London 1720.

1. Sir William Thorold 1 Bt – Grantham 1661-78
2. John Thorold – Grantham 1685-87
3. Sir John Thorold 4 Bt – Grantham 1697-1700 Lincolnshire 1701-05 Grantham 1711-15
4. Sir John Thorold 9 Bt – Lincolnshire 1779-96
5. Sir John Thorold 12 Bt – Grantham 1865-68

Seats: Syston (Old) Hall (Syston Park/Hall), Lincolnshire (built 1766-75 and became chief seat, add. 1822-24, sales of contents 1884 and 1923, unoccupied after 1912, demolished 1928); Marston Hall, Lincolnshire (acq. by 1368, add. later 16th c., abandoned for Syston in the 18th c., reoccupied 1928, held for 600 years, still own); Cranwell Hall, Lincolnshire (built 17th c., demolished c. 1815); Harmston Hall, Lincolnshire (built c. 1700, sold late 19th c., demolished 1892)
Estates: Bateman 12533 (E) 17652. Rubinstein – 9 Bt left £125,000 in probate in 1815.
Title: Baronet 1642- ; 1709-37; 1740-64
Notes: Thorold family has an entry and five others in the ODNB.

THOROTON [Hildyard]

Thoroton

Origins: Yeomen in Nottinghamshire for many centuries. A London businessman (member of the Salters Company), brother of a physician, raised the family to gentry status, purchasing landed estates in 1669 and 1685. They acquired coal mines via marriage to an heiress in the 18th century. Being agent to the 3 Duke of Rutland in the mid-18th century also assisted the family's rise in wealth. Thomas Thoroton married in 1815 the daughter and heiress of the last male Hildyard of Winstead and took the additional name Hildyard.

1. Thomas Thoroton – Boroughbridge 1757-61 Newark 1761-68 Bramber 1769-82
2. Thomas Thoroton – Grantham 1802-12
3. Thomas Thoroton Hildyard – S. Nottinghamshire 1846-52 1861-85

Seats: Flintham Hall, Nottinghamshire (18th c. house, purch. 1789, rebuilt 1798, remod. 1851-57, still own); Screveton Hall (Kirketon Hall), Nottinghamshire (purch. 1685, sold 1918, demolished 1920s)
Estates: Bateman 4262 (E) 6650. Much land sold in the 1960s, but retained some land. Owned 2,100 acres in 2001.
Notes: Four in ODNB.

Hildyard

Origins: Gentry by the reign of Henry III. Kt and warrior at the Battle of Towton in 1461. **First MP 1563. Two additional MPs 1589-1628**.

1. Henry Hildyard – Hedon 1660
2. Sir Robert Hildyard 2 Bt – Hedon 1701-02
3. Sir Robert Hildyard 3 Bt – Great Bedwyn 1754-61

Seats: Winestead Hall (Red Hall), Yorkshire (medieval, acq. by mar. 1431, new house 1579 and c. 1729, sold 1880, demolished 1936); Manor House, Patrington, Yorkshire (acq. c. 1660s and 1829, rebuilt 1743, still owned 1892)
Estates: Worth £2,357 pa in the 1670s. Rubinstein – Henry Hildyard left £140,000 in probate in 1832.
Title: Baronet 1660-1814
Notes: Hildyard male line extinct 1814. Estates passed through mar. to the Thorotons. One in ODNB.

Hildyard

Origins: Descended from a younger son of the Hildyards of Winstead.

1. Robert Hildyard – Whitehaven 1847-57

Seat: Manor House, Catherton, Dorset

THORPE

Origins: Medieval family emerged in 15th century due to office-holding. Estates forfeited but partially restored. Family did not re-enter Parliament until the twentieth century when a barrister, son of an Archdeacon, was elected in 1919. **First MP was a kt of the shire 1449 and 1453**, Speaker of the Commons 1453-54.

1. John Henry Thorpe – Manchester Rusholme 1919-23
2. Jeremy Thorpe – North Devon 1959-79

Seat: Barnwell, Northamptonshire (residence 1447-96)

THROCKMORTON [Carew]

Throckmorton

Origins: Tenants of the Bishops of Worcester from 1182. Prominent in the West Midlands since the 15th century. Treasurer to Henry VI and allied with the Earls of Warwick. Diplomat and statesman under Edward VI and Elizabeth I. **First MP 1402 for Worcestershire. Eighteen additional MPs 1414-1626, eleven kts of the shire**. An important Roman Catholic family.

1. Sir Clement Throckmorton – Warwick 1654 1656 1660 1661-63
2. Robert Throckmorton – Huntingdonshire 1698-99
3. Sir Robert Throckmorton 8 Bt – Berkshire 1831-34

Seats: Coughton Court, Warwickshire (acq. by mar. to the heiress of Sir Guy de Spineto 1409, built 1510-20, remod. c. 1600 and c. 1650, 1668 one wing destroyed, ceased to be main residence 1690, add. 1835, resumed as main seat 1908, NT 1946); (West) Molland Manor, Devon (acq. by mar. 1747, still own); Hail Weston, Huntingdonshire (acq. 1507 and 1552, sold 1720 and 1767); Haseley Manor (The Manor House, Hasley), Warwickshire (purch. c. 1550, built 1560, passed by mar. to Bromleys in 18th c., sold before 1875); Buckland House, Berkshire (acq. by mar. to Courtenay heiress 1690, rebuilt 1755-9, became main residence, sold to Kt of Kerry 1908); Harvington Hall, Worcestershire (medieval, add. c. 1560-75, acq. 1696, remod. 1701, sold 1923, institutional use)
Estates: Bateman 22385 (E) 27092
Title: Baronet 1642-
Notes: The Throckmorton (Throgmorton) family have an entry and seven others in the ODNB.

Throckmorton

Origins: Cadet line. Established in Gloucestershire in the 15th century. **First MP 1553. Three additional MPs 1555-1604, two for Gloucestershire**.

1. Sir Baynham Throckmorton 2 Bt – Gloucestershire 1656 Wootton Bassett 1660 Gloucestershire 1661-64
2. Sir Baynham Throckmorton 3 Bt – Gloucestershire 1664-79

Seat: Clearwell, Gloucestershire (built by Baynhams in 16th c., acq. by mar. to Baynham heiress c. 1609, sold late 17th c. to Wyndhams)
Title: Baronet 1611-82
Notes: The Throckmorton Baronets have an entry in the ODNB.

Carew

Origins: The Carews of Beddington were a cadet line c. 1300 of the Carews of Antony (see Carew I) **First MP 1361 for Surrey. Six additional MPs 1394-1640, four of them for Surrey**. The great-grandfather of the 1 Baronet was Sir Nicholas Throckmorton of Coughton, who married Anne, heiress of Sir Nicholas Carew. The Throckmortons took the name Carew on inheriting the estate in 1611.

1. Sir Nicholas Carew – Gatton 1664-81
2. Sir Nicholas Carew 1 Bt – Haslemere 1708-10 1714-22 Surrey 1722-27

Seat: Beddington Park, Surrey (medieval, acq. 1363, passed to Throckmortons by mar. 1611, who took name Carew, rebuilt 1709, passed to Gees by inher. 1769, passed to Hallowells by inher. 1834 who took name Carew, sold 1859)
Estates: Worth £1,600 pa c. 1660. Rubinstein - Richard Carew left £100,000 in probate in 1816.
Title: Baronet 1715-62
Notes: Three in ODNB.

THURLOW

Baron Thurlow (1778-1806 GB; 1792- GB)

Origins: Professional family from the 17th century onwards. Lord Chancellor 1778, and a brother was Bishop of Durham 1787.

1. Edward Thurlow 1 Baron Thurlow – Tamworth 1765-78

Seats: Ashfield House, Suffolk (acq. by mar. 1770s, new house built c. 1820, sold 1910-12); Dunphail House, Elginshire (medieval castle, rebuilt 1828-29, add. 1842, acq. by mar. from Cumming Bruce family in 1864, resident late 19th c.); Baynards Park, Surrey (medieval, purch. 1832, rebuilt 1832-40, sold 1952, burned 1980)
Estates: Bateman 1529 (E) 2800. 5 Baron inher. 10,500 acres in Scotland worth £1,182 pa
Peers: 5 peers 1778-1829 1835-1945
1 in Cabinet 1778-92
Notes: 1 and 2 Barons and one other in ODNB.

THYNNE [Carteret, Granville (Grenville)]

Marquess of Bath (1789- GB)

Origins: John Thynne, the builder of Longleat, was the son of a farmer from Shropshire who went to London as a kitchen clerk to his uncle, William Thynne, Chief Clerk to Henry VIII's royal kitchens, and rose to become Master of the Household. He moved on and became Steward of the Earl of Hertford's household (later the Duke of Somerset, Lord Protector). He purchased 60 acres at Longleat in 1540, and by the time he was knighted at age 36 he held 6,000 acres. (Rich, *Inherit the Land*, 17) He was elected an **MP 1539 (1559 for Wiltshire). Five additional MPs 1584-1640, one for the county**. The 2 Viscount Weymouth married the daughter and heiress of the 2 Earl Granville. Their younger son was created Baron Carteret.

1. Sir James Thynne – Wiltshire 1640-43 1664-70
2. Sir Thomas Thynne – Hindon 1660
3. Thomas Thynne – Wiltshire 1670-81
4. Thomas Thynne 1 Viscount Weymouth – University of Oxford 1674-79 Tamworth 1679-81
5. John Thynne – Hindon 1681
6. James Thynne – Cirencester 1701
7. Henry Thynne – Tamworth 1701-02 Weymouth & Melcombe Regis 1702-08
8. Henry Thynne Carteret 1 Baron Carteret – Staffordshire 1757-61 Weobley 1761-70
9. Thomas Thynne 2 Marquess of Bath – Weobley 1786-90 Bath 1790-96
10. George Thynne 2 Baron Carteret – Weobley 1790-1812
11. John Thynne 3 Baron Carteret – Weobley 1796 Bath 1796-1832
12. Thomas Thynne Viscount Weymouth – Weobley 1818-20
13. Henry Thynne 3 Marquess of Bath – Weobley 1824-26 1828-32
14. Lord William Thynne – Weobley 1826-31
15. Lord Edward Thynne – Weobley 1831-32 Frome 1859-65
16. Lord Henry Thynne – S. Wiltshire 1859-85
17. Thomas Thynne 5 Marquess of Bath – Frome 1886-92 1895-96
18. Lord Alexander Thynne – Bath 1910-18
19. Henry Thynne 6 Marquess of Bath – Frome Div. Somerset 1931-35

Seats: Longleat, Wiltshire (medieval monastic buildings, purch. 1540, fire 1567, new house built c. 1572-80, remod. 1806-18, 1829-31, 1874-82, still own); Kempsford Manor, Gloucestershire (medieval house, acq. 1549, rebuilt 1630s, ruinous 18th c., sold 1767, demolished 1784); Minsterley Hall, Shropshire (house built c. 1580, purch. 1634, add. 1654, ceased to be a main residence later 17th c., estate offices, sold 1926)
Estates: Bateman 55574 (E) & (I) 68015. Worth £200,000,000 in 1990. Owned 10,000 acres in 2001.

Titles: Viscount Weymouth 1682- E; Baron Carteret 1784-1849 GB; Baronet 1641-
Peers: 10 peers 1685-1714 1731-51 1755-1837 1784-1849 1852-1945
3 Lds Lt 19th, 20th
3 in Cabinet 1702-07 1765 1775-79
3 KG 18th, 19th, 20th
Ntes: 1 Baron Carteret and 1 Viscount Weymouth and 1, 4, and 6 Marquesses and seven others in ODNB.

Earl Granville (1715-76 GB)

Origins: The Carterets held property in Jersey from the 12th century. The first MP was Baliff of Jersey, Treasurer of the Navy 1661, and one of the Proprietors of the Colony of New Jersey, making a fortune out of office. George Carteret 1 Baron Carteret of Haynes Park married Lady Grace Granville, created Viscountess Carteret and Countess Granville in 1715. Their son succeeded to the Carteret and Granville estates as 2 Earl Granville. On the death of the 3 Earl the estates passed to Lady Louisa Carteret, who married the 2 Viscount Weymouth (see above). Lord John Thynne succeeded as 3 Baron Carteret (cr. 1784) in 1838, and was seated at Haynes Park. On his death in 1849 the Barony became extinct. His nephew Lord John Thynne succeeded to the estates.

1. Sir George Carteret 1 Bt – Portsmouth 1661-79
2. Sir Charles Carteret 2 Bt – Milbourne Port 1690-1700
3. Edward Carteret – Huntingdon 1698-1700 Bedford 1702-05 Bere Alston 1717-21
4. Robert Carteret 3 Earl Granville – Yarmouth (IoW) 1744-47

Seat: Haynes (Haines, Hawnes) Park, Bedfordshire (acq. c. 1667, passed by inher. to Thynnes 1849, school from 1929-75)
Estates: 14961 (E) 13459
Titles: Baron Carteret 1681-1776; Baronet 1645-1776; 1670-1715
Peers: 3 peers 1681-95 1711-76
1 Ld Lt 18th
1 in Cabinet 1721-30 1742-44 1746 1751-63
1 KG 18th
Notes: 2 Earl and four others in ODNB.

Earl of Bath (1661-1711 E)

Origins: The Granvilles (Grenville) settled in the West Country soon after the Conquest (Roskill, Clark, and Rawcliffe, *The House of Commons*, III, 236) and held land in Cornwall from the 12th century. Archbishop of York 1304. **First MP 1388 for Devon. Nine further MPs 1529-1642, three for Cornwall**. Acquired large estates after the

Dissolution. The male line became extinct in 1711 and the daughter of the last Earl married the 1 Baron Carteret (see above).

1. Bernard Granville – Liskeard 1661-79 Launceston 1679 Saltash 1681 Plymouth 1685-87 Saltash 1689-90 Launceston 1690-95 Lostwithiel 1695-98
2. Charles Granville 2 Earl of Bath – Launceston 1680-81 Cornwall 1685-87
3. John Granville 1 Baron Granville – Launceston 1685-87 Plymouth 1689-98 Newport 1698-1700 Fowey 1701 Cornwall 1701-03
4. Sir Bevil Granville – Fowey 1685-87 Lostwithiel 1690-95 Fowey 1695-1700
5. George Granville 1 Baron Lansdowne – Fowey 1702-10 Cornwall 1710-12
6. Bernard Granville – Camelford 1710-12 Fowey 1712-13

Seats: Stowe (Hall), Cornwall (there by 16th c., rebuilt c. 1679, passed to Lady Carteret 1711, demolished 1739); Buckland Abbey, Devon (medieval, purch. 1541, remod. 1576, sold 1581)
Titles: Baron Granville and Viscount Lansdowne 1661-1711 E; Baron Granville 1703-07 E; Baron Lansdowne 1712-35 GB
Peers: 4 peers 1661-1701 1689-1701 1703-07 1712-14 1717-18
3 Lds Lt 17th, 18th
Notes: 1 Earl in ODNB and two others.

TIGHE [Fownes] *IRELAND*

Tighe

Origins: The founder emigrated to Ireland c. 1640 from Lincolnshire and became a contractor supplying Cromwell's army. Sheriff of Dublin 1649, Mayor 1651. **First {MP 1656}.** Originally, small landowners. Sheriff 1716. Married the heiress of Woodstock and greatly increased the family fortune. Controlled four parliamentary seats in the later 18th century.

1. Richard Tighe – {Belturbet 1703-13 Newtown 1715-27 Augher 1727-36}
2. William Tighe – {Clomines 1734-60 Wicklow 1761-66}
3. Richard Tighe – {Wicklow 1767-68}
4. William Tighe – {Athboy 1761-76}
5. Edward Tighe – {Belturbet 1763-68 Wicklow 1768-76 Athboy 1776-83 Wicklow 1783-97}
6. Henry Tighe – {Innistiogue 1797-1800}
7. William Tighe – {Banagher 1789-90 Wicklow 1790-97 Innistiogue 1797-1800} Wicklow 1806-16

Seats: Woodstock Park, Kilkenny (built c. 1740s, acq. by mar. 1778, add. late 18th c., burned 1922, still own); Rossanagh (Rossana, Rosana, Upper Rossana, formerly Eccles Grove), Wicklow (built early 18th c., purch. 1741, add. mid-18th c., family departed 1932, moved to England, sold 1940, part demolished 1950s); Coolquill Castle, Tipperary (Gahans acq. 1666, acq. by mar. from Gahans 1800, sold by mid-19th c.); Ballina Park, Wicklow (built late 17th c., add. c. 1840, resident into 20th c.)
Estates: Bateman 21763 (I) 11889 and 3459 (I) 2538
1 Ld Lt 19th
Notes: One in ODNB.

Fownes

Origins: The 1 Baronet, of obscure parentage, was Comptroller of Customs in Youghal 1693, Sheriff of Dublin 1697, and Lord Mayor in 1708. The 2 Bt was a businessman. William Tighe married in 1765 Sarah daughter of Sir William Fownes 2 Bt. The Fownes estates passed to the Tighes in the early 19th century.

1. Sir William Fownes 1 Bt – {Wicklow 1704-13}
2. Sir William Fownes 2 Bt – {Dingle 1749-60 Knocktopher 1761-76 Wicklow 1776-78}

Seat: Woodstock Park, Kilkenny (Sweete family purch. 1702, acq. by mar. from Sweetes mid-18th c., passed to Tighes by mar. of 1778)
Estates: Worth £1,500 pa in 1773.
Title: Baronet 1724-78

Tighe

Origins: Kinsmen of the Tighes of Woodstock. Purchased estates in the late 17th century. Sheriff 1760.

1. Richard Stearne Tighe – {Athy 1761}
2. Robert Tighe – {Roscommon 1769-76 Carrick 1777-83}
3. Robert Tighe – {Carrick 1800}

Seats: South Hill (Southill), Westmeath (built c. 1810, passed by mar. to Chapmans later 19th c.); Mitchelstown, Westmeath (purch. early 18th c., rebuilt early 19th c., passed by mar. to Chapman Bts later 19th c., see Chapman)
Estates: 1809 (I) 1242 in 1878. Worth £624 pa in c. 1704.

TISDALL (Tisdal) *IRELAND*

Origins: Migrated to Ireland in the mid-17th century. Possibly descended from a lawyer in London **MP 1621**. Purchased estates in the 1660s. Granted arms 1679. Richard Tisdall MP was Registrar of the Irish Court of Chancery. Philip Tisdall MP was a judge, Attorney General, and Secretary of State.

1. James Tisdall – {Ardee 1692-93 1695-99 1703-14}
2. Richard Tisdall – {Dundalk 1707-13 County Louth 1713-27}
3. Michael Tisdall – {Ardee 1713-26}
4. James Tisdall – {Dundalk 1721-27}
5. Philip Tisdall – {Dublin University 1739-76 County Armagh 1776-77}

Seats: Charlesfort, Meath (purch. 1668, new house 1740s, add. c. 1800, sold 1968); Bawn, Louth (medieval, acq. 1690, sold by 19th c.); Mount Tisdall (Bloomsbury House), Meath (purch. 1672, built c. 1700, sold 1835, derelict)
Estates: Bateman 5030 (I) 4828. £1,200 and £200 pa in 1713.
Notes: One in ODNB.

TOKE (Tooke)

Origins: Old Kent family, possibly from the 13th century. **First MP in the reign of Henry V. One additional MP 1554.**

1. John Toke – East Grinstead 1702-08

Seat: Godinton Park, Kent (medieval, acq. by mar. r. Henry VII, rebuilt 1628, family departed 1866, sold 1896)
Estates: Bateman 3855 (E) 5232

TOMPKYNS (Tomkins)

Origins: Gentry from the 15th century. **First MP 1614. Two further MPs 1624-40.**

1. Sir Thomas Tomkyns – Weobley 1640-44 1660-74

Seats: Monnington Court (Monyngton), Herefordshire (purch. 1535, built c. 1600, sold later 17th c.); Garnstone, Herefordshire (acq. 1553, sold 1657)
Estates: Worth over £1,000 pa 1636.
Notes: The family suffered declining fortunes in the 17th century.

TOOKER

Origins: Yeomen in the 15th century. Mayor of Salisbury 1493. **The first MP 1601** for Salisbury, a lawyer and recorder, was the son of a yeoman. **Another MP 1628 also for Salisbury.**

1. Edward Tooker – Salisbury 1654 Hindon 1659 Salisbury 1660-64

Seat: Maddington, Wiltshire (purch. 1552, passed out of family 1676, estates divided among heiresses)
Estates: Worth £1,000 pa in the 1660s.
Title: Baronet 1664-76
Notes: Extinct in male line 1676.

TOWER

Origins: Founded by a Collector of Customs for London 1696. Director of the Bank of England 1734. Purchased landed estate 1745. Sheriff 1760.

1. Christopher Tower – Lancaster 1727-34 Aylesbury 1734-41 Bossiney 1741-42
2. Thomas Tower – Wareham 1729-34 Wallingford 1734-41
3. Christopher Tower – Harwich 1832-35
4. Christopher Tower – Buckinghamshire 1845-47

Seats: Weald Hall, Essex (built c. 1550s and c. 1570, remod. c. 1720s, purch. 1745 or 1752, sold 1946, demolished 1950, still own some land); Delaford Park, Buckinghamshire (purch. manorial land 1699, built late 18th c., add. 19th c., purch. house at Delaford 1869, still owned 1925); Huntsmore Park, Buckinghamshire (purch. 1696, sold and demolished 1930s)
Estates: Bateman 5287 (E) 9833

TOWNSEND (Townshend) *IRELAND*

<u>Townsend</u>

Origins: To Ireland as a colonel in 1647. Acquired estates 1666-79. Sheriff 1671.

1. Richard Townsend – {Baltimore 1661-66 1692}
2. Bryan Townsend – {Clonakilty 1695-99}
3. Richard Townsend – {County Cork 1759-83}
4. Richard Townsend – {Dingle 1782-95}
5. John Townsend – {Dingle 1783-97 Castlemartyr 1797-1800}

Seat: Castle Townsend, Cork (acq. and built c. 1660, new house c. 1700, fire 1858, new house c. 1860, still own)
Estates: Bateman 22615 (I & E) 10683

Townsend

Origins: Cadet line.

1. Thomas Townsend – {Belturbet 1797-1800}

TOWNSHEND

Marquess Townshend (1787- GB)

Origins: At Raynham as sheep-farmers at the end of the 14th century. Family fortunes founded by a lawyer, Kt and **MP 1467**, Justice of the Common Pleas 1484. The family did well out of the Dissolution of the Monasteries. (Moreton, *The Townshends and Their World*, 1-27) **First MP 1467. Eight additional MPs, 1529-1628, four of them for Norfolk.**

1. Horatio Townshend 1 Viscount Townshend – Norfolk 1656 1659 1660
2. Roger Townshend – Norfolk 1701-02 1705-08 Great Yarmouth 1708-09
3. Horatio Townshend – Great Yarmouth 1715-22 Heytesbury 1727-34
4. Thomas Townshend – Winchelsea 1722-27 University of Cambridge 1727-74
5. Charles Townshend 3 Viscount Townshend – Great Yarmouth 1722-23
6. William Townshend – Great Yarmouth 1723-38
7. Roger Townshend – Great Yarmouth 1738-47 Eye 1747-48
8. George Townshend 1 Marquess Townshend – Norfolk 1747-64
9. Charles Townshend – Great Yarmouth 1747-56 Saltash 1756-61
10. Charles Townshend 1 Baron Bayning – Great Yarmouth 1756-84 1790-96
11. Henry Townshend – Eye 1758-62
12. Lord John Townshend – University of Cambridge 1780-84 Westminster 1788-90 Knaresborough 1793-1818
13. Lord Charles Townshend – Great Yarmouth 1796
14. Charles Townshend 2 Baron Bayning – Truro 1808-10
15. Lord Charles Townshend – Tamworth 1812-18 1820-34
16. Lord James Townshend – Helston 1818-32 1835-37
17. John Townshend 4 Marquess Townshend – Tamworth 1847-55
18. John Townshend 5 Marquess Townshend – Tamworth 1856-63
19. Charles Townshend – Wrekin Div. Shropshire 1920-22

Seats: Raynham Hall, Norfolk (acq. estates by late 14th c., medieval house, rebuilt 1619-58, remod. 1659-62, remod. 1720-30, still own); Honingham Hall, Norfolk (built 1605, purch. 1702, passed by mar. to Fellowes in 1887 – seat of the Lords Bayning 1797-1887, demolished 1966); Stiffkey Old Hall, Norfolk (built c. 1578, acq. by mar. from the Bacons early 17th c., sold 1911); Balls Park, Hertfordshire (built 1637-40, acq. later 18th c., remod. early 19th c., family departed 1880s, sold 1901, institutional use); Tamworth Castle, Warwickshire (transferred to Staffordshire 1888) (medieval, add. 17th c., acq. by mar. 1751, remod. 1781, sold 1891)
Estates: Bateman 19910 (E) 22560; Bayning 4323 (E) 5419. Worth £5,500 pa in 1687. The 7 Marquess left £54,000,000 in 2010.
Titles: Baron Townshend 1661- E; Viscount Townshend 1682- E; Baron Ferrers 1770-1855 GB; Earl of Leicester 1784-1855 GB; Baron Bayning 1797-1866; Baronet 1617-
Peers: 11 peers 1661-87 1697-1738 1723-1807 1774-1811 1797-1823 1855-1921 1937-45
4 Lds Lt 17th, 18th, 19th
4 in Cabinet 1714-17 1720-30 1739 1761-63 1765-67 1767-68 1767-82
1 KG 18th
Notes: "Lord" John Townshend, "Earl of Leicester" (John Dunn Gardner) sat for Bodmin as an MP 1841. He was the son of the 3 Marchioness Townshend and a bigamously married second husband, and was legally declared not to be a Townshend in 1843 (Fisher, *The House of Commons*, VII, 480). 1 Baron Bayning and 1, 2 and 3 Viscounts and 1, 2, 3, 5, and 7 Marquesses and eleven others in ODNB.

Earl Sydney (1874-90 UK)

Origins: The 1 Viscount Sydney was a grandson of the 2 Viscount Townshend. A combination of inheritances from relatives and income from sinecures enabled the 1 Viscount to set up an independent landed family.

1. Thomas Townshend 1 Viscount Sydney – Whitchurch 1754-83
2. John Townshend 2 Viscount Sydney – Newport (IoW) 1786-90 Whitchurch 1790-1800
3. William Townshend – Whitchurch 1800-16
4. Sir Horatio Townshend – Whitchurch 1816-26 1831-32
5. John Townshend 1 Earl Sydney – Whitchurch 1826-31

Seats: Frognal House, Kent (built early 18th c., purch. 1752, passed to Marshams by inher. 1890, who took name Townshend, sold 1917, institutional use); Scadbury Park, Kent (medieval, acq. by mar. mid-18th c., demolished 1738, passed to Marshams by inher. 1890, who took name Townshend, new house 1914, fire 1976, sold 1983, nature reserve); Matson House, Gloucestershire (built 1575-76, remod. c. 1720, inherited from the Selwyns, 1791, sold 1912)
Estates: Bateman 3112 (E) 6615

Titles: Baron Sydney 1783-1890 GB; Viscount Sydney 1789-1890 GB
Peers: 3 peers 1783-1890
1 Ld Lt 19th
1 in Cabinet 1782-90
Notes: 1 Viscount in ODNB.

TRAFFORD

Origins: The family claimed to have held Trafford before the Conquest. (Beavan, *The Parliamentary Representation of Lancashire 1258-1885*, 15) **First MP 1312 for Lancashire. Two further MPs 1572-93, one for the county.** The Traffords remained Roman Catholic and were thus excluded from Parliament until Emancipation in the 19th century. Created Baronets 1841. Held 9,800 acres listed in Bateman worth £36,570 pa. Trafford was sold in 1896. A cadet line founded by a younger son who married well produced the MP below.

1. Sigismund Trafford – King's Lynn 1689-90

Seats: Dunton Hall, Lincolnshire (acq. by mar. early 17th c., built c. 1720, demolished c. 1768); Wroxham Hall, Norfolk (built c. 1790, acq. c. 1820, add. c. 1890 and 1926, house demolished c. 1950s, estate was retained and family lived in smaller country house, sold 2006)
Estates: Bateman 7110 (E) 16959

TRANT *IRELAND*

Origins: The father of Dominick Trant {MP}, a barrister, was a successful merchant who purchased estates in Kerry and Tipperary. Sheriff 1846. Cousins elected **two {MPs in 1585-1613 for Dingle}**, origins unknown.

1. Dominick Trant – {St. Canice 1781-83}
2. William Trant – Okehampton 1824-26 Dover 1828-30 Okehampton 1831

Seats: Dovea House, Tipperary (medieval castle (Killahara), acq. early 18th c., new house built c. 1760s (Dovea), sold 1940s, business use); Farrincantillon, Kerry (acq. early 18th c., passed out of family 1856); Drumonby, Limerick (purch. early 19th c., passed out of family 1856); Dunkettle, Cork (acq. early 18th c., sold later 18th c.)
Estates: Bateman 2970 (I) 2128. Worth £2,018 pa in 1811.
Notes: William Trant MP served with the East India Company. The family sold most of their property in Dingle and made Dovea their main seat in 1809.
Notes: Two in ODNB.

TREBY

Origins: The family began an upward ascent by marrying a local heiress to Plympton c. 1630s. The first MP became Chief Justice of the Common Pleas 1689. He purchased large estates. His son was a Secretary of State 1718. Paul Ourry married the daughter and heiress of George Treby. The Ourrys were Huguenots who rose through military service in the 18th century.

1. Sir George Treby – Plympton Erle 1677-81 1689-92
2. George Treby – Plympton Erle 1708-27 Dartmouth 1727-42
3. George Treby – Dartmouth 1722-27
4. George Treby – Plympton Erle 1747-61
5. George Treby – Plympton Erle 1761-63
6. Paul Ourry – Plympton Erle 1763-75
7. Paul Treby-Ourry – Plympton Erle 1784

Seat: Plympton House, Devon (acq. by mar. c. 1630, built c. 1700-20, sold 1830)
Title: Baronet 1718-24
Notes: One in ODNB.

TREDENHAM [Scobell]

Tredenham

Origins: Seated for many generations at the small manor of Tredenham. A lawyer purchased larger estates in the 1630s.

1. Sir William Tredenham – St. Mawes 1658 1661-62
2. Sir Joseph Tredenham – St. Mawes 1666-79 Grampound 1679 St. Mawes 1679-81 Grampound 1685-87 St. Mawes 1689-95 1698-1707
3. John Tredenham – St. Mawes 1690-1705 1707-10
4. Seymour Tredenham – St. Mawes 1695-96

Seat: Tregonan, Cornwall (acq. c. 1630, passed by inher. to Scobells 1710)
Estates: Worth £900 pa in the late 17th c.
Notes: Family extinct in the male line 1710, greatly encumbered by debts. One in ODNB.

Scobell

Origins: Grandfather of first MP a Clerk of the Parliament during the Interregnum. First MP was a lawyer.

1. Francis Scobell – Mitchell 1690-95 Grampound 1699-1708 St. Germans 1708-10 Launceston 1710-13 St. Mawes 1713-15

Seats: Menegwins, Cornwall (acq. by inher. mid-17th c., passed out of family later 18th c.); Tregonan, Cornwall (acq. by mar. from Tredenhams 1710, passed out of family later in 18th c.)

TREFFRY (Treffrydwe, Trefrye, Treffy)

Origins: Rich merchants in Fowey in the later Middle Ages. It is unlikely that their claim to have been the standard bearer of the Black Prince at Crécy was true. (See Rowse, *The Little Land of Cornwall*, 112) They supported the Tudors in 1485 and rose high under Henry VII. **First MP 1348. Eight additional MPs 1406-1621, one for Cornwall.**

1. John Treffry – Fowey 1679-81 1685-87

Seats: Place House, Cornwall (acq. by mar. c. 1400, ruinous 18th c., rebuilt mid-19th c., still own); Rooke, Cornwall (sold 1711)
Estates: Owned profitable mines.
Notes: The male line died out in the mid 18th c. Place passed through a succession of heiresses whose husbands took the name Treffry, increasingly impoverished. In the early 19th century the family fortunes were revived by Joseph Austen Treffry (1782-1850), an industrialist (mining, lime kilns, shipbuilding), who rebuilt Place, to which a nephew, Edward Wilcocks succeeded in 1850. One in ODNB.

TRELAWNEY [Brereton, Salusbury]

Trelawney

Origins: The Trelawneys held land in Cornwall from the 12th century and had pre-Conquest ancestors (Shirley, *The Noble and Gentle Men of England*, 27; Bindoff, *The House of Commons*, III, 478). According to family tradition one fought at Agincourt (Roskell, Clark and Rawcliffe, *The House of Commons*, IV, 645). **First MP 1325. Ten additional MPs 1397-1611, three for Cornwall.** The 8 Baronet took the additional name Salusbury under the will of his cousin Owen Salusbury-Brereton in 1802.

1. Samuel Trelawney – Bossiney 1659 Camelford 1660 Plymouth 1660-65
2. Sir Jonathan Trelawney 2 Bt – East Looe 1660 Cornwall 1661-78 East Loee 1679-81
3. John Trelawney – West Looe 1661-81
4. John Trelawney – West Looe 1677-80
5. Charles Trelawney – East Looe 1685-87 1689-98 Plymouth 1698-1713

6. Henry Trelawney – West Looe 1685-87 East Looe 1689-1700 Plymouth 1701-02
7. Sir Harry Trelawney 3 Bt – East Looe 1708-10
8. Sir John Trelawney 4 Bt – West Looe 1713-15 Liskeard 1715-22 West Looe 1722-27 East Looe 1727-34
9. Edward Trelawney – West Looe 1724-32
10. Sir William Trelawney 6 Bt – West Looe 1757-67
11. Charles Trelawney-Brereton – St. Michael 1808-09 1814
12. Sir William Salusbury Trelawney 8 Bt – E. Cornwall 1832-37
13. Sir John Salusbury-Trelawney 9 Bt – Tavistock 1843-52 1857-65 E. Cornwall 1868-74

Seats: Trelawne, Cornwall (medieval, purch. c. 1600, sold c. 1920, institutional use); Hengar House (Manor), Cornwall (medieval, rebuilt 1620, acq. by mar. 1690, passed out of family by mar. later 18th c.); Shotwick Park, Cheshire (inherited from the Salusbury Breretons 1862, built 1872, sold 1906, fire 1907, now an institution)
Estates: Bateman 8000 (E) 6000
Title: Baronet 1618-
1 Ld Lt 19th
Notes: Three in ODNB.

Brereton-Salusbury

Origins: The first Brereton was a saddler and innkeeper in the 17th century. **First MP 1624**. Thomas Brereton married the heiress of Salusbury Lloyd of Leadbrooke, Flintshire and took the additional name Salusbury in 1749. The Salusbury estates later passed to the Trelawneys (see above).

1. Edward Brereton – Denbigh 1698-1705
2. Thomas Brereton-Salusbury – Liverpool 1724-29 1734-56
3. Owen Salusbury Brereton – Ilchester 1775-80

Seat: Shotwick Park, Cheshire (Salusburys purch. 1700, Breretons acq. by mar. from Salusburys c. 1740, passed to Trelawneys 1862, see above)
Notes: Two in ODNB.

Trelawney

Origins: Descended from Sir Jonathan Trelawney (d. 1604), who left Coldrenick to a younger son.

1. Jonathan Trelawney – West Looe 1681 1690-95
2. Darell Trelawney – Lostwithiel 1727
3. Charles Trelawney – Liskeard 1740-54

Seat: Coldrenick (Coldrinnick), Cornwall (built early 18th c., acq. mid-18th c., passed to heiress 1764)
Estates: Bateman 2524 (E) 3184
Note: This branch extinct in male line in 1764 and estates passed via heiresses eventually to Stephens family who took name Trelawney.

Trelawney

Origins: Cousins of the Trelawneys of Trelawne. Plymouth merchants. **First MP 1640 for Plymouth.**

1. John Trelawney – Plymouth 1690-95

Seat: Ham House, Devon (acq. and built 1639, passed via heiress to Collins family 1784 who took add. name Trelawney, donated to Plymouth 1947, flats)

TREMAYNE (Tremaine) [Lemon, Wise]

Tremayne

Origins: An old Cornish family. **First MP 1323. Eight additional MPs 1344-1650s.**

1. Sir John Tremayne – Tregony 1690-94
2. Arthur Tremayne – Launceston 1727-34
3. John Tremayne – Cornwall 1806-26
4. John Tremayne – E. Cornwall 1874-80 S. Devon 1884-85
5. Arthur Tremayne – Truro 1878-80

Seats: Heligan House, Cornwall (purch. 1569, built 1603, rebuilt 1692, add. 1810 and 1830, family departed c. 1916, sold 1970s, flats); Sydenham House, Devon (acq. by marriage from a Wise (see below) heiress 1675, sold 1937); Collacombe, Devon (medieval, acq. 14th c., rebuilt early 15th c., add. mid-16th c. and 1574, sold 1948)
Estates: Bateman 11267 (E) 13997
Notes: The Tremayne family has an entry and two others in the ODNB.

Wise (Wyse)

Origins: The Wise family were landowners in the 11th century. **First MP 1411. Five additional MPs 1432-1641, two for Devon**. The daughter and heiress of Edward Wise MP married Arthur Tremayne, who succeeded to Sydenham.

1. Edward Wise – Okehampton 1659 1660-75

2. Ayshford Wise – Totnes 1812-18
3. John Ayshford Wise – Stafford 1852-60

Seats: Sydenham, Devon (acq. 13th c., passed to Tremaynes 1675); Clayton Hall, Staffordshire (built c. 1600, acq. by mar. 1837, rebuilt 1840s, family departed 1892, sold by 1924)

Lemon

Origins: William Lemon, a poor man's son, founded the family fortunes by becoming a mine manager and discovering a great tin mine of his own. He also mined copper. He purchased landed estates with the profits in the mid-18th century. John Tremayne of Heligan married Matilda, daughter of Sir William Lemon 1 Bt in 1813. His son succeeded to the Lemon estates on the death of the 2 Bt in 1868.

1. Sir William Lemon 1 Bt – Penryn 1770-74 Cornwall 1774-1824
2. John Lemon – West Looe 1784 Saltash 1787-90 Truro 1796-1814
3. Sir Charles Lemon 2 Bt – Penryn 1807-12 1830-31 Cornwall 1831-32 W. Div. Cornwall 1832-57

Seat: Carclew, Cornwall (built 1720s, purch. 1749, rebuilt c. 1750, passed to Tremaynes by mar. 1868, fire 1934, ruin)
Estates: Bateman 8823 (E) 8190
Title: Baronet 1774-1868
Notes: Lemons extinct 1868

TRENCH [Le Poer] *IRELAND*

Earl of Clancarty (1803- I)

Origins: Huguenots who left France for England c. 1575. Migrated to Ireland 1631. The 1 Earl was connected through his mother, Frances Power of Corheen, with Donagh MacCarthy, 4 Earl of Clancarty of the first creation (see Davys).

1. Frederick Trench – {County Galway 1715-52}
2. Richard Trench – {Banagher 1735-60 County Galway 1761-68}
3. William Trench 1 Earl of Clancarty – {County Galway 1768-97}
4. Eyre Trench – {Newtown Limavady 1798-99}
5. Richard Trench 2 Earl of Clancarty – {Newtown Limavady 1796-97 County Galway 1797-1800} 1801-05 Rye 1807
6. Charles Trench – {Newtown Limavady 1799-1800}

7. Sir Frederick Trench – Mitchell 1806 Dundalk 1812 Cambridge 1819-32 Scarborough 1835-47
8. William Le Poer Trench – County Galway 1872-74

Seats: Garbally Court (House), Galway (purch. and built c. 1631, burned 1798, rebuilt 1819, sold 1922, institutional use); Heywood, Queen's County (built 1773, passed by inher. to Domviles early 19th c., fire 1950, demolished)
Estates: Bateman 25510 (I) 12817. Worth £10,000 pa in 1809.
Titles: Baron Kilconnel 1797- I; Viscount Dunlo 1801- I; Baron Trench 1815- UK; Viscount Clancarty 1823- UK
Peers: {1 peer 1797-1800} 1 Irish Rep peer 1808-15
5 peers 1815-1945
1 in Cabinet 1812-18
Notes: Created Marquis of Huesden in the Netherlands in 1818. Resident in England by the 1930s. Trench heiress mar. 1815 to the 1 Domvile Bt. The daughter of the 3 Bt succeeded to Heywood and married a Poë in 1886. 2 Earl and two others in ODNB.

<u>Baron Ashtown</u> (1800- I)

Origins: Descended from a younger son of Frederick Trench of Garbally (d. 1669), ancestor of the Earls of Clancarty.

1. Frederic Trench 1 Baron Ashtown – {Maryborough 1785-90 Portarlington 1798-1800} 1801
2. Francis Trench – {Ballynakill 1800}

Seats: Woodlawn House, Galway (purch. 1702, built 1750s, add. c. 1860, sold 1947); Cangort Park, King's County (acq. by mar. 1798, built 1807, passed to Atkinsons by mar. 1881); Sopwell Hall, Tipperary (old castle, acq. by Sadlier 17th c., rebuilt 1745, passed by mar. to Trench family 1796, remod. 1866-68, sold 1986)
Estates: Bateman 43643 (I & E) 34689 and 12134 (I) 6578. Most of the estate sold in the 1920s and 1930s.
Peer: 1 Irish Rep peer 1908-15
Notes: Trench family inherited the estates of the Sadlier family by mar. of 1745 {**MP 1656**}. Declared bankrupt 1912. Three in ODNB.

TRENCHARD [Henning]

<u>Trenchard</u>

Origins: Unbroken male descent from the reign of Henry I. **First MP 1449. Six additional MPs 1542-1659, four of them for Dorset.**

1. Thomas Trenchard – Poole 1670-71
2. Henry Trenchard – Poole 1679-81
3. Sir John Trenchard – Taunton 1679-81 Thetford 1689-90 Poole 1690-95
4. Thomas Trenchard – Dorchester 1689-95 Wareham 1695-1700 Dorchester 1701 Dorset 1701-02
5. Henry Trenchard – Dorchester 1713-20
6. George Trenchard – Poole 1713-41 1747-54

Seats: Lytchett Maltravers, Dorset (medieval, purch. 1611, rebuilt 17th c., sold 1829, most demolished 20th c.); Wolfeton (Wolveton) House, Dorset (medieval, acq. by mar. 1480, add. early and late 16th c., remod. c. 1600, part demolished 1822, sold 1862); Bloxworth House, Dorset (built 1608, purch. 1689, remod. early 19th c., sold 1964)
Estates: Bateman 2895 (E) 3584
1 in Cabinet 1692-95
Notes: One in ODNB.

Trenchard

Origins: Cadet line.

1. William Trenchard – Westbury 1679-81 Heytesbury 1690-95 Westbury 1702
2. John Trenchard – Taunton 1722-23

Seats: Cutteridge, Wiltshire (purch. 1558, prob. built late 16th c., passed to Hippesleys by mar. who took name Trenchard 1723, passed to Ashfordbys by mar. who took name Trenchard 1787, demolished c. 1800, sold 1807); Leigh Court (Abbot's Leigh), Somerset (built 16th c., acq. by mar. c. 1715, sold 1811, institutional use)
Notes: Male line extinct 1723. One in ODNB.

Viscount Trenchard (1936- UK)

Origins: Cadet line.

No MPs

Seat: Abdale House, Hertfordshire (built 16th and 17th c., purch. early 20th c., still own)
Titles: Baron Trenchard 1930- UK; Baronet 1919-
Peer: 1 peer 1930-45
Notes: 1 Viscount was the father of the RAF. 1 Viscount in ODNB.

Henning

Origins: The Hennings were merchants in Dorchester. They purchased landed estates in 1575. Sheriff 1609. The daughter and heiress of Henry Henning married Thomas Trenchard MP, and he acquired her estates in 1699. An heiress resumed the name Henning 1725. Hennings (Trenchards) were bankers in the 18th c.

1. Henry Henning – Weymouth & Melcombe Regis 1680-81 1685-87 1689-95

Seat: Poxwell Manor, Dorset (purch. 1575, built c. 1600, passed by mar. to Trenchards 1699, passed to Pickards after 1800)
Notes: Henning bank failed c. 1840.

TREVANION [Bettesworth]

Origins: Justice of the Common Pleas under Edward III. **First MP 1407 for Cornwall. Five additional MPs 1529-1642, one for the county**. The sister and heiress of William Trevanion MP married John Bettesworth, and their son succeeded to Caerhayes in 1767 and took the name Trevanion.

1. Charles Trevanion – Grampound 1661-79 Tregony 1679-81
2. John Trevanion – Tregony 1705-08 Bodmin 1708-10 Cornwall 1710-22
3. William Trevanion – Tregony 1747-67
4. John Bettesworth-Trevanion – Penryn 1807

Seat: Caerhayes (Carhayes, Caerhays) Castle (aka Trevanion Park), Cornwall (acq. 1390, demolished c. 1700, passed by mar. 1767, rebuilt 1807-08, family depart 1840, sold 1853)
Estates: 8,000 acres c. 1600. Worth £4,000 pa in 1740.
Notes: The family bankrupt in 1840. One in ODNB.

TROTMAN

Origins: Gentry by the 17th century. A barrister in the mid-17th century purchased Siston, while Bucknell was acquired by cousins at about the same time. The lines merged in the 18th century.

1. Samuel Trotman – Bath 1707-20
2. Samuel Trotman – New Woodstock 1722-34
3. Fiennes Trotman – Northampton 1784-90

Seats: Siston Court, Gloucestershire (built late 16th c., purch. 1651, passed to Dickinsons by marriage 1875); Bucknell, Oxfordshire (medieval, purch. 1652, rebuilt 1702, passed to Hibberts by mar. 1835, sold 1897)
Notes: Male line extinct 1835.

TRUMBULL

Origins: The **first MP 1626,** a lawyer and son of a yeoman, rose through an official career. **Another MP 1656**. He was granted Easthampstead Park for his diplomatic work. His grandson was an ambassador and Secretary of State.

1. Sir William Trumbull – East Looe 1685-87 University of Oxford 1695-98

Seat: Easthampstead Park, Berkshire (acq. 1629, passed to Hills – see Marquess of Downshire - by mar. 1769)
1 in Cabinet 1695-98
Notes: Two in ODNB.

TUCHET (Touchet) [Thicknesse]

<u>Earl of Castlehaven</u> (1616-1777 I)

Origins: The Tuchets were a medieval family who married the Goscelin heiress to Markeaton, whose family had held it from 1086. They rose to greater status by marriage to the daughter of the 2 Baron Audley, heiress of the Audley estates and title (inher. 1405). The Audleys emerged in the 13th century, Barons 1313. Several episodes of forfeiture and restoration of estates took place. **First MP for Sussex 1453**. Active in Ireland in the 16th and 17th centuries. The 2 Earl of Castlehaven was **MP for Dorset 1614**. Mary Tuchet, sister and heiress of the 6 and last Earl of Castlehaven, married in 1749 Philip Thicknesse. Their son, George Thicknesse, succeeded as 19 Baron Audley. The Thicknesse family were Newcastle-under-Lyme burgesses in the 13th century. **First MP 1377 for Newcastle under Lyme. Another MP also for Newcastle 1378**. Ralph Thicknesse MP 1831 was a collier in the coastal trade and banker, the son of a physician.

1. Ralph Thicknesse – Wigan 1831-34
2. Ralph Thicknesse – Wigan 1847-54

Seats: Heleigh (Heighley) Castle, Staffordshire (medieval, demolished 1640s, "Balterley Hall" built early 17th c. remained a residence, inher. from Audley descendents 1777, sold estate and Balterley Hall 1790); Beech Hill, Lancashire (acq. c. 1800, passed

to Coldwells by mar. 1842 who took name Thicknesse, sold 1880s); Markeaton Hall, Derbyshire (Tuchets acq. by mar. in Middle Ages, sold 1516)
Estates: 1 Earl was granted 200,000 acres in Ireland in the later-16th c.
Title: Baron Audley 1313-1872 E
Peers: 9 peers 1660-1740 1744-77 1779-1872
Notes: 7 Baron Audley and 2 and 3 Earls and two other Tuchets and two Thicknesses in ODNB.

TUDWAY

Origins: London merchants and West Indian plantation owners. A barrister later in the 18th century.

1. Charles Tudway – Wells 1754-61
2. Clement Tudway – Wells 1761-1815
3. John Tudway – Wells 1815-30
4. Robert Tudway – Wells 1852-55

Seats: The Cedars, Somerset (built 1760s, sold 1909); Stoberry Park, Somerset (acq. later 19th c., sold mid-20th c.)
Estates: Bateman 2827 (E) 4511. Owned 1,096 acres in Antigua.

TUFNELL [Tyrell (Tirel, Tirrell, Tyrrell)]

<u>Tufnell</u>

Origins: A London salter in the 16th century and a brewer in the 17th century laid the foundations for the family fortune. A barrister in the 18th century purchased Langleys. **First MP 1640 for Southwark.**

1. Samuel Tufnell – Maldon 1715-22 Colchester 1727-34 Great Marlow 1741-47
2. John Tufnell – Beverley 1754-61
3. George Tufnell – Beverley 1761-68 1774-80
4. William Tufnell – Colchester 1806-07
5. Henry Tufnell – Ipswich 1837 Devonport 1840-54
6. Edward Tufnell – S. E. Essex 1900-06
7. Richard Tufnell – Cambridge 1934-45

Seats: Langleys, Essex (built c. 1620, purch. 1711, rebuilt c. 1719, add. c. 1820s, add. 1870s, still own); Pleshey, Essex (inher. from Jolliffes 1750)
Estates: Bateman 7584 (E) 10377
Notes: Two in ODNB.

Tyrell

Origins: The family claimed descent from a landowner listed in the Domesday Book. Tyrell is the "oldest name" in Essex deriving from Norman times. Landed by the 14th century. Twenty-three knights in lineal succession. One was supposedly the unwitting killer of William II, while Sir Thomas Tyrell (d. 1502) was the alleged murderer of the Princes in the Tower. (Fisher, *The House of Commons*, VII, 521) The eighth Knight married the Heron heiress to Heron. (*Country Life*, 36, p. 54) Speaker of the House of Commons 1427. **First MP 1355. Eleven MPs 1365-1558, eight kts of the shire**. A younger son of the Tufnells of Langleys married Elizabeth, daughter and heiress of Sir John Tyrell 2 Bt of Boreham House.

1. Sir John Tyrell – Maldon 1661-76
2. Sir John Tyrell 2 Bt – Essex 1830-31 N. Essex 1832-57

Seats: Boreham House, Essex (built 1728, acq. by Tyrells c. 1800 from heiress of John Higham, passed by mar. to the Tufnells and then in 1912 to 3 Baron Kenyon via an heiress, sold 1930); Heron Hall, Essex (acq. by mar. 15th c. to Heron heiress, demolished 1790)
Estates: Bateman 3078 (E) 4840
Titles: Baronet 1666-1766; 1809-77
Notes: Tyrell family has an entry in the ODNB.

Tyrell

Origins: Cadet of the Essex Tyrells. **First MP 1604**.

1. Sir Thomas Tyrell – Aylesbury 1659 Buckinghamshire 1660
2. Sir Timothy Tyrell – {Fore 1661-62}
3. Sir Peter Tyrell 1 Bt – Buckingham 1679
4. James Tyrell – Boroughbridge 1722-42

Seats: Castle Thorpe, Buckinghamshire (medieval castle, demolished, purch. 1626, sold 1714, most demolished by 1799, farm house); Shotover Park, Oxfordshire (acq. by mar. 1519, rebuilt 1713-18, sold 1839); Oakley, Buckinghamshire (acq. by mar. 1526, sold 1707)
Title: Baronet 1665-1714
Notes: The last Tyrell left Shotover to his cousin Penelope Madan, wife of Augustus Schutz, a second cousin of George II. The Schutz family sold it in 1839.

Tyrell

Origins: Cadet line.

1. Charles Tyrell – Suffolk 1830-32 W. Suffolk 1832-34

Seats: Plashwood (Hall), Suffolk (acq. by mar. to Ray heiress 1801, sold c. 1900?); Polstead Hall, Suffolk (built 16th c., remod. early 17th c. and 1816-19, acq. by mar. to Cooke heiress 1828, passed back to Cookes 1872); Gipping Hall, Suffolk (medieval, acq. 15th c., demolished 1850)
Estates: Bateman 3462 (E) 4534
Notes: One in ODNB.

Brand

Origins: The grandfather of the MP below was a clothier in Boxford, Suffolk who purchased estates including Edwardstone and Polstead. First MP a merchant and Alderman of London. Brand estates passed to Cookes in later 18th c., and hence to Charles Tyrell MP above.

1. Joseph Brand – Sudbury 1660

Seats: Edwardstone Hall, Suffolk (purch. late 16th c., built early 17th c., sold c. 1847, large part demolished 1952); Polstead Hall, Suffolk (purch. 1598, built 16th c., remod. early 17th c., passed to Cookes later 18th c.)

TUFTON

Earl of Thanet (1628-1849 E)

Origins: An old family in the North that moved to Kent in the 13th century. **First MP 1601 (Kent 1624). Two further MPs 1614-48**. They inherited the vast Clifford (peers from 1299 and MPs for Westmorland and Yorkshire) estates centered around Appleby by marriage to the daughter and heiress Anne, 18 Baroness de Clifford, granddaughter of the 3 Earl of Cumberland (see Clifford). On the death of the 6 Earl of Thanet, the de Clifford title passed via his daughter to the Southwells (see Southwell), but the Tuftons retained most of the estates. On the death of the last Earl of Thanet, the estates passed to his illegitimate son, who was created Baron Hothfield.

1. Sir John Tufton 2 Bt – Maidstone 1661-81 1685-87
2. Thomas Tufton 6 Earl of Thanet – Appleby 1668-79
3. Richard Tufton 5 Earl of Thanet – Appleby 1679-80

4. Richard Tufton – Steyning 1679-81
5. Sackville Tufton – Appleby 1681 1685-87
6. Sackville Tufton 7 Earl of Thanet – Appleby 1722-29
7. Henry Tufton 11 Earl of Thanet – Rochester 1796-1802 Appleby 1826-32
8. John Tufton – Appleby 1796-98

Seats: Appleby Castle, Westmorland (medieval, acq. by Cliffords 1269, slighted 1569, restored 1651, passed by mar. to Tuftons 1676, part rebuilt 1686-88, sold 1963, now offices); Hothfield Place, Kent (acq. and built c. 1540, new house c. 1780, sold later 1940s, demolished 1954); Skipton Castle, Yorkshire (built 12th c., granted by Edward II to Cliffords 1310, confiscated 1461, reclaimed 1485, add. c. 1500, add. 1535, passed to 4 Earl of Thanet by mar., still own)
Estates: Bateman 39276 (E) 45987
Titles: Baron de Clifford 1299- E; Baron Tufton 1626-1849 E; Baron Hothfield 1881- UK; Baronet 1611-1849; 1851-
Peers: 11 peers 1660-1786 1790-1849 1881-1945
3 Lds Lt 17th, 19th, 20th
Notes: 9 Earl and one other in ODNB.

TULSE

Origins: Never achieved more than a modest estate, rising in the mid-17th century. **First MP 1640**.

1. Henry Tulse – Christchurch 1659 1660-79
2. William Tulse – Lymington 1698

Seat: Hinton Admiral, Hampshire (acq. mid-17th c., sold 1708)
Notes: Lost estates in the late 17th century.

TURNER I [Dryden, Page]

Page-Turner

Origins: The founding Turner was a barrister (d. 1578). His grandson was a merchant in London. The 1 Bt was Chairman of the East India Company 1733. Sir Gregory Turner 3 Bt inherited the estates of his great uncle Sir Gregory Page 1 Bt and took the additional name Page. The Pages began with a shipwright and ship owner. His son was also a ship owner and Chairman of the East India Company 1716. He sold his stock just before the crash and was worth perhaps £600,000. (Knight, *London's Country Houses*, 77) On the extinction of the senior line of Page-Turner Baronets in 1874, the Baronetcy passed to a cadet line descended from a younger son of the 2 Bt who had married a Dryden heiress and had taken the name Dryden.

1. Sir Gregory Page 1 Bt – New Shoreham 1708-13 1715-20
2. Sir Edward Turner 2 Bt – Great Bedwyn 1741-47 Oxfordshire 1755-61 Penryn 1761-66
3. Sir Gregory Page-Turner 3 Bt – Thirsk 1784-1805

Seats: Battlesden House (Park), Bedfordshire (purch. 1706, rebuilt 1860-64, demolished 1886); Ambrosden, Oxfordshire (purch. and built for reputedly £100,000 in the mid-18th c., demolished and sold c. 1800); Wricklemarsh, Kent (old house, Page purch. 1721 and rebuilt 1723, sold 1784, demolished 1787)
Estates: Bateman 11799 (E) 15050. The 1 Page Bt left £500,000 to 600,000. Rubinstein – 3 Bt left £175,000 in probate 1820.
Titles: Baronet 1714-75; 1733-
Notes: One Page in ODNB.

Dryden

Origins: John Dryden married 1551 Elizabeth Cope, whose father Sir John Cope had acquired Canons Ashby soon after the Dissolution. The Drydens acquired a Baronetcy in 1619. **First MP 1624. Another MP 1640 for Northamptonshire**. In the 18th century Canons Ashby passed by marriage to John Turner in 1791, and he took the name Dryden and was created a Baronet, which was merged with the Page-Turner title in 1874 (see above).

1. John Dryden – Huntingdonshire 1690-95 1699-1708

Seat: Canons Ashby, Northamptonshire (purch. 1538 by Copes by whom it passed by mar. to Drydens later in the 16th c., built c. 1550, add. c. 1570 and 1584, remod. 1708-17, NT 1980)
Title: Baronet 1619-1770; 1795-
Notes: The Huntingdon estates of the Drydens passed to a nephew, Robert Pigott of Chetwynd, Shropshire (see Pigott). The poet Dryden was a member of the family. Six in ODNB.

TURNER II

Origins: An apprentice vintner, son of an attorney, married his master's daughter and founded one of the leading families of King's Lynn in the 17th and 18th centuries. Kt 1684, Bt 1727.

1. Sir John Turner – King's Lynn 1679-81 1685-87 1689-1702

2. Sir Charles Turner 1 Bt – King's Lynn 1695-1738
3. Sir John Turner 2 Bt – King's Lynn 1712-13
4. Sir John Turner 3 Bt – King's Lynn 1739-74

Seat: Warham Hall, Norfolk (purch. 1709, sold 1785, demolished soon afterwards)
Title: Baronet 1727-80

TURNOR

Turnor

Origins: Country gentlemen in the 15th and 16th centuries. A royalist judge and Baron of the Exchequer during the Civil War. Did well after the Restoration. Kt 1663. Continued to expand estates in the 18th and early 19th centuries.

1. Edmund Turnor – Midhurst 1802-06
2. Christopher Turnor – S. Lincolnshire 1841-47
3. Edmund Turnor – S. Lincolnshire 1868-80

Seats: Stoke Rochford Hall, Lincolnshire (purch. 1665 and built a house, demolished late 18th c. and rebuilt, rebuilt again 1839-43, leased out as offices, still own estate); Panton Hall, Lincolnshire (built c. 1719, purch. and add. 1775, sold early 20th c., demolished 1964); Little Ponton Hall, Lincolnshire (built 17th c., acq. 18th c., became principal seat, part destroyed by fire c. 1900, still own); Snitterton Hall, Derbyshire (acq. by mar. 1723, leased out, sold 1910)
Estates: Bateman 20664 (E) 27513. Rubinstein – Edmund Turnor MP left £160,000 in probate in 1829. Held 18,000 acres 1920s.
Notes: Two in ODNB.

Ferne (Fearne)

Origins: Humble origins in the 16th c., granted arms 1580, mayor of Doncaster 1588, Kt 1603. **First MP 1604**, a lawyer and official. A bishop 1662. Estates passed via an heiress to the Turnors.

1. Robert Ferne – Ludgershall 1713-15

Seats: Snitterton Hall, Derbyshire (medieval, remod. 1632, purch. 1690s, passed by mar. to Turnors 1723); Locko House (Park), Derbyshire (built 17th c., purch. 1721, rebuilt c. 1725, sold 1747)
Notes: Two in ODNB.

TURNOUR (Turnor)

Earl of Winterton (1766- I)

Origins: The Turnors were an old Suffolk family raised to prominence by a successful lawyer and judge during the Restoration period. Speaker of the House of Commons 1661. **First MP 1614.** The granddaughter of Sir Edward Turnor married Joseph Garth, bringing with her Shilliglee Park, originally a Gore (London merchants) seat that passed to the Turnors by marriage in the early 18th century. The Garths took the name Turnour.

1. Sir Edward Turnor – Essex 1654 1656 1659 1660 Hertford 1661-71
2. Sir Edward Turnor – Orford 1701-09 1710-21
3. Edward Garth-Turnour 1 Earl of Winterton – Bramber 1761-69
4. Edward Turnour 6 Earl of Winterton – Horsham Div. Sussex 1904-18 Horsham & Worthing Div. Sussex 1918-45 Horsham Div. Sussex 1945-51

Seats: Hallingbury Place, Essex (purch. 1666, sold 1729); Shillinglee Park, Sussex (purch. 1641 by Gores, passed to Turnours by mar., rebuilt 1734-35, add. 1776-78, fire 1943, sold c. 1962, ruin, restored 1976, flats)
Estates: Bateman 5760 (E) 4883
Title: Baron Winterton 1761- I; Baron Turnour 1952- UK
Peers: {2 peers 1761-1800}
1 in Cabinet 1937-39
Notes: 6 Earl and three others in ODNB.

TWYSDEN (Twisden)

Twysden

Origins: The Twysdens were seated at Twysden in Kent from the end of the 13th century. Sheriff in the later 16th century. Kt 1603, Bt 1611. **First MP 1593. Two further MPs 1625-40, one for Kent.**

1. Sir William Twysden 3 Bt – Kent 1685-87 Appleby 1695-97

Seat: Royden Hall, Kent (medieval, acq. mid-15th c. by mar., rebuilt 1535, remod. late 17th c., sold 1834)
Estates: Worth £2,000 pa in the lifetime of the 3 Bt.
Title: Baronet 1611-
Notes: Three in ODNB.

Twisden

Origins: The Twisdens descended from a younger son of Sir William Twysden 1 Bt of Royden, who was a judge in the mid-17th century.

1. Sir Thomas Twisden 1 Bt – Maidstone 1646-48 1660
2. Sir Roger Twisden 2 Bt – Rochester 1689-90
3. Sir Thomas Twisden 3 Bt – Kent 1722-27
4. Sir Roger Twisden 5 Bt – Kent 1741-54

Seat: Bradbourne House (Hall), Kent (medieval, purch. 1656, rebuilt 1713-15, sold 1937)
Title: Baronet 1666-1841 or 1937
Notes: It is uncertain when the male line became extinct. One in ODNB.

TYRWHITT [Bourchier, Jones, Knyvet, Wilson]

Baron Berners (1455- E)

Origins: The Jones family was seated at Uckington, Shropshire since at least the reign of Elizabeth I. The **first MP 1625** was a merchant and Mayor of Shrewsbury 1638. One was Chief Justice of the Common Pleas (Kt) died 1692. The Jones estates passed to a nephew, Thomas Tyrwhitt of Netherlay House in 1782, and he took the additional name Jones. The Tyrwhitts were clergymen in the 18th century. Sir Henry Tyrwhitt 3 Bt married Emma Wilson Baroness Berners in her own right in 1853. Their son succeeded as 13 Baron Berners.

1. Sir Thomas Tyrwhitt-Jones 1 Bt – Weymouth & Melcombe Regis 1790-91 Denbigh 1797-1802 Athlone 1802-06 Shrewsbury 1807-11
2. Thomas Tyrwhitt – Okehampton 1796-1802 Portarlington 1802-06 Plymouth 1806-12
3. Sir Thomas Tyrwhitt-Jones 2 Bt – Bridgnorth 1818-20

Seats: Keythorpe Hall, Leicestershire (purch. by Wilsons 1646-7, fire mid-18th c. and house rebuilt by Lord Berners completed 1842, sold c. 1919); Netherlay House, Somerset; Stanley Hall, Shropshire (purch. by Huxley family, built 1642, devolved to Tyrwhitts by mar. to an heiress 1730, add. c. 1816, sold and much demolished c. 1923)
Estates: Bateman 6922 (E) 11757 and also at Stanley Hall 5889 (E & W) 8445. The 14 Baron left 600 acres, a country house, and £218,000 in 1950.
Title: Baronet 1808-
Peers: 2 peers 1917-45
Notes: 14 Baron and one other in ODNB.

Wilson

Origins: Rowland Wilson was a draper in London who purchased Keythorpe in the 1640s. His great-grandson Henry Wilson married Elizabeth Knyvet (heiress of Catherine Knyvet). She asserted her right to the barony of Berners, which had been in abeyance, as lineal heiress of Sir John Bouurchier 1 Baron Berners. She gained the title in 1720.

1. William Wilson – Ilchester 1761-68 Camelford 1768-74

Seat: Kirby Cane Hall, Norfolk (built 17th and 18th c., acq. c. 1800 by Lord Berners, remod. early 19th c., sold 1851)
Title: Baronet 1858-1921
Peers: 3 peers 1832-71
Notes: William Wilson MP died without male heirs and the Berners title passed by marriage to the Tyrwhitt-Jones family (see above). One in ODNB.

Knyvet (Knyvett, Knevett)

Origins: The Knyvets owned manorial land by the 12th century. The real founder was Lord Chancellor (Kt) 1372-77. **First MP 1397 for Huntingdonshire.** Baron 1455. **Six further MPs 1421-1607, three kts of the shire**. Ashwellthorpe passed to the Wilsons (see above) by marriage along with the Berners lineage.

1. Thomas Knyvet (de jure 7 Baron Berners) – Dunwich 1685-87 Eye 1689-90

Seat: Ashwellthorpe Hall, Norfolk (acq. by Thorpe family 1267, medieval house, passed to Knyvets by mar. 1422, rebuilt 1831-45, passed to Wilsons by mar., sold 1920)
Title: Baron Knyvet 1607-22 E
Notes: The Knyvets inherited the estates of the Green family in the 15th c. **Two MPs 1390-1410, both kts of the shire**. Ashwellthorpe came to the Knyvets from the Thorpe family, Barons Thorpe (1309). **Three MPs 1305-1407, all kts of the shire**. The last male died in 1422 when the estates passed to the Knyvets. Eight in ODNB

Bourchier

Origins: The Bourchiers were great lords between the reigns of Edward III and Henry VIII. Archbishop of Canterbury and Lord Chancellor in the 14th century. The son of William Bourchier Count of Eu (d. 1420) and a granddaughter of Edward III was created Baron Berners in 1455. An illegitimate son of 2 Lord Berners, established a line at Beningborough, Yorkshire. **First MP 1328. Four additional MPs 1472-1646 {2 Irish MPs 1585 and 1613}.**

1. Barrington Bourchier – Thirsk 1660
2. Thomas Bourchier – Malmesbury 1702-05

Seat: Beningborough Hall, Yorkshire (acq. by mar. 1544, built c. 1714-16, passed by non-blood inher. to Dawnays 1827)
Titles: Baron Berners 1455- ; Earl of Bath 1536-1654
Notes: The family became extinct in the male line in 1767 and in the female line in 1827. Beningborough passed by mar. to the Erles and eventually in 1827 to the 6 Viscount Downe (see Dawnay) in 1827. 1 Baron Bourchier and 2 Baron Berners and 1 and 2 Earls of Essex and 5 Earl of Bath and four others in ODNB.

UDNY *SCOTLAND*

Origins: The family is first mentioned in a charter of 1407. **First [MP 1645 for Aberdeenshire].**

1. John Udny – [Kintore 1681 1685-86]
2. John Udny – [Aberdeenshire 1703-07]

Seats: Udny Castle, Aberdeenshire (built 16th c., add. 17th c., abandoned c. 1775, repaired c. 1801, add. 1874, partly demolished 1960s, still own); Knockhall Castle, Aberdeenshire (built 1565, fire 1734, ruin)
Estates: Bateman 9225 (S) 9041
Notes: One in ODNB.

UNIACKE *IRELAND*

Uniacke

Origins: Burgesses of Youghal in the 16th century, Mayor 1556. Another was Mayor in 1723. He purchased landed estates. His eldest son married Elinor Fitzgerald, daughter and heiress of Garret Fitzgerald of Lisquinlan. Their eldest son was seated at Woodhouse, while a younger line lived at Lisquinlan. The Fitzgeralds were a cadet of the Geraldine dynasty (see Fitzgerald I). This branch was living in County Kerry by 1420.

1. Robert Uniacke – {Youghal 1777-1800}

Seat: Woodhouse, Waterford (purch. 1725, rebuilt early 19th c., passed by mar. to Beresfords mid-19th c.)
Estates: In 1878 the estate ran to 2,352 acres worth £1,907 pa.
Notes: The Uniacke property was confiscated in 1658 and restored in 1663. One in ODNB.

Uniacke-Fitzgerald

Origins: Cadet line (see above).

1. Robert Fitzgerald – {Youghal 1692-93 1695-99 Castlemartyr 1703-13}
2. Robert Uniacke-Fitzgerald – {County Cork 1797-1800} 1801-06
3. Sir Robert Uniacke-Penrose-Fitzgerald 1 Bt – Cambridge 1885-1906

Seats: Lisquinlan, Cork (acq. later 16th c., family departed 1850s, still owned late 19th c., now a ruin); Corkbeg Island (Corkbeg House), Cork (castle built 1396, acq. by mar. to Fitzgeralds and took additional name Fitzgerald 1715, new house 18th c., rebuilt mid-19th c., castle collapsed 1915, house sold 1945, demolished)
Estates: Bateman 6071 (I) 4865
Titles: Baronet 1801-17; 1896-1908
Notes: Male line extinct 1908. One in ODNB.

Uniacke

Origins: Descended from a brother of the Uniacke who married the Fitzgerald heiress. Sheriff 1776.

1. James Uniacke – {Youghal 1776-97}

Seat: Mount Uniacke, Cork (purch. early 18th c., burned 1923)
Estate: 1,559 (I) 972 in 1878. Held 7,754 acres worth £2,051 in 1854.

UPTON [Howard, Otway] *IRELAND & ENGLAND*

Viscount Templetown (1806- I)

Origins: The Uptons acquired estates in Devon in the 15th century. Merchant traders in the 17th century. **First English MP 1604. Two further MPs 1625-41**. A younger son emigrated to Antrim 1598 in a military capacity with Essex. **First Irish {MP 1634}.**

1. Arthur Upton – {Carrickfergus 1661-66 Antrim 1692-93 County Antrim 1695-99}
2. Clotworthy Upton – {Newton 1695-99 County Antrim 1703-25}
3. Thomas Upton – {Antrim 1713-14 County Antrim 1716-27 Londonderry 1727-33}
4. John Upton – {County Antrim 1725-40}
5. Arthur Upton – {Carrickfergus 1742-68}
6. John Upton 1 Viscount Templetown – Bury St. Edmunds 1803-12
7. Fulke Greville Upton Howard – Castle Rising 1808-32
8. Arthur Upton – Bury St. Edmunds 1818-26

9. George Upton 3 Viscount Templetown – Antrim 1859-63

Seats: Castle Upton (aka Castle Norton), Antrim (built 1610 c., purch. 1625, remod. 1783-89, remod. 1837, sold early 20th c.); Levens Park, Westmorland (medieval, rebuilt c. 1580-86, add. c. 1690s, acq. by mar. 1817, add. 1820, eventually passed back to the Bagots in 1883)
Estates: Bateman 24769 (I) 19217 and 9252 (E) 5300
Title: Baron Templetown 1776- I
Peers: {2 peers 1777-85 1792-1800} 2 Irish Rep peers 1866-90 1894-1939
Notes: The daughter and heiress of the 11 Earl of Suffolk married Richard Bagot and brought the Levens Park, Westmorland estate in 1817 to the Uptons (see Howard I). Two in ODNB.

Upton

Origins: Cousins of the Viscounts Templetown who remained in England succeeded by marriage of 1693 to the estates of the Otways, Westmorland gentry from the Tudor period onwards (see Cave).

1. John Otway – Preston 1667-81
2. John Upton – Dartmouth 1679-81
3. John Upton – Westmorland 1761-68

Seats: Ingmire Hall, Yorkshire (Otway seat, enlarged 1838, sold 1922, burned 1928, part demolished); Middleton Hall, Westmorland (medieval, add. 16th c., acq. 17th c., remod. 1647 and 1670, ruin in 18th c.); Beckside Hall, Westmorland (Otways acq. early 16th c., resident 17th c., became a farm house)
Estates: Rubinstein – John Upton left £100,000 in probate in 1832. His landed estate passed to the Cottrell-Dormers later in the 18th c. (Bateman 5500 (E) 5800).

URQUHART [Pollard] *SCOTLAND & IRELAND*

Urquhart

Origins: The Urquharts traced themselves back to Adam (*Country Life*, 37, p. 115). Well entrenched in landed society by the 14th century. Sheriffs of Cromarty since 1365. **First [MP 1605 for Cromartyshire]. Two further [MPs 1617-40 both for shires].** The family wealth shrank in the 17th century until Captain John Urquhart (d. 1756), made a fortune as a merchant and planter and repurchased 1739-41 estates alienated earlier.

1. Sir John Urquhart – [Inverness-shire 1661-63]
2. Adam Urquhart – [Aberdeenshire 1665 1667 1669-74 1678]

3. Sir Alexander Urquhart – [Banffshire 1667]
4. Thomas Urquhart – [Cromarty Burgh 1670]
5. John Urquhart – [Cromartyshire 1693]
6. John Urquhart – [Dornoch Burgh 1703-07]

Seats: Craigston Castle, Aberdeenshire (acq. 1597, built 1603-07, add. 1845, still own); Meldrum House, Aberdeenshire (descended for 750 years through Meldrum, Seton, Urquhart, and Duff families, for sale 1991); Cromarty Castle, Cromartyshire (acq. mid-14th c., built 1470, add. 1632, sold 1760s, pulled down 1772)
Estates: Bateman 4014 (S) 3118 and 5837 (S) 6707. 4,200 acres in 1996.
Notes: The male line died out in 1837. An heiress mar. 1846 a Pollard who took the additional name Urquhart, see below. One in ODNB.

Pollard

Origins: A Pollard accompanied the Earl of Essex to Ireland in 1598 as a captain. Acquired estates soon afterwards. Sheriff 1692. Mary Urquhart, the family heiress married in 1846 William Pollard of Castle Pollard.

1. Dillon Pollard – {County Westmeath 1692-93}
2. Walter Pollard – {Fore 1695-99 1703-13}
3. William Pollard – County Westmeath 1852-57 1859-71

Seats: Castle Pollard (Kinturk, Rathyoung), Westmeath (acq. c. 1600, built 18th c., remod. 1821, sold 1935, institution); Craigston Castle, Aberdeenshire (acq. by mar. 1846, and took name Urquhart, still own)
Estates: Bateman 6093 (I) 4782
Notes: One in ODNB.

Urquhart

Origins: Cadet line 15th century.

1. Robert Urquhart – Elginshire 1708-10
2. Duncan Urquhart – Inverness Burghs 1737-41

Seat: Burdsyards, Elginshire (acq. early 15th c., sold 1795)
Estates: Worth £620 pa in 1730.
Notes: The estates were sold by the 13th laird in 1795.

Urquhart

Origins: The MP below claimed to be the Chief of Clan Urquhart after the extinction of the main line in 1837.

1. David Urquhart – Stafford 1847-52

Seats: Mollands House, Perthshire (resident 19th c.); Braelangwell, Cromartyshire (built late 18th c., sold 1839)

VACHELL (Fachell)

Origins: The founder of the family was a wool merchant c. 1300. **The first MP 1324 for Berkshire** was a lawyer who purchased estates**. Five additional MPs 1388-1645, most for Reading**. Kt 14th c.

1. Tanfield Vachell – Reading 1701-05

Seat: Coley Park (aka Vachell House), Berkshire (acq. early to mid 14th c., built c. 1555, remod. c. 1651, sold 1727, demolished and rebuilt 1802)
Notes: The family experienced a financial crisis during the life of the last MP.

VANDELEUR *IRELAND*

Origins: The Vandeleur to emigrate to Ireland was the son of a Dutch merchant who acquired land in Clare in the 1630s and 1640s. He was a maltster and tanner, and his son was a Collector of Taxes in Limerick. High Sheriff of Clare 1664.

1. Crofton Vandeleur – {Ennis 1768-76}
2. Thomas Pakenham Vandeleur – {Granard 1790-97}
3. John Vandeleur – {Granard 1790-97}
4. John Vandeleur – {Carlow 1790-97 Ennis 1798-1800} 1801-02
5. Crofton Vandeleur – {Granard 1798-1800}
6. Crofton Vandeleur – Clare 1859-74

Seats: Kilrush House, Clare (acq. and built 1687, rebuilt early 19th c., fire 1897, ruin); Brickhill, Clare (owned 17th c., passed in 18th c. to Lysaghts); Cahircon (Cahercon), Clare (built 18th c., purch. 1899, sold 1921)
Estates: Bateman 20206 (I) 11596
1 Ld Lt 19th-20th
Notes: One in ODNB.

VANE (Fane) [Aubrey, Fletcher, Luther, Powlett, Stewart, Tempest] *ENGLAND & IRELAND*

Duke of Cleveland (1833-1891 UK)

Origins: Yeomen in the 14th century, Kt 1365, Chamberlain to the Duke of Buckingham at Tonbridge Castle 1456. Richard Fane, the son of John Vane or Fane (both spellings used), had a grandson who married 1574 a Neville heiress, who brought Mereworth with her, for whose son the Earldom of Westmorland was revived. Richard's younger brother, John, had descendents who formed several great estates through marriage, politics, court favor, and inheritance. The Vanes of Fairlawne settled at Raby Castle (purch. 1626) in the reign of Charles I, although they also kept property in Kent. The Dukedom of Cleveland was created for the mistress of Charles II. Her grandson, the 3 Duke of Cleveland (surname Fitzroy, said to be worth £100,000 pa), died without male heirs in 1774 and left his estates to his sister, who married the 1 Earl of Darlington. The Dukedom was revived for the Vanes in 1833. The 3 Duke succeeded to his mother's estates and took the name Powlett; his wife was the heiress of the last Duke of Bolton (see Powlett). He resumed the name Vane on succeeding to the Dukedom. The 1 Duke of the second creation also succeeded to half of the vast Pulteney estates on the extinction of that family. **First MP 1547. Three further MPs 1593-59.**

1. Christopher Vane 1 Baron Barnard – County Durham 1675-79 Boroughbridge 1689-90
2. Thomas Vane – County Durham 1675-79
3. Lionel Vane – County Durham 1698-1702
4. William Vane 1 Viscount Vane – County Durham 1708-10 Steyning 1727-34 Kent 1734
5. Henry Vane 1 Earl of Darlington – Launceston 1726-27 St. Mawes 1727-41 Ripon 1741-47 County Durham 1747-53
6. Henry Vane 2 Earl of Darlington – Downton 1749-53 County Durham 1753-58
7. Raby Vane – County Durham 1758-61 Carlisle 1761-68
8. Frederick Vane – County Durham 1761-74
9. William Vane 1 Duke of Cleveland – Totnes 1788-90 Winchelsea 1790-92
10. Henry Vane 2 Duke of Cleveland – County Durham 1812-15 Winchelsea 1816-18 Tregony 1818-26 Totnes 1826-30 Saltash 1830-31 S. Shropshire 1832-42
11. William Vane Powlett 3 Duke of Cleveland – Winchelsea 1812-15 County Durham 1815-31 St. Ives 1846-52 Ludlow 1852-57
12. Henry Vane Powlett 4 Duke of Cleveland – S. Durham 1841-59 Hastings 1859-64

Seats: Raby Castle, Durham (medieval, purch. 1626, add. c. 1626, remod. c. 1738-60, 1781-85, 1845-49, 1864, still own); Fairlawne, Kent (purch. c. 1630s, rebuilt c. 1680s,

remod. 1739-42, passed out of family 1789); Selaby Hall, Durham (acq. 1626, still own); Battle Abbey, Sussex (medieval, purch. 1857, rebuilt c. 1858, sold 1901)
Estates: Bateman 104,194 (E) 97398. The 1 Duke left over £3,000,000 in non-landed assets. Worth £40,000,000 with 53,000 acres in 1990.
Titles: Baron Barnard 1698- E; Viscount Vane 1720-89 I; Viscount Barnard and Earl of Darlington 1754-1891; Marquess of Cleveland 1827-91 UK; The original Dukedom of Cleveland 1670-1774 E
Peers: 12 peers 1683-1774 1698-1758 1765-1945 {2 peers 1720-89}
5 Lds Lt 18th, 19th, 20th
4 KG 18th, 19th
Notes: 1 and 2 Earls of Darlington and 2 Duke of Cleveland of the 1st creation and 1 Duke of 2nd cr. and four others in ODNB.

Fletcher Vane

Origins: The Fletchers were wealthy Cockermouth merchants in the later 16th century (Hutton estate purchased 1606). Sir George Vane, brother of Sir Henry Vane of Raby, established two lines. One inherited Hutton-in-the-Forest by marriage to an heiress of the Fletcher Baronets. Included in this list are two Fletcher MPs not descended from the Vane line who inherited Clea Hall and for whom the Fletcher Baronetcy was revived. The 1 Bt of this creation was Chairman of the East India Company 1782 and a nabob.

1. Sir George Fletcher 2 Bt – Cumberland 1661-79 1681 1689-1700
2. Sir Henry Fletcher 3 Bt – Cockermouth 1689-90
3. George Fletcher – Cockermouth 1698-1701 Cumberland 1701-02 1705-08
4. Sir Henry Fletcher 1 Bt – Cumberland 1768-1806
5. Sir Frederick Fletcher Vane 2 Bt – Winchelsea 1792-94 Carlisle 1796-1802 Winchelsea 1806-07
6. Sir Henry Aubrey-Fletcher 4 Bt – Horsham 1880-85 Mid Sussex 1885-1910
7. William Fletcher Vane 1 Baron Inglewood – Westmorland 1945-1964

Seats: Hutton-in-the-Forest, Cumberland (built 14th c., purch. 1606, add. c. 1641-45, remod. c. 1680, passed by mar. to Vanes 1741, add. 1826-30, and 1860, still own); Clea Hall, Cumberland (built early 17th c., acq. by mar. from Musgraves 17th c., declined to a farm house 19th c.); Armathwaite Hall (Castle), Cumberland (built early 16th c., purch. 1796, rebuilt c. 1800, sold 1850); Cockermouth Hall, Cumberland (orig. seat of the Fletchers, built mid-16th c., sold late 18th c., demolished c. 1960)
Estates: Bateman 7194 (E) 5102
Title: Baron Inglewood 1963- UK; Baronet 1640-1712; 1786-1934; 1782-
Notes: Richard Fletcher Vane, 2 Baron Inglewood, was an MEP before succeeding to the peerage. 2 Baron Inglewood was an MEP. Two in ODNB.

Marquess of Londonderry (1816- I)

Origins: Another descendent of George Vane (see above), Henry Vane 1 Bt (1782), married the heiress Frances Tempest, and their son inherited large estates in the north of England, taking the name Vane-Tempest. The Tempests held land by 1100. **First MP 1404 for Yorkshire. Four further MPs 1529-1656 (of Bracewell, Yorkshire and Tong Hall, Yorkshire, Bt 1664-1819).** The 2 Baronet's daughter married the 3 Marquess of Londonderry and the family became Vane-Tempest-Stewart. The Stewarts emigrated to Ireland from Scotland and were granted land at Ballylawn in Donegal in 1630. Alexander Stewart, a Belfast and London merchant, married the heiress of an Alderman of Londonderry and nabob. Mount Stewart was purchased with the proceeds of linen manufacturing and the Vane-Tempest marriage in 1744.

1. John Tempest – County Durham 1675-79
2. William Tempest – Durham 1679 1681 1690-95
3. John Tempest – County Durham 1707-08
4. John Tempest – Durham 1742-68
5. Alexander Stewart – {Londonderry 1760}
6. John Tempest – Durham 1768-94
7. Robert Stewart 1 Marquess of Londonderry – {County Down 1771-83}
8. Robert Stewart 2 Marquess of Londonderry – {County Down 1790-1800} Tregony 1794-96 Orford 1796-97 County Down 1801-05 Boroughbridge 1806 Plympton Erle 1806-12 County Down 1812-21 Orford 1821-22
9. Sir Henry Vane-Tempest 2 Bt – Durham 1794-1800 County Durham 1807-13
10. Charles Stewart 3 Marquess of Londonderry – {Thomastown 1800 County Londonderry 1800} 1801-14
11. Alexander Stewart – County Londonderry 1814-18
12. Alexander Stewart – County Londonderry 1818-30
13. Frederick Vane-Tempest-Stewart 4 Marquess of Londonderry – County Down 1826-52
14. George Vane-Tempest-Stewart 5 Marquess of Londonderry – N. Durham 1847-54
15. Lord Adolphus Vane-Tempest – Durham 1852-53 N. Durham 1854-64
16. Charles Vane-Tempest-Stewart 6 Marquess of Londonderry – County Down 1878-84
17. Charles Vane-Tempest-Stewart 7 Marquess of Londonderry – Maidstone 1906-15
18. Edward Vane-Tempest-Stewart 8 Marquess of Londonderry – County Down 1931-45

Seats: Wynyard Park, Durham (medieval, Tempest seat purch. 1742, built 1780s, add. 1803-06, passed to Stewarts by mar. 1819, rebuilt 1822-41, fire 1841 and rebuilt, sold 1987); Mount Stewart, Down (tower house 16th c., Stewarts purch. and built 1744, add. c. 1800, add. 1846, NT 1977); Brancepeth Castle, Durham (medieval, purch. 1776 by

Tempests, sold 1796); Seaham Hall, Durham (built 1791-92, purch. 1821, add. c. 1830, family departed 1922, donated to County Council 1927, now hotel); Ards, Donegal (old house, purch. 1781, rebuilt c. 1830, sold c. 1925, demolished c. 1965); Killynether House, Down (Stewart estate land, built 1875-76, leased or sold by early 20th c., govt. use from 1940, demolished 1966); Plas Machynlleth (Greenfields), Montgomeryshire (built 17th c., acq. by mar. 1850, remod. 1853, donated to County Council c. 1920-30s)
Estates: Bateman 108412 (E, W, & I) 120,688
Titles: Baron Londonderry 1789- I; Viscount Castlereagh 1795- I; Earl of Londonderry 1796- I; Baron Stewart 1814- UK; Earl Vane 1823- UK
Peers: 1 Irish Rep peer 1801-21 6 peers 1814-1945
6 Lds Lt 19th, 20th
3 in Cabinet 1798-1809 1812-22 1886-89 1900-05 1928-29 1931-35
4 KG 18th, 19th
2 KP 19th
Notes: The 2 Marquess of Londonderry spent £60,000 on one election for County Down. The Tempest family has an entry and one other and the 1, 2, 3, 6, and 7 Marquesses and one other in ODNB.

<u>Earl of Westmorland</u> (1624- E)

Origins: For ancestry see under Duke of Cleveland above. The family was called either Fane or Vane until the 17th century. Sir Thomas Fane married Mary Neville, *suo jure* Baroness Le Despencer (cr. 1264, Barony called out of abeyance in her favor with precedence of 1624). Their son was created Earl of Westmorland. He married 1599 the daughter and heiress of Sir Anthony Mildmay of Apethorpe. **First MP 1559. Six additional MPs 1589-1640, three for Kent.** The mid-18th c. MPs Francis and Thomas Fane were businessmen in Bristol, who purchased Brympton in 1730 and Thomas succeeded to the Earldom in 1762.

1. Charles Fane 3 Earl of Westmorland – Peterborough 1660-66
2. Vere Fane 4 Earl of Westmorland – Peterborough 1671-79 Kent 1679-81 1689-91
3. Thomas Fane – Maidstone 1679-81
4. John Fane 7 Earl of Westmorland – Hythe 1708-11 Kent 1715-22 Buckingham 1727-34
5. Mildmay Fane – Kent 1715
6. Francis Fane – Taunton 1727-41 Petersfield 1741-47 Ilchester 1747-54 Lyme Regis 1754-57
7. Thomas Fane 8 Earl of Westmorland – Lyme Regis 1753-62
8. John Fane 9 Earl of Westmorland – Lyme Regis 1762-71
9. Henry Fane – Lyme Regis 1772-1802
10. Thomas Fane – Lyme Regis 1784-1806
11. Sir Henry Fane – Lyme Regis 1802-18 Sandwich 1829-30 Hastings 1830-31
12. John Fane 11 Earl of Westmorland – Lyme Regis 1806-16

13. John Fane – Lyme Regis 1816-32
14. Vere Fane – Lyme Regis 1818-26
15. Henry Sutton Fane – Lyme Regis 1826-32
16. Henry Hamlyn-Fane – S. Hampshire 1865-68

Seats: Apethorpe House (Hall), Northamptonshire (medieval, rebuilt 1490s, add. 16th c., acq. by mar. 1617, add. 1620s, remod. 1693, remod. 1846, sold 1904); Mereworth Castle, Kent (medieval, acq. by mar. 1574, new house built 1720-30, - it is reported the 7 Earl spent £100,000 on Mereworth over 40 years - Hussey, *English Country Houses: Early Georgian 1715-1760*, 58 - passed to Dashwoods by mar. 1762); Fulbeck Hall, Lincolnshire (acq. 1622, built later 17th c., rebuilt 1775, add. 1784 and 1813, still own); Avon Tyrrell, Hampshire (acq. by mar. later 18th c., passed by mar. to Manners-Suttons 1885); Brympton d'Evercy, Somerset (medieval house, built c. 1520s, rebuilt 1650s/60s c., add. 1722-23, purch. 1730, leased to school 1966-74, sold 1992); Burston, Kent (built 16th c., purch. c. 1560s, passed by inher. to Dashwoods 1781, declined to a farm house 18th c.); Clovelly Court, Devon (medieval, inher. by mar. 19th c., fire 1944, partly demolished, family still own estate); Badsell, Kent (medieval, acq. by mar. 1511, rebuilt c. 1600, remod. 17th c., passed by inher. to Dashwoods 1781, sold 1917)
Estates: Bateman 17581 (E) 18705. Worth c. £3,000 pa in 1612.
Titles: Baron Le Despencer 1264-1762 E; Baron Catherlough 1733-62 I
Peers: 12 peers 1660-93 1704-74 1780-1945
5 Lds Lt 17th, 18th, 19th
2 in Cabinet 1719-35 1789-95 1798-1827
1 KG 18th-19th
Notes: 1, 2, 7, 9, 10, 11, and 12 Earls and eleven others in ODNB.

<u>Viscount Fane</u> (1718-66 I)

Origins: A great-grandson of the 1 Earl of Westmorland was created Viscount Fane.

1. George Fane – Callington 1640-43 Wallingford 1661-63
2. Sir Henry Fane – Reading 1689-98
3. Charles Fane 1 Viscount Fane – {Killibegs 1715-18}
4. Charles Fane 2 Viscount Fane – Tavistock 1734-47 Reading 1754-61

Seat: Basildon Park, Berkshire (purch. 1654, sold 1771)
Estates: Property in Ireland acquired from the Countess of Bath who settled some of the Limerick estates of the Bourchiers on the Fanes just prior to 1668.
Peers: {2 peers 1725-66}

Fane

Origins: Descended from a grandson of the 1 Earl of Westmorland. This line acquired Wormsley by marriage to a Scrope heiress.

1. Henry Fane – Lyme Regis 1757-77
2. Francis Fane – Lyme Regis 1777-80 Dorchester 1790-1807
3. John Fane – Oxfordshire 1796-1824
4. John Fane – Oxfordshire 1824-31
5. John Fane – Oxfordshire 1862-68

Seats: Wormsley House, Oxfordshire (acq. by Scropes late 16th c., inher. from Scropes 1720, rebuilt 18th c., sold 1984); Myles's (Manor House), Essex (acq. by mar. 1786, rebuilt 18th c., demolished 1837)
Estates: Bateman 5288 (E) 7217

Luther

Origins: John Luther MP, a barrister inherited wealth from a maternal grandfather, court physician to Queen Anne, left his estates to his sister's son, Francis Fane MP 1777-1807 (see above).

1. John Luther – Essex 1763-84

Seat: Myles's (Manor House), Essex (medieval, acq. late 16th c., passed to Fanes by inher. 1786)
Estates: Rubinstein – Levina Luther, wife of the MP, left £100,000 in probate in 1822.

VANNECK

Baron Huntingfield (1796- I)

Origins: Founded by a merchant in London who arrived from Holland in the 1690s.

1. Sir Gerald Vanneck 2 Bt – Dunwich 1768-90
2. Joshua Vanneck 1 Baron Huntingfield – Dunwich 1790-1816
3. Joshua Vanneck 2 Baron Huntingfield – Dunwich 1816-19
4. William Vanneck 5 Baron Huntingfield – Eye Div. Suffolk 1923-29

Seat: Heveningham Hall, Suffolk (built c. 1700, purch. 1752, rebuilt 1778-84, fire 1949, restored, sold 1970, fire, restored)
Estates: Bateman 16869 (E) 22177

Title: Baronet 1751-
Peers: {1 peer 1796-1800}
Notes: Sir Peter Vanneck, son of the 5 Baron, was Lord Mayor of London 1977 and MEP 1979-89.

VANSITTART [Marwood, Neale, Turner]

Baron Bexley (1823-51 UK) and Baron Vansittart (1941-57 UK)

Origins: A Dutch merchant family that moved to Danzig and then settled in London after 1674. They gained a large fortune in the Baltic trade. Director of the East India Company and nabobs. Purchased estates in the early 18th century. The progenitor of the parliamentary family was Arthur Vansittart of Clewer and Moat Park, Kent. A senior line was seated at Shottesbrooke Park. A younger son married Viscountess Newcommen in her own right. Their daughter succeeded to Kirkleatham Hall through her marriage to Sir Charles Turner Bt. Another younger son became Baron Bexley. A third son was seated at Bisham Abbey.

1. Arthur Vansittart – Berkshire 1757-74
2. Henry Vansittart – Reading 1768-70
3. George Vansittart – Berkshire 1784-1812
4. Nicholas Vansittart 1 Baron Bexley – Hastings 1796-1802 Old Sarum 1802-12 East Grinstead 1812 Harwich 1812-23
5. Arthur Vansittart – Windsor 1804-06
6. George Vansittart – Berkshire 1852-59
7. William Vansittart – Windsor 1857-65

Seats: Shottesbrooke Park, Berkshire (built late 16th c., purch. 1716, rebuilt early 18th c., remod. early 19th c., part demolished 1950s, descendents still own); Bisham Abbey, Berkshire (medieval, rebuilt 1550s, add. 17th c., purch 1780, passed to the Neales 1885 who took the add. name Vansittart, still owned 1920s, sold, conference and sports center); Foots Cray Place, Kent (built 16th c., new house 1754, purch. 1821, sold late 19th c., fire 1949, demolished); Foxley, Berkshire (purch. 1765, resident in 19th c.); Kirkleatham Hall, Yorkshire (built c. 1765, acq. by mar. 1812, passed by mar. to Newcommens 1848, abandoned 1948, demolished 1954); Allesley Park, Warwickshire (built late 17th c., inher. by mar. 1805 from Neales, sold 1870, fire 1897, demolished 1907)
Estates: Bateman 7855 (E) 18728. Rubinstein – Emilia Vansittart left £120,000 in probate 1819.
Peers: 2 peers 1823-51 1941-45
1 in Cabinet 1805 1812-28
Notes: 1 Baron Bexley and 1 Baron Vansittart and six others in ODNB.

Turner

Origins: Country gentlemen by the 17th century with lead mining interests. The elder son of the purchaser of Kirkleatham, was a barrister. A younger son, who launched the line of MPs was a successful woolen draper in the City of London, Lord Mayor 1689. Estates passed to the Vansittarts (see above).

1. Sir William Turner – London 1690-93
2. Cholmley Turner – Northallerton 1715-22 Yorkshire 1727-41 1742-47
3. Sir Charles Turner 1 Bt – York 1768-83
4. Sir Charles Turner 2 Bt – Kingston-upon-Hull 1796-1802

Seat: Kirkleatham (Kirk Leatham), Yorkshire (purch. 1623, built mid-17th c., remodel. 1760s, passed Vansittarts 1812)
Title: Baronet 1782-1810

Marwood

Origins: Entered the gentry in the 16th century by means that are unclear. The Marwood heiress of Busby Hall married Cholmley Turner of Kirkleatham (see above).

1. Sir George Marwood 1 Bt – Malton 1658-59 Northallerton 1660
2. Sir Henry Marwood 2 Bt – Northallerton 1685-87

Seat: Busby Hall, Yorkshire (purch. 1587, still own)
Estates: Bateman 2938 (E) 3636
Title: Baronet 1660-1740

Neale

Origins: Coventry businessmen in the 17th century. One married a landed heiress. Allesley Park passed in 1805 to Edward Vansittart (see above), by maarriage.

1. Henry Neale – Buckinghamshire 1696-98
2. John Neale – Chipping Wycombe 1722 Coventry 1722-34 1737-41

Seats: Allesley Park, Warwickshire (purch. 1692, built late 17th c., passed to Vansittarts 1805); Cherington Park, Gloucestershire (purch. 1724, passed to Turners by mar. 1746, sold 1766, demolished c. 1955); Dean, Bedfordshire (purch. 1545, sold c. 1702); Dinton, Buckinghamshire (acq. mid-17th c., sold 1695)

VAUGHAN I *WALES*

Earl of Lisburne (1776- I)

Origins: Among the first rank of ancient Welsh families, almost without parallel in uninterrupted possession of their original estate, acquired by marriage in the 13th c. Lord Chief Justice of the Common Pleas 1668.

1. Sir John Vaughan – Cardiganshire 1628 1640-45 1661-68
2. Edward Vaughan – Cardiganshire 1669-79 1679-81
3. John Vaughan 1 Viscount Lisburne – Cardiganshire 1694-98
4. John Vaughan 2 Viscount Lisburne – Cardiganshire 1727-34
5. Wilmot Vaughan 1 Earl of Lisburne – Cardiganshire 1755-61 Berwick-on-Tweed 1765-68 Cardiganshire 1768-96
6. Sir John Vaughan – Berwick-on-Tweed 1774-95 {St. Johnstown 1776-83}
7. John Vaughan 3 Earl of Lisburne – Cardigan 1796-1818
8. Ernest Vaughan 4 Earl of Lisburne – Cardiganshire 1854-59

Seats: Trawscoed (Crosswood, Trawsgoed), Cardiganshire (acq. by mar. 13th c., add. mid-16th c., rebuilt mid-17th c., add. 1760s and 1890s, sold 1947, repurch. 1996 and still own some of the original estate); Mamhead Park, Devon (old house, rebuilt c. 1700, acq. by mar. 1754, sold 1822); Buncrana Castle, Donegal (purch. 1716 and new house built, sold c. 1840)
Estates: Bateman 42761 (W) 13676. Worth £1,200 pa in later 17th c. Owned 2,000 acres in 2001. Additional income from lead and zinc mines.
Title: Viscount Lisburne 1695- I
Peers: {3 peers 1695-1721 1764-1800}
5 Lds Lt 18th, 19th, 20th
Notes: The family was in continuous residence at Trawscoed for six centuries until 1947 when it became the headquarters of the agricultural advisory service for Wales (Morgan, *A Welsh House and Its Family*). Two in ODNB.

VAUGHAN II [Nanney] *WALES*

Vaughan

Origins: Medieval family. Married an heiress to Corsygedol (a ward of Llewellyn the Great). Supported the Lancastrian cause. **First MP 1545 for Merioneth. Another MP 1628, for the county**.

1. Richard Vaughan – Merioneth 1701-34
2. William Vaughan – Merioneth 1734-68
3. Evan Vaughan – Merioneth 1774-91

4. Sir Robert Vaughan 2 Bt – Merioneth 1792-1836

Seats: Corsygedol (Cors-y-Gedol) Hall, Merionethshire (acq. by mar. early 13th c., rebuilt 1576-99, passed to Mostyns by mar. 1791); Nannau Hall (House), Merionethshire (acq. by mar. 1733, partly demolished c. 1965, sold 1966); Plas Hengwrt (Hen Gwrt), Merionethshire (medieval, acq. by mar. 16th c., passed to Mostyns by mar. 1791, sold 1850, fire 1885, rebuilt 1892)
Estates: Bateman 16588 (W) 4520
Title: Baronet 1791-1859
1 Ld Lt 18th
Notes: The estates were divided among numerous heirs on the extinction of the Baronetcy 1859. One in ODNB.

Nanney (Nannau)

Origins: Seated in Merionethshire since the 13th century, warriors and gentry. **First MP 1593 for Merioneth.** Janet Nanney, daughter and heiress of the last male Nanney, married in 1719 Robert Vaughan 1 Bt of Corsygedol, who succeeded to Nannau Hall in 1733.

1. Hugh Nanney – Merioneth 1695-1701

Seat: Nannau Hall (House), Merionethshire (medieval, acq. 13th c., rebuilt 1612, rebuilt 1693, passed to Vaughans 1733)

VAUGHAN III *WALES*

Earl of Carbery (1628-1713 I)

Origins: Illegitimate descendents of the medieval Princes of Powys. Settled in Carmarthenshire where they acquired estates in the 16th century. **First MP 1558 (Carmarthenshire 1572). Five additional MPs 1572-1644, four for the county**.

1. Francis Vaughan Lord Vaughan – Carmarthenshire 1661-67
2. John Vaughan 3 Earl of Carbery – Carmarthen 1661-79 Carmarthenshire 1679-81 1685-87
3. Sir Henry Vaughan – Carmarthenshire
4. Altham Vaughan – Carmarthen 1679-81
5. Richard Vaughan – Carmarthen 1685-87 1689-1724
6. John Vaughan – Carmarthenshire 1745-54
7. John Vaughan – Carmarthenshire 1779-84

Seats: Golden Grove, Carmarthenshire (acq. c. 1500, passed to Earls of Cawdor by mar. c. 1700, see Campbell I); Derwydd, Carmarthenshire (acq. by mar. 1610, passed to Stepneys by mar. 18th c., sold 1990s)
Estates: See Welsh property of the Earl of Cawdor (Campbell I) Golden Grove estate in 1980s was 21,000 acres.
Titles: Baron Vaughan 1621-1713 I; Baron Vaughan 1643-1713 E
Peer: 1 peer 1660-86
2 Lds Lt 17th, 18th, 19th
Notes: The last John Vaughan MP left Golden Grove to the Earl of Cawdor even though they were not related (see Campbell I). 1, 2, and 3 Earls and three others in ODNB.

VEITCH *SCOTLAND*

Origins: Lairds by 1296. **First [MP 1630 for Peeblesshire]. One further [MP 1643-48 for the county].**

1. John Veitch – [Peeblesshire 1669-74 1678]

Seat: Dawyck Castle, Peebleshire (built 13th c., acq. 1491, sold c. 1691)

VERNER *IRELAND*

Origins: To Ireland early-mid 17th c. The first MP was a self-made man, an attorney, land agent, and local official who gained an estate worth £4,000 pa. Sheriff 1800.

1. James Verner – {Dungannon 1794-1800}
2. Sir William Verner 1 Bt – County Armagh 1832-68
3. Sir William Verner 2 Bt – County Armagh 1868-73
4. Sir Edward Verner 4 Bt – Lisburn 1863-73 County Armagh 1873-80

Seat: Church Hill (Churchill), Armagh (old house, acq. mid-18th c., rebuilt c. 1830, estate and house sold between 1902 and 1927, demolished 1928)
Estates: Bateman 24257 (I) 13138
Title: Family bankrupt through mismanagement or gambling late 19th c. Baronet 1846-

VERNEY [Calvert, Heath, Peyto]

<u>Earl Verney</u> (1743-91 I)

Origins: The Verneys began with a London merchant, Lord Mayor 1465. They were seated at Claydon by the later 15th century. High Sheriff c. 1500. **First MP 1459, for London. Four additional MPs 1491-1642, three for Buckinghamshire**. The 1

Viscount, son of the 1 Baronet, was bound as an apprentice and spent 12 years in Aleppo as a merchant before returning as a London trader who served on the boards of the Bank of England and the East India Company. On the extinction of the Earldom in 1791 an heiress was created Baroness Fermanagh. Her estates passed 1810 to her half-sister by her mother's second marriage to a Calvert. On the death of this heiress in 1827 Claydon passed to Sir Harry Calvert 2 Bt, a cousin, who took the name Verney.

1. Sir Ralph Verney 1 Bt – Aylesbury 1640-45 Buckingham 1681 1685-87 1689-90
2. John Verney 1 Viscount Fermanagh – Buckinghamshire 1710-15 Amersham 1715-17
3. Ralph Verney 1 Earl Verney – Amersham 1717-27 Wendover 1741-52
4. Ralph Verney 2 Earl Verney – Wendover 1753-61 Carmarthen 1761-68 Buckinghamshire 1768-84 1790-91
5. Sir Harry Calvert Verney 2 Bt – Buckingham 1832-41 Bedford 1847-52 Buckingham 1857-74 1880-85
6. Frederick Calvert – Aylesbury 1850-51
7. Sir Edmund Verney 3 Bt – N. Buckinghamshire 1885-86 1889-91
8. Frederick Verney – N. Buckinghamshire 1906-10
9. Sir Harry Verney 4 Bt – N. Buckinghamshire 1910-18

Seat: Claydon House, Buckinghamshire (medieval, purch. 1463, rebuilt 1620, rebuilt 1754-82, much demolished 1792 and 1860, NT 1956)
Estates: Bateman 13758 (E & W) 17608. Worth £1,078 pa in 1688. Bankrupt later 18th c.
Titles: Baron Verney and Viscount Fermanagh 1703-91 I; Baroness Fermanagh 1792-1810 I; Baronet 1661-1791; 1818-
Peers: {3 peers 1703-91}
Notes: The 1 Viscount Fermanagh was an apprentice and merchant and continued to engage in business even after becoming heir to the Verney title and estates. The 2 Earl died bankrupt 1791, having fled abroad to France to escape his creditors. 1 Viscount Fermanagh 2 Earl and eight others in ODNB.

<u>Calvert</u>

Origins: The Calverts were a brewing family who purchased estates in the late 17th century. They remained brewers into the 19th century, Lord Mayor of London 1748. A considerable cousinage developed all of whom are listed here. They inherited the Verney estates in 1827 (see above).

1. Felix Calvert – Reading 1713-16
2. Sir William Calvert – London 1742-54 Old Sarum 1755-61
3. John Calvert – Wendover 1754-61 Hertford 1761-80 1784-1802 Tamworth 1780-84
4. Nicolson Calvert – Tewkesbury 1754-74

5. John Calvert – Malmesbury 1780-84 Tamworth 1784-90 St. Albans 1790-96 Huntingdon 1796-1831
6. Thomas Calvert – St. Mawes 1792-95
7. Nicolson Calvert – Hertford 1802-26 Hertfordshire 1826-34
8. Charles Calvert – Southwark 1812-32

Seats: Albury Hall, Hertfordshire (purch. c. 1700, rebuilt c. 1780, sold 1847, demolished c. 1950); Marcham, Berkshire (purch. 1691, sold 1717); Ockley Court, Surrey (acq. by mar. 1818, still own); Furneaux Pelham Hall (Pelham Hall), Hertfordshire (old house demolished early-mid.17th c., purch. 1677, sold c. 1910); Mount Mascal, Kent (resident mid-18th c., probably leased); Nine Ashes, Hertfordshire (built 16th c., purch. 1675, demolished and sold by Calverts early 19th c.); Hunsdon, Hertfordshire (built 1446-48, remod. 1630s, decayed 18th c., acq. 1745 by Nicolsons who passed it to the Calverts, rebuilt 1806-10, remod. mid-19th c., sold 1850s); Kneller Hall, Middlesex (purch. 1818, sold 1847, institutional use)
Notes: One in ODNB.

Baron Willoughby de Broke (1491- E)

Origins: Sir Richard Verney of Compton Verney, a younger son of Ralph Verney of Claydon, in the 16th century married Margaret Greville, 6 Baroness Willoughby de Broke (she was a sister of the 1 Baron Brooke of Warwick Castle) in her own right through a descent from a younger son of the 4 Baron Willoughby de Eresby (see Bertie). **First MP 1411 for Lincolnshire. Four Willoughby MPs 1467-1554, three kts of the shire. Two Verney MPs 1589-1621, one for Warwickshire.**

1. Richard Verney 11 Baron Willoughby de Broke – Warwickshire 1685-87 1689-90
2. John Verney – Leicestershire 1685-87 1695-1707
3. John Verney – Downton 1722-34 1741
4. Richard Verney 19 Baron Willoughby de Broke – Rugby Div. Warwickshire 1895-1900

Seats: Compton Verney, Warwickshire (acq. by Verneys 1440, built 1442-3, rebuilt 1714, add. 1736-43, 1762, sold 1921, museum); Allexton Hall, Leicestershire (medieval, acq. 15th c., rebuilt 16th-17th c., sold 19th c.)
Estates: Bateman 18145 (E & W) 23915. The 12 Baron left over one million pounds in 1986. Owned 4,000 acres in 2001.
Peers: 10 peers 1696-1752 1759-1862 1865-1945
1 Ld Lt 20th
Notes: 11, 12, 13, and 19 Barons and one other in ODNB.

Heath

Origins: The son of the 11 Baron Willoughby de Broke married the heiress of John Heath of Brasted Place. The Heaths were a legal family of Tudor origin. Chief Justice of the Common Pleas 1630s, Lord Chief Justice 1641. **First MP 1621.**

1. John Heath – Clitheroe 1661-79

Seat: Brasted Place, Kent (purch. c. 1620, passed by mar. of 1683 to Verneys, sold c. 1800)

Peyto

Origins: Elizabeth Verney, sister of the 11 Baron Willoughby de Broke, married William Peyto of Chesterton House, and the property passed to the Verneys 1746. The Peytos came from Germany to England in the late 13th century, and were prominent in Warwickshire from that time. They rose through the law and marriage. **First MP 1330 for Warwickshire. Four additional MPs 1337-1658, all for the county.**

1. William Peyto – Warwickshire 1715-34

Seat: Chesterton House, Warwickshire (medieval, acq. by mar. 1341, rebuilt 1462-87, rebuilt 1657-62, passed by mar. 1772 to Verneys, demolished 1802)
Notes: Extinct in male line 1734. Peyto family has an entry and one other in ODNB.

VERNON I [Borlase, Hall, Harcourt, Sedley, Slater, Warren]

Baron Vernon (1762- GB)

Origins: An ancient family with many ramifications. Settled in Cheshire since the Conquest. (Bindoff, *The House of Commons*, III, 522) Baron c. 1100. At Haddon Hall, Derbyshire by c. 1200 (latter passed to the Dukes of Rutland by marriage – see Manners), where they mined lead, which was the source of their prosperity. Chief Justice under Henry III. Speaker of the House of Commons 1426. Governor of Prince Arthur under Henry VII. **First MP 1419, for Staffordshire. Seven additional MPs 1432-1626, five kts of the shire**. The 1 Baron Vernon's father succeeded to the Venables estates. **First MP 1553 for Cheshire**.

1. Peter Venables – Cheshire 1640-44 1661-69
2. Edward Vernon – {Carlingford 1661-66}
3. George Vernon – Derby 1679-81 1698-1700
4. Henry Vernon – Staffordshire 1713-15 Newcastle-under-Lyme 1715

5. George Venables-Vernon 1 Baron Vernon – Lichfield 1731-47 Derby 1754-62
6. George Venables-Vernon 2 Baron Vernon – Weobley 1757-61 Bramber 1762-68 Glamorgan 1768-80
7. George Venables Vernon Warren 5 Baron Vernon – Derbyshire 1831-32 S. Derbyshire 1832-35

Seats: Sudbury Hall, Derbyshire (held by Alchers from 1086, to the Montgomerys from whom it passed in the early 16th c. to the Vernons, built 1659-99, add. 1876-83, NT 1963); Kinderton, Cheshire (Venables seat acq. soon after Conquest, passed to Earl of Abingdon late 17th c., demolished c. 1860); Poynton Hall, Cheshire (acq. by mar. to Warren heiress 1826, demolished c. 1830, old hall, Poynton Towers, enlarged 1869, demolished 1935 - see Leicester); Stapleford Hall, Nottinghamshire (Warren house, passed by mar. 1839 to Vernons, demolished 1935); Newick Park, Sussex (built 16th c., rebuilt late 17th c., passed by mar. 1765 to Vernons, sold 1816); Haddon Hall, Derbyshire (medieval, passed to Manners by mar. 1565, see Manners)
Estates: Bateman 9801 (E) 24473
Peers: 9 peers 1762-1898 1909-45
Notes: Archbishop of York 1757. Vernons of Haddon Hall have an entry and the 5 and 6 Barons and three others in ODNB.

<u>Vernon</u>

Origins: Cadet line from the 15th century. Settled in Worcestershire since 1580. Successful lawyer acquired more property (he made £100,000 as a barrister 1654-1721 - Foss, *The National Trust Country House Treasures*, 170).

1. Thomas Vernon – Worcestershire 1715-21
2. Bowater Vernon – Bishop's Castle 1722-26
3. Thomas Vernon – Worcester 1746-61
4. Sir Harry Vernon 1 Bt – E. Worcestershire 1861-68

Seat: Hanbury Hall, Worcestershire (purch. c. 1600, built c. 1701, add. 18th c., NT 1953)
Estates: Bateman 7447 (E) 12828
Title: Baronet 1885-1940
Notes: Family extinct in the male line 1940. One in ODNB.

<u>Hall</u>

Origins: The Hall property passed by marriage to Thomas Vernon MP 1715-21.

1. Thomas Hall – Worcester 1660

Borlase-Warren

Origins: The 4 Baron Vernon married in 1802 Frances Warren, daughter of Sir John Borlase Warren 1 Bt, and took the additional name Warren. Their child was the 5 Baron Vernon. The Warrens were an old Cheshire family, illegitimate descendents of the last Earl of Surrey (Warrene), established at Poynton since the reign of Edward III. **First MP 1589.** Sir John Borlase Warren's grandfather, Arthur Warren of Stapleford Hall, had married Anne Borlase, daughter and heiress of Sir John Borlase 1 Bt of Bockmer. The Borlase family came from France and was granted Borlase, Cornwall by William II. **First MP 1395. Two further MPs 1433-51. Also two Irish {MPs 1634-39}.** A branch acquired estates in Buckinghamshire in 1561. The father of the **first MP (1586 for Buckinghamshire**) of this line was a mercer and supplied wine to Henry VIII. **Four further MPs 1604-44.**

1. Sir John Borlase 1 Bt – Great Marlow 1640 Corfe Castle 1641-44 Chipping Wycombe 1661-72
2. William Borlase – Great Marlow 1659 1661-65
3. Humphrey Borlase – Mitchell 1673-79
4. Sir John Borlase 2 Bt – Chipping Wycombe 1673-81 Great Marlow 1685-87 1689-90
5. John Borlase – Great Marlow 1679-81
6. John Borlase – St. Ives 1705-10
7. Borlase Warren – Nottingham 1713-15 1727-84
8. Sir John Borlase Warren 1 Bt – Great Marlow 1774-84 Nottingham 1797-1806 Buckingham 1807

Seats: Bockmer (Bockmers), Buckinghamshire (Borlase purch. 1561-95, passed to Warrens by mar. 1689, sold 1781, became farm house early 18th c.); Stapleford Hall, Nottinghamshire (built 13th c., acq. first half 17th c., rebuilt 1788, passed to Vernons by mar. 1839); Poynton Lodge, Cheshire (Warrens acq. by mar. mid-14th c., passed to Vernons by mar. 1826)
Titles: Baronet 1642-89; 1775-1822
Notes: Five in ODNB.

Vernon

Origins: Descended from the senior line of the family. Settled in Shropshire since the 15th century. **First MP 1553 for Shropshire. Another MP 1621, also for the county**. A Ludlow heiress married into the family, and the Vernons succeeded to that family's seat at Hodnet. The Ludlows descended from Odo de Hodnet (d. 1201). **First MP 1300. Six additional MPs 1307-1486, five for Shropshire**.

1. Sir Henry Vernon 1 Bt – Shropshire 1660 West Looe 1661-76
2. Sir Richard Vernon 3 Bt – {Monaghan 1703-13}

Seat: Hodnet Hall, Shropshire (medieval castle, Vernons acq. by mar. late 15th c., new house 16th c., passed by mar. 1752 to Hebers, see Percy)
Title: Baronet 1660-1725
Notes: The 3 Baronet was a spendthrift and sold most of the estates except for Hodnet.

Vernon

Origins: The great-grandfather of Henry Vernon married the eventual heiress of Hilton Park. Henry was a great uncle of the 1 Baron Vernon.

1. Henry Vernon – Stafford 1711-15
2. Henry Vernon – Lichfield 1754 1755-61 Newcastle-under-Lyme 1761-62
3. Richard Vernon – Tavistock 1754-61 Bedford 1761-74 Okehampton 1774-84 Newcastle-under-Lyme 1784-90

Seat: Hilton Hall (Park), Staffordshire (medieval, acq. by mar. 1562, rebuilt 1720, sold 1955, offices)
Estates: Bateman 4650 (E) 4000
Notes: The Vernons inherited Wentworth Castle, Yorkshire in 1799 (see Wentworth). Two in ODNB.

Slater-Sedley

Origins: The last Slater of Nuthall left his estates to his great-grandson Sir Charles Sedley 2 Bt. The Slaters were grocers in the 17th century who inherited the Nuthall estate. The Sedleys were small landowners in Kent in the 14th century whose rise to prominence was due to an Auditor of the Exchequer under Henry VIII. He married a City heiress. The last Sedley Baronet had an illegitimate daughter who married a scion of the Lords Vernon, who succeeded to the estates in 1778 and took the name Sedley.

1. Sir Charles Sedley 5 Bt – New Romney 1668-81 1690-1701
2. Richard Slater – Nottingham 1679-81 1690-99
3. Sir Charles Sedley 2 Bt – Nottingham 1747-54 1774-78

Seats: Nuthall (Nuttall) Temple, Nottinghamshire (acq. by Sedleys by mar. to Slater heiress 1718, built 1754-57, passed to Vernons 1778, sold 1819, demolished 1929); Southfleet, Kent (built 14th c., purch. c. 1590, sold sec. half 18th c.)
Estates: Worth £3,000 pa in 1696. In Bateman the new owners (Holders) are listed with 3641 (E) 7204
Titles: Baronet 1611-1701; 1702-78
Notes: Two Sedleys in ODNB.

Earl Harcourt (1749-1830 GB)

Origins: A Norman family that acquired land in the Midlands in the later 11th century. High Sheriff of Warwick 1198. KG 15th century. **First MP 1322 for Oxfordshire. Thirteen additional MPs 1376-1597, nine kts of the shire**. The 1 Baron Vernon married Martha Harcourt, aunt of the 1 Earl Harcourt. A younger brother of the 3 Baron Vernon succeeded to the Harcourt estates in 1830 and took the additional name Harcourt.

1. Sir Philip Harcourt – Boston 1666-79 Oxfordshire 1681
2. Sir Simon Harcourt – Abingdon 1690-1705 Bossiney 1705-08 Abingdon 1708-10 Cardigan 1710
3. Simon Harcourt 1 Viscount Harcourt – Aylesbury 1702-05 1710-15
4. Simon Harcourt – Wallingford 1710-13 Abingdon 1713-15
5. George Harcourt 2 Earl Harcourt – St. Albans 1761-68
6. William Harcourt 3 Earl Harcourt – Oxford 1768-74
7. Richard Harcourt – Sussex 1768-74
8. John Harcourt – Ilchester 1785-86 1790-96 Leominster 1812-18 1819-20
9. George Harcourt – Westbury 1796-1800
10. John Harcourt – Westbury 1800-02
11. George Vernon Harcourt – Lichfield 1806-31 Oxfordshire 1831-61
12. George Harcourt – Buckinghamshire 1837-41
13. Francis Vernon-Harcourt – Isle of Wight 1852-57
14. Sir William Venables Vernon-Harcourt – Oxford 1868-80 Derby 1880-95 W. Monmouthshire 1895-1904
15. Edward Harcourt – Oxfordshire 1878-85 Henley Div. Oxfordshire 1885-86
16. Lewis Harcourt 1 Viscount Harcourt – Rossendale Div. Lancashire 1904-16
17. Robert Venables Vernon-Harcourt – Montrose Burghs 1908-18

Seats: Nuneham Park, Oxfordshire (purch. 1710, built 18th c., sold 1948, institutional use); Stanton Harcourt, Oxfordshire (acq. by mar. 1191, built from 1380, remod. 1460s-80s and c. 1540, ceased to be main residence 1688, decayed by 1718, much demolished by 1760, rebuilt c. 1866-68, resumed as main seat 1948, still own); Malwood Lodge, Hampshire (purch. and built 1883-84, sold 1947, flats); Ankerwycke House, Buckinghamshire (built mid-16th c., inher. by mar. 1725, sold 1807, repurch. 1829, still owned 1925, sold to Bucks CC, demolished late 1970s); Ellenhall, Staffordshire (Noels acq. 12th c., built 17th c., inher. by mar. from Noels 13th c., sold c. 1810, farm house)
Estates: Bateman 8206 (E) 13000. Rubinstein - 3 Earl left £180,000 in probate in 1830. The 2 Viscount left over two and a half million pounds in 1979. Owned 7,000 acres in 2001.
Titles: Baron Harcourt 1713-1830 GB; Viscount Harcourt 1721-1830 GB; Viscount Nuneham 1749-1830 GB; Viscount Harcourt 1917-79 UK

Peers: 6 peers 1713-27 1735-1830 1917-45
1 in Cabinet 1884-85 1886 1892-95 1905-16
Notes: Lord Chancellor 1712. Archbishop of York 1807. Harcourt family has an entry and 1 and 2 Viscounts 1st cr. and 1 and 3 Earls and 1 and 2 Viscounts 2nd cr. and four others in the ODNB.

Vernon

Origins: Granville Vernon was a younger son of Edward Venables Vernon, Archbishop of York, who succeeded to the estates of the 3 Earl Harcourt.

1. Granville Harcourt-Vernon – Aldeburgh 1815-20 East Retford 1831-47
2. Granville Harcourt Vernon – Newark 1852-57

Seat: Grove Hall (Park), Nottinghamshire (medieval, rebuilt 16th c., acq. by mar. 1836, sold 1946)
Estates: Bateman 3886 (E) 4987; Francis Vernon, a younger brother seated at Buxted Park, Sussex (built c. 1720, add. 1810, purch. mid-19th c., sold 1934) 2759 (E) 3425

Earl of Shipbrook (1777-83 I)

Origins: Distantly related to the Barons Vernon. Officials in the 17th century. Secretary of State 1697. Admiral 1745 who gained a fortune through prize money and purchased an estate.

1. James Vernon – University of Cambridge 1679 Penryn 1695-98 Westminster 1698-1702 Penryn 1705-10
2. James Vernon – Cricklade 1708-10
3. Edward Vernon – Penryn 1722-34 Portsmouth 1741 Ipswich 1741-57
4. Francis Vernon 1 Earl of Shipbrook – Ipswich 1761-68
5. Charles Vernon – Tamworth 1768-74

Seat: Orwell Park, Suffolk (purch mid-18th c., sold before 1848)
Titles: Baron Orwell 1762-83 I; Viscount Orwell 1776-83 I
1 in Cabinet 1697-1702
Notes: Three in ODNB.

VERNON II

Origins: Rose in the 17th century through being a bishop's servant, significant gentry by the 1640s. Another Vernon made a fortune as a Turkey merchant and army bread contractor in the later 17th and early 18th century.

1. Sir George Vernon – Haslemere 1685-87
2. Sir Thomas Vernon – London 1690-95
3. George Vernon – Haslemere 1698-1700 1701-05 1713-15
4. Thomas Vernon – Whitchurch 1710-21 1722-26
5. Sir Charles Vernon – Chipping Wycombe 1731-34 1735-41 Ripon 1747-61

Seats: Twickenham Park, Middlesex (purch. 1702, sold 1743); Vernon House, Farnham, Surrey (built 1563, purch. 1693, remod. 1721, sold 1899)

VESEY *IRELAND*

Viscount De Vesci (1776- I)

Origins: Rose in the service of the Church of Ireland. A rector in Ireland in the 1630s. His son was Archbishop of Tuam and Lord Justice of Ireland. His son was a bishop. His son was the 1 Baron.

1. Agmondisham Vesey – {Tuam 1703-39}
2. William Vesey – {Tuam 1715-50}
3. John Vesey 1 Baron Knapton – {Newtown 1727-50}
4. Agmondisham Vesey – {Harristown 1740-60 Kinsale 1765-83}
5. John Vesey 2 Viscount De Vesci – {Maryborough 1796-97}
6. George Vesey – {Tuam 1800}
7. Thomas Vesey 3 Viscount De Vesci – Queen's County 1835-37 1841-52

Seats: Abbey Leix (Abbey Leix) House, Queen's County (acq. via mar. to a Muschamp heiress 1698, built 1773, remod. 1859-60, add. 1902, sold 1995); Lucan House, Dublin (old castle owned by Sarsfields, passed by mar. c. 1700 to Veseys, new house built 1770s, passed by inher. to Colthursts 1819, sold 1932)
Estates: Bateman 16307 (I) 44568. Owned 1,800 acres in 2001.
Titles: Baron Knapton 1750- I; Baron De Vesci 1884-1903 UK; Baronet 1698
Peers: {2 peers 1750-1800} 2 Irish Rep peers 1839-55 1857-75 1 peer 1884-1903
2 Lds Lt 19th, 20th
Notes: Until 1995 the estate was still largely intact because forest and urban land were exempted from the Wyndham Act of 1903 and this estate was rich in both. Three in ODNB.

Muschamp

Origins: Held manorial property in Sussex from 1536. **First MP 1624**. To Ireland as Lord Chancellor 1665, a land speculator.

1. Denny Muschamp – {Swords 1665-66 Blessington 1695-99}

Seats: Abbey Leix (Abbeyleix) House, Queen's County (purch. 1674-75, passed by mar. to Veseys 1698); Rowbarnes House, Surrey (acq. by mar. 1620, passed out of the family 1701)

VILLIERS [Child, Fitzgerald, Hyde, Mason] *ENGLAND & IRELAND*

Duke of Buckingham (1623-87 E)

Origins: Lord Clarendon wrote of the Villiers: "a family of ancient extraction, even from the time of the conquest, and transported then with the conqueror out of Normandy". (Clarendon, *Selections from The History of the Rebellion and Civil Wars*, 91) Settled in Nottinghamshire in the 13th century. **First MP for Nottinghamshire 1307. Another for Leicestershire 1352**. One married the heiress to Brokesby Hall. Remained gentry until the Tudor period. They rose high through royal favor under the early Stuarts. **Two more MPs 1604-1625**. Sir George Villiers was the common ancestor of the various branches. His wife was created Countess of Buckingham in her own right in 1617. The eldest son was made a Baronet 1619. The second son married the niece of the 1 Viscount Grandison (Sir Oliver St. John of Lydiard Tregoze – see St. John). Their son succeeded as the 2 Viscount. One of the 2 Viscount's younger sons was created Earl of Jersey. Sir George Villiers' third son was called to the House of Lords as Viscount Purbeck. The fourth son was made Duke of Buckingham, and the youngest Earl of Anglesey both in 1623.

1. Robert Villiers Danvers Viscount Purbeck – Westbury 1659 Malmesbury 1660 (illegitimate)
2. Sir William Villiers 3 Bt – Leicester 1698-1701

Seats: Brokesby (Brooksby) Hall, Leicestershire (acq. by mar. c. 1235, sold c. 1712); Cliveden, Buckinghamshire (built c. 1665-80, sold 1696); Helmsley Castle, Yorkshire (medieval, add. c. 1580, acq. by mar. 1632, sold 1695)
Estates: Worth £19,000 pa in the late 1660s.
Titles: Baron Whaddon and Viscount Villiers 1616-87 E; Earl of Buckingham 1617-87 E; Marquess of Buckingham 1618-87 E; Baron Ros 1632-87 E; Baronet 1619-1712
Peer: 1 peer 1661-87
1 Ld Lt 17th
1 in Cabinet 1660-74
1 KG 17th
Notes: Robert Danvers MP above was the illegitimate son of Sir Robert Howard, younger son of the 1 Earl of Suffolk. The 2 Duke's estates were sold to pay debts. 1 Earl of Angelsey and 1 and 2 Viscounts Purbeck and 1 and 2 Dukes and two others in ODNB.

Earl of Grandison (1721-21 I; 1746-1800 I)

Origins: The son of the 4 Viscount Grandison (see above) married the ultimate heiress (daughter of John Fitzgerald of the Decies) of the 7 Earl of Desmond (created Baron Dromana and Viscount Decies in 1569, extinct 1572) and the Dromana estate. Their son took the name Fitzgerald and was created Earl of Grandison. The title became extinct in the year of its creation. The Earl's daughter and heiress, Lady Elizabeth Villiers, was created Countess of Grandison in her own right and married Aland Mason of Waterford (see below). Her son succeeded as 2 Earl and took the name Mason-Villiers. His only daughter, Lady Gertrude Villiers, married Lord Henry Stuart, fifth son of the 1 Marquis of Bute (see Stuart I). Their son was created Baron Stuart de Decies. William Stewart {MP 1703-14} is included here because he married Viscountess Grandison and controlled the wealth and influence of the family during his wife's lifetime.

1. John Fitzgerald – {Dungarvon 1661-66}
2. Edward Fitzgerald Villiers – {County Waterford 1692-93}
3. William Stewart – {County Waterford 1703-14} (spouse)
4. James Fitzgerald Villiers Lord Villiers – {County Waterford 1730-32}
5. Edward Villiers – {Kilmallock 1761-68}
6. George Mason-Villiers 2 Earl of Grandison – Ludlow 1774-80

Seat: Dromana, Waterford (medieval castle, passed to Villiers by mar. late 17th c., badly damaged mid-17th c., rebuilt later 17th c. and early 18th c., rebuilt 1780s, passed by mar. 1802 to Stuarts)
Estates: See Stuart I, Baron Stuart de Decies
Titles: Viscount Grandison 1621- I (passed by special remainder to Earls of Jersey); Viscount Grandison 1746-1800 I
Peers: {3 peers 1661-89 1707-66 1784-1800}
Notes: One in ODNB.

Mason

Origins: Sir John Mason {MP 1695-1714} was a Searcher, Waterford Passage and Ross 1671, Mayor of Waterford 1696, Sheriff of County Waterford 1709 (see Grandison above).

1. Sir John Mason – {County Waterford 1695-99 1703-14}
2. John Mason – {Waterford 1715-38}
3. Aland Mason – {County Waterford 1749-59}
4. John Mason – {Blessington 1761-76 St. Canice 1776-1800}

Seat: Newtown House, Waterford (owned 18th c., demolished); Nymph Hall, Waterford (very confused succession, acq. by mar. from Alands 1691, acq. by Alcocks by mar. of 1740, Masons resumed residence, passed to Alands again 1783, demolished)

Earl of Jersey (1697- E)

Origins: See Duke of Buckingham above. The 5 Earl of Jersey married a Child heiress to Osterley Park.

1. William Villiers 2 Earl of Jersey – Kent 1705-08
2. George Villiers 4 Earl of Jersey – Tamworth 1756-65 Aldborough 1765-68 Dover 1768-69
3. George Child-Villiers 6 Earl of Jersey – Rochester 1830-31 Minehead 1831-32 Honiton 1832-34 Weymouth 1837-42 Cirencester 1844-52
4. Frederick Villiers – Weymouth 1847-52
5. Francis Villiers – Rochester 1852-56

Seats: Osterley Park, Middlesex (built c. 1575, purch. by Childs 1711, remod. c. 1763-80, Villiers acq. by mar. 1804, NT 1949); Middleton Park, Oxfordshire (old house, purch. 1750, add. 1806, demolished 1934, rebuilt 1935-38, sold 1946, converted to flats 1974); Upton House, Warwickshire (built 1690s, acq. by mar. 1804, sold with 1,182 acres 1894, NT 1948)
Estates: Bateman 19389 (E & W) 34599. Owned 1,900 acres in 2001 in Middlesex, which have great value.
Titles: Viscount Grandison 1621- I; Viscount Villiers 1690- E
Peers: 9 peers 1697-1721 1729-1859 1866-1923 1931-45
1 Ld Lt 19th-20th
1 in Cabinet 1699-1700
Notes: The 7 Earl was both a colonial governor and a prominent banker (d. 1917). 1, 2, 4, 5, and 7 Earls and one other in ODNB.

Child

Origins: Bankers on a grand scale in the 17th and 18th centuries. Lord Mayor of London 1698, 1731 (see Earl of Jersey above).

1. Sir Francis Child – Devizes 1698-1702 London 1702-05 Devizes 1705-08 1710-13
2. John Child – Devizes 1702-03
3. Robert Child – Helston 1710-13 Devizes 1713-15
4. Sir Francis Child – London 1722-27 Middlesex 1727-40
5. Samuel Child – Bishop's Castle 1747-52
6. Francis Child – Bishop's Castle 1761-63

7. Robert Child – Wells 1766-82

Seats: Upton House, Warwickshire (built 1690s, purch. 1757, passed by mar. to Earl of Jersey 1804); Osterley Park, Middlesex (built c. 1575, acq. 1713, remod. c. 1763-80, passed to Jerseys by mar. 1804)
Estates: See Earl of Jersey above.
Notes: Two in ODNB.

Earl of Clarendon (1776- GB)

Origins: A younger son of the 2 Earl of Jersey married Lady Charlotte Capel, heiress through her mother, Lady Jane Hyde, to the last Earl of Clarendon of the 1 creation.

1. Thomas Villiers 1 Earl of Clarendon – Tamworth 1747-56
2. Thomas Villiers 2 Earl of Clarendon – Christchurch 1774-80 Helston 1781-86
3. John Villiers 3 Earl of Clarendon – Old Sarum 1784-90 Dartmouth 1790-1802 Tain Burghs 1802-05 Queenborough 1807-12 1820-24
4. George Villiers – Warwick 1792-1802
5. Thomas Villiers – Hedon 1826-30 Wootton Bassett 1830-31 Bletchingley 1831-32
6. Charles Villiers – Wolverhampton 1835-98
7. Edward Villiers 5 Earl of Clarendon – Brecon 1869-70
8. Theresa Villiers – Chipping Barnet 2005-

Seat: The Grove, Hertfordshire (built 16th c., rebuilt c. 1720, purch. 1753, rebuilt 1754-61, add. 1841-42, sold 1925, institutional use)
Estates: Bateman 4347 (E) 6766
Title: Baron Hyde 1756- GB
Peers: 6 peers 1756-1945
1 Ld Lt 19th-20th
3 in Cabinet 1771-82 1783-86 1840-41 1846-58 1864-66 1868-70 2012-
2 KG 19th, 20th
Notes: 1, 3, 4, and 6 Earls and nine others in ODNB.

Earl of Clarendon (1661-1753 E)

Origins: The Hydes were minor gentry in Cheshire from the 13th century. One married a Wiltshire heiress in the mid-16th century. His son became Auditor of the Exchequer under Elizabeth I and also married an heiress (Harris, *Clarendon*, 1983). **First MP 1559. Seven further MPs 1584-1642.**

1. Edward Hyde – Wootton Bassett 1640 Salisbury 1664-65

2. Laurence Hyde 1 Earl of Rochester – Newport 1660 University of Oxford 1661-79 Wootton Bassett 1679-81
3. Henry Hyde 2 Earl of Clarendon – Lyme Regis 1660 Wiltshire 1661-74
4. Lawrence Hyde – Winchester 1661-79
5. Sir Frederick Hyde – Haverfordwest 1666-77
6. Robert Hyde – Hindon 1677-79 1685-87 1689-98 Wiltshire 1702-22
7. Edward Hyde 3 Earl of Clarendon – Wiltshire 1685-87 1689-95 Christchurch 1695-1701
8. Henry Hyde 4 Earl of Clarendon – Launceston 1692-1711
9. Henry Hyde Viscount Cornbury – University of Oxford 1732-51

Seats: Cornbury Park, Oxfordshire (acq. c. 1660, rebuilt 1660s, sold 1751); (West) Hatch House, Wiltshire (acq. 1570, decayed in 18th c. and sold before 1805); Vastern(e) Park, Wiltshire (medieval, purch. 1676, declined to a farm house, sold 1866); Hinton Daubeny, Hampshire (purch. 1604, passed out of family by mar. mid-18th c., demolished); Swallowfield Park, Berkshire (old house, acq. by mar. 1678, rebuilt 1680-90, sold 1719)
Estates: Sold off early in the 18th century to pay debts.
Titles: Baron Hyde 1660-1753 E; Viscount Cornbury 1661-1753; Viscount Hyde 1681-1753 E; Earl of Rochester 1682-1753 E
Peers: 7 peers 1660-67 1674-1723 1681-1753 1712-13 1751-53
3 Lds Lt 17th, 18th
3 in Cabinet 1660-67 1679-85 1685-87 1700-03 1710-11
1 KG 17th-18th
Notes: The 1 Earl of Clarendon was father of James II's first wife, mother of Queen Mary II and Queen Anne. The 3 Earl died in deep debt. The 2 Earl inherited the Backhouse estates by mar., a family that produced several **MPs in the early 17th c**. 5 Baron and 1 Earl of Rochester and 1, 2, and 3 Earls of Clarendon and five others in ODNB.

VINCENT [Chiswell]

<u>Viscount D'Abernon</u> (1926-41 UK)

Origins: Held manorial land since the reign of Edward II. Married the Lyfield heiress to Stoke D'Abernon in the later 16th century. **First MP 1584. Two additional MPs 1593-1626, one for Surrey**.

1. Sir Francis Vincent 3 Bt – Dover 1661-70
2. Thomas Vincent – Reigate 1689-90
3. Sir Francis Vincent 5 Bt – Surrey 1690-95 1710-13
4. Sir Henry Vincent 6 Bt – Guildford 1728-34
5. Sir Francis Vincent 7 Bt – Surrey 1761-75

6. Sir Francis Vincent 10 Bt – St. Albans 1831-34
7. Sir Charles Vincent – Central Sheffield 1885-1908
8. Edgar Vincent 1 Viscount D'Abernon – Exeter 1899-1906

Seats: D'Abernon Chase (Stoke D'Abernon), Surrey (medieval, acq. by mar. later 16th c., built mid-18th c., sold 1776, repurch. 1933, sold 1956, school); Debden Hall, Essex (acq. by mar. 1797, passed out of family 1880); Esher Place, Surrey (built 15th c., much demolished c. 1678, add. late 17th c., rebuilt 1730, rebuilt 19th c., purch. 1893, donated 1930 to institution)
Estates: Bateman 3259 (E) 3433
Titles: Baron D'Abernon 1914-41 UK; Baronet 1620-1941
Peer: 1 peer 1914-41
Notes: The 5, 6, and 7 Baronets made advantageous marriages into the London mercantile elite. The lineage that brought Stoke to the family was lengthy. The Lyfields of Stoke D'Abernon elected an **MP 1571 (Surrey 1572)**. They acquired Stoke by marriage to the heiress of the 1 Baron Bray (see Crewe). The Brays had inherited Stoke from a Norbury heiress. **First MP**, Treasurer of England, **1391. Three additional MPs 1445-95, two for Surrey**. The Norburys inherited Stoke from the Croysers, **first MP 1336 for Bedfordshire. Two additional MPs 1338-1404, one for Surrey and one for Bedfordshire.** 1 Viscount and two others in ODNB.

Chiswell

Origins: First MP a Turkey merchant and Director of the Bank of England. Debden descended in 1772 via an heiress to a Dutch merchant (Muilman), who took the name Chiswell. After the death of the second MP it passed in 1797 to Lady Vincent.

1. Richard Chiswell – Calne 1715-22
2. Richard Muilman Chiswell – Aldborough 1790-97

Seats: Debden Hall, Essex (medieval, purch. 1715, passed to Muilman 1772 and to Vincent 1797, add. 1795, passed to Trevilians in 1860, sold after 1882, demolished 1936); Kirby Hall, Essex (Muilman seat – purch. early 18th c.)
Estates: The second MP inherited £470,000 and was said by 1790 to be worth £1 million. However, much of the fortune was later lost in speculative ventures. Muilman Company went bankrupt in 1797.
Notes: The Cely-Trevilians had an estate listed in Bateman 4337 (E) 4500. Three in ODNB.

VIVIAN [Glynn] *ENGLAND & WALES*

Baron Vivian (1841- UK)

Origins: The Vivians came into view in the 16th century. They were heavily involved in banking and smelting copper in the 19th century. In 1840 the Hafod works were the largest copper smelting operation in the world. This entry combines the families of Lord Vivian and Lord Swansea. The 1 Baron Swansea was a nephew of the 1 Baron Vivian.

1. Richard Vivian 1 Baron Vivian – Truro 1820-26 Windsor 1826-31 Truro 1832-34 E. Cornwall 1837-41
2. John Vivian – Swansea 1832-55
3. Charles Vivian 2 Baron Vivian – Bodmin 1835-42
4. John Vivian – Penryn 1841-47 Truro 1857-59 1865-71
5. Henry Vivian 1 Baron Swansea – Truro 1852-57 Glamorganshire 1857-85 Swansea 1885-93
6. Arthur Vivian – W. Cornwall 1868-85

Seats: Glynn House, Cornwall (built 1805, fire 1819, purch. 1825, rebuilt, sold 1947, offices); Singleton Abbey, Glamorganshire (built 1784, purch. 1817, rebuilt mid-19th c., sold 1919, institutional use); The Park, Truro, Cornwall; Caer Beris, Breconshire (owned at least until 1934, hotel); Glanafon, Glamorganshire; Bosahan, Cornwall (built 18th c., add. 1850s, demolished c. 1965); Clyne Castle (Woodlands), Glamorganshire (built 1791, add. 1800, remod. 1819-20, acq. and add. later 19th c., sold 1953); Parc le Breos, Glamorganshire (acq. and built mid-19th c., family departed by 1939, sold 1953); Beechwood House, Hampshire (acq. early 19th c., sold 1840s)
Estates: Bateman 8269 (E & W) 8719. Rubinstein – Alice Vivian left £140,000 in probate in 1825 and John Vivian left £180,000.
Titles: Baron Swansea 1893- UK; Baronet 1828- ; 1882-
Peers: 8 peers 1841-93 1893-1934 1899-1945
1 Ld Lt 19th
Notes: A Cornish family that developed Swansea as their center of smelting operations. Company sold 1927. 1, 2, and 3 Barons Vivian and 1 Baron Swansea and three others in ODNB.

Glynn

Origins: The Glynns were settled on the property from which they took their name in the 14th century. The great-grandfather of the 1 Baron Vivian married in 1712 Lucy Glynn. Through this marriage the Vivians succeeded to Glynn in 1840.

1. Nicholas Glynn – Bodmin 1679-81 1685-87 1689-95
2. Dennys Glynn – Camelford 1698-1705
3. John Glynn – Middlesex 1768-79

Seat: Glynn House, Cornwall (acq. and built 14th c., rebuilt c. mid-18th c., rebuilt 1805, fire 1819, remod. 1833, passed by mar. to Vivians 1840)

VYVYAN (Vivian) [Robyns]

Vyvyan

Origins: Established in Cornwall in the 13th century, as brigands and pirates. The original seat of Trevidren was held by the family for over eight centuries (*Country Life*, 39, p. 450). **First MP 1421. Five additional MPs 1572-1628**.

1. Sir Richard Vyvyan 1 Bt – Penryn 1640 Tregony 1640-44 St. Mawes 1663-65
2. Thomas Vyvyan – Camelford 1660
3. Sir Vyell Vyvyan 2 Bt – Helston 1679-81
4. John Vivian – Mitchell 1685-87
5. Francis Vivian – Mitchell 1689-90
6. Thomas Vivian – Fowey 1695-1700
7. Sir Richard Vyvyan 3 Bt – Mitchell 1701-02 Cornwall 1703-08 1712-13
8. Sir Richard Vyvyan 8 Bt – Cornwall 1825-31 Okehampton 1831-32 Bristol 1832-37 Helston 1841-57

Seats: Trelowarren, Cornwall (medieval, acq. by mar. 1426, held by the previous family since the 13th c., built 15th c., rebuilt later 16th c., add. 1662, remod. 1753-60 and c. 1820, still own); Trewan Hall, Cornwall (acq. 15th c., built c. 1633, remod. 18th c., sold 1920)
Estates: Bateman 9738 (E) 18147
Title: Baronet 1645-
Notes: Two in ODNB.

Robyns (Robins)

Origins: The first MP was a lawyer. His daughter and heiress married 1671 Sir Vyell Vyvyan 2 Bt.

1. James Robyns – Penryn 1660

Seat: Glasney College, Cornwall (Robyns acq. mid-16th c., passed by mar. to Vyvyans c. 1671)

WAKE

Origins: The Wakes were a Norman family that held land in Guernsey c. 1100 and in Lincolnshire by the 12th c. Acquired estates in Northamptonshire by marriage 1138. **Summoned to Parliament as a baron by writ (Lord Wake) 1295-99. The second Lord Wake summoned as a baron 1317-48. First MP 1300 for Northamptonshire. Four further MPs 1407-1624, three kts of the shire.**

1. Sir William Wake 8 Bt – Bedford 1774-84

Seats: Courteenhall, Northamptonshire (built later 16th c., remod. 17th c., inher. by mar. to Jones heiress 1672, rebuilt 1791-95, still own); The Abbey House, Waltham, Essex (built c. 1590, acq. by Jones family 1676 and inher. by Wakes from them 1688, main seat until late 18th c., largely abandoned after 1739, ruinous by 1770)
Estates: Bateman 3141 (E) 5810. Owned 62,500 acres in Scotland in 1970. The Scottish estate was sold. Still owned 2,000 acres in Northamptonshire in 2001.
Title: Baronet 1621-
Notes: The 3rd Wake Bt married the Drury heiress and succeeded to estates in Suffolk 1712-44. The Drurys quite probably accompanied the Conqueror to England. (Roskell, Clark, and Rawcliffe, *The House of Commons*, II, 803) The Drurys produced **eleven MPs 1391-1625, seven kts of the shire**. (See Gordon, *The Wakes of Courteenhall*) 2 Lord Wake and two others in ODNB.

WAKELY (Wackley, Wakeley) *IRELAND*

Origins: Tudor soldier had a patent of lands in Meath 1547. **First {MP 1559}. One additional {MP 1585}**. Sheriff 1570.

1. John Wakeley – {Kilbeggan 1692-93}

Seat: Ballyburley, King's County (acq. 1550, built c. 1700, burned 1888, rebuilt late 19th c., burned 1923)
Estates: In the later 19th century 1,722 (I) 1,462.

WALCOT

Origins: The family can be traced to the reign of Henry II. Acquired Walcot in the 13th century. In the Elizabethan period one was a merchant adventurer. **First MP 1586.**

1. Sir Thomas Walcot – Ludlow 1679-81
2. John Walcot – Shropshire 1685-87
3. George Walcot – Bishop's Castle 1701

4. Humphrey Walcot – Ludlow 1713-22
5. John Walcot – Shropshire 1727-34
6. Charles Walcot – Weymouth & Melcombe Regis 1763-68

Seats: Walcot Hall, Shropshire (acq. 12th c., sold 1763); Bitterley Court, Shropshire (built early 17th c., purch. and became principal seat 1665, rebuilt c. 1700, sold 1899)
Notes: Two in ODNB.

WALDEGRAVE

Earl Waldegrave (1729- GB)

Origins: The earliest known Waldegrave was Sheriff of London 1205. Knightly rank in the 14th century. Speaker of the House of Commons 1381. Member of the King's Council 1390s. Married an illegitimate daughter of James II, which produced a peerage. A Roman Catholic family until they "conformed" in 1722. **First MP 1327 for Northamptonshire. Nine additional MPs 1335-1597, seven kts of the shire**.

1. Thomas Waldegrave – Sudbury 1661-77
2. John Waldegrave 3 Earl Waldegrave – Orford 1747-54 Newcastle-under-Lyme 1754-63
3. George Waldegrave 4 Earl Waldegrave – Newcastle-under-Lyme 1774-80
4. William Waldegrave 8 Earl Waldegrave – Bedford 1815-18
5. George Waldegrave-Leslie – Hastings 1864-68
6. William Waldegrave 1 Lord Waldegrave – Bristol West 1979-97

Seats: Navestock Hall, Essex (built early 16th c., purch. 1554, new house built c. 1720, demolished 1811, abandoned as seat but Dudbrook House, on the estate, was used as a dower house in the 19th century after Navestock was demolished); Bevills (Great Bevills), Suffolk (built c. 1500, abandoned as seat in the first half of the 18th c., became a farm house); Smallbridge Hall, Suffolk (medieval, acq. by mar. 14th c., rebuilt c. 1555, sold c. 1700); Chewton, Somerset (acq. 1550s, Priory demolished c. 1955, still own)
Estates: Bateman 15425 (E & I) 23495. Owned 4,500 acres in 2001.
Titles: Baron Waldegrave 1685- E; Baron Radstock 1800- I; Baron Waldegrave of North Hill 1999- UKLife; Baronet 1643-
Peers: 12 peers 1686-90 1722-89 1806-35 1837-59 1872-1945
1 in Cabinet 1990-97
2 Lds Lt 17th, 18th
2 KG 18th
Notes: 1 Baron Waldegrave and 1, 2, and 3 Earls and 1, 2, and 3 Barons Radstock and five others in ODNB.

WALKER

Origins: Rich merchants (goldsmiths) long prominent in Exeter in the 16th and 17th century. Mayors.

1. Robert Walker – Exeter 1640-43 1661-73
2. Thomas Walker – Exeter 1673-79 1681
3. James Walker – Exeter 1685-87

WALLACE *SCOTLAND*

Origins: **First [MP 1494]. Three further [MPs 1560-1621, one for Ayrshire].**

1. Sir Thomas Wallace 1 Bt – [Ayrshire 1665 1667]

Seat: Craigie House (Castle), Ayrshire (medieval castle, acq. by mar. 1371, family depart c. 1600, ruinous, new house built c. 1730, sold 1783)
Estates: Passed to the Dunlops 1770 who sold out in the 1780s.
Title: Baronet 1638-59; 1670-1770
Notes: The illegitimate son of the 4 Marquess of Hertford who left the nation the "Wallace Collection" was probably mothered by a (Dunlop) Wallace of Craigie (see Seymour). One in ODNB.

WALLER *ENGLAND & IRELAND*

Waller

Origins: Gentry by the 14th century. One served at Agincourt. **The first MP 1453. Three further MPs 1478-1604**. Edmund Waller MP 1624-87 married a City heiress.

1. Edmund Waller – Ilchester 1624 Chipping Wycombe 1626 Amersham 1628 1640 St. Ives 1640-43 Hastings 1661-79 Saltash 1685-87
2. Sir William Waller – Andover 1640 1642-48 Middlesex 1660
3. Sir William Waller – Westminster 1680-81
4. Edmund Waller – Amersham 1689-98
5. Edmund Waller – Great Marlow 1722-41 Chipping Wycombe 1741-54
6. Harry Waller – Chipping Wycombe 1726-47
7. Edmund Waller – Chipping Wycombe 1747-54 1757-61
8. John Waller – Chipping Wycombe 1754-57
9. Robert Waller – Chipping Wycombe 1761-90

Seats: Hall Barn, Buckinghamshire (purch. 1624, sold 1832, partial demolition, 1969); Farmington Lodge, Gloucestershire (built later 18th c., add. 1854, sold c. 1912)
Estates: Bateman 6904 (E) 7972. Worth £3,500 pa in 1616.
Notes: Four in ODNB.

Waller

Origins: A younger son of the Hall Barn line went to Ireland 1630s and became a Cromwellian soldier. **First {MP 1634, County Limerick 1639}.**

1. James Waller – {Tralee 1692-93 Kinsale 1695-99}
2. John Waller – {Doneraile 1727-42}
3. John Waller – {County Limerick 1790-1800} 1801-02

Seats: Castletown Manor, Limerick (acq. by mar. 1636, sold 1936, demolished 1940s); Dromore Castle, County Kerry (built 1839, inher. after 1905, sold 1993)
Estates: Bateman 6996 (I) 5929
Notes: One in ODNB.

WALLOP [Conduitt, Fellowes]

Earl of Portsmouth (1743- GB)

Origins: The Wallops claimed to have held Wallop before the Conquest. This may be true. (*Country Life*, 90, p. 536) Held estates in Hampshire by the 14th century. **First MP 1328 for Hampshire. Five additional MP 1414-1640, four for the county.** Lord Justice of Ireland under Elizabeth I. **One Irish {MP 1585 for County Carlow}.** Operated ironworks in 17th century. Twice declined a peerage under James I. (Thrush and Ferris, *The House of Commons 1604-1629*, VI 655). The 4 Earl of Portsmouth took the name of Fellowes in 1795 on succeeding to the estates of his maternal uncle H. A. Fellowes of Eggesford House.

1. Robert Wallop – Andover 1621 1624 Hampshire 1625 1626 Andover 1628 1640-53 1654 1656 1659 Whitchurch 1660
2. Henry Wallop – Whitchurch 1660-74
3. Henry Wallop – Whitchurch 1679-81
4. John Wallop 1 Earl of Portsmouth – Hampshire 1715-20
5. John Wallop Viscount Lymington – Andover 1741-49
6. Bluett Wallop – Newport (IoW) 1747-49
7. Charles Wallop – Whitchurch 1747-54
8. Henry Wallop – Whitchurch 1768-74
9. Coulson Wallop – Andover 1796-1802

10. Newton Fellowes 4 Earl of Portsmouth – Andover 1802-20 N. Devon 1832-37
11. Henry Wallop Fellowes – Andover 1831-34
12. Newton Wallop 6 Earl of Portsmouth – Barnstaple 1880-85 S. Moulton Div. Devon 1885-91
13. Gerard Wallop 9 Earl of Portsmouth – Basingstoke Div. Hampshire 1929-34

Seats: Hurstborne Priors, Hampshire (purch. 1634, rebuilt c. 1712, demolished c. 1785, rebuilt early 19th c., fire 1870, rebuilt 1894, sold 1934, demolished 1965); Farleigh (Wallop) House, Hampshire (acq. by mar. 1460, rebuilt 1731, remod. 1935-37, still own); Eggesford House, Devon (acq. by mar. 1795, rebuilt 1822, new house c. 1854, sold 1913, gutted 1917); Enniscothy Castle, Wexford (built 1201, purch. 1587, rebuilt 1746, leased out in 19th c., restored c. 1900, now a museum)
Estates: Bateman 46984 (E & I) 36271. Owned 3,000 acres worth 80 million pounds in 2001.
Title: Viscount Lymington 1720- GB
Peers: 9 peers 1720-1945
1 Ld Lt 18th
Notes: The Wallop family amassed a huge estate in Wyoming that they still own. Malcolm Wallop, grandson of the 8 Earl, became a US Senator. 1 and 9 Earls and four others in ODNB.

<u>Conduitt</u>

Origins: Obscure origins. Married an heiress and acquired Cranbury Park 1720. Master of the Mint 1727. The daughter and heiress of John Conduitt MP married John Wallop.

1. John Conduitt – Whitchurch 1721-35 Southampton 1735-37

Seat: Cranbury Park, Hampshire (purch. 1720, sold c. 1740)
Notes: One in ODNB.

WALROND

<u>Baron Waleran</u> (1905-66 UK)

Origins: In Devon since the 12th century. **Two possible MPs 1449-78.** The 1 Baron's grandfather was named Dickerson, a wealthy Turkey merchant who brought two big business fortunes to the Walronds. He married the Walrond heiress in 1815 and took the name Walrond in 1845 on the death of his father-in-law. A Roman Catholic family.

1. Sir John Walrond 1 Bt – Tiverton 1865-68

2. William Walrond 1 Baron Waleran – E. Devon 1880-85 Tiverton Div. Devon 1885-1905
3. William Walrond – Tiverton Div. Devon 1906-15

Seats: Bradfield House, Devon (acq. and built 13th c., rebuilt 16th c., sold to school c. 1966); Dunchideock House, Devon (built mid-17th c., purch. 1690 by Pitmans, rebuilt early 18th c., add. early 19th c., Walronds succeeded to the Pitman estates by mar. 1871, sold 1905); Bovey House, Devon (medieval, rebuilt 1592, purch. c. 1670, sold 1778)
Estates: Bateman 7045 (E) 9364
Title: Baronet 1876-1966
Peers: 2 peers 1905-45
1 in Cabinet 1902-05
Notes: One in ODNB.

<u>Walrond</u>

Origins: Several cadet lines separated in the 16th and 17th centuries produced MPs. They are combined here.

1. Amos Walrond – Tamworth 1661-68
2. Edmond Walrond – Honiton 1685-87 1689-90
3. Bethell Walrond – Sudbury 1826-31 Saltash 1831-32

Seat: Dulford House, Devon (acq. and built late 18th c., sold later 19th c., demolished 1930s)
Estates: Bethell Walrond's father was a West Indian planter and merchant worth £75,000 in 1815, held 3,000 acres in Devon.
Notes: One in ODNB.

WALSH [Benn] *ENGLAND & WALES*

<u>Baron Ormathwaite</u> (1868-1984 UK)

Origins: The 1 Baronet was the son of William Benn a member of a Cumberland family that achieved gentry status in the 18th century. He married in 1778 the daughter of the sister of John Walsh MP who died unmarried in 1795 and left his estates including Warfield Park to John Benn (who made a fortune as a diamond and opium trader in India) who took the name Walsh. The Walsh family had held land in Worcestershire since the reign of Richard I. **First MP 1593 for Worcestershire.** Their fortune was greatly enhanced by a nabob in the 18th century (Habakkuk, *Marriage, Debt and the Estates System: English Landownership 1650-1950*, 449).

1. George Walsh – Eye 1680-81

2. William Walsh – Worcestershire 1698-1705 Richmond 1705-08
3. John Walsh – Worcester 1761-80
4. Sir John Benn-Walsh 1 Bt – Bletchingley 1802-06
5. John Benn-Walsh 1 Baron Ormathwaite – Sudbury 1830-34 1838-40 Radnorshire 1840-68
6. Arthur Walsh 2 Baron Ormathwaite – Leominster 1865-68 Radnorshire 1868-80
7. Arthur Walsh 3 Baron Ormathwaite – Radnorshire 1885-92

Seats: Warfield Park, Berkshire (old house, purch. 1764, fire 1766, rebuilt 1766, remod. 1809-11, passed to Benns by mar. 1795, sold and demolished c. 1955); Ormathwaite Hall, Cumberland (built mid-18th c., sold 1921); Knill Court, Herefordshire (leased, fire 1943); Abberley Hall, Worcestershire (acq. 1531, passed out of family by mar. 1708); Penybont (Pen-y-Bont) Hall, Radnorshire (purch. early 19th c., most of estate sold 1945, house sold 1984)
Estates: Bateman 26261 (E, W, & I) 14667. The Walsh estates were worth £300 pa in 1700.
Title: Baronet 1868-1984
Peers: 5 peers 1868-1945
3 Lds Lt 19th, 20th
Notes: Heavily indebted later 19th c. Irish estates sold early 20th c. 1 Baron and one other in ODNB.

WALTER

Origins: The parentage of the first MP is unknown. The latter was a successful moneylender and agent to many landed families. He foreclosed on mortgages and built up an estate.

1. Peter Walter – Bridport 1715-27 Winchelsea 1728-34
2. Peter Walter – Shaftesbury 1741-47
3. Edward Walter – Milborne Port 1754-74

Seats: Stalbridge Park, Dorset (purch. early 18th c., passed by inher. to Bayly's 1754 of Plas Newyyd, see Paget, sold c. 1854); Bury Hill, Surrey
Estates: Worth £10,000 pa in 1761.

WARBURTON *IRELAND*

Origins: The family lived in Dublin by the 1620s. No known evidence linking them to the Warburtons of Arley (see Egerton). Clerk of the Council of Ireland 1654. Postmaster General of Ireland c. 1690s. Sheriff 1701.

1. John Warburton – {Belturbet 1692-93 1695-99}
2. George Warburton – {Gowran 1692-93 Portarlington 1695-99}
3. Richard Warburton – {Portarlington 1692-93 1695-99 1703-16}
4. Richard Warburton – {Ballyshannon 1697-99 1703-13}
5. Richard Warburton – {Portarlington 1715-27 Ballynakill 1727-47}
6. George Warburton – {County Galway 1750-53}
7. Richard Warburton – {Queen's County 1729-60}
8. John Warburton – {Queen's County 1779-97}

Seats: Garryhinch, Queen's County (acq. 1662, built early 18th c., add. late 18th c., burned c. 1914); Firmount, Kildare (acq. and built late 17th c., resident through 19th c.)
Estates: Bateman 12126 (I) 7087. Worth £1,000 pa in 1713.
Notes: James Warburton (1810-92) was an MP on Prince Edward Island, Canada.

WARD I [Dudley, St. Paul, Sutton]

<u>Earl of Dudley</u> (1827-33 UK; 1860- UK)

Origins: The Dudleys were a medieval family. First summoned to Parliament 1308. **First MP 1342**. Lord Lieutenant of Ireland 1428. Baron 1439. KG 1459. **Five additional MPs 1472-97, three kts of the shire.** They became rich from coal and iron-making. Humble Ward 1 Baron Ward married Frances Sutton 6 Baroness Dudley in her own right (see Lexinton under Manners). Their eldest son succeeded as 7 Baron Dudley and 2 Baron Ward. On the death of the 5 and 10 Baron Dudley the title descended through his sister to her son Ferdinando Lea 11 Baron Dudley. That title fell into abeyance in 1757 and was revived for Ferdinando Lea Smith in 1916. The Ward Barony passed to a descendent of the 1 Baron's younger son, who succeeded as 6 Baron and was created 1 Viscount Dudley. His grandson was made Earl of Dudley. On the death of the 1 Earl that title became extinct and the Barony passed to a junior line descended from a brother of the 6 Baron. The 11 Baron was created an Earl in 1860.

1. William Ward – Staffordshire 1710-13 1715-20
2. John Ward 1 Viscount Dudley – Newcastle-under-Lyme 1727-34
3. John Ward 2 Viscount Dudley – Marlborough 1754-61 Worcestershire 1761-74
4. William Ward 3 Viscount Dudley – Worcester 1780-88
5. John Ward 1 Earl of Dudley – Downton 1802-03 Worcestershire 1803-06 Petersfield 1806-07 Wareham 1807-12 Ilchester 1812-18 Bossiney 1819-23
6. Robert Ward – Crewe Div. Cheshire 1895-1900
7. William Dudley Ward – Southampton 1906-22
8. William Ward 3 Earl of Dudley – Hornsey 1921-24 Wednesbury 1931-32
9. George Ward 1 Viscount Ward of Witley – Worcester 1945-60

Seats: Witley Court, Worcestershire (built early 17th c., add. 1683 and 1735, remod. 1805, purch. for £900,000 in 1837, add. mid-19th c., sold 1920, fire 1937, ruins - *Country Life*, 97, p. 1039); Sedgley Hall (Park), Staffordshire (built 15th c., acq. by mar. 1678, family departed 1757 for Himley, leased house to a school 1763-1873, sold, demolished 1966); Willingsworth Hall, Staffordshire (acq. by mar. 1678, passed to St. Paul family 1810, demolished mid-19th c.); Himley Hall, Staffordshire (built 13th, 15th, and 16th c., purch. by Wards 1537, became main seat of Wards after fire at Dudley Castle 1750, rebuilt mid-18th c., add. 1824-27, sold after WWII, institutional use); Dudley Castle, Staffordshire (built 11th c., add. 13th c., acq. by mar. 1321, add. 1340s-50s, remod. 16th c., partly demolished 1647, add. 1690s, fire 1750, ruin)
Estates: Bateman 25554 (E, S, & W) 123176. Rubinstein – 1 Earl left £350,000 in probate in 1833, the widow of the 3 Viscount left £160,000 in probate in 1833, and the 1 Earl of the second creation left £1,026,000 personality in 1885.
Titles: Baron Dudley 1439-1757 rev. 1916- E; Baron Ward 1643- E; Viscount Dudley and Ward 1763-1833 GB; Viscount Ward of Witley 1960-.
Peers: 15 peers 1660-1701 1704 1735-57 1740-1835 1838-85 1888-1945 1916-45
2 in Cabinet 1827-28 1902-05
Notes: Two cadet branches of the medieval family of Dudley also produced MPs. The line established at Yanwath, Cumberland **three MPs 1553-1601** and the great lords, Duke of Northumberland (1551) and Earl of Leicester (1564), **three MPs 1529-59 all kts of the shire.** The Dudleys operated ironworks as early as the 16th century and prospered greatly later from mining coal. Became holders of one of the largest industrial fortunes of the 19th c. 2 Viscount of 1st cr. and 1 Earl of 1st cr. and 2 Earl in ODNB.

St. Paul

Origins: Members of the Paul family were in business in Coventry in the later 17th century. They were county gentlemen and soldiers in the 18th century. They took the additional name "Saint" by Act of Parliament 1768. Sir Horace St. Paul 1 Bt married the daughter and heiress of the 2 Viscount Dudley and succeeded to Willingsworth Hall.

1. Henry St. Paul – Berwick-on-Tweed 1812-20
2. Sir Horace St. Paul 1 Bt – Bridport 1812-30
3. Sir Horace St. Paul 2 Bt – E. Worcestershire 1837-41

Seats: Ewart Park, Northumberland (purch. 1775, built 1787, add. 1814, add. 1867, derelict 20th c.); Willingsworth Hall, Staffordshire (acq. by mar. 1810, demolished mid-19th c.)
Title: Baronet 1813-91 or 1898
Notes: A younger son served as an officer in the Austrian army and was created Count of the Holy Roman Empire in 1759.

WARD II *IRELAND*

Viscount Bangor (1781- I)

Origins: Emigrated to Ireland in 1570 from Capesthorne, Cheshire (for the stem family, see Bromley). Surveyor General of the Ordnance in Ireland 1599-1602. Acquired estates gradually from the 1580s onwards. Justice of the King's Bench in Ireland 1727. Developed the linen trade in County Down.

1. Nicholas Ward – {Downpatrick 1661-66}
2. Robert Ward – {Bangor 1713-14}
3. Michael Ward – {County Down 1713-27 Bangor 1727}
4. Bernard Ward 1 Viscount Bangor – {County Down 1745-70}
5. Robert Ward – {Bangor 1761-67}
6. Bernard Ward – {Enniskillen 1769-70}
7. Nicholas Ward 2 Viscount Bangor – {Bangor 1771-76}
8. Edward Ward – {Bangor 1776-83 County Down 1783-90}
9. Robert Ward – {Wicklow 1777-83 Killyleagh 1790-97 Bangor 1797-1800} County Down 1812

Seat: Castleward (Castle Ward), Down (built 15th c., purch. 1570, tower house built 1610, rebuilt 1760-73, NT 1950)
Estates: Bateman 9864 (I) 13243. Owned 5,000 acres in 2001.
Baron Bangor 1770- I; Baronet 1682-91
Peers: {2 peers 1770-85} 4 Irish Rep peers 1855-81 1885-1911 1913-45
Notes: Wards of Bangor Castle, Down [Bateman 5830 (I) 8517] descended from a younger son of the 1 Viscount. Property acquired by Wards 1709. House built 1800, rebuilt 1847. One in ODNB.

WARDLAW *SCOTLAND*

Origins: Landed by the late 15th century. **First [MP 1560]. Two other [MPs 1612-25]** (includes a cadet line).

1. Sir Henry Wardlaw 4 Bt – [Fife 1662-63]

Seats: Pitreavie Castle, Fife (purch. 1608, built c. 1630, sold 1703); Balmule House, Fife (acq. c. 1596, sold 1837, hotel)
Title: Baronet 1630-

WARING I (Warren) [Maxwell] *IRELAND*

Waring

Origins: The Warings emigrated to Ireland in the early 17th century. Purchased estates in 1656. Sheriff 1669.

1. Samuel Waring – {Hillsborough 1703-27}
2. Thomas Waring – N. Down 1885-98

Seat: Waringstown House, Down (purch. 1656, built 1667, remod. 1673, remod. c. 1750, remod. 19th c., still own)
Estates: Bateman 3522 (I) 4150. Owned 1,654 acres in 1716.
Notes: A Waring served in the NI Parliament 1929-33. One in ODNB.

Waring-Maxwell

Origins: The great-grandson of William Waring ancestor of the Warings of Waringstown married Dorothea Maxwell, heiress of Finnebrogue, and took the additional name Maxwell. The Maxwells were kinsmen of the Lords Farnham (see Maxwell).

1. John Waring-Maxwell – Downpatrick 1820-30 1832-34

Seats: Finnebrogue (Finnabrogue), Down (Maxwells built c. 1635, add. late 17th c., passed by mar. to Warings 18th c., remod. 1789-95, passed by mar. to Percevals 1809, sold post 1975); Groomsport House, Down (acq. and built 1849, sold 1968, flats)
Estates: Bateman 12428 (I) 12132
Notes: The daughter and heiress of John Waring-Maxwell married William Perceval and the family name was changed to Perceval-Maxwell. John Percival-Maxwell (1896-1963) of Finnebrogue was a member of the NI Commons and Senate.

WARING II

Origins: London grocers early 17th c. A lawyer acquired Owlbury by marriage to an heiress. **First MP 1656**. Sheriff 1724.

1. Edmund Waring – Bishop's Castle 1660-81 1685-87
2. Walter Waring – Bishop's Castle 1689-95
3. Walter Waring – Bishop's Castle 1755-59 Coventry 1773-80

Seats: Owlbury Hall, Shropshire (built c. 1600, acq. by mar. early 17th c., remod. 18th c.); Llandinam Hall, Montgomeryshire (acq. by mar. early 17th c.); Groton, Suffolk (purch. early 17th c., sold early-mid-19th c.)
Notes: One in ODNB.

WARREN I *IRELAND*

Origins: Church of Ireland clergy: Dean of Emly 1620, Dean of Ossory 1647. The first {MP} was a Cromwellian officer and Mayor of Kilkenny 1656. He purchased estates. Sheriff 1694.

1. Abel Warren – {Kilkenny 1661-65}
2. Ebenezer Warren – {Kilkenny 1695-99 1715-21}
3. Edward Warren – {Kilkenny 1721-27}

Seat: Lodge Park ("The Lodge", Balleen Lodge), Kilkenny (purch. 1656, sold 1905)
Estates: 1661 (I) 1246 in 1878.
Notes: Extinct in male line 1898.

WARREN II *IRELAND*

Origins: To Ireland as an army officer 17th century. Cork bankers in the 18th century. Built up estate gradually by small purchases from 1688. (see Johnston-Liik, *History of the Irish Parliament*, VI, 503). Sheriff 1796.

1. Thomas Warren – {Charleville 1776-83 Castlebar 1783-90}
2. Sir Augustus Warren 2 Bt – {Cork City 1784-90}
3. Robert Warren – Dublin University 1867-68

Seats: Warren's Court (Kilbarry), Cork (purch. 1698, built 18th c., burned 1921); Crookstown House, Cork (acq. late 18th c., burned 1921)
Estates: 7787 (I) 3738
Title: Baronet 1784-
Notes: 1 Bt bankrupt due to election expenses 1784.

WARRENDER *SCOTLAND*

Baron Bruntisfield (1942- UK)

Origins: The Warrenders were merchants involved in foreign trade. Purchased landed estates in the later 17th century. Lord Provost of Edinburgh 1713.

1. Sir George Warrender 1 Bt – Edinburgh 1715-21

2. Sir Patrick Warrender 3 Bt – Haddington Burghs 1768-74
3. Sir George Warrender 4 Bt – Haddington Burghs 1807-12 Truro 1812-18 Sandwich 1818-26 Westbury 1826-30 Honiton 1830-32
4. Victor Warrender 1 Baron Bruntisfield – Grantham Div. Lincolnshire and Rutland 1923-42

Seats: Bruntisfield (Bruntsfield) House, Edinburgh (built 16th c., add. 1605, purch. 1675, add. 19th c., sold 1901, now school); Lochend House, Haddingtonshire (purch. 1708, fire 1859, remains demolished 1909, estate sold from 1947 onwards)
Estates: Bateman 3423 (S) 6561. Rubinstein – Hugh Warrender left £203,259 in probate 1820.
Title: Baronet 1715-
Peer: 1 peer 1942-45
Notes: One in ODNB.

WARTON (Wharton)

Origins: Merchants in Hull in the 16th century, although office holding seems to have been the key to their rise. They acquired land at the Dissolution of the Monastaries. Became one of the largest landowners in the East Riding of Yorkshire by the 1630s. (English, *Great Landowners of East Yorkshire*, 21-22) **First MP 1586 for Beverley. One further MP 1640-44 for Beverley**. In the early 18th century a Warton heiress married Ambrose Stevenson. Their daughter, Ann, married John Hall of Skelton Castle. Their son John Hall Stevenson Wharton succeeded to the Hall and much of the Warton estates in 1788 and took the name Wharton.

1. Michael Warton – Beverley 1660-81 1685-87
2. Sir Michael Warton – Boroughbridge 1675-79 Kingston upon Hull 1679-81 Beverley 1689-1702 1708-22
3. Sir Ralph Warton – Beverley 1685-87
4. Ralph Warton – Beverley 1695-1701
5. John Hall Wharton – Beverley 1790-1826

Seats: Skelton Castle, Yorkshire (medieval, Halls acq. 18th c., passed to Whartons 1788, demolished and rebuilt c. 1770 and 1810-17, still own, but land is being sold off); Beverley Parks, Yorkshire (medieval, Wartons occupied from 1573, Lodge remod. 1548, purch. 1628, built c. 1670, estate divided up and manor house demolished c. 1775)
Estates: Bateman 10647 (E) 7659. Estates said to be worth £15,000 pa in c. 1700.
Notes: An heiress inherited Skelton in 1938 and her husband took the name Wharton.

WASON *ENGLAND & SCOTLAND*

Origins: The first MP was a barrister and son of a merchant and ironmonger in Bristol. His maternal grandfather was Mayor of Liverpool in 1774.

1. Rigby Wason – Ipswich 1831-37 1841-42
2. Eugene Wason – S. Ayrshire 1885-86 1892-95 Clackmannan & Kinross 1899-1918
3. John Wason – Orkney & Shetland 1900-21

Seat: Kildinan, Ayrshire; Corwar, Ayrshire (built 1838, demolished 1974)

WATERHOUSE

Origins: Held the manor of Halifax from the 13th century. **First MP 1584. One other MP 1589.**

1. Samuel Waterhouse – Pontefract 1863-80

Seats: Well Head (Wellhead) House, Yorkshire (owned 19th c.); Hope Hall, Halifax, Yorkshire (built 1762-65, purch. c. 1855, sold c. 1881)
Notes: **Two Waterhouse {MPs} in Ireland 1585-1658.** Related? One in ODNB.

WATSON I [Armstrong]

<u>Baron Armstrong</u> (1887-1900 UK; 1903- UK)

Origins: The founder of the Armstrong family was a corn merchant and Mayor of Newcastle in the early 19th century. His son trained as a solicitor. In the later 19th century the 1 Baron Armstrong became a great industrialist. Sir William Watson married the sister of the 1 Baron. Their grandson inherited the Armstrong estates and was created Baron Armstrong.

1. Sir William Watson – Kinsale 1841-47 Hull 1854-56

Seats: Bamburgh Castle, Northumberland (medieval, ruin, restored 1757, purch. 1894, restored and add. 1894-1904, still own); Adderstone Hall, Northumberland (medieval, acq. 1763, rebuilt 1819, sold 1961); Cragside, Northumberland (purch. 1863, built 1864-66, add. 1870-84 and 1895, NT 1977)
Estates: Bateman 2265 (E) 6606. By 1900 Lord Armstrong owned 16,000 acres (Girouard, *The Victorian Country House*, 306).
Peers: 3 peers 1887-90 1903-45
Notes: The 1 Baron spent perhaps 1 million pounds on remodeling Bamburgh Castle in the 1890s (*Country Life*, July 8, 2015, p. 74).

WATSON II *SCOTLAND*

Origins: All three [MPs] were merchants. **The first [MP 1593 for St. Andrews]** was Provost of St. Andrews. **One other [MP 1630].**

1. Alexander Watson – [St. Andrews 1703-07]

Seat: Aithernie, Perthshire (purch 1670, sold c. 1740s)
Notes: The estates were sold in the 1740s leaving the family in penury.

WAY [Hill]

Origins: The Hills were merchants in Taunton in the reign of Henry VIII. **First MP 1571 for Taunton. Two further MPs 1571-1653.** A rich lawyer was Attorney General during the Commonwealth. Director of the South Sea Company in the 18th century. The Hill estates and a fortune of £300,000 passed by inheritance to Lewis Way, son of Benjamin Way MP, in the later 18th century.

1. Sir Roger Hill – Amersham 1679-81 Wendover 1702 1705-22
2. Benjamin Way – Bridport 1765-68
3. Arthur Way – Bath 1859-65

Seats: Denham Place, Buckinghamshire (old manor house, purch. 1673, new house built 1688-1701, passed to Ways by mar. later 18th c., remod. 1771, sold c. 1919, now offices); Stansted Park, Sussex (medieval, rebuilt 1680s, remod. later 18th c., purch. 1804, sold 1840)
Estates: Bateman 2327 (E) 4409
Notes: One Hill and three Ways in ODNB.

WEAVER *IRELAND*

Origins: John Weaver {MP 1692-1727} was a Revenue Commissioner in Ireland 1653. Sheriff 1689.

1. John Weaver – Stamford 1645-59 {King's County 1661-66}
2. John Weaver – {Queen's County 1692-93 1695-99 1703-13 Ballynakill 1715-27}
3. John Weaver – {Queen's County 1692-93 Maryborough 1695-99}
4. Daniel Weaver – {Ballynakill 1692-93}

Seat: Ballymadock, Queen's County (acq. mid. 17th c., sold 18th c.)

WEBB I

Origins: The Webbs rose partly via a marriage to a St. John heiress in the 16th century. A general who fought with Marlborough at Blenheim purchased Biddesden in 1692.

1. Edmund Webb – Cricklade 1679-81 1685-87 1689-98 Ludgershall 1701-05
2. Thomas Webb – Calne 1685-87 Cricklade 1702-05 Devizes 1710-13
3. John Webb – Ludgershall 1695-98 1699-1705 1706-13 Newport (IoW) 1713-15 Ludgersall 1715-24
4. Borlase Webb – Ludgersall 1722-34
5. John Webb – Bossiney 1761-66

Seats: Biddesden House, Wiltshire (purch. 1692, built 1711, sold 1795); Rodbourne Cheney, Wiltshire (acq. by mar. early-16th c., sold by 1800?, engulfed by Swindon in 19th c.)
Notes: One in ODNB.

WEBB II

Origins: Gloucester tradesmen active in the civic life of the city in the 18th century. They purchased landed estates. The second MP worked for the East India Company. Edward Webb MP owned cloth mills and ships.

1. Thomas Webb – Gloucester 1708-13
2. John Webb – Gloucester 1780-95
3. Edward Webb – Gloucester 1816-32

Seats: Norton Court, Gloucestershire (built 1762, add. 1847, sold pre-1880?, destroyed by fire 1959); Cote House, Gloucestershire (built early 17th c., remod. later 18th c., purch. 1775, sold 1797, demolished 1925); Stoke Bishop, Gloucestershire (leased only); Adwell, Gloucestershire (old house, rebuilt 18th c., remod. 19th c., inher. 1818, passed by inher. to Birch family, sold 1959)
Estates: Bateman 6044 (E) 8999 (under Birch-Reynardson)

WEBB III

Origins: A mercantile family. The father of Robert Webb MP 1747-54 made a fortune as a West Indian merchant. Robert Webb bought land in Taunton and the family became civic leaders.

1. John Webb – Ilchester 1705-08
2. Robert Webb – Taunton 1747-54
3. Nathaniel Webb – Taunton 1768-75 Ilchester 1775-80

WEBSTER

Origins: The founder was a wealthy London clothier in the 17th century. Became a supplier of clothing to the army. Kt 1708. Governor of the Bank of England 1710. Purchased landed estates from 1700 onwards.

1. Sir Thomas Webster 1 Bt – Colchester 1705-11 1713-14 1722-27
2. Sir Whistler Webster 2 Bt – East Grinstead 1741-61
3. Sir Godfrey Webster 4 Bt – Seaford 1786-90 Wareham 1796-1800
4. Sir Godfrey Webster 5 Bt – Sussex 1812-20

Seats: Battle Abbey, Sussex (medieval monastic buildings, remod. 1538, purch. 1719, remod. 1810, add. 1850s, sold 1857, repurch. 1901 for £200,000, school (leased) from 1922, fire 1931, sold to Department of the Environment 1976 £690,000); Copped Hall (Copt), Essex (built 16th c., purch. 1700, sold c. 1740); (Great) Nelmes, Essex (built 16th c., add. 17th c., purch. 1700, sold 1780, demolished 1967)
Estates: Sir Godfrey Webster left £23,000 in stock on his death in 1720. Sir Thomas Webster (d. 1751) spent £96,000 purchasing land in Sussex. The Battle Abbey estate was c. 8,000 acres with an income of £5,000 pa in the 19th century. Serious financial downturn in 19th c.; rescued by marriage to an heiress in early 20th c.
Title: Baronet 1703-1923
Notes: The Webster family has an entry in ODNB.

WEDDERBURN [Halkett, Scrymgeour] *SCOTLAND*

Earl of Dundee (1660-68 revived 1953- S)

Origins: The Scrymgeours have been the Standard Bearers of Scotland from 1107. The office Royal Standard Bearer was made hereditary in the 13th century. **First [MP 1461 for Dundee]. Seven further [MPs 1491-1633, five for Dundee and two for Forfarshire].** Created Viscount Dudhope in 1641 and Earl of Dundee in 1660. The titles were declared extinct in 1668, and the estates alienated. The estates should have passed to the cadets at Kirkton and Birkhill (John Scrymgeour of Kirkton [MP 1681-1707] below). David Scrymgeour of Birkhill married the daughter of Sir Alexander Wedderburn and their son succeeded to the Wedderburn estates and clan chieftainship. The Wedderburns were lairds by the 13th century and held important civil and religious office in the early 17th century. **First [MP 1585]. One additional [MP 1628].** Henry Scrymgeour-Wedderburn established the right to carry the royal standard of Scotland at the coronation of Edward VII. His grandson won the right from the House of Lords to revive the Viscountcy and Earldom in 1953.

1. Alexander Wedderburn – [Dundee Burgh 1661-63 1678]
2. John Scrymgeour – [Dundee Burgh 1681 1702 1703-07]
3. Henry Scrymgeour Wedderburn – W. Div. Renfrew 1931-45

Seats: Birkhill Castle, Fife (built 1780, add. 1812-14, still own); Dudhope Castle, Forfarshire (acq. 1298, built 1580, sold 1668, later a mill and barracks); Kirkton, Forfarshire
Estates: Bateman 2051 (S) 6382
Titles: Viscount Dudhope 1641-68 revived 1952- S; Baron Glassary 1954-
Peer: 1 peer 1660-68
1 in Cabinet 1958-61
Notes: 1 and 2 Viscounts Dudhope and 1 Earl of Dundee and one other Scrymgeour in ODNB.

Wedderburn

Origins: The senior line of a cadet branch descended from the main stem in the 16th century. Family was attainted 1745, and escape to Jamaica. A new fortune was made in the West Indies. Regained Ballindean but later sold it.

1. Alexander Wedderburn – [Dundee Burgh 1645-47 1648-52 1661-63]
2. Sir David Wedderburn 1 Bt – Perth Burghs 1805-18
3. Sir David Wedderburn 3 Bt – Ayrshire 1868-74 Haddington District 1879-82
4. Sir William Wedderburn 4 Bt – Banffshire 1893-1900

Seat: Ballindean House, Perthshire (old house, rebuilt 1711, forfeited 1746, repurch. 1768, sold c. 1819, old house demolished c. 1962)
Estates: Bateman 6336 (S) 5734
Titles: Baronet 1704-46; 1803-
Notes: One in ODNB.

Earl of Rosslyn (1801- UK)

Origins: Descended from the junior branch of the Ballindean line. The 1 Earl was a great-nephew of the 1 Baronet. Inherited the Sinclair estates via an Erskine heiress in the later 18th century and acquired Dysart. Became rich through the law. The Earldom later passed to a nephew (see Erskine).

1. Sir Peter Wedderburn – [Haddingtonshire 1661-63 1665 1667 1669-74]
2. John Wedderburn – [Haddingtonshire 1685-86]
3. Sir Peter Wedderburn 1 Bt – [Dumfermline 1705-07] Scotland 1707-08
4. Sir Peter Wedderburn Halkett 2 Bt – Stirling Burghs 1734-41

5. Alexander Wedderburn 1 Earl of Rosslyn – Ayr Burghs 1761-68 Richmond 1768-69 Bishop's Castle 1770-74 Okehampton 1774-78 Bishop's Castle 1778-80

Seats: Dysart House, Fife (acq. 1470, rebuilt 1755-56, passed by mar. to the Erskines 1805); Gosford, Haddingtonshire (purch. mid-17th c., sold 1781); Pitfirrane Castle (Pitfurane, Pitferrane), Fife (married Halkett heiress to Pitfirrane 1694 and took name Halkett on inher. the castle, remod. late 17th c., add. 1854, sold 1951); Castle Rosslyn (Roslin Castle), Edinburghshire (medival, damaged mid-17th c. and 1688, derelict 18th c., Erskines inher. 1789, and inher. Earldom of Rosslyn from Wedderburns 1805, part restored)
Title: Baronet 1697-1904
Peers: 1 peer 1780-1805
1 in Cabinet 1793-1801
Notes: 1 Earl in ODNB.

Halkett

Origins: The first Halkett was recorded in the reign of Robert Bruce. His grandson was designated as of Pitferrane in a charter in 1437. **First [MP 1593]. Another [MP 1649 for Fifeshire]**. Sir Peter Wedderburn 1 Bt (above) married the Halkett heiress and took the additional name Halkett.

1. Sir Charles Halkett 1 Bt – [Fifeshire 1681 Dumfermline Burgh 1689-95]
2. Sir James Halkett 2 Bt – [Dumfermline Burgh 1703-04]

Seat: Pitfirrane Castle, Fife (medieval, acq. 14th c., add. 15th, 1583, passed to Wedderburns by mar. of 1694)
Title: Baronet 1662-1705

WELBY [Gregory]

Baron Welby (1894-1915 UK)

Origins: The Welbys could trace their ancestry back to the Conquest (Fisher, *The House of Commons*, VII, 679). They took their name from the manor of Welby, first recorded there 1216, which they still owned in 1900. **First MP 1421 for Lincolnshire. Three additional MPs 1450-1654, all for the county**.

1. Sir William Welby 1 Bt – Grantham 1802-06
2. Sir William Welby 2 Bt – Grantham 1807-20
3. Sir Glynne Welby-Gregory 3 Bt – Grantham 1830-57
4. Sir William Welby-Gregory 4 Bt – Grantham 1857-68 S. Lincolnshire 1868-84

5. Alfred Welby – Taunton 1895-1906
6. Sir Charles Welby 5 Bt – Newark Div. Nottinghamshire 1900-06

Seat: Denton Hall (House, Manor), Lincolnshire (purch. from Thorolds c. 1523, house built 17th c., rebuilt 18th c., rebuilt 1879-83, burned 1906, demolished 1939, new house post-1945, still own)
Estates: Bateman 16904 (E) 27130
Title: Baronet 1801-
Peer: 1 peer 1894-1915
Notes: Inherited property from Gregory Gregory of Harlaxton and took the additional name Gregory in 1861. 1 Baron in ODNB.

WELLESLEY (Wesley) [Colley, Pole] *ENGLAND & IRELAND*

Duke of Wellington (1814- UK)

Origins: The Wellesleys were landowners in Somerset in the 12th century. They emigrated to Ireland 1226. Sheriff 1312. Summoned to Parliament as a Baron 1371. **First {MP 1372}. Two additional {MP 1585-1634}.** On the death of Garret Wesley of Castle Carbery in 1727, his brother's son, Richard Colley, succeeded to the Wesley estate of Dangan and took the name Wesley. He was created 1 Baron Mornington. The Colleys came from Staffordshire and acquired property in Ireland in 1506. Master of the Rolls in Ireland 1538. **First {MP 1559}. Two additional {MPs 1613-42}.** Acquired enlarged estates 1617. Sheriff 1643. The 4 Earl of Mornington married the Tylney-Long heiress (see Long I). On the death of the 5 Earl his estates went to the descendents of the fourth son of the 1 Earl, who received the title Earl Cowley. The Mornington title passed to the son of the third son of the 1 Earl, Arthur, Duke of Wellington. The 2 Earl, the eldest brother, was created Marquess Wellesley, a title that became extinct on his death. The 3 Earl of Mornington succeeded in 1781 (sold 1812) to the estates of his cousin William Pole of Ballyfin, Queen's County and took the additional name Pole.

1. Dudley Colley – {Philipstown 1661-63}
2. Garret Wesley – {Trim 1692-93 Athboy 1695-99 County Meath 1711-14 Trim 1727-28}
3. Henry Colley – {County Kildare 1698-99}
4. Henry Colley – {Strabane 1723-24}
5. Richard Wesley 1 Baron Mornington – {Trim 1729-46}
6. Garret Wesley 1 Earl of Mornington – {Trim 1757-58}
7. Richard Wellesley 1 Marquess Wellesley – {Trim 1780-81} Bere Alston 1784-86 Saltash 1786-87 New Windsor 1787-96 Old Sarum 1796-97
8. William Wellesley-Pole 3 Earl of Mornington – {Trim 1783-90} East Looe 1790-95 Queen's County 1801-21
9. Henry Wellesley 1 Baron Cowley – {Trim 1795} Eye 1807-09

10. Arthur Wellesley 1 Duke of Wellington – {Trim 1790-97} Rye 1806 St. Michael 1807 Newport 1807-09
11. Richard Wellesley – Queenborough 1810-12 East Grinstead 1812 Yarmouth (IoW) 1812-17 Ennis 1820-26
12. William Pole-Tylney-Wellesley 4 Earl of Mornington – St. Ives 1812-18 Wiltshire 1818-20 St. Ives 1830-31 Essex 1831-32
13. Arthur Wellesley 2 Duke of Wellington – Aldeburgh 1829-32 Norwich 1837-52
14. Lord Charles Wellesley – S. Hampshire 1842-52 Windsor 1852-55
15. Henry Wellesley 3 Duke of Wellington – Andover 1874-80

Seats: Stratfield Saye, Hampshire (old house, rebuilt c. 1630s, remod. 18th c., purch. 1818 for £263,000, remod. 1822, add. 1838, 1846-47, still own); Dangan Castle, Meath (acq. by Cusacks 13-14th c., castle built 13th c., passed by mar. to Wesleys 15th c., fire early 18th c., rebuilt mid-18th c., passed by mar. to Colleys 1727 sold 1793, fire and ruin 1809); Draycot Cerne, Wiltshire (Long family acq. in medieval period, rebuilt mid-18th c., passed to Wellesleys by mar., demolished 1955); Castle Carbery (Carbury Castle), Kildare (medieval castle, acq. by Colleys 1506 or 1562, rebuilt early 17th c., passed to Pomeroys [see Pomeroy] by mar. 1747, abandoned and ruin by 1767); Wanstead House, Essex (acq. by mar. by William Pole-Tilney-Long-Wellesley in 1812 – see Long (Child), sold and demolished 1823, park); Ballyfin, Queen's County (inher. from Poles 1781 and built, sold 1812)
Estates: Bateman 19116 (E) 22162 (Earl Cowley 5900 (E) 23172); Worth £3,500 pa in 1713 and £6,000-8,000 pa c. 1810. Earls of Mornington held 9,000 Irish acres and 12,000 English acres - sold 1816. 1 Earl of Mornington was nearly bankrupt 1781. The 1 Duke was voted £400,000 to purchase an estate in 1814. Worth £40,000,000 with 7,000 acres in 1990. Owned 31,700 acres in 2001. Also still owns an estate in Spain granted to the 1 Duke after the defeat of Napoleon.
Titles: Baron Mornington 1746- I; Viscount Wellesley and Earl of Mornington 1760- I; Baron Wellesley 1797-1842 GB; Marquess Wellesley 1799-1842 I; Viscount Wellington 1809- UK; Earl and Marquess of Wellington 1812- UK; Marquess of Douro 1814- UK; Baron Maryborough 1821-63 UK; Baron Cowley 1828- UK; Earl Cowley 1857- UK
Peers: {3 peers 1746-1800} 15 peers 1797-1842 1814-1945 1821-63 1828-1945
3 Lds Lt 19th, 20th
4 in Cabinet 1807-09 1809-12 1809-12 1814-23 1819-27 1821-28 1828-30 1833-35 1834-35 1841-46
5 KG 18th, 19th, 20th
1 KP 18th-19th
Notes: The heir to the 8 Duke, the Marquess of Duoro, was an MEP 1979-89. 1 Baron and 1 Earl Cowley and 1 Baron Mornington and 1, 3, and 4 Earls of Mornington and 1 Marquess Wellesley and 1 Duke and four others in ODNB.

Pole

Origins: Younger sons of Devonshire Baronets (see Carew I) came to Ireland in 1660.

1. Periam Pole – {Maryborough 1692-93}
2. William Pole – {Queen's County 1761-76}

Seat: Ballyfin, Queen's County (acq. later 17th c., add. 1748, passed to 3 Earl of Mornington by mar. 1781 who took the additional name Pole)
Estates: 11,000 acres worth £4,000 pa in 1853.
Notes: Extinct in male line 1781.

WEMYES *IRELAND*

Origins: Sir Patrick Wemyes, a Scottish soldier under the Earl of Ormonde during the Civil War, participated in the defense of Drogheda 1641. His grandson was the first to own Danes Fort. Sheriff 1695.

1. Sir Patrick Wemyes – {Gowran 1639 Knocktopher 1661}
2. Sir James Wemyes – {Knocktopher 1661-66}
3. Sir Henry Wemyes – {Callan 1692-93 1695-99 County Kilkenny 1703-14}
4. Francis Wemyes – {Harristown 1695-99}
5. Patrick Wemyes – {Gowran 1703-14 County Kilkenny 1721-47}
6. Henry Wemyes – {Callan 1727-50}
7. James Wemyes – {Callan 1751-65}
8. Patrick Wemyes – {Callan 1762 County Kilkenny 1747-60}
9. James Wemyes – {Kilkenny 1793-1800}

Seat: Danes Fort (Danesfort, Dunfert), Kilkenny (acq. and built late 17th c., add. early 18th c., demolished 20th c.)
Estates: 1870 acres worth £1,423 pa in 1870. Worth £400 pa in 1713. £7,000 pa in 1750.

WEMYSS [Charteris, Erskine] *SCOTLAND*

Earl of Wemyss and March (1633- and 1697- S)

Origins: The Wemyss family has been associated with Wemyss in Fife since at least the 12th century. They owned and operated mines from the 13th century. **The first [MP 1596]. One further [MP 1650].** The 5 Earl of Wemyss married Janet, daughter and heiress of Francis Charteris of Amisfield, who left £100,000 and an estate worth £7,000 pa. Their son the 7 Earl succeeded to the Charteris estates and took the name Charteris. **The first Charteris [MP 1621]. One additional [MP 1639], both for**

Dumfriesshire]. He also succeeded to the Douglas Earldom of March in 1810 (see Douglas). The Wemyss Earldom was forfeited between 1746 and 1826.

1. James Wemyss – Fifeshire 1763-68 Sutherlandshire 1768-84
2. Francis Charteris-Wemyss Lord Elcho – Haddington Burghs 1780-87
3. Francis Charteris 10 Earl of Wemyss – E. Gloucestershire 1841-46 Haddingtonshire 1847-83
4. Hugo Charteris 11 Earl of Wemyss – Haddingtonshire 1883-85 Ipswich 1886-95

Seats: Amisfield, Haddingtonshire (Wemyss inher. by mar. from Charteris family 1732, new house c. 1756, demolished 1925); Gosford House, Haddingtonshire (old house, purch. and new house built 1781-1800, remod. 1880s, fire 1940, restored, still own); Neidpath Castle, Peeblesshire (old castle rebuilt 14th c., add. 1654, derelict 1790s, inher. from Douglas 1810, still own); Stanway House (Hall), Gloucestershire (medieval, expanded c. 1530s, add. c. 1580-90, passed to Earl of Wemyss after 1817 by inher., add. 1913, still own); Elcho Castle, Perthshire (acq. 1468, built 1560s-c.1600, ceased regular use 1781 in favor of Gosford, became derelict)
Estates: Bateman 62028 (S & E) 54968. Worth £25,000,000 in 1990. Stanway estate alone composed of 5,000 acres in 1973. Owned 40,100 acres in Scotland in 1996.
Titles: Baron Wemyss 1628- S; Baron Wemyss 1821- UK; Baron Charteris of Amisfield 1978-99 UKLife; Baronet 1625-
Peers: [1 peer 1660-79] 1 Scottish Rep peer 1707-10 5 peers 1821-1945
3 Lds Lt 19th, 20th
Notes: The heiress of Anthony Tracy-Keck of Great Tew married Lord Elcho in 1771 and Stanway descended to the Earl of Wemyss in 1817 (see Hanbury). 2, 4, 6, and 8 Earls and five others in ODNB.

<u>Erskine-Wemyss</u>

Origins: The 5 Earl of Wemyss was a Jacobite who died in France. His sons divided up his estates. The third son succeeded to Wemyss Castle. Marriage to an Erskine heiress of Torry House brought additional estates in 1841, and a younger brother then inherited Wemyss (see Erskine).

1. William Wemyss – Sutherland 1784-87 Fifeshire 1787-96 1807-20
2. James Erskine-Wemyss – Fifeshire 1820-47
3. James Erskine-Wemyss – Fifeshire 1859-64

Seats: Wemyss Castle, Fife (acq. 12th c., built c. 1420, add. early 16th c., add. c. 1600 and 1669, remod. mid. 19th c., still own); Torry (Torrie) House, Fife (built c. 1785, remod. early 19th c., acq. by mar. 1841, ruin, still own)
Estates: Bateman 6925 (S) 12314 + 8492

Title: Baron Wester Wemyss 1919-33 UK
Peer: 1 peer 1919-33
2 Lds Lt 19th
Notes: 1 Baron Wester Wemyss in ODNB.

Wemyss

Origins: Descended from a younger son of David Wemyss of Wemyss (d. 1595). **First [MP 1605].**

1. Sir John Wemyss – [Fifeshire 1644 1645-47 1669-74]

Seat: Bogie House, Fife (acq. 1583, sold mid-18th c., partly demolished 1935)
Title: Baronet 1704-70

WENTWORTH [Armytage, Fitzwilliam, Lee Warner, Miles, Monson, Sondes, Vernon, Watson] *ENGLAND, IRELAND, & SCOTLAND*

Earl of Strafford (1640-95 E; 1711-99 GB)

Origins: The Wentworth family consolidated its position by a marriage of William Wyntword to the heiress of William Wodehouse of Wodehouse, Yorkshire in the reign of Henry III. The senior line, seated at Wentworth Woodhouse (which eventually became the largest private dwelling in the British Isles) gained the Earldom of Strafford. This title was separated from the family estates in a complicated series of developments. A younger son of William Wentworth (d. 1308) established a line that became the Barons Wentworth (1529 E). This title later passed through many families. **First MP 1447. Fourteen further MPs (including cadet lines) 1483-1644, six kts of the shire.** The 1 Earl of Strafford's title was forfeited in 1641 and revived in 1662. The 2 Earl died without children in 1695. Most of the Wentworth property passed to the family of Lady Anne Wentworth, 1 Earl's daughter married to Edward Watson 2 Baron Rockingham (see below). The Earldom was recreated for the grandson of the brother of the 1 Earl in 1711. On the death of the 2 Earl the title passed to a cousin, who died without children in 1799. Wentworth Castle was inherited by the Vernons of Hilton Park, Staffordshire (see Vernon I) by the marriage of Henrietta Wentworth, daughter of the 1 Earl of the second creation, to Henry Vernon. The Vernons took the additional name Wentworth in 1804. The title was recreated a third time for the Byng family, via a remote female descent, in 1847 (see Byng).

1. Sir William Wentworth – Thirsk 1673-79
2. Ruisshe Wentworth – Aldborough 1678-79 Liverpool 1679-81
3. Bruce Vernon-Wentworth – Brighton 1893-1906

Seats: Wentworth Castle (Stainborough), Yorkshire (built later 17th c., purch. 1708, rebuilt 1709-35, add. 1759, sold c. 1951, school); Wentworth Woodhouse, Yorkshire (acq. by end of 13th c., passed by mar. to Watsons 1695, see below); Dall House, Perthshire (built 1854, purch. c. 1900, sold 1951, later school); Toddington Manor, Bedfordshire (acq. by Cheney family via an heiress 1528, built c. 1545, passed to Wentworths by mar. 1614, demolished 1745, sold 1806); Blackheath (Black Heath), Suffolk (built 1890s, still own); Boughton Hall, Northamptonshire (medieval, remod. late 17th c. and 1718, purch. 1717, sold 1791)
Estates: Bateman 22930 (E & S) 20546
Titles: Viscount Wentworth 1628-95 E; Baron Raby 1640-95 E; Baronet 1611-
Peers: 4 peers 1662-1739 1743-99
1 in Cabinet 1712-14
2 KG 17th, 18th
Notes: Wentworth cousins at Nettlestead, Suffolk were cr. Baron Wentworth 1529 and earl of Cleveland in 1626-67. The barony passed through many families via female descent. 1, 2, and 5 Barons Wentworth and Earl of Cleveland and 1 Earl of Strafford of 1st cr. and 1 Earl of 2nd cr. and five others in ODNB.

Marquess of Rockingham (1746-82 GB)

Origins: The grandfather of the **first Watson MP (1601)** was a Receiver to the Bishop of Lincoln and made a fortune. His father acquired Rockingham Castle by marriage to a Montagu heiress. **One further MP 1621**. Sheriff 1591. The son of the first MP was made Baron Rockingham in 1645. The heiress of the 1 Earl of Stafford brought Wentworth Woodhouse to Edward Watson 2 Baron Rockingham in 1695. His eldest son became Earl of Rockingham. The 3 Earl died in 1746 when the Barony passed to Thomas Watson-Wentworth, son of a younger son of the 2 Baron and Lady Anne Wentworth.

1. Lewis Watson 1 Earl of Rockingham – Canterbury 1681 Higham Ferrers 1689
2. Thomas Watson Wentworth – Bossiney 1701 Higham Ferrers 1703-13 Malton 1713-22 Higham Ferrers 1722-23
3. Edward Watson Viscount Sondes – Canterbury 1708-10 New Romney 1713-22
4. Thomas Watson Wentworth 1 Marquess of Rockingham – Malton 1715-27 Yorkshire 1727-28
5. Thomas Watson 3 Earl of Rockingham – Canterbury 1741-45

Seats: Wentworth Woodhouse, Yorkshire (rebuilt c. 1630, inher. by mar. from Staffords 1695, rebuilt c. 1725, add. 1768-1801, passed to Fitzwilliams 1782); Rockingham Castle, Northamptonshire (built by William I, add. 12th and 13th c., decayed 16th c., leased 1530, purch. manor 1551, remod. 1579, purch. castle 1619, add. early 17th c., partly dismantled mid-17th c., remod. mid-19th c., descendents still own); Great Harrowden Hall,

Northamptonshire (purch. 1693, built 1719-23, passed by mar. to the Earls Fitzwilliam 1782, partially leased out from 1947, family departed 1979, sold)
Estates: See Fitzwilliam below. Worth £4,000 pa in 1689 and inherited the Sondes estates of £3,000 pa in 1709. Estimated worth £20,000 pa in 1751.
Titles: Baron Rockingham 1645-1782 E; Baron Throwley, Viscount Sondes, and Earl of Rockingham 1714-46 GB; Baron Malton 1728-82 GB; Earl of Malton 1734-82 GB; Baronet 1621-1782
Peers: 6 peers 1660-1724 1735-82
5 Lds Lt 18th
1 in Cabinet 1765-66 1782
1 KG 18th
Notes: 1 Baron Rockingham and 2 Marquess in ODNB.

Earl Fitzwilliam (1716-1979 I; 1746-1979 GB)

Origins: The family began as merchants, Warden of the Merchant Taylors 1494. One was Cardinal Wolsey's treasurer. Kt c. 1515. Set up as modest landed gentry under Henry VIII, pursuing careers at Court, in state office, and the army over the next century. Lord Deputy of Ireland 1571. (Finch, *The Wealth of Five Northamptonshire Families*, 100-34) **First MP 1553. Five additional MPs 1559-1648.** Baron 1620. The 3 Earl Fitzwiliam married 1744 the daughter of the 1 Marquess of Rockingham. On the death of the 2 Marquess in 1782 Wentworth Woodhouse passed to the Fitzwilliams, who took the additional name Wentworth. They became one of the greatest families of the Industrial Revolution (mines and chemical works) and were active managers of these enterprises into the 20th century. Twelve members of the family represented Peterborough between 1553 and 1889.

1. William Fitzwilliam 1 Earl Fitzwilliam – Peterborough 1667-79 1681
2. Charles Fitzwilliam – Peterborough 1685-87 1689-90
3. John Fitzwilliam 2 Earl Fitzwilliam – Peterborough 1710-27
4. William Fitzwilliam 3 Earl Fitzwilliam – Peterborough 1741-42
5. George Fitzwilliam – Richmond 1781-84
6. Charles Wentworth Fitzwilliam 5 Earl Fitzwilliam – Malton 1806-07 Yorkshire 1807-30 Peterborough 1830 Northamptonshire 1831-32 N. Northamptonshire 1832-33
7. William Wentworth Fitzwilliam Viscount Milton – Malton 1832-33 N. Northamptonshire 1833-35
8. William Wentworth Fitzwilliam 6 Earl Fitzwilliam – Malton 1837-41 1846-47 County Wicklow 1847-57
9. George Wentworth Fitzwilliam – Richmond 1841 Peterborough 1841-59
10. Charles Wentworth Fitzwilliam – Malton 1852-85
11. William Wentworth Fitzwilliam Viscount Milton – S. Div. W. R. Yorkshire 1865-72

12. William Wentworth Fitzwilliam – County Wicklow 1868-74 S. Div. W. R. Yorkshire 1880-85 Doncaster Div. W. R. Yorkshire 1888-92
13. William Wentworth Fitzwilliam – Peterborough 1887-89
14. William Wentworth Fitzwilliam 7 Earl Fitzwilliam – Wakefield 1895-1902

Seats: Milton Park, Northamptonshire (purch. 1502, passed by mar. to Naylor Leylands 1979, still own); Wentworth Woodhouse (rebuilt c. 1630, rebuilt c. 1725, add. 1768, passed to Fitzwilliams 1782, house (only) sold 1980s); Coollattin, Wicklow (acq. 17th c., built 1801-04, sold 1977, golf club); Carnew Castle, Wicklow (old castle was ruin by the end of the 18th c., reroofed and modernized by 4 Earl Fitzwilliam, sold 20th c.); Great Harrowden Hall, Northamptonshire (built 1719-23, passed by inher. 1782 to Fitzwilliams, sold 1895, golf club)
Estates: Bateman 139061 (E & I) 178348. Worth £330 pa in 1534 which had risen to £3,000 pa in 1719. Worth from all estates £60,000 pa by 1790. Rubinstein – the 4 Earl left £180,000 in probate in 1833. Collectively, the descendents of the last Earl may still own as much as 130,000 acres in 2012.
Titles: Baron Fitzwilliam 1620-1979 I; Viscount Milton 1716-1979 I; Viscount Fitzwilliam 1742-1979 GB
Peers: {3 peers 1661-1728 1741-56} 6 peers 1742-56 1769-1945
2 Lds Lt 18th, 19th
1 in Cabinet 1794-95 1806-07
2 KG 19th, 20th
Notes: Sir William Fitzwilliam was Lord Deputy of Ireland 1572-75 and 1588-94, and his descendent the 2 Earl Fitzwilliam was Lord Lieutenant of Ireland in 1795. The male line became extinct in 1979. 1, 2, and 3 Earls and two others in ODNB.

Earl of Feversham (1676-1709 E) and Earl Sondes (1880-1996 UK)

Origins: The 1 Earl of Rockingham married Catherine Sondes, daughter and heiress of the 1 Earl of Feversham of Lees Court. The Sondes family acquired estates by marriage in the 15th century. The family rose further by marriage and by the methodical purchase of land from impoverished neighbors, which they then sold for a profit. (*Country Life*, 52, p. 210) **First MP 1584. One further MP 1601.** On the death of the 3 Earl of Rockingham in 1746 the Sondes estates passed to the family of the daughter of the 1 Earl, Lady Margaret Watson, who married the 1 Baron Monson (see below). They had two sons, one of whom carried on the Monson line and the other was created 1 Baron Sondes. The 2 Baron Sondes married 1785 Elizabeth Miles, heiress of Nackington and Elmham. The 4 Baron took the name Miles. His son was created 1 Earl Sondes. A younger son of the 2 Baron Sondes inherited Rockingham Castle, which later passed by marriage to the Culme-Seymours.

1. George Sondes 1 Earl of Feversham – Higham Ferrers 1626 1628 Ashburton 1661-76

2. Lewis Monson Watson 1 Baron Sondes – Boroughbridge 1750-54 Kent 1754-60
3. Lewis Watson 2 Baron Sondes – Hedon 1776-80
4. George Watson – Canterbury 1800-06
5. Richard Watson – Canterbury 1830-34 Peterborough 1852
6. George Watson Miles 1 Earl Sondes – E. Kent 1868-74

Seats: Lees Court, Kent (purch. 1600, rebuilt 1652, fire 1910, rebuilt, now flats, still own estate); Rockingham Castle, Northamptonshire (medieval, passed by mar. from the Marquess of Rockingham to the 1 Baron Sondes 1746, descendents still own); Nackington House, Kent (Miles purch. c. 1727, 2 Baron Sondes mar. Miles heiress late 18th c., new house built early 19th c., sold and demolished 1921); Elmham Hall, Norfolk (built 1727, passed by mar. to the Miles family and then to Earl Sondes, remod. c. 1825, sold c. 1920 and demolished c. 1947); Gateley Hall, Norfolk (built 1726, purch. 1859, sold c. 1920)
Estates: Bateman 23642 (E) 38164. Rubinstein – Henry Watson left £120,000 in probate in 1830
Titles: Baron Duras 1673-1709 E; Baron Sondes 1760-1996 GB; Viscount Throwley 1880-1996 UK
Peers: 10 peers 1676-77 1673-1709 1760-1806 1813-1945
1 Ld Lt 17th
1 KG 17th-18th
Notes: 1 Earl or Feversham in ODNB.

Lee Warner [Miles] (Milles)

Origins: Henry Lee, a mayor of Canterbury, was a nephew of Bishop John Warner of Rochester (d. 1766), to whose Norfolk estates he succeeded in 1713. The Bishop's father was a merchant tailor in London. Purchased estates in Norfolk in 1660s. Lee's father was also a clergyman and took the name Warner. Henry Lee married the heiress of Samuel Miles MP of Herne and Nackington (from an old Kentish gentry family, PC under James I). Lee's son also inherited the estates of his uncle Sir James Howe 2 Bt in 1736 (see Curzon). Christopher Miles married the daughter of Richard Lee Warner of Walsingham. Christopher's son Richard's daughter and heiress mar. Lewis Thomas Watson, 2 Baron Sondes.

1. Henry Lee – Canterbury 1685-87 1689-95 Hindon 1697-98
   Canterbury 1698-1708 1710-15
2. Henry Lee Warner – Hindon 1711-13
3. Samuel Milles – Canterbury 1722-27

Seats: Nackington House, Kent (purch. by Miles c. 1727, passed to Watsons via the Lee Warner by mar. late 18th c.); Herne, Kent (acq. by Miles early 17th c., passed to Watsons

by mar. 1785, leased out thereafter); Walsingham Abbey (Abbey House), Norfolk (medieval, Warners purch. and built c. 1720s, add. c. 1806, remod. 1842, sold 1921)
Estates: Bateman 11913 (E) 16398

Viscount Oxenbridge (1886-98 UK) (Mounson)

Origins: The Monsons claimed medieval descent, but were merchants in the 1440s. They later purchased land. Kt 1541, Sheriff 1553. Judge 1572. Courtiers and an admiral in the early 17th century. **First MP 1553. Five additional MPs 1597-1640, two for Lincolnshire.**

1. Sir John Monson – Lincoln 1664-74
2. Sir Henry Monson 3 Bt – Lincoln 1675-81 1685-87 1689
3. Sir William Monson 4 Bt – Lincoln 1695-98 Heytesbury 1702-08 Hertford 1708-10 Aldborough 1715-22
4. John Monson 1 Baron Monson – Lincoln 1722-28
5. George Monson – Great Grimsby 1727-34
6. Charles Monson – Lincoln 1734-54
7. George Monson – Lincoln 1754-68
8. William Monson – Lincoln 1806-07
9. William Monson 1 Viscount Oxenbridge – Reigate 1858-62

Seats: Burton Hall, Lincolnshire (built 16th c., purch. 1600, became principal seat in the 18th c. rebuilt 1766, family departed 1949, sold); Carlton Hall, Lincolnshire (acq. early 16th c., built 16th c., main seat until 18th c., became principal seat again after 1945, sold 1963); Gatton Park, Surrey (purch. 1830, sold 1888); Broxbourne, Hertfordshire (acq. by mar. 1645, sold 1790)
Estates: Bateman 10134 (E) 21800. Owned 3,000 acres in 2001.
Titles: Viscount Monson 1628-61 E; Baron Monson 1728- GB; Baronet 1611- ; 1905-
Peers: 10 peers 1728-1809 1830-1945
1 in Cabinet 1737-48
Notes: 1 and 2 Barons and 1 Viscount Monson and seven others in ODNB.

Wentworth

Origins: A cadet branch of the family seated at Woolley since 1599. **First MP 1640.**

1. Sir Michael Wentworth – Aldborough 1685-87 1689-96
2. William Wentworth – Aldborough – 1698
3. Godfrey Wentworth – York 1741-47

Seat: Woolley Park, Yorkshire (acq. 1599, passed by mar. of 1760 to Armytage)
Estates: Bateman 5180 (E) 13002

Armytage

Origins: A prudent and thrifty yeoman founded the family. He purchased Kirklees in 1565 and built a new house. His heirs continued to buy more land. (Cliffe, *The Yorkshire Gentry from the Reformation to the Civil War*, 97-98) Sheriff 1614. Baronet 1641. Sir George Armytage 3 Bt married in 1760 Anna Wentworth, the heiress to Woolley Park. Their third son inherited Woolley and took the name Wentworth.

1. Sir John Armytage – York 1754-58
2. Sir George Armytage – York 1761-68
3. Godfrey Armytage-Wentworth – Tregony 1806-08

Seat: Kirklees Park, Yorkshire (purch. 1565, sold 1988, hotel)
Estates: Bateman 3274 (E) 8700
Titles: Baronet 1641-1737; 1738-
Notes: One in ODNB.

Wentworth

Origins: A cadet line. The 5 Baronet took the name Blackett after his father married the heiress of Sir William Blackett 2 Bt of Wallington and Hexham, Northumberland (see Beaumont I). His illegitimate daughter, Diana Wentworth, succeeded to estates said to be worth £40,000 pa in 1792. She married Thomas Beaumont (see Beaumont I).

1. Sir William Wentworth 4 Bt – Malton 1731-41
2. Thomas Wentworth – Whitchurch 1743-47

Seat: Bretton Park, Yorkshire (acq. 1407, passed out of the family by mar. 1792)
Title: Baronet 1664-1792

WESTERN

Baron Western (1833-44 UK)

Origins: A successful grocer bought estates in the 1650s. His son was a lawyer and first MP. Another family member was an ironmaster who died in 1707 worth £200,000.

1. Samuel Western – Winchelsea 1689-98
2. Thomas Western – Sudbury 1715-22
3. Charles Western 1 Baron Western – Maldon 1790-1806 1807-12 Essex 1812-32
4. Thomas Western – Maldon 1857-68
5. Sir Thomas Western 1 Bt – N. Essex 1865-68

Seats: Felix Hall, Essex (old house purch. 1650s, add. early 18th c., add. c. 1825, part demolished 1925, fire 1939/40, mostly a shell); Rivenhall Place, Essex (built late 16th c., purch. c. 1690s, rebuilt c. 1700, sold 19th c.); Preston Manor, Sussex (medieval and 16th c., purch. c. 1650, remod. 18th c., moved seat to Rivenhall in 1771, sold 1794); Tattingstone Place, Suffolk (built c. 1764, acq. by mar. 1808, sold 1893)
Estates: Bateman 10009 (E) 13535
Title: Baronet 1666-1705; 1864-1917
Peer: 1 peer 1833-44
Notes: Rivenhall Place belonged to the Bollan family heiress who married Charles Western in the later 18th century. The Westerns succeeded to the estates of the Shirley Baronets (related to the Staunton Harold line, see Shirley) of Preston by marriage in the mid-18th century. 1 Baron in ODNB.

WESTFALING

Origins: Emigrated from Germany in the 15th century. Bishop of Hereford 1585.

1. Herbert Westfaling – Hereford 1660-79
2. Herbert Westfaling – Hereford 1717-27
3. Herbert Westfaling – Thetford 1754-61

Seat: Rudhall, Herefordshire (built 14th c. or earlier, add. 16th c., acq. by mar. 1668, sold 1830)
Estates: Worth £800 pa in 1652.
Notes: The Westfalings inherited the Rudhall (Rudhale) estates (acq. in the early 14th c.) in the 17th century by marriage. **First Rudhall MP 1491 for Herefordshire. Two additional MPs 1529-1626, both for the county**. One in ODNB.

WESTON

<u>Earl of Portland</u> (1633-88 E)

Origins: The Westons were established in Surrey in the late 13th century. The great-great-grandfather of the 1 Earl was a mercer in London. Grandfather of the 1 Earl was Justice of the Common Pleas 1559-72. Kt 1602. Baron 1628. **First MP 1553. Four additional MPs 1601-59, one for Essex.**

No post-1660 MPs

Seat: Prestead (Prested) Hall, Essex (medieval, acq. c. 1300, rebuilt c. 1527, sold c. 1678); Skreens, Essex (purch. 1555, sold 1635)
Estates: Worth £6,000 pa in 1635.

Titles: Baron Weston 1628-88
Peer: 1 peer 1660-63
Notes: The last two earls were Roman Catholic and lived abroad. The last Earl died in 1688 leaving little property and no heirs. 1 and 2 Earls and one other in ODNB.

Weston

Origins: Kinsmen of the Earls of Portland. **First MP 1330 (a lawyer) for Surrey. Nine additional MPs 1415-1648, four for Surrey**.

1. John Weston – Guildford 1689-90 Surrey 1698-1702

Seats: Ockham Park, Surrey (tenants 15th c., purch. 1621, sold 1711); Sutton Place, Surrey (acq. 1521, built 1523, fire 1571, rebuilt 17th c., remod. 19th c., sold c. 1900)
Notes: In debt and sold some estates 1710-11. Three in ODNB.

WHALEY (Whalley) *IRELAND & ENGLAND*

Origins: Originally from Staffordshire where they owned land in the 15th century. One married an heiress to Kirton in Nottinghamshire. Comptroller of the Earl of Rutland's household in the first half of the 16th century. **First MP 1547 (for Nottinghamshire 1554). Three additional MPs 1597-1659, one for Nottinghamshire**. A Whalley was the brother-in-law of Oliver Cromwell, and his son was a regicide. To Ireland mid-17th c. Sheriff 1694.

1. Henry Whaley – {Athenry 1661-66}
2. Richard Whaley – {County Wicklow 1747-60}
3. Richard Whaley – {Athenry 1692-93 1695-99 1703-25}
4. Thomas Whaley – {Newcastle 1785-90 Enniscorthy 1798-1800}

Seat: Whaley Abbey, Wicklow (acq. late 17th c., sold early 19th c.)
Estates: 3956 (I) 1919 in 1878. Worth £7,000 pa in 1769.
Notes: Ran up huge debts and sold estates early 19th c. One in ODNB.

Whalley

Origins: Remotely connected to the Whaleys who went to Ireland. George Whalley (MP 1853-78) was the son of a merchant and banker in Gloucester.

1. George Whalley – Peterborough 1853 1859-78
2. George Whalley – Peterborough 1880-83

Seat: Plas Madoc, Denbighshire (purch. 19th c., sold c. 1883)
Estates: Bateman 2554 (E & W) 3499
Notes: George Whalley MP 1853-78 died insolvent and his son the MP was also declared bankrupt in 1883. The latter emigrated to Australia. One in ODNB.

WHARTON [Byerley, Kemys, Tynte, Worth] *ENGLAND, WALES, & IRELAND*

<u>Duke of Wharton</u> (1718-29 GB)

Origins: The Whartons of Westmorland may have been minor gentry from the reign of Edward I, but it is possible that they were a new family at the beginning of the 15th century. (James, *Society, Politics and Culture: Studies in Early Modern England,* 103) Acquired extensive estates in Buckinghamshire by marriage in the 15th century. The 1 Baron rose as a royal official under the Tudors. Baron 1545. **First MP 1419 for Westmorland. Seven additional MPs 1436-1628, four kts of the shire**.

1. Sir Thomas Wharton – Westmorland 1660
2. Thomas Wharton 1 Marquess of Wharton – Wendover 1673-79
3. Goodwin Wharton – East Grinstead 1679-81 Westmorland 1689-90 Malmesbury 1690-95 Cockermouth 1695-98 Buckinghmshire 1698-1704
4. Henry Wharton – Westmorland 1689

Seats: Wharton Hall, Westmorland (acq. and built Middle Ages, add. c. 1559, family moved their seat in 17th c., sold 18th c., ruin by 1770s); (Upper) Winchendon, Buckinghamshire (built c. 1637, acq. by mar. 1643, add. later 17th c., sold c. 1723, demolished); Woodburn, Buckinghamshire (acq. by mar. 1643, sold 1732, demolished 1963); Rathfarnham, Dublin (acq. 1700, sold 1723); Halswell Park (House), Somerset (medieval house, rebuilt 16th c., new house 1689, passed by mar. to 9 Lord Wharton 20th c., fire 1923, repaired, sold 1950)
Estates: Worth £750 pa in 1568 and £8,000 pa in 1700.
Titles: Baron Wharton 1544- E; Earl of Wharton 1706-29 GB
Peers: {1 peer 1717-25} 3 peers 1660-1715 1719-25
1 Ld Lt 17th-18th
1 in Cabinet 1708-10 1714-15
Notes: The 4 Baron married the Goodwin heiress to Upper Winchendon, **two MPs for Buckinghamshire in years between 1586-1643**. Worth £1,000 pa. in 1643. The 1 Duke converted to Roman Catholicism and died bankrupt, a declared outlaw, in exile and his estates confiscated. Most of the 2 Duke's estates were sold to pay debts 1723-40. (Habakkuk, *Marriage, Debt and the Estates System: English Landownership 1650-1950,* 380) 1, 2, and 4 Barons and 1 Marquess and 1 Duke and one other in ODNB.

Baron Wharton (1544- R)

Origins: On the extinction of the Dukedom of Wharton, the Wharton Barony went into abeyance. A daughter of the 4 Baron married Sir Charles Kemys 3 Bt. The Kemyses were a genuine Norman family in Gwent by 1091. They had been seated at Cefn Mabi since the 15th century. **Two MPS 1451, one for Gloucestershire. Two further MPs 1593-1628, both for Monmouthshire**. The daughter of the Wharton-Kemys match, Jane, married Sir John Tynte 2 Bt. The Tyntes were yeomen at Newland, Gloucestershire by the 13th century. They purchased landed estates in the late 16th century. Married a heiress to Wraxall, Somerset. Their daughter married a Halswell in 1637. The latter family was at Halswell Park by 1318. **First MP 1553. Two additional MPs 1604-14**. Jane Halswell, their daughter, married John Johnson, who took the name Kemys-Tynte in 1785. (*Country Life*, 24, p. 702) One of their descendents claimed the dormant Barony of Wharton in 1916, when the title was called out of abeyance.

1. John Tynte – Bridgwater 1661-69
2. Sir Halswell Tynte 1 Bt – Bridgwater 1679-81 1685-87
3. Sir Charles Kemys 3 Bt – Monmouthshire 1685-87 Monmouth 1690-95 Monmouthshire 1695-98
4. Sir Charles Kemys 4 Bt – Monmouthshire 1713-15 Glamorgan 1716-34
5. Edward Kemys – Monmouth 1722-34
6. Sir Halswell Tynte 3 Bt – Bridgwater 1727-30
7. Sir Charles Kemys-Tynte 5 Bt – Monmouth 1745-47 Somerset 1747-74
8. Charles Kemys-Tynte – Bridgwater 1820-37
9. Charles Kemys-Tynte – W. Somerset 1832-37 Bridgwater 1847-65

Seats: Halswell Park (House), Somerset (acq. by Halswells 1318, medieval house, rebuilt 16th c., new house 1689, passed to Tyntes by mar. of 1637, sold 1948-50, flats); Cefn Mably (Mabli) (Cefnmabli), Glamorganshire (medieval, acq. by Kemys by mar. 15th c., rebuilt late 16th c., passes by mar. to Tyntes in 1737, rebuilt c. 1713, sold 1923, partly dismantled c. 1960s, hospital); Llanfair Castle, Monmouthshire (Kemys, medieval castle a ruin, purch. 1614, house demolished, still owned estate in 1901); Burhill, Surrey (acq. and built 1726, Kemys-Tyntes inher. 1841, sold 1851, golf club); Wraxall (Tynte's Place), Somerset (acq. by Tyntes by 1401, family departed later 17th c., declined to farm house, sold 1813); Chelvey Court, Somerset (Tyntes purch early 17th c., built 1618-60, became principal seat, later 17th c., then declined in importance 18th c., part demolished 1805, became farm houses)
Estates: Bateman 20679 (E & W) 37566
Titles: Baronet 1642-1735; 1674-1785
Peers: 2 peers 1916-45
Notes: The Kemys (Kemeys) family has an entry in the ODNB.

Kemmis (Kemys)

Origins: Cadet of the Kemys family (see above) from Monmouthshire. Settled in Ireland in the 18th century.

1. Herman Kemmis – {Tralee 1798-1800}
2. Thomas Kemmis – East Looe 1830-32

Seat: Kimmage, Dublin
Estates: 4159 (I) 1620 in the later 19th c.

Byerley

Origins: The granddaughter of Sir Thomas Wharton (brother of the 4 Baron) married Robert Byerley and brought with her Edlington, Yorkshire. The Byerleys were bankers who became successful in the early 17th century and entered the gentry.

1. Robert Byerley – County Durham 1685-87 1689-90 Knaresborough 1695-1714

Seats: Edlington, Yorkshire (acq. by mar. 1692, sold c. 1700); Midridge (Middridge) Grange, Durham (built c. 1578, acq. early 17th c., remod. c. 1690, remod. c. 1720, passed by mar. to Jervoise family 1692 and the by mar. to the O'Carrolls 1776, who sold it in 1812, fire 19th c., declined to farm house, derelict)
Estates: Worth £600 pa in 1660.
Notes: Family extinct mid-18th century. The family inherited the Hutton estates of Goldsborough, Yorkshire (**one MP 1621-28**). One in ODNB.

Tynte

Origins: The uncle of John Tynte MP (1661-69) emigrated to Ireland c. 1600. Original estates in Cork. Sheriff 1711. James Worth {MP} below succeeded to Tynte estates through his mother and took the name Tynte. He married the Bulkeley heiress (see Bulkeley) to Old Bawn 1702 and succeeded to her estates in 1710.

1. Sir Henry Tynte – {County Cork 1661}
2. James Worth Tynte – {Rathcormack 1716-27 Youghal 1727-58}

Seat: Tynte Park, Wicklow (acq. 18th c., add. c. 1835, sold c. 1974); Old Bawn, Dublin (built c. 1635, succ. by mar. to Bulkeley (see Bulkeley) estates 1710, demolished 1970s)
Estates: Bateman 5013 (I) 4677
Title: Baronet 1778-85

Worth

Origins: The daughter and heiress of Sir Henry Tynte {MP 1661} married William Worth. Their son James Worth (Tynte – MP 1716-58) succeeded to the Tynte estates in 1691 and took the name Tynte. The Worths were originally from Cheshire. The great-grandfather of Edward Worth {MP 1695-1741} emigrated to Ireland. His son was Bishop of Killaloe, and the father of the {MP} was Baron of the Exchequer in Ireland 1681-86.

1. Edward Worth – {Knocktopher 1695-99 1703-41}
2. Edward Worth – {New Ross 1715-27}

Seats: Rathfarnham, Dublin (Whartons - acq. 1700, sold 1723); Blanfield (Blanchfield), Kilkenny (purch. 1703, sold late 18th c.)
Estates: Worth £2,000 pa in 1713 and £3,000 pa in 1741. 5,696 acres worth £1,954 in 1851.
Notes: Extinct in the male line late 18th c. One in ODNB.

Wharton

Origins: A cadet line descended from an ancestor of the Dukes of Wharton. Active colliers and railway entrepreneurs in the 19th century.

1. Humphrey Wharton – Richmond 1679-81
2. Richard Wharton – Durham 1802-04
3. John Wharton – Durham 1871-74 Ripon Div. W. R. Yorkshire 1886-1906

Seats: Dryburn, Durham (medieval, purch. c. 1760, rebuilt 1824, passed to Darwins by mar. late 19th c. and took the additional name Wharton, sold c. 1945, hospital); Kirkby Thore, Westmorland (built 14th c., remod. 16th c. and 17th c., became a farm house)

WHEATE [Barnett]

Origins: "Worthies" in Coventry in the early 17th century, new money. A lawyer purchased Glympton. Sheriff 1696. The 3 Bt was a barrister, the 4th an army officer, the 5th a naval officer, and the 6th a clergyman. Benjamin Barnett married the daughter of Sir John Wheate 6 Bt in 1846 and the Barnetts succeeded to Glympton Park.

1. Sir Thomas Wheate 1 Bt – New Woodstock 1690-95 1708-21
2. Sir Thomas Wheate 2 Bt – New Woodstock 1722-27
3. Henry Barnett – Woodstock 1865-74

Seat: Glympton Park (Manor), Oxfordshire (purch. 1633, rebuilt c. 1750, remod. 1846, sold 1943)
Title: Baronet 1696-1816

WHELER (Wheeler)

Origins: Grocers in the 1560s. The father of the first MP was secretary to the Merchant Adventurers in Holland. Purchased estates in the 1630s. Kt 1649. A Chairman of the East India Company in the 1770s.

1. Sir William Wheler 1 Bt – Westbury 1640-48 Banffshire 1659 Queenbororugh 1660
2. Sir Charles Wheler 2 Bt – University of Cambridge 1667-79
3. Sir Granville Wheler 1 Bt – Faversham Div. Kent 1910-27

Seats: Ledston Hall, Yorkshire (built later 16th c., remod. 1630s, purch. 1653 by Sir John Lewis a lawyer, remod. c. 1670, and passed by mar. after 1789 to the Whelers, now flats); (Westbury) Leigh Manor, Wiltshire (purch. 1638, sold 1772); Leamington Hastings, Warwickshire (acq. 1676 by inher., passed by mar. to Sitwells 1798, still owned 1951); Birdingbury Hall, Warwickshire (built 1st half of the 17th c., passed via the widow of Sir Charles Wheler to the Biddulphs (see that family) in 1687); Otterden Place, Kent (built first half 16th c., purch. 1725, part demolished 1786, add. early 19th c., add. 1886, long lease granted 1958, flats)
Estates: Bateman 5031 (E) 4351
Titles: Baronet 1660- ; 1925-27
Notes: The 1 Baronet of the 1925 creation was a member of a cadet line. Two in ODNB.

WHICHCOTE (Whichcot) [Meres]

Origins: Began with merchants in the 15th century. **First MP 1460-61**. Acquired landed estates in the early 16th century. A barrister from a cadet line was Solicitor General and created a Baronet 1660. The lines later intermarried.

1. George Whichcot – Lincolnshire 1698-1700 1705-10
2. Sir Francis Whichcote 3 Bt – Cambridgeshire 1718-22
3. Thomas Whichcot – Lincolnshire 1740-74

Seats: Harpswell Hall, Lincolnshire (acq. and built early 16th c., family departed 1776, demolished mid-19th c., sold estate 1918); Aswarby Park (Hall), Lincolnshire (built later 17th c., purch. 18th c., rebuilt 1836-38, demolished 1952, stables converted to house for family); Melwood, Lincolnshire (acq. by mar. c. 1683); Quy Hall, Cambridgeshire (purch. 1685, sold 1722)
Estates: Bateman 11218 (E) 16923. 6,000 acres in the 1990s. (Leach, *Lincolnshire Country Houses, Part One*, 44)
Title: Baronet 1660-1949
Notes: Christopher Whichcote MP Berkshire 1658 related? One in ODNB.

Meres

Origins: Rose to prominence as a judge and royal servant 1370s-80s. **First MP 1407 for Lincolnshire. One additional MP 1429 for the county**. The Meres heiress married 1699 George Whichcot MP, and the Meres' estates passed to the family in 1736.

1. Sir Thomas Meres – Lincoln 1659 1660 1661-81 1685-87 1701-10

Seat: Kirton House, Lincolnshire (acq. 14th c., passed by mar. to Whichcots 1736, sold)
Notes: Three in ODNB.

WHITAKER (Whittaker)

Origins: One of the most important families in the Wiltshire wool trade in the 16th century. Granted arms 1560. **First MP 1586. One additional MP 1624-46 for Shaftesbury**. The third MP, below, a lawyer, acquired further estates.

1. Henry Whitaker – Shaftesbury 1659 1661-79
2. Henry Whitaker – Shaftesbury 1711-15

Seat: Motcombe (aka Palmer's Place), Dorset (purch. 1648, sold 1825)

WHITBREAD

Origins: A family of brewers. The firm founded by a member of the Bedfordshire lesser gentry (17th century) with £2,000 in capital in the mid-18th century continued into the 20th. The first MP died worth £1,000,000.

1. Samuel Whitbread – Bedford 1768-74 1775-90 Steyning 1792-96
2. Samuel Whitbread – Bedford 1790-1815
3. William Whitbread – Bedford 1818-34
4. Samuel Whitbread – Middlesex 1820-30
5. Samuel Whitbread – Bedford 1852-95
6. Samuel Whitbread – S. Bedfordshire 1892-95 S. Huntingdonshire 1906-10

Seats: Southill Park, Bedfordshire (built 17th c., rebuilt 1724-32, purch. 1795 for £85,000 and new house cost £54,000 (Hussey, *English Country Houses: Late Georgian 1800-1840*, 27, 29) and £20,000-30,000 on furnishings (Collett-White, *Inventories of Bedfordshire Country Houses*, 218), built 1796-1803, still own); Cardington (Barnes House), Bedfordshire (built mid-16th, purch. 1650-1760s, ceased to be seat in later 18th c.); Loudham Hall, Suffolk (built 16th c., rebuilt c. 1730s, remod. c. 1790, purch. 1792, sold 1921)

Estates: Bateman 13829 (E) 21790. By 1785 held 4,500 acres and by 1796 over 12,000 acres. (Rapp, "Social Mobility", 382-3.) Total income of over £20,000 pa in c. 1800. Rubinstein – Samuel Whitbread left £200,000 probate in 1815. Worth £148,000,000 in 1990 with Southill estate and 32,000 acres in Scotland.
1 Ld Lt 20th
Notes: Three in ODNB.

WHITE I *IRELAND*

Baron Annaly (1863- UK)

Origins: Luke White (MP 1818-24), of unknown parentage, was a lottery operator, bookseller, contractor for government loans, and banker. He spent £200,000 on elections and purchased Lord Carhampton's estate for £180,000 in 1799. Sheriff 1806. He died leaving property worth at least £30,000 pa and £100,000 in liquid assets.

1. Luke White – County Leitrim 1818-24
2. Henry White 1 Baron Annaly – County Dublin 1823-32 County Longford 1837-47 1857-61
3. Samuel White – County Leitrim 1824-47
4. Luke White – County Longford 1832 1836-42
5. Luke White 2 Baron Annaly – County Clare 1859-60 Longford 1861-62 Kidderminster 1862-65
6. Charles White – Tipperary 1866-75

Seats: Luttrellstown Castle, Dublin (renamed Woodlands) (old castle, remod. 18th c., purch. 1799, remod. early 19th c., add. 1850s, sold early 20th c.); Headford, Leitrim (acq. late 18th c., still owned 1870s, demolished by 1940); Lareen House, Leitrim (purch. early 19th c., built 1820s, passed to Massys 1880, fire 1933, ruin); Rathcline(s) Castle, Longford (rebuilt 1660s, damaged 1690, purch. 1770, never adequately repaired, ruinous today); Cahercon, Clare (built 18th c., purch. 1873, sold 1899); Killakee House, Dublin (purch. 1800, house built 1806, passed to Massys 1880, demolished 20th c.)
Estates: Bateman 16514 (I) 14761 and 23957 (I) 9548 and 6152 (I) 2292. Worth £3,000 pa in 1799.
Peers: 4 peers 1863-1945
3 Lds Lt 19th
1 KP 19th

WHITE II *IRELAND*

Earl of Bantry (1816-91 I)

Origins: A farmer, Richard White, settled on Whiddy Island in Bantry Bay in the late 17th century. He took over much of the estate of the Earl of Anglesey. His son was a successful lawyer. His grandson was sent to Harrow and made a peer for helping to organize resistance to the French invasion of 1796. The family continued to acquire land in the 19th century.

No MPs

Seats: Bantry House (Blackrock, Seafield), Cork (built 1710, purch. 1750, add. c. 1770, add. 1845, still own); Macroom Castle, Cork (old castle destroyed in the Civil War, restored post 1660, passed from Eyres to Whites by mar. in 19th c., burned c. 1920); Glengarriffe Castle (Lodge), Cork (acq. c. 1800, sold 1892, reacq. 1899, sold 1960, demolished later 20th c.)
Estate: Bateman 69500 (I) 14561. Owned 2,500 acres in 2001.
Titles: Baron Bantry 1797-1891 I; Viscount Bantry 1800-91 I; Viscount Berehaven 1816-91 I
Peers: {1 peer 1797-1800} 2 Irish Rep peers 1854-68 1869-84

WHITE III

Origins: Descended from a Merchant of Staple at Calais d. 1461. **First MP 1547 for Hampshire. Five additional MPs 1555-71.**

1. William White – Pontefract 1645 Clitheroe 1659 1660

Seats: Bashall Hall, Yorkshire (built c. 1600, acq. by mar. 1629, passed later 17th c. by inher. to Ferrers, remod. early 18th c., sold by 1806); Duffield Park, Derbyshire (sold later 17th c. or early 18th c.)

WHITE IV [Lawrence, Taylor]

White

Origins: Rose through service to Mary I and rewarded with a manor. Married a sister of Lord Burghley.

1. John White – Nottinghamshire 1679-81 1689-90 1691-98
2. Thomas White – East Retford 1701-02 1708-11 1715-32

3. John White – East Retford 1733-68

Seats: Walling Wells (Wallingwells) Hall, Nottinghamshire (acq. by mar. from Taylors 1699, sold 1919, flats); Tuxford Hall, Nottinghamshire (old house, purch. 1545-47 and 1560, rebuilt 1785, sold c. 1850)
Estates: Bateman 3799 (E) 4423
Title: Baronet 1802-

Taylor

Origins: The first MP was the son of an official. His daughter and heiress married Thomas White MP (see above), who inherited Walling Wells.

1. Richard Taylor – East Retford 1690-98

Seat: Walling Wells (Wallingwells) Hall, Nottinghamshire (medieval, rebuilt 16th c., purch. later 17th c., passed to Whites by mar. 1699)

Lawrence

Origins: Sir Edward Lawrence 1 Bt was succeeded by a great nephew, Isaac Wollaston of Loseby, Leicestershire (see Wollaston), whose daughter married Taylor White MP and was mother of the first White Baronet.

1. Sir Edward Lawrence 1 Bt – Stockbridge 1705-10

Title: Baronet 1748-56

WHITELAW *SCOTLAND & IRELAND*

Viscount Whitelaw (1983-99 UK)

Origins: The first MP was an iron master who made a fortune in mining, shipping, and railways.

1. Alexander Whitelaw – Glasgow 1874-79
2. Graeme Whitelaw – N. W. Lanarkshire 1892-95
3. William Whitelaw – Perth 1892-95
4. William Whitelaw 1 Viscount Whitelaw – Penrith and Border 1955-83

Seats: Gartshore House, Dumbartonshire (built 17th c., purch. 1870, new house 1887, demolished 1950s, estate broken up into smaller units); Ennin, Cumberland (add. 1883, purch. 1950s, sold c. 2001)
1 in Cabinet 1970-74 1979-88
1 KT 20th
Notes: 1 Viscount, a leading figure in the Thatcher years, in ODNB.

WHITELEY

Baron Marchamley (1908- UK)

Origins: The first MP was a cotton manufacturer during the first half of the 19th century.

1. George Whiteley 1 Baron Marchamley – Stockport 1893-1900 Pudsey Div. W. R. Yorkshire 1900-08
2. Sir Herbert Whiteley 1 Bt – Ashton-under-Lyne 1895-1906 Mid Worcestershire 1916-18

Seats: Hawkestone Hall (Park), Shropshire (built 1720, add. 1750, purch. 1906, sold 1926, institutional use); Thorngrove, Worcestershire (built c. 1800, acq. early 20th c., sold c. 1945?)
Peers: 2 peers 1908-45
Title: Baronet 1918-

WHITEWAY

Origins: Woolen merchants in Dorchester by 1600. **First MP 1624 and another 1626, both for Dorchester**.

1. John Whiteway – Dorchester 1654 1656 1660

Notes: The last MP died bankrupt. One in ODNB.

WHITLEY [Scriven] *WALES & ENGLAND*

Whitley

Origins: Burgesses, lawyers, and local officials in Chester and Flint in the 16th century. Sheriff 1637. **First MP 1614 for Chester**. Purchased substantial estates in North Wales.

1. Roger Whitley – Flint Boroughs 1600-81 Chester 1681 1689-90 1695-97
2. Thomas Whitley – Flint Boroughs 1681 1690-95

Seat: Peele Hall, Cheshire (acq. c. 1680, passed by mar. to 3 Earl of Plymouth early 18th c., declined to farm house)
Notes: Extinct in male line early 18th c. One in ODNB.

Scriven

Origins: The founder was a scrivener who acquired an estate by marriage in the 14th century. **First MP 1407 for Shrewsbury. One additional MP for Shrewsbury 1586-1601.** Richard Scriven MP had a daughter and heiress who married the son of Roger Whitley (see above).

1. Richard Scriven – Bishop's Castle 1679-81

Seat: Frodesley, Shropshire (acq. by mar. 14th c., passed by mar. to Whitleys 1683)
Notes: Extinct in male line 1683.

WHITLOCK (Whitelocke)

Origins: Recorded in Berkshire in the 15th century. A London merchant's son became a judge in the early 17th century. Kt 1620. **First MP 1609. Three additional MPs 1626-59.**

1. Sir William Whitlock – West Looe 1659 Great Marlow 1689-95 Oxford University 1703-17

Seats: Phyllis Court, Oxfordshire (medieval, purch. 1672, sold 1768, club from 1906); Fawley Court, Buckinghamshire (purch. 1616, sacked 1642, sold 1679, institutional use)
Estates: Spent £9,000 buying land c. 1620. Worth £700 pa in the 1660s.
Notes: Sir Bulstrode Whitlocke MP 1626-56 was a Cromwellian peer and a regicide. Three in ODNB.

WHITMORE [Wolryche]

Origins: Although they can be traced back to the 14th century, the Whitmores acquired Apley with a London-based fortune made as silk merchants in the 16th century, Lord Mayor 1631. Further purchases took place in 1614 and 1621. **First MP 1621 for Brignorth. One other MP 1640 also for Bridgnorth**. From 1621 the family sat for Bridgnorth in every Parliament save five until 1870 (Whiteley, *The Social Composition of the House of Commons, 1868-1885,* 65). Baronets 1641. An election jingle of 1852 ran "Bridgnorth can't remember, No Whitmore for Member." (*Victoria County History, Shropshire*, 1979, p. 334).

1. Thomas Whitmore – Much Wenlock 1659 1660
2. Sir William Whitmore 2 Bt – Shropshire 1660 Bridgnorth 1661-81 1685-87 1689-99
3. Sir Thomas Whitmore – Bridgnorth 1663-81
4. William Whitmore – Bridgnorth 1705-10 1713-25
5. Thomas Whitmore – Bridgnorth 1734-54
6. William Whitmore – Bridgnorth 1741-47 1754-71
7. Thomas Whitmore – Bridgnorth 1771-95
8. John Whitmore – Bridgnorth 1795-1806
9. Thomas Whitmore – Bridgnorth 1806-31
10. William Wolryche-Whitmore – Bridgnorth 1820-32 Wolverhampton 1832-34
11. Thomas Whitmore – Bridgnorth 1832-52
12. Henry Whitmore – Bridgnorth 1852-70
13. Charles Whitmore – Chelsea 1886-1906

Seats: Apley Park, Shropshire (medieval castle, purch. 1582, Georgian house, rebuilt 1811, sold 1867); Dudmaston Hall, Shropshire (built c. 1695-1701, acq. by mar. 1774, remod. 1820s, NT 1978); Lower Slaughter Manor House, Gloucestershire (medieval, acq. 1611, rebuilt 1656-58, add. 1860s and 1891, sold 1964); Orsett Hall, Essex (house built 17th c., remod. 18th c., acq. by mar. 1884, family departed 1964, hotel)
Estates: Bateman 5198 (E) 6272. Worth £1,000 pa in 1620s and £5,000 pa c. 1700.
Title: Baronet 1641-99
1 Ld Lt 20th
Notes: Thomas Whitmore (MP 1806-31) owned an estate worth £20,000 pa and was a London banker. But he spent heavily on electioneering and sold much land in the 1830s and 1840s. He died leaving a debt of £180,000 in 1846, with a net income reduced to £5,000 pa. His son sold Apley for £500,000 to William Foster MP and purchased Gumley, Leicestershire. (Fisher, *The House of Commons*, VII, 742-43). One in ODNB.

Wolryche

Origins: Settled in Shropshire in the 13th century. Succeeded to Dudmaston by marriage in 1403 (an estate that passed by inheritance for 850 years - Negus, *A Tour of Twelve Great Country Houses*, 135). **First MP 1435 for Bridgnorth. Another MP 1621.** Purchased more land in the 16th and 17th centuries. Baronets 1641. The male lineage failed in 1723, when the Wolryche estates passed through the female line via the Welds of Willey (see Forester) to the Whitmores in 1774. Thus Bridgnorth was represented by a member of the Wolyrche-Whitmore dynasty repeatedly between 1435 and 1870.

1. John Wolryche – Much Wenlock 1679-81

Seats: Dudmaston Hall, Shropshire (acq. by mar. of 1403 to an heiress of a family that had held it since the 12th c., rebuilt c. 1730, passed to Whitmores by mar. 1774);

Dinmore Manor, Herefordshire (medieval, purch. 1559, rebuilt c. 1600, add. c. 1700, passed out of family by mar. early 18th c.)
Estate: 4,500 acres by c. 1600. Worth £6,355 pa in 1858.
Title: Baronet 1641-1723
Notes: One in ODNB.

WHITWORTH I [Aylmer, Priestman] *ENGLAND & IRELAND*

Earl Whitworth (1815-25 UK)

Origins: Gentry by mid-17th century. The 1 Baron was a leading diplomat in the first half of the 18th century.

1. Charles Whitworth 1 Baron Whitworth – Newport (IoW) 1722-25
2. Francis Whitworth – Minehead 1723-42
3. Charles Whitworth – Minehead 1747-61 Bletchingley 1761-68 Minehead 1768-74 East Looe 1774 Saltash 1775-78
4. Richard Whitworth – Stafford 1768-80

Seats: Batchacre Hall, Staffordshire (built 18th c., now a farm house); Leyborne Grange, Kent (medieval, purch. 1724, rebuilt c. 1730, sold 1776); Blackford, Somerset (resident 18th c.)
Titles: Baron Whitworth 1721-1825 I; Baron Whitworth 1800-25 I; Viscount Whitworth 1813-25 UK
Peers: 1 peer 1813-25
1 in Cabinet 1813-17
Notes: Extinct in male line 1825. 1 Baron 1st cr. and 1 Earl and one other in ODNB.

Baron Aylmer (1718- I)

Origins: The Aylmers claimed descent from Athelmar, Earl of Cornwall in the reign of Ethelred the Unready. They participated in the Norman invasion of Ireland and settled at Lyons, Kildare c. 1300. (Burke, *A Visitation of Seats and Arms of the Noblemen and Gentlemen of Great Britain and Ireland*, I, p. 82) The founder of the modern family was Lord Chief Justice of Ireland 1535. The sister and heiress of the last Earl Whitworth married the 4 Baron Aylmer. Their son, the 5 Baron, changed his name to Whitworth-Aylmer in 1825. Several branches of Irish Aylmers descended from John Aylmer of Lyons and are combined here.

1. John Aylmer – [Naas 1692-93}
2. Matthew Aylmer 1 Baron Aylmer – Dover 1697-1713 1713-20
3. Henry Aylmer 2 Baron Aylmer – Rye 1722-27

4. Sir Fitzgerald Aylmer 6 Bt – {Roscommon 1761-68 Old Leighlin 1768-76 Kildare 1776-83 Harristown 1783-94}
5. John Aylmer – Maidstone 1880-85

Seats: Lyons Castle, Kildare (medieval castle, acq. c. 1300, sold 1796); Balrath, Meath (acq. 16th c., rebuilt c. 1800, sold 1795); West Cliffe (Westcliffe), Kent (purch. c. 1700, sold mid-18th c.); Donadea Castle, Kildare (castle, acq. 1558, rebuilt 17th c., remod. c. 1800, left to Church of Ireland 1935, later a ruin); Courtown, Kildare (acq. 18th c., burned 1798, rebuilt c. 1815, add. c. 1900, sold 1947)
Estates: Bateman 20007 (I) 11479
Titles: Baronet 1621- ; 1662-
Peers: {5 peers 1718-66 1778-85 1796-1800}
Notes: Attainted 1689-90. The 1 Baron was an admiral 1708. The Aylmers were Roman Catholic until the 1 Baron conformed to the Church of Ireland. The Lords Aylmer were poor in the 18th century, having sold all their estates. Moved to Canada in 20th c. 1 Baron and two others in ODNB.

Priestman

Origins: The MP below was a Lord of the Admiralty of unknown parentage. His daughter and heiress married the 2 Baron Aylmer and brought the Priestman property to the Aylmer family.

1. Henry Priestman – New Shoreham 1695-98

WHITWORTH II [Aylmer] *IRELAND & ENGLAND*

Origins: Manchester merchants and manufacturers in the 19th century, with interests in Drogheda.

1. Benjamin Whitworth – Drogheda 1865-69 Kilkenny 1875-80 Drogheda 1880-85
2. Thomas Whitworth – Drogheda 1869-74
3. William Whitworth – Newry 1874-80

Seat: The Sycamores (Sycamore House), Louth (built c. 1880, remod. c. 1910)
Estates: 11 (I) 560 in 1878

WHORWOOD

Origins: The founder of the family was Attorney General to Henry VIII, who purchased land in Staffordshire. **First MP 1529. One further MP for Staffordshire 1572.**

1. Brome Whorwood – Oxford 1661-68

Seats: Holton, Oxfordshire (old house, acq. by mar. 1613 from a family that held it from the 15th c., rebuilt 17th c., sold 1801 for £54,000); Sandwell Hall (Park), Staffordshire (medieval, purch. c. 1560s, sold 1701, demolished c. 1920); Stourton Castle, Staffordshire (medieval, add. mid to late 16th c., acq. c. 1590, sold c. 1660)
Notes: Estates passed to an illegitimate son in 1701. One in ODNB.

WICKHAM

Origins: Descended from an Elizabethan Bishop of Winchester of a family long settled in Yorkshire. The first MP was an official who purchased estates in Hampshire in 1815. Henry Wickham (MP 1852-67) was a partner in an iron works.

1. William Wickham – Heytesbury 1802 Cashel 1802-06 Callington 1806-07
2. Henry Wickham – Bradford 1852-67
3. William Wickham – Petersfield Div. Hampshire 1892-97

Seats: Cottingley House (Hall), Yorkshire (built early 17th c., acq. by mar. of 1761, sold 1804, demolished 1872); Binsted Wyck, Hampshire (purch. 1815, sold early 20th c.); Cookham Elms, Berkshire (purch. c. 1800, sold c. 1830)
Notes: Three in ODNB.

WIGGIN

Origins: The first MP was apprenticed to a draper as a boy and later founded a great metal refining firm in Birmingham.

1. Sir Henry Wiggin 1 Bt – E. Staffordshire 1880-85 Handsworth Div. Staffordshire 1885-92
2. Sir Jerry Wiggin – Weston-super-Mare 1969-97
3. William Wiggin – Leominster 2001-10 N. Herefordshire 2010-

Seat: Metchley Grange, Staffordshire
Estates: The 1 Bt left £475,000 in probate in 1906.
Title: Baronet 1892-
Notes: One in ODNB.

WIGRAM (Fitzwygram)

Baron Wigram (1935- UK)

Origins: The son of a master of a privateer lost at sea was raised by his uncle, a doctor. He started out as a surgeon, became a drug importer and East India merchant, making a great fortune. He invested £100,000 in a brewery and £100,000 in docks and ships. Baronet 1805, Sheriff 1812. His son was Director of the Bank of England 1807. A younger son became Chairman of the East India Company.

1. Sir Robert Wigram 1 Bt – Fowey 1802-06 Wexford 1806-07
2. Sir Robert Fitzwygram 2 Bt – Fowey 1806-18 Lostwithiel 1818-26 Wexford 1829-30
3. William Wigram – New Ross 1807-12 Wexford 1820-26 New Ross 1826-30 Wexford 1830-31 New Ross 1831-32
4. Sir James Wigram – Leominster 1841
5. Loftus Wigram – University of Cambridge 1850-59
6. Sir Frederick Wigram 4 Bt – S. Hampshire 1884-1900
7. Alfred Wigram – S. Essex 1894-97

Seats: Leigh Park, Hampshire (built 1802, add. mid-19th c., new house 1861, purch. 1874, family departed 1936, sold 1944); Belmont Lodge, Worcestershire (purch. mid-19th c., sold late 19th c., hotel); Benington (Place) Park, Hertfordshire (purch. mid-19th c., sold later 19th c.); Walthamstow House, Essex (purch. 1782, sold 1842)
Estates: 1 Bt est. worth over £500,000 in 1809.
Title: Baronet 1805-
Peers: 1 peer 1935-45
Notes: The name change to Fitzwygram adopted by the 2 Bt was entirely fanciful. 1 Baron and six others in ODNB.

WILBRAHAM [Bootle]

Wilbraham

Origins: Knight and Sheriff in the 13th century. **First MP 1553, for Cheshire 1554. Two further MPs 1571-1614**. The common ancestor of the families below was Thomas Wilbraham of Woodhey, an estate that passed to the eldest son. The youngest son was the ancestor of the lines at Delamere and Lathom. The Cheshire estates passed to the Tollemaches (Earls of Dysart – see Tollemache) in the early 18th century. On the death of the 6 Earl in 1821 the Suffolk and Cheshire estates passed by mar. to John Halliday.

1. Sir Thomas Wilbraham 3 Bt – Stafford 1679-81

Seat: Woodhey, Cheshire (built c. 1600, rebuilt c. 1690, passed by mar. to 2 Earl of Dysart, demolished c. 1740); Tilstone Hall, Cheshire (built c. 1600, damaged 1640s, ceased to be main seat, passed to 2 Earl of Dysart, demolished c. 1740, passed to Hallidays and new house c. 1821)
Estates: Worth £4,000 in the 17th century.
Title: Baronet 1621-91
Notes: See Manners (Tollemache, Earls of Dysart)

Wilbraham

Origins: See above.

1. Roger Wilbraham – Helston 1786-90 Bodmin 1790-96
2. George Wilbraham – Bodmin 1789-90
3. George Wilbraham – Stockbridge 1826-31 Cheshire 1831-32 S. Cheshire 1832-41

Seats: Delamere House (Lodge, Manor), Cheshire (new house built 1784 and became main seat 1780s, demolished 1938, rebuilt as Delamere Manor 1939, family departed 1940, sold after 1945, business use); Townsend House, Cheshire (original seat built 1575, moved seat to Delamere House 1780s, demolished)
Estates: Bateman 4321 (E) 8426

Earl of Lathom (1880-1930 UK)

Origins: Descended from a younger brother of Roger Wilbraham of Delamere. This line was seated at Rode Hall. Richard Wilbraham married Mary, daughter and heiress of Robert Bootle of Lathom House. Their eldest son was created Baron Skelmersdale in 1828. His younger brother succeeded to Rode Hall. The first Bootle MP was a lawyer, and the Lathom estates included valuable coal mines.

1. Sir Thomas Bootle – Liverpool 1724-34 Midhurst 1734-53
2. Randle Wilbraham – Newcastle-under-Lyme 1740-47 Appleby 1747-54 Newton 1754-68
3. Richard Wilbraham Bootle – Chester 1761-90
4. Edward Bootle-Wilbraham 1 Baron Skelmersdale – Westbury 1795-96 Newcastle-under-Lyme 1796-1812 Clitheroe 1812-18 Dover 1818-28
5. Richard Bootle-Wilbraham – S. Lancashire 1835-44

Seats: Lathom House, Lancashire (medieval house, ruined 1644, purch. 1714 by the Bootles from the Stanleys, new house 1725-30, remod. early 19th c. and 1866, sold early 1925, demolished soon after through to 1960); Rode Hall, Cheshire (purch. 1669, built c. 1700, add. 1752 and c. 1800, passed by mar. to Baker Bts who took the name Wilbraham 1878, remod. 1920s, still own); Blythe Hall, Lancashire (built later 16th c., acq. by mar. 1826, became principal seat c. 1920, sold after 1930)

Estates: 7213 (E) 21869 (at Rode Hall 2032 (E) 4514) Rubinstein – 2 Wilbraham Baker Bt left £120,000 in probate 1830.
Title: Baron Skelmersdale 1828- UK
Peers: 5 peers 1828-1910 1916-45
Notes: First Baker Bt was Physician to George III. One in ODNB.

WILDE

Baron Truro (1850-99 UK)

Origins: The 1 Baron was the son of an attorney. The family acquired wealth and status through the law in the 18th and 19th centuries.

1. Thomas Wilde 1 Baron Truro – Newark 1831-32 1835-41 Worcester 1841-46

Seat: Falconhurst, Kent (acq. and built 1864-67, still resident 1879, sold 1890s, hotel, demolished c. 1955)
Estates: Under 2000 acres in Bateman
Peers: 3 peers 1850-99
1 in Cabinet 1850-51
Notes: 1 Baron in ODNB.

WILDMAN

Origins: The first MP was a London attorney and gained wealth through exploiting the Beckford estates of which he was agent and manager. The second MP owned a West Indian plantation.

1. Thomas Wildman – Hindon 1795
2. James Wildman – Hindon 1796-1802
3. James Wildman – Colchester 1818-26

Seats: Chilham Castle, Kent (medieval, rebuilt 1616, purch. 1794, sold 1861); Yotes Court, Kent (built 1656-58, purch. 1861, sold 1948)
Notes: The estates of Stephen Lushington (MP 1807-37, see Lushington) of Norton Court, Kent passed in 1868 to his grandson James Lushington Wildman, son of his daughter and heiress Mary Ann and James Beckford Wildman (MP 1818-26 above).

WILLES

Origins: The father of the first MP was a Canon of Lichfield. The son was Lord Chief Justice 1737.

1. Sir John Willes – Launceston 1724-26 Weymouth & Melcombe Regis 1726-27 West Looe 1727-37
2. John Willes – Banbury 1746-54 Aylesbury 1754-61
3. Edward Willes – Old Sarum 1747 Aylesbury 1747-54 Leominster 1767-68

Seats: Astrop, Northamptonshire (purch. 18th c, sold 1901, demolished); Newbold Comyn Hall, Warwickshire (purch. 1539, built mid-16th c., family departed after 1945, sold and demolished 1965)
Estates: Bateman 2631 (E) 4255
Notes: Four in ODNB.

WILLIAMS I [Powell, Symonds, Wood] *WALES & ENGLAND*

Williams

Origins: The father of the first MP was a substantial yeoman descended from an obscure branch of an ancient lineage. The first MP was a lawyer and then a Judge of the King's Bench. Purchased a significant landed estate in 1612. **First MP 1584. Two further MPs 1601-29, one for Breconshire**. Sir Edward Williams of Elham 1 Bt made a fortune as a court physician to Charles II. He married 1675 the daughter of Sir Henry Williams 2 Bt of Gwernyfed, uniting the two families.

1. Sir Henry Williams 2 Bt – Breconshire 1660-61
2. Sir Thomas Williams 1 Bt – Weobley 1675-78
3. Sir Edward Williams – Breconshire 1697-98 1705-21
4. Sir John Williams 2 Bt – Herefordshire 1701-05

Seats: Gwernyfed, Breconshire (purch. 1600, passed to another Williams family by mar. of 1675, passed to Woods by mar. 1804, sold 1922, see below); Elham, Kent (purch. 1681, sold c. 1730); Llangoed Castle (Hall), Radnorshire (purch. and built 1632, passed to other Williams family by mar. of 1675, passed to Woods by mar. and sold 1804)
Estates: Worth £700 pa in the 1660s.
Titles: Baronet 1644-95; 1674-1804

Williams

Origins: Cousins of the Williams family of Gwernyfed. **First MP 1659.**

1. Richard Williams – Radnorshire 1677-79 Breconshire 1679-81 Radnorshire 1685-87 New Radnor Boroughs 1689-90 Radnorshire 1690-92

Seat: Cabalfa, Radnorshire
Notes: This line became extinct in 1704.

Powell

Origins: The daughter and heiress of William Powell MP (born Hinson) of Pengethley married Sir John Williams 2 Bt. **First Hinson MP 1586** was a lawyer. The daughter and heiress of Sir John Williams 2 Bt married Thomas Symonds, whose descendants held the Pengethly estate into the 20th century.

1. William Powell – Herefordshire 1660
2. Thomas Powell Symonds – Hereford 1800-19

Seat: Pengethley, Herefordshire (older house rebuilt c. 1826, sold mid-20th c., now a hotel)
Estates: Worth £2,000 pa in the 17th century.
Notes: Was the (John) Powell (Powle) MP for Leominster 1604-11 related?

Wood

Origins: The Woods were in business in the 18th century and investors in the East India Company. On the extinction of the Williams Baronetcy in 1804 their estates passed to the last Baronet's daughter who married in 1743 Thomas Wood of Littleton.

1. Thomas Wood – Middlesex 1779-80
2. Thomas Wood – Breconshire 1806-47
3. Thomas Wood – Middlesex 1837-47

Seats: Littleton Park (House), Surrey (purch. 1660 and 1780, built 1689, destroyed by fire 1874, restored, sold 1931, movie studio); Gwernyfed Park, Breconshire (acq. by mar. 1804, sold 1922); Coxhoe Hall, Durham (built 1725, purch. 1850, sold 1938, demolished c. 1956)
Estates: Bateman 9978 (E & W) 12419. Rubinstein – Thomas Wood left £180,000 in probate in 1835.
Notes: One in ODNB.

WILLIAMS II [Addams] *WALES*

Origins: The Williams family was of ancient lineage but rose to importance during the 16th century as clients of the Earls of Pembroke. **First MP 1621 for Monmouthshire**. Baronet 1642. On the extinction of the male line in 1758 the estates passed to a niece, Ellen Williams, who married William Addams of Anchor Hill, Monmouthshire, who took the additional name Williams.

1. Sir Trevor Williams 1 Bt – Monmouth 1660 Monmouthshire 1667-79 Monmouth 1679 Monmouthshire 1679-81 1689-90
2. Sir John Williams 2 Bt – Monmouth 1689-90 Monmouthshire 1689-1704
3. Sir Hopton Williams 3 Bt – Monmouthshire 1705-08
4. William Addams-Williams – Monmouthshire 1831-41

Seats: Llangibby (Llangybi) Castle House, Monmouthshire (medieval castle, purch. and built new house 1554, slighted 1640s, ruin, new house later 17th c., passed to Addams family by mar. 1739, sold and demolished 1951, still own estate); Anchor Hill, Monmouthshire (Addams seat in 18th c.)
Estates: Bateman 2827 (W) 2981
Title: Baronet 1642-1758
Notes: One in ODNB.

WILLIAMS III *ENGLAND & WALES*

Origins: The first MP began as a country solicitor and became a self-made king of the copper trade. He set up his own smelting works and manufactured brass as well. The firm had capital of £1,000,000 in 1799. His personal fortune was half a million pounds in 1802 (Gash, *Politics in the Age of Peel*, 219; Jenkins, *The Foundations of Modern Wales: Wales 1642-1780*, 291,293).

1. Thomas Williams – Great Marlow 1790-1802
2. Owen Williams – Great Marlow 1796-1832
3. John Williams – New Windsor 1802-04
4. Thomas Williams – Great Marlow 1820-68
5. Owen Williams – Great Marlow 1880-85

Seats: Temple House, Berkshire (purch. 1788, built c. 1790, sold and demolished c. 1922); Craig-y-don (Craigydon), Anglesey (purch. and built 1790s, sold 20th c.?); Llanidan Hall, Anglesey (built 1631, leased by 1772 to early 19th c.)
Estates: Bateman 14434 (E, W, & I) 21855. Rubinstein – Owen Williams left £120,000 in probate in 1832 (his father, Thomas Williams MP was said to have left £500,000).

WILLIAMS IV

Origins: Began as merchants in Dorchester who purchased landed estates in the early 16th century. Sheriff under Henry VII. Said to have been the richest family in Dorset in the mid-16th century. **First MP for Dorset 1604**. Kt 1607. A member of a cadet line sought his fortune in London in the late 18th century as an apprentice cabinet-maker and then shipbuilder. He became a banker and Director of the East India Company leaving a fortune of £500,000 in 1814. Kept active in the family bank into the 20th century.

1. Robert Williams – Wootton Bassett 1802-07 Grampound 1808 Kilkenny 1809-12 Dorchester 1812-34
2. Robert Williams – Dorchester 1807-12
3. William Williams – Weymouth & Melcombe Regis 1818-26
4. Robert Williams – Dorchester 1835-41
5. Sir Robert Williams 1 Bt – W. Dorset 1895-1922

Seats: Herringston(e) (House), Dorset (medieval, purch. 1513, built c. 1500, remod. c. 1803, still own); Bridehead, Dorset (built 16th c., purch. 1798, add. 1850s, part demolished, still own); Moor Park, Hertfordshire (built 1460s, remod. c. 1617, rebuilt 1679-84, rebuilt c. 1720-28 at a cost of £150,000 - Hussey, *English Country Houses: Early Georgian 1715-1760*, 44 - add. 1763-65, purch. 1801, sold 1828)
Estates: Bridehead line Batemen 4934 (E) 7000; Herringstone line 7349 (E & I) 2259
Title: Baronet 1915-
Notes: One in ODNB.

WILLIAMS V

Origins: A Welsh family that moved to Cornwall in the early 18th century. The founder was John Williams, an eighteenth-century mining engineer and shrewd investor who rose in wealth and status as the price of tin rose. The first MP was the head of a copper smelting firm and a banker.

1. Michael Williams – W. Cornwall 1853-58
2. Sir Frederick Williams 2 Bt – Truro 1865-78
3. Charles Williams (Basset) – Barnstaple 1868-73
4. John Williams – Truro Div. Cornwall 1892-95
5. Charles Williams – Tavistock Div. Devon 1918-22 Torquay Div. Devon 1924-55
6. Alfred Williams – N. Cornwall 1924-29

Seats: Burncoose House, Cornwall (purch. 1715, still own); Heanton Court (House), Devon (purch. c. 1852, declined to a farm house, now hotel); Scorrier House, Cornwall (purch. and built 1778, enlarged 1845, fire 1908, rebuilt, still own); Tregullow, Cornwall (built mid-19th c.); Caerhayes (Caerhays) Castle, Cornwall (medieval, demolished c. 1700, rebuilt 1807-08, purch. 1855, add. 1890s, still own)
Estates: Bateman 18322 (E) 26705. Owned 20,000 acres worth 75 million pounds in 2001.
Title: Baronet 1866-
1 Ld Lt 20th
Notes: The Bassets were seated at Heanton Court (see Basset) The Williams family purchased the house, but one of them married a Bassett and took the additional name Basset. The Williams family remained active in the mining business into the 1890s. One in ODNB.

WILLIAMS-WYNN (Gwynne, Wynne) [Vaughan] *WALES & ENGLAND*

Williams-Wynn

Origins: The Williams were chieftains in Wales from at least the 14th century. They were a great dynasty during the Tudor period. The modern line had modest beginnings with a seventeenth-century younger son who was a clergyman. His son who married well and emerged in English politics thanks to a career as a lawyer and Speaker of the House of Commons under Charles II. The Speaker's son was adopted as heir by Sir John Wynn of Wynnstay, being the son of a brother's granddaughter, who had married Sir William Williams 2 Bt. The Williams family took the additional name Wynn. The Wynns were also of ancient lineage, princes in North Wales in the Middle Ages and claimed to have been kings as early as the 9th century. They built up great estates in the 14th and 15th centuries. **First MP 1542 for Caernarvonshire. Eight further MPs 1553-1649, five of them for the county**.

1. Henry Wynn – Merioneth 1624 1625 1640 1661-71
2. Sir Richard Wynn 4 Bt – Caernarvonshire 1647-48 1661-81
3. Sir William Williams 1 Bt – Chester 1675-81 Montgomery 1685 Beaumaris 1689-90 1695-98
4. Sir John Wynn 5 Bt – Merioneth 1679-81 1685-87 1689-95 Caernarvon 1698-1705 Caernarvonshire 1705-13
5. Sir William Williams 2 Bt – Denbigh 1708-10
6. Sir Watkin Williams-Wynn 3 Bt – Denbighshire 1716-41 Montgomeryshire 1741-42 Denbighshire 1742-49
7. Robert Williams – Montgomeryshire 1740-41 1742-47
8. Richard Williams – Flint Boroughs 1742-47
9. Watkin Williams – Montgomeryshire 1772-74 Flint Boroughs 1777-1806
10. Sir Watkin Williams-Wynn 4 Bt – Shropshire 1772-74 Denbighshire 1774-89
11. Robert Watkin Wynn – Denbighshire 1789-96
12. Sir Watkin Williams-Wynn 5 Bt – Beaumaris 1794-96 Denbighshire 1796-1840
13. Charles Watkin Williams-Wynn – Old Sarum 1797-99 Montgomeryshire 1799-1832 S. Montgomeryshire 1832-50
14. Sir Henry Watkin Williams-Wynn – Midhurst 1807
15. Sir Watkin Williams-Wynn 6 Bt – Denbighshire 1841-85
16. Herbert Williams-Wynn – Montgomeryshire 1850-62
17. Charles Watkin Williams-Wynn – Montgomeryshire 1862-80
18. Herbert Williams-Wynn 7 Bt – Denbighshire 1885

Seats: Wynnstay (originally Watstay), Denbighshire (old house, acq. by mar. to Wynn heiress 1684, rebuilt mid-18th c., fire 1858, new house 1859-65, family departed after 1918, sold 1948, school then flats, still own estate); Llangedwyn Hall, Denbighshire

(old house, acq. and rebuilt by mar. 1718, became main seat after WWI, partly demolished 1952, still own); Llanforda, Shropshire (built early 18th c., new house 1780, destroyed by fire before completion, acq. by mar. to cousins 1852, old house remod. 1813, demolished 1949, still own estate); Glascoed Hall, Denbighshire (acq. by mar. 2nd half 17th c., owned in 19th c.); Nantanog, Anglesey (original Williams seat 16th c., became a farm); Gwydir Castle, Caernarvonshire (acq. by mar. to a Wynn heiress 1675 (Wynns acq. c. 1500), left by Sir Richard Wynn 4 Bt to his daughter Mary who married the 1 Duke of Ancaster, see Bertie); Plas Glanllyn (Glan-llyn), Merionethshire (passed from Vaughans by mar. to Williams-Wynns 1718, sold 1950, institutional use)
Estates: Bateman 145770 (W & E) 54575. Worth £25,000,000 with 17,000 acres in 1990.
Titles: Baronet 1611-1719; 1688-
6 Lds Lt 17th, 18th, 19th, 20th
1 in Cabinet 1822-28 1834-35
Notes: The Wynns inherited the estates of the Loyds of Rhiwgoch, Merionethshire c. 1640, **two MPs 1586-1614, both for the county**. Wynn family and six others have an entry in ODNB. One Williams of Nantanog in ODNB.

Williams

Origins: A cadet line of the Williams (see above).

1. Hugh Williams – Anglesey 1725-34
2. Kyffin Williams – Flint Boroughs 1747-53

Seats: Bodelwyddan Castle, Flintshire (built 15th c., rebuilt c. 1600, purch. c. 1690, remod. 18th c., remod. c. 1800, add. c. 1830s-50s, remod. 1880s, sold 1920-25, museum); Plas Rhianfa (Rhinava), Angelsey (built 1849-51, passed out of family by mar. 1930, hotel)
Estates: Bateman 9371 (W) 8871
Title: Baronet 1798-
Notes: One in ODNB.

Wynne

Origins: Descended from a younger son of the Bodelwyddan line. Jane Williams, heiress of Penairth, married in 1771 William Wynne of Wern.

1. William Wynne – Merioneth 1852-65
2. W. R. Wynne – Merioneth 1865-68

Seat: Penairth House, Merionethshire (acq. by mar. to Williams heiress in 1800, sold late 19th c.)
Estates: Bateman 10556 (W & E) 6229
1 Ld Lt 19th-20th

Baron Newborough (1776- I)

Origins: Descended from a junior line of the Wynns (see above). **First MP 1621.**

1. John Wynne – Denbighshire 1664-79
2. Owen Wynne – New Radnor Boroughs 1685-87
3. John Wynne – Denbigh 1713-15
4. Sir Thomas Wynn 1 Bt – Caernarvon Boroughs 1713-49
5. Sir John Wynn 2 Bt – Caernarvonshire 1740-41 Denbigh Boroughs 1741-47 Caernarvonshire 1754-61 Caernarvon Boroughs 1761-68
6. Sir William Wynn – Cernarvon Boroughs 1749-54
7. Thomas Wynn 1 Baron Newborough – Caernarvonshire 1761-74 St. Ives 1775-80 Beaumaris 1796-1807
8. Glyn Wynn – Caernarvon Boroughs 1768-90
9. Glynn Wynn – Westbury 1807-09
10. Thomas Wynn 2 Baron Newborough – Caernarvonshire 1826-30

Seats: Glynnllivon (Glynliffon) Park, Caernarvonshire (acq. by mar. c. 1700, rebuilt 1751, rebuilt 1836, sold 1954); Melai, Denbighshire (acq. and built, late 14th c., leased to tenants from the 18th c., rebuilt mid-19th c., still own); Belan Fort (Fort Belan), Caernarvonshire (acq. earlier, built 1775, converted to a house 1820s, add. 1890s, sold 1987-92); Bodvean (Bodfean, Bodvan), Caernarvonshire (built 1726, add. late 19th c., sold 1967); Rûg (Rhug), Merionethshire (built late 18th c., acq. by mar. 19th c., partly demolished 1974, still own)
Estates: Bateman 28800 (W) 22726 and 10504 (W) 8905. Owned 22,000 acres worth 12 million pounds in 2001.
Title: Baronet 1742-
Peers: {1 peer 1776-1800}
1 Ld Lt 18th
Notes: The 1 Bt married the Glyn(ne) heiress to Glynnllivon c. 1700 (see Gladstone [Glynne]).

Wynne

Origins: Cadet line in the 16th century.

1. Robert Wynne – Caernarvon Boroughs 1754-61

Seat: Bodyscallen, Caernarvonshire (medieval, passed out of family 1776)
Notes: The estates passed to the Salusburys (see Cotton I) via an heiress in 1776.

Vaughan

Origins: Descended from the Princes of Powys (*Dictionary of Welsh Biography*). Held property in Montgomeryshire since the 14th century. Came to prominence in the Tudor period. Sheriff 1594. The estates passed by the marriage of an heiress, Ann Vaughan, to Watkin Williams-Wynn in 1718.

1. Edward Vaughan – Merionethshire 1626 Montgomeryshire 1647-48 1659 1661
2. Edward Vaughan – Montgomeryshire 1679-81 1685-87 1689-1718
3. John Vaughan – Montgomery 1701-05

Seats: Llwydiarth Park, Montgomeryshire (acq. by mar. 14th c., passed by mar. to Williams-Wynns 1718); Llangedwyn, Denbighshire (passed by mar. to Williams-Wynns 1718); Glanllyn, Merionethshire (acq. Middle Ages, passed by mar. to Williams-Wynns 1718)
Estates: Worth £2,500 pa in 1650. Owned 100,000 acres of upland pasture in northern Montgomeryshire mid-17th c.

WILLIS-FLEMING

Origins: The Flemings were merchants in Southampton, Mayor in the 15th century. They came to prominence due to an Elizabethan lawyer whose career culminated as Lord Chief Justice 1607. He purchased Stoneham. **First MP 1449 for Southampton. Five additional MPs 1504-1628, four of them for Southampton, one sitting for Hampshire in 1597**. The family represented Southampton for three and a half centuries. The Fleming male line became extinct in 1802, when the estates passed by marriage to the Willis family. Arising from a dynasty of physicians, Browne Willis MP made a fortune as a doctor. His grandson John took the additional name Fleming.

1. Edward Fleming – Southampton 1689
2. Browne Willis – Buckingham 1705-08
3. Richard Fleming – Southampton 1710-22
4. John Willis-Fleming – Southampton 1774-80 1784-90
5. John Willis-Fleming – Hampshire 1820-31 1835-42
6. Thomas Willis-Fleming – Winchester 1864-65

Seats: (North) Stoneham Park, Hampshire (Flemings purch. 1595, demolished c. 1948, sold 1953); Chilworth Manor, Hampshire (built 17th c., add. 18th c., purch. 1825, rebuilt 1904, sold 1947, institutional use); Whaddon Hall, Buckinghamshire (medieval, remod. 16th c., Willis purch. 1698, remod. early 18th c., sold 1760)

Estates: Bateman 11610 (E) 16000. The Willis estate was worth £2,000 pa in 1700 (although reported as half that in 1728). The Willis-Flemings owned 8,000 acres in the 1820s; Rubinstein – John Willis, royal physician, left £250,000 in probate in 1835.
Notes: One Fleming and two Willises in ODNB.

WILLS

Baron Winterstoke (1906-11 UK)

Origins: The Wills were long established Bristol merchants. They entered the tobacco trade 1786 and became the owners of Imperial Tobacco. The company generated profits of £788,000 in 1901. The family produced more wealth holders than any other industrial dynasty (Rubinstein, *Men of Property*, 69). They acquired four baronetcies and two peerages within 36 years. The family remained active in the management of the company well into the 20th century.

1. William Wills 1 Baron Winterstoke – Coventry 1880-85 E. Bristol 1895-1900
2. Sir Frederick Wills 1 Bt – N. Bristol 1900-06
3. Gilbert Wills 1 Baron Dulverton – Taunton 1912-18 Weston-super-Mare 1918-22

Seats: Coombe Lodge, Somerset (purch. 1882, rebuilt 1930-32, family departed 1960, leased out for institutional use); East Court (Eastcourt), Kent (medieval, purch. early 20th c., family departed 1932, business use); Northmoor House, Somerset (built 1856-9, purch. 1874, sold 1926); Batsford Park, Gloucestershire (built 1888-92, purch. 1918, still own); Hazelwood, Somerset (purch. sec. half 19th c., sold c. 1945?); Applecross House, Ross-shire (built c. 1675, rebuilt c. 1730-40, purch. 1924, now in a trust); Meggernie Castle, Perthshire (built c. 1585, purch. c. 1912, sold c. 1960); Littlecote House, Berkshire (medieval, rebuilt 16th c., add. 1673, purch. 1929, sold 1985)
Estates: Northmoor estate formed 2,000 acres. The Littlecote estate was 8,000 acres in 1914. The Meggernie Castle estate consisted of 45,000 acres. The Applecross estate of 62,000 acres was purchased by the Wills family in 1924. Owned 263,000 acres in total in Scotland in 1970. Most sold off by 2001 except for Applecross. Members of the family who died between 1909 and 1911 left £13,000,000. Purchased Ditchley Park and 3,000 acres in 1953.
Titles: Baron Dulverton 1929- UK; Baronets 1893- ; 1897- ; 1904- ; 1923-
Peers: 2 peers 1906-11 1929-45
2 Ld Lt 20th
Notes: The Wills family and 1 Baron Winterstoke and two others have entries in the ODNB.

WILMOT (Wylmot) [Childers, Chetwode, Eardley, Gideon, Horton, Smith] *ENGLAND & IRELAND*

Wilmot

Origins: The Wilmots were drapers in Derby and acquired land at the Dissolution of the Monasteries. A physician to George II added to the family fortune.

1. Sir Henry Wilmot 5 Bt – S. Derbyshire 1869-85

Seats: Chaddesdon Hall, Derbyshire (purch. 1539, built 1626, rebuilt 1727-28, add. c. 1790 and 1870s, sold and demolished 1926); Stubton Hall, Lincolnshire (built 1813-14, acq. by inher. later 19th c., sold c. 1918, school)
Title: Baronet 1759-
Notes: One in ODNB.

Wilmot-Horton

Origins: Little is known about the origins of the Hortons. They were gentry by the Tudor period. **First MP 1559.** Robert Wilmot 3 Bt of Osmaston married 1806 the Horton (extinct 1823) heiress and took the additional name Horton on inheriting Catton Hall. He descended from Nicholas Wilmot, younger son of Robert Wylmot of Chaddesden. This line had gained its own baronetcy in 1772.

1. Robert Wilmot – Derby 1690-95
2. Sir Robert Wilmot-Horton 3 Bt – Newcastle-under-Lyme 1818-30

Seats: Osmaston Hall, Derbyshire (purch. c. 1600, built 1630s, new house built 1696, leased out 1814-87, sold 1888, demolished 1938); Catton Hall, Derbyshire (acq. by Hortons 1404, built new house 1740s, acq. by mar. by Wilmots in 1823, add. 1907, passed to the Ansons by mar. 1931, still own); Sudbrook Park, Surrey (built 1715-19, purch. by Hortons 1825, sold 1842)
Estates: Bateman 6036 (E) 12055. Rubinstein – 2 Bt left £100,000 in probate in 1834.
Title: Baronet 1772-1931
Notes: Two in ODNB.

Eardley-Wilmot

Origins: The son of Nicholas Wilmot (see above) married the heiress of Edward Eardley.

1. John Eardley-Wilmot – Tiverton 1776-84 Coventry 1784-96
2. Sir John Eardley-Wilmot 1 Bt – N. Warwickshire 1832-42
3. Sir John Eardley-Wilmot 2 Bt – S. Warwickshire 1874-85

Seat: Berkswell Hall, Warwickshire (acq. by Marow family 1557, built 1663-74, passed. by mar. late 17th c. to Wilmots, sold 1862, now flats)
Title: Baronet 1821-
Notes: Four in ODNB.

Chetwode (Chetwood)

Origins: Migrated to Ireland during the second half of the 17th century and acquired estates. Lawyer involved with forfeited estates. Sheriff 1781. The estates passed in 1839 by marriage of a Chetwood heiress to the Eardley-Wilmots one of whom took the name Chetwode.

1. Benjamin Chetwood – {Harristown 1713-14}
2. Jonathan Chetwood – {Downpatrick 1790-97}

Seat: Woodbrook, Queen's County (acq. and built early 18th c., add. early 19th c., passed to Wilmots 1839, sold 1963)
Estates: 1,389 acres worth £603 in 1878. Worth £1,200 pa in 1713.

Baron Eardley (1789-1824 I)

Origins: A Jewish Portuguese West Indian merchant named Gideon launched the family in the early 18th century. His son, Sampson Gideon, was a financier in London who left £500,000 to his son, the first Baron. Sampson married in 1766 the daughter of Sir John Eardley Wilmot of Berkswell (see above). Their son took the name Eardley in 1789 and was created an Irish peer.

1. Sampson Gideon Eardley 1 Baron Eardley – Cambridgeshire 1770-80 Midhurst 1780-84 Coventry 1784-96 Wallingford 1796-1802

Seats: Abington Hall, Cambridgeshire (medieval, new house 1712, leased by 1 Baron Eardley 1770s); Belvedere, Kent (built c. 1775, passed by mar. to Smiths below 1842)
Title: Baronet 1759-1824
Notes: One in ODNB.

Childers

Origins: A daughter of the 1 Baron Eardley married John W. Childers, and their son inherited one-third of the Gideon fortune. The first Childers of importance was Mayor of Doncaster in 1604. His property passed via an heiress to the Walbankes, who took the name Childers.

1. John W. Childers – Cambridgeshire 1832-35 Malton 1836-46 1847-52
2. Hugh Eardley Childers – Pontefract 1859-85 S. Edinburgh 1886-92

Seats: Cantley Hall, Yorkshire (medieval, purch. 1610, passed to Walbankes by mar. mid-18th c., sold 1901); Carr House, Yorkshire (acq. and built early 17th c., family departed mid-18th c.)
Estates: Bateman 13333 (E) 18769
1 in Cabinet 1868-71 1872-73 1880-82 1882-85 1886
Notes: Four in ODNB.

Smith

Origins: Another daughter and co-heriess of the 1 Baron Eardley married Sir Culling Smith 2 Bt. Their grandson succeeded to the Belvedere estate in 1842. The Smiths were Huguenots originally named Lefevre who came to England in the later 16th century and took the name Smith. Merchants in London in the 18th century.

1. Sir Culling Eardley Eardley (Smith) 3 Bt – Pontefract 1830-31

Seats: Belvedere, Kent (acq. by mar. 1842, demolished 1957); Bedwell Park, Hertfordshire (medieval, rebuilt late 17th c., Culling Smith purch. 1807, remod. 1840s and 1860s, passed by mar. to Hanbury 1865 who took the additional name Culling, sold 1920s, institutional use); Hadley, Middlesex (Smith purch. 18th c., sold 19th c.)
Estates: Bateman 3970 (E) 7096
Title: Baronet 1802-75
Notes: On the death of the 3 Bt in 1863 the estates were broken up among his children and some went to a Childers nephew, which explains the relatively small size of the Eardley Smith property listed in Bateman. One in ODNB.

WILSON

Baron Nunburnholme (1906- UK)

Origins: A Hull shipping dynasty founded in the 1820s and 1830s by a junior clerk and then salesman for an iron merchant who was the son of a lighter owner. Also involved in mining. He left £200,000 at his death in 1869.

1. Charles Wilson 1 Baron Nunburnholme – Kingston-upon-Hull 1874-85 W. Div. Hull 1885-1905
2. Arthur Wilson – Holderness Div. E. R. Yorkshire 1900-02
3. Charles Wilson 2 Baron Nunburnholme – W. Div. Hull 1906-07
4. Guy Wilson – W. Div. Hull 1907-18

Seats: Arthingworth, Northamptonshire (built mid-18th c., Wilsons owned 1st half 20th c., ruin 1967); Warter Priory (Hall), Yorkshire (built c. 1700, add. 1872, purch. 1878, rebuilt 1885-95, sold 1929, demolished 1972); Tranby Croft, Yorkshire (purch. and built c. 1874, family departed c. 1940, sold c. 1945, school); Ferriby Hall, Yorkshire (purch. 1904)
Estates: Bateman 8500 (E) 8000. The 1 Baron left a fortune of nearly one million pounds and the shipping firm was worth two and a half million in the 1890s. Estate was 14,500 acres in the 20th c.
Peers: 3 peers 1906-45
1 Ld Lt 20th
Notes: Arthur Wilson of Tranby Croft married the heiress of the last Filmer Baronet. Their son inherited the Filmer estates in 1916 (see Filmer). 1 Baron and two others in ODNB.

WINGFIELD *IRELAND & ENGLAND*

Viscount Powerscourt (1618-34, 1665-1717, 1744- I)

Origins: Knights at Wingfield Castle in Suffolk from the 13th century until 1385 and then Letheringham in the later 14th century. A younger son went to Ireland as a soldier of high rank under Elizabeth I. Acquired the Powerscourt estate in 1609. **First MP 1376 for Suffolk. 22 additional English MPs 1449-1628, five for Suffolk and three other kts of the shire. First Irish {MP 1559}. One additional {2 MPs 1613-38}.**

1. Folliott Wingfield 1 Viscount Powerscourt – {County Wicklow 1616-66}
2. Edward Wingfield – {County Sligo 1692-93 1695-99 1703-13}
3. Richard Wingfield 1 Viscount Powerscourt – {Boyle 1727-44}
4. Edward Wingfield 2 Viscount Powerscourt – Stockbridge 1756-61
5. Richard Wingfield 3 Viscount Powerscourt – {County Wicklow 1761-64}
6. Richard Wingfield 6 Viscount Powerscourt – Bath 1837-41

Seats: Powerscourt, Wicklow (old castle, acq. 1609, built from 1731-40, add. 19th c., sold 1961, burned 1974); Luggala, Wicklow (built 1790, purch. 1857, sold 1937)
Estates: Bateman 53258 (I) 16385. At Addington 17470 (E & I) 11338. At Barrington 18761 (E & W) 35389
Title: Baron Powerscourt 1885- UK
Peers: {5 peers 1665-1718 1744-51 1762-1800} 2 Irish Rep peers 1821-23 1865-85 2 peers 1885-1945
1 Ld Lt 20th
2 KP 19th, 20th
Notes: A younger son of the 4 Viscount inherited Addington Park (Place), Kent (medieval, demolished – see Leigh II). Descendents of a younger brother of the 5 Viscount succeeded by inheritance in 1869 to Barrington Park, Oxfordshire from the Rice family (still own), see Talbot I. 1 Viscount and nine others in ODNB.

Wingfield

Origins: Descended from a younger son of Sir Robert Wingfield of Letheringham, Suffolk

1. Francis Wingfield – Stamford 1660

Seat: Tickencote Hall, Rutland (acq. by mar. 1594, rebuilt c. 1705, Parry's inher. by mar. and took name Wingfield 1931, demolished 1949)
Estates: Bateman 3047 (E) 5339

WINN [Allanson] *ENGLAND & IRELAND*

Baron St. Oswald (1885- UK)

Origins: London merchants and aldermen. The founder was Queen Elizabeth I's draper. Granted arms 1604. His son purchased landed estates in the mid-17th century. Sheriff 1657.

1. Sir Rowland Winn 5 Bt – Pontefract 1768
2. Rowland Winn 1 Baron St. Oswald – N. Lincolnshire 1868-85
3. Rowland Winn 2 Baron St. Oswald – Pontefract 1885-93

Seats: Nostell Priory, Yorkshire (monastic buildings, purch. 1655, new house built 1733-50, add. 1765-85, NT 1953); Thornton Hall, Lincolnshire (acq. mid-16th c., built 1690s, sold 1919)
Estates: Bateman 7983 (E) 18587
Peers: 3 peers 1885-1945
Notes: 4 Baron in ODNB.

Baron Headley (1797-1994 I)

Origins: Descended from a younger son of the first Winn Baronet of Nostell Priory. The 1 Baron Headley succeeded by marriage 1775 to the Allanson estates and took the additional name Allanson. **The first Allanson MP 1640-53**, Sir William Allanson, was the son of a yeoman. Sir William was a draper in York, Mayor of York 1633.

1. Charles Allanson – Westbury 1715-22
2. Charles Allanson – Ripon 1768-75
3. George Allanson-Winn 1 Baron Headley – Ripon 1789-98
4. Charles Winn-Allanson 2 Baron Headley – Ripon 1806-07 Malton 1807-08 Ludgersall 1811-12
5. George Allanson-Winn – Maldon 1826-27

Seats: Aghadoe House, Kerry (acq. by mar. to Blennerhasset of Ballyseedy heiress 1793, rebuilt 1828, burned 1922, rebuilt, sold before WWII, institutional use); Warley Lodge, Essex (Winn acq. part by inher. 1763 and purch. 1772, built c. 1800, sold 1919); Glenbeigh (Castle) Towers (Wynne's [or Winn's] Castle, Headley Towers), Kerry (built 1867-71, sold to a relative 1886, burned 1922, ruin); Bramham Biggin, Yorkshire (built 17th c., Allansons resident (lease?) mid-18th c., now derelict)
Estates: Bateman 16042 (E & I) 13388
Titles: Baronets 1660-1994; 1797-1994
Peers: 2 Irish Rep peers 1868-77 1883-1913
Notes: 4 Baron declared bankrupt 1883 and 5 Baron bankrupt 1922. Possible Allanson **MP 1656-58** for Leeds. 5 Baron in ODNB.

WINNINGTON [Jeffries, Salwey]

Winnington

Origins: The family claimed medieval descent. The immediate ancestry of the first MP was obscure. He built a fortune through the law. Solicitor General 1674. Kt 1672. Edward Winnington married the niece and heiress of Henry Jeffries of Ham Castle and took the name Jeffries.

1. Sir Francis Winnington – Windsor 1677-79 Worcester 1679-81 Tewkesbury 1692-98
2. Salwey Winnington – Bewdley 1694-1708 1710-15
3. Edward Winnington Jeffries – Droitwich 1708-25
4. Thomas Winnington – Droitwich 1726-41 Worcester 1741-46
5. Francis Winnington – Droitwich 1747-54
6. Sir Edward Winnington 1 Bt – Bewdley 1761-68 1769-74
7. Sir Edward Winnington 2 Bt – Droitwich 1777-1805
8. Sir Thomas Winnington 3 Bt – Droitwich 1807-16 Worcestershire 1820-30 Droitwich 1831-32 Bewdley 1832-37
9. Henry Winnington – W. Worcestershire 1833-41
10. Sir Thomas Winnington 4 Bt – Bewdley 1837-47 1852-68

Seats: Stanford Court, Worcestershire (inher. by mar. in portions from 1668 through early 18th c., Georgian, fire 1882, rebuilt 1886-88, still own); Broadway, Worcestershire (purch. late 17th c., still own); Ham Castle, Worcestershire (medieval castle and house, fire 1605, ruined 1646, new house built, acq. by mar. 1709 from family who held it since mid-16th c., became a farm house, still own)
Estates: Bateman 4622 (E) 6418
Title: Baronet 1755-
Notes: Two in ODNB.

Salwey

Origins: An old landed family. (*Victoria County History Shropshire*, 1979) The first MP was the son of an official in the Exchequer. **First MP 1640 for Worcestershire. Two further MPs 1645-59, one for the county**. Sir Francis Winnington married the heiress Elizabeth Salwey of Stanford Court. A Salwey cadet line produced the MP below.

1. Henry Salwey – Ludlow 1837-52

Seats: Haye Park, Herefordshire (acq. and built later 17th c., add. 19th c., declined to a farm house, still own); The Lodge, Richard's Castle, Herefordshire (medieval castle, acq. by mar. of 1558, rebuilt lodge 18th c., declined to farm house, still own); Moor Park, Shropshire (built c. 1720, sold 1874, school); Stanford Court, Worcestershire (acq. by mar. 1420, passed by mar. to Winningtons later 17th c., see above)
Estates: Bateman 3193 (E) 3617
Notes: Two in ODNB.

WISEMAN

Origins: The Wiseman family held land in Essex from c. 1430. The first MP was a lawyer and official. **First MP 1554. Two additional MPs 1571-1604.** A cadet line produced a London goldsmith in the early 17th century that also purchased landed estates and produced the MPs below.

1. Sir Richard Wiseman – Maldon 1661-79
2. Sir William Wiseman 1 Bt – Maldon 1677-81

Seats: Rivenhall Place, Essex (purch. 1590, built late 16th c., sold 1692); Torrell's Hall, Essex (purch. early 17th c., passed out of family by mar. 1712)
Estates: Worth £1,200 pa in 1660s.
Titles: Baronet 1628-54; 1660-88
Notes: One in ODNB.

WODEHOUSE (Woodhouse)

Earl of Kimberley (1866- UK)

Origins: The first MP was a royal servant and Chancellor of the Duchy of Lancaster who purchased landed estates in Norfolk in the later 14th century. **First MP 1410 for Norfolk. Five additional MPs 1545-1653, one for the county**. Five hundred years separated the first and last member of the family sitting for Norfolk with at least one MP sitting in each century between 1410 and 1910.

1. Sir Philip Wodehouse 3 Bt – Norfolk 1654 1656 Thetford 1660
2. Sir John Wodehouse 4 Bt – Thetford 1695-98 1701-02 1705-08 Norfolk 1710-13
3. William Woodhouse – Norfolk 1734-37
4. Sir Armine Wodehouse 5 Bt – Norfolk 1737-68
5. John Wodehouse 1 Baron Wodehouse – Norfolk 1784-97
6. John Wodehouse 2 Baron Wodehouse – Great Bedwyn 1796-1802 Marlborough 1818-26
7. Edmond Wodehouse – Norfolk 1817-30 E. Norfolk 1835-55
8. Edmund Wodehouse – Bath 1880-1906
9. Armine Wodehouse – Saffron Walden Div. Essex 1900-01
10. John Wodehouse 3 Earl of Kimberley – Mid Norfolk 1906-10

Seats: Kimberley Hall, Norfolk (acq. c. 1384, built by 1402, ruinated 17th c., rebuilt 1712, add. c. 1754 and 1835, sold 1958); Barnham Broom Hall, Norfolk (built early 16th c., add. 1614, purch. 1644, sold 1960s); Lexham Hall, Norfolk (purch. 1673, built early 18th c., sold 1800); Witton Park (Hall), Norfolk (purch. 1770 by Norris family and passed by mar. 1796 to Wodehouses, sold c. 1920, demolished later); Sennowe Park, Norfolk (built 1774, sold c. 1850)
Estates: Bateman 11147 (E) 25000. Worth £2,000 pa under Elizabeth I. Worth £5,000 pa c. 1700.
Titles: Baron Wodehouse 1797- GB; Baronet 1611-
Peers: 6 peers 1797-1941 1945
1 Ld Lt 19th
1 in Cabinet 1864-66 1868-74 1880-86 1892-95
1 KG 19th-20th
Notes: Sir Thomas Wodehouse son of the 3 Bt and father of the 4 Bt married the heiress of Sir William Armyn 2 Bt of an old and rich Lincolnshire family in the mid-17th century. **First MP 1382 for Lincolnshire. Four additional MPs 1589-1653, two kts of the shire**. 1 Earl and three others in ODNB.

WOGAN *WALES*

Origins: An old gentry family at Wiston Castle from the 14th century. Gained significant wealth from the 1770s developing their coal mines. (Howell, *Patriarchs and Parasites*, 11) **First MP 1545 for Pembrokeshire. Three additional MPs 1571-1659, all for the county.** The MPs below were cousins.

1. Sir William Wogan – Haverfordwest 1679 1685-87 1689-1700 Pembrokeshire 1681
2. Lewis Wogan – Pembroke Boroughs 1712-15

Seats: Wiston Castle, Pembrokeshire (medieval castle acq. before 1324, ruin, medieval manor house, enlarged in 16th c., forfeited 1661, recovered, sold 1794, fell into ruin); Llanstinan (Hall), Pembrokeshire (orig. owners the Lloyds, passed by mar. to Wogans 1588, rebuilt later 17th c., passed by mar. 1710 to Symmons family, sold 1783, burned

1940); Hean Castle, Pembrokeshire (medieval, passed to Wogans by mar. to Lewis heiress mid-17th c., passed by mar. out of the family late 18th c.)
Estates: Llanstinan estate was 3,200 acres in 1856.
Notes: William Wogan was a regicide, arrested and fled into exile after the Restoration. Last Wogan of Llanstinan died 1710. The Wogan male line at Wiston failed 1793. Successor family (Symmons) extinct c. 1800. One in ODNB.

WOLFE *IRELAND*

Viscount Kilwarden (1800-30 I)

Origins: The Wolfes went to Ireland c. 1658 from Durham. Rose by marriage and office holding. Sheriff 1756. 1 Viscount was Chief Justice of the King's Bench in Ireland 1798.

1. Arthur Wolfe 1 Viscount Kilwarden – {Coleraine 1783-90 Jamestown 1790-97 Dublin 1797-98}
2. John Wolfe – {County Kildare 1783-90 Killibegs 1790-97 Carlow 1798-1800}
3. John Wolfe 2 Viscount Kilwarden – {Ardee 1790-97}
4. George Wolfe – {TD Kildare 1923-32}

Seats: Forenaghts, Kildare (acq. by mar. 1699, built early to mid-18th c., add. c. 1831, remod. early 20th c., sold post 1976); Newlands Castle, Dublin (built early 18th c., purch. later 18th c., remod. c. 1800, sold 1837, demolished 1976)
Estates: Bateman 2762 (I) 2351. Worth £1,330 pa c. 1803.
Title: Baron Kilwarden 1795 and 1798-1830 I
Notes: Page family acq. Forenaghts in 17th c. The estate passed to the Wolfes by mar. of 1699. 1 Viscount and one other in ODNB.

WOLLASTON

Wollaston

Origins: Gained wealth as wool merchants in London. Purchased landed estates in the mid 17th century.

1. William Wollaston – Ipswich 1733-41
2. William Wollaston – Ipswich 1768-84

Seats: (Great) Finborough Hall, Suffolk (purch. 1656, built soon afterwards, sold before 1795, fire 1795); Shenton Hall, Leicestershire (purch. and built 1625, add. 1862, family departed 1940, sold 1951)
Estates: Bateman 2196 (E) 3430

Wollaston

Origins: Cadet line descended from a younger son in the mid-17th century.

1. Richard Wollaston – Whitchurch 1698-1710

Seat: Wormley, Hertfordshire (purch. later 17th c., sold 1727)
Title: Baronet 1748-56
Notes: Became indebted in the 18th century.

WOLSELEY *IRELAND & ENGLAND*

Viscount Wolseley (1885-1936 UK)

Origins: The Wolseleys held the manor of Wolseley since the 12th century. Baron of the Exchequer under Edward IV. Official under James I. Baronet 1628. Member of Cromwell's House of Lords. **First MP 1449. One additional MP 1478**. A younger son of the 2 Bt moved to Ireland as a soldier late 17th c., Sheriff 1722. Baronet 1745.

1. Sir Charles Wolseley 2 Bt – Oxfordshire 1653 Staffordshire 1654 1656 Stafford 1660
2. William Wolseley – {Longford 1692-93 1695-97}
3. Robert Wolseley – {Taghmon 1695-97}
4. Richard Wolseley – {County Carlow 1703-13 1715-24}
5. Sir Richard Wolseley 1 Bt – {Carlow 1727-68}
6. Charles Wolseley – Milborne Port 1775-80

Seats: Wolseley Hall (House), Staffordshire (acq. and built late 12th c., add. 1469, add. 18th and 19th c., new house 1820-21, demolished 1967); Mount Wolseley, Carlow (purch. 1703, add. 19th c., sold 20th c., institutional use)
Estates: Bateman 2111 (E) 2789 and 5190 (I) 3027. Worth £1,000 pa in 1670s.
Titles: Baron Wolseley 1882-1913 UK; Baronet 1628- ; 1745-
Peer: 1 peer 1885-1913
1 KP 19th-20th
Notes: 1 Viscount and 2 Viscountess and six in ODNB.

WOLSTENHOLME (Worsnam) [Raynton]

Origins: The 1 Baronet was a farmer of customs whose father also held that position in which he amassed a fortune and lived at Nostell Priory, Yorkshire. **First MP 1625. An additional MP 1628.**

1. Sir John Wolstenholme 3 Bt – Middlesex 1695-1700 1705-09

Seats: Nostell Priory, Yorkshire (monastic buildings, purch. 1629, sold 1654); Forty Hall, Middlesex (acq. by mar. 1696, sold 1740)
Estates: The Forty Hall estate totaled 1,440 acres in the 18th c.
Title: Baronet 1665-1762
Notes: Forty Hall was purch. by Sir Nicholas Raynton, a City merchant and Lord Mayor 1632. His property passed to the Wolstenholmes by marriage. Sir John Wolstenholme was declared bankrupt in the 1650s. The family was in trouble financially in the early 18th century. Three in ODNB.

Raynton (Rainton)

Origins: A haberdasher and Lord Mayor of London 1632 founded the family. The first MP purchased Enfield Manor and rebuilt Forty Hall. He left his estates to his daughter Mary who married Sir John Wolstenholme 3 Bt.

1. Nicholas Raynton – Middlesex 1681

Seat: Forty Hall, Middlesex (built 16th c., rebuilt 1629-32, purch. 1629 or 1641, passed by mar. to Wolstenholmes 1696)
Notes: One in ODNB.

WOOD I

Earl of Halifax (1944- UK)

Orgins: Merchants in York in the 16th century. Owned land by 1610 but not yet gentry. Some dabbling in manufacturing was followed by a law practice in Barnsley. Three of the four sons of Francis Wood (d. 1775) went into the military or clergy. The second son made a fortune in Canton with the East India Company and after returning home married an heiress. Baronet 1784. (Roebuck, *Yorkshire Baronets 1640-1760*, 29) The discovery of large coal seams in the 19th century made the Woods really rich.

1. Charles Wood 1 Viscount Halifax – Great Grimsby 1826-31 Wareham 1831-32 Halifax 1832-65 Ripon 1865-66
2. Edward Wood 1 Earl of Halifax – Ripon Div. W. R. Yorkshire 1910-25
3. Charles Wood 2 Earl of Halifax – York 1937-45
4. Frederick Wood Baron Holderness – Bridlington Div. E. R. Yorkshire 1950-79

Seats: Hickleton Hall, Yorkshire (built 16th c., rebuilt 1745-48, add. 1777, purch. 1828, family departed 1947, leased, sold 2015, flats); Garrowby, Yorkshire (purch. 1803 for £23,000, new house 1892, still own); Hemsworth Hall, Yorkshire (purch. 1760s,

resident in 18th c., engulfed by Sheffield 19th c., demolished?); Bolling Hall, Yorkshire (medieval, add. 16th c., remod. early 17th c., acq. mid-18th c., add. 1779-80, family departed early 19th c., leased out, given to Barnsley Corporation 1912, museum)
Estates: Bateman 10142 (E) 12169. Owned 15,000 acres worth 90 million pounds in 2001.
Titles: Viscount Halifax 1866- UK; Baron Irwin 1925- UK; Baron Holderness UK Life 1979-2002; Baronet 1784-
Peers: 3 peers 1866-1934 1925-45
3 in Cabinet 1846-66 1870-74 1922-29 1935-40 1963-64 1970-74
1 KG 20th
Notes: An unusually active political family in the 19th and 20th centuries. The first Earl was the alternative candidate to Winston Churchill as Prime Minister in 1940. 1 and 2 Viscounts and 1 Earl in ODNB.

WOOD II

Baron Hatherley (1868-81 UK)

Origins: The first MP was the son of a serge maker in Tiverton. He became a chemist's traveler and made a fortune in copper mines. Lord Mayor of London in the 1830s. His son was Lord Chancellor 1868.

1. Sir Matthew Wood 1 Bt – London 1817-43
2. William Wood 1 Baron Hatherley – Oxford 1847-52
3. Western Wood – London 1861-63

Seat: Hatherley Court, Gloucestershire (built mid-17th c., add. late 18th c., acq. 1828, sold 1857, hotel)
Estates: The 1 Bt received £100,000, including the Hatherley estates, from an unrelated Gloucester banker named Wood in 1836, a notorious miser.
Title: Baronet 1837-81
Peer: 1 peer 1868-81
1 in Cabinet 1868-72
Notes: 1 Baron and four others in ODNB.

WOODRUFFE (Woodroffe)

Origins: A London haberdasher, Lord Mayor 1579, purchased Poyle in 1581. **First MP 1584 for London.**

1. Sir George Woodruffe – Haslemere 1681 1685-87
2. George Woodruffe – Haslemere 1695-98 1701-02 1705-08

Seat: Poyle Park, Surrey (purch. 1581, passed to Chester family 1854 by inher., sold 1913, demolished)
Estates: Worth £1,500 pa in 1660. In serious financial trouble 19th c.

WORSLEY [Holmes, Pennyman]

Worsley

Origins: The Worsleys were an old Lancashire family split into two branches in the early Tudor period. A younger son who rose due to court favor as Groom of the Wardrobe to Henry VIII, purchased Appledurcombe from the main line in 1527 while the other branch was seated in Yorkshire. **First MP 1539 for Hampshire. One additional MP 1614.**

1. Sir Henry Worsley 2 Bt – Newport 1640-48 (IoW) Newtown (IoW) 1661-66
2. Sir Robert Worsley 3 Bt – Newport 1666-75
3. Sir James Worsley 5 Bt – Newtown 1695-1701 1705-22 1727-29 1734-41
4. Henry Worlsey – Newport 1705-15
5. Sir Robert Worsley 4 Bt – Newtown 1715-22
6. Charles Worsley – Newtown 1722-27
7. Edward Worsley – Yarmouth (IoW) 1774-75 Newtown 1775-82
8. Sir Richard Worsley 7 Bt – Newport 1774-79 1780-84 Newtown 1791-93 1796-1801
9. James Worsley – Yarmouth 1775-80 Newtown 1784
10. Sir Leonard Worsley-Holmes 9 Bt – Newport 1809-25
11. Richard Worsley-Holmes – Newport 1812-14

Seats: Appuldurcombe House, Hampshire (IoW) (medieval, acq. by mar. 1527, rebuilt c. 1600, rebuilt 1710-13, add. 1773-82, passed by mar. to Anderson-Pelhams 1825, sold 1854, became a school, bomb damage WWII, ruin by 1952); Pylewell Park, Hampshire (old house, purch. 1609, rebuilt 1677, sold 1781); Chilton Candover, Hampshire (purch. mid-17th c., passed by inher. to Earl Granville 1747, who passed it to the Thynnes, sold 1818); Westover House, Hampshire (IoW) (purch. and built 1760s by Holmes, rebuilt early 19th c., sold early 20th c.)
Estates: 7 Bt heavily indebted.
Title: Baronet 1611-1825
Notes: On the death of the 7 Bt in 1805, Appledurcombe passed by the marriage of a niece and heiress, who married the 2 Baron Yarborough, later created Barons Worsley (see Pelham). The Baronetcy went to a cousin whose mother was the daughter of the 1 Baron Holmes of the second creation. The Holmes estates passed to the A'Court family (see Ashe). (see also Leigh III) Four in ODNB.

<u>Worsley</u>

Origins: The senior line of the family that acquired Hovingham in the mid-16th century. **First MP 1386 for Lancashire. Four additional MPs 1512-1654, one for Lancashire.**

1. Thomas Worsley – Malton 1685-87 1698-1700
2. Thomas Worsley – Thirsk 1711-13
3. Thomas Worsley – Orford 1761-68 Callington 1768-74
4. Sir Marcus Worsley 5 Bt – Keighley Div. W. Yorkshire 1959-64 Chelsea 1966-74

Seat: Hovingham Hall, Yorkshire (acq. mid-16th c., built 1750-60, still own)
Estates: Bateman 2558 (E) 3225
Title: Baronet 1838-
Notes: Katharine Worsley married 1961 the Duke of Kent. One in ODNB.

<u>Pennyman</u>

Origins: Rose by land purchases 1580s-1610. Granted arms 1599. Kt 1642. Lord Privy Seal under William III. **First MP 1640.** On the extinction of the Baronetcy in 1852 the estates went to James White Worsley a younger son of the Hovingham line, who was the grandson of the last Pennyman Bt's sister. He took the name Pennyman.

1. Sir James Pennyman 6 Bt – Scarborough 1770-74 Beverley 1774-96

Seat: Ormesby Hall, Yorkshire (acq. 1599, passed by mar. to Pennymans early 18th c., built early 1740s, remod. 1770s, passed to Worsleys by mar. 1852, NT 1963, family resident until 1983)
Estates: Bateman 3163 (E) 3801
Titles: Baronet 1628-43; 1664-1852

WREN

Origins: Founded by a London mercer, whose son was Clerk of the Closet to Charles I, followed by a Bishop of Ely.

1. Matthew Wren – Mitchell 1661-72
2. Sir William Wren – Cambridge 1685-87
3. Sir Christopher Wren – Plympton Erle 1685-87 New Windsor 1689-90 Weymouth and Melcombe Regis 1701-02
4. Christopher Wren – New Windsor 1713-15

Seat: Wroxall Abbey, Warwickshire (built 1580s, purch. 1713, sold 1861)

Notes: The male line of the Wrens became extinct in 1828 when the estates passed by marriage to the Hoskyns family. They sold Wroxall 1861. (See Hoskyns) Five in ODNB.

WREY (Wray)

Origins: Held land in the 15th century. Married a Cornish heiress in the reign of Elizabeth I. **First MP 1593. One further MP 1624.** The 3 Bt married Anne, daughter and heiress of Edward Bourchier 4 Earl of Bath (whose ancestors had held Tawstock since the early 12th century) (see Tyrwhitt). The Earldom became extinct in 1654 and the Wreys succeeded to the estates in that year.

1. Sir Chichester Wrey 3 Bt – Lostwithiel 1661-68
2. Sir Bourchier Wrey 4 Bt – Liskeard 1678-79 Devon 1685-87 Liskeard 1689-96
3. Chichester Wrey – Liskeard 1685-87
4. Sir Bourchier Wrey 5 Bt – Camelford 1712-15
5. Sir Bourchier Wrey 6 Bt – Barnstaple 1748-54

Seats: Tawstock Court, Devon (medieval, acq. by mar. from holders since early 12th c. in 1654, fire 1787, rebuilt 1789, add. 1885, family departed c. 1914, leased out, sold 1970s); Trebeigh (Trebigh), Cornwall (acq. later 16th c., family departed for Tawstock mid-17th c., in 19th c. declined to a farm house)
Estates: Bateman 7985 (E) 9269. Estate was over 6,000 acres in the mid-17th c. Held about 7,000 acres until sold in the 1970s.
Title: Baronet 1628-
Notes: Two in ODNB.

WRIGHT

<u>Wright</u>

Origins: Began as ironmasters in the early 18th century in Nottinghamshire and then founded a bank in 1761, but continued in iron industry throughout the 19th c. The capital value of the iron company was approaching half a million pounds in 1858. Married the heiress to Osmaston in 1791. Sheriff 1811.

1. Henry Wright – Leominster Div. Herefordshire 1912-18

Seat: Osmaston Manor, Derbyshire (17th c. house, acq. by mar. of 1791, rebuilt 1846-52 at a cost of £50,000 – Franklin, *The Gentleman's Country House*, 265 – sold 1883, demolished 1965)
Estates: Bateman 6637 (E) 12611. Francis Wright left £1,400,000 in 1874.
Notes: One in ODNB.

Wright

Origins: Cadet line descended from a younger brother of the founder of the iron works.

1. Charles Wright – Nottingham 1868-69
2. Henry Wright – S. Nottinghamshire 1886-95

Seat: Mapperley Hall, Nottinghamshire (purch. and built 1792, remod. 1845 and 1889-90, sold c. 1900, institutional use)
Notes: One in ODNB.

WRIGHTSON

Origins: The first MP married the daughter of a wealthy Newcastle merchant family c. 1700. The property passed to their daughter, whose husband took the name Wrightson and continued the family.

1. William Wrightson – Newcastle-upon-Tyne 1710-22 Northumberland 1723-24
2. William Wrightson – Aylesbury 1784-90
3. William Battie-Wrightson – East Retford 1826-27 Hull 1830-32 Northallerton 1835-65

Seat: Cusworth Park (House), Yorkshire (medieval, purch. 1669, built 1740-53, passed to Battie family by mar. 1760 who took name Wrightson, passed 1891 by mar. to Thomases who took the name Battie-Wrightson, sold contents 1952, sold hall 1961)
Estates: Bateman 6260 (E) 10610

WROTH (Wrothe)

Origins: Merchants in London. Lord Mayor 1361. Acquired a manor in Somerset in Richard I's reign and Enfield Manor in Middlesex by marriage to the heiress Margaret Enfield. Purchased further estates in Wiltshire and Essex. **First MP 1332 for Middlesex. Twelve additional MPs 1362-1610, eight of them for Middlesex.**

1. Sir Thomas Wroth – Bridgwater 1628 1646 1656 1659 1660
2. John Wroth – Essex 1689
3. Sir Thomas Wroth 3 Bt – Bridgwater 1701-08 Somerset 1710-13 Wells 1713-15
4. Robert Wroth – Guildford 1705-08 1717-20

Seats: Petherton Park, Somerset (foresters at Petherton 12th c., purch. later 16th c., built c. 1671, passed by mar. to Aclands 1721, sold 1834, declined to a farm house); Blendon

Hall, Kent (purch. c. 1630, sold 1672, demolished 1934); Durants (Place), Middlesex (acq. by mar. 1353 and 1401, sold 1672, part demolished 18th c. and 1910)
Estates: Worth between £500 and £1,000 pa in 1648.
Title: Baronet 1660-1721
Notes: The 3 Bt left the Wroth estates to his daughter in 1721, the wife of Sir Hugh Acland 2 Bt (see Acland). The father of John Wroth MP for Essex 1689, a lawyer, was from a cadet line, and the MP was a member of several merchant trading companies. Four in ODNB.

WROTTESLEY

Baron Wrottesley (1838- UK)

Origins: Enfeoffed at Wrottesley c. 1164. Kt c. 1250. Made a KG at Crécy by Edward III. **First MP 1460 for Staffordshire. One further MP 1491.**

1. Sir John Wrottesley 4 Bt – Staffordshire 1708-10
2. Sir Richard Wrottesley 7 Bt – Tavistock 1747-54
3. Sir John Wrottesley 8 Bt – Newcastle-under-Lyme 1768 Staffordshire 1768-87
4. John Wrottesley 1 Baron Wrottesley – Lichfield 1799-1806 Staffordshire 1823-32 S. Staffordshire 1832-37
5. Henry Wrottesley – Brackley 1810-25

Seat: Wrottesley Hall, Staffordshire (acq. c. 1164, rebuilt 16th c., rebuilt 1689, fire 1897, new house 1923, sold 1963, flats)
Estates: Bateman 5785 (E) 11021
Title: Baronet 1642-
Peers: 4 peers 1838-1945
1 Ld Lt 19th
Notes: The 5 Baron moved to S. Africa in 1963. 1 and 2 Barons and three others in ODNB.

WYKEHAM [Coleper, Cornwallis, Fairfax, Mann, Martin, Wenman]

Marquess Cornwallis (1792-1823 GB)

Origins: The daughter and heiress of the 5 and last Earl Cornwallis (d. 1852) married Charles Wykeham Martin of Leeds Castle, Kent who was descended from a younger son of Richard Wykeham of Swalcliffe Park, Oxfordshire. William of Wykeham was Chancellor of England 1368-71 and 1389-91. The family produced **two MPs 1402-42**. The first notable Wykeham of the Swalcliffe line was a vicar in the 18th century whose mother was the sister and co-heiress of the last Viscount Saye and Sele (see Fiennes).

The Wykehams accumulated an exceptional kinship network through marriage to heiresses. The Cornwallis family began with a London vintner who married an heiress of the Sheriff of London 1378. **First MP 1449 for Suffolk. Six further MPs 1553-1625, two for Suffolk and one for Norfolk.** The son of Charles Wykeham Martin and the Cornwallis heiress took the name Cornwallis, and his son was created Baron Cornwallis in 1927.

1. Frederick Cornwallis 1 Baron Cornwallis – Eye 1640-42 Ipswich 1660
2. Charles Cornwallis 2 Baron Cornwallis – Eye 1660-62
3. Charles Cornwallis – Eye 1662-75
4. Charles Cornwallis 4 Baron Cornwallis – Eye 1695-98
5. James Cornwallis – Eye 1722-27
6. John Cornwallis – Eye 1727-47
7. Stephen Cornwallis – Eye 1727-43
8. Edward Cornwallis – Eye 1743-49 Westminster 1753-63
9. Charles Cornwallis 1 Marquess Cornwallis – Eye 1760-62
10. Henry Cornwallis – Eye 1761
11. William Cornwallis – Eye 1768-74 1782-84 Portsmouth 1784-90 Eye 1790-1807
12. Charles Cornwallis 2 Marquess Cornwallis – Eye 1795-96 Suffolk 1796-1805
13. James Mann Cornwallis 5 Earl Cornwallis – Eye 1799-1806 1807
14. Philip Wykeham-Martin – Rochester 1856-78
15. Charles Wykeham-Martin – W. Kent 1857-59 Newport (IoW) 1865-70
16. Fiennes Wykeham-Martin-Cornwallis 1 Baron Cornwallis – Maidstone 1885-95 1898-1900

Seats: Brome Hall, Suffolk (medieval, acq. by mar. early 15th c., rebuilt 1561, remod. 1815, sold 1823, demolished 1963); Culford Hall, Suffolk (built 17th c., acq. by mar. 17th c., remod. 1790-96 and 1806-08 and became main seat, sold 1823, school); Leeds Castle, Kent (medieval, Martins inher. by mar from Fairfaxes c. 1800 and then passed on to Wykehams, restored and add. 1822-24, sold 1927); Linton Park, Kent (rebuilt 1730, inher. by mar. 1814, add. 1825, passed by mar. to the Amherst family (see) 1852, but returned to the Cornwallises in the 1880s, sold 1937)
Estates: Bateman 18053 (E) 30744. Rubinstein – Sir William Cornwallis left £100,000 in probate 1819, the 2 Marquess Cornwallis left £120,000 in 1823 and the 4 Earl left £200,000 in 1824. Rubinstein – Philip Martin left £200,000 in probate 1821.
Titles: Baron Cornwallis 1661-1852 E; Viscount Brome and Earl Cornwallis 1753-1852 GB; Baron Cornwallis 1927-35 UK; Baronet 1627-1852
Peers: 11 peers 1661-1853 1927-35
1 in Cabinet 1795-1801
1 KG 18th-19th

Notes: The Wykeham-Martin-Cornwallis estates were temporarily alienated (1856-83) to the Amherst family but then returned. 4 Earl and 1 and 2 Marquesses and ten other Cornwallises and one Wykeham in ODNB.

Mann

Origins: The Manns gained a fortune in commerce in the early 18th century and purchased Linton. Sir Horatio Mann 2 Bt left his estates to his nephew, James Cornwallis 5 Earl Cornwallis in 1814.

1. Sir Horatio Mann 2 Bt – Maidstone 1774-84 Sandwich 1790-1807

Seats: Linton Park, Kent (purch. early 18th c., rebuilt 1730, passed to Cornwallis family 1814); Sissinghurst, Kent (built c. 1490, add. 1558-60, purch. 1764, passed to Cornwallis family 1814, most of house demolished, family never resident, sold 1903)
Estates: The Mann fortune stood at £100,000 plus landed property in c. 1800.
Title: Baronet 1755-1814
Notes: Two in ODNB.

Baron Fairfax of Cameron (1627- S)

Origins: The family shared a common descent from the Viscounts Fairfax (see Fairfax). Merchants in York who acquired manorial property in the 13th century. **First MP 1324**. This cadet branch produced a Justice of the King's Bench, Kt 1477. Barons 1627. Governor of Virginia 1675 where the family acquired gigantic tracts of land (over 300,000 acres). **First MP 1586 for Yorkshire. Two additional MPs 1586-1648.** The 5 Baron Fairfax married the heiress of the 2 Baron Colepeper. She inherited Leeds Castle, Kent and Virgina estates. On the death of the 7 Baron Fairfax, Leeds Castle devolved on the issue of his sister Frances and her husband the Rev. Denny Martin, who assumed the name Fairfax. Their son, Fiennes Wykeham of Leeds Castle, took the additional name Martin in 1821 on the death of his kinsman General Martin. His grandson was created Baron Cornwallis in 1927.

1. Thomas Fairfax 3 Baron Fairfax – Cirencester 1649 W. R. Yorkshire 1654 Yorkshire 1659 1660
2. Henry Fairfax 4 Baron Fairfax – Yorkshire 1679-81
3. Thomas Fairfax 5 Baron Fairfax – Malton 1685-87 Yorkshire 1689-1702 1707
4. Henry Fairfax – Aldborough 1696
5. Robert Fairfax – York 1713-15
6. Robert Fairfax 7 Baron Fairfax – Maidstone 1740-41 1747-54 Kent 1754-68

Seats: Leeds Castle, Kent (built c. 1119, add. 17th c., inher. from Colepepers 1725, decayed 18th c., passed to Martins and hence Wykehams 1800, see above); Nun Appleton Hall,

Yorkshire (medieval, acq. 1540s, built late 17th c., sold 1708, derelict); Denton Hall, Yorkshire (medieval, acq. by mar. 1515, sold 1717, offices); Steeton Castle, Yorkshire (acq. 1557, sold 1716); Newton Kyme Hall (Newton Hall), Yorkshire (medieval castle, ruin, purch. 1602, new house later 17th c., sold later 19th c.); Bilbrough Hall, Yorkshire (purch. 1556, rebuilt 1670, fire 1832, became a farm, new house 1902, sold 1943); Toulston Hall, Yorkshire (acq. by mar. 1685, sold 1711)
Estates: Bateman 10649 (E) 17062. 300,000 acres in Virginia in the 18th century.
Peers: [3 peers 1660-1707]
1 Ld Lt 17th
Notes: In 1747 the 6 Baron moved permanently to America. The 8 Baron Fairfax was an American clergyman. The Virginia estates were devastated during the American Revolution. Even so, the 6 Baron died one of America's richest men. 1, 2, 3, and 6 Barons and fourteen others in ODNB.

<u>Baron Colepeper</u> (1644-1725 E) [Culpepper, Culpeper]

Origins: Held landed property from the 12th century. **First MP 1361 for Kent. Seven additional MPs 1365-1642, three of them for Kent.** Estates passed to the Fairfaxes via an heiress of the 2 Baron Colepeper 1725.

1. Sir Thomas Colepeper 3 Bt – Maidstone 1705-13 1715-23

Seats: Preston Hall, Kent (acq. c. 1300, passed out of the family 1734); Leeds Castle, Kent (acq. 1632, passed to Fairfaxes 1725)
Title: Baronet 1622-1723
Peers: 4 peers 1660-1725
Notes: The Culpeper family and the 1 Baron and two others in ODNB.

<u>Viscount Wenman</u> (1628-86 I; 1683-1800 I)

Origins: The Wenmans started as clothiers in the 15th century; then came fortunate marriages. The grandson of one of these was knighted and married Isabella Williams the heiress of Thame. Their grandson became the 1 Viscount. Acquired further property chiefly by marriage. **First MP 1547. Four additional MPs 1555-1640, all kts of the shire**. Sophia Wenman, heiress of the last Viscount married in 1768 William Wykeham, son of Richard Wykeham of Swalcliffe (see above). Their granddaughter was created Baroness Wenman in 1834. She was succeeded by cousins descended from the Wykeham-Musgraves of Barnsley Park, Gloucestershire.

1. Thomas Wenman 2 Viscount Wenman – Brackley 1621 1624 1625 Oxfordshire 1626 Brackley 1628 1640 {Mallow 1634?} Oxfordshire 1640-48 1660
2. Sir Francis Wenman 1 Bt – Oxfordshire 1664-79

3. Richard Wenman 1 Viscount Wenman – Brackley 1679-81 1685-87 1689-90
4. Philip Wenman 3 Viscount Wenman – Oxford 1749-54
5. Philip Wenman 4 Viscount Wenman – Oxfordshire 1768-96
6. Thomas Wenman – Westbury 1774-80

Seats: Thame Park, Oxfordshire (medieval, acq. by Williams family 1639, add. 16th c., acq. by mar. from Williams family late 16th, new house 1745, passed by inher. to Wykehams 1800, family departed 1914, contents sold 1919, house sold 1925); Caswell House, Oxfordshire (acq. and built c. 1500 and 1550, family departed later 18th c., sold 1930s); Twyford Lodge, Buckinghamshire (medieval, acq. by mar. 1550, new house built 16th-17th c., became a farm house 18th c., passed by inher. to Wykehams 1800, demolished 1857, sold by 1873)
Estates: Bateman 16495 (E) 24091 (under Wykeham-Musgrave)
Titles: Baron Wenman 1834-70 UK; Baronet 1662-1800
Peers: {4 peers 1665-86 1683-90 1740-60 1763-1800}
Notes: The Williams family of Thame rose via the career of a royal official, the 1 Baron Williams of Thame (cr. 1559), who worked with Cromwell and acquired 26 manors as a result of the Dissolution. Lord President of Wales under Elizabeth I. **Two MPs 1542-53, both knights of the shire**. Thame Park came to William King, a yeoman, at the Dissolution (through his elder brother who was a gentleman of Worminghall). William King married Anne Williams, whose brother John became the 1 Baron in 1559 and the owner of Thame in 1547. He divided his estates amongst two daughters. His seat at Ryecot went to the younger one who married Sir Henry Norreys (see Bertie). Thame went to the elder, Isabella (see above). (*Country Life*, 26, pp. 94ff.) 1, 2, and 6 Viscounts and one other in ODNB.

WYLDE (Wilde)

Origins: Prominent Worcestershire clothiers from the mid-16th century. Lawyers in the 17th century. **First MP 1547. Four additional MPs 1584-1659**.

1. Thomas Wylde – Worcester 1701-27

Seat: The Commandery, Worcestershire (acq. by 1541, sold 1785, since 1977 museum)

WYNDHAM (Windham) [Ashe, Campbell, Edwin, Quin] *ENGLAND, WALES, & IRELAND*

<u>Earl of Egremont</u> (1749-1845 GB)

Origins: The Wyndhams took their name from the Norfolk town of Wymondham. They were merchants in Norwich in the early 15th century. **First MP 1439** purchased first manorial land in the same year. At the same time the family married into the gentry. Associated with the Duke of Norfolk in the 1480s. They migrated to Somerset in the first half of the 16th century and married the Sydenham heiress of Orchard Sydenham c. 1526 (renamed Orchard Wyndham 1528, held by the Orchards and then Sydenhams from at least 1287). All the Wyndhams shared a common descent from Sir John Wyndham of Orchard Wyndham. (Wyndham, *A Family History 1410-1688*, 1-3) The Earls of Egremont descended from the senior line. The 3 Bt of Orchard Wyndham married Catherine Seymour, daughter of 6 Duke of Somerset and Lady Elizabeth Percy, heiress of the last Earl of Northumberland (see Seymour). The 7 Duke was created Earl of Egremont with special remainder to his nephew the fourth Wyndham Baronet of Orchard Wyndham, who succeeded as 2 Earl in 1750. He inherited Petworth, Sussex and large estates elsewhere. On the death of the 4 Earl, the estates passed in 1859 to the illegitimate son of the 3 Earl, George Wyndham, 1 Baron Leconfield. Percy Wyndham, brother of the 2 Earl succeeded by marriage to the estates of the 7 Earl of Thomond (see O'Brien) and was created Earl of Thomond in 1756 (I).

1. Sir William Wyndham 1 Bt – Somerset 1656 Taunton 1659 1660-79
2. Sir Edward Wyndham 2 Bt – Ilchester 1685-87 1689-95
3. Hopton Wyndham – Wells 1690-95
4. Sir William Wyndham 3 Bt – Somerset 1710-40
5. Charles Wyndham 2 Earl of Egremont – Bridgwater 1735-41 Appleby 1742-47 Taunton 1747-50
6. Percy Wyndham O'Brien 1 Earl of Thomond – Taunton 1745-47
7. Percy Wyndham – Chichester 1782-84 Midhurst 1790-96
8. Charles Wyndham – Midhurst 1790-95 New Shorham 1795-1802 Sussex 1807-12
9. Charles Wyndham – W. Sussex 1841-47
10. Sir Henry Wyndham – Cockermouth 1852-57 W. Cumberland 1857-60
11. Henry Wyndham 2 Baron Leconfield – W. Sussex 1854-69
12. Percy Wyndham – W. Cumberland 1860-85
13. George Wyndham – Dover 1889-1913

Seats: Petworth House, Sussex (Percy family acq. 1150, built 1260s and 1309-15, rebuilt 1688-96, passed to Wyndhams 1750, add. c. 1780, remod. 1869-72, NT 1947); Cockermouth Castle, Cumberland (built mid-13th c., add. c. 1360-70, passed via the mar. of Lady Elizabeth Percy to the Dukes of Somerset and then in 1750 to the Wyndhams, restored c. 1800, add. late 19th c., still own); Orchard Wyndham, Somerset (medieval house, expanded repeatedly from 1470s, acq. by mar. c. 1526, add. 1550s, remod. 1816, add. 1830s, passed to Dinton line below 1876, still own); Clouds, Wiltshire (purch. 1876, built 1876-85, fire 1889, rebuilt, sold 1937, much demolished 1938); Witham Friary (Witham Hall), Somerset (medieval, rebuilt mid-16th c., inher. by mar from Hoptons 1652, rebuilt 1717, sold 1761); Silverton Park (Egremont House), Devon (built 1839-45, sold 1880s, demolished 1900)

Estates: Bateman 114142 (E & I) 92276. Rubinstein – 3 Earl of Egremont left £250,000 in probate in 1837. Owned 22,000 acres worth 120 million pounds in 2001.
Titles: Baron Leconfield 1859- UK; Baronet 1661-1845
Peers: 6 Peers 1750-63 1772-1845 1859-1945
1 Ld Lt 20th
3 in Cabinet 1712-14 1761-63 1900-05
Notes: Hopton estate of Witham Friary, Somerset passed to Wynhams by mar. 1652. The Hoptons, gentry of medieval origins, produced **six MPs 1539-1642 (all but one kts of the shire)**. The 1 Baron Leconfield was the illegitimate son of the 3 Earl of Egremont. The 6 Baron was Private Secretary to Prime Minister Harold Macmillan for which he received a peerage in 1963. 6 Baron Leconfield and 2 and 3 Earls of Egremont and three others in ODNB.

Windham

Origins: Felbrigg Hall (acquired in the mid-15th century) passed to a younger brother, Thomas Windham, of John Wyndham of Orchard Wyndham. **First MP 1439. Two further MPs mid-16th century, both for Norfolk.** On the death of William Windham in 1810 Felbrigg passed to William Lukin, who took the name Windham, a cousin by marriage. This line became extinct in 1896. A Windham daughter married a distant cousin of a junior line of the Wyndhams seated at Cromer, Norfolk. Her sister-in-law married Cremer Cremer. The son of that marriage, Thomas Cremer, married the daughter of John Ketton, who had purchased Felbrigg in 1863. Their son Wyndham Ketton-Cremer inherited Felbrigg.

1. Ashe Windham – Norfolk 1708-10
2. William Windham – Sudbury 1722-27 Aldeburgh 1727-30
3. Joseph Windham Ashe – Downton 1734-41 1742-46
4. William Windham – Aldeburgh 1747-61 Helston 1766-68
5. William Windham – Norwich 1784-1802 St. Mawes 1802-06 New Romney 1806-07 Higham Ferrers 1807-10
6. William Windham – E. Norfolk 1832-35
7. Charles Windham – E. Norfolk 1857-59

Seats: Felbrigg Hall, Norfolk (Wyndhams acq. c. 1450, rebuilt c. 1620, add. 1686, sold 1863 to Kettons, passed by mar. to the Wyndham Cremers 1924, descendents of the builder of the house, given to NT 1969); Earsham, Norfolk (built 1704-08, purch. c. 1720 add. 1750 and 1785, passed by mar. to Dallings and Meades, sold 1973); Hanworth Hall, Norfolk (built c. 1700, purch. 1844, sold 1896)
Estates: Bateman 10924 (E) 12945 (Ketton and Windham- Walker)
1 in Cabinet 1783 1794-1801 1806-07
Notes: Eight in ODNB.

Earl of Dunraven and Mount Earl (1822-2011 I)

Origins: The Quin family claimed descent back to the 3rd century as Kings of Munster (*Country Life*, 145, p. 1231). The first reliable evidence of the emergence of the family came with a Bishop of Limerick in the reign of Henry VIII. A great-nephew (d. 1671) married the heiress of the O'Riordans. Their son purchased Adare in 1683 and added more estates. Conformed to the Established Church 1739. Thomas Wyndham of Cromer, Norfolk, descended from a junior line of the Windhams of Felbrigg, married his cousin Jane Wyndham (d. 1723) daughter and heiress of William Wyndham of Dunraven Castle, Glamorganshire. He married secondly Ann, daughter of Samuel Edwin of Llanmihangel Plas, Glamorganshire. The Edwins were London merchants, Lord Mayor 1696, and acquired a great fortune. His son took the name Edwin. A descendent, Caroline Wyndham, heiress to the Welsh estates, married William Quin in 1810. His father, Valentine Quin, was created Earl of Dunraven. A daughter of the 1 Earl married the 1 Marquess of Headfort, and their second son succeeded to the family seat of Quinborough, Clare and took the name Quin (see Taylour).

1. Samuel Edwin – Minehead 1717
2. Thomas Wyndham – Truro 1721-27 Dunwich 1727-34
3. Charles Edwin – Westminster 1741-47 Glamorgan 1747-56
4. Windham Quin – {Kilmallock 1768-76}
5. Charles Wyndham Edwin – Glamorgan 1780-89
6. Thomas Wyndham – Glamorgan 1789-1814
7. Richard Quin 1 Earl of Dunraven – {Kilmallock 1799-1800}
8. Windhan Wyndham-Quin 2 Earl of Dunraven – County Limerick 1806-20
9. Edwin Wyndham 3 Earl of Dunraven – Glamorganshire 1837-51
10. Windham Wyndham-Quin 5 Earl of Dunraven – S. Glamorganshire 1895-1906

Seats: Dunraven Castle, Glamorganshire (medieval, purch. mid-17th c., new house built early 19th c., demolished c. 1962); Adare Manor, Limerick (purch. 1683, built c. 1720-30, remodelled 1780s, rebuilt from 1820-62 through 1860s, sold with 1,000 acres in 1987, hotel); Llanmihangel Plas, Glamorganshire (medieval, new house built mid-16th c., purch. by Edwin family c. 1681, passed to Wyndhams by mar. of 1810, leased out from that time forward); Kenry House, Surrey (purch. and built 19th c., family departed 1914, sold after WWI, institutional use); Clearwell Castle, Gloucestershire (built 16th c., Wyndhams inher. by mar. 1727, rebuilt c. 1730, passed to Earl of Dunraven 1820, sold 1907); Castletown Cox, Kilkenny (built 1767-71, purch. 1909, sold 1928)
Estates: Bateman 39745 (E, W, & I) 35478. Quins worth £6,000 pa c. 1800.
Titles: Baron Adare 1800-2011 I; Viscount Mount Earl 1816-2011 I; Baron Kenry 1866-1926 Uk; Baronet 1781-2011
Peers: 1 Irish Rep peer 1839-50 2 peers 1866-1926
2 Lds Lt 19th, 20th

2 KP 19th, 20th
Notes: The contents of Adare were sold by the 7 Earl in 1982 for £945,000. (Hicks, *Irish Country Houses*, 62). 3 and 4 Earls and one Edwin in ODNB.

Baron Windham (1731-45 I)

Origins: Descended from Sir Wadham Wyndham ancestor of the most junior line of the descendents of Sir John Wyndham of Orchard Wyndham. Several branches descended from Sir Wadham are combined here.

1. John Wyndham – Salisbury 1681 1685-87
2. Thomas Wyndham – Wells 1685-87 1689
3. Thomas Wyndham – Wilton 1689-95
4. Henry Wyndham – Wiltshire 1795-1812
5. Wadham Wyndham – Salisbury 1818-43

Seats: St. Edmund's College (aka The College and also Wyndham House), Salisbury, Wiltshire (medieval, purch. 1660, remod. early 18th c., remod. 1788-90, sold 1871, offices); Wyld Court, Devon (built 1593, acq. by mar. of 1693, sold early 19th c., became a farm house); Corhampton (Carhampton) House, Hampshire (purch. c. 1750, remod. 1750s, passed by mar. to Campbells (see below) 1843 who took name Wyndham)
Estates: Bateman 7067 (E) 7802. Rubinstein – Wadham Wynham left £125,000 probate in 1812.
Peer: {1 peer 1731-45}
Notes: 1 Baron and one other in ODNB.

Windham

Origins: A junior line descended from Sir Wadham Wyndham (see above). The Dinton line succeeded to Orchard Wyndham on the death of the last Countess of Egremont in 1876, an amazing descent of property to remote cousins (*Country Life*, 177, p. 816).

1. William Wyndham – Calne 1691-95
2. William Wyndham – S. Wiltshire 1852-59

Seats: Dinton House (Philipps House, Park), Wiltshire (purch. 1689, rebuilt 1817, sold 1917, NT 1943); Orchard Wyndham, Somerset (see above, inher. 1876, still own); Norrington Manor, Wiltshire (built late 14th c., partly rebuilt later 16th c., purch. 1659, sold 1952)
Estates: Bateman 23708 (E) 37420. Rubinstein – Laetitia Wyndham left 100,000 in probate in 1837.
Notes: Two in ODNB.

Wyndham

Origins: Descended from a younger son of an earlier Sir John Wyndham of Orchard Wyndham, grandfather of the Sir John, who was the common ancestor of the other lines. The branches seated at Kentsford and Cranbury House are combined here.

1. Sir Edmund Wyndham – Minehead 1625 1628 Bridgwater 1640-41 1661-79
2. Sir Francis Wyndham 1 Bt – Minehead 1640 Milbourne Port 1660-76
3. Sir Hugh Wyndham – Minehead 1661-71
4. Thomas Wyndham – Minehead 1673-79 Yarmouth (IoW) 1679-81 1685-87
5. Sir Charles Wyndham – Southampton 1679-81 1685-87 1689-98 St. Ives 1698-1700
6. Sir Francis Wyndham 3 Bt – Ilchester 1695-1705
7. Francis Wyndham – Gloucester 1709-10
8. Thomas Wyndham – Poole 1732-41

Seats: Kentsford, Somerset (acq. mid-16th c., sold 1697); Cranbury House, Hampshire; Tale, Devon; Cathanger, Somerset (acq. by Pynes c. 1620, acq. by mar. from Pyne family 1639)
Estates: Worth £2,500 pa in the 17th century.
Titles: Baronet 1641-63; 1673-1719
Notes: Pyne family rose by law early 17th c. **First MP 1624. Two other MPs 1625-53.** Held at least 3,000 acres in 1620s. One in ODNB.

Campbell

Origins: The father of John Henry Campbell MP married sister of Wadham Wyndham MP 1818-43 (above). The Campbells succeeded to the Wyndham estates 1843. The Campbells of Dunoon were a cadet of the Ardkinglas line (see Campbell I).

1. John Henry Campbell – Salisbury 1843-47

Seats: Corhampton (Carhampton) House, Hampshire (acq. by mar. 1843, see above, passed via mar. several lines to the Longs by mar. 1894, taking the name Campbell-Wyndham-Long, sold 1950); Dunoon Castle, (Dunoar), Argyllshire (acq. medieval period, family departed 1649, destroyed 1685, ruin, donated to town 1924, park); Inellan House, Argyllshire (built 1650, family departed 1840s, unroofed, ruin); Blunham Court (House) (Lawlesses), Bedfordshire (old house, purch. 1768, rebuilt early 19th c., sold 1835)
Estates: 7062 (E) 7802
Note: This line carried the title of Captain of Dunoon.

WYNNE *IRELAND*

Origins: A gentleman from a Welsh family that emigrated to Ireland in 1658 as a Cromwellian soldier. Sheriff 1659.

1. Owen Wynne – {Carrick 1692-93 Ballynakill 1715-27}
2. James Wynne – {County Leitrim 1692-93}
3. Owen Wynne – {Sligo 1713-56}
4. Eugene Wynne – {Ballyshannon 1713-14}
5. Owen Wynne – {Ballyshannon 1713-27 County Sligo 1727-37}
6. James Wynne – {County Sligo 1737-48}
7. John Wynne – {Castlebar 1727-47}
8. Owen Wynne – {County Sligo 1749-76 Sligo 1776-89}
9. James Wynne – {Sligo 1751-60 County Leitrim 1761-68 Sligo 1761-68}
10. Owen Wynne – {County Sligo 1778-90 Sligo 1790-1800} 1801-06 1820-30
11. Robert Wynne – {Sligo 1789-99}
12. William Wynne – {Sligo 1798-1800}
13. John Wynne – Sligo 1830-32 1856-60

Seat: Hazlewood (Hazelwood), Sligo (purch. 1722, built 1731, add. 19th c., abandoned 1923, sold 1937, now business site)
Estates: Bateman 28418 (I) 14091. Estates purch. for £20,000 in 1722. (F. Jones, *The Wynnes*, 30)
Notes: The male line became extinct in 1910. One in ODNB.

WYNTER (Winter) [Blathwayte]

Origins: The Wynters were Bristol merchants who moved to London in the 16th century. One became First Treasurer of the Navy in 1545, followed by another naval official. **First MP 1559 (Gloucestershire 1586). One other MP also sat for the county 1589 and 1601**. The politician William Blaythwayte MP, the son of a barrister from a merchant family, married in 1686 the heiress Mary Wynter.

1. William Blaythwayte – Newtown (IoW) 1685-87 Bath 1693-1710

Seats: Dyrham Park, Gloucestershire (built 15th and 16th c., purch. 1571, passed to Blathwaytes by mar. and rebuilt 1692-1704, sold 1956, NT 1971); Lydney Park, Gloucestershire (acq. 1588, built c. 1590, rebuilt c. 1670, sold 1723)
Estates: Bateman 7349 (E) 8705
1 in Cabinet 18th c.
Notes: Last Blathwayte died 1936. One Wynter and one Blathwayte in ODNB.

WYVILL

Origins: The family claimed to have fought with the Conqueror at Hastings (*Dictionary of National Biography*, xxi, 1193). Their fortune was founded in the 15th and early 16th centuries and augmented by marriage. The son of the founder entertained Elizabeth I at Constable Burton and was Vice Chamberlain of the Household. **First MP 1553. One additional MP 1584-97.**

1. Sir Christopher Wyvill 3 Bt – Richmond 1659 1660
2. Sir Marmaduke Wyvill 5 Bt – Richmond 1695-98
3. Sir Marmaduke Wyvill 6 Bt – Richmond 1727-28
4. Marmaduke Wyvill – York 1820-30
5. Marmaduke Wyvill – Richmond 1847-65 1866-68
6. Marmaduke Wyvill – Otley Div. W. R. Yorkshire 1895-1900

Seats: Constable Burton, Yorkshire (built 1338, acq. c. 1550, remod. later 16th c., new house 1762-68, still own); Denton Hall (Park), Yorkshire (Ibbetsons purch. 1717, passed by mar. to Wyvills 1861, family departed c. 1902, sold 1920, business use)
Estates: Bateman 8309 (E) 9141
Title: Baronet 1611-1774
Notes: Three in ODNB.

YELVERTON *IRELAND & WALES*

<u>Viscount Avonmore</u> (1800-1910 I)

Origins: Possibly related to the Yelvertons of Easton Maudit, Northamptonshire (see Grey II), but no proof. To Ireland in the later 17th c. The 1 Viscount rose by merit beginning as an usher in a boarding school (Malcolmson, *John Foster: the Politics of the Anglo-Irish Ascendancy,* 5). He became a successful lawyer and judge.

1. Barry Yelverton 1 Viscount Avonmore – {Donegal 1774-76 Carrickfergus 1776-83}
2. Walter Yelverton – {Tuam 1797-1800}
3. William Yelverton – Carmarthen 1832-35

Seats: Belle Isle, Tipperary (acq. and built c. 1790-1800, sold 1879 or c. 1910); Hazle Rock (Hazelrock), Mayo (acq. and built early 19th c., sold 1879, ruin); Fortfield House, Dublin (acq. later 18th c., built c. 1785, sold mid-19th c., demolished 1940s); Whitland Abbey, Carmarthenshire (acq. by mar. of 1825, passed by inher. to Blakes 1920, who took name Yelverton in 1927, sold c. 1930s and 1951)
Estates: 3260 (I) 1102 in 1878; Bateman 2837 (W) 3040
Title: Baron Yelverton (1795-1910 I)
Notes: 1 and 4 Viscounts in ODNB.

YERBURGH

Baron Alvingham (1929- UK)

Origins: The Yerburghs acquired land in the 12th century. **First MP 1325. One additional MP 1450**. Robert Yerburgh MP 1886-1916 was a barrister and politician.

1. Robert Yerburgh – Chester 1886-1906 1910-16
2. Robert Yerburgh 1 Baron Alvingham – S. Dorset 1922-29

Seats: Caythorpe Court, Lincolnshire (built 1899-1901, purch. 1907, sold 1948, institutional use); Woodfold Park (Hall), Lancashire (acq. by mar. from Thwaites 1888, family departed 1945, house sold 1949, unroofed and partly demolished 1955, still own but a ruin, now flats)
Peer: 1 peer 1929-45
Notes: First 20th-century MP married the Thwaites brewery heiress, who managed the business herself and whose money purchased Caythorpe. The family continued to manage the business until most of it was sold for 25 million pounds in 2015. One in ODNB.

Thwaites

Origins: The Thwaites were brewers in Blackburn (company founded 1807). The Thwaites heiress married Robert Yerburgh MP who succeeded to the company and estates.

1. Daniel Thwaites – Blackburn 1875-80

Seats: Woodfold Park (Hall), Lancashire (built 1796-99, purch. 1865, passed by mar. to the Yerburghs 1888); Billinge Scarr, Lancashire (purch. and built 1876, passed by mar. to Yerburghs 1888, sold c. 1907, demolished 1947)
Estates: Bateman 4569 (E) 24828

YONGE (Young)

Origins: Mayor of Bristol under Henry IV. A younger son went to London, Lord Mayor 1453. Justice of the King's Bench (d. 1476). Merchants and landowners under Elizabeth I. **First MP 1413 for Bristol (Gloucestershire 1460). Five further MPs 1435-1649 one other for Bristol**.

1. Sir John Yonge 1 Bt – Plymouth 1642 Honiton 1654 Devon 1656 Honiton 1660
2. Sir Walter Yonge 2 Bt – Honiton 1659 Lyme Regis 1660 Dartmouth 1667-70
3. Sir Walter Yonge 3 Bt – Honiton 1679-81 Ashburton 1689-90 Honiton 1690-1710

4. Sir William Yonge 4 Bt – Honiton 1715-54 Tiverton 1754-55
5. Sir George Yonge 5 Bt – Honiton 1754-61 1763-96 Old Sarum 1799-1801

Seats: Colyton House, Devon (purch. 16th c., sold 1789); Escott House, Devon (purch. 16th c., sold 1794)
Title: Baronet 1661-1812
1 in Cabinet 1735-41
Notes: 5 Bt was bankrupt at the end of his life (d. 1812). Five in ODNB.

YORKE I [Freman] *ENGLAND & WALES*

Earl of Hardwicke (1754- GB)

Origins: The founder of the family was a merchant in Dover (d. 1682). His son was a solicitor. His son became Lord Chancellor 1736.

1. Philip Yorke 1 Earl of Hardwicke – Lewes 1719-22 Seaford 1722-23
2. Philip Yorke 2 Earl of Hardwicke – Reigate 1741-47 Cambridgeshire 1747-64
3. Charles Yorke – Reigate 1747-68 University of Cambridge 1768-70
4. Joseph Yorke 1 Baron Dover – East Grinstead 1751-61 Dover 1761-74 Grampound 1774-80
5. John Yorke – Higham Ferrers 1753-68 Reigate 1768-84
6. Philip Yorke 3 Earl of Hardwicke – Cambridgeshire 1780-90
7. Charles Yorke – Cambridgeshire 1790-1810 St. Germans 1810-12 Liskeard 1812-18
8. Sir Joseph Yorke – Reigate 1790-1806 St. Germans 1806-10 West Looe 1812 Sandwich 1812-18 Reigate 1818-31
9. Philip Yorke Viscount Royston – Reigate 1806-08
10. Joseph Yorke – Reigate 1831-32
11. Charles Yorke 4 Earl of Hardwicke – Reigate 1831-32 Cambridgeshire 1832-34
12. Eliot Yorke – Cambridgeshire 1835-65
13. John Yorke – Tewkesbury 1864-68 E. Gloucestershire 1872-85 Tewkesbury 1885-86
14. Charles Yorke 5 Earl of Hardwicke – Cambridgeshire 1865-73
15. Eliot Yorke – Cambridgeshire 1873-79

Seats: Wimpole Hall, Cambridgeshire (built c. 1640-70, remod. 1693-1705, add. 1713-30, purch. 1740, remod. 1742-47 and 1791-1806, add. c. 1840, sold 1894, NT 1976); Forthampton Court, Gloucestershire (medieval, remod. 1540s and 1643-47, purch. 1762, remod. c. 1788 and 1889-92, still own); Hardwicke Court, Gloucestershire (medieval, rebuilt later 16th c., remod. early 18th c., purch. c. 1726, sold 1808, demolished c. 1815)
Estates: Bateman 19382 (E) 27121. The 5 Earl squandered much of the family wealth (d. 1897).
Titles: Baron Hardwicke 1733- GB; Baron Dover 1788-92 GB
Peers: 10 peers 1733-1945 1788-92

3 Lds Lt 18th, 19th
5 in Cabinet 1737-56 1770 1801-06 1803-04 1810-12 1852 1858-59
1 KG 19th
Notes: The Wimpole estate was sold to pay debts in the late 19th century. The 2 Earl married Lady Jemima Campbell, daughter of he 3 Earl of Breadalbane (see Campbell I). She succeeded as Marchioness Gray in 1740 and was a great heiress. On the death of the 2 Earl his wife's estates, which descended from the Dukes of Kent, went to his daughters. The elder was created Countess de Grey and the younger married the 2 Lord Grantham (see Grey II under Grey de Ruthin and Robinson). The 5 Earl bankrupted the estate and the 6 Earl had to earn a living as a stockbroker. 1 Baron Dover and 1, 2, 3, 4, 5, and 6 Earls and eight others in ODNB.

Blount

Origins: Thomas Pope was the son of a small Oxfordshire landowner. He was a lawyer and became a petty official at the Court of Chancery in 1532. He worked for Thomas Cromwell, purchased twenty manors at the Dissolution, including Tyttenhanger, was granted arms, and was knighted. He was succeeded by his wife's brother's son, Sir Thomas Pope Blount in 1591. Tittenhanger passed in 1747 to the Yorkes and in the 19th century to the Alexander Earls of Caledon (see Alexander).

1. Sir Thomas Pope Blount 1 Bt – St. Albans 1679-81 Hertfordshire 1689-97

Seat: Tittenhanger (Tyttenhanger) House, Hertfordshire (acq. by Popes 1547, built 16th c., passed by mar. to Blounts 1591, rebuilt 1654-55, remod. early and late 18th c., passed by mar. to the Freemans 1757 and then to the Yorkes later 18th c., and to Alexanders 1834, commercial use)
Title: Baronet 1680-1757
Notes: Five in ODNB.

Yorke

Origins: Descended from a younger son of the grandfather of the 1 Earl of Hardwicke. He married the daughter and heiress of John Meller of Erdigg.

1. Philip Yorke – Helston 1775-81
2. Simon Yorke – Grantham 1793-1802

Seat: Erdigg (Erthig), Denbighshire (built 1680s, add. 1724, acq. by mar. 1733, remod. 1770s, remod. 1826, donated 1973 NT)
Estates: Bateman 2341 (W) 4503
Notes: One in ODNB.

Freeman

Origins: The founder was Ralph Freeman, merchant and Lord Mayor of London d. 1634. In 1772 Aspenden passed by inheritance to the Earls of Hardwicke.

1. Ralph Freeman – Hertfordshire 1685-87 1690-95
2. Ralph Freeman – Hertfordshire 1697-1727

Seats: Tyttenhanger House, Hertfordshire (acq. by mar 1757, passed by mar. in the later 18th c. to the Yorkes, see above); Hamels Park, Hertfordshire (built c. 1580, purch. 1712, passed by inher. to Yorkes mid-18th c., sold by Yorkes 1796, rebuilt early 19th c., flats and offices); Aspenden Hall, Hertfordshire (purch. 1607, passed by inher. to Yorkes 1772, sold 1782)
Notes: Extinct in male line 1772.

YORKE II

Origins: Merchant in York and of Staple in Calais in the 15th century. Also served as administrators in York. **First MP 1472 for York.** Successful speculators in monastic property after the Dissolution. Kt 1485. **Two further MPs 1559-89.**

1. Sir John Yorke – Richmond 1661-63
2. Thomas Yorke – Richmond 1689-90 1695-1710 1713-16
3. John Yorke – Richmond 1710-13 1717-27 1728-57
4. Thomas Yorke – Richmond 1757-61

Seats: Bewerley Hall, Yorkshire (purch. 1674, enlarged 1815-21, sold 1923 for £150,000 - Waterson & Meadows, *Lost Houses of the West Riding*, 11 - demolished c. 1965); Gouthwaite Hall, Yorkshire (acq. 16th c., submerged in a reservoir c. 1900); Halton Place, Yorkshire (owned property previously, built house 1770, add. c. 1900, still own)
Estates: Bateman 14499 (E) 11000
Notes: Three in ODNB.

YOUNG

Baron Kennet (1935- UK)

Origins: The founder of the family was an 18th-century admiral. His son served in the East India Company and was created a Baronet.

1. Charles Young – Christchurch 1885-92
2. Edward Young 1 Baron Kennet – Norwich 1915-23 Sevenoakes Div. Kent 1929-35

3. Sir George Young Baron Young – Ealing Acton 1974-97 N. W. Hampshire 1997-2015

Seat: Formosa Place, Berkshire (purch. 1785 and built 1810, demolished c. 1949, still own estate)
Estates: Worth est. £1,000,000 in 2012.
Title: Baron Young of Cookham 2015- UKLife; Baronet 1813-
Peer: 1 peer 1935-45
1 in Cabinet 1995-97 2010-12
Notes: 1 and 2 Barons and six others in ODNB.

YOUNGER *SCOTLAND*

Viscount Younger of Leckie (1923- UK)

Origins: Brewers from the 18th century onwards.

1. George Younger 1 Viscount Younger – Ayr District 1906-22
2. Kenneth Younger – Grimsby 1945-59
3. George Younger 4 Viscount Younger – Ayr 1964-92

Seats: Leckie House (Watson House), Stirlingshire (Leckie House built 16th c., Watson House built mid-19th c., purch. 1906, family departed 1939, Watson House sold c. 1946, new house built and Old Leckie House restored, still own these houses and estate); Auchen Castle, Dumfriesshire (medieval castle, ruin, new house built 1869, passed by inher. from Butler-Johnstones (see Butler I) late 19th c./early 20th c., sold, now hotel)
Estates: Own 1,700 acres at Leckie 2015. 4 Viscount died worth three and a half million pounds in 2003.
Titles: Baron Blanesburgh 1923-46 UK; Baron Younger of Prestwick 1992-2003 UK Life; Baronet 1911-
Peers: 3 peers 1923-45 1923-45
1 in Cabinet 1979-89
1 Ld Lt 20th
Notes: Baron Blanesburgh and 1 and 4 Viscounts and three others in ODNB.

Bibliography

Many more works than listed here were consulted – mostly at the Cambridge University Library, the British Library, the Institute of Historical Research (London), the Library of Congress, and the University of Delaware. The sources listed below are those either cited in the text or particularly useful to the task of collecting data on the subject. I was also fortunate to be able to consult some unpublished material at the History of Parliament in London, and in the office of the late Professor Edith Johnston-Liik, editor of the history of the Irish Parliament, at Queen's University, Belfast.

The magazine *Country Life* contains over a century's worth of history relating to the British landed elite (generally of a high scholarly standard) that is frequently consulted by those interested in architecture but neglected by social and political historians.

Reference Works

The following three sources are usually not cited. Much important information has been derived from them.

DNB – *Dictionary of National Biography* (original edition)
ODNB – *Oxford Dictionary of National Biography*
VCH – *Victoria County Histories*

Bateman, John, *The Great Landowners of Great Britain and Ireland*, ed. David Spring, Leicester, 1971 [1876, 1883].
Bindoff, S. T., *The House of Commons 1509-1558*, London, 1982, 3 vols.
Burke's Landed Gentry, various editions.
Burke's Landed Gentry of Ireland, various editions.
Burke's Peerage and Baronetage, London, various editions.
Burke, John and John Bernard Burke, *The Extinct and Dormant Baronetcies of England*, London, 1841.
Burke, J. B., *A Visitation of Seats and Arms of the Noblemen and Gentlemen of Great Britain and Ireland*, sec. series, 1854.
Cockayne, G. E., *The Complete Baronetage*, 1900-06 [1983].
Cockayne, G. E., and Vicary Gibbs, *The Complete Peerage*, [1887-98] and 1910-59 and 2000, 14 vols.
Dictionary of Welsh Biography, 1959.
Fisher, David, *The House of Commons 1820-1832*, Cambridge, 2009, 7 vols.
Hasler, P. W., *The House of Commons 1558-1603*, London, 1981, 3 vols.
Hayton, D. W., *The House of Commons 1690-1715*, Cambridge, 2002, 5 vols.
Henning, Basil Duke, *The House of Commons 1660-1690*, London, 1983, 3 vols.
Johnston-Liik, Edith Mary, *History of Irish Parliament 1692-1800*, Belfast, 2002, 6 vols.
Lists of Sheriffs for England and Wales from the Earliest Times to AD 1831, New York, 1963 [1898].
Namier, Sir Lewis and John Brooke, *The House of Commons 1754-1790*, London, 1964, 3 vols.
Official Return of Members of Parliament, London, 1878-79.
Paley, Ruth, ed., *The House of Lords 1660-1715*, Cambridge, 2016, 5 vols.

Return of Owners of Land of One Acre and Upwards ... in Ireland, Baltimore, 1988 [1876].
Roskell, J. S., Linda Clark and Carole Rawcliffe, *The House of Commons 1386-1421*, Stroud, 1992, 4 vols.
Rubinstein, William D., *Who Were the Rich?: A Biographical Directory of British Wealth-holders, Volume I, 1809-1839*, London, 2009.
Sainty, J. C., *Lists of Lieutenants of Counties 1585-1642 and 1660-1974* (IHR, London) 1970, 1979.
Sedgwick, Romney, *The House of Commons 1715-1754*, London, 1970, 2 vols.
Stenton, Michael and Stephen Lees, *Who's Who of British Members of Parliament, 1832-1979*, Hassocks, 1976-81, 4 vols.
Thrush, Andrew and John P. Ferris, *The House of Commons 1604-1629*, Cambridge, 2010, 6 vols.
Wedgwood, Josiah C., and A. D. Holt, *History of Parliament: Biographies of Members of the Commons House 1439-1509*, London, 1936, 2 vols.
Young, Margaret D., ed., *The Parliaments of Scotland, Burgh and Shire Commissioners*, Edinburgh, 1992, 2 vols.

Journals

Country Life
The Irish Genealogist

Online Sources

History or Parliament, www.historyofparliamentonline.org/research/members
Timothy William Ferres, "Lord Belmont in Northern Ireland", www.*lordbelmontinnorthernireland,blogspot.com*
Moore Institute for Research in the Humanities and Social Science, NUI Galway, "Landed Estates Database", www.landedestates.nuigalway.ie
Nick Kingsley, "Landed Families of Britain and Ireland". *www.landedfamilies.blogspot.com/*

Books and Articles

Acheson, Eric, *A Gentry Community: Leicestershire in the Fifteenth Century, c. 1422-1485*, Cambridge, 1992.
Adams, Maxwell, "Some Notes on the Churches at the Manors of East and West Ogwell", *Report and Transactions of the Devonshire Association*, xxxii, 1900, 229-48.
Anderson, James, *Members of Parliament for Glasgow, Glasgow & District: From the Union to the Reform Bill*, 1928.
Angus-Butterworth, Lionel, *Old Cheshire Families*, Manchester, 1932.
Bardon, Jonathan, *A History of Ulster*, Belfast, 1992.
Batt, Elisabeth, *The Moncks and Charleville House: a Wicklow Family in the Nineteenth Century*, Dublin, 1979.
Beard M., *Acres and Heirlooms, the Survival of Britain's Historical Estates*, New York, 1989.
Beastall, T. W., *A North Country Estate: the Lumleys and Saudersons as Landowners* 1600-1900, London, 1975.
Beckert, Sven, *Empire of Cotton: A Global History*, 2014.
Beckett, J. V., *The Aristocracy in England, 1660-1914*, Oxford, 1986.

Beckett, John, *The Rise and Fall of the Grenvilles: Dukes of Buckingham and Chandos, 1710 to 1921*, Manchester, 1994.
Beckett, J. C., *The Anglo-Irish Tradition*, Ithaca, 1976.
Bence-Jones, Mark, *The Catholic Families*, London, 1992.
Bennett, H. S., *The Pastons and Their England*, Cambridge, 1968.
Beresford, Philip, *The Book of the British Rich*, New York, 1990.
Bevan, Alfred B., *The Parliamentary Representation of Lancashire, 1258-1885*, London, 1889.
Blake, Tarquin, *Abandoned Mansions of Ireland*, Wilton, Cork, 2010-12, 2 vols.
Bourke, Eamon, *Burke, Bourke, and De Burgh*, Dublin, 1990.
Brown, D., "'Cotton Lord' to Landed Aristocrat: the Rise of Sir George Philips," *Historical Research*, lxix, 1996, 62-82.
Brunton, D. and D. H. Pennington, *Members of the Long Parliament*, London, 1954.
Bunbury, T., *The Landed Gentry & Aristocracy: Kildare*, Dublin, 2004.
Burns, Robert E., *Irish Parliamentary Politics in the Eighteenth Century: Volume 1 1714-1730 and Volume 2 1730-1760,* Washington, 1989 and 1990.
Burtchell, G. D., *Genealogical Memoirs of the Members of Parliament for the County and City of Kilkenny*, Dublin, 1888.
Cahill, Kevin, *Who Owns Britain*, Edinburgh, 2001.
Callander, Robin Fraser, *A Pattern of Landownership in Scotland: with Particular Reference to Aberdeenshire*, Finzean, 1987.
Cannadine, David, *Aspects of Aristocracy: Grandeur and Decline in Modern Britain*, New Haven, 1994.
Cannadine, David, *The Decline and Fall of the British Aristocracy*, New Haven, 1990.
Cannadine, David, *Lords and Landlords: the Aristocracy and the Towns, 1774-1967*, Leicester, 1980.
Cannadine, David, ed., *Patricians, Power and Politics in Nineteenth-Century Towns*, New York, 1982.
Cannon, John, *Aristocratic Century: the Peerage of Eighteenth-century England*, Cambridge, 1984.
Carpenter, Christine, *Locality and Polity: a Study of Warwickshire Landed Society 1401-1499*, Cambridge, 1992.
Cecil, Lord David, *Some Dorset Country Houses: a Personal Selection*, Stanbridge, 1988.
Chambers, Anne, *Chieftain to Knight: Tibbott-ne-Long Bourke (1567-1629)*, Dublin, 1983.
Christie, Ian R., *British 'Non-Elite' MPs, 1715-1820*, Oxford, 1995.
Christie, Ian R., *Myth and Reality in Late Eighteenth Century British Politics*, London, 1970.
Clarendon, Earl of, *Selections from The History of the Rebellion and Civil Wars and the Life by Himself*, ed., G. Huehns, Oxford, 1968.
Clark, Desmond, *Arthur Dobbs, 1689-1765*, Chapel Hill, 1957.
Clemenson, H. A., *English Country Houses and Landed Estates*, London, 1982.
Cliffe, J. T., *The Yorkshire Gentry from the Reformation to the Civil War*, London, 1969.
Cliffe, J. T., *The World of the Country House in Seventeenth-Century England*, New Haven, 1999.
Collett-White, James, *Inventories of Bedfordshire Country Houses: 1714-1830*, Bedford, 1995.
Colyear, R. J., "Decline of a Great Estate", *Welsh History Review*, ix, 1979, 418.
Connolly, S. J., *Religion, Law, and Politics: the Making of Protestant Ireland, 1660-1760*, Oxford, 1992.
Cooke, Robert, *West Country Houses*, Bristol, 1957.
Coss, Peter, *The Origins of the English Gentry*, Cambridge, 2003.
Country Houses in Great Britain, New Haven, 1979
Coward, Barry, *The Stanleys, Lord Stanley, and Earls of Derby, 1385-1672*, Manchester, 1983.
Cragoe, M., *An Anglican Aristocracy: the Moral Economy of the Landed Estates in Carmarthenshire, 1832-1895*, Oxford, 1996.
Craven, Maxwell and Michael Stanley, *The Derbyshire Country House*, Derby, 1991.

Cronin, Denis A., *A Galway Gentleman in the Age of Improvement: Robert French of Monivea 1716-79*, Dublin, 1995.
Crosleigh, Charles, *Descent and Alliances of Crosleigh and Coddington and Evans*, London, 1904
Dakers, Caroline, *Clouds: The Biography of a Country House*, New Haven, 1993.
Dashwood, Sir Francis, *The Dashwoods of West Wycombe*, London, 1987.
Davies, R. R., *The Age of Conquest: Wales, 1063-1415*, Oxford, 1992.
Delderfield, E. R., *West Country Historic Houses and Their Families*, Vol. 2, Newton Abbot, 1970.
Denholm-Young, N., *The Country Gentry in the Fourteenth Century*, Oxford, 1969.
De Vere, Joan, *The Ruin Reconciled: A Memoir of Anglo-Ireland: 1913-1959*, Dublin, 1990.
Dickson, John, "The Colvill Family of Ulster", *Ulster Journal of Archeology*, 2nd ser., vol. 5, 139-45.
Donnelly, Eithne, "The Roches, Lords of Fermoy", *Journal of the Cork Historical and Archeological Society*, 1933, xxxviii, pp. 86-91 and ff.
Dunboyne, Lord, *Butler Family History*, 7th ed., Dublin, 1991.
Dunning, Robert, *Some Somerset Country Houses*, Wimborne, 1991.
Elton, Arthur and Brett Harrison and Keith Wark, *Researching the Country House: a Guide for Local Historians*, London, 1992.
Emery, Anthony, *Dartington Hall*, Oxford, 1970.
Emery, Anthony, *Greater Medieval Houses of England and Wales: 1300-1500, Volume III, Southern England*, Cambridge, 2006.
English, Barbara, *The Great Landowners of East Yorkshire 1530-1910*, New York, 1990.
Figueirdo, Peter de and Julian Treuherz, *Cheshire Country Houses*, Chichester, 1998.
Finch, Mary E., *The Wealth of Five Northamptonshire Families 1540-1640*, Northampton, 1966.
Forman, Sheila, *Scottish Country Houses and Castles*, Collins, Glasgow, 1967.
Foss, Arthur, *The National Trust Country House Treasures*, London, 1980.
Franklin, Jill, *The Gentleman's Country House and Its Plan 1835-1914*, London, 1981.
Fraser, W. Hamish and R. J. Morris, *People and Society in Scotland*, 2 vols., Edinburgh, 1990.
Gash, Norman, *Politics in the Age of Peel: A Study in the Technique of Parliamentary Representation, 1830-1850*, London, 1953.
Ginter, Donald E., *A Measure of Wealth: The English Land Tax in Historical Analysis*, Montreal, 1992.
Girouard, Mark, "Enmore Castle" in *Decantations*, ed. Agnes Bernelle, Dublin, 1992, 39-46.
Girouard, Mark, *The Victorian Country House,* revised and enlarged edition, New Haven, 1979.
Given-Wilson, C., *The English Nobility in the Late Middle Ages*, London, 1987.
Gordon, Peter, *The Wakes of Northamptonshire*, Northampton, 1992.
Guinness, Desmond and William Ryan, *Irish Houses and Castles,* Thames and Hudson, London, 1973.
Gwynn, Denis, *The Life of John Redmond*, Freeport, NY, 1932.
Habakkuk, John, *Marriage, Debt and the Estates System: English Landownership 1650-1950*, Oxford, 1994.
Hancock, David, *Citizens of the World: London Merchants and the Integration of the British Atlantic Community, 1735-1785*, Cambridge, 1995.
Harris, B. E., ed., *Victoria County History of the County of Cheshire*, Oxford, 1979, ii, 102.
Harris, Paul, *Life in a Scottish Country House: the Story of A. J. Balfour and Whittingehame House,* Whittingehame, 1989.
Harris, R. W., *Clarendon and the English Revolution*, Stanford, 1983
Hawkins, Desmond ed., *The Grove Diaries: The Rise and Fall of an English Family 1809-1925*, Newark, 1995.
Heal, F. and C. Holmes, *The Gentry in England and Wales, 1500-1700*, London, 1994.
Heward, John and Robert Taylor, *The Country Houses of Northamptonshire*, London, 1996.
Hicks, David, *Irish Country Houses: A Chronicle of Change*, Wilton, Cork, 2012.
A History of Northumberland, Newcastle, 1896, vol. iii.

Howell, David W., *Patriarchs and Parasites: The Gentry of South-West Wales in the Eighteenth Century*, Cardiff, 1986.
Hussey, Christopher, *English Country Houses: Early Georgian 1715-1760*, London, 1955.
Hussey, Christopher, *English Country Houses: Late Georgian 1800-1840*, London, 1955.
Hussey, Christopher, *English Country Houses: Mid Georgian 1760-1800*, London, 1955.
Jackson, Alvin, *Colonel Edward Saunderson, Land and Loyalty in Victorian Ireland*, Oxford, 1995.
Jackson-Stops, Gervase, *The Country House in Perspective*, London, 1990.
James, Mervyn, *Family, Lineage, and Civil Society: a Study of Society, Politics and Mentality in the Durham Region 1500-1640*, Oxford, 1974.
James, Mervyn, *Society, Politics and Culture: Studies in Early Modern England*, Cambridge, 1986.
Jenkins, Geriant, *The Foundations of Modern Wales: Wales 1642-1780*, Oxford, 1987.
Jenkins, P., *The Making of a Ruling Class: the Glamorgan Gentry 1640-1790*, Cambridge, 1983.
Johnson, Joan, *The Gloucestershire Gentry*, Gloucester, 1989.
Johnston, Edith Mary, *Great Britain and Ireland, 1760-1800: A Study in Political Administration*, Edinburgh, 1963.
Jones, Clyve, ed., *A Short History of Parliament: England, Great Britain, The United Kingdom, Ireland, and Scotland*, Rochester, 2009.
Jones, Francis, *Historic Houses of Pembrokeshire and Their Families*, Pembrokeshire, 1996.
Jones, *Views of the Seats of Noblemen and Gentlemen in England, Wales, Scotland and Ireland*, sec. ser., London, 1829.
Jones, Winston G., *The Wynnes*, Manorhamilton, Sligo, 1994.
Keeler, Mary, *The Long Parliament, 1640-41: a Biographical Study of Its Members*, Philadelphia, 1954.
Kennedy, Carol, *Harewood: the Life and Times of an English Country House*, London, 1982.
Kenworthy-Browne, John and Peter Reid, Michael Sayer, David Watkin, *Burke's and Savills Guide to Country Houses: East Anglia*, Volume III, London, 1971.
Kingsley, Nicholas, *The Country Houses of Gloucestershire, Volume I 1500-1660*, Cheltenham, 1989.
Kingsley, Nicholas, *The Country Houses of Gloucestershire, Volume II 1660-1830*, Chichester, 1992.
Kingsley, Nicholas and Michael Hill, *The Country Houses of Gloucestershire, Volume III 1830-2000*, Chichester, 2001.
Knight, Caroline, *London's Country Houses*, Chichester, 2009.
Knox, James, *The Scottish Country House*, London, 2012.
Ladd, Frederick J., *Architects at Corsham Court*, Bradford on Avon, Wilts., 1987.
A Landlord's Garden: Derreen Demesne, County Kerry, sec. ed., Bantry, 2005.
Larmine, Vivienne, *Wealth, Kinship and Culture: The Seventeenth-Century Newdigates of Arbury and Their World*, Boydell Press, Woodbridge, 1995
Laslet, Peter, "The Rise and Fall of an English Family" *History Today*, III, 1953, 535-43.
Lawrence, W. T., *Parliamentary Representation of Cornwall*, Truro, n.d., 34-52
Leach, Terence R., *Lincolnshire Country Houses & Their Families, Parts One and Two*, Lincoln, 1990-91.
Lees-Milne, James, *English Country Houses: Baroque 1685-1715*, London, 1970.
Legg, Rodney, *Dorset Families*, Tiverton, 2002.
Lloyd, Thomas, *The Lost Houses of Wales*, London, 1989.
Lubenow, William, *Parliamentary Politics and the Home Rule Crisis: the British House of Commons in 1886*, Oxford, 1988.
Lyons, Mary Cecelia, *Illustrated Incumbered Estates, Ireland, 1850-1905*, Whitegate, Clare, 1993.
MacDonagh, Oliver, *O'Connell: The Life of Daniel O'Connell 1775-1847*, London, 1991.
Maguire, W. A., *The Downshire Estates in Ireland 1801-1845*, Oxford, 1972.
Malchow, H. L., *Gentleman Capitalists: the Social and Political World of Victorian Businessmen*, Stanford, 1992.

Malcolmson, A. P. W., *John Foster: the Politics of the Anglo-Irish Ascendancy*, Oxford, 1978.
Masters, Brian, *The Dukes: The Origins, Ennoblement and History of Twenty-six Families*, London, 2001.
McCord, Norman, *British History 1815-1906*, Oxford, 1991.
McPhee, John, *The Crofter and the Laird*, New York, 1992.
Meisel, Janet, *Barons of the Welsh Frontier 1066-1272*, London, 1980
Millar, A. H., *The Historical Castles & Mansions of Scotland*, London, 1890.
Mingay, G. E., *English Landed Society in the Eighteenth Century*, London, 1970 [1963].
Mingay, G. E., *The Gentry: The Rise and Fall of a Ruling Class*, London, 1976.
Mitchell, Anthony, *Kingston Lacy*, London, 1994.
Montgomery-Massingberd, Hugh, *The Field Book of Country Houses and Their Owners: Family Seats of the British Isles*, London, 1988.
Moody, T. W. and Vaughan, W. E., *A New History of Ireland, IV, Eighteenth-Century Ireland 1691-1800*, Oxford, 2009.
Morgan, Gerald, *A Welsh House and Its Family, The Vaughans of Trawsgoed*, Ceredigion, 1997.
Morris, R. J., *Class, Sect, and Party: The Making of he British Middle Class: Leeds 1820-1850*, Manchester, 1990.
Morris, F. O., *A Series of Picturesque Views of Seats of Noblemen and Gentlemen of Great Britain and Ireland*, London, 1880, 7 volumes.
Moreton, C. E., *The Townshends and Their World: Gentry, Law, and Land in Norfolk, c. 1450-1551*, Oxford, 1992.
Mullin, T. M., *Coleraine in Bygone Centuries*, Belfast, 1976.
Neave, David and Edward Waterson, *Lost Houses of East Yorkshire,* Beverley, 1988.
Negus, Arthur, *A Tour of Twelve Great Country Houses*, London, 1985.
Nicolson, Harold, *The Desire to Please*, New York, 1943.
O'Byrne, Robert, *Luggala Days*, New York, 2012.
O'Connell, Maurice, *Daniel O'Connell*, Dublin, 1990.
Oswald, Arthur, *Country Houses of Dorset*, London, 1959.
Paley, Ruth and Paul Seaward, eds., *Honor, Interest and Power: An Illustrated History of the House of Lords, 1660-1715*, Rochester, 2010.
Parker, Matthew, *The Sugar Barons*, London, 2011.
Payling, Simon, *Political Society in Lancastrian England: the Greater Gentry of Nottinghamshire*, Oxford, 1991.
Pearman, Robert, *The Cadogan Estate: A History of a Landed Family*, London, 1986.
Perceval-Maxwell, M., *The Scottish Migration to Ulster*, London, 1973.
Pevsner, Nicklaus and David Lloyd, *Hampshire and the Isle of Wight*, Penguin, 1967.
Phillips, John A., *The Great Reform Bill in the Boroughs: English Electoral Behavior: 1818-1841*, Oxford, 1992.
Pielou, Pierce Leslie, *The Leslies of Tarbert*, Dublin 1935.
Plumb, J. H., *Sir Robert Walpole: The Making of a Statesman*, Boston, 1956.
Quiney, Anthony, *Kent Houses*, Woodbridge, 1993.
Rampini, Charles, *A History of Moray and Nairn*, Edinburgh, 1897.
Rapp, Dean, "Social Mobility in the Eighteenth Century: the Whitbreads of Bedfordshire – 1720-1815", *Economic History Review*, 27 1974, 380-94.
Rich, Lawrence, *Inherit the Land: Landowners in the 'Eighties*, London, 1987.
Richards, Eric, *The Leviathan of Wealth: the Sutherland Fortune in the Industrial Revolution*, London, 1973.
Roberts, W. M., *Lost Country Houses of Suffolk*, Woodbridge, 2010.
Robinson, John Martin, *The Dukes of Norfolk*, Oxford, 1983.

Robinson, John Martin, *Felling the Ancient Oaks: How England Lost Its Great Country Estates*, London, 2011.
Robinson, John Martin, *A Guide to the Country Houses of the North-West*, London, 1991.
Roebuck, Peter, ed. *Macartney of Lisanoure 1737-1806*, Belfast, 1983.
Roebuck, Peter, *Yorkshire Baronets 1640-1760: Families, Estates and Fortunes*, London, 1980.
Rosenheim, James M., *The Emergence of a Ruling Order: English Landed Society, 1650-1750*, London, 1997.
Rowse, A. L., *The Early Churchills*, New York, 1956.
Rowse, A. L., *The Little Land of Cornwall*, Gloucester, 1986.
Rubinstein, W. D., *Men of Property: the Very Wealthy in Britain since the Industrial Revolution*, London, 1981.
Rubinstein, W. D. "New Men of Wealth and the Purchase of Land in the Nineteenth-Century Britain", *Past and Present*, 1981, 92, 132.
Rubinstein, W. D., "The Structure of Wealth-holding in Britain 1809-39", *Historical Research*, 65, 1992, 74-89.
Russell, Una and Audey Grindrod, *The Manor Houses of Dorset*, Stanbridge, 2007.
Saul, Nigel, *Knights and Esquires: The Gloucestershire Gentry in the Fourteenth Century*, Oxford, 1981.
Sayer, Michael, *The Disintegration of a Heritage: Country Houses and Their Collections 1979-1992*, Norwich, 1993.
Scott, John, *Who Rules Britain?*, Cambridge, 1991.
Scriven, Marcus, *Splendour and Squalour: The Disgrace and Disintegration of Three Aristocratic Dynasties*, London, 2010.
Shirley, E. P., *The Noble and Gentle Men of England*, London, 1866.
Simms, J. G., David Hayton, and Gerald O'Brien, *War and Politics in Ireland 1649-1730*, London, 1986.
Skidmore, Warren, *The Scudamores of Upton Scudamore*, Akron, 1982.
Smith, R. B., *Land and Politics in the England of Henry VIII: The West Riding of Yorkshire, 1530-46*, Oxford, 1970.
Smythe, Colin, *Guide to Coole Park Co. Galway: Home of Lady Gregory*, 4th ed., 2011.
Spring, D. and E. Spring, "Social Mobility and the English Landed Elite", *Canadian Journal of History*, 21 (1986), 333-51.
Spring, D. and E. Spring, "The English Landed Elite, 1540-1880", *Albion*, 17 (1985) 149-80 and 393-96.
Spring, E., *Law, Land, and Family: Aristocratic Inheritance in England 1300 to 1800*, Chapel Hill, 1993.
Stevenson, John, *Two Centuries in Life in Down 1600-1800*, Belfast, 1920.
Stone, Lawrence, *The Crisis of the Aristocracy 1558-1641*, Oxford, 1979.
Stone, Lawrence and Jeanne F. Stone, *An Open Elite? England 1540-1880*, Oxford, 1984.
Stringer, K. J., *Essays on the Nobility of Medieval Scotland*, Edinburgh, 1985.
Strong, Roy and Marcus Binney and John Harris, *The Destruction of the Country House 1875-1975*, London, 1974.
Taylor, James, *Great Historic Families of Scotland, Baltimore, 1995.*
Thompson, F. M. L., "Desirable Properties", *Historical Research*, 64, 1991.
Thompson, F. M. L., *English Landed Society in the Nineteenth Century*, London, 1971.
Thompson, F. M. L., "Life after Death: How Successful Nineteenth-Century Businessmen Disposed of Their Fortunes", *Economic History Review*, sec. ser., 43, 1990, 40-61.
Thompson, H. L., "The Poyntz Family", *Transactions of the Bristol and Gloucestershire Archeological Society*, 4, 1879-80, 73-85.
Thorold, Henry, Harland Walshaw, and Peter Burton, *Lincolnshire Houses*, Norwich, 1999.

Turner, M. E., J. Beckett, B. Afton, *Agricultural Rent in England, 1690-1914*, Cambridge, 2004.
Tyack, Geoffrey, *Warwickshire Country Houses*, Chichester, 1994.
Wagner, Anthony, *English Genealogy*, Oxford, 1972.
Ward, J. T. and R. G. Wilson, *Land and Industry: The Landed Estates and the Industrial Revolution*, Newton Abbot, 1971.
Warrand, Duncan, *Hertfordshire Families*, *Victoria County History*, London 1907, 243-51.
Wasson, Ellis, *Aristocracy and the Modern World*, Basingstoke, 2006.
Wasson, Ellis, *Born to Rule: British Political Elites*, Stroud, 2000.
Waterson, Edward and Peter Meadows, *Lost Houses of the West Riding*, York, 1998.
Wedgwood, Josiah, *Staffordshire Parliamentary History*, London, 1920-22, 3 vols.
Whiteley, William Henry, *The Social Composition of the House of Commons, 1868-1885*, unpublished Ph.D thesis, Cornell University, 1960, 2 volumes.
Wiener, Martin J., *English Culture and the Decline of the Industrial Spirit 1850-1980*, Cambridge, new ed., 2004.
Wightman, Andy, *Who Owns Scotland*, Edinburgh, 1996.
Williams, Glanmor, ed., *Glamorgan County History*, IV, Cardiff, 1974.
Williams, W. R., *The Parliamentary History of the City of Oxford 1313-1899*, Breknock, 1899.
Williams, W. R., *The Parliamentary History of the Principality of Wales, 1541-1895*, Brecknock, 1895.
Willson, F.M.G., *A Strong Supporting Cast: the Shaw Lefevres 1789-1936*, London, 1993.
Wilson, R. G., *Gentlemen Merchants: the Merchant Community in Leeds, 1700-1830*, Manchester, 1971.
Winter, C. W. R., *The Manor Houses of the Isle of Wight*, Stanbridge, 1984.
Wood, Florence and Kenneth, eds., *A Lancashire Gentleman, The Letters and Journals of Richard Hodgkinson 1763-1847*, Stroud, 1992.
Worsley, Giles, *England's Lost Houses*, London, 2011.
Wright, William Ball, *The Ussher Memoirs*, Dublin, 1889.
Wyndham, H. A., *A Family History 1410-1688*, Oxford, 1939.
Ziegler, Philip, *The Sixth Great Power: A History of One of the Greatest of All Banking Families: The House of Barings 1762-1929*, New York, 1988.

Appendices

Appendix I
Families not Included in the Main List

This list contains the names of families that did not manage to elect three MPs or secure a peerage that sustained family representation in Parliament over several generations 1660-1945 and yet were substantial landowners or otherwise potential candidates for inclusion in the ruling class. It encompasses all the landowning families of the British Isles who owned over 5,000 acres or possessed an income from land of over 5,000 pounds listed in Bateman (1876) not included in the main section of these volumes.[1] I have also tried to identify families extinct by the mid-nineteenth century in possession of resources sufficient to enter parliamentary life on a regular basis and who did not and others who purchased large estates after 1876.[2]

Many families managed to elect one or two MPs but did not have the time or opportunity to gain enough traction in the electoral system to become a full-blown parliamentary dynasty. These and other families may also have fielded candidates in elections but were unsuccessful. (Over two-thirds of losing candidates in eighteenth-century elections, however, were MPs at some other time or were members of established parliamentary families.[3]) They were often sheriffs and chairs of county councils, which offered them the prestige and influence suitable to their relatively modest resources. Many reasons explain why rich families did not achieve the three MP/peer minimum. Among these are the following:

1. They acquired wealth too late in the 19th century, after the Reform Acts began to make gaining election more challenging for those who relied mainly on status rather than merit or ideology to earn votes.
2. They lacked sufficient wealth to launch a sustained parliamentary presence – due perhaps to estates divided up among multiple heirs rather than descending by primogeniture. Virtually all families listed with 10,000 acres/income or more in Bateman were parliamentary families.
3. They possessed a blood connection or clientage with a parliamentary family where the latter dynasty reserved the parliamentary seats over which it had influence for members of the stem family.

---

1 Some families with less than 5,000 acres in Bateman nonetheless have sustained ownership of land and houses for many centuries but elected few or no MPs. The Fursdons of Fursdon, Devon have held their estate since 1259 (757 years) and the Kellys at Kelly, Devon since around 1100 (900 years) (*Country Life*, 25 May 2016, 76-83).

2 For further information about these families, see Ellis Wasson, *Born to Rule*, 2000, 37-40.

3 Wasson, *Born to Rule*, 9.

4. They purchased land in an area with few parliamentary seats and/or where a large number of magnate families anxious to dominate the available seats for their own benefit prevailed in elections.
5. They became extinct in the male line by the early 18th century.
6. They remained Roman Catholic in faith, which meant legal exclusion from office until 1829.
7. They were members of a "Dissenting" church, which also legally, although not necessarily in practice, excluded them from Parliament until "Emancipation".
8. Various unique quirks or kinks in the genealogical development of the family that produced a sequence of adult males uninterested in or incapable (minors, insane, bankrupt, traitors, etc.) of gaining election to Parliament or a sequence of heiresses who were legally ineligible for election.
9. They lacked interest in parliamentary participation (most common after the Second Reform Act among newly risen families).
10. Rising hostility to Protestant candidates for Parliament in Ireland in the second half of the 19th century brought an end to Ascendancy participation in the south. Also the drastic decrease in the number of Irish seats after 1800 had a negative effect on the parliamentary participation of many families.
11. Abandonment of engagement in the political life of Wales by the traditional landowning class during the course of the 19th century and rising hostility towards them among electors due to class, religious, and nationalist feeling.
12. Declining finances or bankruptcy necessitating the sale of estates early in the history of the family.

It should be noted that even after the Reform Acts some new families continued to follow traditional pathways to status and power. A good example is the line in descent from James Watt (1736-1819) of Birmingham. The immortal Watt invented improvements to the steam engine that made the rest of the Industrial Revolution possible. Like many British businessmen before him, he purchased a landed estate. This began with 500 acres around Doldowold in Radnorshire in 1803. By 1876 the Watts had accumulated 11,036 acres. The inventor's son, although an excellent man of business, retired in 1840 from the partnership his father had founded and began building a proper great house to match the size of the estate. This was inherited by James Gibson, grandson of Watt's daughter, who took the name Watt and became High Sheriff of the county. His son was sent to Eton, and his son served in the Welsh Guards and as MP for Hereford 1956-74. He gained a peerage (Lord Gibson-Watt cr. 1979). His daughter married the 5th Lord Biddulph. One of her sons bears the name Watt and the family continues to reside at Doldowlod. (*Country Life*, Jan. 8, 2004, pp. 40-45). Another example of continued traditional aspirations and methods of ascent is the Profumo family. Founded by a Piedmontese Baron who served as an aide to Cavour, they migrated to London and in 1877 founded the Provident Life Association, which made them millions of pounds. A country house was acquired in Derbyshire at

Avon Dassett. The 4th Baron (use of the Italian title was gradually discontinued) stood unsuccessfully for Parliament in 1892 and on several subsequent occasions his hopes met a similar fate. However, his son Jack, sent to Harrow and Oxford, gained election for Kettering in 1940. He served as an army officer and was one of those Conservatives in the Commons whose votes brought down the Chamberlain government in May of that year. He achieved the rank of Minister of War before being enveloped in a celebrated scandal in the 1960s involving sex and spies that helped undermine the Macmillan administration.[4] That catastrophe and the ever-increasing difficulty of finding a seat brought an end to the family's political ambitions. One can cite numerous similar instances. Most recently, the supermarket Sainsburys have shown every sign, from purchasing very large estates to planting themselves in Parliament, of following the traditional pathway to power and status, but they are now the exception, not the rule.

Note: I have not deeply pursued research into the origins of many of these families and have not always discovered the origins of their wealth. This list is a rough outline.

ENGLAND

Aldersey of Aldersey Hall, Cheshire
(medieval gentry, modest estate)
Allan of Blackwell Grange, Durham (**1 MP**)
(16th c. gentry)
Allcroft of Stokesay, Shropshire
(19th c. manufacturer)
Anderson of Lea Hall, Lincolnshire
(related to Anderson-Pelhams, Earls of Yarborough)
Askew of Pallinsburn, Northumberland
(18th c., physicians, clergy)
Austen of Brandeston Hall, Suffolk
(19th c., lawyer)
Bragge of Stradsett Hall, Norfolk
(inher. estate 18th c.)
Barbour of Bolesworth Castle, Cheshire
(19th c. Manchester businessman)
Barneby of Saltmarshe Castle, Herefordshire
(old gentry, inher. estate 19th c.)
Barton of Stapleton Park, Yorkshire
(19th c. estate owned for a brief tenure and sold)

4 David Profumo, *Bringing the House Down: A Family Memoir*, London, 2006.

Bazley of Eyford Park, Gloucestershire
(19th c. Lancashire cotton manufacturers)
Bengough of The Ridge, Gloucestershire
(19th c. Bristol bankers and publishers)
Berners of Woolverstone Park, Suffolk
(inher. estate 18th c.)
Bevan of Fosbery House, Wiltshire
(18th c. Quaker bankers, brewers)
Blount of Mapledurham House, Oxfordshire (**ROMAN CATHOLIC**)
(medieval gentry)
Blundell of Ince-Blundell, Lancashire (**ROMAN CATHOLIC**)
(old gentry family)
Blundell of Crosby Hall, Lancashire (**ROMAN CATHOLIC**)
(acq. 17th c.)
Boileau of Ketteringham Park, Norfolk
(Huguenots, merchants 18th c.)
Bolitho of Trengwainton, Cornwall (1 MP)
(18th c. merchants, later tin mining, banking)
Borough (Borrow) of Chetwynd Park, Shropshire (**1 MP**)
(18th c. Derbyshire iron founders)
Garnett-Botfield of Norton Hall, Northamptonshire (**1 MP**)
(18th c. iron industry)
Bourne of Cowarne Court, Herefordshire
(19th c. owned estate for a short tenure)
Brocklebank of Haughton Hall, Cheshire
(mid-19th c. ship owners)
Brooke of Sarawak (**1 MP**)
(hereditary rulers of Sarawak in Borneo 19th-20th c.)
De Capell-Brooke of Oakley Hall, Northamptonshire
(old gentry)
Brooksbank of Healaugh Manor, Yorkshire
(18th c. London bankers)
Stapleton-Bretherton of Lackham, Wiltshire (**ROMAN CATHOLIC**)
(founded by a stage-coach proprietor)
Prideaux-Brune of Prideaux Place, Cornwall
(old gentry, declining finances)
Brymer of Ilsington House, Dorset (**1 MP**)
(18th c. merchant in Canada, returned to UK 19th c., held landed estate for a short period 1861-1921)
Buckworth of Cockley Cley Hall, Norfolk
(18th c. grain merchants, inher. landed estate 19th c., bankrupt early 20th c.)

Burroughes of Burlingham Hall, Norfolk (**1 MP**)
(18th c. solicitor, inher. land 19th c., sold off estates later 19th c. and early 20th.)
Cave of Cleve Hill House, Gloucestershire (**1 MP**)
(Quaker bankers Bristol 19th c.)
Scott-Chad of Thursford Hall, Norfolk
(18th c. lawyer, sold estates early 20th c.)
Chafy-Chafy of Rous Lench Court, Worcestershire
(19th c. clergyman, purch. estate 1876, sold 50 years later)
Charlton of Hesleyside, Northumberland (**ROMAN CATHOLIC**)
(medieval gentry)
Childe-Pemberton of Millichope Park, Shropshire
(inher. 1848, sold 1896)
Clarke of Swakeleys, Middlesex
(18th c. clergyman, 19th c. passed to Thornhills, leased, sold)
Clayton of The Chesters, Northumberland
(coal merchants and lawyers 18th-19th c. Newcastle)
Stracey-Clitherow of Hotham Hall, Yorkshire
(17th c. London commerce, East India trade)
Cookson of Meldon, Northumberland
(18th c. Newcastle bankers, mines, manufacturing)
Cooper of Toddington Manor, Bedfordshire
(early 19th c. brewer, sold early 20th c.)
Courtauld of Gosfield Hall, Essex
(19th c. industrialists)
Craster of Craster Tower, Northumberland
(medieval gentry, not rich)
Cresswell (Baker) of Cresswell, Northumberland (**2 MPs**)
(medieval gentry)
Davenport of Foxley Hall, Herefordshire (**2 MPs**)
(19th c. pottery manufacturer)
Kevill-Davies of Croft Castle, Herefordshire (**1 MP**)
(inher. estate late 18th c., sold early 20th c.)
Dent of Ribston Hall, Yorkshire (**1 MP**)
(19th c. property speculator, money-lender)
Cottrell-Dormer of Rousham Hall, Oxfordshire
(17th c. gentry)
Drummond of Cadland House, Hampshire
(related to Earls of Perth, banking)
Duckworth of Orchardleigh, Somerset (**1 MP**)
(fortune in Manchester real estate 19th c.)
Balantine-Dykes of Doverby Hall, Cumberland
(medieval gentry)

Enys of Enys, Cornwall
(medieval gentry)
Errington of Beaufort Castle, Northumberland (**ROMAN CATHOLIC**)
(old gentry – see under Massey **S**tanley in the main list)
Evans of Allestry Hall, Derbyshire (**2 MPs**)
(19th c. mill owners and bankers)
Every of Eggington Hall, Derbyshire (**1 MP**)
(17th c. gentry)
Farquharson of Eastbury, Dorset (**1 MP**)
(18th c. East India Company merchant)
Fenton Boughey of Betley Court, Staffordshire (**1 MP**)
(18th c. minerals and land)
FitzGerald of Boulge Hall, Suffolk
(Irish family inher. English business fortune 19th c.)
Foster of Anstey Hall, Cambridgeshire
(Cambridge bankers 19th c.)
Fountaine of Narford Hall, Norfolk
(Master of the Mint 18th c.)
Fox of Stratham Lodge, Cheshire
(19th c. Manchester banker)
Frampton of Moreton House, Dorset (**3 MPs** – all pre 1660)
(old gentry)
France-Hayhurst of Bostock Hall, Cheshire
(Liverpool merchants 18th c.)
Rokewood-Gage of Hengrave Hall, Suffolk
(16th c. gentry)
Garnett of Bleasdale Tower, Lancashire
(19th c. Russia merchants in Manchester, cotton mill owners)
Garnier of Rooksbury Park, Hampshire (**1 MP**)
(18th c., owned salt mines)
Giffard of Chillington Hall, Staffordshire (**ROMAN CATHOLIC**)
(medieval gentry)
Gilstrap of Fornham Hall, Suffolk
(Nottinghamshire brewer 19th c.)
Gist of Wormington Grange, Gloucestershire
(Bristol merchants 18th c.)
Glegg (Baskervyle) of Withington Hall, Cheshire
(medieval gentry)
Gooch of Benacre Hall, Suffolk (**2 MPs**)
(18th c. bishop)
Gosling of Hassobury, Essex
(18th c. bankers)

Greene of Whittington Hall, Lancashire (**1 MP**)
(19th c. barristers, modest resources, sold estate 1925)
Greg of Coles Park, Cheshire
(18-19th c. Cheshire merchants and mill owners)
Gregory of Harlaxton Manor, Lincolnshire
(Huguenots, business fortune, became landed 18th c.)
Grimston of Kilnwick Hall, Yorkshire
(medieval gentry)
Gunning of Horton House, Northamptonshire (**2 MPs**)
(17th c. bishop, 18th c. diplomat, held estate for about a century, sold later 19th c.)
Haggerston of Haggerston Castle, Northumberland (**ROMAN CATHOLIC**)
(medieval gentry)
Haigh of Grainsby Hall, Lincolnshire
(19th c. Halifax mill owners)
Hall of High Hall, Yorkshire
(Liverpool merchants 17th c.)
Hall of The Hall, Six Mile Bottom, Cambridgeshire
(19th c., three generals, inher. estate, owned for only about 70 years, sold 1912)
Hamond of Westacre High House, Norfolk
(17th c. gentry, sold estate later 19th c.)
Hanbury of Holfield Grange, Essex
(18th c. merchants)
Harford of Blaise Castle, Gloucestershire
(Bristol Quaker bankers 18th c.)
Hargreaves of Ormerod House, Lancashire
(18th c. coal mine owners)
Harrison of Snelston Hall, Derbyshire
(owned foundry in Derby 18th c.)
Hasell of Dalemain, Cumberland (**1 MP**)
(steward of noble estate 17th c.)
Hulton-Harrop of Lythwood Hall, Shropshire
(old gentry)
Hemming of Bentley Manor, Worcestershire
(19th c. manufacturer in Worcestershire, purch. landed estate 1831, passed to an heiress 1891)
Heywood of Cloverley, Shropshire (**2 MPs**)
(19th c. Manchester bankers, later railways, multiple heirs divided up estate)
Holbech of Farnborough Hall, Warwickshire (**1 MP**)
(17th c. lawyer)
Holden of Nuthall Temple, Nottinghamshire
(19th c., real estate speculation and marriage to heiresses, sold 1920s)

Hollond of Benhall Lodge, Suffolk (**1 MP**)
(East India Co. fortune 19th c.)
Hornby of Dalton Hall, Westmorland (**2 MPs**)
(19th c. barrister, mar. heiress)
Hornyold (Gandolfi) of Blackmore Park, Worcestershire (**ROMAN CATHOLIC**)
(old gentry)
Hulton of Hulton Park, Lancashire (**1 MP**) (**ROMAN CATHOLIC**)
(old gentry)
Humfrey-Mason of Heggatt Hall, Norfolk
(16th c. gentry)
Holdich-Hungerford of Dingley Park, Northamptosnhire (**1 MP**)
(18th c. lawyer and estate official)
FitzClarence-Hunloke of Wingerworth Hall, Derbyshire (**ROMAN CATHOLIC**)
(Hunlokes 16th c. gentry, mar. son of a royal bastard in 19th c., heavily indebted, extinct 1856)
Hurt of Alderwasley Hall, Derbyshire
(18th c. iron forge owners, manufacturing)
Hussey of Scotney Castle, Kent
(London property owners 19th c.)
Jeafferson (Robinson) of Dullingham House, Cambridgeshire
(17th c., West Indies fortune, complicated inheritance after 1824)
Jones of Cramer Hall, Norfolk (**1 MP**)
(18th c., Welsh gentry, mar. Norfolk heiress)
Kennaway of Estcot Lodge, Devon (**1 MP**)
(woolen merchant in Exeter 18th c., East India Co.)
King of Ashby-de-la-Launde, Lincolnshire
(16th c. gentry)
Kingscote of Kingscote, Gloucestershire (**1 MP**)
(medieval gentry)
Laslett of Abberton Hall, Worcestershire (**1 MP**)
(bankers in Worcester 18th c., owned estate for about70 years)
Leche of Carden Park, Cheshire
(medieval gentry)
Lee (Hanning) of Dillington Park, Somerset (**2 MPs**)
(successful tenant farmer 19th c.)
Lever of Thornton Manor, Cheshire
(Viscount Leverhulme, 19th c. industrialist owned 34,700 acres in 2001)
Lindow (Burns) of Ehen Hall, Cumberland
(industrialists in iron-making 19th c.)
Cann-Lippincott of Over Court, Gloucestershire
(19th c., owned for about 50 years)

Livesey of Stourton Hall, Lincolnshire
(18th c. business)
Lomax (Trappes) of Clayton Hall, Lancashire (**ROMAN CATHOLIC**)
(old gentry)
Long of Dunston Hall, Norfolk
(17th c.)
Drury-Lowe of Locko Park, Derbyshire
(coal mine owners 18th c.)
Barneby-Lutley of Brockhampton Park, Herefordshire
(16th c. gentry)
Lyon of Ashfield Hall, Cheshire
(urban development 19th c.)
Mackenzie of Fawley Court, Buckinghamshire
(canal and railway contractors 18th - 19th c.)
Marker of Combe House, Devon
(19th c. inher.)
Marling of Sedbury Park, Gloucestershire (**1 MP**)
(cloth manufacturers 19th c.)
Mason of Necton Hall, Norfolk
(16th c. gentry)
Micklethwaite of Taverham Hall, Norfolk
(inher. 19th c.)
Middleton of Stockfield Park, Yorkshire (**ROMAN CATHOLIC**)
(medieval gentry)
Miller of Singleton Hall, Lancashire
(Preston cotton mill owner 19th c.)
Mills of Hilborough Hall, Norfolk (**1 MP**)
(textile manufacturers 18th-19th c., purch. estate 1861)
Monypenny of Great Maytham Hall, Kent
(RN Captain 18th c., financial trouble second half 19th c.)
Moore of Appleby Hall, Derbyshire
(London merchants 16th-17th c.)
Palmer-Morewood of Alfreton Hall, Derbyshire
(Manchester businessmen 18th-19th c.)
Morritt of Rokeby, Yorkshire (**2 MPs**)
(emerged 18th c., source of wealth unknown)
Mott of Barningham Hall, Norfolk (**1 MP**)
(18th c. lawyer and inher.)
Musters of Colwick, Nottinghamshire
(London grocer 17th c., mar. heiress 18th c.)

Naylor (Leyland) of Hooton Hall, Cheshire
(Liverpool businessmen 19th c., Leyland ship owners who began by winning a lottery 1768)
Neave of Dagnam Park, Essex (**2 MPs**)
(West India merchant 18th c.)
Neeld of Grittleton House, Wiltshire (**2 MPs**)
(silversmith, jeweler 19th c.)
Newall of Forest Hall, Essex
(19th c., resident for about 40 years in later part of century)
Newcome (Wyche) of Feltwell Hall, Norfolk (**2 MPs**)
(17th c. gentry)
Newton of Barrells Hall, Warwickshire
(Birmingham industrialists 19th c.)
Newton of Croxton Park, Cambridgeshire (**1 MP**)
Baron Eltisley 1934
(Liverpool merchant 18th c.)
Norman of Bromley Common, Kent (**1 MP**)
Baron Norman 1944
(London timber merchant, banking, insurance 18th c.)
Pares of Hopwell Hall, Derbyshire (**1 MP**)
(18th-19th c. Leicester manufacturers and bankers)
Townley-Parker of Cuerden Hall, Lancashire (**1 MP**)
(16th c. gentry)
Pemberton of Hawthorne Towers, Durham
(medieval gentry)
Pinney of Bettiscombe Manor, Dorset (**1 MP**)
(owned plantation on Nevis, 17th-18th c.)
Plowden of Plowden, Shropshire (**ROMAN CATHOLIC**)
(medieval gentry)
Chandos-Pole of Radburne Hall, Derbyshire (**1 MP**)
(medieval gentry)
Powell (Grigby) of Drinkstone Park, Suffolk (**1 MP**)
(18th c., lawyer and estate steward)
Pratt of Ryston Hall, Norfolk
(16th c., architect 17th c.)
Preston of Beeston Hall, Norfolk
(17th c. lawyers and landowners)
Preston of Moreby Hall, Yorkshire
(Leeds merchants 18th c.)
Prideaux of Prideaux Place, Cornwall
(old gentry)

Wegg-Prosser of Belmont House, Herefordshire (**2 MPs**) (**ROMAN CATHOLIC**)
(18th c. senior clergy)
Radcliffe (Percival, Pickford) of Rudding Park, Yorkshire
(Manchester merchant 17th c.)
Rankin of Bryngwyn, Herefordshire (**1 MP**)
(19th c. Glasgow timber and shipbuilding)
Reeve of Leadenham House, Lincolnshire
(inher. 18th c.)
Richardson of Honingham Hall, Norfolk (**2 MPs**)
Baron Cramond 1628-1715 S
(Chief Justice KB 1630s, suffered under Commonwealth, sold estates, none elected Scottish Rep. peers)
Riddell of Felton Park, Northumberland (**ROMAN CATHOLIC**)
(17th c. inher.)
Rogers (Coxwell) of Dowdeswell Court, Gloucestershire
(16th c. gentry, sold c. 1900)
Rogers of Penrose, Cornwall (**2 MPs**)
(tin mines and urban property 18th c.)
Roundell of Gledstone Hall, Yorkshire
(inher. three fortunes in 18th-19th c.)
Rowley of Harston Manor House, Cambridgeshire
(inher. 19th c.)
Watts-Russell of Biggin Grange, Northamptonshire
(London soap boiler late 18th c., mar. heiress) (**1 MP**)
Ryland-Smith of Barford House, Warwickshire
(Birmingham industrialist 19th c.)
Sainsbury
Baron Sainsbury
(19th c. grocery stores, later supermarkets, **1 MP** 1973-97, billionaires, large landed estates, 1 KG, 1 in Cabinet, several peerages)
Sartoris (Tunno) of Rushden Hall, Northamptonshire (**2 MPs**)
(19th c. bankers)
Scarisbrick of Scarisbrick Hall, Lancashire (**ROMAN CATHOLIC**)
(medieval family, very rich)
Selby of Biddlestone Hall, Northumberland (**ROMAN CATHOLIC**)
(medieval family)
Seymer of Hanford House, Dorset
(old gentry family)
Sheppard of Campsea Ashe High House, Suffolk
(17th c. agriculturalists)

Sherbrooke (Lowe) of Oxton Hall, Nottinghamshire (**1 MP**)
  Viscount Sherbrooke 1880
  (16th c. gentry)
Smyth of Elkington Hall, Lincolnshire
  (medieval gentry)
Smythe of Acton Burnell, Shropshire (**ROMAN CATHOLIC**)
  (aristocratic connection 18th c.)
Sowerby of Putteridge Park, Bedfordshire
  (insurance in London 18th c.)
Sparke of Gunthorpe Hall, Norfolk
  (19th c. inher.)
Stephens of Tregenna Castle, Cornwall (**2 MPs**)
  (Fisheries, mines and copper smelting in Wales 18th c.)
Stocks of Wood Hall, Norfolk
  (coal mining and brewing from 17th c. Yorkshire)
Stracey of Rackheath Hall, Norfolk (**1 MP**)
  (18th c. lawyer)
Stratford of Hawling Manor, Gloucestershire
  (medieval gentry, financial crisis 18th c., most land sold)
Streatfield of Chiddingstone Castle, Kent
  (16th c. gentry)
Symons of The Mynde, Herefordshire (**2 MPs**)
  (London merchant 18th c. purch 1740, estate passed through a number of families by inher.)
Tabor of Great Codham Hall, Essex
  (agricultural rise 19th c. big purchases)
Tatton of Wythenshawe, Lancashire
  (old gentry)
Tayleur of Buntingsdale Hall, Shropshire (**1 MP**)
  (18th c. gentry, second fortune 19th c. railways)
Taylor of Strensham Court, Worcestershire (**1 MP**)
  (banker and button manufacturer Birmingham 18th c.)
Tempest of Broughton Hall, Yorkshire (**ROMAN CATHOLIC**)
  (medieval family)
Thornton of Brockhall, Northamptonshire (**1 MP**)
  (17th c. lawyer)
Todd (Wilson) of Halnaby Hall, Yorkshire (**1 MP**)
  (17th c. acq. estates, Hull merchants?)
Trafford of Wroxham Hall, Norfolk (**1 MP**) (**ROMAN CATHOLIC**)
  (19th c. inher. part of 18th c. Boehm banking fortune)
De Trafford of Trafford Park, Lancashire (**ROMAN CATHOLIC**)
  (medieval family)

Tryon of Bulwick Hall, Northamptonshire
(16th c., Flemish refugee merchants, landed gentry from 17th c.)
Turbutt of Ogston Hall, Derbyshire
(inher. 18th c.)
Wakefield of Sedgwick House, Westmorland (**2 MP**)
Baron Wakefield 1963
(19th c. Quaker merchants)
Walker of Berkswell Hall, Warwickshire
(ironmaster from Staffordshire 19th c., bankrupt)
Walker of Sand Hutton, Yorkshire (**1 MP**)
(Manchester merchants 18th c.)
Watt of Speke Hall, Lancashire
(Liverpool West Indies merchants 18th c.)
Watson of North Seaton Hall, Northumberland
(18th c. coal mine owners, sold 1880s)
Webb of Newstead Abbey, Nottinghamshire
(inher. part of Belasyse estates via heiresses in 18th c.)
Wilkes of Lofts Hall, Essex
(18th c. agricultural)
Willson of Rauceby Hall, Lincolnshire
(bankers 19th c.)
Williams (Greswolde) of Malvern Hall, Warwickshire
(19th c. inher., sold c. 1900)
Willyams of Carnanton, Cornwall
(inher. 16th c.)
Wilson of Rigmaden, Westmorland
(bankers 19th c.)
Wilson of Stowlangtoft Hall, Suffolk
Baron Wilson 1945
(19th c. silk manufacturer)
Maryon-Wilson of Charlton House, Kent (**1 MP**)
(17th c. gentry, valuable London estate)
Wingfield of Onslow Hall, Shropshire
(17th c. gentry)
Wise of Woodcote, Warwickshire (**1 MP**)
(royal gardener 18th c., urban property)
Wood of Newbold Revel. Warwickshire
(railway promoter 19th c.)
Woodward of Arley Castle, Worcestershire
(19th c., Liverpool merchants)
Wright of Mottram Hall, Cheshire
(16th c. gentry)

WALES

Bowen of Llwyngwair, Pembrokeshire (**1 MP**)
(old gentry famiy, 1 Ld Lt)
Colby of Bletherston, Pembrokeshire
(18th c. gentry)
Crawshay of Cyfarthfa Castle, Glamorganshire
(Ironmasters 18th-19th c.)
De Winton (Wilkins) of Maesllwych Castle, Radnorshire
(**2 MPs**)
(East India Co. 18th c., banks, canals, iron works)
Hughes of Kinmel Park, Denbighshire (**1 MP**)
(19th c. copper mine owners)
Jenner of Wenvoe Castle, Glamorganshire (**1 MP**)
(19th c. inher. land by mar. and railways)
Lloyd of Bronwydd, Cardiganshire
(old gentry)
Mynors of Evancoyd, Radnorshire
(medieval gentry)
Nichol of Merthyr Mawr, Glamorganshire (**2 MP**)
(19th c. judge)
Roch of Butter Hill, Pembrokeshire (**1 MP**)
(17th c. gentry)

SCOTLAND

Alexander of Ballocmyle House, Ayrshire (**2 MPs**)
(18th c. East India Fortune)
Allen of Inchmartine House, Perthshire
(17th c. gentry)
Balfour of Balfour Castle, Orkney (**2 MPs**)
(18th-19th c. nabob)
Brook of Hoddom Castle, Dumfriesshire
(Huddersfield mill owner 19th c.)
Tyndall-Bruce of House of Falkland, Fife
(Bristol Quaker bankers and slave traders 18th c.)
Butter of Faskally, Perthshire
(old gentry)
Cameron of Lochiel of Achnacarry Castle, Inverness (**1 MP**) (**ROMAN CATHOLIC**)
(ancient clan chiefs, "out" in 1715 and 1745 and then exile in France, owned 76,000 acres in 2001)

Cuninghame of Lainshaw, Ayrshire (**1 MP**)
(old gentry)
Finlay of Castle Toward, Argyllshire (**2 MPs**)
(19th c. Glasgow merchants)
Fletcher (Jack) of Rosehaugh, Ross-shire
(Liverpool merchants 19th c.)
Forbes of Callendar House, Stirlingshire
(18th c. business fortune, copper)
Dingwall-Fordyce of Brucklay Castle, Aberdeenshire
(16th c. gentry)
Gammell of Drumtochty Castle, Kincardineshire
(19th c. Greenock banker)
Guthrie of Torosay Castle, Argyllshire
(London business fortune 19th c.)
Hall of Dunglass, Haddingtonshire (**2 MPs**)
(17th c. gentry)
Hay of Duns Castle, Berwickshire (**2 MPs**)
(medieval gentry)
Hay of Seaton House, Aberdeenshire
(younger son inher. an estate by mar. 19th c.)
Innes of Raemoir House, Kincardineshire
(18th c., aristocratic descent)
Mitchell-Innes of Ayton Castle, Berwickshire (**1 MP**)
(banker 19th c.)
Irvine of Drum, Kincardineshire
(medieval gentry)
Jardine of Jardine Hall, Dumfriesshire (**1 MP**)
(19th c. merchants in the Far East, several lines)
Johnstone of Lathrisk, Fife
(18th c. Baltic merchants)
Leslie of Balquhain, Aberdeenshire (**ROMAN CATHOLIC**)
(English lead mines 18th c.)
Crawford-Leslie of Rothie House, Aberdeenshire
(aristocratic connections, 18th c. house)
Mackenzie of Glenmuick, Aberdeenshire
(Aberdeen silk merchant 19th c.)
Mackintosh, The Mackintosh of (**1 MP**)
(ancient family)
Paterson of Castle Huntly, Forfarshire
(18th c. nabob)
Porteous of Lauriston Castle, Kincardineshire
(jute merchant in Dundee, railways 19th c.)

Preston of Valleyfield, Fife (**1 MP**)
(East India Co., broker, shipowner London 18th c.)
Ramsay of Bamff, Perthshire
(medieval gentry)
Ramsay of Kildalton Castle, Argyllshire (**1 MP**)
(Islay distiller 19th c.)
Russell of Aden House, Aberdeenshire
(medieval gentry)
Smythe of Methven Castle, Perthshire
(16th c. gentry)
Johnston-Stewart of Physgill House, Wigtownshire (**1 MP**)
(17th c. inher.)
Stirling of Kippencross, Stirlingshire
(medieval gentry)
Traill of Castlehill House, Caithness-shire (**1 MP**)
(Flagstone quarries, lawyer 19th c.)
Trotter of Morton Hall, Midlothian
(old family)
Young of Durris House, Kincardineshire
(inventor and manufacturer 19th c.)

IRELAND

Adair of Rathdaire, Queen's County
(Scots to Ire. c. 1690, mar. heiress 18th c.)
Agnew of Kilwaughter Castle, Antrim
(19th c. business fortune)
Alen of St. Wolstan's Priory, Kildare {**2 MPs**}
(Archbishop of Dublin 16th c., estates sold 1752)
Bagot of Ballymoe, Galway
(medieval gentry, large inher. 18th c.)
Balfe of South Park, Roscommon
(19th agriculture - grazier)
Barrington of Glenstal Castle, Limerick
(18th c. merchants)
Barton of Straffan House, Kildare
(19th c. wine merchants)
Batt of Purdysburn, Down
(19th c. Belfast bakers)
Wrixon-Beecher of Castle Hyde, Cork (**1 MP**)
(16th c. gentry)

Bernard of Castle Bernard, King's County (**1 MP**)
(17th c. gentry)
Bond of Farragh, Longford {**1 MP**}
(18th c.- 19th c.)
MacGeough-Bond of Drumshill, Armagh
(17th c. gentry)
Keown-Boyd of Ballyduggan, Down (**1 MP**)
(18th c. gentry)
Browne of Aughentaine Castle, Tyrone
(18th c. gentry, inher.)
Burges of Parkanaur, Tyrone
(17th c. gentry)
Burke of Marble Hill, Galway (**2 MPs**)
(17th c. gentry, large estate)
Burrowes of Stradone House, Cavan {**1 MP**} (**1 MP**)
(17th c. gentry)
Carden of Templemore Abbey, Tipperary
(17th c. gentry)
Chaine of Ballycraigy, Antrim (**1 MP**)
(19th c., shipping, ferries, railroads)
Chearnley of Salterbridge, Waterford
(17th c. gentry)
Clarke of Bushy Park, Tipperary
(19th c., textile merchant Macclesfield)
Cleland of Stormont Castle, Down
(19th c. clergyman and agent for an estate mar. an heiress)
Cliffe of Bellevue, Wexford
(17th c., converted to Roman Catholicism 1856)
Close of Drumbanagher, Armagh (**1 MP**)
(17th c. gentry and mar. heiresses later)
Congreve of Mount Congreve, Waterford {**2 MPs**}
(17th c. gentry)
Corbally of Corbalton Hall, Meath (**ROMAN CATHOLIC**)
(18th c. gentry)
Hall-Dare of Newtownbarry House, Wexford
(English family, inher. 19th c.)
Delap of Monella, Donegal
(17th c. merchants)
De Robeck (Fock) of Gowran Grange, Kildare
(Swedish mar. heiress late 18th c.)
De Salis, Count, of the Grange, Limerick
(Count of Holy Roman Empire, mar. heiress 18th c.)

Dickson of Croom Castle, Limerick
(19th c. English inher. Irish estate)
Blacker-Douglas of Grace Hall, Down
(17th c. gentry)
Duckett of Duckett's Grove, Carlow
(17th c. gentry)
Eccles of Ecclesville, Tyrone
(17th gentry)
Ennis of Ballynahowen Court, Westmeath (**2 MP**)
(19th c. Dublin banker)
Farrell of Moynalty, Meath (**ROMAN CATHOLIC**)
(18th c. Dublin business)
Fowler of Rahinston House, Meath
(18th c. Archbishop of Dublin)
Gerrard of Gibbstown, Meath
(17th c. gentry, 19th c. banker in Canada)
Gervais of Cecil, Tyrone
(Huguenots, to Ireland 18th c., military and officials)
Gordon (Crawford) of Florida Manor, Down {**1 MP**}
(19th c. banker, 18th inher. land)
Gray of Graymount, Antrim
(19th c. linen merchants)
Hall of Narrow Water, Down {**1 MP**}
(17th c. gentry)
Hayes of Drumboe Castle, Donegal {**1 MP**} (**1 MP**)
(18th c. gentry, mar. heiress)
Blakiston-Houston of Orangefield, Down (**1 MP**)
(19th c. bankers)
Humphrys of Ballyhaise House, Cavan
(19th c. wood trade merchant from Dublin)
Hutchins of Ardnagashel, Cork
(17th c. military, gentry)
Ievers of Mount Ievers, Clare {**1 MP**}
(17th c. gentry)
Johnston of Kinlough House, Leitrim
(18th c. Dublin businessman)
Hamilton-Jones of Moneyglass House, Antrim
(18th c. Welsh to Ireland, mar. heiress 19th c.)
Kelly of Rockstown Castle, Limerick (**1 MP**) (**ROMAN CATHOLIC**)
(18th c. gentry)
Kemmis of Shaen Castle, Queen's County (**2 MPs**)
(18th c. gentry)

Knox of Creagh, Mayo
(17th c., mar. heiress 18th c.)
Leader of Dromagh Castle, Cork (**2 MPs**)
(coal mine owner 19th c.)
Wallace-Legge of Malone House, Antrim
(19th c. Belfast businessmen)
Leslie of Leslie Hill, Antrim
(17th c. bishop, cadet of Earl of Rothes)
Lloyd of Croghan House, Roscommon (**1 MP**)
(16th c. to Ireland, West Indies 17th c.)
Lloyd of Rockville, Roscommon
(18th c. mar. heiress)
Dames-Longworth of Glynwood, Westmeath
(18th c. inher.)
Lowry of Pomeroy House, Tyrone
(aristocratic connections)
McMahon of Facarry House, Tyrone
(Master of the Rolls 19th c.)
Madden of Hilton Park, Monaghan {**1 MP**}
(17th c. official)
Magan of Clonearl, King's County (**1 MP**)
(17th c. gentry)
Magenis of Finvoy Lodge, Antrim {**2 MPs**}
(18th c., agriculture? business?)
Mahon of Castlegar, Galway {**2 MPs**}
(17th c. gentry)
Martin of Ballynahinch Castle, Galway (**1 MP**) (**ROMAN CATHOLIC**)
(17th c. gentry)
Montgomery of Benvarden, Antrim
(bankers and fruit merchant 18th-19th c.)
Moore of Mooresfort, Tipperary (**2 MPs**) (**ROMAN CATHOLIC**)
(18th c. merchants in Liverpool)
Moutray of Favour Royal, Tyrone {**2 MPs**}
(inher. 17th c.)
Murphy of Mount Merrion, Dublin
(19th c.)
Murphy of Ballinacloon, Westmeath (**ROMAN CATHOLIC**)
(19th c. Dublin cattle dealers)
Musgrave of Tourin, Waterford (**2 MPs**)
(18th c. gentry)
Musgrave of Drumglass, Donegal
(19th c. Belfast tea, sugar, and a big iron foundry)

Downing-Nesbitt of Leixlip House, Kildare
(18th c. gentry, 19th c. inher.)
Nicholson of Balrath Burry, Meath
(17th c. military)
Nugent (O'Reilly) of Ballinlough Castle, Westmeath (**ROMAN CATHOLIC**)
(medieval gentry)
O'Connor of Rockfield House, Dublin
(19th c. inher.)
O'Donnell of Newport House, Mayo {**2 MPs**}
(18th c. gentry and linen manufacturing)
O'Shee of Gardenmorris, Waterford (**1 MP**)
(merchants 16th c.)
Palmer of Palmerstown, Mayo {**1 MP**} (**1 MP**)
(17th c. gentry)
Persse of Moyode Castle, Galway
(clergy 17th c., whisky-making 19th c., emigrate to Australia)
Phibbs of Lisheen (Seafield), Sligo
(16th c. military)
Pollok of Lismany House, Galway
(Glasgow merchant 19th c.)
Porter of Belle Isle, Fermanagh
(18th c. bishop)
Power of Newtown House, Waterford (**1 MP**)
(18th c. gentry)
Power of Edermine House, Wexford (**1 MP**)
(distillers in Dublin 19th c.)
Putland of Bray Head House, Wicklow
(Dublin merchants 18th c.)
Redington of Kilcoran, Galway (**ROMAN CATHOLIC**)
(17th c., mar. heiress 19th c.)
Richardson of Moyallon House, Down (**1 MP**)
(Spinning mill 18th c.)
Richardson of Somerset, Londonderry
(Edinburgh merchants 17th c.)
Rotheram of Crossdrum, Meath
(19th c., estate manager)
Rowe of Ballycross, Wexford
(17th c. gentry)
Smyth of Gaybrook, Westmeath
(17th c. bishop)
Smyth of Masonbrook, Galway
(19th c. grazier)

Stronge of Tynan Abbey, Armagh (**2 MPs**)
(17th c., gentry 2 NI MPs 20th c.)
Synge of Glanmore Castle, Wicklow {**1 MP**}
(17th c. 4 bishops and an Archbishop)
Tuite of Sonna, Westmeath (**1 MP**)
(medieval family)
Usborne of Blackrock, Cork (**1 MP**)
(19th c. corn merchant in Cork)
Wade of Clonebraney, Meath {**1 MP**}
(17th c. gentry)
Waldron of Helen Park, Tipperary (**2 MP**) (**ROMAN CATHOLIC**)
(Dublin merchant 19th c.)
Waller of Newport, Tipperary {**1 MP**}
(17th c. military, 18th c. gentry, emigrated to US)
Wilson of Lisnadill, Armagh
(19th c.)
Woods of Milverton Hall, Dublin
(18th c. commercial Dublin)
Young of Bailieborough Castle, Cavan (**1 MP**)
Baron Lisgar 1870-76
(East India Co. 19th c.)

Appendix II

List of Parliamentary Families Organized by Country

Families in **BOLD** possessed cross-border peerages/ MPs/ property that made them significant bi-national or tri-national straddlers.

Families with a significant but secondary political and/or economic interest in one country with primary interest in one of the other countries are indicated by underlining.

The seat listed is not necessarily the most important in the family. These often shifted over time. Sometimes a city is listed (Baines of Leeds) rather than a house.

If data was unavailable about the size of an estate, the orientation of the family's social and political activities was used to determine the country with which they were principally associated.

Stem families in upper case.
Subsidiary or cadet families in lower case.

When land was also held in another country, this is noted in parenthesis.

When the orientation of the family in the Commons post-1660 was divergent from its pre-1660 experience, the entry is weighted towards post-Restoration activity and ownership of land in terms of placement.

A single MP may be counted twice if he or she sat for constituencies in two different countries.

ENGLAND

ABBOT Baron Colchester
ABBOTT Baron Tenterden
ABDY of Albyns
Abney-Hastings of Willesley (RAWDON HASTINGS)
ACLAND of Killerton
ACTON Baron Acton (10 English MPs/ 1 Irish MP)
ADAIR Baron Waveney (large Irish estates) (1 Scottish MP/ 2 Irish MPs/ 2 English MPs)
ADDERLEY Baron Norton
ADDINGTON Viscount Sidmouth
ADEANE of Brabraham

AFFLECK of Dalham
[AGAR Viscount Clifden] - IRELAND
Agar Earl of Normanton (AGAR) (large Irish estates)
AGLIONBY of The Nunnery
Aislabie of Studley Royal (GREY II)
AITKEN Baron Beaverbrook
[AKERS-DOUGLAS Viscount Chilston] - SCOTLAND
Aldworth of Stanlake (NEVILLE)
ALFORD of Offington (some Welsh land)
Allanson (Winn) Baron Headley (substantial Irish estate) (WINN)
ALLESTRY of Darley
ALLSOPP Baron Hindlip
ALSTON of Odell Castle
AMCOTTS (Cracroft, Hall) of Hackthorn
AMHERST Earl Amherst
Amherst Baron Amherst of Hackney
Anderson-Pelham Earl of Yarborough (PELHAM)
ANNESLEY Earl of Anglesey (2 Welsh MPs/ 11 English MPs/ 6 Irish MPs) (substantial Irish estate)
ANSON Earl of Lichfield
ANTROBUS of Eaton
APSLEY of Thakenham
ARCHER Baron Archer
Arden Baron Alvanley (HAMILTON I)
ARKWRIGHT of Hampton Court
Armytage (Wentworth) of Kirklees (WENTWORTH)
[ARNOLD of Llanthony] - WALES
Arundell Baron Arundell of Trerice (MONCKTON)
Arundell Baron Arundell of Wardour (MONCKTON)
ARSCOTT of Tetcott
ARTHINGTON of Arthington
ASHBURNHAM Earl of Asburnham (some Welsh land)
Ashburnham of Broomham (ASHBURNHAM)
ASHBY of Quenby
ASHE Baron Heytesbury (A'Court, Repington) (some Irish land)
Ashe of Heywood (ASHE)
ASSHURST of Waterstock
ASHLEY-COOPER Earl of Shaftesbury (substantial Irish land)
Assheton Baron Clitheroe (CURZON)
ASTLEY of Patshull
Astley Baron Hastings (ASTLEY)
Aston of Aston (HERVEY)

[Aston Baron Aston] - IRELAND
ASTOR Viscount Astor
ATHERTON (Gwillym) of Atherton
ATKINSON of Hill Hall
ATKYNS of Sapperton (4 English MPs/ 1 Welsh MP)
ATTWOOD of Sion Hill
AUBREY of Boarstall (5 English MPs/ 1 Welsh MP) (some Welsh land)
AUSTEN of Hall Place
AYSCOUGH of South Kelsey
BABINGTON of Rothley Temple
BACON of Thonock
Bacon of Shrubland (BACON)
BAGOT of Blithfield (16 English MPs/ 1 Welsh MP) (large Welsh estate)
[BAILEY – Baron Glanusk] - WALES
[Baillie-Hamilton Earl of Haddington] - SCOTLAND
BAINES of Leeds
BAKER of Ranston
Baker Holroyd Earl of Sheffield (STANLEY)
BALCH of Bridgwater
BALDWIN Earl Baldwin
BALDWYN (Childe) of Kinlet
Balle of Mamhead (HUSSEY)
BAMPFYLDE Baron Poltimore
BANKES of Kingston Lacy
BANKS of Winstanley Hall
Banks Stanhope of Revesby (STANHOPE)
Barclay of Eastwick (BARCLAY)
BARING Earl of Northbrook
Baring Earl of Cromer (BARING)
Baring Baron Ashburton (BARING)
BARKER I of Grimston
BARKER II of Sonning
BARKER III of Fairford
BARNARDISTON of Ketton
BARNE of Sotterley
BARNES Baron Gorell
BARRAN of Sawley (2 English MPs/ 1 Scottish MP)
BARRINGTON I (Shute, Wildman) Viscount Barrington
BARRINGTON II of Swainstown
BARTTELOT of Stopham
BASS Baron Burton
BASSET of Heanton

Basset Baron Dunstanville (BASSET)
BASSETT I of Claverton
BASTARD of Kitley
Bateman Viscount Bateman (HANBURY)
BATHURST Earl Bathurst (15 English MPs/ 1 Welsh MP)
Bathurst of Clints (BATHURST)
BAYNTUN-ROLT of Spye
BEAUCHAMP (Proctor) of Langley
BEAUCLERK Duke of St. Albans (some Irish land)
BEAUMONT I Viscount Allendale
BEAUMONT II Baron Beaumont
Beaumont Viscount Beaumont of Swords (BEAUMONT II)
BECKETT Baron Grimthorpe
BECKFORD of Stepleton (PITT)
BEDINGFIELD of Oxburgh
BEECHER of Howbury
BEKE of Whiteknights (3 English MPs/1 Scottish MP)
BELASYSE Earl of Fauconberg (8 English MPs/ 1 Irish MP)
BELLOT of Great Moreton
BENCE of Benhall
BENETT of Pythouse
BENN Viscount Stansgate (4 English MPs/ 1 Scottish MP)
Bennet Earl of Tankerville (GREY I)
Benyon of Englefield (FELLOWES)
BERKELEY Earl of Berkeley
Berkeley Baron Botetourt (BERKELEY) (7 English MPs/ 1 Welsh MP)
Berkeley Earl of Falmouth (BERKELEY) (12 English MPs/ 1 Irish MP)
BERNARD II of Brampton
Berney of Langley (BRAMSTON)
BERRY I Viscount Camrose
BERRY II of Burrough
BERTIE Duke of Ancaster
Bertie Earl of Lindsey (BERTIE)
Bertie Earl of Abingdon (BERTIE)
BEST Baron Wynford
BETHELL I of Rise
BETHELL II Baron Westbury
BETHEL III Baron Bethell
Biddulph of Lebury (MYDDELTON)
Bilson of West Mapledurham (LEGGE)
BIRCH of Garnstone
BISSE of Martlock

BISSHOPP Baron Zouche
BLACKBURNE of Orford
BLAGRAVE of Southcote
Blackett of Matfen (BEAUMONT I)
BLAKISTON of Blakiston
BLAND of Kippax
[BLIGH Earl of Darnley] - IRELAND
BLOIS (Brooke) of Grundisburgh
BLOOMFIELD Baron Bloomfield
BLOUNT of Sodington
Blount Earl of Newport (BLOUNT)
BLUDWORTH of Thorncroft
Bockland of Standlynch (DILLINGTON)
Bold (Patten, Wilson) Baron Winmerleigh (HOGHTON)
BOLES of Rackenford
BOLLES of Scampton
BOND of Creech Grange (small Welsh estate)
BONHAM of Titness
Boone of Rook's Nest (EVELYN)
Booth Earl of Warrington (GREY II)
Bootle-Wilbraham Earl of Lathom (WILBRAHAM)
Borlase-Warren of Bockmer (VERNON I)
BOSCAWEN Earl of Falmouth
BOTELER of Woodhall
Boteler of Biddenham (BOTELER)
BOUGHTON of Downton
Bourchier of Beningborough (TYRWHITT)
Bowes of Streatlam (LYON)
BOWYER Baron Denham (11 English MPs/ 1 Irish MP)
Bowyer of Norton (ADDERLEY)
BOYNTON of Burton Agnes
BRADDYLL (Gale) Highhead Castle
Bradshaigh of Haigh (LINDSAY)
BRADSHAW I of Lifton
BRADSHAW II of Risby
BRAMSTON of Skreens
Brand (Trevor) Viscount Hampden (HILL I)
BRANDLING of Gosforth
BRASSEY Earl Brassey
[Bray (Morgan) of Llantaram] - WALES
Brereton Baron Brereton of Laghlin (7 English MPs/ 1 Welsh MP) (some Welsh land) (HOLTE)

Brereton-Salusbury of Shotwick (3 English MPs/ 1 Welsh MP) (TRELAWNEY)
BRETT Viscount Esher
BRIDGEMAN (Newport) Earl of Bradford (28 English MPs/ 1 Welsh MP) (small amount of Welsh land)
Bridges of Goodnestone (PLUMPTRE)
BRIGHT I of Brockbury
BRIGHT II The Ash
BRINCKMAN (Broadhead) of Monk Bretton
BRISCOE of Crofton
BRISTOW of Micheldever
BROADLEY of Welton
BROCKLEHURST Baron Rankesborough
[BRODRICK Earl of Midleton] - IRELAND
BROKE of Broke
BROMLEY Baron Montfort
Bromley of Baginton (BROMLEY)
Bromley Wilson of Dallam Tower (SMITH I)
BROOKE II Baron Brooke
BROOKE-PECHELL of Pagglesham (small Irish estate)
BROOKS of Whatton
BROUGHAM Baron Brougham
BROUGHTON (Delves) of Broughton
Brouncker Viscount Brouncker (LYTTELTON)
BROWN (Clifton) Viscount Ruffside
BROWNE I of Frampton
BROWNE II Viscount Montague
Browne of Betchworth (BROWNE II)
BROXHOLME of Broxholme
[Bruce Earl of Elgin] - SCOTLAND
BRUDENELL (Montagu) Earl of Cardigan
Brudenell-Bruce Marquess of Ailesbury (BRUDENELL)
Brydges Duke of Chandos (GRENVILLE)
Bucknall of Oxhey (ESTCOURT)
Bulkeley of Nether Burgate (BULKELEY)
BULLER of Downes
Buller (Yarde, Manningham) Baron Churston (BULLER)
BULLOCK of Faulkbourne
Bulteel of Flete (HELE)
Bunbury of Barton (NORTH)
BURDETT I of Foremark
BURGOYNE of Sutton Park
BURKE of Gregories (4 English MPs/ 1 Irish MP)

BURRARD (Neale) of Walhampton
Burrell Baron Gwydir (BERTIE)
BURRIDGE of Thorn Falcon
[Burton of Pollacton] - IRELAND
BUSFIELD (Ferrand) of St. Ives (2 English MPs/ 1 Irish MP)
BUTLER II of Warminghurst
BUTLER III Baron Butler of Saffron Walden
[BUTLER IV Earl of Lanesborough] - IRELAND
BUTTON of Buckland
BUXTON I Earl Buxton
BUXTON II of Shadwell
BYNG Viscount Torrington
Byng Earl of Strafford (substantial Irish estate) (BYNG)
Byron Baron Byron (MILBANKE)
BYSSHE of Smallfield
CADOGAN Earl Cadogan
CAESAR of Bennington
CALCRAFT of Rempstone
CALMADY of Langdon
Calthorpe of East Barsham (ASTLEY)
Calverley (Blackett) of Calverley (BEAUMONT I)
Calvert Baron Baltimore (EVELYN)
Calvert of Albury (VERNEY)
[CAMPBELL II Baron Stratheden] - SCOTLAND
CAMPION of Danny
CANNING Earl Canning (7 English MPs/ 2 Irish MPs) (substantial Irish estate)
CAPEL Earl of Essex (some Irish land)
CAREW I of Antony
Carew of Beddington (THROCKMORTON)
Carey Earl of Dover (MORDAUNT)
Carey Viscount Falkland (13 English MPs/ 1 Irish MP) (MORDAUNT)
CARLETON I Baron Dorchester (some Irish land)
Carpenter Earl of Tyrconnel (5 English MPs/ 1 Irish MP) (TALBOT I)
CARR ELLISON of Hebburn
Carr of Dunston (CARR ELLISON)
CARTER II of Kinmel (2 English MPs/ 1 Welsh MP) (Welsh land)
CARTER III (Bonham) of Adhurst St. Mary
Carteret Earl Granville (THYNNE)
CARTWRIGHT of Aynhoe
Cary of Clovelly (MORDAUNT)
CASWALL of Sacombe
CATELYN of Kirby Cane

CAVE Baron Bray
CAVENDISH Duke of Devonshire (33 English MPs/ 3 Irish MPs) (large Irish estate)
Cavendish Baron Waterpark (3 English MPs/ 5 Irish MPs; Irish peers 1792-) (substantial Irish estate) (CAVENDISH)
Cavendish Baron Chesham (CAVENDISH)
Cavendish-Bentinck Duke of Portland (22 English MPs/ 1 Scottish MP) (large Scottish estate) (CAVENDISH)
CAWLEY Baron Cawley
CAYLEY of Brompton (some Welsh land)
CAYZER Baron Rotherwick (large Scottish estate)
CECIL Marquess of Exeter
Cecil Marquess of Salisbury (CECIL)
CHAFIN of Chettle
Chaloner Baron Gisborough (LONG I)
CHAMBERLAIN of Birmingham
Champernowne of Dartington (FOWELL)
CHAPLIN Viscount Chaplin
Charlton of Ludford (LECHMERE)
[Charlton Meyrick of Bush] - WALES
CHAWORTH Viscount Chaworth
CHAYTOR of Witton Castle
CHEETHAM of Eastwood
CHERNOCK of Holcot
Chester of Chicheley (BAGOT)
CHETWODE of Chetwode
Chetwynd Viscount Chetwynd (TALBOT I)
Chetwynd of Grendon (some Welsh land) (TALBOT I)
CHEYNE Viscount Newhaven
Chichester Baron Templemore (1 Irish MP/ 1 English MP) (substantial Irish estate) (CHICHESTER)
Chichester of Youlston (CHICHESTER)
Chicheley of Wimpole (GRIFFITH II)
Child of Upton (VILLIERS)
Child-Tylney Earl Tylney (LONG I)
Cholmeley of Easton (CHOLMONDELEY)
Cholmley of Whitby (CHOLMONDELEY)
CHOLMONDELEY Marquess of Cholmondeley (10 English MPs/ 1 Welsh MP)
Cholmondeley Baron Delamere (5 English MPs/ 1 Welsh MP) (CHOLMONDELEY)
CHOWNE of Horsham
CHRISTIE (Burton, Peters) of Hull Bank
Chudleigh of Ashton (OXENDEN)
CHUTE (Wiggett) of The Vyne

CLARGES of Stoke Poges (5 English MPs/ 1 Scottish MP)
CLARK of Saltwood
CLARKE of Somershall
Clarke-Jervoise of Idsworth (JERVOISE)
Clerke of Ulcombe (CLARKE)
CLAVELL of Smedmore
Clavering of Axwell (COWPER)
CLAYTON II of Adlington
CLAYTON III of Harleyford
CLERKE of Shabbington
CLEVLAND of Tapeley
CLIFFORD (Constable) Baron Clifford of Chudleigh
CLIFTON Baron Clifton
Clifton of Lytham (RAWDON HASTINGS)
CLIVE Earl of Powis (11 English MPs/ 1 Welsh MP) (large Welsh estates)
Clive of Whitfield (6 English MPs/ 1 Welsh MP) (some Irish land)
CLOPTON of Clopton
COBBOLD Baron Cobbold
COCKS (Somers) Earl Somers
COCKAYNE Viscount Cullen
CODRINGTON of Dodington
COKE I Earl of Leicester
COKE II of Trusley
COKER of Hill Deverill
COLBORNE Baron Seaton (some Irish land)
[COLEBROOKE Baron Colebrook] - SCOTLAND
Colepper Baron Colepepper (WYKEHAM)
COLERIDGE Baron Coleridge
COLLETON of Haines Hill
COLLETT of Lochers
COLLIER Baron Monkswell
Collingwood of Dissington (STANHOPE)
COLMAN of Gornhay
COLSTON Baron Roundway
COLT of Colt
COLYEAR Earl of Portmore (2 English MPs; Scottish peers 1699-1835) (some Scottish land)
COMPTON Marquess of Northampton (some Scottish land)
Compton of Minstead (COMPTON)
CONNOCK of Tregworgey
Coningsby Earl Coningsby (CAPEL)
CONYERS of Copt Hall

[Conyngham Marquess Conyngham] - IRELAND
COOKE I of Wheatley
COOKE II of Highnam
[Coote of Portrane] - IRELAND
COPE of Bramshill
CORBET Viscount Corbet
Corbet of Adderley (4 English MPs/ 1 Welsh MP) (CORBET)
Corbet of Longnor (CORBET) (a little Welsh land)
Corbet of Sprowston (CORBET)
CORDELL of Melford
CORNEWALL of Berrington
Cornewall of Delbury (2 English MPs/ 1 Welsh MP) (CORNEWALL)
Corneall (Amyard) of Moccas (CORNEWALL)
CORRANCE of Parham
CORYTON of Pentillie Castle
COTES of Woodcote
COTTON I (Salusbury) Viscount Combermere (5 English MPs/ 1 Wesh MP/ 1 Irish MP)
COTTON II of Madingley
COTTON III of Alkington
Cotton of Conington (COTTON I)
COURTENAY Earl of Devon (large Irish estate)
Courtenay of Trethurfe (COURTENAY)
Courthorpe Baron Courthorpe (4 English MPs/ 1 Irish MP) (CLAYTON I)
COVENTRY Earl of Coventry
COVERT of Slaugham
COWPER Earl Cowper
Coxe of Kemble (GORDON I)
COZENS-HARDY Baron Cozens-Hardy
CRADOCK of Cradock
[CRAUFURD of Auchenames] – SCOTLAND
[Craufurd of Newark Castle] - SCOTLAND
CRAVEN Earl of Craven
CRAWLEY of Stockwood
Cresswell (Estcourt) of Pinkney (ESTCOURT)
CREWE (Offley) Marquess of Crewe
Crewe Baron Crew (CREWE)
CRIPPS Baron Parmoor
CROFT Baron Croft
CROFTS Baron Crofts
Croke of Marston (FRANKLAND)
CROMPTON of Wood End
CROMWELL Earl of Ardglass (3 English MPs/ 1 Irish MP) (substantial Irish estate)

Cromwell of Bodsey (CROMWELL)
CROSS Viscount Cross
CROSSLEY Baron Somerleyton
CROWLE of Fryston
CUBITT Baron Ashcombe
CUNLIFFE-LISTER Earl of Swinton
CURRIE Baron Currie
CURTEIS of Windmill Hill
CURWEN of Workington
CURZON Marquess Curzon
Curzon Baron Zouche (CURZON)
CUST (Brownlow) Earl Brownlow
CUTTS Baron Cutts
DALSTON of Dalston
DAMER Earl of Dorchester (7 English MPs/ 3 Irish MPs/ 1 Scottish MP)
DANBY of Farnley
DANIEL I of Trelissick
DANIEL II of St. Margaret's
Darcy Earl of Holdernesse (OSBORNE I)
Darcy (Nassau) Earl of Rochford (PITT)
DARELL of Calehill
DARRELL of Lillingstone
DASHWOOD Baron Le Despencer
Dashwood of Kirtlington (6 English MPs/ 1 Scottish MP) (DASHWOOD)
Davenport (Bromley) (BROMLEY)
Davers of Rougham (HERVEY)
DAVIE of Creedy
Dawkins of Over Norton (COLYEAR)
DAWNAY Viscount Downe
DE CRESPIGNY of Ufford
DE GREY Baron Walsingham
DE LA BERE of Rotherwas
De Saumarez of Shrubland (BROKE)
De Vere Earl of Oxford (BEAUCLERK)
DEEDES of Saltwood Castle
Delaval (Blake) Baron Delaval (ASTLEY)
DENISON Viscount Ossington
Denison (Conyngham) Earl of Londesborough (CUNNINGHAME)
DENMAN Baron Denman
DENNE of Denne Hill
DENTON (Chamberlayne) of Hillesdon (15 English MPs/ 1 Irish MP)
DERING of Surrenden Dering (12 English MPs/ 3 Irish MPs)

De Ros (Fitzgerald) Baron De Ros (1 English MP) (entireEstate Irish land) (FITZGERALD I)
[Devereux Viscount Hereford] - WALES
DICKINSON I of Kingweston
DICKINSON II Baron Dickinson
DIGBY Earl Digby (Irish peers 1620-/ English peers 1618-98 GB peers 1765-) (large Irish estate)
DILKE of Wolston
DILLINGTON of Knighton Gorges
[DILLON Viscount Dillon] - IRELAND
DIMSDALE of Essenden
Dixwell of Broome (OXENDEN)
DOCMINIQUE of Chipstead
DODINGTON (Bubb) Baron Melcombe (4 English MPs/ 1 Irish MP)
DODSON Baron Monk Bretton
Dolben of Finedon (MACKWORTH)
Dormer Earl of Carnarvon (STANHOPE)
DOWDESWELL of Pull Court
DOWNING of Gamlingay (3 English MPs/ 1 Scottish MP)
DOYLEY of Chiselhampton
DRAKE of Shardeloes
Drake of Ashe (DRAKE)
Drake of Buckland (ELLIOT)
DREWE of Broadhembury
[DRUMMOND Earl of Perth] - SCOTLAND
Dryden of Canons Ashby (TURNER I)
DUCANE of Braxted
DUCKETT of Hartham
DUGDALE of Merevale
DUKE I of Benhall
DUKE II (Heath) of Otterton
DUMMER (Chamberlayne) of Cranbury
DUNCH of Down Ampney
DUNCOMBE Earl of Feversham
Duncombe of Battlesden (DUNCOMBE)
DUNDAS Marquess of Zetland (14 English MPs/ 6 Scottish MPs/ 1 Welsh MP) (large Scottish estate)
DUNNE of Gatley
DU PRE of Wilton
Dutton Baron Sherborne (LEGGE)
DYKE of Lullingstone
DYMOKE of Scrivelsby
DYOTT of Freeford

Eardley-Wilmot of Berkswell (WILMOT)
EARLE of Eastcourt
Eden Earl of Auckland (HENLEY)
EDGCUMBE Earl of Mount Edgcumbe
[Edwardes Baron Kensington] - WALES
Edwards Freeman of Wingfield (MITFORD)
EGERTON Duke of Bridgewater (18 English MPs/ 1 Scottish MP)
Egerton Earl Egerton of Tatton (EGERTON)
Egerton Earl of Wilton (EGERTON)
Egerton-Warburton of Arley (EGERTON)
ELFORD of Bickham
ELIOT Earl of St. Germans
ELLICE of Glenquoich (4 English MPs/ 1 Scottish MP) (large Scottish estate)
[ELLIOT Earl of Minto] - SCOTLAND
ELLIS Baron Howard de Walden
Ellys of Nocton (HILL I)
ELTON of Clevedon
ELWES of Stoke College
ENGLAND of Stokesby
Erle (Ernle, Drax, Grosvenor, Plunkett) of Charborough (15 English MPs/ 1 Irish MP) (GROSVENOR)
[Erskine Baron Erskine] - SCOTLAND
ESTCOURT Baron Estcourt
EURE Baron Eure
EVELYN of Nutfield
EVERARD I of Langleys
EVERSFIELD of Denne
EWER of The Lea
EYRE I of Newhouse
EYRE II of Rampton
Eyre of Brickworth (EYRE I)
Eyles of Earnshill (EGERTON)
FABER Baron Faber
Fagge of Wiston (GORING)
FAIRFAX Viscount Fairfax of Emley
Fairfax Baron Fairfax of Cameron (WYKEHAM)
Fane Earl of Westmorland (VANE)
Fane Viscount Fane (3 English MPs/ 1 Irish MP) (substantial Irish estate) (VANE)
Fane of Wormsley (VANE)
FANSHAWE Viscount Fanshawe (8 English MPs/ 1 Scottish MP)
FARMER (Wilshere) of Nonsuch and The Frythe
FARNHAM of Quorndon

FARQUHAR (Townshend) Earl Farquhar
FARRINGTON of Farrington
FAWKES of Farnley
FEILDEN of Witton
FEILDING Earl of Denbigh (4 English MPs/ 1 Irish MP) (substantial Welsh estate)
FELLOWES Baron De Ramsey
FELTON of Playford
FENWICK of Wallington
Fenwick of Burrow (FENWICK)
Fermor Earl of Pomfret (HESKETH)
FETHERSTONHAUGH of Stanhope
FFOLKES of Hillington
FIELDEN of Grimston
FIENNES (Twisleton, Wykeham) Viscount Saye and Sele
FILMER of East Sutton
FINCH Earl of Winchilsea and Nottingham
Finch Earl of Aylesford
FITZCLARENCE Earl of Munster
FitzHerbert (1 English MP/ 1 Irish MP) (HOWARD I)
Fitzjames of Leweston (STRODE)
Fitzmaurice Earl of Orkney (3 English MPs/ 1 Irish MP) (substantial Irish estate/ some Welsh land) (FITZGERALD I)
Fitzroy (Bennet) Duke of Grafton (GREY I)
Fitzroy Baron Southampton (GREY I)
[FITZWILLIAM Earl of Tyrconnel] - IRELAND
FLEETWOOD of Penwortham
Fleetwood of Aldwinkle (FLEETWOOD)
Fleetwood of Great Missenden (FLEETWOOD)
FLEMING I of Rydal
Fletcher Vane of Jutton-in-the-Forest (VANE)
FLUDYER of Lee Place
FOLEY Baron Foley
Foljambe of Aldwarke (JENKINSON)
FONNEREAU of Christchurch Mansion
FOOT Baron Caradon (3 English MPs/ 1 Welsh MP)
FORESTER Baron Forester
FORSTER I of Adderstone
Forster of Aldermaston (LEGGE)
FORT of Read Hall
FORTESCUE Earl Fortescue (25 English MPs, 1 Welsh MP) (some Irish land)
FOSTER I of Hornby Castle
FOSTER II of Trecwm (some Welsh land)

FOSTER III of Apley
FOWELL of Fowellscombe
FOWNES (Luttrell) of Dunster Castle
FOX I of Caynham
FOX III (Strangways) Earl of Ilchester
Fox Baron Holland (5 English MPs/ 1 Scottish MP) (FOX III)
FRANKLAND (Russell) of Thirkleby
Fraser of Carlton Curlieu (FRASER II)
FREDERICK of Burwood
FREEMAN-THOMAS Marquess of Willingdon
Freke of Shroton (PITT)
FREMANTLE Baron Cottesloe (5 English MPs/ 1 Scottish MP/ 1 Irish MP)
FRERE of Roydon
FRESCHEVILLE Baron Frescheville
FREWEN of Brickwall
FULFORD of Fulford
Fullarton of Fullaton (3 Scottish MPs/ 1 English MP) (substantial Scottish estate)
Fuller of Rosehill (ELLIOT)
Furnese of Waldershare (NORTH)
FURNESS Viscount Furness
FYDELL of Kirton
GAGE Viscount Gage
GAPE
GARDNER Baron Gardner
GARLAND (Lester) of Leeson
Garrard of Lamer (DRAKE)
Gascoigne of Parlington (OLIVER)
Gascoyne of Childwall (CECIL)
GAWDY of Crow's Hall
GAYER of Stoke Park
GEERS (Winford) of Glasshampton
GELL of Hopton
GERARD Earl of Macclesfield
Gerard Baron Gerard of Gerard's Bromley
Gerard Baron Gerard
Gerard of Flambards
GIBBS Baron Aldenham
GIFFORD I Baron Gifford
GINKEL Earl of Athlone
GIPPS of Hall Place
[GLADSTONE Viscount Gladstone] - SCOTLAND
GLANVILLE of Catchfrench

GLEANE of Hardwick
GLEMHAM of Glemham
GLYN Baron Wolverton (8 English MPs/ 1 Scottish MP)
Glynn of Glynn (VIVIAN)
GODDARD I of The Lawns
GODDARD II of Etchilhampton
Godolphin Earl Godolphin (OSBORNE I)
GOLDSMID of Somerhill
GOODRICKE of Ribston
GOODWIN of Rowfant
[Gordon Marquis of Huntly] - SCOTLAND
Gordon-Lennox Duke of Richmond and Gordon (very large Scottish estate) (GORDON I)
GORE II of Tring
[Gore (Ormsby) Baron Harlech] - IRELAND
Gore-Langton Earl Temple of Stowe (GRENVILLE)
GORGES of Charlton
Gorges of Batcombe (GORGES)
GORING Earl of Norwich
GOTT of Battle
GOUGH-CALTHORPE Baron Calthorpe
GOULD I of Upway
GOULD II of Woodford
Gounter Nicoll of Racton (LEGGE)
GRAHAM III Viscount Preston
Graham of Netherby (3 English MPs/ 1 Welsh MP) (GRAHAM III)
[Graham-Foster-Pigott of Kinross House] - SCOTLAND
GRANTHAM of Goltho
Granville Earl of Bath (THYNNE)
GRATWICK of Tortington
GRAVES Baron Graves
Graves-Sawle of Penrice (GRAVES)
GREENALL Baron Daresbury
GREENE II of Nether Hall
GRENFELL Baron Desborough
GRENVILLE (Temple, Brydges) Duke of Buckingham and Chandos
Grenville Baron Glastonbury (GRENVILLE)
Gresham of Titsey (LEVESON GOWER)
Gresley of Drakelow (ADDERLEY)
GREVILLE Earl of Brooke and Warwick (22 English MPs/ 1 Irish MP) (substantial Irish estate)
GREY I Earl of Tankerville
GREY II Duke of Kent

Grey Earl Grey (GREY I)
Grey Earl of Stamford and Warrington (GREY II)
Grey-Egerton of Oulton (EGERTON)
GRIMSTON Earl of Verulam
GROSVENOR Duke of Westminster (15 English MPs/ 1 Welsh MP/ 1 Irish MP) (some Welsh land)
GROVE of Ferne
GUEST Viscount Wimborne (7 English MPs, 4 Welsh MPs) (large and valuable Welsh estate/ large but not valuable Scottish estate)
GUISE of Elmore
GULLY Viscount Selby
Gulston of Wyddial (GULSTON)
GUMLEY of Gumley
GURDON (Rebow) Baron Cranworth
GURNEY of Sprowston
GUYBON of Thursford
Gwyn of Llansannor (3 English MPs/ 1 Welsh MP) (some Welsh land) (PRIDEAUX)
HADDOCK of Wrotham
HALE of King's Walden
HALES of Bekesbourne
Hales of Hales Place (HALES)
Halford of Edith Weston (FREMANTLE)
Hall of Bradford-on-Avon (PIERREPONT)
HALSEY of Gaddesden
HAMBRO Baron Hambro
[Hamilton Duke of Abercorn] – IRELAND
[Hamilton Viscount Boyne] - IRELAND
[HANBURY of Pontypool] - WALES
Hanbury-Tracy Viscount Tracy (12 English MPs/ 2 Welsh MPs) (large Welsh estate) (HANBURY)
HANDLEY of Newark
HANKEY of Fetcham
[Hanmer Baron Hanmer] - WALES
HARBORD Baron Suffield
Harcourt (Vernon) Earl Harcourt (30 English MPs/ 2 Welsh MPs/ 1 Scottish MP) (VERNON I)
HARDINGE Viscount Hardinge (3 English MPs/ 2 Irish MPs)
HARDRES of Hardres Court
HARDY (Gathorne) Earl of Cranbrook
Hare Baron Coleraine (PAKENHAM)
Hare of Stow Bardolph (PAKENHAM)

HARLEY Earl of Oxford and Mortimer (12 English MPs/ 4 Welsh MPs) (small Welsh estate)
HARMSWORTH Viscount Northcliffe (2 English MPs/ 1 Scottish MP)
Harpur of Calke (CREWE)
HARRINGTON Baron Harrington
HARRIS I of Hayne
HARRIS II Earl of Malmesbury
HARRIS III Baron Harris (1 English MP/ 1 Welsh MP) (small Irish estate)
HARRISON II of Balls Park
Hart of Lullingstone (DYKE)
HARTLEY (Packer) of Bucklebury
HARTOPP (Cradock) of Four Oaks (4 English MPs/ 1 Irish MP)
HARVEY of Rolls Park
Hatton Viscount Hatton (FINCH)
HAWKE Baron Hawke
HAWKINS of Trewithen
HAWLEY Baron Hawley (4 English MPs/ 1 Irish MP)
Hawtrey of Chequers (FRANKLAND)
Hay of Little Horsted (CLEVLAND)
Hayes of Bedgebury (ST. LEGER)
HAZLERIGG Baron Hazelrigg
HEATH of Biddulph Grange
Heathcote Baron Aveland (BERTIE)
Heathcote of Hursley (BERTIE)
HEATHCOTE-AMORY Viscount Amory
HEBBLETHWAITE of Norton
HEDGES of Shipton Moyne
HELE of Flete
HENDERSON I Baron Faringdon
HENDERSON II Baron Henderson
HENEAGE Baron Heneage
HENLEY Earl of Northington
Henley Baron Henley
HENNIKER (Major) Baron Henniker
HENRY II of Woodlands
HERBERT Earl of Pembroke and Montgomery (many Welsh MPs pre-1660 but only 1 Welsh MP post 1660/ 9 English MPs post 1660) (no Welsh estate post 1660 but valuable Irish estate from 1833)
[Herbert Marquess of Powis] - WALES
Herbert Earl of Carnarvon (HERBERT)
Herbert of Tythrop (HERBERT)

Herbert Baron Herbert of Cherbury (post-1660 3 English MPs/ 2 Welsh MPs) (large Welsh estate) (HERBERT)
Herbert Earl of Torrington (2 English MPs/ 1 Welsh MP) (some Welsh land) (HERBERT)
HERLE of Prideaux
HERNE of Luton Hoo
HERON of Moor Hall
Heron of Cressy (2 English MPs/ 1 Irish MP) (HERON)
HERSCHELL Baron Herschell
HERVEY Marquess of Bristol
Hervey of East Betchworth (HERVEY)
HESKETH Baron Hesketh
HEVENINGHAM of Heveningham
HEWITT I Viscount Hewitt of Gowran (2 English MPs/ 1 Irish MP)
[HEYGATE of Bellarena] - IRELAND
HEYSHAM of Stagenhoe
Hickman of Gainsborough (CLIVE)
HICKS-BEACH Earl of St. Aldwyn
Hildyard of Winstead (THOROTON)
HILL II Viscount Hill
Hill Baron Berwick (HILL II)
HILLERSDEN of Elstow
HIPPISLEY COXE of Ston Easton
HOARE II of Stourhead
Hoare Viscount Templewood (HOARE I)
Hobart Earl of Buckinghamshire (small Irish estate) (HILL I)
HOBHOUSE Baron Broughton
HOBY of Bisham (6 English MPs/ 1 Welsh MP)
HODGE Baron Wyfold
HODSON (Cardwell) of Ellerbeck
HODY of Northover
HOGG Viscount Hailsham (6 English MPs) (an Irish estate)
HOGHTON of Hoghton
HOLDEN Baron Holden
HOLLAND I Viscount Knutsford
HOLLAND II of Quidenham
Holles Marquess of Clare (PELHAM)
Holmes Baron Holmes (ASHE)
HOLTE of Aston
HONYWOOD of Evington
Honywood of Marks Hall (HONYWOOD)
HOOD Viscount Hood
Hood Viscount Bridport (HOOD)

Hood (Fuller-Acland) Baron St. Audries (HOOD)
HOOKE of King's Weston
HOPKINS of Oving
HOPTON of Cannon ffrome
HORDE of Horde
HORNBY of Poole Hall
Horner of Mells (FOX III)
HOSKYNS of Harewood
HOTHAM Baron Hotham
Houblon (Archer) of Hallingbury (EYRE II)
HOWARD I Duke of Norfolk (20 English MPs/ 1 Irish MP)
Howard Earl of Suffolk and Berkshire (HOWARD I)
Howard Earl of Carlisle (HOWARD I)
Howard Earl of Effingham (HOWARD I)
Howard-Vyse of Stoke Place (HOWARD I)
Howe (Curzon) Earl Howe (CURZON)
Howe Baron Chedworth (CURZON)
HUBBARD Baron Addington
HULSE (Lethieullier) of Breamore
Hume of Wormleybury (CUST)
HUNGERFORD Baron Hungerford
Hungerford of Studley (HUNGERFORD)
Hunt (Ward) of Mollington (AGAR)
HURD Baron Hurd
HURST of Horsham Park
HUSSEY Baron Hussey
HUTCHINSON I of Owthorpe
HUTTON of Marske
Hyde Earl of Clarendon (16 English MPs/ 1 Welsh MP) (VILLIERS)
Ingibly of Ripley (AMCOTTS)
INGOLDSBY of Waldridge
Ingram Viscout Irvine (SEYMOUR)
Irby Baron Boston (PAGET I)
Ireland of Hale (BLACKBURNE)
Ireton of Attenborough (POWLE)
ISHAM of Lamport
JACKSON II Baron Allerton
JAMES Baron Northbourne
JANSSEN of Wimbledon
JENISON of Walworth
JENKINSON Earl of Liverpool
JENNINGS I of Ripon

JENNINGS II of Duddleston
Jenyns of Bottisham (SPENCER I)
Jermyn Earl of St. Albans (HERVEY)
JERVIS Earl St. Vincent
Jervis of Darlaston (JERVIS)
JERVOISE of Herriard
JODRELL of Bayfield
Johnson of Friston (MILBANKE)
[Johnstone of Westerhall] – SCOTLAND
[Johnstone of Alva] - SCOTLAND
JOICEY Baron Joicey
JOLLIFFE Baron Hylton
JONES III of Cerreghwfa (5 English MPs) (Welsh land)
Jones of Ramsbury (2 English MPs/ 1 Welsh MP) (BULLER)
KAYE of Woodsome
KEKEWICH of Peamore
KEMP of Gissing
Kemys-Tynte Baron Wharton (12 English MPs/ 4 Welsh MPs) (large Welsh estate) (WHARTON)
KENDALL of Pelyn
KENNARD of Fernhill
KENT I of Fornham
KENT II of Winsley
KENYON Baron Kenyon (4 English MPs/ 1 Welsh MP) (large Welsh estate)
Kenyon-Slaney of Hatton (KENYON)
KEPPEL Earl of Albemarle (7 English MPs/ 1 Scottish MP) (some Irish land)
[Kerr Marquis of Lothian] - SCOTLAND
KILLIGREW of Arwenick (10 English MPs/ 1 Scottish MP)
KINGSMILL of Sydmontan
KIRKBY of Kirkby
KITSON Baron Airdale
Knatchbull (Hugesson) Baron Brabourne
KNIGHT Earl of Catherlough
Knight of Chawton (PEACHEY)
KNIGHTLEY Baron Knightley
KNOLLYS Earl of Banbury
Knollys of Thame (KNOLLYS)
Kynaston of Hardwick (13 English MPs/ 1 Welsh MP) (small Welsh estate) (CORBET)
Knyvet of Ashwellthorpe (TYRWHITT)
Kyrle of The Homme (GROSVENOR)
LIDDELL Earl of Ravensworth
Lake Viscount Lake (GERARD)

Lamb Viscount Melbourne (5 English MPs/ 2 Irish MPs) (some Irish land) (COKE II)
LAMBART Earl of Cavan (4 English MPs/ 1 Irish MP) (small Irish estate)
Lambert of Boyton (BENETT)
LAMBTON Earl of Durham
LAMPLUGH of Lamplugh
LANE-FOX Baron Bingley (large Irish estate)
LANGFORD of Langford
LANGHAM of Cottesbrooke
LASCELLES Earl of Harewood
LAW Earl of Ellenborough
Lawley Baron Wenlock (THOMPSON I)
LAWRENCE I of King's Ride
LAWRENCE II Baron Lawrence
LAWSON I of Brayton
LAWSON II Viscount Burnham
LAWSON III of Alborough
LAWTON of Lawton
LEADER (Maberly) of Putney
LECHMERE Baron Lechmere
LEE of Hartwell
Lee Earl of Lichfield (DILLON)
Lee Warner (Milles) of Nackington (WENTWORTH)
LEGGE Earl of Dartmouth
LEGH Baron Newton
LEICESTER Baron de Tabley
LEIGH II of Hawley
LEIGH III of North Court
Leigh Baron Leigh (LEGH)
Leigh (Egerton) of High Leigh (LEGH)
LEIGHTON of Loton
LEKE Earl of Scarsdale
Lemon of Carclew (TREMAYNE)
LENNARD (Barrett) Earl of Sussex (6 English MPs/ 2 Irish MPs) (large Irish estate)
LENTHALL of Burford
LESTRANGE of Hunstanton
LEVESON GOWER Duke of Sutherland (30 English MPs/ 4 Scottish MPs) (very large Scottish estate)
Lewknor of West Dean (PEACHEY)
Lewis of St. Fagan's (large Welsh estates) (CLIVE)
Ley Earl of Marlborough (SPENCER I)
Leycester of Toft (LEICESTER)
[LINDSAY Earl of Crawford and Balcarres] - SCOTLAND

LINGEN of Stoke Edith
Lisle of Moyles (PHILLIPPS DE L'ISLE)
LISTER Baron Ribblesdale
Littleton Baron Hatherton (LYTTELTON)
Littleton Baron Lyttelton
LLOYD III Baron Loyd (some Welsh land)
LLOYD IV of Aston Hall
LOCKWOOD Baron Lambourne
Lockyer of Mapperton (PHELIPS)
LODER Baron Wakehurst
LONG I Viscount Long (small Welsh estate)
LONG II Baron Farnborough (4 English MPs/ 1 Scottish MP)
Long of Draycot Cerne (LONG I)
Long of Whaddon (PARKER II)
LONGVILLE of Bradwell
LOPES Baron Ludlow
LOVELACE of Lovelace Place
Lovelace Earl of Lovelace (MILBANKE)
Lovelace Baron Lovelace (MILBANKE)
LOWE of Calne
LOWNDES of Whaddon
LOWTHER Earl of Lonsdale (47 English MPs/ 1 Scottish MP)
Lowther of Holker (LOWTHER)
[Lowther of Shrigley] - IRELAND
LUBBOCK of High Elms
LUCY of Charlecote
Ludlow Earl Ludlow (7 English MPs/ 2 Irish MPs) (some Irish land) (RUSSELL I)
LUKE of Woodend
LUMLEY Earl of Scarborough
LUSHINGTON of Park House
Lushington of South Hill (LUSHINGTON)
[LUTTRELL Earl of Carhampton] - IRELAND
LUTWYCHE of Lutwyche
LYGON Earl Beauchamp
[LYON (Bowes) Earl of Strathmore and Kinghorne] - SCOTLAND
Lyster of Rowton Castle
LYTTELTON of Frankley
Lyttelton Viscount Cobham (LYTTELTON)
LYTTON Earl of Lytton
MACARTHUR of London
MACKINNON of Acryse
MACKWORTH of Normanton

[Mackworth of Gnoll Castle] - WALES
Mackworth-Praed of Trevethoe (MACKWORTH)
[MADOCKS of Tan-yr-allt] - WALES
MAINWARING of Peaover
Mainwaring of Oteley (8 English MPs/ 1 Welsh MP) (substantial Welsh estate) (MAINWARING)
MAITLAND II of Stansted (3 English MPs/ 1 Welsh MP) (some Welsh land and some Scottish land)
[MALCOLM Baron Malcolm] - SCOTLAND
MALET of Poyntington
MALLALIEU of Larkwood
MALLOCK of Cockington
MANATON of Trecarrell
MANGLES of Poyle
[MANLEY of Bryn y Ffynnon] - WALES
MANNERS Duke of Rutland
Manners Sutton Viscount Canterbury (MANNERS)
MANSFIELD Viscount Sandhurst
MARKHAM of Markham
MARSHALL of Leeds
MARSHAM Earl of Romney
MARTIN I of Overbury (11 English MPs/ 1 Irish MP)
MARTIN II of Little Farm
MARTON of Capernwray
MARTYN I of Plympton Erle
MASHAM Baron Masham
MASON of Rockley
MASSEY of Coddington
MASTER of Cirecester Abbey
Mauleverer of Allerton Mauleverer (MONCKTON)
[MAXWELL Earl of Nithsdale] - SCOTLAND
May of Rawmere (PEACHEY)
MAYNARD I of Clifton Reynes
Maynard Viscount Maynard (GREVILLE)
Mayne of Arnos Grove (ALLEN) (substantial Irish land) (1 Irish MP/ 2 English MP)
MEDLYCOTT of Ven House (6 English MPs/ 1 Irish MP)
MELLISH of Blyth
MELLOR of Culmhead
MEREDITH II
Meres of Kirton (WHICHCOTE)
METHUEN Baron Methuen
MEYNELL of Hoar Cross

Meysey-Thompson Baron Knaresborough (THOMPSON I)
MICHELL of Kingston Russell (5 English MPs/ 1 Irish MP)
Michell of Field Place (MICHELL)
MICKLETHWAIT Viscount Micklethwait
MIDDLETON II of Belsay Castle
MIDDLETON III of Hills Place
MILBANKE of Thorpe Perrow
MILBORNE-PILKINGTON of Chevet (small Welsh estate)
Mildmay Earl of Fitzwalter (ST. JOHN)
MILES of Kings Weston
Mill of Mottisfont (KNOLLYS)
MILLER II of Little Bredy
MILLER III
MILLS Baron Hillingdon
MILNER of Nun Appleton
Milnes Baron Houghton (CREWE)
Milnes-Gaskell of Clifton Hall (CREWE)
MITFORD Earl of Redesdale
MOHUN of Flete
Mohun Baron Mohun (GERARD)
Morley of Glynde (HILL I)
Molesworth of Pencarrow (MOLESWORTH)
[Molineux-Montgomerie of Garboldisham] - SCOTLAND
MOLYNEUX I Earl of Sefton
Molyneux of Teversal (MOLYNEUX I)
MOMPESSON of Mompesson House
MONCK Duke of Albemarle
MONCKTON Viscount Galway
MONOUX of Wotton
Monson Viscount Oxenbridge (WENTWORTH)
MONTAGU I Duke of Montagu
MONTAGU II Baron Swaythling
Montagu Baron Montagu of Beaulieu (2 English MPs/ 1 Scottish MP) (MONTAGU I)
Montagu Duke of Manchester (MONTAGU I)
Montagu Earl of Halifax (MONTAGU I)
Montagu Earl of Sandwich (MONTAGU I)
Montagu (Fountayne-Wilson) of Papplewick (MONTAGU I)
[Montagu-Douglas-Scott Duke of Buccleuch and Queensbery] – SCOTLAND
MORDAUNT Earl of Peterborough
Mordaunt of Walton D'Eiville (MORDAUNT)
MORE I of Bank Hall
MORE II of Linley

More Molyneux of Loseley (MOLYNEUX I)
MORETON Earl of Ducie
MORGAN II of Kinnersley (4 English MPs/ 1 Welsh MP)
MORICE of Werrington
MORLEY I Baron Hollenden (2 English MPs/ 1 Welsh MP)
MORLEY II of Droxford
Morley of Halnaker (STANLEY)
MORRISON Baron Margadale (large Scottish estate)
Morton of Milborne St. Andrew (PLEYDELL-BOUVERIE)
MOSLEY of Rolleston (3 English MPs/ 1 Irish MP)
MOUNT of Wasing Place
MOYLE of Bake
MUNDY of Markeaton
Mundy of Shipley (MUNDY)
MUNTZ of Umberslade
[Murray Earl of Dunsmore] – SCOTLAND
[Murray Earl of Mansfield and Mansfield] - SCOTLAND
MUSGRAVE of Edenhall
Musgrave of Hayton Castle (MUSGRAVE)
[MUSSENDEN of Larchfield] - IRELAND
[MYDDELTON of Chirk Castle] - WALES
MYTTON of Halston
Nanfan of Birts Morton (COOTE)
Napier of Puncknowle (NAPIER I)
Napier of Middlemarsh (NAPIER I)
[NEEDHAM Earl of Kilmorey] - IRELAND
Nelson Earl Nelson (EYRE I)
[NESBITT of Lismore] - IRELAND
NEVILLE Marquess of Abergavenny (7 English MPs/ 1 Welsh MP) (small Welsh estate)
Neville (Griffin, Grey, Aldworth, Grenville) Baron Braybrooke (NEVILLE)
NEWDIGATE of Arbury
NEWLAND of Gatton
NEWMAN Baron Mamhead
NEWNHAM of Newtimber
NEWTON of Barr's Court
NICHOLAS of West Horsley
Nicholas of Ashton Keynes (NICHOLAS)
NICHOLSON of Basing
NICOLL of Penvose
Nicolson Baron Carnock (1 Scottish MP/ 2 English MPs) (some Scottish land) (SHAW STEWART)
[Nisbet-Hamilton of Biel] - SCOTLAND

NOEL earl of Gainsborough (16 English MPs/ 1 Scottish MP)
Norreys Baron Norreys (BERTIE)
NORRIS I of Utkinton
NORRIS II of Hemsted
NORTH Earl of Guildford
NORTHCOTE Earl of Iddesleigh
NORTHEY of Compton Bassett
NORTON I Baron Grantley
NORTON II of Ashe
Norton of Rotherfield (POWLETT)
NOSWORTHY of Ince Castle
Nugent (Craggs) Earl Nugent (some Irish land) (NUGENT)
[O'BRIEN Marquess of Thomond] - IRELAND
Oglander of Nunwell
Ogle Baron Ogle (11 English MPs/ 2 Irish MPs) (CAVENDISH)
OGLETHORPE of Westbrook
OKEOVER of Okeover
ONGLEY Baron Ongley
ONSLOW Earl of Onslow
ORD of Whitfield
Orde-Powlett Baron Bolton (4 English MPs/ 1 Irish MP) (large Scottish estate) (POWLETT)
OSBALDESTON of Hunmanby
OSBORN of Chicksands (8 English MPs/ 1 Scottish MP)
OSBORNE I Duke of Leeds
OWEN II of Condover
[Owen of Clenennau] - WALES
OXENDEN of Deane
Packe of Prestwold (HUSSEY)
PAGET I Marquess of Anglesey (15 English MPs/ 10 Welsh MPs) (large Welsh estate)
PAGET II of Meadow House
PAKINGTON Baron Hampton (small Welsh estate)
PALK Baron Haldon
PALMER I Baron Palmer
PALMER II Earl of Selborne (5 English MPs/ 1 Scottish MP)
PALMER III of Carlton
Palmer of Fairfield (HOOD)
Palmer Earl of Castlemaine (HOOD)
PALMES of Lindley
Papillon (Cressett, Pelham) (PELHAM)
PARKER I Earl of Macclesfield
PARKER II of Erwarton

PARKER III Earl of Morley
PARKER IV of Ratton
PARKER V of Brownsholme
Parker of Melford (PARKER III)
PARKHURST of Catesby
PARKYNS of Bunny
PARSONS of Reigate
[Parsons Earl of Rosse] - IRELAND
PARTHERICH of Bridge
PARTINGTON Baron Doverdale
PASTON Earl of Yarmouth
PAUNCEFORT Baron Pauncefote
Payne (Gallwey) of Tempsford (FRANKLAND)
PEACHEY Baron Selsey
PEARSON Viscount Cowdray
PEASE Baron Gainford
PEDLEY of Abbotsleigh
PEEL Earl Peel (14 English MPs/ 1 Irish MP)
Peirse-Beresford (BERESFORD) (4 English MPs/ 2 Irish MPs)
PELHAM Duke of Newcastle
Pelham Earl of Chichester (20 English MPs/ 1 Irish MP) (PELHAM)
PELLEW Viscount Exmouth
PEMBERTON I Baron Kingsdown
PEMBERTON II of Rushden
PENDARVES of Pendarves
PENDER Baron Pender
PENN of Laleham
PENNINGTON Baron Muncaster
PENRUDDOCKE of Compton
PEPYS Earl of Cottenham
[PERCEVAL Earl of Egmont] - IRELAND
PERCY (Smithson) Duke of Northumberland
[Perrott of Haroldston] - WALES
Pershall of Horsley (PIGOTT)
Petty-Fitzmaurice Marquess of Lansdowne (12 English MPs/ 7 Irish MPs) (large Irish estate and large Scottish estate) (FITZGERALD I)
PETO of Cheddington
PETRE Baron Petre
Peyto of Chesterton (VERNEY)
PEYTON of Knowlton
Peyton of Doddington (DASHWOOD)
PHELIPS of Montacute

PHILIPS I of Welcombe
[Philipps Viscount St. Davids] - WALES
PHILLIMORE Baron Phillimore
PHILLIPPS of Berwick House
PHILLIPPS DE L'ISLE of Garendon
PHIPPS I of Leighton
PHIPPS II Marquess of Normanby
PICKERING I of Whaddon
PICKERING II of Titchmarsh
PIERREPONT Duke of Kingston
PIGOT Baron Pigot
[PIGOTT of Knapton] - IRELAND
PITT Baron Rivers
Pitt Earl of Chatham (PITT)
Pitt Earl of Londonderry (4 English MPs/ 2 Irish MPs) (some Irish land) (PITT)
PLEYDELL-BOUVERIE Earl of Radnor (17 English MPs/ 1 Scottish MP)
PLUMER of Blakesware
PLUMMER
PLUMPTRE of Plumptre
Pleydell of Coleshill (PLEYDELL-BOUVERIE)
Pole (CAREW I)
POLEY of Badley
POLHILL of Howbury
POLLARD of Eggesford
POLLEN of Rodbourne
Pollexfen of Nutwell (ELLIOT)
POLLOCK of Hanworth
Pomeroy of Sandridge (POMEROY)
[PONSONBY Earl of Bessborough] - IRELAND
POOLE of Kemble
POPE of Woolstaston
Pope Earl of Downe (NORTH)
Popham of Littlecote (MUNDY)
Popham of Winterbourne Monkton (MUNDY)
PORTER of Newent
Portman Viscount Portman (BERKELEY)
POTTER I of Buile Hill
POTTER II of Ridgmont
Poulett Earl Poulett (POWLETT)
Powell (Hinson) of Pengethley (WILLIAMS I)
POWLE of Williamstrip
POWLETT Duke of Bolton

POWNEY of Ives
POWYS Baron Lilford
Poyntz of Cowdray (BROWNE II)
PRATT Marquess Camden (6 English MPs/ 1 Welsh MP) (substantial Welsh estate)
PRETYMAN (Tomline) of Orwell
PRICE III of Foxley
PRICE V of Tibberton
PRIDEAUX of Netherton
Prideaux of Theuborough (PRIDEAUX)
PRIESTLEY of Hungerton
[PRIMROSE Earl of Rosebery] - SCOTLAND
PROBY Earl of Carysfort (8 English MPs/ 2 Irish MPs) (large Irish estate)
PUCKERING of Warwick
PULTENEY Earl of Bath
PYE of Faringdon
PYM of The Hasells (4 English MPs/ 1 Welsh MP)
Pym of Brymore (HALES)
Pytts of Kyre (BALDWYN)
RADCLIFFE Earl of Derwentwater
Rainsford of Dallington (NEVILLE)
RALEIGH of Downton
RAMSDEN of Byram (8 English MPs/ 1 Welsh MP) (large Scottish estate)
RASHLEIGH of Menabilly
RATHBONE of Greenbank (5 English MPs/ 1 Welsh MP)
RAWDON HASTINGS Marquess of Hastings (15 English MPs/ 4 Irish MPs) (large Irish estate)
RAWLINSON Baron Rawlinson
READE of Shipton
Rebow (Martin) of Wivenhoe (GURDON)
REYNELL of Ogwell (10 English MPs/ 2 Irish MPs)
RICARDO of Gatcombe (4 English MPs/ 1 Irish MP)
RICH I of Sonning
RICH II Earl of Warwick and Holland
Rich of Roos (RICH II)
RIDER (Barham) of Boughton Monchelsea
RIDLEY Viscount Ridley
RIGBY of Middleton
RIVERS of Chafford
RIVETT-CARNAC of Mapleton
Robartes Earl of Radnor (AGAR)
ROBARTS
ROBERTS of Queen's Tower

ROBINSON I of Treveneage
ROBINSON II of Cranford
Robinson Marquess of Ripon (9 English MPs/ 1 Irish MP) (GREY II)
Robinson (Montagu) Baron Rokeby (MONTAGU I)
RODNEY Baron Rodney
ROGERS Baron Blachford
ROLLE Baron Rolle
ROLLESTON of Watnall
ROMILLY Baron Romilly (Welsh estate)
Roper Baron Teynham (LENNARD)
ROSCARROCK of Trevenna
ROSE II Baron Strathnairn
ROTHSCHILD Baron Rothschild
ROUND of Birch Hall
ROUS I Earl of Stradbroke
ROUS II of Halton
Rouse of Rous Lench (BOUGHTON)
[Rowley of Tendring] - IRELAND
RUDGE of Evesham
RUMBOLD of Woodhall
RUNCIMAN Viscount Runciman
RUSHOUT Baron Northwick
RUSSELL I Duke of Bedford (35 English MPs/ 3 Irish MPs) (some Irish land)
RUSSELL II of Strensham
RUSSELL III of Chippenham
Russell of Swallowfield (RUSSELL II)
RYDER Earl of Harrowby
Sacheverell of Morely (4 English MPs/ 2 Irish MPs) (SITWELL)
SACKVILLE Duke of Dorset
Sackville-West Earl De La Warr (9 English MPs/ 1 Welsh MP) (SACKVILLE)
St. Aubyn Baron St. Levan (MOLESWORTH)
ST. JOHN Earl of Bolingbroke
St. John Viscount Bolingbroke (ST. JOHN)
St. John Mildmay of Dogmersfield (ST. JOHN)
ST. LOE of Knighton
St. Paul of Ewart
ST. QUINTIN of Scampston
Salwey of Haye (WINNINGTON)
SAMBROOKE (Vanacker) of Bush Hill
SAMUELSON of Hatchford
Sandford of Howgill Castle (HONYWOOD)
Sandys Baron Sandys (HILL I)

SASSOON Baron Sassoon
Saunderson Earl of Castleton (LUMLEY)
Savage Earl Rivers (9 English MPs/ 1 Irish MP) (PITT)
SAVILE Marquess of Halifax
Savile Earl of Mexborough
Sawbridge (Erle-Drax) of Holnest (GROSVENOR)
SAYER of Pett Place
SCARLETT Baron Abinger (large Scottish estate)
SCAWEN of Carshalton
SCHOMBERG Duke of Schomberg
SCOTT II of Rotherfield
SCOTT III of Lytchet Minster (3 English MPs/ 1 Irish MP)
SCOTT V Earl of Eldon
[Scott of Dunninald] - SCOTLAND
Scriven of Frodesley (WHITLEY)
SCROPE of Cockerington
SCUDAMORE Viscount Scudamore
Scudamore of Kentchurch (SCUDAMORE)
SEBRIGHT of Besford
Sedley (Slater) of Nuthall Temple (VERNON I)
SEELY Baron Sherwood
SELWYN of Matson
SEVERNE of Thenford (small Welsh estate)
SEYMOUR Duke of Somerset
Seymour of Sherborne (SEYMOUR)
Seymour Conway Marquess of Hertford (16 Irish MPs/ 14 English MPs/ 2 Welsh MPs) (large Irish estate) (SEYMOUR)
SHAFTO (Duncombe) of Whitworth
SHAKERLEY of Hulme (some Welsh land)
SHAW LEFEVRE Viscount Eversley
Sheffield Duke of Buckingham and Normanby
SHELDON of Braile's House
SHELLEY of Michelgrove
SHEPHEARD of Exning
SHERARD Earl of Harborough
Sheridan of Frampton (2 English MPs/ 2 Irish MPs) (BROWNE)
SHIRLEY (Ferrers) Earl Ferrers (28 English MPs/ 1 Irish MP)
Shuckburgh (Evelyn) of Shuckburgh (JENKINSON)
SHUTTLEWORTH Baron Shuttleworth
SIBTHORP (Waldo) of Canwick
SIDEBOTTOM of Etherow
Sidney Earl of Leicester (SHELLEY)

Simeon of Walliscote (BARRINGTON II)
SITWELL of Renishaw
SKIPPON of Foulsham
SKIPWITH of Newbold Revel
SLANNING of Maristow
SLINGSBY of Scriven
Sloane-Stanley (6 English MPs/ 1 Irish MP)(CADOGAN)
SLOPER of West Woodhay
SMITH I (Carington) Marquess of Lincolnshire
SMITH II of Hatherton
SMITH III Viscount Hambledon
SMITH IV Baron Mount Stephen (large Scottish estate)
SMITH V of Ashton
SMITH VI (Bowyer-Smijth) of Hill Hall
SMITH VII (Assheton) of Vaynol (4 English MPs/ 2 Welsh MPs) (large Welsh estate)
Smith of Woodhall (SMITH I)
Smith of Dale Park (SMITH I)
SMYTH II of Trehenick
SMYTH III of Heath Hall
SMYTH IV of Upton (3 English MPs/ 1 Welsh MP)
SMYTH V Viscount Carrington
SNEYD of Keele
SOAME of Dereham
SOMERSET Duke of Beaufort (15 Welsh MPs/ 7 English MPs) (large Welsh estate)
SOUTHBY of Carswell
SOUTHCOTE of Buckland Tout Saints
Southwell (Coussmaker) Baron de Clifford (4 English MPS/ 4 Irish MPs) (large Irish estate) (SOUTHWELL)
Sparke of Plymouth (SPECCOT)
SPECCOT of Penheale
SPEKE of White Lackington
SPELMAN of Narborough
SPENCER I (Churchill) Duke of Marlborough
Spencer Viscount Churchill (SPENCER I)
Spencer Earl Spencer (SPENCER I)
SPRING of Pakenham
Stafford Jerningham Earl of Stafford (HOWARD I)
STANDISH of Standish
STANHOPE Earl of Chesterfield (23 English MPs/ 1 Irish MP)
Stanhope Earl Stanhope (small Irish estate) (STANHOPE)
Stanhope Earl of Harrington (STANHOPE)
STANTON of The Thrupp

STANLEY (Smith) Earl of Derby
Stanley Baron Stanley of Alderley (STANLEY)
STAPLEY (Springlet) of Broyle
Stapylton of Myton (BEAUMONT II)
STARKIE of Huntroyde
Stawell Baron Stawell (LEGGE)
STEPHENS I of Lypiatt
STEPHENS II of Bowcombe
STERN Baron Wandsworth
STEWARD I of Weymouth
STEWARD II of Hartley Mauditt
[Stewart (Tempest, Vane) Marquess of Londonderry] - IRELAND
STOCKDALE of Bilton
Stonhouse of Radley (BOWYER)
STONOR Baron Camoys
STOURTON Baron Mowbray and Stourton
STRACHEY Baron Strachie (2 English MPs/ 1 Scottish MP)
[STRAHAN (Spottiswoode) of Spottiswoode] - SCOTLAND
Strangways of Melbury (FOX III)
STRICKLAND Baron Strickland
Strickland of Hildenley (STRICKLAND)
Stringer of Durrants (PARKER V)
STRODE of Harrington
Strode of Newnham (HILL II)
STRUTT I Baron Belper
STRUTT II Baron Rayleigh
[Stuart Earl of Castle Stewart] – IRELAND
[STUART (Crichton) Marquis of Bute] - SCOTLAND
STUCLEY of Moreton
Sturt (Alington) Baron Alington (NAPIER I)
STYLE of Wateringbury
SUCKLING of Woodton
SUGDEN Baron St. Leonards
SULLIVAN of Imber
SURTEES of Redworth
Sutton Baron Lexinton (MANNERS)
SWANTON of Salisbury
SWINBURNE of Capheaton
SYDENHAM of Brympton d'Evercy
SYKES of Sledmere
TALBOT I Duke of Shrewsbury (19 English MPs/ 2 Welsh MPs/ 2 Irish MPs) (substantial Welsh estate)

TALBOT II of Thornton-le-Street
Talbot (Ivory, Fox) of Lacock Abbey (TALBOT I)
Tate of Delapre (BISSHOPP)
TAVERNER (Harris) of Soundness
TAYLOR I of Burcott
TAYLOR III of Bifrons
[TAYLOUR Marquess of Headfort] - IRELAND
Temple Viscount Palmerston (5 English MPs/ 4 Irish MPs) (substantial Irish estate) (GRENVILLE)
TENNYSON Baron Tennyson
THELLUSSON Baron Rendlesham
THESIGER Viscount Chelmsford
THISTLETHWAYTE of Southwick
THOMPSON I of Humbleton
THOMPSON II Baron Haversham
Thompson of Long Marston (THOMPSON I)
Thornhaugh of Osberton (JENKINSON)
THORNHILL of Riddlesworth
THORNTON of Albury
THOROLD of Syston
THOROTON of Flintham
THORPE of Barnwell
THROCKMORTON of Coughton
Throckmorton of Clearwell (THROCKMORTON)
Thurbane of Chequers (FRANKLAND)
THURLOW Baron Thurlow
THYNNE Marquess of Bath
TOKE of Godinton
Tollemache (Manners) Earl of Dysart (MANNERS)
Tollemache Baron Tollemache (small Welsh estate) (MANNERS)
TOMPKYNS of Monnington
TOOKER of Maddington
TOWER of Weald Hall
Towneley of Towneley (3 English MPs/ 1 Irish MP) (LEGH)
Towneley of Fulbourn (LEGH)
Townsend of Honington (PAKENHAM)
TOWNSHEND Marquess Townshend
Townshend Earl Sydney (TOWNSHEND)
Tracy Keck of Stanway (HANBURY)
TRAFFORD of Dunton
TREBY of Plympton
TREDENHAM of Tregonan

TREFFRY of Place House
Trefusis Baron Clinton (ROLLE)
TRELAWNEY of Trelawne
Trelawney of Coldrenick (TRELAWNEY)
TREMAYNE of Heligan
TRENCHARD of Lytchett Maltravers
TREVANION of Caerhayes Castle
Trevelyan of Nettlecombe (BEAUMONT I) (4 English MPs/ 1 Irish MP)
Trevor (Hampden) Viscount Hampden of Glynde (25 English MPs/ 1 Welsh MP) (small Welsh estate) (HILL I)
Trollope Baron Kesteven (MYDDELTON)
TROTMAN of Siston
TRUMBULL of Easthampstead
TUCHET Earl of Castlehaven
TUDWAY of Wells
TUFNELL of Langleys
TUFTON Earl of Thanet
TULSE of Hinton Admiral
TURNER I (Page) of Battlesden
TURNER II of Warham
Turner of Kirkleatham (VANSITTART)
TURNOR of Stoke Rochford
TURNOUR Earl of Winterton
Turton of Upsall (LEESON)
Twisden of Bradbourne (TWYSDEN)
TWYSDEN of Royden
Tyrell of Boreham (TUFNELL)
Tyrell of Castle Thorpe (TUFNELL)
Tyringham-Backwell of Tyringham (MACKWORTH)
TYRWHITT (Jones) Baron Berners (4 English MPs/ 1 Welsh MP/ 1 Irish MP)
Tyrwhitt of Stainfield (DRAKE)
Upton (Otway) of Ingmire (UPTON)
[UPTON Viscount Templetown] - IRELAND
VACHELL of Coley
Vanden-Bempde (Johnstone) Baron Derwent (HOPE)
VANE Duke of Cleveland
VANNECK Baron Huntingfield
VANSITTART Baron Bexley
Vaux (Mostyn) Baron Vaux of Harrowden (Irish and Welsh estates) (MOSTYN)
VERNEY Earl Verney
Verney Baron Willoughby de Broke (VERNEY)
VERNON I (Venables) Baron Vernon (15 English MPs/ 1 Irish MP/ 1 Welsh MP)

VERNON II of Twickenham
Vernon of Hanbury (VERNON I)
Vernon of Hodnet (2 English MPs/ 1 Irish MP) (VERNON I)
Vernon of Hilton (VERNON I)
Vernon Earl of Shipbrook (VERNON I)
Vernon Smith Baron Lyvedon (2 English MPs/ 1 Irish MP/ 1 Scottish MP) (FITZPATRICK)
VILLIERS Duke of Buckingham
Villiers (Child) Earl of Jersey (VILLIERS)
Villiers Earl of Clarendon (7 English MPs/ 1 Welsh MP/ 1 Scottish MP)(VILLIERS)
VINCENT Viscount D'Abernon
Vincent of Trelavan (NUGENT)
VIVIAN Baron Vivian (5 English MPs/ 2 Welsh MPs) (substantial Welsh estate)
Vyner of Newby (GREY II)
VYVYAN of Trelowarren
WAKE of Courteenhall
WALCOT of Walcot
WALDEGRAVE Earl Waldegrave
WALKER of Exeter
Wallace Baron Wallace (HOPE)
WALLER of Hall Barn
WALLOP Earl of Portsmouth
Wallwyn of Longworth (PHILLIPPS)
Walpole Earl of Orford (8 English MPs/ 1 Irish MP) (COLMONDELEY)
Walpole Earl of Orford of Wolterton (CHOLMONDELEY)
WALROND Baron Waleran
Walrond of Dulford (WALROND)
WALSH Baron Ormanthwaite (7 English MPs/ 3 Welsh MPs) (large Welsh estate) (large Irish estate)
WALTER of Stalbridge
Walter of Sarsden (ROLLE)
[Wandesford Earl of Wandesford] - IRELAND
WARD I Earl of Dudley
WARING II of Owlbury
Warre of Hestercombe (BAMPFYLDE)
WARTON of Skelton Castle
WASON of Kildinan (2 Scottish MPs/ 1 English MP)
WATERHOUSE of Well Head
WATSON I Baron Armstrong (1 English MP/ 1 Irish MP)
Watson (Sondes) Earl of Feversham (WENTWORTH)
Watson Wentworth Marquess of Rockingham (WENTWORTH)
WAY (Hill) of Denham
WEBB I of Biddesden

WEBB II of Norton Court
WEBB III of Taunton
WEBSTER of Battle Abbey
WELBY Baron Welby
Weld of Willey (FORESTER)
WELLESLEY (Colley) Duke of Wellington (17 Irish MPs/ 9 English MPs) (substantial Irish estate)
[WEMYSS Earl of Wemyss and March] - SCOTLAND
Wenman Viscount Wenman (WYKEHAM)
WENTWORTH (Vernon) Earl of Strafford (substantial but not valuable Scottish estate)
Wentworth Viscount Wentworth (NOEL)
Wentworth of Woolley (WENTWORTH)
Wentworth Fitzwilliam Earl Fitzwilliam (20 English MPs/ 2 Irish MPs) (large Irish estate) (WENTWORTH)
WESTERN Baron Western
WESTFALING of Rudhall
WESTON Earl of Portland
Weston of Ockham (WESTON)
WHALLEY of Plas Madoc
WHARTON Duke of Wharton
Wharton of Dryburn (WHARTON)
WHEATE of Glympton
WHELER of Ledston (3 English MPs/ 1 Scottish MP)
WHICHCOTE of Harpswell
WHITAKER of Motcombe
WHITBREAD of Southill
WHITE III of Bashall
WHITE IV of Walling Wells
[WHITELAW Viscount Whitelaw] - SCOTLAND
WHITELEY Baron Marchamley
WHITEWAY of Dorchester
WHITLEY of Peele Hall (2 English MPs/ 2 Welsh MPs) (substantial Welsh estate)
WHITLOCK of Phyllis Court
WHITMORE of Apley
WHITWORTH I Earl Whitworth
WHORWOOD of Holton
WICKHAM of Cottingley
Widdrington of Widdrington (GRAHAM III)
WIGGIN of Metchley
WIGRAM Baron Wigram (6 English MPs/ 3 Irish MPs)
WILBRAHAM of Woodhey
Wilbraham of Delamere (WILBRAHAM)

WILDE Baron Truro
WILDMAN of Chilham Castle
Wilkinson of Aldborough (LAWSON III)
WILLES of Astrop
WILLIAMS III of Temple House (large Welsh estate) (some Irish land)
WILLIAMS IV of Herringston
WILLIAMS V of Burncoose
WILLIS-FLEMING of Stoneham
Willoughby Baron Middleton (BERTIE)
Willoughby Baron Willoughby of Parham (BERTIE)
WILLS Baron Winterstoke (very large Scottish estate)
WILMOT (Horton) of Chaddesdon
WILSON Baron Nunburnholme
Windham of Felbrigg (WYNDHAM)
Windsor-Clive Earl of Plymouth (14 English MPs/ 3 Welsh MPs) (large Welsh estate) (CLIVE)
[WINGFIELD Viscount Powerscourt] - IRELAND
Wingfield-Digby of Sherborne (DIGBY)
WINN Baron St. Oswald
WINNINGTON of Stanford Court
Wise of Sydenham (TREMAYNE)
WISEMAN of Rivenhall
[Wishart of Pittarrow] - SCOTLAND
WODEHOUSE Earl of Kimberley
WOLLASTON of Finborough
Wolryche of Dudmaston (WHITMORE)
WOLSELEY Viscount Wolseley (4 English MPs/ 4 Irish MPs) (substantial Irish estate)
WOLSTENHOLME (Rayton) of Nostell Priory
WOOD I Earl of Halifax
WOOD II Baron Hatherley
Wood of Gatton (LOCKWOOD)
Wood of Littleton (2 English MPs/ 1 Welsh MP) (WILLIAMS I)
WOODRUFFE of Poyle
WORSLEY of Appldurcombe
Worsley of Hovingham (WORSLEY)
Wortley-Montagu (Stuart) Earl of Wharncliffe (14 English MPs/ 1 Scottish MP) (substantial Scottish estate) (MONTAGU I)
Wray of Ashby (LUMLEY)
WREN of Wroxall
WREY of Tawstock
WRIGHT of Osmaston
WRIGHTSON of Cusworth

WROTH of Petherton
WROTTESLEY of Wrottesley
WYKEHAM-MARTIN-CORNWALLIS Marquess Cornwallis
WYNDHAM (O'Brien) Earl of Egremont (large Irish estate)
Wyndham Baron Windham (WYNDHAM)
Wyndham of Kentsford (WYNDHAM)
[Wyndham-Quin Earl of Dunraven] - WALES
WYNTER (Blathwayte) of Dyrham
WYVILL of Constable Burton
Yarde of Churston Ferrers (BULLER)
Yelverton Earl of Sussex (GREY II)
YERBURGH Baron Alvingham
YONGE of Colyton
YORKE I Earl of Hardwicke
YORKE II of Bewerley
YOUNG Baron Kennet

WALES

ARNOLD of Llanthony (3 Welsh MPs/ 3 English MPs) (No information on the size of the estates but held land in England and Wales)
BAILEY Baron Glanusk (3 English MPs/ 2 Welsh MPs) (substantial English estate)
Barlow of Slebech (6 Welsh MPs/ 1 English MP) (OWEN I)
BASSETT II of Beaupré Castle
Bayly of Plas Newydd (2 Irish MPs/ 2 Welsh MPs/ 1 English MP) (held Irish and English land) (PAGET I)
BODVELL of Bodvel Castle
Bray (Morgan) of Llantaram (7 Welsh MPs/ 1 English MP) (some English land) (MORGAN I)
BRUCE Baron Aberdare
BULKELEY Viscount Bulkeley
[Campbell Earl of Cawdor] – SCOTLAND
[CARTER II of Kinmel] - ENGLAND
Charlton Meyrick of Bush (2 Welsh MPs/ 3 English MPs) (substantial English estate) (MEYRICK)
[CLIVE Earl of Powis] - ENGLAND
Conway (Shipley) of Bodrhyddan (4 Welsh MPs/ 1 English MP) (TAYLOUR)
Cunliffe (Offley) of Acton (2 English MPs/ 1 Welsh MP) (only Welsh land) (CUNLIFFE-LISTER)
Devereux Viscount Hereford (2 Welsh MPs/ 1 English MPs) (some English land) (SHIRLEY)
DILLWYN (Venables, Llewelyn) of Penllergare

Edwardes Baron Kensington (4 Welsh MPs/ 1 English MP) (valuable estate in London) (RICH II)
EYTON of Leeswood and Eyton
[FEILDING Earl of Denbigh] - ENGLAND
Glynne of Harwarden (5 Welsh MPs/ 2 English MPs) (GLADSTONE)
[Gore (Ormsby) Baron Harlech] - IRELAND
GRIFFITH I (Wynne, Finch) of Cefnamwlch (some English land)
[GUEST Viscount Wimborne] - ENGLAND
GULSTON of Dirleton (3 English MPs) (some English land)
GUNTER of Abergavenny
[Gwyn of Lansannor] - ENGLAND
GWYNNE of Garth (3 Welsh MPs/ 1 English MP)
HALL (Herbert) Baron Llanover (3 Welsh MPs/ 2 English MPs)
HAMLYN of Edwinsford (some English land)
HANBURY of Pontypool (4 Welsh MPs/ 4 English MPs)
Hanmer Baron Hanmer (9 Welsh MPs/ 7 English MPs/ 1 Irish MP) (small English estate) (NORTH)
[Hanbury-Tracy Viscount Tracy] - ENGLAND
Herbert Marquess of Powis (6 English MPs/ 2 Welsh MPs) (some English land) (HERBERT)
Herbert of Coldbrook (HERBERT)
[Herbert Baron Herbert of Chirbury] - ENGLAND
HOWARTH of Maesllwch Castle (2 English MPs/ 1 Welsh MP) (some English land)
JEFFREYS (5 Welsh MPs/ 3 English MPs)
Johnes of Llanfair (BOUGHTON) (some English land)
JONES II of Buckland
JONES-PARRY of Wernfawr
[Kemys-Tynte Baron Wharton] – ENGLAND
[KENYON Baron Kenyon] - ENGLAND
LEWIS I of Coedmawr
LEWIS II Baron Merthyr
Lewis of Harpton (5 Welsh MPs/ 1 Irish MP) (FRANKLAND)
[Lewis of St. Fagan's] - ENGLAND
LLOYD II of Peterwell
LLOYD GEORGE Earl Lloyd George of Dwyfor (3 Welsh MPs/ 1 English MP)
Mackworth of Gnoll Castle (3 English MPs/ 3 Welsh MPs) (MACKWORTH)
MCLAREN Baron Aberconway (2 Scottish MPs/ 5 English MPs)
MADOCKS of Tan-yr-allt (2 English MPs/ 1 Welsh MP) (some English land)
[Mainwaring of Peaover] – ENGLAND
[MAITLAND II of Stansted] - ENGLAND
MANLEY of Bryn y Ffynnon (1 Welsh MP/ 1 English MP/ 1 Irish MP)
Mansel (Phillips, Talbot) Baron Mansel (13 Welsh MPs/ 2 English MPs) (TALBOT I)

MEYRICK of Bodorgan
MORGAN I Viscount Tredegar (small English estate)
MOSTYN Baron Mostyn (14 Welsh MPs/ 3 English MPs)
MYDDELTON of Chirk Castle (14 Welsh MPs/ 3 English MPs) (substantial English estate)
OWEN I of Orielton
Owen of Clenennau (4 English MPs/ 1 Welsh MP) (substantial English estate) (GORE I)
[PAGET I Marquess of Anglesey] - ENGLAND
Pennant (Dawkins, Douglas) Baron Penrhyn (3 English MPs/ 2 Welsh MPs) (substantial English estate) (DOUGLAS)
Perrott of Haroldston (4 Welsh MPs/ 1 English MP) (some English land) (PAKINGTON)
PHILIPPS Baron Milford
Philipps Viscount St. Davids (2 Welsh MPs/ 2 English MPs/ 1 Scottish MP) (some English land) (PHILIPPS)
POWELL of Nanteos
[PRATT Marquess Camden] - ENGLAND
PRICE I of Norton (3 Welsh MPs/ 1 English MP)
PRICE IV of Rhiwlas
PRICE VI of Park Penprice
Price of Brecon Priory (4 Welsh MPs/ 2 English MPs) (JEFFREYS)
PRYSE of Plas Gogerddan
PUGH of Mathafarn
PULESTON of Emral
Purcell of Natcribba (MOYLE)
Ravenscroft of Harwarden (5 Welsh MPs/ 1 English MP) (GLADSTONE)
Rice-Talbot Baron Dynevor (6 Welsh MPs/ 2 English MPs) (small English estate) (TALBOT I)
Salusbury of Llewenny (COTTON I)
[SMITH VII (Assheton) of Vaynol] – ENGLAND
[SOMERSET Duke of Beaufort] - ENGLAND
Stepney of Dirleton (Cowell) (GULSTON)
[Stewart (Tempest, Vane) Marquess of Londonderry] - IRELAND
Stradling of St. Donat's Castle (DRAKE)
[STUART (Crichton) Marquis of Bute] – SCOTLAND
[TALBOT I Duke of Shrewbury] - ENGLAND
THOMAS of Wenvoe Castle (3 Welsh MPs/ 1 English MP)
VAUGHAN I Earl of Lisburne (7 Welsh MPs/ 2 English MPs/ 1 Irish MP) (some English land) (some Irish land)
VAUGHAN II of Corsygedol
VAUGHAN III Earl of Carbery
Vaughan of Llwdiarth (WILLIAMS-WYNN)
[VIVIAN Baron Vivian] – ENGLAND

[WALSH Baron Ormanthwaite] – ENGLAND
[WHITLEY of Peele Hall] - ENGLAND
WILLIAMS I of Gwernyfed (5 Welsh MPs/ 2 English MPs) (some English land)
WILLIAMS II of Llangibby Castle
Williams of Nant (BULKELEY)
WILLIAMS-WYNN of Wynnstay (26 Welsh MPs/ 4 English MPs) (some English land)
[Windsor-Clive Earl of Plymouth] - ENGLAND
WOGAN of Wiston
Wyndham-Quin Earl of Dunraven and Mount Earl (5 Welsh MPs/ 3 Irish MPs/ 3 English MPs) (large Irish estate) (some English land) (WYNDHAM)
Wynn Baron Newborough (10 Welsh MPs/ 1 English MP)
[YELVERTON Viscount Avonmore] - IRELAND

SCOTLAND

ABERCROMBY of Forglen (some Irish land) (5 Scottish MPs)
Abercromby Baron Abercromby (9 Scottish MPs/ 1 English MP) (ABERCROMBY)
ADAM of Blair Adam (4 Scottish MPs/ 1 English MP)
AGNEW of Lochnaw
AKERS-DOUGLAS Viscount Chilston (3 English MPs) (substantial English land)
ANSTRUTHER of Carmichael House
Anstruther of Balcaskie (ANSTRUTHER) (some English land) (5 Scottish MPs/ 1 English MP)
ARBUTHNOT Viscount Arbuthnot (Maitland)
BAILLIE of Dochfour (5 English MPs/ 1 Irish MP/ 4 Scottish MPs)
Baillie of Polkemmet (3 Scottish MPs/ 1 Irish MP/ 1 English MP) (BAILLIE)
Baillie of Lamington (COCHRANE)
Baillie-Hamilton Earl of Haddington (5 Scottish MPs/ 4 English MPs) (large English estate) (HAMILTON I)
BAIRD I Viscount Stonehaven (5 Scottish MPs/ 1 English MP)
BAIRD II of Newbyth
BALFOUR I Earl Balfour (2 Scottish MPs/ 3 English MPs)
BALFOUR II Baron Balfour of Burleigh (5 Scottish MPs/ 1 English MP)
BANNATYNE of Kames
BARCLAY of Ury (Allardice)
BAYNE of Tulloch
BELL of Glasgow
Belsches of Fettercairn (FORBES)
Bethune of Balfour (BALFOUR II)
BORTHWICK Baron Borthwick
Boyle Earl of Glasgow
BRODIE of Brodie Castle

Brodie of Lethen (BRODIE)
Bruce Earl of Elgin (2 Scottish MPs/ 9 English MPs) (BRUDENELL)
Bruce of Balcaskie (BRUDENELL)
Bruce of Blairhall (BRUDENELL)
Buchan-Hepburn of Smeaton (HOME)
BUCHANAN of Buchanan
BUCHANAN-SMITH Baron Balerno
BURNS Baron Inverclyde
[Butler Baron Dunboyne] - IRELAND
CAMPBELL I Duke of Argyll (13 Scottish MPs/ 3 English MPs) (Scottish peers 1445- / English peers 1705-43)
Campbell of Auchinbreck (CAMPBELL I)
Campbell Earl of Cawdor (10 Scottish MPs/ 7 Welsh MPs) (large Welsh estate) (CAMPBELL I)
Campbell of Lochnell (CAMPBELL I)
Campbell Marquis of Breadalbane (5 Scottish MPs/ 2 English MPs) (CAMPBELL I)
Campbell Baron Blythswood (CAMPBELL I)
Campbell of Garscube (CAMPBELL I)
Campbell (Muir) Earl of Loudon (CAMPBELL I)
Campbell of Ardkinglas (CAMPBELL I)
Campbell of Shawfield (CAMPBELL I)
CAMPBELL II Baron Stratheden (2 Scottish MPs/ 2 English MPs)
Carmichael Earl of Hyndford (ANSTRUTHER)
Carmichael Baron Carmichael (ANSTRUTHER)
CARNEGIE Earl of Southesk
Carnegie Earl of Northesk (1 Scottish MP/ 2 English MPs; Scottish peers 1639-) (some English land) (CARNEGIE)
CATHCART Earl of Cathcart (some English land)
[CAYZER Baron Rotherwick] - ENGLAND
CLARK (1 Scottish MP/ 1 English MP) (some English land)
CLERK of Penicuik (3 Scottish MPs/ 1 English MP)
COATS Baron Glentanar (1 Scottish MP/ 1 English MP)
COCHRANE Earl of Dundonald (8 Scottish MPs/ 4 English MPs)
Cochrane-Wishart-Baillie Baron Lamington (1 Scottish MP/ 2 English MPs) (COCHRANE)
COCKBURN (5 Scottish MPs/ 2 English MPs)
Cockburn of Ormiston (COCKBURN)
COLEBROOKE Baron Colebrooke (4 English MPs/ 1 Scottish MP) (small English estate)
Colquhoun of Rossdhu (GRANT)
COLVILLE Viscount Colville
Colville Baron Colville of Ochiltree (COLVILLE)
CRAIGIE of Langskaill

CRAUFURD of Auchenames (3 Scottish MPs/ 4 English MPs)
Craufurd of Newark Castle (2 English MPs) (CRAUFURD)
Cumming (Gordon, Bruce) of Altyre (GORDON I)
CUNINGHAM of Caprington
Cuninghame of Craigends (CUNNINGHAME)
CUNNINGHAME Earl of Glencairn
CUNYNGHAME of Livingston
DALRYMPLE Earl of Stair (11 Scottish MPs/ 1 Irish MP)
Dalrymple (Hamilton) of Leuchie (7 Scottish MPs/ 2 English MPs) (DALRYMPLE)
Dalrymple-Elphinstone of Logie (1 Scottish MP/ 1 English MP) (DALRYMPLE)
DAVIDSON of Tulloch (2 Scottish MPs/ 1 English MP)
DEWAR Baron Dewar (2 Scottish MPs/ 1 English MP)
DOUGLAS Duke of Queensberry
Douglas Marquis of Queensberry (DOUGLAS)
Douglas of Cavers (DOUGLAS)
Douglas of Springwood (3 Scottish MPs/ 1 English MP) (DOUGLAS)
Douglas (Steuart) Duke of Douglas (DOUGLAS)
Douglas of Spynie Castle (DOUGLAS)
Douglas Earl of Morton (small English estate) (DOUGLAS)
DRUMMOND Earl of Perth (5 Scottish MPs/ 4 English MPs)
Drummond of Blair Drummond (DRUMMOND)
Drummond of Riccarton (DRUMMOND)
Drummond of Megginch (3 Scottish MPs/ 2 English MPs) (DRUMMOND)
DUFF Duke of Fife (11 Scottish MPs/ 1 English MP)
Duff-Gordon of Drummuir Castle (DUFF)
DUNBAR of Hempriggs Castle
Dunbar of Westfield (DUNBAR)
Dunbar of Dalvey (DUNBAR)
Duncan Earl of Camperdown (1 Scottish MP/ 1 English MP) (HALDANE)
[DUNDAS Marquess of Zetland] - ENGLAND
Dundas Viscount Melville (11 Scottish MPs/ 4 English MPs) (small Irish estate) (DUNDAS)
Dundas of Dundas (DUNDAS)
DUNLOP of Dunlop
EDMONSTONE of Duntreath Castle (7 Scottish MPs/ 1 Irish MP)
[ELLICE of Glenquoich] - ENGLAND
ELLIOT Earl of Minto (9 Scottish MPs/ 6 English MPs)
Eliott Baron Heathfield (ELLIOT)
ELPHINSTONE Baron Elphinstone (2 Scottish MPs/ 1 English MP) (Scottish peers 1510- / Irish peers 1797-1867)
Elphinstone Baron Balmerino (ELPHINSTONE)
ERSKINE Earl of Mar (7 Scottish MPs/ 1 English MP)

Erskine Earl of Buchan (4 Scottish MPs/ 1 English MP) (ERSKINE)
Erskine Baron Erskine (2 English MPs) (ERSKINE)
Erskine (St. Clair) Earl of Rosslyn (7 Scottish MPs/ 2 English MPs) (ERSKINE)
Erskine of Dun (ERSKINE)
Erskine-Wemyss of Wemyss Castle (WEMYSS)
FERGUSON of Pitfour
Ferguson of Kilkerran (DALRYMPLE) (4 Scottish MPs/ 2 English MPs)
FERGUSSON of Craigdarroch
FLEMING II Earl of Wigtown
FLETCHER of Dundee
FORBES Baron Forbes
Forbes Baron Sempill (FORBES)
Forbes of Culloden (FORBES)
Forbes Baron Forbes of Pitsligo (FORBES)
FORRESTER Baron Forrester
FOTHERINGHAM of Powrie Castle
FOULIS of Colinton (6 Scottish MPs/ 1 English MP)
FRASER I of Philorth
FRASER II Baron Lovat (4 Scottish MPs/ 1 English MP)
[Fullarton of Fullarton] - ENGLAND
GILMOUR Baron Gilmour (4 Scottish MPs/ 1 English MP)
GLADSTONE Viscount Gladstone (6 English MPs/ 2 Scottish MPs/ 1 Irish MP) (large Welsh estate)
GORDON I Duke of Gordon (5 Scottish MPs/ 3 English MPs)
Gordon Marquis of Huntly (3 Scottish MPs/ 2 English MPs) (substantial English estate) (GORDON I)
Gordon of Gordonstoun (GORDON I)
Gordon of Embo (GORDON I)
Gordon Viscount Kenmure (GORDON I)
Gordon Marquis of Aberdeen and Temair (7 Scottish MPs/ 2 English MPs) (GORDON I)
GORDON II of Invergordon
[Gordon-Lennox Duke of Richomond and Gordon] - ENGLAND
Graeme of Orchill (GRAHAM I)
GRAHAM I Duke of Montrose (9 Scottish MPs/ 3 English MPs)
Graham of Fintry Castle (GRAHAM I)
Graham-Foster-Pigott of Kinross House (some English land) (MONTGOMERIE)
GRANT Earl of Seafield
Grant Baron Glenelg (3 Scottish MPs/ 1 English MP) (GRANT)
Gray Baron Gray (STUART)
GRIERSON of Rock Hall
HALDANE of Gleneagles
Halkett of Pitfirrane Castle (WEDDERBURN)

Halyburton of Pitcur (GORDON I)
HAMILTON I Duke of Hamilton and Brandon (23 Scottish MPs/ 5 English MPs) (some English land)
Hamilton Earl of Selkirk (HAMILTON I)
Hamilton of Silverton Hill (3 Scottish MPs/ 1 Irish MP) (HAMILTON I)
Hamilton Baron Hamilton of Dalzell (3 Scottish MPs/ 1 English MP) (HAMILTON I)
Hamilton Earl of Carnwarth (HAMILTON I)
Hamilton Baron Belhaven and Stenton (2 English MPs) (HAMILTON I)
[Hamilton Duke of Abercorn] - IRELAND
HARDIE (3 Scottish MPs/ 1 English MP/ 1 Welsh MP)
HAY Marquis of Tweeddale (6 Scottish MPs/ 5 English MPs)
Hay Earl of Erroll (some English land) (HAY)
Hay Earl of Kinnoull (2 Scottish MPs/ 3 English MPs) (HAY)
Hay of Smithfield Castle (HAY)
Hepburn-Scott Baron Polwarth (HOME)
HOME Earl of Home
Home (Milne) of Wedderburn Castle (2 English MPs/ 1 Scottish MP) (HOME)
Home Earl of Dunbar (HOME)
Home of Blackadder (HOME)
HONYMAN of Armadale
HOPE of Culdraines
Hope Marquis of Linlithgow (13 Scottish MPs/ 5 English MPs) (HOPE)
Hope-Johnstone of Raehills (HOPE)
Hope-Vere of Craigie (2 Scottish MPs/ 1 English MP) (HOPE)
[HORE (Ruthven) Earl of Gowrie] - IRELAND
Houston of Houston (SHAW STEWART)
Hume Earl of Marchmont (HOME)
HUNTER BLAIR of Abbotshill
HUTCHINSON II of Eriska
IRVINE I of Dumfries
Johnstone Marquis of Annandale (HOPE)
Johnstone of Westerhall (6 Scottish MPs/ 6 English MPs) (HOPE)
Johnstone of Alva (2 Scottish MPs/ 1 English MP)
KEITH-FALCONER Earl Marischal
KENNEDY Marquis of Ailsa (4 Scottish MPs/ 1 English MP)
KERR (Innes) Duke of Roxburghe (9 Scottish MPs/ 1 English MP)
Kerr Marquis of Lothian (3 Scottish MPs/ 5 English MPs) (large English estate)
Kerr of Greenhead (KERR)
KINNAIRD Baron Kinnaird (3 Scottish MPs/ 2 English MPs) (small English estate)
KIRKPATRICK of Closeburn
LAMONT of Ardlamont
Lamont of Knockdow (2 Scottish MPs/ 1 English MP) (LAMONT)

LAURIE of Maxwelton
LEITH (Hay, Forbes) Baron Leith of Fyvie (2 Scottish MPs/ 1 English MP)
LESLIE Duke of Rothes
Leslie Baron Lindores (LESLIE)
Leslie Earl of Leven and Melville (LESLIE)
[LEVESON GOWER Duke of Sutherland] - ENGLAND
LINDSAY Earl of Crawford and Balcarres (6 Scottish MPs/ 10 English MPs) (large and valuable English estate) (some Welsh land)
Lindsay of Edzell (LINDSAY)
LIVINGSTON I Earl of Linlithgow and Callender
LIVINGSTON II Viscount Kilsyth
LOCH Baron Loch (2 Scottish MPs/ 2 English MPs) (some English land)
LOCKHART of Lee Castle
Lockhart of Cleghorn (LOCKHART)
LYELL Baron Lyell (2 Scottish MPs/ 1 English MP)
LYON (Bowes) Earl of Strathmore and Kinghorne (5 Scottish MPs/ 1 English MP) (large English estate)
MCBRIAR of Almagill
MCCULLOCH of Myrton Castle
MACDONALD Baron MacDonald (2 English MPs/ 2 Scottish MPs) (some English land)
MCDOUGAL of Makerstoun
MacDowall of Castle Semple (GRANT)
MCKAY Baron Reay
MACKAY Earl of Inchcape (some English land)
MACKENZIE Earl of Seaforth
Mackenzie of Kintail (MACKENZIE)
Mackenzie Earl of Cromartie (MACKENZIE)
Mackenzie of Inchcoulter (MACKENZIE)
MACKIE of Larg
Mackie of Bargaly (MACKIE)
[MCLAREN Baron Aberconway] - WALES
MacLean Baron MacLean of Duart (2 Scottish MPs/ 1 English MP) (COMPTON)
MACLEOD of Dunvegan Castle (4 Scottish MPs/ 1 English MP)
MacLeod of Cadboll Castle (MACLEOD)
MacPherson-Grant of Ballindalloch Castle (GRANT)
MAITLAND I Duke of Lauderdale (8 Scottish MPs/ 3 English MPs)
[MAITLAND II of Stansted] - ENGLAND
MALCOLM Baron Malcolm (3 English MPs/ 1 Scottish MP) (some English land)
MARJORIBANKS Baron Marjoribanks (3 Scottish MPs/ 1 English MP) (small English estate)
Marjoribanks Baron Tweedmouth (1 Scottish MP/ 2 English MPs) (MARJORIBANKS)
MATHESON of Ardross (2 English MPs/ 1 Scottish MP)

Maule Earl of Panmure
MAXWELL Earl of Nithsdale (large English estate)
Maxwell of Monreith
Maxwell-Heron of Springkell (MAXWELL)
MENZIES of Castle Menzies
MIDDLETON I Earl of Middleton (1 Scottish MP/ 1 English MP)
MILLER I of Glenlee
MILNE of Barnton
MITCHELLHILL of Selkirk
Molineux-Montgomerie of Garboldisham (1 Scottish MP/ 2 English MPs) (only English land) (MONTGOMERIE)
MONCREIFF Baron Moncreiff
Moncreiff of Sauchope (MONCREIFF)
Montagu-Douglas-Scott Duke of Buccleuch and Queensberry (9 Scottish MPs/ 2 English MPs) (large English estate) (MONTAGU I)
Montgomerie Earl of Eglinton and Winton
Montgomery of Stobo Castle (5 Scottish MPs/ 1 Irish MP) (MONTGOMERIE)
MUNRO of Foulis Castle
Munro-Ferguson Viscount Novar (5 Scottish MPs/ 1 English MP) (BUTLER I)
MURE of Caldwell
MURRAY I Duke of Atholl (13 Scottish MPs/ 1 English MP)
MURRAY II of Philiphaugh
MURRAY III of Edinburgh
MURRAY IV of Touchdam Castle
Murray Earl of Dunmore (3 English MPs) (MURRAY I)
Murray Earl of Mansfield and Mansfield (7 Scottish MPs/ 2 English MPs) (small English estate) (MURRAY I)
Murray (Stewart) of Cally (MURRAY I)
Murray Viscount Elibank (16 Scottish MPs/ 1 English MPs) (MURRAY I)
Murray of Murrayfield (3 Scotish MPs/ 1 Welsh MP) (MURRAY I)
Murray of Ochtertyre (MURRAY I)
Murray of Stanhope (MURRAY II)
NAPIER I Baron Napier and Ettrick (5 Scottish MPs/ 1 English MP/ 1 Irish MP)
NAPIER II Baron Napier of Magdala
[Nicolson Baron Carnock] - ENGLAND
Nisbet-Hamilton of Biel (4 Scottish MPs/ 2 English MPs) (large English estate) (HAMILTON I)
Ogilvie Earl of Findlater (GRANT)
Ogilvie of Boyne Castle (GRANT)
Ogilvy Baron Banff (ABERCROMBY)
Ogilvy Earl of Airlie (GRANT)
Ogilvy of Inverquarity Castle (GRANT)

OLIPHANT Baron Oliphant
ORR-EWING of Cardross (3 Scottish MPs/ 2 English MPs)
OSWALD I of Dunnikier
OSWALD II of Auchincruive
[Petty-Fitzmaurice Marquess of Lansdowne] - ENGLAND
PINKERTON of Rutherglen
PORTERFIELD of Porterfield
PRIMROSE Earl of Rosebery (6 Scottish MPs/ 2 English MPs/ 1 Irish MP) (large English estate)
PRINGLE of Torwoodlee
Pringle of Newhall (PRINGLE)
Pringle of The Haining (PRINGLE)
RAMSAY I Marquis of Dalhousie (10 Scottish MPs/ 1 English MP)
RAMSAY II of Balmain (8 Scottish MPs/ 1 English MP)
RIDDELL of Riddell
ROLLO Baron Rollo
ROSE I of Kilravock Castle
ROSS II Baron Ross
RUTHERFURD Earl of Teviot
SANDILANDS Baron Torphichen
SCOTT IV of Logie
Scott of Dunninald (3 Scottish MPs/ 2 English MPs) (SCOTT IV) (some English land)
Scott of Whitslade (MONTAGU I)
Scott of Thirlestane Castle (NAPIER I)
Scott-Blair of Blair Castle (MONTAGU I)
Seton Earl of Winton (MONTGOMERIE)
Seton of Touch (GORDON I)
SHAW STEWART of Ardgowan Castle (14 Scottish MPs/ 2 English MPs)
SINCLAIR I of Stevenson
SINCLAIR II Earl of Caithness
Sinclair Baron Sinclair (SINCLAIR II)
Sinclair Viscount Thurso (SINCLAIR II)
Sinclair Baron Pentland (SINCLAIR II)
SMOLLETT of Bonhill (4 Scottish MPs/ 1 English MP)
SOMERVILLE II Baron Somerville
SPEIRS of Elderslie (3 Scottish MPs/ 1 English MP)
SPENCE of Stonelaw Tower
STEUART of Coltness
STEWART I Earl of Galloway (20 Scottish MPs/ 4 English MPs)
Stewart Earl of Traquair (MAXWELL)
Stewart of Allanbank (STEUART) (2 Scottish MPs/ 1 English MP) (STEUART)
Stewart of Castle Stewart

Stirling of Keir (MAXWELL)
Stirling-Hamilton of Preston Tower (HAMILTON I)
Stirling-Maxwell of Pollock (MAXWELL)
STRAHAN (Spottiswoode) of Spottiswoode (3 English MPs/ 1 Irish MP)
STRATON of Lauriston Castle
STUART (Crichton) Marquis of Bute (19 Scottish MPs/ 8 English/ 6 Welsh MPs) (substantial English estate) (large and valuable Welsh estate)
Stuart (Stewart) of Torrance (6 Scottish MPs/ 1 English MPs) (STUART)
Stuart Earl of Moray (3 English MPs/ 2 Scottish MPs) (STUART)
Sutherland Earl of Sutherland (LEVESON GOWER)
Sutherland Baron Duffus (LEVESON GOWER)
SWINTON of Swinton
TENNANT Baron Glenconner (2 Scottish Mps/ 1 English MP) (some English land)
UDNY of Udny Castle
URQUHART of Craigston Castle
Vans (Agnew) of Barnbarroch (AGNEW)
VEITCH of Dawyck
WALLACE of Craigie
WARDLAW of Pitreavie
WARRENDER Baron Bruntisfield (3 Scottish MPs/ 2 English MPs)
WATSON II of Aithernie
WEDDERBURN Earl of Dundee
Wedderburn of Ballindean (WEDDERBURN)
Wedderburn Earl of Rosslyn (5 Scottish MPs/ 1 English MP) (WEDDERBURN)
WEMYSS Earl of Wemyss and March (Charteris) (8 Scottish MPs/ 2 English MPs) (substantial English estate)
WHITELAW Viscount Whitelaw (3 Scottish MPs/ 1 English MP)
Wishart of Pittarrow (2 Scottish MPs/ 1 English MP) (COCHRANE)
YOUNGER Viscount Younger of Leckie (2 Scottish MPs/ 1 English MP)

IRELAND

In the case of Ireland, if a preponderance of MPs elected after 1660 was Irish, a history of electing English MPs before that date is not taken into consideration when determining the country of principal association.

Not noted are Irish peerages clearly conferred as honorific on English, Welsh, or Scottish families without the holders intending to take their seats in the Dublin Parliament.

ACHESON Earl of Gosford (1 Scottish MP/6 Irish MPs)
[ADAIR Baron Waveney] - ENGLAND

AGAR Viscount Clifden (Ellis, Robartes) (substantial English land) (7 Irish MPs/ 5 English MPs)
[Agar Earl of Normanton] - ENGLAND
ALCOCK of Wilton Castle
ALEXANDER Earl of Caledon (6 Irish MPs/ 4 English MPs) (some English land)
[Allanson (Winn) Baron Headley] - ENGLAND
ALLEN Viscount Allen (8 Irish MPs/1 English MP)
Annesley Earl Annesley (ANNESLEY) (9 Irish MPs/ 2 English MPs)
[ANNESLEY Earl of Anglesey] - ENGLAND
ARCHDALL of Castle Archdale
ARMSTRONG of Mount Heaton (2 Irish MPs/ 1 English MP) (sold Irish estates mid-19th c.)
Ashe of Ashfield (ASHE)
Aston Baron Aston (4 English MPs/ 2 Irish MPs) (substantial English estates) (CLIFFORD)
Aylmer Baron Aylmer (2 Irish MPs/ 3 English MPs) (some English land) (WHITWORTH I)
AYLWARD of Shankill Castle
Bagenall of Mount Bagenall (4 Irish MPs/ 2 English MPs/ 1 Welsh MP) (some Welsh land) (PAGET I)
BAGWELL of Marlfield
BALL
BARNEWALL Baron Trimleston
Barnewall Viscount Barnewall (BARNEWALL)
Barnewall of Crickstown (BARNEWALL)
BARRINGTON III of Cullenagh
BARRY Earl of Barrymore (8 Irish MPs/ 4 English MPs) (some English land)
Barry Baron Barry of Santry (BARRY)
BATESON Baron Deramore (3 Irish MPs/ 1 English MP) (some English land)
BELLEW Baron Bellew (6 Irish MPs/ 1 English MP)
BELLINGHAM of Castle Bellingham (5 Irish MPs/ 10 English MPs) (some English land)
BERESFORD Marquess of Waterford (16 Irish MPs/ 4 English MPs) (some English land/ some Scottish land)
Berkeley (BERKELEY)
BERMINGHAM Earl of Louth
BERNARD I Earl of Bandon
BINDON of Clooney
BINGHAM Earl of Lucan (13 Irish MPs/ 4 English MPs) (some English land)
Bingham Baron Clanmorris (BINGHAM)
Blake of Menlough (BLAKE)
BLAKENEY Baron Blakeney
BLAYNEY Baron Blayney (4 Irish MPs/ 1 English MP)
BLENNERHASSETT of Blennerville
Blennerhassett of Ballyseedy (BLENNERHASSETT)

BLIGH Earl of Darnley (7 Irish MPs/ 2 English MPs) (substantial English land)
Blundell Viscount Blundell (4 Irish MPs/ 1 English MP) (HILL I)
BLUNDEN of Castle Blunden
BORROWES of Gilltown
Bourke Viscount Mayo (BURGH)
Bourke Earl of Mayo (5 Irish MPs/ 2 English MPs) (BURGH)
BOYLE Earl of Cork (16 Irish MPs/ 11 English MPs; Irish Peers 1616-/ English peers 1644-1753/ GB peers 1711-) (some English land)
Boyle Earl of Shannon (11 Irish MPs/ 2 English MPs; Irish Peers 1756- / GB peers 1786-) (BOYLE)
BOYSE of Bannow
BRABAZON Earl of Meath
BRODRICK Earl of Midleton (11 Irish MPs/ 7 English MPs) (Irish peers 1715-/ GB peers 1796-) (substantial English estate)
BROOKE I Viscount Brookesborough
Browne Baron Kilmaine (BROWNE II)
Browne Marquess of Sligo (10 Irish MPs/ 2 English MPs) (BROWNE II)
BROWNE III Baron Oranmore and Browne (substantial Scottish estate)
BROWNE IV Earl of Kenmare (4 Irish MPs/ 3 English MPs)
BROWNLOW Baron Lurgan
BRUEN of Oak Park
Bunbury of Moyle (MCCLINTOCK)
BURDETT II of Longtown
BURGH Marquess of Clanricarde
Burgh (Downes, De Burgh, Bagnel) Baron Downes (8 Irish MPs/2 English MPs) (BURGH)
Burgh of Oldtown (BURGH)
Burton of Burton Hall (CUNNINGHAME)
Burton of Pollacton (1 Irish MP/ 1 English MP) (some English land) (CUNNINGHAME)
BUSHE of Kilmurry
BUTLER I Duke of Ormonde (18 Irish MPs/ 3 English MPs) (Irish peers 1328- / English peers 1673-86 1694-1758)
Butler Viscount Galmoye (BUTLER I)
Butler Earl of Carrick (BUTLER I)
Butler Earl of Kilkenny (BUTLER I) (substantial English land)
Butler of Ballin Temple (BUTLER I)
Butler Baron Dunboyne (2 English MPs; Irish peers 1324-1660 1827-) (some Scottish land) (BUTLER I)
Butler Earl of Glengall (BUTLER I)
BUTLER IV Earl of Lanesborough (substantial English estate)
Cairns Earl Cairns (CUNNINGHAME)
[CANNING Earl Canning] - ENGLAND

CAREW II Baron Carew
CARLETON II Viscount Carleton
CARR of Donore
CARTER I of Castle Martin
CARY of Pellipar
CAULFIELD Earl of Charlemont
[Cavendish Baron Waterpark] - ENGLAND
Chambre of Carnowe (BRABAZON)
CHAPMAN of Killua Castle
CHICHESTER Marquess of Donegal (13 Irish MPs/ 1 English MP) (some English land)
[Chichester Baron Templemore] - ENGLAND
CHRISTMAS of Whitfield
CLAYTON I of Mallow
CLEMENTS Earl of Leitrim
Clements of Ashfield (CLEMENTS)
COBBE of Newbridge (2 Irish MPs/ 1 English MP)
CODDINGTON of Oldbridge
COGHILL of Glen Barrahane (3 Irish MPs/ 1 English MP)
Coghlan of Garry Castle (DALY)
COLCLOUGH of Tintern
COLE Earl of Enniskillen
COLTHURST of Blarney Castle
Colvill of Mount Colvill (COLVILLE)
Conolly of Castle town (3 Irish MPs/ 2 English MPs) (some English land) (PAKENHAM)
CONNER of Connerville (3 Irish MPs/ 1 English MP)
Conyngham Marquess Conyngham (10 Irish MPs/ 2 English MPs) (large English estate) (CUNNINGHAME)
COOPER of Markree Castle
COOTE Earl of Mountrath (13 Irish MPs/ 2 English MPs) (some English land)
Coote of Portrane (2 Irish MPs/ 1 English MP) (large English estate) (COOTE)
Coote Earl of Bellamont (4 Irish MPs/ 1 English MP)
Cope of Loughgall (COPE)
CORRY of Derrymore (4 Irish MPs/ 1 English MP)
COSBY Baron Sydney
COTTER of Rockforest
Cox of Castletown Cox (STUART)
Crichton earl of Erne (STUART)
Crofton Baron Crofton (LOWTHER)
CROOKSHANK Viscount Crookshank (2 Irish MPs/ 1 Scottish MP/ 2 English MPs)
CROSBIE Earl of Glandore
CUFFE Earl of Desart (7 Irish MPs/ 2 English MPs)
Cuffe Baron Tyrawley (CUFFE)

Cusack-Smith of Newton (BARRY) (3 Irish MPs/ 1 English MP)
DALWAY of Bella Hill
DALY Baron Dunsandle
[DAMER Earl of Dorchester] - ENGLAND
DAWSON Earl of Dartrey
Dawson (Chichester-Clark) Baron Moyola (6 Irish MPs/ 1 English MP) (CHICHESTER)
Dawson of Riverstown (DAWSON)
Dawson (Damer) Earl of Portarlington (6 Irish MPs/ 1 English MP) (DAMER)
DAVYS I Viscount Mountcashell
DAVYS II of Carrickfergus
DE COURCY Baron Kingsale
Dean Baron Muskerry (5 Irish MPs/ 1 English MP) (FITZGERALD I)
DENNIS Baron Tracton
DENNY Earl of Norwich (12 Irish MPs/ 5 English MPs)
[De Ros (Fitzgerald) Baron De Ros] - ENGLAND
[DIGBY Earl Digby] - ENGLAND
Digby of Laundenstown (DIGBY)
DILLON Viscount Dillon (7 Irish MPs/ 3 English MPs) (substantial English estate)
Dillon Earl of Roscommon (DILLON)
Dillon Baron Clonbrock (DILLON)
Dillon of Lismullen (DILLON)
DIXON Baron Glentoran
Dixon of Colverstown (BORROWES)
DOBBS of Castle Dobbs
DOMVILE (Pocklington) of Santry (6 Irish MPs/ 2 English MPs)
DONNELAN of Ballydonellan Castle
DOPPING (Hamilton) of Dopping Court
DOYNE of Wells
DUNN
ECHLIN of Clonagh Castle (3 Irish MPs/ 1 English MP)
EDGEWORTH of Edgeworthstown
ESMONDE of Ballynastragh
EUSTACE Viscount Baltinglass
EVANS (Freke) Baron Carbery (11 Irish MPs/ 3 English MPs) (small English estate)
EVERARD II of Fethard
Eyre Baron Eyre (EYRE I)
Freke of Castle Freke (EVANS)
FALKINER of Anne Mount
[Fane Viscount Fane] - ENGLAND
Fetherston of Ardagh (FETHERSTONHAUGH)
FFOLLIOTT Baron Ffolliott
FITZGERALD I Duke of Leinster (14 Irish MPs/ 4 English MPs)

FITZGERALD II of Carrigoran
Fitzgerald Knight of Kerry (FITZGERALD I)
FITZGIBBON Earl of Clare
FITZPATRICK Earl of Upper Ossory (5 Irish MPs/ 3 English MPs) (substantial English estate)
FITZWILLIAM Earl of Tyrconnel (4 English MPs/ 1 Irish MP)
FLOOD of Farmley (7 Irish MPs/ 1 English MP) (some English land)
FLOWER of Castle Durrow
Forbes Earl of Granard (7 Irish MPs, 1 Scottish MP/ 1 English MP) (FORBES)
FORDE of Seaforde
FORSTER II of Clonsagh
Fortescue Earl of Clermont (FORTESCUE)
Foster Viscount Ferrard (7 Irish MPs/ 2 English MPs) (SKEFFINGTON)
FOX II of Fox Hall
FRENCH Baron De Freyne
Ffrench of Monivea Castle (FRENCH)
GAHAN of Coolquill Castle
Gardiner Earl of Blesington (BOYLE)
GIBSON Baron Ashbourne (1 Irish MP/ 1 English MP)
GIFFORD II of Castle Jordan
GILBERT of Kilminchy
GORE I Earl of Ross
Gore Earl of Arran (GORE I)
Gore (Ormsby) Baron Harlech (9 Irish MPs/ 5 English MPs/ 2 Welsh MPs) (small English estate, large Welsh estate) (GORE I)
Gore Baron Annaly (GORE I)
Gore of Clonroad (GORE II)
Gore-Booth of Lissadell (GORE I)
Gorges of Rathbele (GORGES)
GOUGH Viscount Gough
Grace of Mantua (PHIPPS II)
GRAHAM II of Platten
Grattan of Tinnehinch (BELLLEW) (5 Irish MPs/ 1 English MP)
GRAYDON of Russelltown
GREENE I of Greenville
GREGORY of Coole (2 Irish MPs/ 1 English MP)
Greville Baron Greville (4 Irish MPs/ 1 English MP) (some English land)
Grogan of Johnstown Castle (FITGERALD I)
GUINNESS Earl of Iveagh (3 Irish MPs/ 6 English MPs) (substantial English estate)
HAMILTON II Earl of Clanbrassil (4 Irish MPs/ 2 English MPs)
HAMILTON III of Castle Hamilton
Hamilton Duke of Abercorn (14 Irish MPs/ 8 English MPs)

(Irish peers 1616-/ Scottish peers 1603-)
(some Scottish land/ some English land) (HAMILTON I)
Hamilton of Dunnamonagh (HAMILTON I)
Hamilton Viscount Boyne (Russell) (7 Irish MPs/ 3 English MPs) (large English estate/ some Welsh land) (HAMILTON I)
Hamilton of Hampton (HAMILTON I)
Hamilton Marquess of Dufferin and Ava (7 Irish MPs/ 1 English MP) (HAMILTON II)
Hamilton Baron Holm Patrick (8 Irish MPs/ 1 English MP) (HAMILTON II)
HANDCOCK Viscount Castlemaine
HARE Earl of Listowel (2 Irish MPs/ 2 English MPs)
HARLAND of Glenfarne (2 Irish MPs/ 1 English MP)
Harman of Rockingham (9 Irish MPs/ 1 English MP) (KING I)
HARRISON I of Castlemartin
HARTPOLE of Shrule Castle
HARTSTONGE of Bruff
HATTON of Clonard
Hawkins-Magill of Gill Hall (MEADE)
HELY-HUTCHINSON Earl of Donoughmore (7 Irish MPs/ 2 English MPs)
HENRY I of Straffan
Herbert of Muckross (5 Irish MPs/ 4 English MPs) (HERBERT)
HEWITT II Viscount Lifford (1 Irish MP/ 1 English MP)
HEYGATE of Bellarena (1 Irish MP/ 2 English MPs) (English Estates)
HILL I Marquess of Downshire (17 Irish MPs/ 5 English MPs) (substantial English estate)
HILL III of Brook Hall
HOARE I of Annabella
HOEY of Cotlandstowne
[HOGG Viscount Hailsham] - ENGLAND
HOLMES of Peterfield
HORE (Ruthven) Earl of Gowrie (6 Irish MPs/ 2 Scottish MPs) (some Scottish land)
HOWARD II Earl of Wicklow
Hume (Dick) of Humewood Castle (HOME)
HYDE of Castle Hyde (5 Irish MPs/ 5 English MPs)
Ingoldsby of Beggstown (INGOLDSBY)
IRVINE II of Castle Irvine
JACKSON I of Jackson Hall
Jephson of Mallow (BERTIE) (14 Irish MPs/ 4 English MPs)
Jocelyn Earl of Roden (6 Irish MPs/ 4 English MPs) (small English estate) (HAMILTON II)
JONES I of Headfort
Jones Earl of Ranelagh (4 Irish MPs/ 2 English MPs) (some English land) (HALL)
KAVANAGH of Borris
KEANE Baron Keane

KEATING of Millicent
KER of Montalto (5 Irish MPs/ 1 English MP)
KING I Earl of Kingston
KING II of Charlestown
KNOX Earl of Ranfurly (14 Irish MPs/ 2 English MPs)
Knox of Prehen (KNOX)
LA TOUCHE of Marley
[LAMBART Earl of Cavan] - ENGLAND
Lambart of Beauparc (LAMBART)
Lane Viscount Lanesborough (LANE-FOX)
LAWLESS Baron Cloncurry
LE HUNTE of Artramont
LEESON Earl of Milltown
LEIGH I of Rosegarland
[LENNARD (Barrett) Earl of Sussex] - ENGLAND
Leslie of Glasslough (LESLIE)
Lestrange of Moystown (LESTRANGE)
LEVINGE of Knochdrin (4 Irish MPs/ 2 English MPs) (some English land)
LLOYD I of Gloster (some Welsh land)
LOFTUS Marquess of Ely (23 Irish MPs/ 3 English MPs) (small English estate)
LONGFIELD Viscount Longueville
LOWRY-CORRY Earl of Belmore
Lowther of Shrigley (some English land) (LOWTHER)
Lucas of Castle Shane (CLEMENTS)
LUTTRELL Earl of Carhampton (4 Irish MPs/ 5 English MPs) (some English land)
LYNCH of Athaville
LYNDON of Carrickfergus
LYONS of Ledwithstown
LYSAGHT Baron Lisle
M'Adam Barry The M'Adam Barry (BARRY)
MACARTNEY of Mountjoy Grange
Macartney Earl Macartney (8 Irish MPs/ 1 English MP/ 1 Scottish MP) (HOME)
MACARTY Earl of Clancarty
MCCAUSLAND of Woodbank
McDonnell Marquess of Antrim (1 Irish MP/ 1 English MP) (KERR)
MCCLINTOCK Baron Rathdonnell
MACNAGHTEN of Dunderave
MACNAMARA of Doolen Castle
MAHER of Ballinkeele
Mahon Baron Hartland (PAKENHAM)
MALONE Baron Sunderlin
Marlay of Belvedere (2 Irish MPs/ 1 English MP) (ROCHFORT)

MARTYN II (Hemphill) of Tulira Castle
Mason of Newtown (VILLIERS)
MASSY Baron Massy
MASSEY Baron Clarina (1 Irish MP/ 2 English MPs)
MATHEW Earl of Landaff
MAUDE Earl de Montalt
MAUNSELL of Plassey
[Mayne of Arnos Grove] - ENGLAND
Maxwell Earl of Farnham (9 Irish MPs/ 2 English MPs) (MAXWELL)
MAY of Mayfield
MAYNARD II of Curryglass
MEADE Earl of Clanwilliam
Meade-Ogle (Smythe) of Barba Villa (SMYTH I)
MEREDITH I of Dollardstown (11 Irish MPs/ 1 English MP)
MERVYN of Trelick
METGE of Athlumney
MOLESWORTH Viscount Molesworth (4 Irish MPs/ 1 English MP) (some English land)
MOLYNEUX II of Castle Dillon (8 Irish MPs/ 1 English MP)
Monck Earl of Rathdown (8 Irish MPs/ 1 English MP) (MONCK)
MONSELL Baron Emly
Montgomery Earl of Mount Alexander (MONTGOMERIE)
Montgomery of Ballyleek (MONTGOMERIE)
MOORE I Marquess of Drogheda (14 Irish MPs/ 2 English MPs)
MOORE II Earl of Mount Cashel
Moore of Drumbanagher (MOORE I)
Moore (Bury) Earl of Charleville (4 Irish MPs/ 1 English MP) (MOORE I)
Moore of Croghan (MOORE I)
Moore of Barne (MOORE II)
More O'Ferrall of Ballyna
MORRES Viscount Mountmorres
MORRIS Baron Killanin
MOSSOM (Hewetson) of Mount Eland
MULLHOLLAND Baron Dunleath
MULLINS Baron Ventry
MUSSENDEN of Larchfield (2 English MPs/ 1 Irish MP) (some English land)
Naper of Loughcrew (6 Irish MPs/ 1 English MP) (LEGGE)
NEEDHAM Earl of Kilmorey (7 Irish MPs/ 5 English MPs) (large English estate)
NESBITT of Lismore (4 Irish MPs/ 4 English MPs) (small English estate)
NETTERVILLE Viscount Netterville
NEVILL of Furness
NEWCOMMEN Viscount Newcommen
NEWENHAM of Belcamp

NUGENT Marquess of Westmeath
Nugent of Donore (NUGENT)
O'BRIEN Marquess of Thomond (16 Irish MPs/ 5 English MPs) (substantial English estate)
O'Byrne of Cabinteely (LEICESTER)
Ogle of Bellevue (Moore) (CAVENDISH)
O'CALLAGHAN Viscount Lismore (6 Irish MPs/ 2 English MPs)
O'CONNELL of Derrynane
O'CONOR O'Conor Don
O'HAGAN Baron O'Hagan
O'HARA (Cooper) of Annaghmore
OLIVER of Castle Oliver
O'LOGLEN of Drumconora
O'MAHONY of Kilmorna
O'NEILL Earl O'Neill
ORMSBY of Tobervady
OSBORNE II of Beechwood (9 Irish MPs/ 1 English MP)
PAKENHAM Earl of Longford (14 Irish MPs/ 2 English MPs)
PARNELL of Avondale
Parsons Earl of Rosse (substantial English estate) (KING I)
PAUL of Ballyglan
PENNEFATHER of Ballyowen
PEPPER of Ballygarth
PERCEVAL Earl of Egmont (7 Irish MPs/ 9 English MPs) (large English estate)
PERY Earl of Limerick
[Petty-Fitzmaurice Marquess of Lansdowne] - ENGLAND
PHILIPS II of Castle Dawson
PIGOTT of Knapton (8 Irish MPs/ 5 English MPs) (substantial English estates)
PLUNKET Baron Plunket (2 Irish MPs/ 1 English MP)
PLUNKETT Earl of Fingall
Plunkett Baron Dunsany (2 Irish MPs/ 2 English MPs) (some Welsh land) (PLUNKETT)
Plunkett Earl of Louth (PLUNKETT)
Plunkett of Rathbeale (PLUNKETT)
Pollard of Castle Pollard (URQUHART)
POMEROY Viscount Harberton (substantial English estate)
PONSONBY Earl of Bessborough (19 Irish MPs/ 12 English MPs) (some English land)
Power Earl of Tyrone (BERESFORD)
Power of Gurteen la Poer (BERESFORD)
Power of Clashmore (BERESFORD)
Pratt of Cabra Castle (MORRES)
PRENDERGAST (Vereker) Viscount Gort (8 Irish MPs/ 1 English MP)
PRESTON I Baron Tara

PRESTON II Viscount Gormanston
PRICE II of Saintfield
PRITTIE Baron Dunalley (4 Irish MPs/ 1 English MP)
[PROBY Earl of Carysfort] - ENGLAND
Purdon of Ballyclough (BARRY)
PUREFOY of Purefoy's Place
RAM of Ramsfort
[RAWDON HASTINGS Marquess of Hastings] - ENGLAND
READING of Rathfarnham
REDMOND of Aughavanagh
[REYNELL of Ogwell] - ENGLAND
REYNOLDS of Loughscur Castle
RICHARDSON of Rich Hill
Richardson of Springtown (MERVYN)
RIGGS of Riggsdale
ROCHE I of Carrass
ROCHE II Baron Fermoy (2 Irish MPs/ 2 English MPs)
ROCHFORT Earl of Belvedere
ROGERSON of Glasnevin (2 Irish MPs/ 1 English MP)
ROSS I of Rostrevor
Rowley (Langford) Viscount Langford (10 Irish MPs/ 1 English MP) (TAYLOUR)
Rowley of Tendring (3 Irish MPs/ 2 English MPs) (TAYLOUR) (large English estate)
RUXTON of Ardee
ST. GEORGE Baron St. George
St. George of Kilrush (ST. GEORGE)
St. George of Woodsgift (ST. GEORGE)
ST. LAWRENCE Earl of Howth
ST. LEGER Viscount Doneraile (14 Irish MPs/ 7 English MPs) (some English land)
SANDES of Carrigfoyle
SANDFORD Naron Mount Sandford
SANKEY of Coolmore
SAUNDERS of Saunders Grove
SAUNDERSON of Castle Saunderson
SCOTT I Earl of Clonmell (1 Irish MP/ 1 English MP)
[Seymour Conway Marquess of Hertford] - ENGLAND
SHARMAN-CRAWFORD of Crawfordsburn
SHEE of Dunmore
Shirley of Lough Fea (3 Irish MPs/ 2 English MPs) (some English land) (SHIRLEY)
SINGLETON of Mell
SKEFFINGTON Earl of Massreene (10 Irish MPs/ 7 English MPs) (some English land)
SMYTH I of Drumcree
SMYTH VI of Ballynatray

SOMERVILLE I Baron Athlumney (5 Irish MPs/ 1 English MP)
[Southwell (Coussmaker) Baron de Clifford] - ENGLAND
SMYTHE Viscount Strangford
SOUTHWELL Viscount Southwell (10 Irish MPs/ 7 English MPs)
SPENCER II of Tremary
SPRING RICE Baron Monteagle (7 Irish MPs/ 1 English MP)
Stafford of Mount Stafford (ECHLIN)
Stanley of Grange Gorman (MONCK)
STANNUS of The Elms
STAPLES of Lissan
STAUNTON of Holbrook (some English land)
Stevenson of Ash Park (HAMILTON II)
STEWART II of Athenree
STEWART III of Bailieborough
Stewart Earl of Blesington (BOYLE)
Stewart (Tempest, Vane) Marquess of Londonderry (14 English MPs/ 9 Irish MPs) (large English estate) (large Welsh estate) (VANE)
STOPFORD Earl of Courtown (6 Irish MPs/ 5 English MPs/ 1 Scottish MP) (small English estate)
STOYTE
STRATFORD Earl of Aldborough (6 Irish MPs/ 1 English MP) (some English land)
Stuart Earl of Castle Stewart (2 Scottish MPs/ 1 English MP) (STUART)
TALBOT III of Talbot Hall
Talbot Earl of Tyrconnel (TALBOT I)
TAYLOR II of Ballynort
TAYLOUR Marquess of Headfort (10 Irish MPs/ 2 English MPs) (large English estate)
[Temple Viscount Palmerston] - ENGLAND
Tenison of Kilronan (KING I)
Tichborne of Beaulieu (MONTGOMERIE)
TIGHE of Woodstock
Tighe of South Hill (TIGHE)
TISDALL of Charlesfort
Tonson Baron Riverdale (LEGGE)
Tottenham of Tottenham Green (LOFTUS)
Townley-Balfour of Townley (BALFOUR II)
TOWNSEND of Castle Townsend
TRANT of Dovea (3 Irish MPs/ 1 English MP)
TRENCH Earl of Clancarty (8 Irish MPs/ 2 English MPs)
Trench Baron Ashtown (TRENCH)
Trevor Viscount Dugannon (7 Irish MPs/ 2 English MPs/ 1 Welsh MP) (small English and Welsh estates) (HILL I)
UNIACKE of Woodhouse

Uniacke-Fitzgerald of Lisquinlan (2 Irish MPs/ 1 English MP) (UNIACKE)
UPTON Viscount Templetown (7 Irish MPs/ 6 English MPs) (some English land)
Ussher of Mount Ussher (ST. GEORGE)
VANDELEUR of Kilrush
VERNER of Church Hill
VESEY Viscount De Vesci
Vesey-Fitzgerald Baron Fitzgerald (2 Irish MPs/ 2 English MPs)
Villiers (Fitzgerald, Stewart, Mason) Earl of Grandison (5 Irish MPs/ 1 English MP) (VILLIERS)
Villiers-Stuart Baron Stuart de Decies (3 Irish MPs/ 1 English MP) (some English land) (STUART)
WAKELY of Ballyburley
Waller of Castletown Manor (WALLER)
[WALSH Baron Ormanthwaite] - ENGLAND
Wandesford Earl of Wandesford (7 Irish MPs/ 5 English MPs) (substantial English land) (BUTLER I)
WARBURTON of Garryhinch
WARD II Viscount Bangor
WARING I (Maxwell) of Waringstown
WARREN I of Lodge Park
WARREN II of Warren's Court
WEAVER of Ballymaddock (4 Irish MPs/ 1 English MP)
Weldon of Kilmorony (BURDETT II)
[WELLESLEY (Colley) Duke of Wellington] - ENGLAND
WEMYES of Danes Fort
[Wentworth Fitzwilliam Earl Fitzwilliam] - ENGLAND
Westenra Baron Rossmore (Cairns, Cuninghame) (11 Irish MPs/ 1 English MP) (CUNNINGHAME)
WHALEY of Whaley Abbey
WHITE I Baron Annaly (6 Irish MPs/ 1 English MP)
WHITE II Earl of Bantry
Whitshed of Killincarrig (MEADE)
WHITWORTH II of Drogheda
[WILLIAMS III of Temple House] - ENGLAND
WINGFIELD Viscount Powerscourt (many pre-1660 English MPs/ 4 Irish MPs/ 2 English MPs)
WOLFE Viscount Kilwarden
[WOLSELEY Viscount Wolseley] - ENGLAND
[Wyndham-Quin Earl of Dunraven] - WALES
WYNNE of Hazlewood
YELVERTON Viscount Avonmore (2 Irish MPs/ 1 Welsh MP) (some Welsh land)

Indexes

Index I

Index of Titles and Family Names

[Names in capitals not followed by a hyphen are for main entries. Names after a hyphen are the title of the entry under which the initial item is to be found.]

Index II

Seats of Parliamentary Families Organized by Country

[Seats may have multiple entries under different spellings. Names after the hyphen are the designation under which the seat is to be found. Names in parenthesis are the cadet or subordinate family under which the seat is to be found within a main entry.]

ENGLAND

WALES

SCOTLAND

IRELAND

Index III

Seats of Parliamentary Families Organized by County

[Each seat has only one entry. Names after the hyphen designate the entries where the seat can be found. Names in parenthesis are the cadet or subordinate family under which the seat is to be found within a main entry.]

ENGLAND

BEDFORDSHIRE

BERKSHIRE

BUCKINGHAMSHIRE

CORNWALL

CUMBERLAND

DERBYSHIRE

DEVON

DORSET

DURHAM

ESSEX

GLOUCESTERSHIRE

HAMPSHIRE

HEREFORDSHIRE

HERTFORDSHIRE

HUNTINGDONSHIRE

KENT

LEICESTERSHIRE

LINCOLNSHIRE

NORTHAMPTONSHIRE

NORTHUMBERLAND

NOTTINGHAMSHIRE

OXFORDSHIRE

RUTLAND

SHROPSHIRE

SOMERSET

STAFFORDSHIRE

SUFFOLK

SURREY

SUSSEX

WARWICKSHIRE

WESTMORLAND

WILTSHIRE

WORCESTERSHIRE

YORKSHIRE

WALES

ANGLESEY

BRECONSHIRE (Brecknockshire)

CAERNARVONSHIRE

CARDIGANSHIRE

CARMARTHENSHIRE

DENBIGHSHIRE

FLINTSHIRE

GLAMORGANSHIRE

RADNORSHIRE

SCOTLAND

ABERDEENSHIRE

ARGYLLSHIRE

BUTESHIRE

CAITHNESS-SHIRE

CLACKMANNANSHIRE

CROMARTYSHIRE

DUMBARTONSHIRE

FIFE

FORFARSHIRE [Angus]

KERRY

KILDARE

KILKENNY

KING'S COUNTY [Offaly]

LEITRIM

LIMERICK

LONDONDERRY

LONGFORD

LOUTH

WEXFORD

WICKLOW